# HUDSON's
## HISTORIC HOUSES & GARDENS
### MUSEUMS & HERITAGE SITES

HUDSON's

# Bringing Britain's Heritage to You

Published by Hudson's Media Ltd
35 Thorpe Road, Peterborough PE3 6AG
Telephone: 01733 296910
Email: info@hudsons-media.co.uk
www.hudsonsheritage.com

## 2014
### 27
years of
HUDSON's

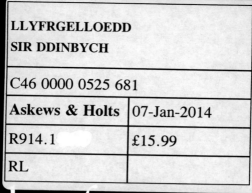

**Smith & Williamson**

# A wealth of experience

## Award-winning private client advisers to owners of historic houses and landed estates.

Smith & Williamson has been looking after the financial affairs of private clients, their families and business interests for over a century. Our family wealth management team includes tax, trusts, financial planning and investment management specialists and has over £14 billion of funds under management and advice*.

The value of investments and the income derived from them may fall as well as rise. Investors may not get back their original investment. Past performance is not a guide to future performance.

*as at 31.07.13

**Smith & Williamson Investment Management LLP** Authorised and regulated by the Financial Conduct Authority.

**Smith & Williamson Financial Services Limited** Authorised and regulated by the Financial Conduct Authority.

**Smith & Williamson LLP** Regulated by the Institute of Chartered Accountants in England and Wales for a range of investment business activities. A member of Nexia International.

The Financial Conduct Authority does not regulate all the products and services referred to here.

**Salisbury**

Andrew Lockwood
01722 434809

Susan Shaw
01722 434831

**Bristol**

Jerry Barnes
0117 376 2044

John Erskine
0117 376 2189

**London**

Joss Dalrymple
020 7131 4297

Charles Gowlland
020 7131 4635

Email: firstname.surname@smith.williamson.co.uk

www.smith.williamson.co.uk

**Principal offices:** London, Belfast, Birmingham, Bristol, Dublin, Glasgow, Guildford, Jersey Manchester, Salisbury, Southampton and Worcester

accountancy | financial planning | investment management | private banking | tax

# Foreword

It seems extraordinary that only a hundred years ago the idea of government both protecting beautiful old buildings and opening them to the public was new. Private owners had, of course, for centuries, done both: landowners had welcomed visitors into their ancestral seats and many had carefully maintained buildings that they no longer lived in but valued and admired for their history. But in 1913 the government formed the national heritage collection: the magnificent array of 850 sites and monuments now in the care of CADW, Historic Scotland and English Heritage.

In the period between the wars, the government's Ancient Monuments Department which then looked after these buildings established what we know today as the heritage industry: the whole panoply of ticket offices, guidebooks, souvenirs and tea rooms. Just about the only thing they didn't invent was the ubiquitous heritage Tea Towel!  At the same time the government introduced listing, the protection of the nation's most important buildings. Without these two century old innovations our country would be so much poorer and, of course, this book would be a great deal thinner.

**Simon Thurley**
**Chief Executive, English Heritage**

# Inside

**Pictures:** Top, left to right: Dalemain, Cumbria; State Drawing Room, Alnwick Castle, Northumberland; Dunvegan Castle Gardens, Isle of Skye. Centre: Audley End, Essex. Bottom: Fortunio Matania's painting of The Menin Crossroads 1914, on show at Kiplin Hall, Yorkshire; Inveraray Castle, Argyll.

# Welcome t

Thanks to everyone at Cadw, Churches Conservation Trust, English Heritage, the Historic Houses Association, Historic Royal Palaces, Historic Scotland, the National Trust, the National Trust for Scotland, the Royal Collection, private owners and local authorities who help us compile Hudson's and keep it accurate and up to date. All images are copyright to Hudson's Media Ltd, the owner or property depicted.

Hudson's Historic Houses & Gardens team:
Editorial: Sarah Greenwood; Neil Pope
Production Manager: Deborah Coulter
Account Manager: Rebecca Owen-Fisher
Creative team: Neil Pope; Jamieson Eley
Publishing Manager: Sarah Phillips
Advertising: Rebecca Owen-Fisher; Matthew Pinfold; Rose Stowell
Printer: Stephens & George, Merthyr Tydfil CF48 3TD
Distribution: Compass, London W4 1RX
Hudson's Media Ltd, 35 Thorpe Road, Peterborough PE3 6AG. 01733 296910

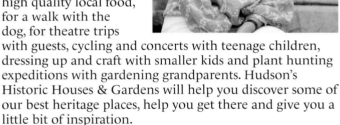

Last year we went on about 20% more day trips in the UK, reflecting not just that many of us enjoy visiting historic houses and gardens, but also that there is much more on offer. For me, my local great house has become a place for regular visits, for coffee with friends, for shopping for special gifts and high quality local food, for a walk with the dog, for theatre trips with guests, cycling and concerts with teenage children, dressing up and craft with smaller kids and plant hunting expeditions with gardening grandparents. Hudson's Historic Houses & Gardens will help you discover some of our best heritage places, help you get there and give you a little bit of inspiration.

The continuing popularity of Downton Abbey has brought a new generation to our historic houses and increased their appeal abroad. For Lady Carnarvon at Highclere Castle, it has brought much more change and helped make the future look more secure. Also more secure is a house rescued from dereliction by Lord Shaftesbury in Dorset; a challenging legacy from his forbears. We will all be thinking about the outbreak of war in 1914 this year and many historic places will have a lot to share with you. We sent Jules Hudson to look at some houses in Yorkshire. And what a delight to discover that Alan Bennett has memories of visiting houses, many of which inform his latest play, *People*. We have given you lots of food for thought wherever you go out for the day this year.

*Sarah Greenwood,*
*Publisher*

# What's new?

## Watch out for some highlights of the heritage year in 2014.

# Stirling Achievement

Astley Castle, Warwickshire, was the 2013 winner of the Royal Institute of British Architects' prestigious Stirling Prize. The prize, awarded each year to the best new building in the UK, is associated with cutting edge modern architecture so it is particularly pleasing for the Landmark Trust that the bold blend of old and new they commissioned from architects Witherford Watson Mann for Astley Castle has been recognised.

*"We are tremendously proud of a scheme which represents an original way of reviving a ruined building."* commented Anne Keay, Director of the Landmark Trust. *"Neither a traditional restoration, nor a brutal modernist juxtaposition, WWM's approach is utterly contemporary and yet in real harmony with the medieval castle. As a result, a historic building that seemed completely unsaveable and close to collapse, has been given a whole new life."*

The project was made possible thanks to the support of many individuals and institutions, including the Heritage Lottery Fund and English Heritage. The castle has been saved from ruin and can now be enjoyed by everyone, through short stays within the castle itself like other Landmark Trust properties, and permanent public access to the site. The Landmark Trust 2014 Handbook is available from Hudson's eShop at www.hudsonsheritage.com.
*Astley Castle, The Landmark Trust (p.277)*

*"Even the familiar statue of axe-wielding Robert the Bruce has been restored to its original bronzed magnificence"*

# Bannockburn remembered

### The Battle of BANNOCKBURN

1314 is a date of crucial importance in British history; this year will mark 700 years since the decisive victory of Robert the Bruce over King Edward II at Bannockburn near Stirling that ended 25 years of English attempts to dominate Scotland. To mark the anniversary, the National Trust for Scotland and Historic Scotland are opening a new visitor centre on the battlefield. Expect not only a building that enhances the landscape but an experience that makes sense of the confusion of a long lost battlefield. Opening every day from March, it promises a 3D interactive battle experience in a realistic medieval battle with lifesize virtual figures of the main protagonists. If that doesn't get you excited it will also provide more sedate interpretation of the battle to help you relive the moment when the Scots, outnumbered 3 to 1, beat back the English knights until *'men could pass dryshod upon the drowned bodies'* in the steep sided burn. Even the familiar statue of axe-wielding Robert the Bruce has been restored to its original bronzed magnificence.

# Stonehenge

At last a new dawn breaks for Stonehenge, unquestionably Britain's most important heritage site, as it enters the modern era with an environmentally sensitive new visitor centre and the restoration of the landscape setting. For the first time at the site, visitors will be able to learn more about this complex, enigmatic monument in a stunning, museum-quality permanent exhibition. The approach to the stones can be made gradually on foot or by a 10 minute ride in a new visitor shuttle. Stonehenge's ancient processional route, guided by new interpretation panels specially developed with the National Trust, will be reconnected to the stone circle after being severed by the A344 for centuries. The new facilities at Airman's Corner will finally restore the dignity of the prehistoric monument and associated landscape and, at last, visitors to Stonehenge will have space to park, shop, eat and use the loo in style. You will still be able to drive past the stones on the A303 but now you'll really be drawn to stop here and enjoy them. The visitor centre opens in December 2013 and the landscape will be gradually revealed by works to continue through 2014.
*Stonehenge is open daily under the care of English Heritage.*

# Literary Laugharne

*Pale rain over the dwindling harbour*
*And over the sea wet church the size of a snail*
*With its horns through mist and the castle*
*Brown as owls...*

So Dylan Thomas, author of *Under Milk Wood* and one of Wales' best loved poets, describes Laugharne Castle, Dyfed (pronounce it like barn) as he looked down on it from the wooded slopes above the town on his 30th birthday. In 2014 to mark his 100th birthday, Cadw are organising a series of events through the year at Laugharne Castle. Dylan Thomas knew the castle well, during the 1940s he wrote *Portrait of the Artist as a Young Dog* in a gazebo built into the Castle's curtain wall with a sweeping view of the estuary mudflats. The castle formed part of the gardens which belonged to his friend the author, Richard Hughes, who also found this magical site a literary inspiration. Earlier visitors to this medieval and tudor ruin include Henry II and the Welsh prince, Llywelyn ap Gruffudd.
*Laugharne Castle, Cadw (p.365)*

# 20th anniversary of Heritage Open Days

The Heritage Open Days movement has really taken off over the last few years. 2014 is the 20th anniversary of the start of the scheme which sees historic buildings opening to the public, sometimes without charge and often where they are not normally open at all. Last year, 4,560 buildings were open for the weekend of 12-15 September and many of you will have discovered buildings in your own district whose secrets were unknown to you. Hadlow Tower in Kent, Britain's tallest Gothic folly, once home to Victorian artist G F Watts and beautifully restored by the Vivat Trust, was one of the most popular. Get ready for Heritage Open Day weekend 2014 from Thursday 11 September to Sunday 14 September and look out for places to visit near you.

**heritage open days**

# Into the kitchens at Kelmarsh

Kelmarsh Hall in Northamptonshire, a virtuoso example of James Gibbs' architecture further enhanced by classic interiors designed by Nancy Lancaster, partner in society decorators Colefax and Fowler.

The Kelmarsh Hall Preservation Trust plans to rescue its domestic range of rooms for a new restoration project aimed at involving visitors in the downstairs history of the house. Dating back to 1800, the basement of the main house contains a butler's pantry, brew house, wine cellar, bakehouse and footman's bedroom.

A separate laundry block - which is accessed from the basement via a long underground tunnel - includes a wash house along with ironing and fuel rooms. While some of these areas are in extremely poor condition, well-preserved original cupboards and fittings remain. These, along with other features from different phases of occupation, will be retained and conserved.

*"Kelmarsh Hall has a rich history both upstairs and downstairs. As well as learning about the families who owned and lived in the hall, we want visitors to gain an insight into the lives of those who worked behind-the-scenes so their stories are heard too,"* said Lesley Denton, General Manager for the Kelmarsh Hall Preservation Trust.
*Kelmarsh Hall, The Kelmarsh Trust (p.260)*

PHOTO: ©KELMARSH HALL

# Drum Castle's secret chamber

There is nothing quite like the legend of a secret chamber so archaeologists were excited to find two hidden rooms inside the medieval tower of Drum Castle in Aberdeenshire last summer. "We were surprised that when we carefully unblocked the windows and peered in by the dim light of a torch through the mists of dust trapped for centuries, to find a perfectly preserved medieval chamber, complete with the guarderobe including the remains of the original toilet seat and the original entrance doorway for the medieval hall," explained Dr Jonathan Clark who led the investigation on behalf of the National Trust for Scotland. A second chamber is almost certainly where Mary Irvine hid her brother for 3 years after the defeat of the 1745 rebellion at the Battle of Culloden.

*Drum Castle, National Trust for Scotland* (*p.355*)

# Mrs Hudson's Holiday

ILLUSTRATION: CLARE MACKIE

*Mrs Hudson's diary of a late summer weekend in the historic city of Lancaster finds her on the trail of witches and fine furniture.*

## September 2013

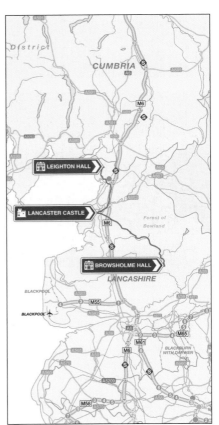

Adopting a red rose for a weekend in the Duchy of Lancaster, less well known on the tourist trail than its rival York. My base was the old quayside inn, the Waggon & Horses in Lancaster, once a beer den for the dockers but now gone up-market with comfortable rooms, interesting pub food and just enough room to park a car outside. Walpole the dog made lots of friends at the bar and slept peacefully in the car.

### Friday

Off the M6, through winding lanes to Leighton Hall. Stop for a shady picnic at Warton Old Rectory, the ruins of a little 14th century manor house tucked behind the village street. Rolling down the drive to Leighton, the long grey gothic house is dwarfed by vistas of the blue hills of Cumbria. All lightness in the charming airy porch and hall, lifted by a delicate flying staircase and graceful pillars. Here's a portrait of Richard Gillow, enriched by the success of three generations of his family furniture business and ready to be a country gent by purchasing the estate and Gothicising the house in 1822. His descendants are still here and the house is filled with early Gillow furniture. Sitting on one of 18 fine walnut chairs to admire simple elegant Gillow pieces crafted for the dining room, from the patented extending table to a fancy

pair of carved griffins holding up a sideboard; the whole room a gleam of polished woodwork. More Gillow pieces in the Drawing Room contrast with fancier French inlaid tables, and oh, the view! There's glowing woodwork in the Bedroom too, this time a maple set brought to the house as a bridal suite in 1931, the bed still garlanded for the bride. Down the hall, a perfect art deco survival in the black and green bathroom. Outside for a stroll in the lovely walled garden with plums dropping plumply from the trees and a chance to try

the weight of a falcon on my arm, though distracted from the majesty of the birds of prey by a phalanx of pheasants rushing across the parkland for their supper. Luckily Walpole is out of sight.

Back to Lancaster in the early evening to stay beside Lancaster's once bustling quay on the River Lune. Now restored, the line of inns and warehouses recall the days when Lancaster was Britain's fourth busiest port before Liverpool stole its pre-eminence. Best view is from the Millenium Bridge.

Leighton Hall. The gothic hall and cantilevered staircase (top left). Known in the family as the Battlefield Bedroom; the present owner and his 11 siblings were all born in this room (top right).

# Saturday

Up the hill into the historic heart of Lancaster. In the small and steep old town, 18th century streets hint at its former prosperity. Here to see medieval Lancaster Castle, now open to the public after 200 years as a grim public prison. Walk in through Henry IV's double towered gatehouse built in 1399, the year he took the throne from his cousin Richard II, a raw demonstration of his Lancastrian power. The first convicts arrived in 1794, the last left 2 years ago and the atmosphere of the prison somehow adds an air of spurious authenticity to the place. Inside the massive square keep (like Dover without the towers) we look through the prison basketball court to a newly revealed gothic inscription 'Come Unto Me' on what was once the chapel wall. Other medieval towers survive, one once held the Lancashire witches who were tried and condemned here in 1612, most celebrated of all English witch trials thanks to a firsthand account. Most of the buildings are Georgian, several fine pieces of Gillow furniture here too in rooms around the crown court, including the fanciful gothic canopy over the judge's seat; impressive but not as excessive as the frilly Coade stone gallery running the whole length of the Shire Hall, today's civil court.

The priory Church of St Mary's next door boasts 14th century choir stalls and carved miserichords while there's more evidence of Lancaster's boomtime at the Georgian church of St John the Evangelist, on a busy road at the foot of the old town with a remarkably complete interior of boxed pews and curved wooden gallery. Ironic that St Mary's survived invasion by the Scots and Dissolution with its medieval interior intact while this Georgian delight is no longer maintained as a church.

Take Walpole for a run to conjure up the ghosts of shipping that once crowded this peaceful wharf, past an early 19th century cotton mill to the mudflats of the river Lune as it slips towards Morecambe Bay.

John of Gaunt, father of Henry IV, stares down from the handsome restored gatehouse at Lancaster Castle.

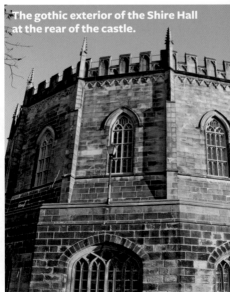

The gothic exterior of the Shire Hall at the rear of the castle.

The 18th century cells look forbidding.

St John the Evangelist and St Mary's Priory Church (below right).

The central courtyard with the 12th century keep to the right.

# Sunday

South into the Forest of Bowland, reputedly the Queen's favourite part of Britain – she's today's Duke of Lancaster. A detour to Dunsop Bridge for Walpole the dog to stretch his legs and for a glimpse back to the Bowland Fells. On to Browsholme Hall, (pronounced like bruise) home of the Parker family. Sun emerges as I come into the park through a charming arch and see the dark block of the house across an ornamental lake below. Mostly Tudor, best bit is the columned and pillared porch that stretches up three stories to the roof. In through the front door to the Hall and a mass of accumulated curios; a real antiquarian's den. All surfaces hold groups of objects; antlers and pot shards, guns and ancient uniform, glass and bronze busts and a skull from the Pilgrimage of Grace. The character of the collector, Thomas Lister Parker, is contained right here, a man of taste and curiosity. He also amassed a remarkable collection of paintings including a fine portrait by Northcote of two waistcoated young men hunting in the Forest of Bowland and a charming little pastel of Oliver Cromwell, warts and all, by Sir Peter Lely. Furniture too, Parker snapped up a Rococco side table, the top held up by three gilded cherubs and a goat, that belonged to famed collector William Beckford of Fonthill. Stained glass was a passion, there's armorial glass in many windows and a patchwork window on the stairs combining fragments from medieval Whalley Abbey, once Lancashire's richest monastery. Browsholme also boasts some remarkable Parker family portraits and a series of comfortable panelled 17th century rooms. A stroll

**Thomas Lister Parker painted by James Northcote.**

**Browsholme Hall.**

**One of the atmospheric 17th century rooms upstairs.**

in the gardens, then past the lake to the beamed 17th century barn, now restored as a venue for weddings and parties. I feel delighted with my weekend, both the elegant Georgian town and open countryside of Lancashire.

*Mrs Hudson is a pseudonym; she is neither the landlady of 221B Baker Street nor related to Jules Hudson on p.40 (who is also not related to this publication). The dog is real but doesn't answer to Walpole.*

**The intriguing dolls in this courtroom scene date from 1700; did the Lancashire witch trial look like this?**

Roman pottery found in the locality.

A medley of salvaged medieval glass on the stairs.

T L Parker's dining room provided a place to show his collection of pictures as well as family portraits.

*Mrs Hudson and Walpole travelled by car and stayed at The Waggon & Horses, St George's Quay, Lancaster 01524 896524 www.visitor-guides.com. They visited Warton Old Rectory, English Heritage; Leighton Hall, the Reynolds family (p.317); Lancaster Castle, Lancashire County Council (p.319); St Mary's Priory Church, St John the Evangelist, Churches Conservation Trust(p.319); Browsholme Hall, the Parker family (p.318)*

Blenheim Palace, Oxfordshire

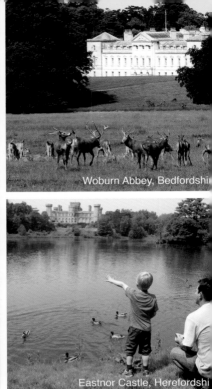
Woburn Abbey, Bedfordshi

Eastnor Castle, Herefordshi

Blair Castle, Pitlochry, Scotland

Highclere Castle, Berkshi

Arley Hall Gardens, Cheshire

Sausmarez Manor, Guernsey

Benvarden, Northern Ireland

Bolton Castle, Yorksh

The Walled Garden at Goodnestone Park, Kent, George Plumptre's family home which has opened for the NGS since the 1970s.

# Cultivating Care

George Plumptre, well known as a writer on gardens for nearly 30 years, is now Chief Executive of the National Gardens Scheme. Under his guidance, the scheme is growing rapidly both in terms of the number of gardens involved and the scale of funding provided to its charitable partners.

In 1927, the first year of the National Gardens Scheme, 600 gardens opened in England and Wales, they all charged a standard entrance fee of one shilling and they raised £8000 for the Queen's Nursing Institute who managed district nurses. In 2013, 3800 gardens opened and the NGS donated £2.2m to its group of beneficiary charities in nursing and caring. In just over 80 years the charity (officially set up in 1980 as the National Gardens Scheme Charitable Trust) has given away some £40m and has become the largest cumulative funder of its annual beneficiaries. These include Macmillan Cancer Support and Marie Curie Cancer Care – two of the largest and best known health charities in the UK.

Over the years many of England's best known gardens have first opened their gates to visitors in aid of the NGS and today we are still fortunate enough to be supported by a host of the country's most admired gardens, including those created by leading contemporary designers and revealed for the first time through the NGS. One key to the NGS's sustained success has been how the types of gardens that open under the scheme have evolved to keep in step with changing social and gardening trends. In the early years the gardens were in rural locations, predominantly they belonged to substantial houses and were maintained by gardeners. Today the scheme embraces all manner of gardens including small town and city ones, allotments, school gardens and, particularly popular with visitors, groups of gardens in one village or city location that open together on the same day. Moreover, the majority of gardens are maintained by their owners for whom 'open day' is a milestone in their annual calendar, looked forward to with a mixture of trepidation and excitement.

Promoting the constant succession of garden openings, that start in February and continue right through to October, demands a range of marketing exercises which the NGS has focused on developing

*"In 2013, 3800 gardens opened and the National Gardens Scheme donated £2.2m to its group of beneficiary charities in nursing and caring"*

**Under the scheme you can view gardens like this one in Dulwich, London, designed by Christopher Bradley-Hole.**

## The National Gardens Scheme Charitable Donations 2013

|  |  |
| --- | --- |
| Macmillan Cancer Support | £450,000 |
| Marie Curie Cancer Care | £450,000 |
| Help the Hospices | £400,000 |
| Carers Trust | £300,000 |
| Queen's Nursing Institute | £200,000 |
| NT Gardening Careership | £120,000 |
| Perennial | £100,000 |
| The Garden Museum | £8,000 |
| Parkinson's UK | £100,000 |
| **Total** | **£2,128,000** |

Broughton Grange, Oxfordshire, designed by Tom Stuart-Smith.

in recent years. Local and national PR work together to balance promoting of individual gardens with raising awareness of the whole scheme and its role as a healthcare funding charity. Long established print outlets, in particular the famous Yellow Book, published annually and still extending to a print run of 40,000 copies, now work hand-in-hand with a sophisticated website and the most recent developments, the NGS App and social media. The fact that visiting gardens is a social, community activity and that it also depends on accurate up-to-the minute information, makes it ideal for promotion via Twitter and Facebook where comment and conversation bring an immediacy to people's activities.

In 2013 the NGS organised the first National Gardens Festival Weekend when some 800 gardens opened in two days and launched the largest garden opening event ever held. The festival brought unprecedented media exposure including national television and a week-long campaign on Classic FM and raised in excess of £400,000. It enabled the NGS to raise awareness of its activities as a major healthcare funder and strengthen its charitable profile, both crucial priorities for the future.

It also gave us the opportunity to work closely with our beneficiary charities with whom we are developing an exciting strategy on promoting the benefits of visiting gardens and gardening for people's health and wellbeing. This will go hand-in-hand with the growing importance of gardens for tourism, confirmed in 2012 when VisitEngland gave their most prestigious annual award, for Outstanding Contribution to Tourism to The English Garden and chose the National Gardens Scheme to be the recipient. Together they will underpin the development of the NGS to celebrating its 90th anniversary in 2017 and ensure that its contribution continues to grow.

www.ngs.org.uk

Brechin Castle, Angus.

Langwell, Caithness.

North of the Border is *Scotland's Gardens,* headed by Chief Executive Paddy Scott, formerly Scotland's Gardens Scheme but renamed in a successful rebranding exercise in 2011.

*Scotland's Gardens* has continued its development and facilitated an increased number of garden openings in order to raise funds for charity.

Approximately six hundred gardens from Shetland to the English border, ranging from extensive castle/country house gardens to tiny village gardens, participate in our annual programme which begins with the Snowdrop Festival and ends with the superb autumn colours. All have horticultural interest and welcome visitors who are able to enjoy their glories at leisure. Fabulous home made teas along with interesting plant stalls are normally available whilst other

SINCE 1931
SCOTLAND'S
GARDENS
GROWING AND GIVING

stalls, children's activities and musical entertainment are often on hand.

Over the last three years more than £1,000,000 has been raised at the garden openings. 40% of this figure has been donated to registered charities of each garden owner's choice and over 250 large and small charities have benefited. 60% net is given to *Scotland's Gardens* beneficiaries, which are Maggie's Cancer Caring Centres, The Queen's Nursing Institute Scotland, The Gardens Fund of the National Trust for Scotland and Perennial.

www.scotlandsgardens.org

Carolside, Berwickshire.

# Heritage in chains

Lady Elizabeth Lindsay and Dido Belle painted in 1779, attributed to Johannes Zoffany. The portrait hangs in the Ambassadors' Room at Scone Palace in Perthshire. Dido, the daughter of Admiral John Lindsay and an enslaved African woman, Maria Belle, was brought up by her father's uncle, William Lindsay, 1st Earl of Mansfield as a companion to her legitimate cousin, Elizabeth. Lord Mansfield left her £500 and a £100 annuity in his will shortly before her marriage to John Davinier. She had three sons and died in 1804. Without this charming painting it is likely that her history would have been largely forgotten, but Scone Palace are mounting a special exhibition exploring her life in 2014.

PHOTO: ©SCONE PALACE

**Baroness Young of Hornsey** sits on the cross benches in the House of Lords and is a campaigner for minority rights in Britain. She has been a Commissioner for English Heritage for the past 2 years. She talked to Sarah Greenwood about the relationship between the slave trade and country houses and what they can tell us about black history.

*What has slavery to do with country houses in Britain?*

The bicentenary of the abolition of the slave trade in 2007 gave us a chance to correct people's assumptions that slaving is all about slaves held on British ships. Because enslavement didn't take place on British soil there is a sense that Britons can occupy a higher moral ground than, say, North Americans. The emphasis is mostly on Britain ending the trade rather than being a major player: the economic landscape of slavery here at home is complex and ingrained.

I am much more interested in this context in the presence of people of African descent in this country over hundreds of years. To me there is a danger of only thinking about the history of Africans in this country as being about enslavement. It posits that the relationship between Britain, Africa and the Caribbean has only one dimension. Instead it is part of a wider colonial history of engagement, exchange, travel and trade.

Contemporaries of the abolitionist William Wilberforce were making links between Africans who were enslaved over there and people here who lived in poor conditions. Similarly today, there is a shift in interest from what goes on upstairs, in the staterooms and the huge drawing rooms, to the servants quarters and what goes on below stairs. If the builder of a country house made money directly or indirectly through the slave trade, we need to know if and how that is marked on the property.

PHOTO: © HAREWOOD HOUSE

**Edward Lascelles was the junior partner to his brother Henry in the sugar business which founded the Harewood fortune.**

**Harewood House, one of England's great treasure houses, was built with wealth generated by the slave plantations of the West Indies. More than any other historic house, Harewood and the Lascelles family have reached out to communities who have a stake in this shared past.**

So do you think we find it hard to understand the attitudes to race in the 18th century?

Despite the fact that it is rarely taught as part of history or art history there are recurrent images of black people in 18th century portraiture but they are often very enigmatic. In the Lansdowne Club the other day, I saw some 18th century political cartoons and in one is a black man. It did not look to me as if he was there to make a particular point about race, he was just included as part of the contemporary reality.

I think of Kenwood House which was home to Lady Elizabeth Lindsay and Dido Belle, who were painted together by Zoffany. Dido had a superior position in Lord Mansfield's household and went on to make a respectable marriage. Lord Mansfield, who effectively adopted her, was instrumental in establishing the law around freedom at the time. Lord Mansfield judged that since you couldn't be a slave on British soil, you couldn't be imprisoned for running away.

Few would have been unaware of the slave trade, so the idea that slavery was happening hundreds of miles away in which most people had no interest cannot have been the case. Likewise, estimates that a significant percentage of the population in London was of African origin in the late 18th century suggest that the presence of black people was not unfamiliar. The government offered enslaved black Americans the chance of freedom by fighting for Britain during the American War of Independence as a way of destabilising the colony.

**Palladian Marble Hill House, built in the 1720's for Henrietta Howard, Countess of Suffolk, mistress to George II, was the model for innumerable plantation houses in the American colonies.**

PHOTO: © ENGLISH HERITAGE

PHOTO: © FRAMPTON COURT

**Frampton Court, built by Richard Clutterbuck, Head of the Bristol Customs House, in the 1730s. His descendents still live here and open the house for groups and house parties.**

Is there enough opportunity for people of African-Caribbean heritage to visit historic houses and gardens?

I think if you are brought up in the middle class you are more likely to have a sense of ownership; historic buildings and art galleries can be very intimidating places. More and more people of African or Indian or Caribbean heritage have developed the confidence to be curious and lay claim to their role in British history.

Here is an anecdote, probably apocryphal, to illustrate some of the alienation we need to get away from. A black family visits a grand mansion somewhere in Britain and walks past the entrance desk without a pause. *"Wait, you haven't paid,"* calls the guy at the reception. *"Oh yes,"* says the father. *"We've already paid."*

Do you know of many historic houses that have dealt well with their slavery heritage?

David Lascelles, the Earl of Harewood at Harewood House has embraced this thoroughly. Harewood is one of the greatest 18th century mansions in England. The family fortune that allowed the house and collection to be commissioned from some of the greatest artists of the day – Robert Adam, Thomas Chippendale, Thomas Gainsborough – was founded on sugar estates in the West Indies. Given modern attitudes, this history can be quite guilt inducing but David Lascelles poses the question: *What is my responsibility given the history for which I was not personally responsible?*

Harewood publish literature explaining the connections and in 2007 staged a huge public event, *Carnival Messiah*, a musical extravaganza written by Trinidad-born playwright, the late Geraldine Connor. David Lascelles is on record saying that facing up to this history has been quite liberating and the success of these initiatives is helping Harewood fully absorb its history into the community.

Does our education give us a clear guide on how to think about this history?

For me, too much of this history has been omitted from conventional curricula. When I started to discover this hidden history for myself, I felt angry and bewildered. I remember learning about the slave trade at school but not being told that any black people came to this country. Black history doesn't fit well with the traditional linear way history is taught. The slave trade is not an abstract that happened far away, we have evidence of the impact on the society around us right here, and we can visit it and help ourselves to understand it.

What do you bring to your role as a Commissioner for English Heritage?

I think what I can help with is in finding ways of making heritage more accessible to different communities through my wide range of contacts and in communicating and helping to facilitate alliances.

Do you think that the current interest in ancestry research will result in a change in the way people view the past?

Yes, it encourages people to be curious about their personal histories. The National Archives have published a series of pamphlets to help British people of Indian and Caribbean origin to trace their ancestors. Names are often revealing. The Royal Shakespeare Company actor David Harewood has an association with Harewood House, for example. Slaves were often given the names of their owners or their overseers as more convenient than their African names so the connections may still be very apparent. Insights gained from stories told at heritage sites help reinforce family history, identity and belonging.

What is the challenge facing all owners and managers of historic houses?

To go back to Harewood House and the approach taken by the Lascelles family, it is significant to notice how they defined their local public. Harewood is a country house, they didn't have to reach out to the people of Leeds and Bradford but they saw a clear responsibility to do so and to make that great house more accessible to a wider range of local people.

**Carnival Messiah spectacularly combined the musical and theatrical traditions of Europe and the Caribbean at Harewood in 2007.**

Is the history of slavery in country houses particularly relevant in certain parts of the UK?

The great slave trade ports were Bristol, Liverpool and London and all are surrounded by country houses built with the profits of the trade but there are other insights into slavery which are not necessarily as obvious. The blockade of the cotton trade in the 19th century to support the abolition of slavery in the cotton plantations of the southern states of America had a terrible effect on Lancashire for example. The cotton spinning industry collapsed and the economic fallout was significant for the area. Yorkshire wool was made into caps exported to the slave plantations for slave labourers to wear when carrying loads on their heads. Birmingham was the source of manacles and chains and had a brief economic boom associated with that metal industry. All of these economic threads can be traced in the rise and fall of country houses, but sometimes you have to shift your perspective.

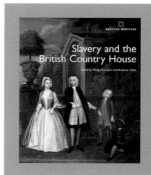

*Slavery and the British Country House*, the newly published record of a conference hosted by English Heritage and the National Trust, which inspired this interview is published by English Heritage, priced £50 and available from Hudson's eShop on www.hudsonsheritage.com

# Bennett's

Alan Bennett's latest play, *People*, was first performed at the National Theatre in London in October 2012 before touring England in October 2013. Its setting is a shabby but important country house in the North of England, now lived in by a middle aged lady and her companion. The play asks obvious questions about what will happen to the house. Will its contents and collections be scattered and sold? Will it be taken on by the National Trust? Will it be sold to a sinister charity as a convention centre? But it also asks wider questions about taste, commercialism, the influence of the 1980s and taking things for granted. For those who missed it on stage, here is an extract from Alan Bennett's introduction to the Faber & Faber edition of the play and a couple of snippets of the action to give a taste of the pithy views of one of our greatest living playwrights.

*"I saw Temple Newsam as a wonderfully ancient and romantic place, which it wasn't really, having been heavily restored and remodelled in the 19th century"*

# People

S ome plays seem to start with an itch, an irritation, something one can't solve or a feeling one can't locate. With *People* it was a sense of unease when going around a National Trust house and being required to buy into the role of reverential visitor.

The first stately home I can remember visiting was Temple Newsam, a handsome early 16th-century house given to Leeds by the Earl of Halifax. While aged nine or ten I didn't wholly appreciate its contents, I saw Temple Newsam as a wonderfully ancient and romantic place, which it wasn't really, having been heavily restored and remodelled in the 19th century. Still, it gave me a lifelong taste for enfiladed rooms and for Leeds pottery. As a boy

though, for me its most numinous holding was a large felt hat reputed to be that of Oliver Cromwell with a bullet hole in the crown to prove it. Visiting Temple Newsam was always a treat, as it still is more than half a century later.

I have never been entirely confident that the glimpses one is allowed in stately homes of the family's 'real life' always ring true. Years ago, I was filming at Penshurst Place, the home of Lord de Lisle and Dudley, and I wrote in my diary (15 December 1984):

> *The house is everything one imagines an English country house should be...a hotchpotch of different periods...*
>
> *'Ah,' one thinks. 'A glimpse here of a private life.' But is it? Is this really a private room or just a private room for public consumption? These drinks (and the bottle of vitamin pills beside them), have they been artfully arranged to suggest a private life? Is there, somewhere else, another flat which is more private? And so on. And so on.*

The links between these private musings and what happens in the play are obvious.

Privacy or at any rate exclusivity is increasingly for hire. I had written the play when I read that Lichtenstein in its entirety could be hired for the relatively modest sum of £40,000 per night. Everywhere nowadays has its price and the more inappropriate the setting the better. In the management and presentation of 'Stacpoole House' I imagined the (National)Trust as entirely without inhibition, ready to exploit any aspect of the property's recent history to draw in the public, wholly unembarrassed by the seedy and disreputable.

→

**The Still Room at Temple Newsam with the fine collection of Leeds Creamware pottery which impressed the young Alan Bennett but not as much as Cromwell's hat, which the curators are currently trying to track down.**

**Furniture by Chippendale in Mr Wood's Adam library at Temple Newsam, designed by Robert Adam in the 1770s. Alan Bennett's idea of Stacpoole House was inspired by interiors like this.**

It has been said (by Kathryn Hughes in the Guardian) that nowadays *'it is the demotic and the diurnal that matter to us when thinking about the past'* and what are generally called 'bygones' make a brief appearance in the play, as they regularly do in the below-stairs rooms of country houses. Fortunate in having had a relatively long life, I have grown used to seeing everyday items from my childhood featuring in folk museums. Even so, I was surprised this summer when going around Blickling to see

a young man rapt in contemplation of a perfectly ordinary aluminium pan.

Still he was doubtless a dab hand at the computer, which I'm not, even though to me aluminium pans are commonplace. Other vintage items which were in common use when I was young would be: a wicker carpet beater; a wooden clothes horse; a tidy betty; a flat iron; pottery eggs; spats; black lead; vitriol. The danger of making such a list is that one will in due course figure on it.

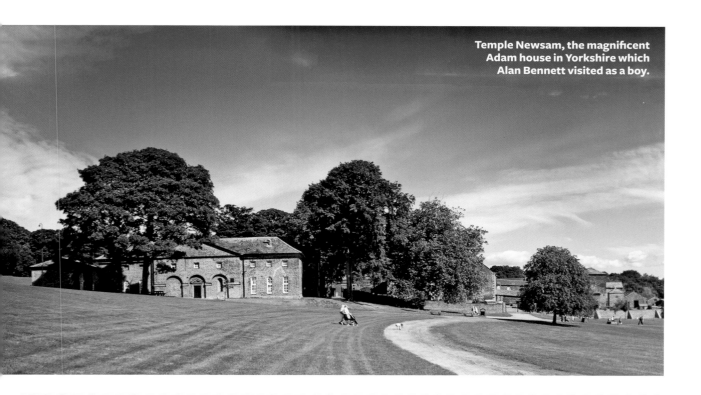

Temple Newsam, the magnificent Adam house in Yorkshire which Alan Bennett visited as a boy.

PHOTO: © PENSHURST PLACE

PHOTO: © PENSHURST PLACE

The Queen Elizabeth Room at Penshurst Place, a room planned for Elizabeth I to hold audiences when she visited her friend Mary Sidney in the 1580s. It is a room built for display to impress visitors (the first paying members of the public came in the late 18th century) that still has the desired effect today. The study referred to in Alan Bennett's diaries was the late Lord de l'Isle's private room away from the grander state rooms. Clearly, the division between the private and the public at great country houses has existed for centuries.

Frances de la Tour as Dorothy and
Linda Bassett at Iris in the National
Theatre production of *People*,
directed by Nicholas Hytner with
designs by Bob Crowley.

# People
## An edited extract

**Dorothy Stacpoole,** resident owner of Stacpoole House
**June Stacpoole,** her sister and an ordained archdeacon
**Iris,** Dorothy's companion at the house
**Ralph Lumsden,** from the National Trust

**June**     People are unavoidable.

**Dorothy**  I thought the clergy were supposed to like people?

**June**     No, we're supposed to love them. Not the same.

**Dorothy**  But do you believe in God?

**June**     This is the Church of England, that's not an issue.

**Dorothy**  So do you still say your prayers?

**June**     You used to say yours with that terrible rosary. Where is that? Where's that got to?

**Dorothy**  I don't know, in a drawer somewhere.

**June**     Because the Trust will want to know. That would be a star attraction, particularly in these days?

**Dorothy**  It won't be lost. It's got a luggage label on it.

**June**     Where's Charles I's shirt?
            *Dorothy shrugs*
            Don't you care?

**Dorothy**  Yes, but they've survived because nobody did care. If they'd cared they'd have been sold years ago. I take them for granted. Not caring is what's preserved them.

**June**     But wouldn't you like to see the place made presentable? The Adam rooms restored, the rubbish cleared out?

**Dorothy**  Not if it means people traipsing around. There was a letter in the paper yesterday saying that the writer had been to York Minster and it was like King's Cross in the rush hour. None of them praying, needless to say. Just looking. And not even looking. Snapping it. Ticking it off. I don't want to be ticked off.

→

PHOTO: CATHERINE ASHMORE/NATIONAL THEATRE

**Lumsden** Forgive me if I enthuse, but I see this house and your family's continuous occupancy of it as a metaphor. Tell a child a story of England and it is all here.

**Dorothy** Yes, I would be deceiving you, Mr Lumsden, if I said I had not heard such twaddle before. I particularly abhor metaphor. Metaphor is fraud. England with all its faults. A country house with all its shortcomings. The one is not the other... however much the Trust would like us to think so. I will not collaborate in your conceit of country. It is a pretend England.

**Lumsden** Oh. This is a surprise. I must marshal my forces. I suppose I would say that we...the Trust, its houses, its coastline, its landscape....are, if not the model of England, at least its mitigation.

**Dorothy** Country houses are window dressing. They mitigate nothing.

**Lumsden** Does this affect your donation?

**June** *(returning with the bottle)* No, of course it doesn't. My sister sits alone in this mouldering house and gets some cockeyed ideas.

**Lumsden** Now, Lady Dorothy, we like to debrief our donors. I want you to tell me everything.

**Dorothy** Nothing to tell. This is not the Cotswolds, Mr Lumsden, and South Yorkshire is not conducive to anecdote. We lived as we live now, in a fraction of the house. We did not hunt. The miners had a livelier time than we did, our one excitement when the Festival Ballet came to Sheffield.

**Iris** And open cast mining. That came right up to the terrace.

**Dorothy** But no legends. No idylls. Nothing you could market. And no one the least larger than life.

**Lumsden** There's one legend. I've always understood that what is reputed to be here is the rosary belonging to Henry VIII.

**June** It's here somewhere.

**Dorothy** Yes, I saw it when I was a child and indeed used to play with it. Now...

*She shakes her head.*

**June** It must be here

**Iris** Everything is here somewhere.

**Lumsden** I'm sure, and of course the first thing we would want to do is make an inventory about what we've... what you've got. But not aspic. Not aspic at all. Back in the day, yes, red ropes. 'Do not touch'. Everything in its place. Nowadays the scullery and the still room are as important as the drawing room. And

PHOTO: CATHERINE ASHMORE/NATIONAL THEATRE

Linda Bassett (Iris), Frances de la Tour (Dorothy) and Selina Cadell as June in a scene in the final scenes of *People* at the National Theatre.

we interact...racks of costumes, frock coats, doublets....Visitors can feel themselves a part of the house.

But no pretence.  I noticed for instance as I went round the ragged footings of the tapestries...gnawed by mice, and wet by centuries of dogs. What we would hope to do is to have our experts clean them, obviously with a degree of stabilisation but making no attempt at repair. Or even

disguise. Rather we would draw visitors' attention to them, focus on them as part of the history of the house. They are after all a testament to time and its abrasions. And we cannot halt time... but we can put it on hold – while we live in the present.

*Penshurst Place, The Lord d'Isle (p.150)*
*Temple Newsam, National Trust (p.303)*

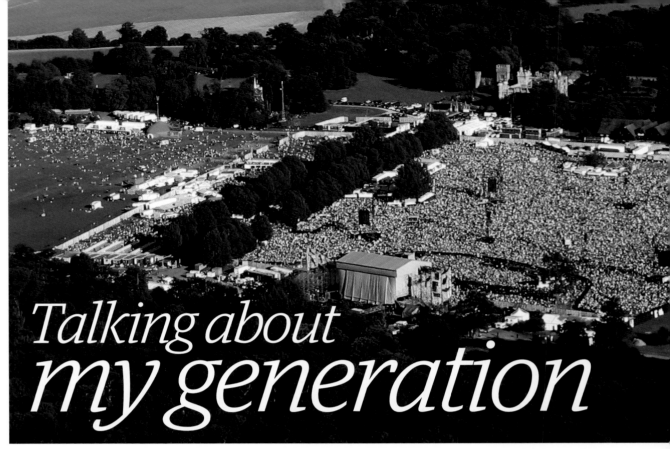

# Talking about
# *my generation*

Knebworth House in Hertfordshire, one time home of the Victorian novelist, Edward Bulwer-Lytton and Lord Lytton, Viceroy of India, has one of the most distinctive rooflines of any country house. While house and garden have their fair share of visitors, a larger number of people by far know its towers and pinnacles as a backdrop to some of the key music events of the last 4 decades, pioneered by the Lytton-Cobbold family.

The best attended music event to date as 375,000 people gather to hear Robbie Williams in 2003.

Sunshine in the park for the crowd of nearly 400,000 Robbie Williams fans in 2003 cannot fail to appreciate the setting as well as the star.

Queen arrive by helicopter and head for a safe landing on the Knebworth lawns.

The series of Sonisphere concerts between 2004 and 2009 have brought the steady beat of rock back to Knebworth.

*Knebworth House, The Lytton-Cobbold family (p.232)*

It's been 40 years since Knebworth House held its first rock concert and in that time the greats of rock, jazz and pop have all played there. From the first show in 1974 with the Allman Brothers, Van Morrison and the Doobie brothers, to the Sonisphere rock and Eastern Electric dance events of the past few years to the plans for a landmark 40th anniversary rock event in 2014; the gothic house backdrop has become emblematic of the best in music.

For many music lovers, the Knebworth concert they attended in their youth defined their generation. In the 1970s, Pink Floyd, The Rolling Stones, Frank Zappa, Genesis and Led Zeppelin all played Knebworth. In 1986 Queen played their last ever gig with Freddie Mercury at Knebworth. The 1990 charity concert *'Live at Knebworth'* featured every major British rock act, including Paul McCartney, Elton John and Eric Clapton, and was broadcast live around the world on MTV. In 1996 Oasis booked a 250,000 ticket show over two-nights, defining the Britpop era in a weekend.

Today's concerts are organised by Martha Lytton-Cobbold and her team, including the record-breaking Robbie Williams concert in 2003. The Robbie Williams concert remains the largest music event ever held in the UK, attracting a staggering 375,000 people over the three nights of the concert.

The Park's natural bowl and easy access from the A1M makes an ideal venue for large events. Most performers and bands with ambition want to play Knebworth. And once you've played Knebworth, as Robbie said, *"Where do you go from here?"*

# War House

Jules Hudson is a familiar face to millions of TV viewers as a presenter of *Countryfile* and *Escape to the Country*. His involvement with the BBC1 archaeology series *Dig 1940* tapped into a personal interest in military history, so *Hudson's* asked him to mark the anniversary of the outbreak of the First World War with a visit to *Duty Calls*, a series of exhibitions and events at country houses in Yorkshire.

**Photos:** Nigel Gibson & Linda Croose-Smith

**Jules and curator Chris Ridgway discuss the changes in the park at Castle Howard during WWI with the Atlas Fountain and Hawksmoor's Pyramid in the background.**

The First World War touched every community in Britain. Thousands of memorials in our towns, cities, villages and churches are a silent testament to the sacrifice made by a generation who found themselves caught up in the tragedy of the first truly global conflict the world has ever seen. Men and women were drawn into factories, farming, the mines, forests and, of course, the misery of the front lines both on land, at sea and, for the first time, in the air. They came from every corner of the British Isles and its commonwealth, and from all walks of life: butchers, bakers, butlers, housemaids, engineers, teachers, the unemployed and who had just left school. The rich, the poor and the privileged were plunged into a national effort that mobilised itself for a new kind of conflict, that of Total War. Every aspect of Britain's society and industry became committed to

victory despite the most appalling losses. Some 9 million men died from all sides along the tortured ribbon of the Western Front, which stretched for some 485 miles from the sand dunes of Belgium to the Swiss Alps.

The casualty lists paid no regard to class or fortune; throughout history, warfare itself has always been a brutal and unforgiving leveller. When we look back at the enormous changes in society that the First World War ushered in, it is perhaps the often-rarified world of the country house, based as it was upon the remnants of Britain's former feudal system, that has become the barometer for that change. ITV's hit fictional series *Downton Abbey* has introduced a new generation to the stark divisions between those 'upstairs', and those who served them from below. In reality, by the War's end these divisions were so

**James Paine's classical Palladian facade at Nostell Priory.**

altered, that for many country estates it marked the beginning of the end.

Preparations are well underway to commemorate the centenary of the start of the war in 2014. The changing fortunes of many of our greatest country houses and their families are once again the subject of much re-appraisal and study. The *Duty Calls* initiative in Yorkshire has set about the task of revisiting many of the stories that can still teach us much about the role our country houses and those who lived and worked in them played in the conflict and other wars as well. Earlier this year I had the chance to see four of them for myself, spread about a county that has long been home to some of our oldest and finest family seats. Castle Howard, Nostell Priory, Kiplin Hall and Brodsworth Hall have different stories to tell which offer a fascinating insight into the country house at war.

**Brodsworth's Curator, Caroline Carr-Whitworth, tells the story of Amy Tyreman, aged 11, whose tireless knitting for the troops was rewarded with 28 letters from grateful soldiers at the front.**

Castle Howard, for all the grace that the architect John Vanbrugh conferred upon it, is in many ways an enigma. The common story of a family brought to a standstill with the loss of its heir is not the one played out here. Nonetheless, of the 9th Earl of Carlisle's six sons, only two were alive in 1914 and in 1917, his youngest, Michael, was killed at Passchendaele.

The estate itself was reluctantly given over to producing food as enemy U-boats in the Atlantic wrought an increasingly appalling toll on allied shipping. Although Castle Howard itself was never requisitioned, its horses were, a common feature of many country estates and one familiar from the critically acclaimed *War Horse*. Remarkably however, archive correspondence reveals that they expected them back.

Refugees from Belgium also moved onto the estate, and their letters and diaries reflect another side of the human cost of the war in Europe that is often overlooked, as we focus on the front lines.

**Curator Chris Ridgway shows Jules Hudson a First World War bugle with papers, diaries and letters in the Muniment Room at Castle Howard.**

**Above: The soaring splendour of Vanbrugh's Great Hall at Castle Howard captures the imagination of every visitor. Jules is looking up to the Venetian frescoes by Pellegrini, damaged by fire in 1940, and the restored dome.**

**Left: Part of Castle Howard's *Duty Calls* exhibition chronicles the wartime story of Michael Howard, killed in 1917. Both surviving Howard sons fought in France.**

**Red Poppies & White Butterflies,** the exhibition at Nostell Priory, aims to capture the wartime memories of visitors with stories of participants written on poppies (those killed) and butterflies (survivors) by their descendants.

**Robert Adam's cool interior sets off Chippendale's chairs in the Top Hall at Nostell Priory.**

Nostell Priory was a house that also saw its fair share of upheaval within the Winn family. Their eldest son Rowland was thought to have been killed in action, but survived and fell in love with chorus girl Nellie Greene. Despite the obvious society questions, he married her in 1915 amidst a flurry of newspaper gossip. He joined the Royal Flying Corps in 1916 and survived the war, eventually becoming the 3rd Baron St Oswald. Today, the family records have been re-assessed under the enthusiastic eye of Exhibition Curator Sarah Burnage. I joined a group for a seminar exploring the effects of the war on the family and the house, as well as providing access to the service records held by the National Archives online. I tapped on the keys and found the report of my grandmother's brother, killed whilst serving with the Navy in the eastern Mediterranean. Opening the archives and inviting locals to come forward with their tales of life at Nostell has revealed much that is new, and has sparked plans to extend the appeal for yet more information from the public in piecing together the Priory's wider history. →

**Book a special Duty Calls mid-week stay at the National Trust's Middlethorpe Hotel & Spa from March to September 2014, Sunday to Thursday. Quote Hudson's for special rate of £149pp per night or £169pp single occupancy. Included is a deluxe period double or twin room, early morning tea, breakfast, Luxury Spa facilities, parking and three course candlelit dinner for £43pp. The deal includes a 2 for 1 entry at Brodsworth Hall, Kiplin Hall, Nostell Priory and Newby Hall and a free one-day York Pass for entry to Fairfax House, Castle Howard or NT Beningbrough Hall. Book now and discover some of the secrets of wartime country houses. Subject to availability.**

Both Castle Howard and Nostell Priory are, to most eyes, archetypal country houses. Grand and imposing, they dominate the landscapes that have been so carefully created around them. Kiplin Hall, however, is an altogether different proposition. Built back in the early 1600s, its looks have changed little, even if its size has somewhat altered thanks to later re-modelling. Nonetheless, this pretty building is a welcoming house that was home to an extraordinary woman. In 1916 Bridget Talbot became a nurse and served with Mrs Watkins in Italy, looking after the wounded and running canteens. Fiercely independent, she never married, despite her beguiling looks, yet she eventually returned to live at Kiplin and bequest it to the Trust that now maintains it. The attic rooms provide a fascinating exhibition of Bridget and Kiplin's history.

The loss of garden staff at Kiplin to the trenches in 1914 was to herald the decline of the kitchen garden in the 20th century.

A tin sailor from HMS Dreadnought, the archetypal battleship of WWI, from Kiplin Hall's toy collection.

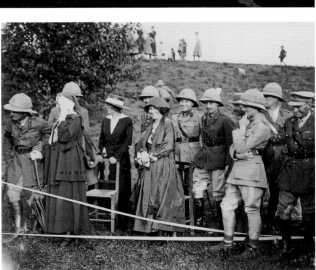

Bridget Talbot (smiling, centre left) in Italy, and (above) Jules holds her WWI medals amidst other memorabilia on display in Kiplin Hall.

**Actor Naomi Broadhead in the part of Molly Hindle, parlour maid during the Second World War. Acting out period roles from Broadworth's wartime history has proved an important channel for sharing memories for the oral history programme.**

Brodsworth Hall is the youngest of the great houses I visited. Classically Victorian, it was designed from the outset as a family seat that borrowed much from the architecture of its neighbours. With service quarters, a library, great hall and dining room, it represents the Victorian ideal of a new-build country home. Curator Caroline Carr-Whitworth looks after one of the country's biggest oral history records from former owners and estate workers. The staff lists were much depleted, first by those who volunteered in 1914 for their part in a war 'that would all be over by Christmas', and then by those conscripted in 1916. However it is the fortunes of Brodsworth's young chauffeur and cowman that I found particularly intriguing. Having joined up as privates and survived the trenches, they both rose through the ranks to become Captains. Catapulted into a different class, neither could have returned to their old jobs 'below stairs'. The last records of them are requests for references as post war London Cab drivers. It is a sobering thought that, having been decorated and promoted in the struggle for freedom, they were unable to conquer the class system upon their return.

*Duty Calls* is the perfect title for these exhibitions. Duty and an individual's sense of it, no matter which level of society they were drawn from, is writ large across the horizon of so many personal accounts. At the start of the War, the country house represented a microcosm of all that was good and bad about British society 100 years ago. At its end four years later, once again the country house served as a window on a world that had changed forever, for better and for worse. So next time you find yourself with an afternoon to spare, drop by and visit one of the houses featuring *Duty Calls* exhibitions. As you'll discover, whilst those who lived through the First World War have now sadly passed away, there remains much to see that we should remember.

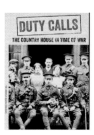
*Duty Calls: the Country House in Time of War. A series of exhibitions exploring the impact of war on country houses and their communities, funded by the Heritage Lottery fund.*

**LOTTERY FUNDED**

PHOTO: JUSTIN BARTON

# A future for St Giles

Nick Ashley-Cooper is the 12th Earl of Shaftesbury, current senior member of one of our great political dynasties. But in 2005, he was a music promoter and DJ in New York with no expectation of returning to the UK, let alone of embarking on the biggest restoration of an important English country house this century at St. Giles House in Dorset.

**Nick and Dinah Ashley-Cooper, the Earl & Countess of Shaftesbury at St Giles today.**

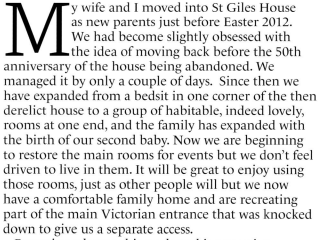

My wife and I moved into St Giles House as new parents just before Easter 2012. We had become slightly obsessed with the idea of moving back before the 50th anniversary of the house being abandoned. We managed it by only a couple of days. Since then we have expanded from a bedsit in one corner of the then derelict house to a group of habitable, indeed lovely, rooms at one end, and the family has expanded with the birth of our second baby. Now we are beginning to restore the main rooms for events but we don't feel driven to live in them. It will be great to enjoy using those rooms, just as other people will but we now have a comfortable family home and are recreating part of the main Victorian entrance that was knocked down to give us a separate access.

Restoring a house this neglected is a massive undertaking. Nothing had been touched since Victorian times. Our ambition was to re-establish the relationship between our family and the house which had begun as far back as the 14th century. It was the spark of an idea built around the feeling that I did not want the house to fall down on my watch.

The house was in a pretty terrible state. The roofs leaked and dry rot had savaged many rooms in the house destroying large sections of plasterwork. But we were lucky. Miraculously, some of the remarkable 17th century decorative plasterwork ceilings had

survived, even in the Dining Room where much of the room around had disintegrated. This ceiling gave us hope. In certain areas we found supporting beams that were nearly 50% rotten; we knew we were intervening just in time.

The St Giles House that is emerging from the scaffolding is roughly the house built by the 1st Earl of Shaftesbury in 1650. Parts of it belong to an earlier 16th century manor house; parts of it are much later and date from the larger house which stood here until the 1970s. But as a whole it conveys the character of a family house where every generation has added or subtracted something.

I was aware of the house as I was growing up - my father, the 10th Earl, moved the estate office into the basement – but it was a shuttered house, empty since 1961. My father was consumed with the problem of what to do with the house. His own father had died when he was 8 and he spent much of his time with his grandparents at St Giles. These grandparents, my great-grandparents, were born in the 1870s and lived through the final flowering of the English country house. From the Edwardian heyday to the period after the Second World War came massive social change, the sale of other family properties and the advent of death duties. The world inhabited by my great-grandfather at his death in 1961 was a very different one from his inheritance in 1886. I have

The restored South Front, stripped of early 19th century render, shows the beauty of the 17th century brickwork. New bricks for the restoration had to be sourced in Suffolk, where clay from the other end of the same clay beds as the originals were fired in a traditional oak-fired kiln to achieve a perfect match.

Controversially, the Dining Room, where only the ceiling, doorcases and overmantel survive will be stabilised in its current state rather than reconstructed, putting back the pictures and bringing the room alive and remembering not only the glory of the original interior but also the years of neglect, dust and grime that interceded.

The double Drawing Room retains much of the remarkable 17th century plasterwork commissioned by the 1st Earl of Shaftesbury, founder of the Whig party.

The North Drawing Room, where a copy of the original red silk damask will replace a later green wallpaper. For the new generation, authenticity is a way of exercising personal taste.

the impression that the house had become a series of grand rooms stuffed with furniture which had outlived their usefulness. For my father, it must have been impossible to imagine a modern role for a house like St Giles. I have a sense that his was the generation caught in the middle and he could only see that places like this had lost their purpose.

He took two major decisions. The first was drastically to reduce the size of the house by knocking down part of the south wing and the entire north wing as well as many of the Victorian embellishments. It was clearly difficult for him and he never talked about it but his careful photographic documenting of the work suggests a view to the future. He also removed the 1820 render, which was austere and trapped moisture, revealing the mellow 17th century brickwork.

He sold around 80% of the contents of the house, keeping examples of furniture, paintings and tapestries that would represent the house and the family history. Even so, when we arrived, the rooms were filled with debris; we moved 60 bags of rubbish from above the ceiling of the South Drawing Room. The Library was the first room we tackled. It was painful to see books dating back to the philosopher 3rd Earl scattered all over the floor, but thankfully their condition was relatively stable. We thought our first plans were ambitious, but we have done far more than we thought possible already. We didn't think we'd be seeing the Brussels tapestries rehung in The Tapestry Room; but it is nearly ready for them again.

My personal connection with this place now is stronger because I have made a choice to embrace it and discovered the house and its history for myself.

Most people have to deal with their parents' plans. For me, it was all fresh. We are a more pragmatic generation and can get stuck in in a way my father's generation never could and we have new technologies to make it all cheaper to run. We have begun to solve the problem of heating and lighting this big house with the help of a ground source heating system which employs several kilometres of piping under the lake.

For the future we are learning from how other people have revitalised great houses. We like bringing people together in this beautiful secluded setting and we have some strong family themes to follow: philosophy, politics and social reform. I am passionate about running so we organised the first Grand Shaftesbury Run in 2013. We had 600-800 people in park this year and would like 10 times that number. In the house, we want to host weddings, parties, bespoke events, dinners and group visits though we have no plans for general public opening. We do everything ourselves. My wife Dinah is a vet and we are very much a team; she has embraced all the uncertainties with open arms and has followed her dreams by founding the St Giles stud.

My children will never know life without this house and will be the first generation to grow up here since my great-grandparents' time. When I put myself in my father's shoes, I sympathise with the decisions he made. The work he undertook must have taken as much energy as we are now putting into restoring the house but at the end, the house still had no future. It is a huge satisfaction that we are now able to give it one.

*St Giles House, The Earl of Shaftesbury (p.219)*

Much of the 18th century landscape garden designed by the 4th Countess and Henry Flitcroft survives and is being restored with help from Natural England.

The Triumphal Arch once formed part of a route through the pleasure grounds and an eyecatcher across the lake.

The Sunken Garden (above), a creation of the 9th Earl, is now restored and looks to a long beech avenue which may one day be finished with a memorial to Nick Ashley-Cooper's brother Anthony who died unexpectedly in 2005. Centre stage will be a copy of the statue of 'Eros' from Piccadilly Circus, erected in memory of 7th Earl, whose social reform programme transformed Victorian working conditions. The statue is one of 10 cast from the original mould found in the V&A.

Stirling Castle, one of Scotland's grandest castles and its most strategic, dominating the central lowlands and the crossing of the River Forth (*p.348*).

# The Apprentice

Craft skills, so essential to the traditional maintenance of historic buildings, have always needed a traditional apprentice system to allow experience to pass from one generation to another. Historic Scotland are investing in a new generation of apprentices.

From the materials used to the skills employed, those who work to conserve Scotland's built heritage take a very traditional approach. Modern methods may be quicker and cheaper at times, but historic buildings have very specific requirements when it comes to conservation and it is essential that any work carried out on the existing fabric of a building takes a 'like-for-like' approach.

This is an approach which is of particular importance to Historic Scotland, one of the largest employers of traditional skills apprentices in the UK. The government agency recently took on 18 new traditional skills apprentices – the biggest single intake in Historic Scotland's history – all of whom get to work on some of Scotland's most

The Engine Shed in Stirling is the site of the new Scottish National Conservation Centre after the confirmation of a £3.5 million grant from the Heritage Lottery Fund. Pictured here with Fiona Hyslop, Cabinet Secretary for Culture and External Affairs (centre) are Historic Scotland apprentices Danny Garrity, Kieran Whyte and Paul Montgomery (Stirling Castle) and Michael Doy (Doune Castle), Jack Suthers (Perth Depot), Michael Renshaw (St Andrews Cathedral) and Liam Grubb (Aberdour Castle).

Historic Scotland apprentice stonemason Danny Garrity at the Engine Shed with drawings of the proposed design.

important historic buildings, from Fort George and Melrose Abbey to Edinburgh Castle and Glasgow Cathedral.

*"It is essential that the traditional skillsets which Historic Scotland already utilises are kept alive by being passed on to the next generation,"* says Ian Walker, Building Crafts Development Manager at Historic Scotland. *"It is wonderful to see such enthusiasm from our young apprentices to pick up these skills and use them to help safeguard our built heritage. They all have promising careers ahead of them."*

Historic Scotland has a National Conservation Centre – with bases in Elgin and in Stirling – which champions traditional skills in areas including stonemasonry and joinery. Dedicated lecturers, training officers and mentors ensure that apprentices receive the best qualifications in their area and while most go on to work for Historic Scotland, many have set up their own businesses after graduating.

Twenty-year-old Ross Kennedy from Stromness is a first-year apprentice stonemason with Historic Scotland and works on a number of properties within Orkney's UNESCO World Heritage Site. He says: *"I grew up on Orkney so it's great to be able to give something back and it feels special to work on these amazing sites. I've been learning so much. Recently I was helping to remove some light graffiti which had been scratched onto the Dwarfie Stane on Hoy. We used a brush of dried heather to remove it which is an amazing traditional technique."*

After gathering at the National Conservation Centre at Forth Valley College in Stirling for an induction, the 18 apprentices have been posted to every corner of Scotland, with most of them working on sites near to where they live. They are learning their trade at Historic Scotland properties including Blackness, Rothesay, Doune and Stirling Castles.

Orkney's Dwarfie Stane dates from 3,000 BC.

# Garden for All Seasons

Lawrence and Elizabeth Banks are some of the most influential gardeners of their generation. Elizabeth retired as President of the Royal Horticultural Society in July 2013 where her husband is an honorary Vice-President. Lawrence describes how they continue the family gardening tradition at Hergest Croft in Herefordshire, which is at once a collectors' garden, a famous arboretum, a plantsman's paradise and a delight at all times of year.

# Four Top Trees

*Pterycarya macroptera*

*Davidia involucrata var. vilmoriniana*

*Acer pectinatum ssp. forrestii*

*Betula albo sinensis*

**W**hilst Hergest Croft is most important as a garden of trees and shrubs, it is unusual, if not unique, among private gardens in that we still maintain the Edwardian garden created by my grandparents, William and Dorothy, from 1895 onwards in all its aspects including borders, bedding, rockery, bulbs and a traditional kitchen garden.

# *Spring*

Spring is a good place to start as we have a letter from Dorothy in 1895 about planting bulbs for their new garden saying *"the great planting time of Autumn has arrived and we have been busy burying for their winter sleep all kinds of daffodils, crocuses, snowdrops, tulips, blue squilly hepaticas, anemones and aconites with which we hope to see a new Garden radiant in spring"*. These plantings have developed for 120 years and are a joy with a mixture of fritillaries, dog tooth violets, daffodils, snowdrops and anemones under the 200-year-old beech trees. Another of the pleasures of spring are the double borders under the 100-year-old apple avenue in the Kitchen garden. Such borders can be something of a horticultural cliché but the succession of hellebores, daffodils and tulips, finishing with a wild

riot of self sown columbines, is an exceptional pleasure.

William Banks' great passion was collecting new and rare trees. He was fortunate to live at a time when the rush of introductions from western China, many found by Ernest 'Chinese' Wilson, was reaching British gardens. The most romantic of these is the pocket handkerchief tree *Davidia involucrata* which was involved in a race between the nurseries of Veitch in England and Vilmorin in France to be the first to offer this literally fabulous plant. Wilson's first attempt to collect seed was thwarted as the tree had been cut down the previous week. We have both the Veitch and Vilmorin collections both planted in 1905 from the original Chinese seeds. They may well be amongst the largest specimens in the world. They give constant delight to children seeing the origin of paper tissues!

Azaleas are bankers' taste often planted in clashing colours on a grand scale and my grandfather, himself a banker, did just that following William Robinson's view that *"nature is a good colourist"*. However my father, Dick, not being a banker, could not stand the effect and spent many hours with my mother reorganising the planting to produce the soothing colour scheme that we have today. The colours are complemented by ravishing scents in mid May. He also planted a valley of rhododendrons in Park Wood that has been described as the closest thing to the Himalayas in Britain; it benefits from our generous rainfall that prompted one visitor, a collector of Himalayan plants, to say to my father during a downpour, *"Dick, I can see why rhododendrons do so well here – you have a monsoon climate."*

# Summer

High summer is not a good season for flowering trees and shrubs so other plants take over. The double herbaceous borders, 30 yards long, date from the 1930s and start with huge old clumps of oriental poppies, possibly 'Beauty of Livermere', that look startling under a thundery sky. They continue through July and August with a succession of different plants, including one of my special favourites, the often-neglected herbaceous *Clematis recta purpurea* with its tall head of feathery flowers. There is a good selection of old fashioned roses and more recently David Austin's English roses that do especially well here though we are certainly not natural rose country.

# Autumn

In the autumn the National Collections of birch and maples come into their own with a blaze of colour. The birches are all shades of yellow shimmering in the late sunshine whilst the maples add the red tones, the best of which for me is *Acer maximowiczianum* (*nikoense*), a seedling of a plant probably collected by Augustine Henry in China. There are many other great autumn trees and shrubs that add to the effect; some years ago we found that one of our *Stewartia monodelpha* had almost black autumn colour and we immediately named it after our local ghost as 'Black Dog' and others tempt me to add to the kennel with 'Red Dog' and 'Hot Dog' a riot of red and gold. The collection of Sorbus adds berries to the meal. Finally amongst the best are the dark red *Neoshirakia japonica*, the Japanese tallow tree, and the brilliant scarlet *Disanthus cercidifolius* that shines like rubies in the low autumn sunshine.

*Hergest Croft Gardens, Herefordshire (p.269)*

# *Winter*

For something entirely different, Elizabeth created a parterre in a place where almost everything refused to grow. We call it the Slate Garden as it is centered on a giant fir cone created by Joe Smith from Welsh slate and surrounded by box and *Lonicera nitida* with not a flower in sight.

# The Downton Effect

Francine Stock, novelist, writer, broadcaster and presenter of Radio 4's The Film Programme talks to The Countess of Carnarvon about what the popularity of Downton Abbey has done for Highclere Castle.

*"My husband has said many times we are stewards and that's how we think of it, we are tenants for our life"*

Fiona, Countess of Carnarvon, is the confident chatelaine of Highclere Castle alongside her husband Geordie, the 8th Earl, and their teenage son, Edward. Millions around the world recognise the house with its distinctive Gothic turrets for a parallel fictional existence, as the seat of the Grantham family in television drama Downton Abbey.

That hugely successful narrative is for Lady Carnarvon, the latest of many. *"This house spins on stories. History is really important to me, both the timeline and the different stories, because you learn so much."* The Victorian exterior conceals earlier structures, Georgian and medieval. For 800 years the owners were the Bishops of Winchester, including William of Wykeham, founder of Winchester College and New College, Oxford. The Carnarvon family have lived at Highclere since 1679, including the 5th Earl and his heiress wife, Almina, who financed Howard Carter's 1922 excavation of the tomb of Tutankhamun. The house is steeped in tales of generosity, sacrifice and intrigue.

The present incumbents are old friends of Downton's creator, Julian (Lord) Fellowes. Lady Carnarvon always leaves guidebooks in guestrooms so Fellowes maybe dreamt up Downton's American heiress Cora when reading about Lady Almina. The illegitimate daughter of Sir Alfred de Rothschild, Almina brought a generous dowry to the Castle; during the First World War she turned Highclere into a hospital for wounded soldiers.

Up to 1600 visitors a day now trace parallels between the fictional Granthams and the Carnarvons. They can wander through the library where Hugh Bonneville as Lord Grantham muses on his tenure, as the real inhabitants must, looking out over the thousand acres of Capability Brown designed parkland. *"My husband has said many times we are stewards and that's how we think of it, we are tenants for our life,"* says Lady Carnarvon.

From the moment visitors arrive, though, history must be divided from fiction. *"The guides welcome them and say 'this is where Maggie Smith sits when she's*

## "When the ratings for Downton Abbey beat X-Factor we knew there'd be a second series"

*filming Downton Abbey but it's also the library where Disraeli and Salisbury had many discussions' to keep the distinction."*

Once Downton Abbey was declared a success (*"when the ratings beat X-Factor, we knew there'd be a second series"*) the house adjusted to an annual schedule of January to July preparations and filming, alongside the staple earners of weddings, charity events and open days. The location required little modification, with filming mainly in the expansive saloon, drawing-room and library; kitchen scenes were shot at Ealing studios. Potted palms were imported for Edwardian ambiance and the odd contemporary lampshade replaced with something more 'droopy' but Lady Carnarvon maintains most furnishings onscreen are as found. She keeps a watchful eye lest powerful lights damage precious paintings or original wallpaper. Crowds of crew and visitors mean extra wear and tear both inside to carpets and out in the garden. *"Footpaths end up getting trodden because that's where someone (in the series) sat!"*

In her biography of Almina, Lady Carnarvon chronicled Highclere during the First World War and the excitement and tragedy of the Egyptian discoveries. She later studied the decline in fortunes after World War II. Finances improved once Lady Carnarvon's husband and father-in-law began to trade on the Tutankhamun connection but the continuing international success of Downton Abbey

→

is of a different order, funding essential repairs and bringing activity back to levels the 5th Earl might have appreciated. *"As they went into the First World War, there were about 250 families round and about for whom he felt responsible"*. And now? *"It's different but there's probably 40-50 (paid) guides part-time in shifts for whom Highclere is a big part of their lives and then there's the team in the gift shop, the gardeners, the chefs, the banqueting ….builders, plumbers, all local people."*

An online ticketing service allows visitors from the USA, Australia, Europe and Japan and more to book timed entry up to six months in advance. *"Now we know we're consistently full and it's probably going to be the same for the next few years so my husband and I can spend money today knowing that it's going to be replaced. We can also continue to employ people here and even support the older members of the staff… that's what these communities are about…We've never got any more cash in the bank than before, you simply spend it at a faster rate".*

For all her enthusiasm, Lady Carnarvon, an accountant by training, is also a strategist. *"You have to look 30 years ahead because you're trying to make this house relevant to today's local and national community in order that it has a future. If it's a white elephant, just lived in by rich toffs, it won't have a future, not long-term, it will just pass from hand to hand and then be destroyed."*

That wider perspective is what she believes differentiates the Carnarvons from the fictional Granthams, obsessed with family, romance and inheritance: *"Almina and her husband looked out: they took the house and thought what could they do for other people. In a drama you're naturally looking in to the small trivia of life. Almina would have dealt with (scheming lady's maid) O'Brien in a matter of seconds and moved on! In that way I find it slightly smaller in scale and when I look at the house and what happened in the 20s and 30s – the beauty, the pageantry and glamour of the parties here was beyond the budget of a TV company".*

Away from the lustrous history, the present fame of Highclere entails instant recognition for the Carnarvons and some loss of personal privacy. *"For sure… now I'm more conscious that I should have brushed my hair... Geordie and I were pulling out ragwort from a bank yesterday and chopping down brambles and we were dressed in old trousers and T-shirts...and that to me is absolute heaven!"* Such off-duty moments are rare; for now, that's the inevitable cost of success.

The Downton Abbey Christmas Special in 2012 spread the Downton effect north of the Border. The Duke of Argyll reports a significant increase in visitors at his home, Inveraray Castle, in summer 2013 as fans continue to come in search of Duneagle Castle where the fictional Crawley family spent a Christmas sporting holiday.

Photographs from the series courtesy of Carnival Films and Television. Highclere series images, photographer: Nick Briggs. Inveraray series images, photographer: Nick Wall. Interview images, photographer: Charlie Hopkinson. Other images ©Highclere Castle.

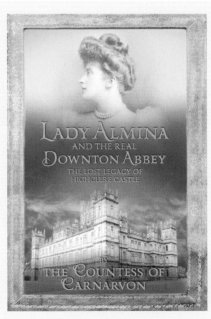

**Lady Almina and the Real Downton Abbey is available from Hudson's eShop at www.hudsonsheritage.com**

# TARR ON THE ROAD

# Chalking up the Miles

Derek Tarr rambles around chalk downs and country houses of the West Sussex and Hampshire border.

Goodwood House.

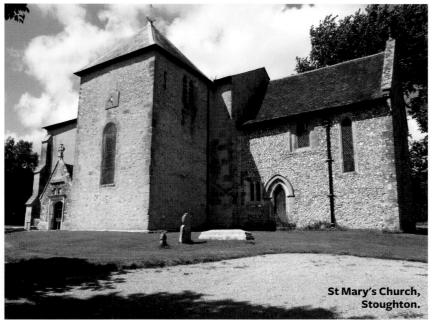

St Mary's Church, Stoughton.

## WALK 1

### East Lavant to Rowland's Castle

**12 miles approx**

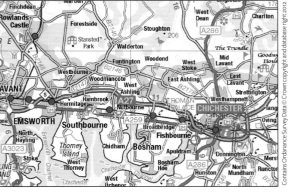

I began in the pretty village of East Lavant and headed north on the West Sussex Literary Trail, a route opened in 2007 to link places associated with famous poets and authors such as Shelley and Galsworthy.

After a mile and a half of pleasant walking between hedgerows entwined with flowering bindweed, I turned west and followed the Binderton Lane track and reached the Kingley Vale National Nature Reserve. This Site of Special Scientific Interest managed by Natural England is one of the finest yew forests in Europe. Climbing beneath the canopy of ancient trees, I passed below the summit of Bow Hill and arrived at a clearing where I came across the Devil's Humps, two Bronze Age round barrows.

## DEREK'S WALKS
## DAY BY DAY

The gentle countryside north of Chichester, with hills, forests, views and heritage grand or commonplace, was the setting for my circular walk.

**Photos:** Nicola Burford

Woodland path near Stoughton.

> ## *"I walked through fields of ripening corn and along leafy lanes until I arrived at the splendid Stansted Park"*

From here there are splendid views over Chichester and its harbour. After a downhill walk I approached the village of Stoughton where I came across a reminder of past conflicts; a memorial to a Polish RAF pilot who crashed his Hurricane in a field by the village following aerial combat with a German Me 109 in 1940.

As it was lunchtime I stopped at The Hare and Hounds where I enjoyed a ploughman's washed down with a superb pint of Dark Star Brewery's Hophead. A short stroll brought me to the beautiful 11th century church before I continued on my route.

For the next hour I walked through fields of ripening corn and along leafy lanes until I arrived at the splendid Stansted Park. The estate has had many owners since it was recorded in the Domesday Book a thousand years ago and is currently managed by the Stansted Park Foundation whose Chairman is Myles, 12th Earl of Bessborough.

As I approached the house I saw, to my delight, a game of cricket in progress on the front lawn, a tradition on summer Sundays since the 1750s. The original house was destroyed by fire in 1900 and rebuilt in 1903. Among the fascinating contents are the Lumley Tapestries hanging on the staircase depicting scenes from the Duke of Marlborough's campaigns and in the Music Room, a chandelier holding unusual black candles.

The Waygood-Otis passenger lift, one of the earliest surviving examples of its kind and installed when the house was rebuilt, connects the upper floors to the basement.

These rooms were state-of-the-art servants quarters when built and the design improved the quality of their lives. Today they give us an insight into life below stairs a hundred years ago.

In the grounds stands the beautiful chapel of St Paul with its stunning blue and gold ceiling, where the poet John Keats was inspired to write The Eve of St Agnes in 1819.

I departed Stansted in the late afternoon sunshine and walked the mile long Avenue to the town of Rowland's Castle and the comfortable Robin Hood Inn, my resting place for the night.

The Golden Gates at Uppark.

Above: Stansted House and Keats' plaque at Stansted Chapel. Below, from left to right: A servant's bedroom and kitchen at Stansted House. The beautiful ceiling decoration at Stansted Chapel.

## WALK 2
### Rowland's Castle to South Harting
**9 miles approx**

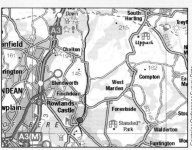

Contains Ordnance Survey Data
© Crown copyright and database right 2012

Following a hearty breakfast, I headed north on the Sussex Border Path and after passing through the village of Finchdean I arrived at Chalton. This delightful village has a 13th century church and the thatched Red Lion is thought to be the oldest inn in Hampshire. Continuing north easterly I passed through Harehurst Wood before arriving at Uppark, home to the Meade-Fetherstonhaugh family but donated to the National Trust in 1954.

After a hot climb up the steep driveway, I entered through The Golden Gates and reached The Eastern Pavilion, now the restaurant and shop, which is connected to the house by an underground tunnel. The house was once home to Lady Emma Hamilton, the mistress of Lord Nelson. It was also familiar to the author H G Wells, whose parents worked at the estate in the mid 19th century.

The 30th August 1989 was a bleak day in Uppark's history as fire ravaged the building. At the height of the blaze 27 fire-engines and 156 firemen from 3 county brigades were at the scene and volunteers formed a human chain to rescue the precious contents from the flames. Remarkably, much of the Georgian interior and the fine Grand Tour collection was saved or able to be restored. However the Meade-Fetherstonhaugh family possessions were entirely destroyed. The National Trust undertook the mammoth task of rebuilding Uppark and restoring it to its original splendour. The doors were opened to the public again in 1995. Today, many rooms have photographs of the damage caused to them so that visitors can compare their current condition with that following the devastation.

From here I walked an easy mile downhill to the delightful town of South Harting to end the day.

Derek at Uppark and the church at Chalton (right).

South Harting from the South Downs Way. Left: The entrance to West Dean Gardens.

## WALK 3
## South Harting to Charlton
### 10 miles approx

That easy downhill walk of the previous evening became the stiff uphill walk to begin the day. On the ridge I headed east along the South Downs Way, a trail which follows the line of a former drove road, eventually reaching Beacon Hill. Here I lingered for a while and surveyed the magnificent views.

The Spinnaker Tower in Portsmouth was clearly visible with the Isle of White standing proud beyond. I continued on The Way for about a mile before turning south through Buriton Farm and close by Telegraph House

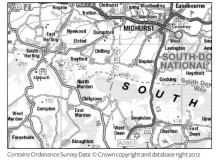

Contains Ordanance Survey Data © Crown copyright and database right 2012

where the philosopher Bertrand Russell lived and founded his experimental Beacon Hill School.

Walking through peaceful countryside of field and forest, I passed by The Royal

Oak at Hooksway and the White Horse Inn at Chilgrove, both excellent venues for refreshment, and arrived at West Dean via the Whitedown Plantation. It was time for lunch and the newly refurbished Dean Ale and Cider House was the perfect setting.

During the afternoon I visited the West Dean Gardens. In 1964 Edward James, the hereditary owner of the West Dean estate, set up a trust to transform the Edwardian house into a college offering courses in horticulture, arts and crafts as well as the maintaining and developing the gardens and managing 6000 acres of land. During the great storm of 1987 winds of over 100 miles an hour battered Britain. Eighteen people lost their lives and 15 million trees were uprooted in the worst storm since 1703. West Dean was badly damaged by the magnitude of the winds.

Once the storm abated, the trustees took stock of the damage and decided to use the opportunity to develop the gardens and to expand visitor numbers.

A visitor centre was opened in 1996 and a programme of events has been introduced including a renowned three day festival, 'The Chilli Fiesta', dedicated to the fiery pepper.

I continued my journey east and after passing through the village of Singleton I arrived at Charlton and my stop for the night, The Fox Goes Free. This charming 17th century inn was the venue in 1915 for the first ever meeting of the Women's Institute in England.

**Derek outside the Fox Goes Free in Charlton.**

**Above (clockwise): The old water pump at South Harting; Singleton's pub signpost; Chillies in the Victorian Garden at West Dean.**

**West Dean Gardens.**

# HUDSON's HERITAGE *Explorer*

Hatfield House, Hertford

# An exciting touring pass

## Opening the door to the country's heritage attractions

2014

**HUDSON's HERITAGE Explorer**
Supported by THE TREASURE HOUSES OF ENGLAND
**CHILD 14-DAY PASS**

**HUDSON's HERITAGE Explorer**
2014
Supported by THE TREASURE HOUSES OF ENGLAND
**ADULT 28-DAY PASS**

3, 7, 14 or 28-day passes

Visit as many participating attractions as you wish during the fixed-day period

Prices start from just £49.00 per Adult

Complimentary full-colour guidebook

Available to buy online and in person at selected outlets

*Amazing value! Visit heritage attractions for less than £6.40 per day\* SAVE MORE WITH EVERY VISIT*

### *www.hudsons-explorer.com*

RHS Garden Wisley, Surrey    Bamburgh Castle, Northumberland    Roman Baths, Somerset    Portsmouth Historic Dockyard

**STATELY HOMES • HISTORIC HOUSES • CASTLES • GARDENS • ABBEYS & CATHEDRALS • WORLD HERITAGE SITES**

\*Based on average daily use of a 28-day Adult Hudson's Heritage Explorer pass (£179). All details correct at time of going to press (December 2013). Please check website www.hudsons-explorer.com from January 2014 for more information. The images and the pass shown here are for illustrative purposes only.

**Above: A cart and the smithy at Weald & Downland Museum.**
**Left: The museum's mill pond, and below, the Stables at Goodwood.**

Horses and riders gather at Goodwood.

## WALK 4
## Charlton to East Lavant
**8 miles approx**

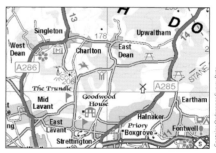

Following a superb breakfast I left Charlton and retraced my steps back to Singleton. Here I visited the Weald & Downland Open Air Museum which was created to preserve threatened vernacular buildings from the South East of England by dismantling and moving them to this 50 acre site. In a fascinating group of buildings, I watched craftspeople demonstrate their skills, keeping alive age-old traditions such as the milling of flour at the old water mill and the forging of metal in the smithy forge.

→

The racecourse at Goodwood from the Trundle.

My route now led me south as I ascended Knight's Hill. My only companions were the many pheasants that waddled along in front of me unperturbed. After a mile or so I reached the top of the Trundle, a hill from where I had a superb view of the Goodwood racecourse. It is fair to say that this loop shaped course has one of the finest locations in Britain. As well as horse racing, Goodwood is renowned for many other sporting occasions including the motoring events 'The Festival of Speed' and 'The Goodwood Revival Meeting'.

From here I walked the mile or so to Goodwood House and its famed art collection, the home of the Dukes of Richmond and Lennox for over 300 years. Originally it was a hunting lodge for the dukes to participate in the fashionable Charlton Hunt. Purchased by the illegitimate son of Charles II in 1697, it was greatly extended following the destruction by fire of the Duke's main residence, Richmond House in London, to house the family's many rescued treasures. In the Entrance Hall hang three magnificent paintings of scenes on the estate by a young George Stubbs. Of the many other superb works the haunting portrait of the 3rd Duke by Sir Joshua Reynolds in the Yellow Drawing Room particularly moved me, and the two

views of London from the old Richmond House by Canaletto are so crisp and fresh they could have been painted yesterday.

Goodwood House is open infrequently but is well worth making the effort to visit. August is the best time as it is usually open five days a week.

Sauntering through the grounds, I noticed a number of cork trees; wonderful pieces of Mother Nature's sculpture and an unexpected treat.

Opposite the Kennel Lodges' entrance to the estate is a lane which brought me back to East Lavant and the smart Royal Oak Inn. With my circular walk complete I settled down for a meal and a pint.

As I contemplated my journey I considered the connections between the places I had seen. Several have faced destruction but the effect was a triumph rather than a tragedy. The consequences of fires at Stansted, Uppark and Richmond were innovative, extended or restored

Derek leans on the cork tree at Goodwood.

houses and of storm damage at West Dean was a replanted and well planned arboretum. Each has risen like a glorious phoenix from the ashes.

# PRIORY BAY
## HOTEL

### the Country House Hotel by the sea

**"You don't have to get on a plane to find a slice of paradise"** *London Evening Standard*

**"It (Priory Bay) offers the elegance and luxury associated with country house hotels in Britain, but without the stuffiness"** *The New York Times*

**"Food is one of the main reasons to visit Priory Bay"** *Daily Express*

**"Set within wooded and landscaped grounds leading down to a beautiful private beach... the hotel combines understated elegance with a warm, welcoming atmosphere and fantastic service"** *Daily Telegraph*

Just off the South Coast of England and two and a half hours from London, The Isle of Wight's Priory Bay Hotel is a quintessential English country house boasting: spectacular views across The Solent sea; a picturesque private beach; a 70 acre estate (a haven for wildlife, red squirrels, flora and fauna); an outdoor pool; an excellent six-hole golf course, falconry courses and wonderful coastal walks. The hotel features two award-winning restaurants: the fine dining Regency-muralled Island Room, and the brasserie-style Priory Oyster with alfresco terrace. Both showcase seasonal cuisine featuring foraged, home-grown and local produce, alongside an innovative wine list which includes an excellent selection of bio-dynamic and organic wines.

Renowned for its outstanding natural beauty, world-famous sailing (the first America's Cup was raced around the Island), beach resorts and rich history, the Island was much loved by Charles Dickens and Alfred Lord Tennyson. Queen Victoria's favourite royal family residence and final home Osborne House is also situated just 20 minutes away from the hotel.

Priory Bay Hotel • Priory Drive • Seaview • Isle of Wight • PO34 5BU
Tel: 01983 613 146 • Fax: 01983 616 539
www.priorybay.co.uk • email: enquiries@priorybay.co.uk

# Join 1 the clan

Visit Scotland has declared 2014 the Year of Homecoming but Lucy Denton discovered that clan links are always a powerful motive for visitors to Scottish houses and castles.

Scotland's cultural genius is rooted in a remarkable history of castles and clans, landscape and literary brilliance, invention and endeavour. Migration, as a result of Highland Clearances or through the expansion of the British Empire, is a significant aspect of its past and many people around the world have deep emotional associations with this extraordinary country.

The clan connection is an ancient political and administrative arrangement based on networks of, mostly Highland, families proclaiming loyalty to a particular chief. Surnames may have been taken as a mark of fidelity, rather than as an indication of common blood. Clans are still legally recognised by the Court of the Lord Lyon despite the defeat of 1745 when the Jacobite rising was crushed by William, Duke of Cumberland, son of George II.

Symbols of identity, such as distinguishing dress and tartans, were forbidden in anti-clan legislation, much of which was not repealed until the end of the 18th century. But, when it was, it lead to the resurgence of interest in clan culture, uplifted by James Macpherson's epic Celtic poems and Sir Walter Scott's romanticised recreation of Highland rituals.

**Culzean Castle, Ayrshire, home of Clan Kennedy.**

**Left: Highland clansman of 1745 at Inverary.**

*"The clan connection is based on networks of families proclaiming loyalty to a chief"*

**Dunvegan Castle.**

**Dame Flora MacLeod and, right, the Dunvegan Clan Parliament in 1956.**

The prototype of the clan society was founded by the formidable Dame Flora MacLeod, the 28th – and first woman – Chief of Clan MacLeod. Born in 10 Downing Street in 1878, she went on to travel the Commonwealth establishing societies which flourished. The seat of the MacLeods for 800 years, Dunvegan Castle, on the Isle of Skye, is the oldest continuously inhabited castle in Scotland. It was opened by Dame Flora to visitors, and is known as a family – or Clan Chief – home, each Chief's custodianship represented in stages of its architectural evolution. Here there are two visitors' books to sign, one of which is dedicated solely to those of MacLeod descent.

The MacArthur bedroom
at Inveraray Castle.

**Inveraray Castle, the seat of the Duke of Argyll and Chief of Clan Campbell.**

Blair Castle in Perthshire, the ancestral home of Clan Murray, tells the story of the Dukes of Atholl, interwoven with the narrative of Scotland's past, from the ultimately doomed Mary Queen of Scots to Culloden, the final full-scale battle on British soil. This striking white-washed edifice, with parts dating back to 1269, is at the heart of one of the largest estates in the country and is the base for the only private army in Europe permitted to carry the Queen's Colours, granted such status on account of Queen Victoria's approval of their proficiency during a stay in 1844.

The Atholl Highlanders now perform ceremonial duties, including opening the Atholl Gathering and Highland Games at Blair each year where traditional sports such as putting the shot and throwing the hammer, each based on ancient fighting techniques, take place. Visitors can also see the Derby Suite in which the monarch stayed with its exquisite bed hangings embroidered in 1650 – as well as muskets and targes (shields) used at Culloden.

The powerful bond of the clan is commemorated at Inveraray Castle, the seat of the Duke of Argyll and Chief of Clan Campbell. At today's castle, rebuilt in the 18th century, a vast architectural fusion of

the Palladian, the Baroque and the Gothic, the story of this most remarkable of families and its accomplishments and ordeals is told, including the fatal fight of the 2nd Earl when leading his Clan against the English at Flodden Field in 1513. Clan Campbell, one of the largest, has strong links with societies around the world including those in New Zealand, Australia and America.

Dunrobin Castle will see a gathering of members of Clan Sutherland in 2014 to co-incide with Homecoming Scotland; its Clan society has members from around the world including Canada and the United States, proud of their Scottish lineage. The Earldom of Sutherland is one of the seven ancient earldoms of Scotland, whose seat at Dunrobin was rebuilt in 1845 to designs by Sir Charles Barry, designer of the Houses of Parliament, and restored in the early 20th century by the prolific Scottish architect Sir Robert Lorimer.

An entry in Queen Victoria's diary remarks that in 1872 the Duke of Sutherland once drove her in his train to his privately-owned station along the 30 miles of tracks he had laid to get to the Castle.

Culzean Castle, on the Ayrshire coast, the former

**Main picture: Blair Castle. Above: Blair Farthing and Blair Highlanders' Dash. Right: Family portraits on the staircase at Blair.**

seat of the Kennedy Clan (not to be confused with the Irish Kennedys), is one of the masterpieces of architect Robert Adam and is now in the care of the National Trust for Scotland. The Castle, built in 1777 and commemorated on the Scottish five pound note, is of particular interest to visitors from the US, since, in 1945, the Kennedy family offered the tenancy of a specially-created apartment to General Eisenhower. Home to one of the largest collections of armoury outside Windsor, Culzean is just one of a number of properties associated with Clan Kennedy including Cassillis House near Maybole, Dunure Castle, Cruggleton Castle and Dunduff Castle.

Ruined Huntly Castle in Aberdeenshire was once the seat of the Gordon family. The red sandstone carved heraldry on the facade, dating to 1602 and commissioned by the 1st Marquis of Huntly, is matchless for its craftsmanship. Clan Gordon went from strength to strength and north eastern Scotland became 'Gordon Country'; the Clan is also associated with Auchindoun and Corgarff Castle. Corgarff, a 16th century tower house, was reputedly burned by the Gordons, in support of Mary Queen of Scots, even though the lady of the house and 24 of her staff were

still inside. Haddo House in Aberdeenshire, another work by William Adam, was another stronghold of the Gordon family for 400 years. For Homecoming 2014, Huntly Castle are producing an online version of *Following in the Family Footsteps*, a guide linking Scottish surnames to historic sites.

Clans are not only associated with the Highlands, Lowland families too adopted the symbols of their Highland neighbours so that they could be distinguished by tartans and other emblems. Thirlestane Castle, south of Edinburgh on the Scottish borders, and built to defend the capital, is the seat of Clan Maitland. The Earls of Lauderdale arrived in Britain with William the Conqueror but Thirlestane was rebuilt to designs by Sir William Bruce at the request of the 2nd Earl of Lauderdale, a Royalist who was Secretary of State for Scotland at the Restoration. The current chief, the 18th Earl of Lauderdale feels the clan provides a valuable fixed point for Maitlands researching family history and has members around the world, especially in the United States.

Other prominent Lowland families include the Hopes at Hopetoun House, the seat of the Earls of Hopetoun and Clan Hope, and the Primroses at

**Thirlestane Castle.**

Dalmeny House, the seat of the Earls of Rosebery and Clan Primrose. Clan symbols were much in evidence when George IV was received at Hopetoun in 1822, the first reigning British monarch to visit the country in 170 years, during a state visit directed by none other than Sir Walter Scott. Hopetoun House demonstrates the global reach of familial ties: visitors come from Australia, where the 7th Earl was Governor-General, and India, where the 8th Earl was Viceroy.

For today's visitors to Scotland's great castles and country houses, the close ties provided by shared genealogy or a common surname, give a connection with the past. For many, it is a true Homecoming.

**Top: Ruined Huntly Castle, still one of Scotland's most impressive medieval buildings. Above: Inveraray Castle.**

# Game on

The sporting estate is still a vital component in the commercial survival of many historic houses and gardens. Game appears frequently on country house menus and is now regularly available in farm shops and supermarkets. With growing recognition of the health benefits of lean naturally grown meat, **Hudson's** asked for some original recipes. All serve 4.

## RAGLEY PARTRIDGE
### INGREDIENTS
3 partridges
500g new potatoes
Baby spinach and watercress leaves, washed
200ml balsamic vinegar
100ml olive oil

### METHOD
Pre-heat oven to 475°F/240°C/Gas 9. Mix oil and vinegar and warm in a pan. Cover new potatoes with water, bring to boil and simmer for 5 minutes. Drain and run under cold water. Cut into 1cm slices, sprinkle with olive oil and sea salt and lay on baking tray.

Place prepared partridges in roasting tin and cover with butter. Roast in oven for 15 minutes. Remove and leave to rest. Reduce oven temperature to 400°F/200°C/Gas 6, put in sliced potatoes and roast until crisp.

Remove meat from partridges and shred. Arrange salad leaves on serving plate, layer potatoes over, then shredded partridge, drizzling dressing over each layer as you go. Serve.

*Ragley Hall, Warwickshire, The Marquess & Marchioness of Hertford (p.278)*

## BRAISED PHEASANT WITH APPLE AND CELERIAC MASH

### INGREDIENTS

4 pheasant breasts
1 tbsp oil
Knob of butter
4 rashers smoked bacon, chopped
1 medium onion, sliced
2 cloves garlic, crushed
1 sprig thyme
1 tbsp plain flour
1 tbsp brown sugar
150ml dry cider
500ml chicken stock
1 tbsp red wine vinegar
500g old potatoes, cubed
350g celeriac, cubed
1 large Bramley apple, chopped
Butter, salt & pepper for mash

### METHOD

Pre-heat oven to 400°F/200°C/Gas 6. Melt butter and oil in a heavy pan and fry the pheasant until browned. Remove and place in an oven-proof dish. Add onion, garlic and bacon to the pan and cook gently until soft. Blend in flour and stir for a minute. Add all the liquids, sugar and thyme and stir until bubbling. Pour over the pheasant, cover and place in oven for 45 minutes.

Boil the potatoes and celeriac in salted water until soft, adding the apples in the last 10 minutes. Mash with butter and seasoning.

Remove the pheasant from the oven, check seasoning and serve with mash and green vegetables.

*Rockingham Castle, Northamptonshire, Mr & Mrs James Saunders Watson (p.261)*

## DIJON PHEASANT WITH GREEN PEPPERCORNS

### INGREDIENTS

4 pheasant breasts
3 tbsp olive oil
1 medium onion
1 celery stalk
1 large mushroom
2 cloves garlic
1 tbsp chopped fresh tarragon
2 tsp Dijon mustard
1 tsp green peppercorns
25g butter
50g plain flour
500ml chicken stock
300ml white wine
250ml crème fraiche
Salt & pepper

### METHOD

Pre-heat oven to 400°F/200°C/Gas 6. Melt butter in frying pan with olive oil, brown pheasant and place in oven-proof dish.

Finely chop onion, celery, mushroom and garlic and fry briefly in same pan until slightly soft, before adding flour. Stir continuously for 1 minute. Add stock, mustard, tarragon, peppercorns and wine and stir until thick and smooth. Add extra stock if too thick. Remove from the heat, season and stir in crème fraiche. Pour sauce over pheasant, cover with foil and put into oven. Cook for 40 minutes. Serve with new potatoes, spinach and braised fennel.

*Mellerstain, Berwickshire, The Countess of Haddington (p.334)*

## RABBIT WITH TAMARIND & YOGHURT

### INGREDIENTS

1.5kg rabbit joints, skinned
2 red or yellow peppers
25g tamarind paste
4 cloves garlic, chopped
1 stalk lemon grass, finely sliced
1 tbsp fresh coriander, chopped
1 tsp coriander seeds, ground
3 tbsp oil
225g natural yoghurt
1 tsp sugar
Salt and pepper

### METHOD

Mix together tamarind, garlic, coriander, lemon grass, ground coriander seeds and oil to a smooth paste. Beat in yoghurt, seasoning and sugar. Make deep cuts in the meat and marinade in an oven-proof dish for at least 4 hours, turning occasionally.

Pre-heat oven to 190°F/375°C/Gas 5. Cover dish and cook in oven for 30 minutes. Add sliced peppers and return to oven, uncovered, for a futher 30-40 minutes. Serve hot with rice or cold with salad.

*Newby Hall, Yorkshire, Mr & Mrs Richard Compton (p.292)*

**Facing page: Newby Hall Gardens, no rabbits here. Bottom: Braised Pheasant with Apple & Celeriac Mash. Above: The Old Kitchen at Rockingham Castle where game dishes have been prepared for centuries.**

# One in a Million

What is your favourite thing in an historic house?
There are millions of wonderful objects to choose
from. **Hudson's** asked a group of heritage
insiders to pick just one.

## THE MARCHIONESS OF SALISBURY'S CHAIRS
### Hatfield House, Hertfordshire

*Hatfield House, home of the Marquess & Marchioness of Salisbury, is a grand Jacobean mansion built to entertain royalty by James I's first minister, Robert Cecil, whose descendants have filled it with paintings, fine furniture and tapestries.*

It is hard to choose a favourite object at Hatfield, whether textiles, paintings, decorative carvings, furniture or archives, which does not reflect the history of the house, the government of the day and the Salisbury of the time.

I am choosing an elegant set of carved and gilded back stools which stretch down the length of the Long Gallery. They were made for the 5th Earl's State Bedroom in 1710. The elaborate bed and the whole room were furnished with cloth of gold and with crimson silk damask in an unusual bizarre design of a decorative triumphal arch with pavilions and flowering palm trees set in a garden with flower beds and an elaborate three tier fountain. The design is finished with a garland.

This original design has been copied precisely by the silk weaver Richard Humphries in a two-colour blue silk damask. Using two complete repeats of the design for each back stool it is satisfying to see how this design fits the shape of the inner back with the large leaves echoing the curve of the lower edge and the two central flowers from the upper garland fitting the double curve at the top of the back.

The fountain fits neatly on the seat with the lower garland to encase it. An especially welcome economy was using the shorter second repeat for the outer back and removing two narrow side strips from the lower fountain area of the double repeat to form the sides of the seat covering. This left a narrower central section of the lower fountain area which was used to cover one of the cushions on the 17th century chairs on the opposite side of the Long Gallery. The 12 back stools have now been re-covered over the original upholstery by the House Textile Conservation Group.

*Hatfield House, Hertfordshire* (p.231)

**www.hudsonsheritage.com**

"It is hard to choose a favourite object at Hatfield, whether textiles, paintings, decorative carvings, furniture or archives, which does not reflect the history of the house, the government of the day and the Salisbury of the time"

## DAVID ADSHEAD'S DRAGONS
### Wallington, Northumberland

*The house at Wallington was remodelled in fashionable Palladian style by Sir Walter Calverley Blackett but today also retains the spirit of the Pre-Raphaelites through the patronage of his descendants the Trevelyans. David Adshead is Head Curator at the National Trust.*

The four massive dragons' heads on the East Lawn at Wallington, Northumberland never fail to delight me. Disembodied and grinning, with lips curled and nostrils flared, they have a surreal, Cheshire Cat quality.

The dragons, not griffins as they are sometimes mistakenly called, served originally as supporters to the badge of the City of London and were supplied by the mason Christopher Horsnaile the Elder for the attic sculpture of Bishopsgate, a 1730s replacement of the ancient gate that commanded Ermine Street, the principal road leading north from the capital. Seen as nuisances in a rapidly expanding city, London Wall's great gates were demolished in the early 1760s and their building materials and ornamental sculpture sold off.

Sir Walter Calverley Blackett bought fragments from Aldersgate and Bishopsgate, and incorporated them in an embattled gothic folly, Rothley Castle, sited high on the moors above his new house at Wallington. In the late 19th century the dragons migrated to a rockery in the gardens, where their wings survive in a mossy pile, before coming to rest on Wallington's green lawns.

Despite their best efforts to fulfil their intended role as fierce guardians, they smile and stare inscrutably, charming visitors young and old.

*Wallington, Northumberland (p.329)*

*"Despite their best efforts to fulfil their intended role as fierce guardians, they smile and stare inscrutably, charming visitors young and old"*

## ALEX MACDONALD'S BOOKCASE
### Dumfries House, Ayrshire

*Palladian Dumfries House was rescued complete with its neo-classical interiors by the Adam brothers and its unrivalled collection of Georgian furniture by The Great Steward of Scotland's Dumfries House Trust, headed by HRH the Prince of Wales, in 2007. Alex MacDonald is Head Guide and Volunteer Co-ordinator.*

This bookcase, for me, sums up the drama and passion of the saving of Dumfries House by HRH Prince Charles in 2007, when we came within 3 weeks of losing the house and all its contents. Thomas Chippendale supplied this bookcase to the 5th Earl of Dumfries in 1759 at a cost of £47 and 5 shillings but it's now described as one of the most valuable pieces of furniture in the world.

It's a stunning, flamboyant example showcasing the variety of Chippendale's Director period and it's difficult to comprehend how avant-garde it must have been in Georgian Britain.

Accounts of its potential value vary but guests gasp when we reveal the estimates. For me, it's a daily delight to see it and the reaction our visitors have to it. These moments give me a connection to the ageing Earl. I picture him earnestly, hopefully, gauging the reaction of potential brides gazing upon it (he may have bought it as a carrot in his attempt to attract a new wife). It would certainly become a key piece in a lady's bedroom to treasure and show.

Did the Earl win a new wife? What might it have achieved at auction? This bookcase is a gateway to so many of the stories we tell at Dumfries House.

*Dumfries House, Dumfriesshire* (*p.335*)

## ANNA EAVIS' FIREPLACE
### Bolsover Castle, Derbyshire

*Bolsover Castle combines the Little Castle, a tower containing tiers of luxurious 17th century staterooms, the now ruined Terrace Range and Britain's finest surviving indoor riding school, on a dramatic site overlooking the Vale of Scarsdale. Anna Eavis is Curatorial Director at English Heritage.*

This extraordinary chimneypiece belongs to one of England's most magical and enigmatic historic interiors, that of the early 17th century Little Castle at Bolsover, in Derbyshire.

Exquisitely carved in smooth, polished stones of a cool and distinctive palette - cream, black, brown and a delicate pink - its projecting rectangular hood is reminiscent of a medieval fireplace. Its elegant ornaments - the columns, strapwork and foliate friezes - are, however, classically inspired. The chimneypiece was probably designed by the architect John Smythson (d.1634), who adapted engravings by the Italian architect Sebastiano Serlio to create a total of 15 decorative fireplaces at Bolsover, each one quite unique. They are made of local stones which, when polished, give the appearance of marble: Ashford Black, quarried in the nearby Chatsworth estate, Speckled Cockleshell, found in the coal measures, and pink alabaster.

This chimneypiece bears the arms of Sir William Cavendish and his first wife Elizabeth Bassett, who fitted out the house in the 1620s. Begun by William's father in 1612, it stood on the site of a medieval castle, high on a hilltop overlooking the Cavendish estates. Described by an early visitor as 'a delicate little house', it was never intended to be a home for the family, whose principal residence was at Welbeck Abbey, only a short horse-ride away. Lavishly decorated and furnished, it was instead a 'high sweet retreat', used solely for the pursuit of pleasure and culture. Here, William Cavendish entertained noble guests, including King Charles I, with banquets, music and theatrical displays. This chimneypiece stands in the Pillar Parlour, or dining room, where visitors ate amid paintings of the five senses and gilded panelling copied from the royal palace at Theobalds.

Although many of the Little Castle's fittings have disappeared, its fireplaces, with their distinctive, jewel-encrusted appearance, evoke the richness of this little palace.

*Bolsover Castle, Derbyshire* (*p.264*)

## JAMES FRYER-SPEDDING'S SKETCHES
### Mirehouse, Cumbria

*In the heart of the Lake District, Mirehouse is an unassuming 17th century house, home of the Spedding family. But Mirehouse has a secret, a series of connections with some of the greatest literary figures of the 19th century: Alfred Lord Tennyson, Edward Fitzgerald, William Makepeace Thackeray, Thomas Carlyle and William Wordsworth.*

When my ancestor, James Spedding attended Trinity College, Cambridge from 1829 to 1832, two of his close friends there were Alfred Tennyson and William Makepeace Thackeray.

Spedding was a skilled sketcher. He regularly drew his subjects unawares. There are at Mirehouse a number of folders of his drawings. One contains drawings (many not much more than doodles) which may well have been made during meetings of the Cambridge Apostles, a debating club to which both Spedding and Tennyson belonged.

The sheet of drawings that I particularly love shows sketches of Tennyson and his friend, the poet Arthur Hallam (A. H. H., the subject of *In Memoriam*). The identity of the third subject is unknown. The sketch of Tennyson shows the poet actually 'pulling a face'. This is likely to be the poet's talent described by Robert Martin in his biography, *Tennyson: The Unquiet Heart*:

*"He discovered that the gift of mimicry with which he amused the family at Somersby entertained his friends. He would do the sun emerging from a cloud by a gradual opening of his eyes and mouth and whole countenance, and then initiate its return into obscurity by slowly closing up once more."*

It is rare to get such a personal glimpse of the past and one that reveals so much of the poet's character. When I look at it, I understand why these men were friends and see what fun they must have had in their years together as students at Cambridge. This invitation into the intimate world of some of the giants of 19th century literature is one of the pleasures of life at Mirehouse.

*Mirehouse, Cumbria* (*p.316*)

# LLEW GROOM'S SEVERED HEADS
## Plas Mawr, Gwynedd

*Plas Mawr claims to be the best preserved Elizabethan townhouse in Britain and shows what life was like for the Tudor gentry of the wealthy merchant town of Conwy. Llew Groom (third from left) is a Volunteer Steward for Cadw, the Welsh Government's historic environment service.*

I love the house; it's been part of my life since I was 10 years old when I was sent to help with the weeding between the cobblestones. Let's go straight to the parlour on the ground floor where we can see a plaster shield that bears three severed heads of Englishmen, proudly displayed as part of the wall decoration. This is the grisly coat of arms of Ednyfed Fychan, Chief Counsellor to the Gwynedd prince, Llywelyn ap Iorwerth (Llywelyn the Great). It is said that Ednyfed killed three of the chief captains of Ranulf, Earl of Chester in battle in the 1200s.

In the 1570s a gentleman named Robert, third son of Robert Wynn of Gwydir, began to amass a fortune through trading interests in Conwy. At the ripe old age of 50 he decided to marry. The lady of his choice was Dorothy, daughter of Sir William Griffith of Penrhyn. Dorothy came from a longer and better established pedigree than that of the Wynns and counted Ednyfed Fychan, an ancestor of the new Tudor dynasty, among her ancestors.

These walls tell the story of ancient Welsh families whose descendants rose to wealth, power and status in Tudor Wales. Today I have the pleasure and privilege of sharing this story with the many visitors who come to marvel at our hidden gem here in Conwy. And we do remind visitors that we no longer cut off Englishmen's heads – we play rugby instead!

*Plas Mawr, Gwynedd* (*p.363*)

# HUDSON'S HERITAGE AWARDS

*Hudson's Heritage Awards* are our way of recognising what is best about visiting heritage sites in the UK each year. The award scheme is independently judged by **Norman Hudson**, heritage expert and founder of *Hudson's*, **Lucinda Lambton**, TV presenter and author, **Jeremy Musson**, writer and broadcaster on country houses, **Simon Foster**, consultant on Channel 4's Country House Rescue and presented by **Loyd Grossman**. **Norman Hudson** told *Hudson's* about this year's winners.

**Lord Montagu of Beaulieu has been distinguished by two awards for a lifetime's achievement in the same year, Hudson's Heritage Award for 60 years at the forefront of the heritage movement and the Octane Award for his contribution to motoring.**

SPECIAL JUDGES AWARD

### LORD MONTAGU OF BEAULIEU

Lord Montagu of Beaulieu is an outstanding figure in the heritage movement. At his home, Beaulieu Abbey in Hampshire, he has been a leading innovator, opening Palace House to the public in 1956, establishing the Montagu Motor Museum in 1959 and then the National Motor Museum in 1972. He revolutionised the idea of public access to heritage, employing ideas first researched with the US National Parks Service and was generous in sharing his knowledge with other owners and managers. He was instrumental in the establishment of the Historic Houses Association and the Heritage Education Trust and was the first Chairman of English Heritage. It is a privilege for Hudson's to be able to recognise Lord Montagu's lifetime contribution with a Special Judges Award.

*Beaulieu Abbey, Lord Montagu of Beaulieu (p141)*

**Lord Montagu's home Palace House, Beaulieu as it is today.**

**The 1972 National Motor Museum housed in an iconic building by architect Leonard Massaneh.**

**Cavalcade to celebrate the opening of the Montagu Motor Museum in 1959.**

## BEST FAMILY DAY OUT

**STOCKELD PARK**, Yorkshire
While Stockeld Park, the classic Palladian villa designed by James Paine in 1758 at the centre of this 2,000 acre estate, is open to groups by appointment, the real crowd-pullers have been the seasonal adventure and activity days which make use of the estate's beautiful woodland. Our judges were looking for a great day out for a mix of age groups – and especially children – including play areas, interactive displays, guides, games, trails and activities. While there are February Fun and Summer and Halloween Adventures staged at Stockeld, it was the 12 week Christmas Adventure that set it apart. There is nothing quite like it in Britain – the adventure zones of the Enchanted Forest, Ice Skating, Nordic Skiing and Illuminated Maze, encourage outdoor active fun. Interactive art and music sculptures encourage children to learn and play.
*Stockeld Park, the Grant family (p.296)*

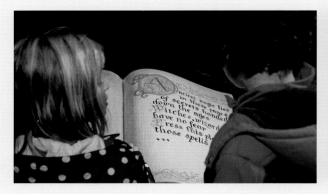

**KIPLIN HALL**, Yorkshire

Kiplin Hall, the 17th century country home of George Calvert, founder of Maryland USA, is little known, notwithstanding its convenient situation less than 5 miles off the A1. This beautiful Jacobean building was left virtually derelict following requisition during the Second World War but since then has been refurbished, with nearly everything displayed in the house belonging to one of the four families who owned it between 1620-1971. The gardens are in the process of being restored. A small dedicated staff and well informed volunteers work tirelessly to keep this building and its grounds as an informative but informal and enjoyable experience. Visitors really feel that they have stumbled on something that has been hidden and undiscovered – which, at the moment, is still the case.

There is little more satisfying for anyone involved with caring for an historic collection of objects than the return of a prodigal, particularly an unexpected and previously unrecognised one. One day in 2012, The Kiplin Hall Trust was offered the chance to buy back a chronometer which had belonged to the 4th Earl of Tyrconnel, Kiplin's owner in the 1840s. He refers to it frequently in his diary for 1844 and had ordered it for use on his yacht, *Intrepid*. His widow then passed it to his nephew, Captain the Hon Walter Talbot who was in the Royal Navy and whose name is inscribed on the box. The offer was to purchase the chronometer at roughly twice its market value, the new owner having just acquired it in a sale at Christies. By serendipity, Nick Ellis, a Kiplin volunteer, found a pile of correspondence in the Kiplin archive describing a burglary in 1976 when a number of items were stolen including this very chronometer. Thanks to the intervention of the North Yorkshire police, the chronometer has now been returned to its rightful home at Kiplin Hall where it rejoins a group of Lord Tyconnel's navigational instruments in the Travellers' Bedroom.
*Kiplin Hall, the Kiplin Hall Trust* (p.291)

**Dorothy Pearce, a Kiplin Hall volunteer, shows a visitor a painted leather chinoiserie screen made in London c1750 in the newly restored Travellers' Bedroom, one of many objects that recall its globe-trotting previous owners.**

**The Kiplin Chronometer pictured here with curator, Dawn Webster and volunteer Nick Ellis, was made in London by Edward J Dent and is no. 1800; David Livingstone took no.1803 to Africa and Charles Darwin took one on HMS Beagle.**

## BEST SHOPPING & BEST WEDDING VENUE

**MOUNT STUART**, Isle of Bute

Mount Stuart, once seen, is never forgotten. A 19th century Gothic Revival house, a feat of Victorian engineering, and one of the most technologically advanced houses of its age. With its opulence and oddity and incongruity, it is like coming upon a Doge's palace in the desert, or the Palace of Westminster rising out of a plain. The well-designed shop is no less innovative, with flexible fixtures and fittings which enable it to be converted from a contemporary retail space to a blank canvas in a matter of minutes. Over 75% of the retail lines are from local and regional sources. There is also an exclusive range of Mount Stuart's own goods incorporating the heritage of the house, inspired by the 3rd Marquess' favourite architect, William Burgess.

In the view of one of the Judges, there could be no more marvellous place to be married in the world, let alone the United Kingdom. Where more extraordinary could you entertain your friends than in the Great Hall with walls and pillars of rarest marble and alabaster, all rushing up to a vaulted ceiling that is emblazoned with the constellations and with the ghostly figures of the zodiac coursing through glinting mirrored stars. Here, more magnificent than most parish churches in Britain, is its immense bright white marble chapel permanently aglow with the blood red of its clerestory glass. The catering features the freshest local produce available and with the addition of new accommodation in sympathetically-converted historic buildings in close proximity to the main house, this was considered an exceptional wedding venue.

*Mount Stuart, the Mount Stuart Trust (p.347)*

# OFFICIAL TOURIST BOARD GUIDE

## New 39th edition

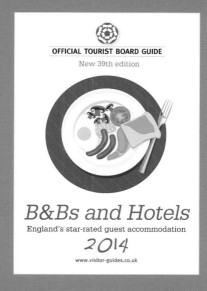

OFFICIAL TOURIST BOARD GUIDE

New 39th edition

**B&Bs and Hotels**

England's star-rated guest accommodation

*2014*

www.visitor-guides.co.uk

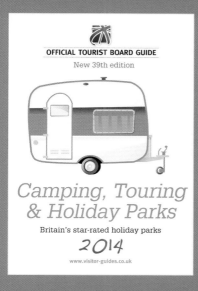

OFFICIAL TOURIST BOARD GUIDE

New 39th edition

**Camping, Touring & Holiday Parks**

Britain's star-rated holiday parks

*2014*

www.visitor-guides.co.uk

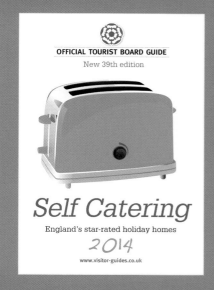

OFFICIAL TOURIST BOARD GUIDE

New 39th edition

**Self Catering**

England's star-rated holiday homes

*2014*

www.visitor-guides.co.uk

## THE official national guide to quality-assessed B&Bs, Hotels and other guest accommodation in England

Packed with information and easy to use
it's all you need for the perfect English break

- Web-friendly features for easy booking
- Events, attractions and other tourist information
- National Accessible Scheme accommodation at a glance

Available from all good bookshops and online retailers

Now book your star-rated accommodation online at

## www.visitor-guides.co.uk

**BEST NEW COMMISSION**

### WOBURN ABBEY GARDENS,
Bedfordshire

Although strictly an historic recreation, the building of Repton's Chinese Temple and Rockery of the early 1800s has been a dream come true. Created with the original plans from Repton's famed Red Book, the project took six years to come to fruition. The 6th Duke of Bedford, inheriting Woburn, commissioned Humphrey Repton in 1804 to create designs to improve the gardens and park. In the early 19th century there was a great obsession with all things Chinoiserie, inspired by the whimsical landscapes observed on imported Chinese porcelain and lacquered chests. The English chose to embrace the Chinese style to a colourful extent, though such fantasies seldom took flight in Scotland and never in Northern

Ireland or Wales. This European version of Chinese style, mocked by so many for its unruly flights of fancy was, by its very nature, invigoratingly original. To have what was planned 200 years ago eventually installed at Woburn is new but not new.
*Woburn Abbey Gardens, The Duke of Bedford* (*p.222*)

## BEST ACCOMMODATION

**ISCOYD PARK**, Shropshire

Iscoyd Park, on the borders of North Wales, Shropshire and Cheshire, has been home to six generations of the same family but the most recent occupiers, Phil and Susie Godsal, have adapted it so that it still functions as their family home but also as a stylish and top-quality wedding venue with associated self-catering and B&B accommodation. This is a grand country house with urban spin combining old and contemporary with brightness and modernity. There is no 'shabby chic' here but it retains a family feel. The recent refurbishment is a breath of fresh air, moving things forward so as to provide country house elegance and style with all the panache of a top boutique hotel.

*Iscoyd Park, Mr & Mrs Philip Godsal (p.362)*

**BEST COMMERCIAL INNOVATION**

**BLENHEIM PALACE**, Oxfordshire

Blenheim Palace, the great Vanbrugh-designed house just outside Oxford, was a gift from Queen Anne and a grateful Nation to John Churchill, 1st Duke of Marlborough, following his famous victory at the Battle of Blenheim in 1704. The Palace, with its 2,000 acres of 'Capability' Brown parkland and award-winning formal gardens, is a UNESCO World Heritage Site and one of Britain's foremost historic attractions. Recently completed at Blenheim is one of the largest developments for over 200 years, involving a significant investment of over £2.3 million as part of a strategy to improve dramatically visitor facilities. Part has been the creation of a sublimely sensitive and indeed beautiful

redevelopment of a new Visitor Centre – the stone colonnade, the Butter Cooler, the Oxfordshire Pantry, the lighting – all and everything is a triumphant mixing of the very best of modernism with the greatness of its 18th century buildings. The number of visitors to Blenheim Palace has grown, and part is in response to the introduction in 2009 of a 'Free Annual Pass' offer, a concept being emulated by many others. This brought an additional 200,000 visitors a year which provided a strong case for the development of the East Courtyard Visitor Centre.
*Blenheim Palace, The Duke of Marlborough (p.156)*

## BEST PICNIC SPOT

**PORT ELIOT**, Cornwall

Port Eliot has many magical picnic spots in the grounds but the calm and dappled shade of the Woodland Garden leading down to the secret estuary, leads to a special spot. Here, sitting on the grass slope, with the Beech Maze to shelter you, you can gaze to the nine-arched Roman Viaduct designed by Isambard Kingdom Brunel for the Great Western Railway in 1864. It is still part of the present line that connects London to Penzance. Here is romance and history combined. Who, you might ask, has sat here to watch the trains as they pass on to London or further? What did this look like when it was an Augustinian monastic fort? Who were the cannons aimed at? The Brunel viaduct spans the river estuary and the picnic spot has Pampas Grass to frame it. A perfect place to eat and for children to roll down the slope or play pirates around the cannons. It is an easy walk from the house but there is an atmosphere of calm in this sylvan setting.
*Port Eliot, The Earl of St Germans (p.191)*

## BEYOND THE CALL OF DUTY

**DAVID MACLEAN, DUNVEGAN CASTLE**, Isle of Skye

The winner, David MacLean, largely created the gardens in which he works at Dunvegan Castle. He was Head Gardener for over 30 years and, after a spell as Head Gardener for the National Trust of Scotland, returned to Dunvegan for the last 12 years. He was responsible for redesigning and replanting the many distinct gardens and glades and it was he who created the famed Water Garden with its giant Gunnera, pools and waterfalls. Not only that, he has developed cut flower beds for the Castle and a vegetable plot for the café – always in the somewhat hostile environment of the Isle of Skye. He leads garden tours and is generous with his time and knowledge to his team and to visitors. He works tirelessly through prolonged heavy rain, clouds of midges and gale-force winds but finds time each month to label a Plant of the Month, specifically to engage the public's attention.
*Dunvegan Castle Gardens, Hugh MacLeod of MacLeod (p.352)*

**David MacLean (left) with his team at Dunvegan.**

# HUDSONS HERITAGE AWARDS

PHOTOS: HERMIONE HASELL-MCCOSH

## BEST EVENT

**DALEMAIN**, Cumbria

Dalemain, a medieval Tudor and early-Georgian house with award-winning gardens, has been home to the same family since 1679. Eight years ago, the current chatelaine, Jane Hasell-McCosh, founded an international competition, the World's Original Marmalade Festival. This quirky and original event is the quintessence of innovation and creativity. It has been a triumphant success, growing from the judging of 60 locally produced jars of marmalade in 2006 to a startling 1,700 jars from all over the world. The Marmalade Awards and Festival has raised over £100,000 for local charities. As if this was not enough, there are such new and delightful diversions as a Marmalade Cat competition as well as a literary competition for prose or poetry related to marmalade. All this takes place in a beautiful 18th century house set against the grandeur and picturesque splendour of the Lakeland fells and parkland and with the award-winning 5 acre plantsman's gardens.

*Dalemain, the Hasell-McCosh family (p.315)*

**Bamburgh Castle.**
© VISIT BRITAIN

# Pick your favourite picnic spot!

## Win a fabulous Hudson's hamper and an invitation to the Hudson's Heritage Awards.

*Five runners up will receive a Blenheim Palace coolbag or a bottle of finest Abbotsford Scotch Whisky. Winners and runners up will all receive a free copy of Hudson's Historic Houses & Gardens 2015.*

**H**elp us find the best heritage picnic site in the UK and you could enjoy your very own picnic with a range of delicious products in a traditional lined wicker hamper fitted out for 6 people as well as an invitation for two to the 2015 Hudson's Heritage Awards.

Nominate any picnic site at any heritage property in the UK. Your favourite might be found in the grounds of a busy stately home or at a remote Neolithic burial mound. Just tell us where you will be spreading your picnic rug this summer and enter your choice for the prize.

Send us a photograph (or up to 4) of your picnic place telling us where it is and in no more than 150 words describe why your chosen spot is so special to you and why it is such a wonderful place to picnic.

If yours is the winning entry you will receive a special **Hudson's hamper** loaded with delicious goodies as well as an invitation for two to attend the prestigious Hudson's Heritage Awards, held each year in London. Your winning entry will also feature in next year's Hudson's Historic Houses and Gardens.

Five runners up will receive either a coveted **Blenheim Palace coolbag** or a bottle of finest **Abbotsford Scotch Whisky**. Winners and runners up will receive a free copy of Hudson's Historic Houses & Gardens 2015.

All entries received will be independently judged by our Awards panel chaired by Norman Hudson. Details can be found at www.hudsons-awards.co.uk. Either give us your nominations online, or send them to us along with your name, address, email and contact telephone number to: Hudson's (Picnic prize), 35 Thorpe Road, Peterborough, PE3 6AG.

● The closing date for all entries to this competition is 31 August 2014;
● Winners will be advised by 30 November 2014;
● The judges' decision is final and no correspondence will be entered into;
● Hudson's reserve the right to reproduce all images provided for use in publicity materials.

© VISIT BRITAIN

**Eastnor Castle.**

© VISIT BRITAIN

## Competition winners 2014

**Congratulations to Douglas Ginn, aged 10, for his winning picture of The Golden Hinde, a reconstruction of Sir Francis Drake's ship, in Hudson's heritage drawing competition for children.**

**The winner of the best picnic spot award for 2014 will be announced at a ceremony in London in February 2014. Thank you to everyone who nominated their favourite spot, there were obviously some great picnics in last year's sunshine. Keep picnicking!**

# Historic House Hotels of the National Trust

National Trust

# Past, Present & Future Perfect

Hartwell House & Spa

Bodysgallen Hall & Spa

Middlethorpe Hall & Spa

**The three Historic House Hotels which became part of the National Trust by donation in 2008 were each rescued from an uncertain future in the 1980's. They, with their gardens and parks, were restored and converted to hotels, combining historically accurate standards with the provision of traditional and up-to-date comfort for guests.**

**STAY IN AN HISTORIC HOUSE HOTEL OF THE NATIONAL TRUST......**

...and enjoy not only the comfort of these restored former homes to eminent persons but also the very best of British hospitality! The service you will receive is characteristic of the traditions of such houses in the past, now well suited to their present role. However, guests should not expect them to be modern hotels like new built establishments in town or country: on the other hand few allowances need to be made for the fact that the building is more than 300 years old.

**Hartwell House & Spa**
Buckinghamshire
Aylesbury,
HP17 8NR
Tel: 01296 747444
www.hartwell-house.com

**Bodysgallen Hall & Spa**
Llandudno,
North Wales,
LL30 1RS
Tel: 01492 584466
www.bodysgallen.com

**Middlethorpe Hall & Spa**
Bishopthorpe Road,
York
YO23 2GB
Tel: 01904 641241
www.middlethorpe.com

# Regional Directory

Glamis Castle

We want to make Hudson's easy for you to use. Turn to our maps on pages 395 for all sites and another for Churches Conservation Trust properties on pages 417. Do check opening times before you visit. Many properties are open regularly, but others only occasionally and some may only open for weddings and special events.

## Key to Symbols

| | |
|---|---|
| **i** | Information |
| 🛍 | Shop |
| 🌱 | Plant Sales |
| 🍸 | Corporate Hospitality / Functions |
| ♿ | Suitability for the Disabled |
| ☕ | Refreshments / Cafe / Tearoom |
| 🍴 | Restaurant |
| 🏃 | Guided Tours |
| 🎧 | Audio Tours |
| **P** | Parking Available |
| 🖼 | Education - School Visits |
| 🐕 | Suitability for Dogs |
| 🚫🐕 | No Dogs |
| 🛏 | Accommodation |
| 🔔 | Civil Wedding Licence |
| ❄ | Open All Year |
| 🎭 | Special Events |
| € | Accept Euros |
| **R** | Special offers/discounts available to Hudson's readers |
| 🏛 | Member of the Historic Houses Association but does **not** give free access to Friends |
| 🏛 Ⓕ | Member of the HHA giving free access under the HHA Friends Scheme |
| 🌿 | Property owned by National Trust. |
| ⌗ | Property in the care of English Heritage |
| ⚜ | Property owned by The National Trust for Scotland |
| 🏯 | Property in the care of Historic Scotland |
| ✿ | Properties in the care of Cadw, the Welsh Government's historic environment service |

575 Wandsworth Road
© National Trust/Christian Barrett/Westminster

# *London*

London

London, a city crowded with historic buildings where iconic sites and palaces vie for attention with modest country houses subsumed by the sprawling city.

*New Entries for 2014:*
• 575 Wandsworth Road

London - England

## VISITOR INFORMATION

### ■ Owner
Chiswick House and Gardens Trust and English Heritage

### ■ Address
Chiswick House
Burlington Lane
London
W4 2RP

### ■ Location
Map 19:C8
OS Ref. TQ210 775
Burlington Lane, London W4.
**Rail:** ½m NE of Chiswick Station.
**Underground:** Turnham Green, ¾m.
**Bus:** 190, E3.

### ■ Contact
The Estate Office
**Tel:** 020 8742 3905

### ■ Opening Times
**Gardens**
7am - dusk all year round.
**Chiswick House**
1 April - 30 September
Sun - Wed 10am - 6pm.
1 October - 31 October
Sun - Wed 10am - 5pm.
1 November - 29 March
Closed.
24 - 26 December,
1 January
Closed.

Open Bank Holiday Mondays in the season.

**Café**
Open every day from 9am.

### ■ Admission
**Gardens**
Entry                              Free

**House**
Adult                            £6.10
Conc.                            £5.50
Child                            £3.70
Family                          £15.90
Discount for groups 11 +
EH Members                       Free

**Garden Tours & Group Bookings:**
Chiswick House
020 8995 0508.
Garden Tours and Camellia Festival Group Boookings
020 8742 3905.

### ■ Special Events
**Camellia Festival 2014**
1- 30 March (closed Mondays)
There are year-round events from garden and family activities to open-air performances after dark - see www.chgt.org.uk.

### Conference/Function

| ROOM | Size | Max Cap |
|---|---|---|
| Chiswick House | | 150 |
| Burlington Pavilion | | 350 |
| The Conservatory | | 120 |
| The Cafe | | 80 |

© Clive Boursnell

# CHISWICK HOUSE AND GARDENS ⌗
www.chgt.org.uk

## Chiswick House is a magnificent neo-Palladian villa set in 65 acres of beautiful historic gardens.

Chiswick House is internationally renowned as one of the first and finest English Palladian villas. Lord Burlington who designed and built the villa from 1725 – 1729, was inspired by the architecture and gardens of ancient Rome and this house is a masterpiece. His aim was to create an impressive setting to show his friends his fine collection of art and his library. The opulent interior features gilded decoration, velvet walls and painted ceilings.

The important 18th Century gardens surrounding Chiswick House have, at every turn, something to surprise and delight the visitor from the magnificent cedar trees to the beautiful Italianate gardens with their cascade, statues, temples, urns and obelisks. 2010 saw the culmination of a major project to restore the historic gardens to their former glory, including the Conservatory and its world famous Camellia collection. The Chiswick House

Camellia Festival held every year during February and March brings a burst of glorious colour to the winter season.

There is also a children's play area and a modern café within the gardens. Judged to be the best new building in London by RIBA in 2011 the cafe is open all year and offers a light airy space to enjoy a seasonal menu and refreshments.

Chiswick House once acted both as a gallery for Lord Burlington's fine art collection and as a glamorous party venue where he could entertain. With exclusive use, the lavishly gilded interiors today provide a stunning setting for civil weddings ceremonies and Chiswick House provides an impressive backdrop for corporate and private events that can be held within the Burlington Pavilion.

## KEY FACTS

ⓘ WCs. Filming, plays, photographic shoots. Weddings, corporate and private events and party hire - please call 020 8742 3905 or events@chgt.org.uk or see website for brochure.

🖥 Private & corporate hospitality.

♿ Gardens only.

☕ 

🚶 Personal guided tours must be booked in advance.

🎧 House. (Downloadable tours-Garden).

🅿 Contact Estate Office.

🐕 
🔔 
♻ 

© Clive Boursnell

© Richard Bryant

## VISITOR INFORMATION

■ **Owner**
Historic Royal Palaces

■ **Address**
London
W8 4PX

■ **Location**
**Map 20:I8**
**OS Ref. TQ258 801**
In Kensington Gardens.
**Underground:**
Queensway on Central
Line, High Street
Kensington on Circle &
District Line.

■ **Contact**
**Tel:** 0844 482 7777
**Venue Hire and**
**Corporate Hospitality:**
020 3166 6115
**E-mail:** kensingtonpalace
@hrp.org.uk

■ **Opening Times**
**Nov-Feb:** daily, 10am-5pm
(last admission 4pm).
**Mar-Oct:** daily, 10am-6pm
(last admission 5pm).
Closed 24-26 Dec.

■ **Admission**
Call 0844 482 7777 or visit
www.hrp.org.uk for more
information.

# KENSINGTON PALACE
www.hrp.org.uk/kensingtonpalace

## Kensington Palace has been transformed and now has so much more for you to see and do.

Discover stories from Queen Victoria's life in her own words, as queen, wife and mother in the Victoria Revealed exhibition, told through extracts from her own letters and diaries. Follow in the footsteps of courtiers from the past in the sumptuous King's State Apartments which show some breathtaking examples of the work of architect and painter William Kent, such as the Cupola Room and King's Grand Staircase. Explore the intimate Queen's State Apartments which lift the curtain on the lives of William III, Mary II, Queen Anne and Anne's little son William, the last member of the Stuart dynasty.

Explore the new landscaped gardens, inspired by the famous lawns that existed in the 18th Century, relax in the wild flower meadow and stroll down the Wiggly Walk. Discover the majestic, 17th Century inspired, Sunken Garden and wander through the restored Cradle Walk offering unmatched views of the palace and gardens. Spoil yourself and enjoy a leisurely lunch or an indulgent afternoon tea while you admire the tranquil splendour of Queen Anne's Orangery, once the setting for the most lavish of court entertainments.

Tempted by some more recent glamour? You'll love the new stylish displays celebrating modern royals. Featuring rare and exquisite dresses from HM Queen Elizabeth II, Princess Margaret and Diana Princess of Wales, this elegant exhibition will provide a feast for the eyes and a nostalgic glance back at recent decades.

## KEY FACTS

ℹ️
🖼️
🍸 Tel: 020 3166 6115.
☕
🍴
🎧
🅿️ Nearby.
🎫 Please book, 0844 482 7777.
✂️
🔔
❄️

## VISITOR INFORMATION

■ **Address**
Spencer House
27 St James's Place
London SW1A 1NR

■ **Location**
Map 20:L8
OS Ref. TQ293 803
**Central London:**
off St James's Street,
overlooking Green Park.
**Underground:**
Green Park.

■ **Contact**
Jane Rick, Director
**Tel:** 020 7514 1958
**Fax:** 020 7409 2952
**Recorded Info Line:**
020 7499 8620.
**E-mail:**
tours@spencerhouse.co.uk

■ **Opening Times**
**2014**
**Open on Sundays from:**
10.30am-5.45pm.
Last tour 4.45pm.
Regular tours throughout
the day.
Max number on each tour
is 20.
**Monday mornings:** for
pre-booked groups only.
**Group size:** min 15-60.
**Closed:** January & August.
Open for private and
corporate hospitality except
during January & August.

■ **Admission**
Adult:              £12.00
Conc*:              £10.00
*Students, Members of the
V&A, Friends of the Royal
Academy, Tate Members
and senior citizens (only on
production of valid
identification), children
under 16. No children
under 10 admitted.
Prices include guided tour.

**For further information
please view the website:**
www.spencerhouse.co.uk
**or telephone the Tours
Administrator:** 020 7514
1958 (Mon-Fri only) or the
**Recorded Information
Line:** 020 7499 8620.

All images are copyright of
Spencer House Limited and
may not be used without
the permission of Spencer
House Limited.

### Conference/Function

| ROOM | Size | Max Cap |
|------|------|---------|
| Receptions | | 400 |
| Lunches & Dinners | | 126 |
| Board Meetings | | 40 |
| Theatre-style Meetings | | 100 |

The Great Room

# SPENCER HOUSE
www.spencerhouse.co.uk

## London's most magnificent 18th Century private palace.

Spencer House, built 1756-66 for the first Earl Spencer, an ancestor of Diana, Princess of Wales (1961-97), is London's finest surviving 18th Century town house. The magnificent private palace has regained the full splendour of its late 18th Century appearance after a painstaking ten-year restoration programme.

Designed by John Vardy and James 'Athenian' Stuart, the nine State Rooms are amongst the first neo-classical interiors in Europe. Vardy's Palm Room, with its spectacular screen of gilded palm trees and arched fronds, is a unique Palladian set-piece, while the elegant mural decorations of Stuart's Painted Room reflect the 18th Century passion for classical Greece and Rome. Stuart's superb gilded furniture has been returned to its original location in the Painted Room by courtesy of the V&A and English Heritage. Visitors can also see a fine collection of 18th Century paintings and furniture, specially assembled for the House, including five major Benjamin West paintings, graciously lent by Her Majesty The Queen.

The State Rooms are open to the public for viewing on Sundays. They are also available on a limited number of occasions each year for private and corporate entertaining during the rest of the week.

## KEY FACTS

ⓘ No photography inside House or Garden.

🍽 House only, ramps and lifts. WC.

👤 Obligatory. Comprehensive colour guidebook.

🐕 Guide Dogs only.

🔔

The Palm Room

The West Facade

# SYON PARK ® 🏛ⓕ
www.syonpark.co.uk

## London home of the Duke of Northumberland with magnificent Robert Adam interiors, 40-acres of gardens, including the spectacular Great Conservatory.

Described by John Betjeman as the 'Grand Architectural Walk', Syon House and its 200-acre park is the London home of the Duke of Northumberland, whose family, the Percys, have lived here for 400 years. Originally the site of a late medieval monastery, excavated by Channel 4's Time Team, Syon Park has a fascinating history. Catherine Howard was imprisoned at Syon before her execution, Lady Jane Grey was offered the crown whilst staying at Syon, and the 9th Earl of Northumberland was imprisoned in the Tower of London for 15 years because of his association with the Gunpowder Plot. The present house has Tudor origins but contains some of Robert Adam's finest interiors, which were commissioned by the 1st Duke in the 1760s. The private apartments and State bedrooms are available to view.

The house can be hired for filming and photo shoots subject to availability. Within the 'Capability' Brown landscaped park are 40 acres of gardens which contain the spectacular Great Conservatory designed by Charles Fowler in the 1820s. The House and Great Conservatory are available for corporate and private hire. The Northumberland Room in Syon House is an excellent venue for conferences, meetings, lunches and dinners (max 60). The State Apartments make a sumptuous setting for dinners, concerts, receptions, launches and wedding ceremonies (max 120). Marquees can be erected on the lawn adjacent to the house for balls and corporate events. The Great Conservatory is available for summer parties, launches, filming, photoshoots and wedding receptions (max 150).

## KEY FACTS

- ℹ️ No photography in the House.
- 🛍
- 🎋 Garden Centre.
- 🍷
- ♿ WCs. House - Limited access . Gardens and Great Conservatory - fully accessible.
- 🍽 The Refectory in the Garden Centre.
- 🍴
- 🚶 By arrangement.
- 🅿️ Free parking.
- 🐾
- ✖️
- 🔊
- 💷 See website for details.

## VISITOR INFORMATION

### ■ Owner
The Duke of Northumberland

### ■ Address
Syon House
Syon Park
Brentford
Middx
TW8 8JF

### ■ Location
Map 19:B8
**OS Ref. TQ173 767**
Between Brentford & Twickenham, off A4, A310 in SW London.
**Sat Nav:** TW7 6AZ
**Public Transport:**
Gunnersbury Station then bus 237 or 267. Brentford Rail, Ealing Broadway or Boston Manor Underground, then bus E8. Minicab companies available at the stations.
**Air:** Heathrow 8m.

### ■ Contact
Estate Office
**Tel:** 020 8560 0882
**Fax:** 020 8568 0936
**E-mail:**
info@syonpark.co.uk

### ■ Opening Times
**Syon House:**
**19 Mar-2 Nov**
Weds, Thurs, Suns and BHs 11am-5pm, last entry 4pm.

**Gardens only:**
**17 Mar-2 Nov**
Daily 10.30am-5pm, last entry at 4pm.
House, Gardens and Great Conservatory closed from 3 Nov 2014- 15 Mar 2015.

### ■ Admission
**House, Gardens & Conservatory:**
| | |
|---|---|
| Adult | £11.50 |
| Child | £5.00 |
| Conc. | £10.00 |
| Family (2+2) | £26.00 |

Booked groups (25+)
| | |
|---|---|
| Adult | £10.00 |
| Conc. | £9.00 |
| School Group | £3.00 |

**Gardens & Great Conservatory:**
| | |
|---|---|
| Adult | £6.50 |
| Child | £3.50 |
| Conc. | £5.00 |
| Family (2+2) | £14.00 |
| School Group | £2.00 |

Syon House Ventures reserves the right to alter opening times. Please phone or check website for up to date details and special events.

### Conference/Function

| ROOM | Size | Max Cap |
|---|---|---|
| Great Hall | 50'x30' | 120 |
| Great Conservatory | 60'x40' | 150 |
| Marquee | | 800 |

London - England

## VISITOR INFORMATION

■ **Owner**
Historic Royal Palaces

■ **Address**
London
EC3N 4AB

■ **Location**
**Map 20:P7**
**OS Ref. TQ336 806**
**Bus:** 15, 25, 42, 78, 100, D1, RV1.
**Underground:** Tower Hill on Circle/District Line. Docklands Light Railway: Tower Gateway Station.
**Rail:** Fenchurch Street Station and London Bridge Station.
**Boat:** From Embankment Pier, Westminster or Greenwich to Tower Pier. London Eye to Tower of London Express.

■ **Contact**
**Tel:** 0844 482 7777
**Venue Hire and Corporate Hospitality:** 020 3166 6226
**E-mail:** visitorservices.tol @hrp.org.uk

■ **Opening Times**
**Summer:**
Mar-Oct, Tues-Sat 9am-5.30pm (last admission 5pm).
Mons & Suns 10am-5.30pm (last admission 5pm).
**Winter:**
Nov-Feb, Tues-Sat 9am-4.30pm (last admission 4pm).
Mons & Suns 10am-4.30pm (last admission 4pm).
Closed 24-26 Dec and 1 Jan.

■ **Admission**
Call 0844 482 7777 or visit www.hrp.org.uk for more information.

ENTRY TO THE TRAITORS GATE

# TOWER OF LONDON
www.hrp.org.uk/toweroflondon

## The ancient stones reverberate with dark secrets, priceless jewels glint in fortified vaults and pampered ravens strut the grounds.

The Tower of London, founded by William the Conqueror in 1066-7, is one of the world's most famous fortresses, and one of Britain's most visited historic sites. Despite a grim reputation for a place of torture and death, there are so many more stories to be told about the Tower and its intriguing cast of characters.

This powerful and enduring symbol of the Norman Conquest has been enjoyed as a royal palace, served as an armoury and for over 600 years even housed a menagerie! Don't miss the re-presented Crown Jewels in the famous Jewel House, unlocking the story behind the 23,578 gems in the priceless royal jewels. Marvel at the Imperial State Crown and the largest diamond ever found and see the only treasure to escape destruction in 1649, after the Civil War. For centuries, this dazzling collection has featured in royal ceremonies, and it is still in use today.

Join Yeoman Warder tours to be entertained by captivating talks of pain, passion, treachery and torture at the Tower. Visit Tower Green and see the memorial to the people who died within the Tower walls. Find out why the last execution at the Tower was in 1941 and see how instruments of torture were used to extract 'confessions' from prisoners. Discover what life was like in the surprisingly luxurious Medieval Palace, and explore the stories of Henry II, Edward I and their courts at work.

See one of the Tower's most famous sights, the ravens. Legend has it Charles II believed that if the ravens were ever to leave the Tower, the fortress and the kingdom would fall. Step into 1000 years of history every day at the Tower of London.

## KEY FACTS

ℹ️ No Photography in Jewel house.

📷

☎ Tel: 020 3166 6226.

🚻 WCs.

🍴 Licensed.

🚶 Yeoman Warder tours are free and leave front entrance every ½ hr.

🅿 None for cars. Coach parking nearby.

🎟 To book 0844 482 7777.

## HAM HOUSE AND GARDEN ❧
### HAM ST, RICHMOND-UPON-THAMES, SURREY TW10 7RS
www.nationaltrust.org.uk/hamhouse

One of London's best kept secrets, this atmospheric Stuart mansion nestles on the banks of leafy Richmond-upon-Thames. It has remained virtually unchanged for 400 years and is internationally recognised for its superb collection of textiles, furniture and art which have remained in the house for centuries. Largely the vision of Elizabeth Murray, Countess of Dysart, who was deeply embroiled in the politics of the English Civil War and subsequent restoration of the monarchy, Ham House and Garden is an unusually complete survival of the 17th Century. It is reputed to be one of the most haunted houses in Britain.
**Location:** Map 19:B8. OS Ref TQ172 732. On S bank of the Thames, W of A307 at Petersham between Richmond and Kingston.

**Owner:** National Trust
**Contact:** The Property Administrator
**Tel:** 020 8940 1950 **Fax:** 020 8439 8241
**E-mail:** hamhouse@nationaltrust.org.uk
**Open:** House and Garden opening times vary throughout the year, please see website for further details.
**Admission:** National Trust members free. Prices vary throughout the year, please see website for further details.
**Key facts:** ⓘ No flash photography. ▣▣▣▣ WCs. ▣ Licensed. ▣ Licensed. ⅺ By arrangement. ▣ Ltd for coaches. ▣▣ Guide dogs only. ▣▣

© UK Parliament

## HOUSES OF PARLIAMENT
### WESTMINSTER, LONDON SW1A 0AA
www.parliament.uk/visiting

Inside one of London's most iconic buildings, tours of the Houses of Parliament offer visitors a unique combination of one thousand years of history, modern day politics, and stunning art and architecture.

Tours start by following the route taken by The Queen at the State Opening of Parliament; from The Queen's Robing Room, through the Royal Gallery and Prince's Chamber, and into the majestic Lords Chamber. Tours then move on to Central Lobby, Members' Lobby and one of the voting lobbies before entering the Commons Chamber, scene of many lively debates. Passing through St Stephen's Hall, the tours end in 900 year old Westminster Hall.

**Location:** Map 20:M8. OS Ref TQ303 795. Central London, 1km S of Trafalgar Square. Underground: Westminster.
**Tel:** 0844 847 1672 or +44 161 425 8677 if calling from outside the UK.
**Open:** Saturdays year round and on weekdays when Parliament is not sitting during major holiday periods (Easter, summer and Christmas).
**Admission:** Adults £16.50, Concessions (seniors, students, armed forces) £14.00, Children one child free with each paying adult otherwise £7.00.
**Key facts:** ⓘ Searches, similar to those used in airports, are conducted on entry. Cameras cannot be used except in Westminster Hall. ▣ Souvenir shop in Westminster Hall. ▣▣ Jubilee Cafe serves light refreshments. ⅺ▣▣▣▣

© National Trust Images / Andrew Butler

# OSTERLEY PARK AND HOUSE ❧
## JERSEY ROAD, ISLEWORTH, MIDDLESEX  TW7 4RB
### www.nationaltrust.org.uk/osterley

Created in the late 18th Century by architect Robert Adam, Osterley is one of the last surviving country estates in London. From the tree lined driveway, spot the Charolais cattle and ponies lazing away the day. Just around the lake the magnificent House awaits; presented as it would have been in its 1780s heyday. Three floors of rooms, from the classical grandeur of the Entrance Hall to the contrasting servants' quarters. Spot the animals in the immaculately preserved tapestries in the state apartments and imagine sleeping in the eight poster bed, reserved for visits from the monarch. The grounds are perfect for picnics or leisurely strolls. Or relax in the serenity of the restored 18th Century pleasure grounds, full of herbaceous borders, roses and ornamental vegetable beds as well as the original Robert Adam summer house with its lemon trees and highly scented shrubs. **Location:** Map 19:C7. OS Ref TQ146 780. A4 between Hammersmith and Hounslow. Main gates at Thornbury & Jersey Road junction. SatNav: TW7 4RD. **Owner:** National Trust **Tel:** 020 8232 5050 **E-mail:** osterley@nationaltrust.org.uk

**Open:** Whole property * ^ : Mon–Sun. 1 Mar-4 Apr, 12-4pm, 5 Apr-30 Sep, 11-5pm, 1-31 Oct, 12-4pm. Last entry one hour before stated closing time. *Basement floor only every Mon & Tues, half price admission. ^ Cafe opens 1hr earlier. Garden & cafe: 1 Nov-31 Dec Mon–Sun, 12-4pm. Shop & second-hand bookshop: 1 Nov-14 Dec, Sat & Sun, 12-4pm. House: 29 Nov-14 Dec, Sat & Sun, 12-4pm. Park & Car Park open daily.
**Admission:** *House & Garden: Adult £10.25, Child £5.15, Family £25.50. Groups (15+) £8.50. Garden: Adult £4.50, Child £2.30, Family £11.30. *includes a voluntary 10% Gift Aid donation. Car Park: £4.00, free to NT Members. Park and grounds: Free. **Key facts:** ℹ️ No flash photography inside House. 📷 Wide range of goods, handmade gifts to books & toys. 🌱 Second-hand bookshop sells plants grown on site in peat-free soil. ☎️ Contact the property for information. ♿ WCs. 🍽️ Seasonal menus, freshly baked cakes & cream teas. Family friendly. Kids' lunchboxes. 🛏️ 📷 By arrangement only. 🎧 Audio-visual guides. 🅿️ Limited for coaches. 🚗 🐕 Guide dogs only. 🏰 ❋ ♿

# SOUTHSIDE HOUSE 🏛️ⓕ
## 3 WOODHAYES ROAD, WIMBLEDON, LONDON  SW19 4RJ
### www.southsidehouse.com

Described by connoisseurs as an unforgettable experience, Southside House provides an eccentric backdrop to the lives and loves of generations of the Pennington Mellor Munthe families. Maintained in traditional style, without major refurbishment, and crowded with family possessions of centuries, Southside offers a wealth of fascinating family stories.
John Pennington-Mellor's daughter, Hilda, married Axel Munthe, the charismatic Swedish doctor and philanthropist. The preservation of the house was left to their youngest son who led a life of extraordinary adventure during the Second World War. Malcolm Munthe's surviving children continue to care for Southside House with its sister property Hellens (www.hellensmanor.com).
**Location:** Map 20:D8. OS Ref TQ234 706. On S side of Wimbledon Common (B281), opposite Crooked Billet Inn.

**Owner:** The Pennington-Mellor-Munthe Charity Trust
**Contact:** The Administrator
**Tel:** 020 8946 7643
**E-mail:** info@southsidehouse.com
**Open:** Easter Sat-3 Oct, Weds, Sats, Suns, BH Mons. Closed during Wimbledon fortnight. Guided Tours on the hour 2, 3 & 4 pm. Special group and candlelit evening tours, and private event bookings throughout the year, by arrangement.
**Admission:** Adults £9.00, Student £6.00, Child £4.50 (to be accompanied by an adult), Family £15.00 (max 4).
Concert and Event Programme – see webpage (www.southsidehouse.com).
**Key facts:** ℹ️ No Photography inside house.
ⓕ Obligatory. 🚗 🐕 ♿

## STRAWBERRY HILL ® 🏛
### 268 WALDEGRAVE ROAD, TWICKENHAM  TW1 4ST
**www.strawberryhillhouse.org.uk**

Strawberry Hill is Britain's finest example of Gothic Revival architecture and interior decoration. It began life in 1698 as a modest house, later transformed by Horace Walpole, the son of England's first Prime Minister. Between 1747 and 1792 Walpole doubled its size, creating extraordinary rooms and adding towers and battlements in fulfilment of his dream. Following an £8.9 million restoration with the support of the Heritage Lottery Fund, the show rooms on the ground and first floors have been fully restored to take the house back to the 1790s when Walpole had completed his creation. Strawberry Hill was a tourist site in its own day and like their 18th Century predecessors, modern visitors can enjoy this little gothic castle's charm which remains undiminished. **Location:** Map 19:C8. OS Ref TQ158 722. Off A310 between Twickenham and Teddington.

**Owner:** Strawberry Hill Trust
**Contact:** Laura Teale
**Tel:** 020 8744 1241  **E-mail:** general@strawberryhillhouse.org.uk
**Open:** House: 1 Mar-9 Nov Mon-Weds 2pm-4.20pm (last admission). Sat and Sun 12 noon-4.20pm (last admission). Cafe, shop museum, and temporary exhibitions (free admission) from 11am. Garden (free admisson): Open year-round at all reasonable hours.
**Admission:** Adult £12.00, Under 18's Free, Concessions £6.00. Please visit our website for the full list of concessions and discounts that may apply.
**Key facts:** 🖼 📶 📺 ⚕ WCs. 🍴 Licensed. 🎫 By arrangement. 🅿 Limited for cars. No coaches. ▦ 🐕 Guide dogs only. ⚘ ♨ 🎗

## SUTTON HOUSE 🍃
### 2 & 4 HOMERTON HIGH STREET, HACKNEY, LONDON  E9 6JQ
**www.nationaltrust.org.uk/suttonhouse**

A rare example of a Tudor red-brick house, built 1535 by Sir Ralph Sadleir, Principal Secretary of State for Henry VIII, with 18th Century alterations and later additions. Restoration revealed 16th Century detail, even in rooms of later periods. Notable features include original linenfold panelling and 17th Century wall paintings. Peel back the layers of time in this Hackney home and discover some unexpected occupants. Open Georgian Panels to reveal Tudor arches or see the squatters' artwork. Delve into family treasure chests or experience the sights and smells of a Tudor Kitchen.
**Location:** Map 20:P3. OS Ref TQ352 851. At the corner of Isabella Road and Homerton High St.
**Owner:** National Trust  **Contact:** The Custodian
**Tel:** 020 8986 2264
**E-mail:** suttonhouse@nationaltrust.org.uk

**Open:** Historic Rooms: 7 Apr-15 Apr Mon, Tues. 28 Jul-26 Aug Mon, Tues. 10.30am-5pm. 8 Feb-21 Dec Weds, Thurs & Fri 10.30am-5pm. 8 Feb-21 Dec Sat & Sun 12pm-5pm.
**Key facts:** 🛍 National Trust Gift Shop & Second-hand book shop. 📺 From lectures and talks to team building and workshops, our barn area provides you with privacy, while our adjoining café can provide you with refreshments throughout the day. ⚕ Ground floor only. WC.
🍴 Open all year round and everyday in the summer, indulge in a cream tea served on vintage crockery in our tearoom. 🚶 Guided Tours are held at weekends. Please call ahead for times. ▦ 🐕 Assistance dogs only. ♨ From February to December, whether you're looking for a ceremony only, or an all day reception, enjoy a perfect wedding day at Sutton House.
❄ Closed in January for Conservation. 🎗

## 18 STAFFORD TERRACE
### 18 Stafford Terrace, London  W8 7BH
www.rbkc.gov.uk/museums

From 1875, 18 Stafford Terrace was the home of Punch cartoonist Edward Linley Sambourne, his wife Marion, their two children and live-in servants. Originally decorated by the Sambournes in keeping with fashionable Aesthetic principles, the interiors evolved into wonderfully eclectic artistic statements within the confines of a typical middle-class home. **Location:** Map 20:I8. OS Ref TQ252 794. Parallel to Kensington High St, between Phillimore Gardens & Argyll Rd.
**Owner:** The Royal Borough of Kensington & Chelsea **Contact:** Curatorial staff **Tel:** 020 7602 3316 **Fax:** 0207371 2467 **E-mail:** museums@rbkc.gov.uk
**Open:** Mid Sep-Mid Jun. Visits are by guided tours only; Weds 11.15am, 2.15pm, Sats and Suns 11.15am, 1pm, 2.15pm, 3.30pm (weekend afternoon tours are costumed). **Admission:** Adult £8.00, Concession £6.00, Child (under 18yrs) £3.00. Groups (12+): Min 96. Joint group (12+) guided tour with Leighton House Museum £17.00pp. **Key facts:** ⓘ No photography. ▣ ⓧ Obligatory. ▣ None. ▣ ▣ Guide dogs only. ✳

## BANQUETING HOUSE
### Whitehall, London  SW1A 2ER
www.hrp.org.uk/banquetinghouse

This revolutionary structure was the first in England to be built in a Palladian style. It was designed by Inigo Jones for James I, and work finished in 1622. Intended for the splendour and exuberance of court masques, the Banqueting House is probably most famous for one real life drama: the execution of Charles I which took place here in 1649 to the 'dismal, universal groan' of the crowd. One of Charles's last sights as he walked through the Banqueting House to his death was the magnificent ceiling, painted by Peter Paul Rubens in 1630-4. **Location:** Map 20:M8. OS Ref TQ302 80. **Owner:** Historic Royal Palaces **Tel:** 0844 482 7777 **E-mail:** banquetinghouse@hrp.org.uk
**Open:** Mon-Sun 10am-5pm. Last adm 4.15pm. Closed BHs & 24 Dec–1 Jan (inc). With very few exceptions, the Banqueting House is guaranteed to open from 10am-1pm Mon-Sun, but we often close at short notice for functions & events. Please check times before your visit by calling +44 (0)203 166 6154/5. **Admission:** Enquiry line 0844 482 7777.
**Key facts:** ⓘ ▣ ⓣ ▣ WCs. ▣ Video and audio guide. ▣ ▣ ▣ ✳

© National Trust/Cristian Barnett

## 575 WANDSWORTH ROAD ❧
### Lambeth, London  SW8 3JD
www.nationaltrust.org.uk/575wandsworthroad

The hand-carved fretwork interior of this modest, early 19th Century, terraced house is enthralling and inspiring. Created by Khadambi Asalache, a Kenyan-born poet, novelist, philosopher of mathematics and British civil servant, who, over 20 years, turned his home into a work of art. Prompted initially by the need to disguise persistent damp he embellished almost every wall, ceiling and door in the house with fretwork patterns and motifs, The house stands as he left it, with his painted decoration on walls, doors and floors and with rooms furnished with his handmade fretwork furniture and carefully arranged collections of objects. **Location:** Map 20:L12. OS Ref 176:292761. 220 Yards from Wandsworth Road Overground Station **Tel:** 020 7720 9459
**E-mail:** 575wandsworthroad@nationaltrust.org.uk
**Open:** Sat 1 Mar–Sun 2 Nov, Wed evening, Fri, Sat & Sun.
**Admission:** By guided tour only, booking essential as placed are limited.

Capel Manor Gardens

© Britainonview

## BUCKINGHAM PALACE
### London  SW1A 1AA
www.royalcollection.org.uk

Buckingham Palace serves as both the office and London residence of Her Majesty The Queen. During the summer, when the Palace is not being used in its official capacity, visitors can tour the nineteen spectacular State Rooms, which are furnished with some of the greatest treasures from the Royal Collection.

**Location:** Map 20:L8. OS Ref TQ291 796.
Underground: Green Park, Victoria, St James's Park.
**Owner:** Official Residence of Her Majesty The Queen
**Contact:** Ticket Sales and Information Office
**Tel:** +44 (0)20 7766 7300
**E-mail:** bookinginfo@royalcollection.org.uk
**Open:** Selected dates in the year.
Contact for details or visit website.
**Admission:** Visit www.royalcollection.org.uk for details.
**Key facts:** ⊡ 🐾 Assistance dogs welcome.

## FOUNDLING MUSEUM ®
### 40 Brunswick Square, London  WC1N 1AZ
www.foundlingmuseum.org.uk

The Foundling Museum explores the history of the Foundling Hospital, the UK's first children's charity and first public art gallery. Through a dynamic programme of exhibitions and events we celebrate the ways in which artists of all disciplines have been inspired to improve children's lives since 1740. The Museum houses a significant collection of 18th Century art, interiors, music and social history, including works by William Hogarth and George Frideric Handel.

**Location:** Map 20:L6. OS Ref TQ303 822. Tube or Train Russell Square, Kings Cross St Pancras, Euston.
**Owner:** Foundling Museum
**Tel:** 020 7841 3600  **Fax:** 020 7841 3607
**E-mail:** enquiries@foundlingmuseum.org.uk
**Open:** Mon Closed. Tues–Sat 10am-5pm. Sun 11am-5pm.
**Admission:** £7.50, Concessions £5.00, Children up to 16yrs and Foundling Friends Free. National Trust members half price.
**Key facts:** ⅈ ⊡ 🍴 ♿ 🖥 🎞 📖 🐾 Guide dogs only. ⚑ ✳ ⚱

## CAPEL MANOR GARDENS
### Bullsmoor Lane, Enfield  EN1 4RQ
www.capelmanorgardens.co.uk

Set in a beautiful 30 acre estate, with over 60 gardens and landscapes to explore, including previous RHS Chelsea Flower Show gold medal winners, Capel Manor Gardens offers a tranquil oasis in a busy world. Come and enjoy the stunning scenery, picnic by the lake or relax in the restaurant and finish with a visit to the garden gift shop.

**Location:** Map 19:E4. OS Ref TQ344 997. Minutes from M25/J25. Tourist Board signs posted.
**Owner:** Capel Manor Charitable Organisation
**Contact:** Customer Services
**Tel:** 0845 6122 122  **Fax:** 01992 717 544
**Open:** Daily in summer: 10am-6pm. Last ticket 4pm, Gardens 5.30pm. Check for winter times.
**Admission:** Adult £5.50, Child £2.50, Conc. £4.50, Family £13.50. Charges alter for special show weekends and winter months.
**Key facts:** ⅈ ⊡ 🍴 ♿ Grounds. WC. 🖥 🍴 🎞 🅿 🐾 In grounds, on leads. ✳ ⚱

© Dr Johnson's House Trust

## DR JOHNSON'S HOUSE
### 17 Gough Square, London  EC4A 3DE
www.drjohnsonshouse.org

Dr Johnson's House is a charming 300-year-old townhouse, nestling amongst a maze of courts and alleys in the historic City of London. Samuel Johnson, the writer and wit, lived and worked here during the eighteenth century, compiling his great 'Dictionary' in the Garret. Today, the House is open to the public with restored interiors and a wealth of original features. **Location:** Map 20:N7. OS Ref TQ313 812. North of Fleet Street. **Owner:** The Trustees
**Contact:** The Curator  **Tel:** 020 7353 3745
**E-mail:** curator@drjohnsonshouse.org
**Open:** 11am-5pm Oct-Apr. 11am-5.30pm May-Sep.
**Admission:** Adults £4.50, Conc. (over 60, students, registered unemployed) £3.50, Child (up to 17) £1.50, Family £10.00. National Trust members discount.
**Key facts:** ⊡ Small shop-books, gifts & souvenirs. 🍴 Available for private events evenings & Sundays. ♿ Many unavoidable steps. 🎞 Pre-booked groups of 10+. ⊡ £2. 🅿 Disabled parking bays only in Gough Square & neighbouring streets. 🖥 English & History workshops, tours/talks schools, A-level groups & univeristies. ✳ ❄ Check website for Christmas closures. ⚱

St Paul's Cathedral
© Britain On View

## KEATS HOUSE
### Keats Grove, Hampstead, London NW3 2RR
www.cityoflondon.gov.uk/keatshousehampstead

This Grade I listed Regency house is where the poet John Keats lived from 1818 to 1820. Here he wrote 'Ode to a Nightingale' and met and fell in love with Fanny Brawne. Suffering from tuberculosis, Keats left for Italy, where he died at the age of 25. Fanny wore his engagement ring until her death, and it is now displayed at the house. Their love story was immortalised in Jane Campion's film 'Bright Star', released in 2009. The museum runs regular poetry readings, talks and events suitable for families throughout the year.
**Location:** Map 20:K3. OS Ref TQ272 856. Hampstead, NW3. Nearest Underground Belsize Park & Hampstead.
**Owner:** City of London **Contact:** The Manager
**Tel:** 020 7332 3868 **E-mail:** keatshouse@cityoflondon.gov.uk
**Open:** Our opening hours are 1 Mar-31 Oct: Tues-Sun, 1pm-5pm; 1 Nov-28 Feb: Fri-Sun, 1pm-5pm. School parties and pre-booked groups by arrangement. The house is also open on Bank Holiday Mondays.
**Admission:** Adults £5.00, Concessions £3.00, Children 16 and under are free. Tickets are valid for one year.
**Key facts:** ⬚ ⬚ WCs. ▣ None. ▣ ▣ Guide dogs only. ▣

## ST PAUL'S CATHEDRAL
### St Paul's Churchyard, London EC4M 8AD
www.stpauls.co.uk

St Paul's Cathedral, with its famous dome, is England's architectural masterpiece and place of national celebration. Enter and explore the beauty of Christopher Wren's St Paul's; the cathedral floor, crypt and famous whispering, stone and golden galleries. Included are touch-screen multimedia guides, scheduled guided tours and the Oculus film experience.
**Location:** Map 20:N7. OS Ref TQ321 812. Central London.
**Owner:** Chapter of St Paul's Cathedral
**Tel:** 020 7246 8350 / 020 7246 8348
**Fax:** 020 7248 3104
**E-mail:** reception@stpaulscathedral.org.uk
**Open:** Mon-Sat, 8.30am-4.30pm. Last admission for sightseeing 4.00pm. Once inside the cathedral, the galleries are open from 9.30am-4.15pm.
**Admission:** Please contact us or view the website for up to date details of the admission prices as well as discounts for groups and online booking.
**Key facts:** ⓘ No photography or videos permitted inside the Cathedral. ⬚ ⬚ ⬚ Wheelchair accessible throughout, except galleries. ▣ ▣ ▣ ⬚ ▣ None for cars, limited for coaches in surrounding area. ▣ ▣ Assistance dogs only. ❄ ▣

## KENWOOD HOUSE ⌗
### Hampstead Lane, London NW3 7JR
www.english-heritage.org.uk/kenwoodhouse

Set in tranquil parkland in fashionable Hampstead, with panoramic views over London, Kenwood has undergone an extensive programme of repairs with striking re-presentations of its fabulous interior and outstanding art collections. View the sumptuous Robert Adam rooms and admire famous paintings.
**Location:** Map 20:K1. OS Ref TQ270 874. M1/J2. Signed off A1.
**Owner:** English Heritage
**Tel:** 020 8348 1286 **E-mail:** customers@english-heritage.org.uk
**Open:** Please visit www.english-heritage.org.uk for opening times, admission prices and the most up-to-date information.
**Key facts:** ⓘ WCs. Concerts, exhibitions, filming. No photography in house. ⬚ ⬚ Exclusive private and corporate hospitality. ▣ ▣ Available on request (in English). Please call for details. ▣ West Lodge car park (Pay & Display) on Hampstead Lane. Parking for the disabled. ▣ Free when booked in advance on 020 7973 3485. ▣ Guide dogs only. ❄ ▣

## SOMERSET HOUSE
### Strand, London WC2R 1LA
www.somersethouse.org.uk

Somerset House is a spectacular neo-classical building in the heart of London. During summer 55 fountains dance in the courtyard, and in winter you can skate on London's favourite ice rink. Somerset House also hosts open-air concerts and films, contemporary art and design exhibitions, learning events and free guided tours.
**Location:** Map 20:N7. OS Ref TQ308 809. Sitting between the Strand and the north bank of the River Thames. Entrances on Strand, Embankment and Waterloo Bridge.
**Owner:** Somerset House Trust **Contact:** Visitor Communications
**Tel:** 020 7845 4600 **Fax:** 020 7836 7613 **E-mail:** info@somersethouse.org.uk
**Open:** For opening times, please see website.
**Admission:** For admission prices, please see website.
**Key facts:** ⬚ ⬚ ⬚ WCs. ▣ Licensed. ⬚ Licensed. ▣ By arrangement. ▣ ▣ On leads. ▣ ❄ ▣

## BURGH HOUSE

**New End Square, Hampstead, London NW3 1LT**

Grade I listed building (1703) in the heart of Hampstead with original panelled rooms, 'barley sugar' staircase banisters and music room. Hampstead Museum, permanent and changing exhibitions. Prize-winning terraced garden. Regular programme of concerts, art exhibitions, and events. Special facilities for schools visits. Rooms for hire. Wedding receptions and ceremonies.

**Location:** Map 20:J2. OS Ref TQ266 859. New End Square, E of Hampstead Underground station. **Owner:** London Borough of Camden

**Contact:** General Manager **Tel:** 020 7431 0144

**Fax:** 020 7435 8817 **Buttery:** 0207 794 2905 **E-mail:** info@burghhouse.org.uk

**Website:** www.burghhouse.org.uk **Open:** Wed-Fri & Sun 12-5pm. Closed Christmas fortnight. Groups by arrangement. Buttery: Wed-Fri 11am-5.30pm, Sat & Sun 9.30am-5.30pm. **Admission:** Free.

**Key facts:** ⬜ 🎥 ♿ Suitable. WCs. 🍽 Licensed. 🍴 Licensed. 🎦 By arrangement. 📷 By arrangement. 🐕 In grounds. ▲ ❄ 💷

## CHELSEA PHYSIC GARDEN

**66 Royal Hospital Road, London SW3 4HS**

Tucked away beside the Thames, the Garden was founded in 1673 by the Worshipful Society of Apothecaries and is London's oldest botanic garden. With over 5,000 different plants, notable features include: Europe's oldest pond rockery; Garden of Edible and Useful Plants and new for 2014, remodelled Garden of Medicinal Plants. **Location:** Map 20:K10. OS Ref TQ276 778. Underground: South Kensington or Sloane Square. Rail: Victoria or Clapham Junction **Owner:** Chelsea Physic Garden Company **Tel:** 020 7352 5646 **Fax:** 020 7376 3910

**E-mail:** enquiries@chelseaphysicgarden.co.uk

**Website:** www.chelseaphysicgarden.co.uk **Open:** Apr-Oct: Tues-Fri, Suns & BHs 11am-6pm. Late opening on Weds Jul-Aug until 10pm. Check website for winter openings. **Admission:** Please see website for latest admission prices.

**Key facts:** 🎦 No bicycles, ball games or wheeled toys. Under 16s must be accompanied (max 2 per adult). ⬜ 🎥 🎦 ♿ Suitable. WCs. 🍽 Licensed. 📷 Free. 📷 Free. 🐕 🐾 Guide dogs only. 💷

## HONEYWOOD MUSEUM

**Honeywood Walk, Carshalton SM5 3NX**

Local history museum in a 17th Century listed building next to the picturesque Carshalton Ponds, containing displays on the history of the house and local area, plus a changing programme of exhibitions and events on a wide range of subjects. Attractive garden at rear.

**Location:** Map 19:D9. OS Ref TQ279 646. A232 approximately 4m W of Croydon. **Owner:** London Borough of Sutton

**Contact:** The Curator **Tel:** 020 8770 4297

**E-mail:** lbshoneywood@btconnect.com

**Website:** www.sutton.gov.uk / www.friendsofhoneywood.co.uk

**Open:** Weds-Fri, 11am-5pm. Sat, Suns & BH Mons, 10am-5pm. Tea room closes 4.30pm.

**Admission:** Free admission.

**Key facts:** ⬜ ♿ WCs. 🍽 📷 By arrangement. 🅿 Limited. 📷 🐾 Guide dogs only. ❄ 💷

## LITTLE HOLLAND HOUSE

**40 Beeches Avenue, Carshalton SM5 3LW**

Step back in time and visit the former home of Frank Dickinson (1874-1961) who dreamt of a house which would follow the ideals of Morris and Ruskin. Dickinson designed, built and furnished the house himself from 1902 onwards. The Grade II* interior features handmade furniture, metalwork, carvings and paintings produced by Dickinson in an eclectic mix of the Arts and Crafts and Art Nouveau styles.

**Location:** Map 19:D9. OS Ref TQ275 634. On B278 1m S of junction with A232. **Owner:** London Borough of Sutton **Contact:** Ms V Murphy

**Tel:** 020 8770 4781 **Fax:** 020 8770 4777 **E-mail:** valary.murphy@sutton.gov.uk

**Website:** www.sutton.gov.uk

**Open:** First Sun of each month & BH Suns & Mons (excluding Christmas & New Year), 1.30pm-5.30pm.

**Admission:** Free. Groups by arrangement, £5.00pp (includes talk & guided tour).

**Key facts:** 🎦 No photography in house. ⬜ ♿ Partial. 📷 By arrangement. 🐾 Guide dogs only. ❄

Pitzhanger Manor-House

## WESTMINSTER CATHEDRAL

**Victoria, London SW1P 1QW**

The Roman Catholic Cathedral of the Archbishop of Westminster. Spectacular building in the Byzantine style, designed by J F Bentley, opened in 1903, famous for its mosaics, marble and music. Bell Tower viewing gallery has spectacular views across London. Exhibition displaying vestments, rare ecclesiastical objects and sacred relics.

**Location:** Map 20:L9. OS Ref TQ293 791. Off Victoria Street, between Victoria Station and Westminster Abbey. **Owner:** Diocese of Westminster

**Contact:** Revd Canon Christopher Tuckwell **Tel:** 020 7798 9055

**Fax:** 020 7798 9090 **Website:** www.westminstercathedral.org.uk

**Open:** All year: 7am-7pm. Please telephone for times at Easter & Christmas.

**Admission:** Free. Tower lift/viewing gallery charge: Adult £5.00 Family (2+4) £11.00 Conc. £2.50. Exhibition prices as those for viewing gallery. Telephone 020 7798 9028 for opening times of Tower and exhibition.

**Key facts:** ⬜ ♿ 🍽 📷 Booking required. 📷 Worksheets & tours. 🐾 ❄

## WHITEHALL

**1 Malden Road, Cheam SM3 8QD**

A Tudor timber-framed house, c1500, in the heart of Cheam Village. Displays on the history of the house and the people who lived here, Nonsuch Palace, Cheam School and Dr. Syntax (William Gilpin). Changing exhibitions and special events throughout the year. Garden with medieval well. Homemade cakes in tearoom.

**Location:** Map 19:C9. OS Ref TQ242638. Approx. 2m S of A3 on A2043 just N of junction with A232.

**Owner:** London Borough of Sutton **Contact:** The Curator

**Tel/Fax:** 020 8643 1236 **E-mail:** whitehallmuseum@sutton.gov.uk

**Website:** www.sutton.gov.uk

**Open:** Wed-Fri, 2-5pm; Sat 10am-5pm; Sun & BH Mons, 2-5pm. Tearoom closes 4.30pm.

**Admission:** Free; Groups by arrangement £4.00pp (includes talk and tour).

**Key facts:** ⬜ ♿ Partial. 🍽 📷 By arrangement. 📷 🐾 Guide dogs only. ❄ 💷

## PITZHANGER MANOR-HOUSE

**Walpole Park, Mattock Lane, Ealing W5 5EQ**

A Grade I listed restored Georgian villa **Location:** Map 19:C7. OS Ref TQ176 805. Ealing, London. **Tel:** 020 8567 1227 **Fax:** 020 8567 0595

**E-mail:** pmgallery&house@ealing.gov.uk **Website:** www.ealing.gov.uk/pmgalleryandhouse **Open:** All year: Tue-Fri, 1-5pm. Sat, 11am-5pm. Summer Suns: ring for details. Closed Christmas, Easter, New Year & BHs. **Admission:** Free.

### APSLEY HOUSE ⌗
**Apsley House, Hyde Park Corner, London  W1J 7NT**
**Tel:** 020 7499 5676 **E-mail:** customers@english-heritage.org.uk

### CHANDOS MAUSOLEUM ⌂
**Whitchurch Lane, Little Stanmore, London  HA8 6RB**
**Tel:** 0845 303 2760 **E-mail:** central@thecct.org.uk

### ELTHAM PALACE AND GARDENS ⌗
**Eltham Palace, Court Yard, Eltham, London  SE9 5QE**
**Tel:** 020 8294 2548 **E-mail:** customers@english-heritage.org.uk

### FITZROY HOUSE ⌂
**37 Fitzroy Street, Fitzrovia, London  W1T 6DX**
**Tel:** 020 7255 2422 **E-mail:** info@fitzroyhouse.org

### GUNNERSBURY PARK & MUSEUM
**Gunnersbury Park, London  W3 8LQ**
**Tel:** 020 8992 1612 **E-mail:** gp-museum@cip.org.uk

### HOGARTH'S HOUSE
**Hogarth Lane, Great West Road, London  W4 2QN**
**Tel:** 020 8994 6757 **E-mail:** victoria.northwood@cip.org.uk

### JEWEL TOWER ⌗
**Abingdon Street, Westminster, London  SW1P 3JX**
**Tel:** 020 7222 2219 **E-mail:** customers@english-heritage.org.uk

### KNELLER HALL
**Kneller Road, Whitton, Twickenham  TW2 7DU**
**Tel:** 020 8744 8633

### MARBLE HILL HOUSE ⌗
**Richmond Road, Twickenham  TW1 2NL**
**Tel:** 020 8892 5115 **E-mail:** customers@english-heritage.org.uk

### MYDDELTON HOUSE GARDENS
**Myddelton House, Bulls Cross, Enfield  EN2 9HG**
**Tel:** 0845 677 0600 **E-mail:** scrow@leevalleypark.org.uk

### RANGER'S HOUSE ⌗
**Chesterfield Walk, Blackheath, London  SE10 8QX**
**Tel:** 020 8853 0035 **E-mail:** customers@english-heritage.org.uk

### ST ANDREW'S CHURCH ⌂
**Old Church Lane, Kingsbury, London  NW9 8RU**
**Tel:** 0845 303 2760 **E-mail:** central@thecct.org.uk

### SANDYCOMBE LODGE
**40 Sandycombe Road, Twickenham  TW1 2NQ**
**E-mail:** turnerintwickenham@gmail.com

### TERRACE GARDENS
**Petersham Road, Richmond, Surrey  TW10**
**Tel:** 08456 122 660

### WELLINGTON ARCH ⌗
**Hyde Park Corner, London  W1J 7JZ**
**Tel:** 020 7930 2726 **E-mail:** customers@english-heritage.org.uk

### WILLIAM MORRIS GALLERY
**Lloyd Park, Forest Road, Walthamstow, London  E17 4PP**
**Tel:** 020 8527 9782

Chiswick House Gardens - The Classic Bridge

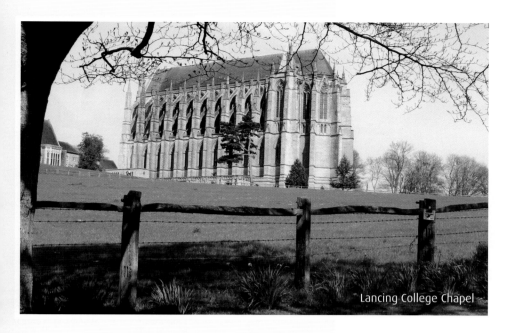

Lancing College Chapel

Berkshire
Buckinghamshire
Hampshire
Kent
Oxfordshire
Surrey
Sussex
Isle of Wight

# South East

South coast castles, sleepy manor houses in the Weald and Palladian mansions and palaces in the home counties; the range of historic houses and gardens in the South East is unsurpassed.

*New Entries for 2014:*
• St John's Jerusalem
• Lancing College Chapel
• Tonbridge Castle

• Claydon House
• Glynde Place
• Clandon Park and Hatchlands Park

**Find stylish hotels with a personal welcome and good cuisine in the South East. More information on page 372.**

• Deans Place Hotel
• Drakes Hotel
• Flackley Ash Hotel & Spa
• Hotel Una
• The Marquis at Alkham
• The Millstream Hotel

• Newick Park Hotel
• The Priory Bay Hotel
• Romney Bay House Hotel
• Stone House
• White Horse Hotel & Brasserie

## SIGNPOST
SELECTED PREMIER HOTELS 2014

www.signpost.co.uk

135

# DORNEY COURT 🏛 Ⓕ
## NR. WINDSOR, BERKSHIRE  SL4 6QP
### www.dorneycourt.co.uk

"One of the finest Tudor Manor Houses in England" - Country Life. Grade I listed and noted for its outstanding architectural and historical importance. Home of the Palmers since the early 16th Century, passing from father to son over thirteen generations. Highlights include the magnificent Great Hall, oak and lacquer furniture and artwork which spans the lifetime of the house. The stunning Old Coach House Barn, set next to Dorney Court, opens on 1 January 2014 and provides a beautiful and flexible space for weddings as well as private and corporate events.

**Location:** Map 3:G2. OS Ref SU926 791. 5 mins off M4/J7, 10mins from Windsor, 2m W of Eton

**Owner/Contact:** Mr James Palmer
**Tel:** 01628 604638
**E-mail:** enquiries@dorneycourt.co.uk
**Open:** May Bank Holidays (4 & 5 May; 25 & 26 May) and every day in Aug. 1.30pm with last admissions at 5pm.
**Admission:** Adult: £8.00, Child (10yrs+) £5.00. OAP's: £7.50 Groups (10+): £7.50 when house is open to public. Private group rates at other times.
**Key facts:** ℹ Film & photographic shoots. No stiletto heels. 🏵 Garden centre. ⛩ Wedding receptions. 🛈 🍽 Licensed. 🍴 Licensed. 🚶 Obligatory. 🅿 🖼 ✂ Guide dogs only. ♿ ❄ ♨ €

# ST THOMAS' CHURCH
## East Shefford, Hungerford, Berkshire RG17 7EF
### www.visitchurches.org.uk

This simple little church, with pre-Norman origins, stands in an idyllic spot beside a water meadow next to the River Lambourn. Its village has long since vanished, but the spirit of the villagers shines through in the church's simple craftsmanship, glorious medieval wallpaintings and fabulous tombs. The alabaster statue of local noble Sir Thomas Fettiplace lies alongside that of his wife and gives a rare glimpse of 15th Century fashion. Look out for the lovely Norman tub font, an early medieval tomb, and fragments of early stained glass.
**Location:** OS Ref SU391 747. 2 miles north east of M4 junction 14, off A338 (Wantage Road).
**Open:** Open daily.

## ETON COLLEGE
### Windsor, Berkshire SL4 6DW
Eton College, founded in 1440 by Henry VI, is one of the oldest schools in the country. The original and historic buildings of the Foundation are part of the heritage of the British Isles and visitors are invited to experience the beauty of the precinct, which includes the College Chapel.
**Location:** Map 3:G2. OS Ref SU967 779. Off M4/J5. Access from Windsor by footbridge only. Vehicle access from Slough 2m N
**Owner:** Provost & Fellows  **Contact:** Rebecca Hunkin
**Tel:** 01753 671177/671157  **Fax:** 01753 671029
**E-mail:** r.hunkin@etoncollege.org.uk  **Website:** www.etoncollege.com
**Open:** During school holidays and Wed, Fri, Sat & Sun during term time between Mar-Oct. Please check with the Visits Office. Pre-booked groups welcome all year.
**Admission:** Please check with Visits Office. Groups by appointment only. Rates vary according to tour type.
**Key facts:** ▢ ⊤ ⬚ Ground floor. WC. 𝄪 🅿 Limited. ⬚ Guide dogs only. ⬚

## ST BARTHOLOMEW'S CHURCH
### Lower Basildon, Reading, Berkshire RG8 9NH
This striking flint-and-brick 700-year-old church stands in a pretty churchyard shaded by fine trees near a beautiful stretch of the Thames. It is filled with memorials to past parishioners and, in early spring, a host of daffodils. Jethro Tull, the father of modern farming, has a memorial here and there is a moving marble statue of two young brothers who drowned in the Thames in 1886. The church itself is simple and serene. The nave and south door were built in the 13th Century, while the ornate roof timbers were installed in the 15th Century, when parishioners grew rich from the local wool and corn trade. Inside, there are several stunning memorials including brass effigies of John Clerk and his wife Lucie, both in medieval costume. The 19th Century memorial for Sir Francis Sykes has a statue of a woman weeping by John Flaxman, famous for his Wedgewood designs.
**Location:** OS Ref SU612 793. 7 miles south of Wallingford, off A329, adjacent to the River Thames and the railway.
**Website:** www.visitchurches.org.uk  **Open:** Open daily 9am to 5pm.

# WINDSOR CASTLE
## Windsor, Berkshire SL4 1NJ
### www.royalcollection.org.uk

Established in the 11th Century by William the Conqueror, Windsor Castle is the oldest and largest occupied castle in the world. Visitors can enjoy the magnificent State Apartments, Queen Mary's Dolls' House, changing exhibitions in the Drawings Gallery, and St George's Chapel. In winter months, the sumptuous Semi-State Rooms are also open to visitors.
**Location:** Map 3:G2. OS Ref SU969 770. M4/J6, M3/J3. 20m from central London. **Owner:** Official Residence of Her Majesty The Queen
**Contact:** Ticket Sales and Information Office
**Tel:** +44 (0)20 7766 7304 **E-mail:** bookinginfo@royalcollection.org.uk
**Open:** Please see website for opening times.
**Admission:** Visit www.royalcollection.org.uk for details.
**Key facts:** ⓘ Photography and filming (for private use only) is permitted in the Castle Precincts. ⬚ Most public areas are accessible for wheelchair-users, including the State Apartments. 𝄪 Guided tours of the Castle Precincts are available at regular intervals throughout the day. ▢ ⬚ Assistance dogs only.

St Bartholomew's Church, Lower Basildon

## VISITOR INFORMATION

### ■ Owner
Mrs E. MacLeod Matthews & Mr C. MacLeod Matthews

### ■ Address
Chenies
Buckinghamshire
WD3 6ER

### ■ Location
Map 7:D12
OS Ref. TQ016 984
N of A404 between
Amersham &
Rickmansworth M25-Ext
18, 3m.

### ■ Contact
Chenies Manor House
**Tel:** 01494 762888
**E-mail:**
macleodmatthews@
btinternet.com

### ■ Opening Times
2nd April–30th October
Inclusive 2014, Weds,
Thurs and Bank Holiday
Mons 2-5pm (last entry to
the house 4.15pm).

### ■ Admission
**House & Garden:**
Adult          £7.00
Child          £4.00
**Garden only:**
Adult          £5.00
Child          £3.50
Groups (20+) by
arrangement throughout
the year.

### ■ Special Events
**21 Apr–Easter Mon**
House & Garden 2-5pm.
The first mention of the
distribution of Easter Eggs
was at Chenies. Children's
Egg Races, Chenies
Resident Magician–Dee
Riley, plants for sale,
homemade teas.

**5 May–BH Mon**
House & Garden 2-5pm.
"Tulip Festival". Bloms
Tulips throughout house &
gardens. Homemade teas,
shop, plants for sale,
Chenies Magician–Dee
Riley.

**26 May–BH Mon**
House & Garden 2-5pm.
Carriage Driving Day
10am-4pm (contact Shirley
Higgins 01923 267919).
Homemade teas, shop,
plants for sale, Chenies
Magician–Dee Riley.

**20th Jul–Sun**
Famous Plant & Garden
Fair 10-5pm. (House 2pm).
75 Specialist Nurseries from
around the country.
Gardens from 10am.
Refreshments all day.

**25 Aug-BH Mon**
House & Garden open
2-5pm. "Dahlia Festival".
Large number of different
varieties of Dahlias
throughout the house and
gardens. Chenies Magician
– Dee Riley.

**29-30 Oct 2-5pm**
"Spooks and Surprises".
Special scary tour of house
for children. Visit the
difficult Yew Maze.
Homemade teas, shop.

# CHENIES MANOR HOUSE Ⓕ
www.cheniesmanorhouse.co.uk

## The Manor House is in the picturesque village of Chenies and lies in the beautiful Chiltern Hills.

The picturesque village of Chenies lies in the beautiful Chiltern Hills. The Manor House is approached by a gravel drive leading past the church. Home of the MacLeod Matthews family, this 15th and 16th Century manor house with fortified tower is the original home of the Earls of Bedford, visited by Henry VIII and Elizabeth I. Elizabeth was a frequent visitor, first coming as an infant in 1534 and as Queen she visited on several occasions, once staying for six weeks. The Bedford Mausoleum is in the adjacent church. The house contains tapestries and furniture mainly of the 16th and 17th Centuries, hiding places and a collection of antique dolls. Art exhibitions are held throughout the season in the restored 16th Century pavilion. The Manor is surrounded by five acres of enchanting gardens which have been featured in many publications and on television. It is famed for the Spring display of tulips. From early June there is a succession of colour in the Tudor Sunken Garden, the White Garden, herbaceous borders and Fountain Court. The Physic Garden contains a wide selection of medicinal and culinary herbs. In the Parterre is an ancient oak and a complicated yew maze while the Kitchen Garden is in Victorian style with unusual vegetables and fruit. Attractive dried and fresh flower arrangements decorate the house. Winner of the Historic Houses Association and Christie's Garden of the Year Award, 2009.

## KEY FACTS

Gardens only.

Delicious homemade teas in the Garden Room.

# HUGHENDEN ❧
## HIGH WYCOMBE, BUCKINGHAMSHIRE HP14 4LA
### www.nationaltrust.org.uk/hughendenmanor

Amid rolling Chilterns countryside, discover the hideaway and colourful private life of Benjamin Disraeli, the most unlikely Victorian Prime Minister. Follow in his footsteps, stroll through his German forest, relax in his elegant garden and imagine dining with Queen Victoria in the atmospheric manor. Uncover the Second World War story of Operation Hillside, for which unconventional artists painted maps for bombing missions - including the famous Dambusters raid. Discover the story of the map makers in our basement exhibition. Outdoors, get tips for growing your own vegetables in our walled garden. Don't miss our ancient woodland, where you may spot red kites soaring overhead.

**Location:** Map 3:F1. OS Ref SU866 955. 1½ m N of High Wycombe on the W side of the A4128.

**Owner:** National Trust **Contact:** The Estate Office

**Tel:** 01494 755573 **Fax:** 01494 474284 **Infoline:** 01494 755565
**E-mail:** hughenden@nationaltrust.org.uk
**Open:** Garden, shop & restaurant: 1 Jan-14 Feb, daily, 11am-3pm, 15 Feb-31 Dec, daily, 10am-5.30pm, or dusk if earlier. Manor: 1 Jan-14 Feb, daily, 11am-3pm, 15 Feb-31 Dec, daily, 11am-5.00pm, or dusk if earlier. Closed 24 and 25 Dec.

**Admission:** House & Garden: Adult £9.40, Child £4.70, Family £25.00. Garden only: Adult £3.60, Child £2.50, Family £10.00. Woodlands Free. Groups: Adult £7.40. Free to NT Members. Includes a voluntary 10% donation but visitors can choose to pay the standard prices advised at the property.

**Key facts:** ▢ ▢ ▢ Partial. WCs. ▢ ▢ Daily. ▢ ▢ ▢ Guide dogs only in the formal and walled gardens. ▢ ▢

Nether Winchendon House

# ASCOTT ✿

## Wing, Leighton Buzzard, Buckinghamshire LU7 0PR
www.ascottestate.co.uk

Originally a half-timbered Jacobean farmhouse, Ascott was bought in 1876 by the de Rothschild family and considerably transformed and enlarged. It now houses an exceptional collection of fine paintings, Oriental porcelain and English and French furniture. The extensive gardens are a mixture of the formal and natural. **Location:** Map 7:D11. OS Ref SP891 230. ½m E of Wing, 2m SW of Leighton Buzzard, on A418. **Owner:** National Trust
**Contact:** Estate Manager **Tel:** 01296 688242
**Fax:** 01296 681904 **E-mail:** info@ascottestate.co.uk
**Open:** House and Garden: 25 Mar-1 June: Tue-Sun, 2-6pm. 3 June-24 July: Tue-Thur, 2-6pm. 29 July-12 Sep Tue-Sun, 2-6pm. Last admission 5pm. Open on Bank Holiday Mondays. **Admission:** House and garden: Adult £10.00, Child £5.00. Garden only: £5.00, Child £2.50. No reduction for groups. Groups must book prior to visit. NT members free, except NGS days, 5 May and 25 Aug, where normal admission fees apply.
**Key facts:** ⓘ Wheelchairs available from the Entrance Kiosk. 🖼 WC's located in the National Trust car park only 🅿 220 metres. Limited for coaches. 🚫

# WOTTON HOUSE

## Wotton Underwood, Aylesbury Buckinghamshire HP18 0SB

The Capability Brown Pleasure Grounds at Wotton, currently undergoing restoration, are related to the Stowe gardens, both belonging to the Grenville family when Brown laid out the Wotton grounds between 1750 and 1767. A series of man-made features on the 3 mile circuit include bridges, temples and statues.
**Location:** Map 7:B11. OS Ref 468576, 216168. Either A41 turn off Kingswood, or M40/J7 via Thame.
**Owner/Contact:** David Gladstone
**Tel:** 01844 238363
**Fax:** 01844 238380
**E-mail:** david.gladstone@which.net
**Open:** 2 Apr-3 Sep: Weds only, 2-5pm. Also: 5 Apr, 21 Apr, 26 May, 5 Jul, 30 Aug: 2-5pm.
**Admission:** Adult £6.00, Child Free, Conc. £3.00. Groups (max 25).
**Key facts:** 🖼 ⓘ Obligatory.
🅿 Limited parking for coaches. 🚫 On leads.

# CLAYDON HOUSE ✿

**Claydon House, Middle Claydon, Buckinghamshire MK18 2EY**

Nestled in the heart of Buckinghamshire countryside lies the beautiful mansion, Claydon House. Here, visitors can enjoy walks along the lake, get to know the family home, browse the shops and catering outlets, and much, much more. Home to the Verneys for 500 years there are lots of interesting characters to uncover, from Barbary pirates to Florence Nightingale, plus a beautiful and unqiue 17th Century costume exhibition to see. **Location:** Map 7:C11. OS Ref SP719 253. M40 J9, signposted off A413 (Buckingham) & A41 (Waddesdon crossroads) **Owner:** National Trust
**Contact:** House Manager **Tel:** 01296 730349
**E-mail:** claydon@nationaltrust.org.uk **Website:** www.nationaltrust.org.uk/claydon **Open:** House: please visit our website. Garden: please call 01296 730252 for opening times and admission prices.
**Key facts:** 📷 💻 01296 730004. 📠 01296 730004. 🖼 🅿 🖼
🐕 On leads in park. 🖼 House & garden. 🔔 📖

# NETHER WINCHENDON HOUSE 🏛®

**Nether Winchendon, Nr Thame, Buckinghamshire HP18 0DY**

Mediaeval Manor Strawberry Hill Gothick. Home last Royal Governor Massachussetts. Continuous family occupation since 1559.
**Location:** Map 7:C11. **Tel:** 01844 290101 **Website:** www.nwhouse.co.uk
**Open:** Apr 22-May 23 (not Sats), May 26 & Aug 25, 2.30-5.30pm. Tours ¼ to each hour. **Admission:** £8.00, Art Fund £6.00, HHA Free, Conc. £5.00, not Sun or BH's. No conc to Art Fund or HHA when open for NGS.

Hughenden

### VISITOR INFORMATION

■ **Owner**
Lord Montagu

■ **Address**
Beaulieu
Hampshire
SO42 7ZN

■ **Location**
**Map 3:C6**
**OS Ref. SU387 025**
M27 to J2, A326, B3054
follow brown signs.
**Bus:** Local service within
the New Forest.
**Rail:** Station at
Brockenhurst 7m away.

■ **Contact**
John Montagu Building,
Beaulieu, Hants SO42 7ZN
**Tel:** 01590 612345
**E-mail:**
info@beaulieu.co.uk

■ **Opening Times**
Summer Whitsun -
September Daily,
10am-6pm. Winter
October-Whitsun Daily,
10am-5pm Please check
website for exact dates.
Closed Christmas Day.

■ **Admission**
All year Individual rates
upon application. Groups
(15+) Rates upon
application.

■ **Special Events**
Apr 27 Boatjumble.
May 17/18 Spring
Autojumble.
Jun 14/15 Custom and Hot
Rod Festival.
Jul 13 Motorcycle
Ride-In Day.
Sept 6/7 International
Autojumble.
Oct 25 Fireworks
Spectacular.
All ticket enquiries to our
Special Events Booking
Office. Tel 01590 612888.

**Conference/Function**

| ROOM | Size | Max Cap |
|---|---|---|
| Brabazon (x3) | 40' x 40' | 85 (x3) |
| Domus | 69' x 27' | 150 |
| Palace House | | 60 |
| Motor Museum | | 250 |

# BEAULIEU 🏠Ⓕ
### www.beaulieu.co.uk

**Voted 2013 Large Visitor Attraction Gold Winners in the England for Excellence Awards, Beaulieu has been owned by the same family since 1538 and is still the private home of Lord Montagu.**

Palace House, overlooking the Beaulieu River, was once the Great Gatehouse of Beaulieu Abbey with its monastic origins reflected in the fan vaulted ceilings of the 14th Century Dining Hall and Lower Drawing Room.

The rooms are decorated with furnishings, portraits and treasures collected by past and present generations of the family. Visitors can enjoy the fine gardens or take a riverside walk around the Monks' Mill Pond.

Beaulieu Abbey was founded in 1204 when King John gave the land to the Cistercians and although most of the buildings have now been destroyed, much of the beauty and interest remains.

The former Monks' Refectory is now the local parish church and the Domus, which houses an exhibition and video presentation of monastic life, is home to beautiful wall hangings.

Beaulieu also houses the world famous National Motor Museum which traces the story of motoring from 1894 to the present day. 250 vehicles are on display including legendary world record breakers plus veteran, vintage and classic cars and motorcycles.

New from Easter 2014 will be 'For Britain and for the Hell of it' featuring the story of human endeavour, national prestige and technical challenges creating world land speed vehicles.

# KEY FACTS

- ⓘ Allow 3 hrs or more for visits. Helicopter landing point.
- Palace House Kitchen Shop & Main Reception Shop.
- Please see http://www.beaulieu.co.uk/hospitality
- WC. Wheelchairs in Visitor reception by prior booking.
- Part of the Brabazon Restuarant- sandwiches to cooked meals and tea & cold drinks.
- Seats 250.
- Attendants on duty.
- P Unlimited. Free admission for coach drivers plus voucher.
- Professional staff available to assist.
- In grounds, on leads only.
- Please see http://www.beaulieu.co.uk/hospitality
- Only closed Christmas Day

© Fergus Baird

## AVINGTON PARK 🏛ⓕ
### WINCHESTER, HAMPSHIRE  SO21 1DB
www.avingtonpark.co.uk

Charles II and George IV both stayed here. It dates back to the 11th Century, was enlarged in 1670 and now enjoys magnificent painted and gilded state rooms. The house and its parkland are perfect for seminars, exhibitions, weddings and private parties, as well as filming and photo shoots. The conservatories and the orangery make a delightful location for summer functions, whilst log fires offer a welcome during winter. All bookings at Avington are individually tailormade and only exclusive use is offered. Several rooms are licensed for Civil wedding ceremonies and a delightful apartment is available for short stays. **Location:** Map 3:D4. OS Ref SU534 324. 4m NE of Winchester ½m S of B3047 in Itchen Abbas.

**Owner/Contact:** Mrs S L Bullen
**Tel:** 01962 779260
**E-mail:** enquiries@avingtonpark.co.uk
**Open:** May-Sep: Suns & BH Mons plus Mons in Aug, 2.30-5.30pm. Last tour 5pm. Other times by arrangement. Coach parties welcome by appointment all year.
**Admission:** Adult £7.50, Child £3.00.
**Key facts:** ⓘ Conferences. ⓣ
🔲 Partial. WC. 🔲 ⓕ Obligatory. 🅿
🐾 In grounds, on leads. Guide dogs only in house. 🔲 🔲 🔲 By arrangement 🔲

## JANE AUSTEN'S HOUSE MUSEUM
### Chawton, Alton, Hampshire  GU34 1SD
www.jane-austens-house-museum.org.uk

17th Century house where Jane Austen wrote or revised her six great novels. Contains many items associated with Jane and her family, documents and letters, first editions of the novels, pictures, portraits and furniture. Recreated Historic kitchen. Pleasant garden, suitable for picnics. Bakehouse with brick oven and wash tub, Jane's donkey carriage. Learning Centre.
**Location:** Map 3:E4. OS Ref SU708 376. Just S of A31, 1m SW of Alton, signposted Chawton.
**Owner:** Jane Austen Memorial Trust
**Contact:** Ann Channon
**Tel:** 01420 83262 **E-mail:** enquiries@jahmusm.org.uk
**Open:** Jan-13 Feb: Sats & Suns, 10.30am-4.30pm. 14 Feb-end May: daily, 10.30am-4.30pm. June-Aug: daily, 10am-5pm. Sep-end Dec: daily, 10.30am-4.30pm. Closed 24-26 Dec.
**Admission:** Fee charged.
**Key facts:** 🔲 Bookshop. ⓣ 🔲 Ground floor & grounds. WC. 🔲 Opposite house. 🅿 Opposite house. 🔲 🔲 Guide dogs only. 🔲 🔲

Avington Park

Jane Austen's House

© Dave Zabraski

## EXBURY GARDENS & STEAM RAILWAY
### Exbury, Southampton, Hampshire SO45 1AZ
www.exbury.co.uk

A tranquil 200-acre woodland garden showcasing the world-famous Rothschild Collection of rhododendrons, azaleas and camellias. Summer brings shady river walks and herbaceous borders. Rock, Heather and Bog Gardens ensure year-round interest. Stunning autumn colour and Gallery display of Nerine sarniensis. The 1¼ mile steam railway is sure to delight visitors of all ages.
**Location:** Map 3:D6. OS Ref SU425 005. 20 mins Junction 2, M27 west. 11m SE of Totton (A35) via A326 & B3054 & minor road. In the New Forest.
**Owner:** Exbury Gardens Ltd. **Contact:** Estate Office
**Tel:** 023 8089 1203 **Fax:** 023 8089 9940 **E-mail:** info@exbury.co.uk
**Open:** 15 Mar-2 Nov 2014, 10am-5pm last admission.
Gates close 6pm or dusk if earlier.
**Admission:** Adults £11.00*; Children U16 £2.75*; Family £24.75*; Railway tickets extra. *Inclusive of Gift Aid. Prices and opening dates subject to variations. Please visit www.exbury.co.uk.
**Key facts:** ⬚ ⬚ ⬚ ⬚ ⬚ ⬚ Licensed. ⬚ By arrangement. ⬚ ⬚ ⬚ In grounds, on short leads. ⬚ ⬚

## BREAMORE HOUSE & MUSEUM ⬚Ⓕ
### Breamore, Fordingbridge
### Hampshire SP6 2DF
www.breamorehouse.com

Elizabethan manor house with fine collections of pictures and furniture as well as tapestries and unique James I pile carpet. Countryside Museum shows life when a village was self-sufficient with shop, blacksmith, brewery, wheelwright, cottage, dairy and many more trades. Large collection of tractors, implements, tools and a traction engine.
**Location:** Map 3:B5. OS Ref SU152 190. Off the A338, between Salisbury and Ringwood.
**Owner:** Michael Hulse **Tel:** 01725 512858 **E-mail:** breamore@btinternet.com
**Open:** Apr: Tues & Sun & Easter Weekend; May–Sep: Tues, Wed, Thurs, Sun & BHs; Oct: Tues & Sun. Tea Barn: 12-5.30pm, Countryside Museum: 1-5.30pm, House: 2-5pm last tour of house 4pm.
**Admission:** Combined ticket for house and museum: Adult £9.50, Child £6.00, OAP £8.00, Family £24.00.
**Key facts:** ⬚ ⬚ Ground floor & grounds. WCs. ⬚ ⬚ Around Breamore House. ⬚ Free. Unlimited. ⬚ ⬚ ⬚

## HIGHCLERE CASTLE, GARDENS & EGYPTIAN EXHIBITION ⬚Ⓕ
### Highclere Castle, Newbury, Berkshire RG20 9RN
www.highclerecastle.co.uk

This spectacular Victorian Castle is currently the setting for Downton Abbey. Visit the splendid State Rooms; admire the masculine opulence of the Library; the lovely south facing Drawing Room. Explore the Egyptian Exhibition in the Castle Cellars; the Antiquities Room and an amazing recreation of the discovery of Tutankhamun's tomb. Gardens inspired by Capability Brown including; Monk's Garden, Secret Garden and new Arboretum.
**Location:** Map 3:D3. OS Ref SU445 587. M4/J13 - A34 south. M3/J8 - A303 - A34 north. **Owner:** Earl of Carnarvon **Contact:** The Castle Office
**Tel:** 01635 253210 **Fax:** 01635 255315
**E-mail:** theoffice@highclerecastle.co.uk **Open:** 13-17; 19-26 Apr. 4-6; 25-27 May. 13-28 Jul; 6 Aug-17 Sep (Sun-Thur). Information correct at time of publication. **Admission:** Group Rates, Concessions, Family Tickets for Castle, Exhibition & Gardens; each element available separately, please check website for admission prices. **Key facts:** ⬚ ⬚ ⬚ Partial. WCs. ⬚ Licensed. ⬚ By arrangement. ⬚ ⬚ ⬚ Guide dogs only. ⬚ ⬚

## HINTON AMPNER
### Bramdean, Alresford, Hampshire SO24 0LA
www.nationaltrust.org.uk

This elegant country manor and tranquil garden sit so harmoniously within the landscape that one cannot exist without the other. Enjoy the exquisite collection of ceramics and art and avenues of sculptured topiary leading to breathtaking views across the South Downs. With newly opened parkland, one can experience all Hinton Ampner has to offer.

**Location:** Map 3:E5. OS Ref SU597 275. M3/J9 or A3 on A272, 1m W of Bramdean **Owner:** National Trust **Contact:** Property office
**Tel:** 01962 771305 **E-mail:** hintonampner@nationaltrust.org.uk
**Open:** Gardens, Tearoom, Shop and Estate: 1 Jan-28 Feb 10am-4pm, 1 Mar-2 Nov 10am-6pm, 3 Nov-31 Dec 10am-4pm. House: 1-26 Jan & 1-28 Feb 10am-4pm, 1 Mar-2 Nov 11am-5pm, 3 Nov-02 Dec & 6-14 Dec 10am-4pm, 27 Dec-31 Dec 10am-4pm, Closed Christmas Eve and Christmas day.
**Admission:** Adult £9.35, Child £4.50, Family £23.10, Groups (15+) £7.25. Dec-Feb entry: Adult £5.60, Child £2.85, Family £14.05.
**Key facts:** ⬚ 🖼 🎦 WCs. 🍴 Licensed. 🎦 By arrangement. 🅿 Limited for coaches. 🐕 Dogs are welcome on parkland, estate and tea-room courtyard. ⬚ ❄ Closed Christmas Eve and Christmas day. ⬚

## HOUGHTON LODGE GARDENS 🏚Ⓕ
### Stockbridge, Hampshire SO20 6LQ
www.houghtonlodge.co.uk

An 18th Century Grade II* listed Gothic 'Cottage Orne' idyllically set above the tranquil River Test. Peaceful formal and informal gardens with fine trees. Chalk Cob walls enclose a traditional Kitchen Garden with new themed Herb Garden, espaliers, hydroponics and stunning orchid house. 14 acres of picturesque countryside, meadow walks and 3 charming Alpacas.

**Location:** Map 3:C4. OS Ref SU344 332. 1½m S of Stockbridge (A30) on minor road to Houghton village.
**Owner/Contact:** Captain & Mrs Martin Busk
**Tel:** 01264 810502/912 **Fax:** 01264 810063
**E-mail:** info@houghtonlodge.co.uk
**Open:** 1 Mar-31 Oct, Thur-Tue, 10am-5pm. Weds by appointment. Tours of the House welcome to pre-booked groups.
**Admission:** Adult £5.00. Additional £2.50 for meadow walk/alpacas. Children under 14 Free. Coach Tours and Groups welcome on any day by appointment - special rates if booked in advance.
**Key facts:** 🎦 🍴 🎦 By arrangement. 🅿 Hard standing for 2 coaches. 🖼 🐕 On short leads. ⬚

## HOLY TRINITY CHURCH 🏛
### Merepond Lane, Privett, Alton, Hampshire GU34 3PE
www.visitchurches.org.uk

The spire of Holy Trinity soars high above the trees, visible for miles around in an idyllic corner of Hampshire. It is an extraordinary experience to find this lavishly decorated medieval-style church with Italian marble mosaic floors in such a rural location. Built in 1876-78, the church was funded by William Nicholson - a local benefactor and gin distiller - and designed by Gothic architect Sir Arthur Blomfield, later responsible for the Royal College of Music. Blomfield used the best craftsmen of the day to produce the magnificent stonework, mosaics and stained glass. The walls are made from warm-toned Ham Hill stone with bands of Bath stone. Marble mosaic floors run across the church and are particularly colourful in the chancel. If you are lucky, you may hear the lovely peal of eight bells ringing out - but at any time you can soak in the wonderful views all over Hampshire.

**Location:** OS Ref SU677 270. 5 miles west from Petersfield, off A272.
**Open:** Open daily from 10am-3pm.

Houghton Lodge Gardens

# KING JOHN'S HOUSE & HERITAGE CENTRE
## Church Street, Romsey, Hampshire SO51 8BT
www.kingjohnshouse.org.uk

Three historic buildings on one site: Medieval King John's House, containing 14th Century graffiti and rare bone floor, Tudor Cottage complete with traditional tea room and Victorian Heritage Centre with recreated shop and parlour. Beautiful period gardens, special events/exhibitions and children's activities. Gift shop and Tourist Information Centre. Receptions and private/ corporate functions.

**Location:** Map 3:C5. OS Ref SU353 212. M27/J3. Opposite Romsey Abbey, next to Post Office.
**Owner:** King John's House & Tudor Cottage Trust Ltd **Contact:** Anne James
**Tel:** 01794 512200 **E-mail:** annerhc@aol.com
**Open:** Main house: Mar-Oct: Mon-Sat, 10am-4pm. Heritage Centre only: Nov-Feb. Limited opening on Sundays. Evenings also for pre-booked groups.
**Admission:** Adult £2.50, Child 50p, Conc. £2.00. Heritage Centre only: Adult £1.50, Child 50p, Conc. £1.00. Discounted group booking by appointment.
**Key facts:** ⬚ ⬚ ⬚ Partial. ⬚ ⬚ By arrangement. ⬚ Off Latimer St with direct access through King John's Garden. ⬚ ⬚ Guide dogs only. ⬚ ⬚

# ST MARY'S CHURCH ⬚
## Itchen Stoke, Alresford, Hampshire SO24 0QU
www.visitchurches.org.uk

St Mary's was built in 1866, by Henry Conybeare for his brother, the Rector of the church, and felt the previous church was cold and damp. He himself bore most of the cost, with the parishioners contributing £50 towards the cost of the windows, as a mark of their regard for him. This dazzling and colourful Victorian jewel of a church overwhelms the senses - tall and imposing, especially as you approach it up a steep path from the road. Its design is clearly inspired by the soaring elegance of the 13th Century Sainte Chapelle in Paris, chapel of French kings. The church is a dazzling kaleidoscopic wonderland of pattern and colour with the richly painted roof, the floor near the altar decorated with sparkling tiles and the pulpit displaying five panels filled with scrollwork and foliage. Best of all is the stained glass, especially in the west window. The elegant arched windows contain small pieces of clear red, blue and green glass arranged in geometrical patterns.

**Location:** OS Ref SU559 323. 6m E of Winchester, on B3047; 1.5m from Alresford. **Open:** Open daily, 10am-4pm.

# STRATFIELD SAYE HOUSE ⬚⬚
## Stratfield Saye, Hampshire RG7 2BZ
www.stratfield-saye.co.uk

After the Duke of Wellington's victory against Napoleon at the Battle of Waterloo in 1815, the Duke chose Stratfield Saye as his country estate. The house contains many of the 1st Duke's possessions and is still occupied by his descendents being a family home rather than a museum.

**Location:** Map 3:E2. OS Ref SU700 615. Equidistant from Reading (M4/J11) & Basingstoke (M3/J6) 1½m W of the A33.
**Owner:** The Duke of Wellington
**Contact:** Estate Office
**Tel:** 01256 882694
**Open:** Thurs 17-Mon 21 Apr. Thurs 31 Jul-Mon 25 Aug.
**Admission:** Weekends: Adult £10.00, Child £5.00, OAP/Student £9.00. Weekdays: Adult £9.00, Child £4.00, OAP/Student £8.00. Groups by arrangement only.
**Key facts:** ⬚ ⬚ WC. ⬚ ⬚ Obligatory. ⬚ ⬚ Guide dogs only.

# WINCHESTER CITY MILL ⬚
## Bridge Street, Winchester SO23 9BH
Winchester City Mill is a working watermill dating back to at least Saxon times. Now fully restored by the National Trust, the City Mill is probably the oldest working watermill in the UK. Visitors can discover more about the mill's long and fascinating history as well as see the mill in action and learn how we produce traditional stone-ground wholemeal flour using the power of the River Itchen.
**Location:** Map 3D:4. OS Ref SU486 293. M3/J9 & 10. City Bridge near King Alfred's statue. 15 min walk from station.
**Owner:** National Trust **Contact:** Anne Aldridge **Tel:** 01962 870057
**E-mail:** winchestercitymill@nationaltrust.org.uk
**Website:** www.nationaltrust.org.uk/winchestercitymill
**Open:** Open Daily: 1 Jan-16 Feb 11am-4pm, 17 Feb-30 Nov 10am-5pm, 1 Dec-24 Dec 10.30am-4pm, Closed 25 & 26 Dec, 27-31 Dec 12noon-4pm.
**Admission:** Adults £4.40, Children £2.20, Family £11.00.
**Key facts:** ⬚ ⬚ ⬚ ⬚ Obligatory. By arrangement. ⬚ Nearby public car park. ⬚ ⬚ Guide dogs only. ⬚ ⬚

# BROADLANDS
## Romsey, Hampshire SO51 9ZD
Broadlands is the historic home of the Brabourne family.
**Location:** Map 3:C5.
**Tel:** 01794 529750 **Website:** www.broadlandsestates.co.uk
**Open:** Jun to Sep. Please see our website for details.

## VISITOR INFORMATION

### ■ Owner
The Denys Eyre Bower Bequest, Registered Charitable Trust

### ■ Address
Chiddingstone Castle
Nr Edenbridge
Kent
TN8 7AD

### ■ Location
**Map 19:G12**
**OS Ref. TQ497 452**
10m from Tonbridge, Tunbridge Wells and Sevenoaks. 4m Edenbridge. Accessible from A21 and M25/J5. London 35m.
**Bus:** Enquiries: Tunbridge Wells TIC 01892 515675.
**Rail:** Tonbridge, Tunbridge Wells, Edenbridge then taxi. Penshurst then 2m walk.
**Air:** Gatwick 15m.

### ■ Contact
**Tel:** 01892 870347
**E-mail:** events@ chiddingstonecastle.org.uk

### ■ Opening Times
Sunday, Monday, Tuesday, Wednesday & Bank Holidays from 1st April until 29th October (check the website for any unforeseen alterations to this).

**Times:** 11am to 5pm. Last entry to house 4:15pm.

### ■ Admission
| | |
|---|---|
| Adults | £8.00 |
| Children (5-13) | £4.00 |
| Family (2 adults + 2 children or 1 adult + 3 children) | £21.50 |
| Admission to Grounds and Tea Rooms | Free |
| Parking | £2.00 |

### ■ Special Events
We have a series of event days - Egyptian and Japanese Days and the Country and Christmas Fairs. Please visit the website What's On page for more information.

# CHIDDINGSTONE CASTLE 🏛 Ⓕ
www.chiddingstonecastle.org.uk

## Chiddingstone Castle is a hidden gem in the Garden of England; a unique house with fascinating artefacts and beautiful grounds.

Situated in an historic village in the heart of the idyllic Kentish Weald, Chiddingstone Castle has Tudor origins and delightful Victorian rooms. Lying between Sevenoaks and Tunbridge Wells, it is conveniently located close to the M25 (Junction 5 - Sevenoaks or Junction 6 - Oxted). We welcome individuals, families and groups - guided tours are available. There is ample parking available and a cosy Tea Rooms set in the Old Buttery for delicious light lunches, cakes and traditional cream teas, all served on vintage china.

Set in 35 acres of informal gardens, including a lake, waterfall, rose garden and woodland, this attractive country house originates from the 1550s when High Street House, as the Castle was known, was home to the Streatfeild family. Several transformations have since taken place and the present building

dates back to 1805 when Henry Streatfeild extended and remodelled his ancestral home in the 'castle style' which was then fashionable. Rescued from creeping dereliction in 1955 by the gifted antiquary Denys Eyre Bower, the Castle became home to his amazing and varied collections - Japanese Samurai armour, swords and lacquer, Egyptian antiquities, Buddhist artefacts, Stuart paintings and Jacobite manuscripts. Visitors can also visit Bower's Study and learn of his eccentric and complicated life, which featured a notorious scandal.

Further exhibition rooms are open showing the Victorian history of the Castle - the Victorian Kitchen and Scullery and the fascinating Housekeeper's Room. From the Servants' Hall, visitors can climb the secret back stairs and discover the Servant's Bedroom in the attic – a real 'upstairs downstairs' experience!

## KEY FACTS

- ℹ Museum, weddings, business and private functions, scenic gardens and lake, picnics, fishing available.
- 🛍 Well stocked gift shop.
- 🍽 Available for special events. Licensed for Civil Ceremonies. Wedding receptions.
- ♿ WCs.
- Cream teas a speciality.
- 🍴
- 🚶 By arrangement.
- 🅿
- 🏫 We welcome visits from schools who wish to use the collections in connection with classroom work.
- 🐕 In grounds and Tea Room courtyard on leads.
- 🔔
- ⬆

## VISITOR INFORMATION

### ◼ Owner
English Heritage

### ◼ Address
Dover Castle
Castle Hill
Dover
Kent
CT16 1HU

### ◼ Location
**Map 4:O4**
**OS Ref. TR325 419**
Easy access from A2 and
M20. Well signposted from
Dover centre and east side
of Dover. 2 hrs from
central London.
**Bus:** 0870 6082608.
**Rail:** London St. Pancras
Intl (fast train); London
Victoria; London Charing
Cross.

### ◼ Contact
Visitor Operations Team
**Tel:** 01304 211067
**E-mail:** customers@
english-heritage.org.uk

### ◼ Opening Times
Please visit www.english-
heritage.org.uk for
opening times, admission
prices and the most up-to-
date information.

### ◼ Special Events
Please visit www.english-
heritage.org.uk for the
most up-to-date
information on our exciting
days out and events.

# DOVER CASTLE ✚
www.english-heritage.org.uk/dovercastle

## Explore over 2,000 years of history at Dover Castle.

Immerse yourself in the medieval world and royal court of King Henry II as you climb the stairs into the Great Tower and meet the first of the many life like projected figures which will guide you round the six great recreated rooms and several lesser chambers of the palace. On special days throughout the year interact with costumed characters as they bring to life the colour and opulence of medieval life.

Take an adventurous journey into the White Cliffs as you tour the maze of Secret Wartime Tunnels. Children will love dressing up in wartime uniforms, exploring the tunnels, the interactive displays and virtual tour. Through sight, sound and smells, re-live the wartime drama of a wounded pilot fighting for his life. Discover what life would have been like during the dark and dramatic days of the Dunkirk evacuation with exciting audio-visual experiences. See the pivotal part the Secret Wartime Tunnels played in Operation Dynamo.

Above ground, enjoy magnificent views of the White Cliffs from Admiralty Lookout and explore the Fire Command Post, re-created as it would have appeared 90 years ago in the last days of the Great War. Also see a Roman Lighthouse and Anglo-Saxon church, as well as an intriguing network of medieval underground tunnels, fortifications and battlements.

Dover Castle was used as a film location for The Other Boleyn Girl starring Natalie Portman and Scarlett Johanssen and Zaffirelli's Hamlet amongst others.

## KEY FACTS

| | |
|---|---|
| ℹ️ | WCs. No flash photography within the Great Tower. |
| 📷 | Two. |
| 🍴 | Licensed. |
| 🚶 | Tour of tunnels. Last tour 1 hr before closing. |
| 🅿️ | Ample. |
| | Free visits available for schools. Education centre. Pre-booking essential. |
| 🐕 | Dogs on leads only. |

## VISITOR INFORMATION

### Owner
Hever Castle Ltd

### Address
Hever Castle
Hever
Edenbridge
Kent
TN8 7NG

### Location
**Map 19:G12**
**OS Ref. TQ476 450**
Exit M25/J5 & J6 M23/J10
30 m from central London,
1½m S of B2027 at Bough
Beech, 3m SE of
Edenbridge.
**Rail:** Hever Station 1m (no
taxis), Edenbridge Town
3m (taxis).

### Contact
Ann Watt
**Tel:** 01732 865224
**Fax:** 01732 866796
**E-mail:**
mail@hevercastle.co.uk

### Opening Times
**15 Feb–24 Dec**
Gardens open at 10.30am
Castle opens at 12 noon
**Half Term Holiday 1–23
Feb Daily**
Last admission 4pm
Final exit 5pm
**Main Season (Wed–Sun)
1-31 March**
Last admission 4pm
Final exit 5pm
**1 Apr–31 Oct Daily**
Last admission 5pm
Final exit 6pm
**Winter Season
(Wed-Sun)**
**1 Nov–24 Dec**
(See website for opening
times).

### Admission
**INDIVIDUAL**
| | |
|---|---|
| Adult | £15.50 |
| Senior | £13.25 |
| Child | £8.70 |
| Family | £39.70 |

**Gardens only**
| | |
|---|---|
| Adult | £13.00 |
| Senior | £11.25 |
| Child | £8.20 |
| Family | £34.20 |

**GROUP**
| | |
|---|---|
| Adult | £12.25 |
| Senior | £11.25 |
| Student | £9.90 |
| Child | £6.90 |

**Gardens only**
| | |
|---|---|
| Adult | £10.25 |
| Senior | £9.75 |
| Student | £8.50 |
| Child | £6.60 |

**Groups (15+)**
Available on request.
Pre-booked private guided
tours are available before
opening, during season.

### Special Events
Special Events throughout
the year including Rose
Week and Jousting
Tournaments.

### Conference/Function
| ROOM | Size | Max Cap |
|---|---|---|
| Dining Hall | 35' x 20' | 70 |
| Breakfast Rm | 22' x 15' | 12 |
| Sitting Rm | 24' x 20' | 20 |
| Pavilion | 96' x 40' | 250 |
| Moat Restaurant | 25' x 60' | 75 |

# HEVER CASTLE & GARDENS 🏰Ⓕ
www.hevercastle.co.uk

## Experience 700 years of colourful history and spectacular award-winning gardens at the childhood home of Anne Boleyn.

Hever Castle dates from 1270, when the gatehouse, outer walls and inner moat were first built. 200 years later the Boleyn family added the Tudor manor house constructed within the walls. This was the childhood home of Anne Boleyn, Henry VIII's second wife and mother of Elizabeth I. There are many Tudor artefacts including two Books of Hours signed and inscribed by Anne Boleyn. The Castle was later given to Henry VIII's fourth wife, Anne of Cleves.

In 1903, the estate was bought by the American millionaire William Waldorf Astor, who became a British subject and the first Lord Astor of Hever. He invested an immense amount of time, money and imagination in restoring the castle and grounds. Master craftsmen were employed and the castle was filled with a fine collection of paintings, furniture and tapestries. The Miniature Model Houses exhibition, a collection of 1/12 scale model houses, room views and gardens, depicts life in English Country Houses.

### Gardens

Between 1904-1908, 125 acres of formal and natural gardens were laid out and planted; these have now matured into one of the most beautiful gardens in England. The unique four acre walled Italian Garden contains a magnificent collection of statuary. The glorious Edwardian Gardens include the Rose Garden, Tudor Garden, traditional yew maze and a 110 metre herbaceous border. There are several water features, a 38 acre lake with rowing boats, a water maze, lake walk, adventure playground, gift and garden shops and special events throughout the season.

## KEY FACTS

ⓘ Filming, residential conferences, Corporate hospitality and Golf.

Gift, garden & book.

Weddings, receptions and private banqueting.

Partial. WCs.

Licensed.

By Arrangement. Pre-booked tours in French, German, Dutch, Italian and Spanish (min 20).

Free parking.

English, French, German & Dutch.

Well behaved dogs on lead in grounds.

B&B in Astor Wing of the Castle.

# LEEDS CASTLE 🏰

www.leeds-castle.com

## "The Loveliest Castle in the World"

Set in 500 acres of beautiful Kent parkland, there's something to discover every day at "the loveliest castle in the world" . The historic castle, glorious gardens, attractions and programme of events awaits visitors.

During its 900 year history, Leeds Castle has been a Norman stronghold, the private property of six of England's medieval Queens and a palace used by Henry VIII. In the 1930s the castle was a playground for the rich and famous, as Lady Baillie, the last private owner, entertained high society down from London for the weekends.

During your visit, the whole family will enjoy exploring the gardens and grounds, getting lost in the maze, watching a falconry display, riding on Elsie the Castle Land Train and crossing the Great Water on the Black Swan Ferry Boat. Children will love letting off steam in one of our playgrounds and toddler's turf maze.

After all that excitement, the Fairfax Restaurant offers an excellent choice of freshly prepared hot and cold dishes and Costa Coffee is now open in the Courtyard. For unusual, quality gifts and souvenirs, visit the two Leeds Castle shops before you leave.

Our golf course also has a fully stocked golf shop with advice from our PGA Professional.

## KEY FACTS

 Residential and day conferences, weddings, team building days, falconry, golf, croquet and helipad.

WCs.

Licensed.

Licensed.

Free parking.

Guide dogs only.

€

## VISITOR INFORMATION

### ■ Owner
Leeds Castle Foundation

### ■ Address
Leeds Castle
Maidstone
Kent
ME17 1PL

### ■ Location
Map 4:L3
OS Ref. TQ835 533
From London to A20/M20/ J8, 40m, 1 hr. 7m E of Maidstone, ¼m S of A20.
**Bus:** Spot Travel operate a shuttle bus from Bearsted Train station during hire season.
**Rail:** South Eastern Trains available, London-Bearsted.
**Air:** Under an hour from Kent International Airport and London Gatwick airport.
**Ferry:** Under an hour from the Dover Channel Ports.

### ■ Contact
**Tel:** 01622 765400
**Fax:** 01622 735616
**E-mail:** enquiries@leeds-castle.co.uk

### ■ Opening Times
**Summer**
1 Apr-30 Sept Daily, 10.30am-4.30pm (last adm).
**Winter**
1 Oct-31 Mar Daily, 10.30am-3pm (last adm).

### ■ Admission
Key to the Castle tickets. (valid for 1 year)*
| | |
|---|---|
| Adult | £21.00 |
| Child (4-15yrs) | £13.50 |
| OAP/Student | £18.50 |
| Disabled (1 carer Free) | £18.50 |

Groups rates for 15+ available. Visit our website or call 01622 767865.

### ■ Special Events
Special events held throughout the year. See website for details.

### Conference/Function

| ROOM | Size | Max Cap |
|---|---|---|
| Fairfax Hall | 19.8 x 6.7m | 180 |
| Garden House | 9.8 x 5.2m | 30 |
| Terrace | 8.9 x 15.4m | 80 |
| Castle Boardroom | 9.7 x 4.8m | 30 |
| Castle Dining Rm | 13.1 x 6.6m | 70 |
| Maiden's Tower | 8 x 9m | 120 |

South East - England

## VISITOR INFORMATION

**■ Owner**
Viscount De L'Isle

**■ Address**
Penshurst
Nr Tonbridge
Kent
TN11 8DG

**■ Location**
Map 19:H12
OS Ref. TQ527 438
From London M25/J5 then A21 to Hildenborough, B2027 via Leigh; from Tunbridge Wells A26, B2176.
**Bus:** 231, 233 from Tunbridge Wells and Edenbridge.
**Rail:** Charing Cross/ Waterloo East-Hildenborough, Tonbridge or Tunbridge Wells; then bus or taxi.

**■ Contact**
**Tel:** 01892 870307
**Fax:** 01892 870866
**E-mail:** enquiries @penshurstplace.com

**■ Opening Times**
**House & Grounds:**
**15 Feb-30 Mar:**
Sats & Suns only, 10.30am-6pm or dusk if earlier.
**31 Mar-2 Nov:**
Daily, 10.30am-6pm.
**House**
12 noon. Last entry 4pm.
**Grounds**
10.30am-6pm.
Last entry 5pm.
**Shop & Porcupine Pantry**
Open all year.
**Winter**
Open to Groups by appointment only.

**■ Admission**
For 2014 individual prices see website for details.
**2014 Group prices:**
(pre-booked 15+).
Freeflow.
Adult £8.00
Child £5.00
**House Tours**
Adult £10.00
Child £5.50
**Garden Tours**
(pre-booked 15+).
Adult £10.00
Child £5.50
**House & Garden Tours**
Adult £16.00
Child (5-16 yrs) £10.00
*under 5s Free.

**■ Special Events**
**Weald of Kent Craft Show:** First May Bank holiday and a weekend in September Friday – Sunday.
**Glorious Gardens Week:** First week in June.
Please see www.penshurstplace.com /whatson

### Conference/Function

| ROOM | Size | Max Cap |
|------|------|---------|
| Sunderland Room | 56' x 120 | 100 |
| Baron's Hall | 64' x 39' | 250 |
| Buttery | 23' x 22' | 50 |

# PENSHURST PLACE & GARDENS
www.penshurstplace.com

## One of England's greatest family-owned historic houses with a history spanning nearly seven centuries.

In some ways time has stood still at Penshurst; the great House is still very much a medieval building with improvements and additions made over the centuries but without any substantial rebuilding. Its highlight is undoubtedly the medieval Baron's Hall, built in 1341, with its impressive 60ft-high chestnut-beamed roof. A marvellous mix of paintings, tapestries and furniture from the 15th, 16th and 17th Centuries can be seen throughout the House, including the helm carried in the state funeral procession to St Paul's Cathedral for the Elizabethan courtier and poet, Sir Philip Sidney, in 1587. This is now the family crest.

### Gardens
The Gardens, first laid out in the 14th Century, have been developed over generations of the Sidney family, who first came to Penshurst in 1552. A twenty-year restoration and re-planting programme under-taken by the 1st Viscount De L'Isle has ensured that they retain their historic splendour. He is commemorated with an Arboretum, planted in 1991.

The gardens are divided by a mile of yew hedges into 'rooms', each planted to give a succession of colour as the seasons change, with the completion of a major restoration project on the Jubilee Walk in 2012. There is also an Adventure Playground, Woodland Trail, Toy Museum and Garden Restaurant, with the Porcupine Pantry cafe and a Gift Shop open all year. A variety of events in the park and grounds take place throughout the season.

## KEY FACTS

- ℹ Guidebook available to purchase. No photography in house.
- 🏠 Gift Shop outside paid perimeter.
- 🌱 Small plant centre.
- 🍽 Conference and private banqueting facilities.
- ♿ Partial. Contact for details.
- ☕ Porcupine Pantry outside paid perimeter.
- 🍴 Garden Restaurant in the grounds.
- 🚶 Guided tours available by arrangement before the House opens to the public. Garden tours available 10.30am-4.30pm.
- 🅿 Ample for cars and coaches.
- 🎓 All year by appointment, discount rates, education room and teachers' packs.
- 🐕 Guide dogs only.
- 🔔 Wedding ceremonies and receptions.
- ❄ See opening times.
- 🗓 See www.penshurstplace.com/whatson

## RESTORATION HOUSE 🏛Ⓕ
### 17-19 CROW LANE, ROCHESTER, KENT ME1 1RF
#### www.restorationhouse.co.uk

Fabled city mansion deriving its name from the stay of Charles II on the eve of The Restoration. This complex ancient house has beautiful interiors with exceptional early paintwork related to decorative scheme 'run up' for Charles' visit. The house also inspired Dickens to create 'Miss Havisham' here. 'Interiors of rare historical resonance and poetry', Country Life. Fine English furniture and strong collection of English portraits (Mytens, Kneller, Dahl, Reynolds and several Gainsboroughs). Charming interlinked walled gardens and ongoing restoration of monumental Renaissance water garden. A private gem. 'There is no finer pre-Civil war town house in England than this' - Simon Jenkins, The Times.
**Location:** MAP 4:K2 OS Ref TQ744 683. Historic centre of Rochester, off High Street, opposite the Vines Park.

**Owner:** R Tucker & J Wilmot   **Contact:** Robert Tucker
**Tel:** 01634 848520   **Email:** robert.tucker@restorationhouse.co.uk
**Open:** 29 May - 26 Sept, Thur & Fri, 10am-5pm. Sats 31 May & 12 Jul, 12-5pm.
**Admission:** Adult £7.50 (includes 36 page illustrated guidebook), Child £3.75, Conc £6.50. Booked group (8+) tours: £8.50pp.
**Tea Shop:** 1st, 2nd & 4th Thurs in month and other days by arrangement (see website for updates).
**Key Facts:** ℹ No stiletto heels. No photography in house.
🌳 Garden by appointment. 🍴 1st, 2nd & 4th Thurs in month & other days by arrangement. 🚻 By arrangement. 🅿 None. 🐕 Guide Dogs Only.

## BELMONT HOUSE & GARDENS 🏛Ⓕ
### Belmont Park, Throwley, Faversham ME13 0HH
#### www.belmont-house.org

Belmont is an elegant 18th Century house with views over the rolling Kentish North Downs. Its hidden gardens range from a Pinetum complete with grotto, a walled ornamental garden and a walled kitchen garden with Victorian greenhouses. Belmont also has the finest private collection of clocks in Britain to explore.
**Location:** Map 4:M3. OS Ref TQ986 564. 4½m SSW of Faversham, off A251.
**Owner:** Harris (Belmont) Charity
**Tel:** 01795 890202 **E-mail:** administrator@belmont-house.org
**Open:** April-Sep. Weds tours 11am & 1pm, Sat tours 2.15pm & 3.15pm, Sun & BH Mon tours 2.15pm, 3pm & 3.45pm. Gardens open every day 10am-6pm or dusk if earlier. Groups Tues & Thurs by appointment. Pre-booked specialist clock tours last Sat of the month (April-Sep). For Special Events visit our website.
**Admission:** House & Garden: Adult £8.00, Child (Under 12's free) £5.00, Conc. £7.00. Garden Only: Adult £5.00, Child (12-16yrs) £2.50, Conc. £4.00. Pre-booked Clock Tour £15.00.
**Key facts:** ℹ No photography in house. 🅿 🚻 Partial. WCs.
🍴 Tearoom open from 2pm on Sat & Sun for afternoon tea & cakes. Self-service Mon-Fri. 🚶 Obligatory. 🅿 Limited for coaches.
🐕 In the gardens, on lead only. ⚘ 🛈

## CHARTWELL 🌿
### Chartwell, Mapleton Road, Westerham, Kent TN16 1PS
#### www.nationaltrust.org.uk/chartwell

Chartwell was the much-loved Churchill family home and the place from which Sir Winston drew inspiration from 1924 until the end of his life. With its magnificent views over the Weald of Kent. The Mulberry Room at the restaurant can be booked for meetings, weddings, conferences, lunches and dinners.
**Location:** Map 19:F11. OS Ref TQ455 515. 2m S of Westerham, forking left off B2026. **Owner:** National Trust **Contact:** Visitor Experience Manager
**Tel:** 01732 868381 **Fax:** 01732 868193
**E-mail:** chartwell@nationaltrust.org.uk
**Open:** House: 1 Mar-2 Nov, Daily, 11am-5pm. Garden, Shop, Restaurant, Exhibition, & Studio, everyday 1 Jan-31 Dec, times vary please call 01732 868381 for further details.
**Admission:** House, Studio: Adult £13.80, Child £6.90, Family £34.50. Garden, Exhibition, Studio & Winter season only: Adult £6.90, Child £3.45, Family £17.25. Gift Aid prices. Groups (15+) Adult £10.70, Child £5.35.
**Key facts:** ℹ Conference, wedding & function facilities. 📷 🛈 New extended plant area. 🚻 Partial. WCs. 🍴 Licensed. 🚶 By arrangement. 🅿 Free for NT members, £3 for non-members. ⚘ 🐕 In grounds on leads. 🛈 ⚘ 🛈

## EMMETTS GARDEN 🌿
### Ide Hill, Sevenoaks, Kent TN14 6BA
www.nationaltrust.org.uk/emmetts

Charming Emmetts - an Edwardian estate owned by Frederic Lubbock - was a plantsman's passion and a much loved family home. Influenced by William Robinson, the delightful garden was laid out in the late 19th Century and contains many exotic and rare trees and shrubs from across the world. After exploring the rose and rock gardens, you can take in the spectacular views and enjoy the glorious shows of spring flowers and shrubs, followed by vibrant autumn colours. **Location:** Map 19:G11. OS Ref TQ477 524. 1½m N of Ide Hill off B2042. M25/J5, then 4m.
**Owner:** National Trust **Contact:** Property Operations Manager
**Tel:** 01732 750367 **Fax:** 01732 750489
**E-mail:** emmetts@nationaltrust.org.uk
**Open:** Garden, shop and tearoom: 1 Mar-31 Dec, Daily, 10am-5pm. Closed Christmas Eve and Christmas Day. Last entry 45 minutes before closing.
**Admission:** Standard admission: Adult £6.80, Child £3.40, Family £17.00. Gift Aid admission: Adult £7.60, Child £3.80, Family £19.00. Groups (15 or more) Adult £5.80, Child £2.50. **Key facts:** 🖼 🅿 🎏 🔲 WCs. 📷 🎬 By arrangement. 🅿 🚌 🐕 Dogs on leads only. 🏫

## IGHTHAM MOTE 🌿
### Mote Road, Sevenoaks, Kent TN15 0NT
www.nationaltrust.org.uk/ighthammote

Moated manor dating from 1320, reflecting seven centuries of history, from the medieval Crypt to a 1960s Library. Owned by knights, courtiers to Henry VIII and society Victorians. Highlights include Great Hall, Drawing Room, Tudor painted ceiling, Grade 1 listed dog kennel and apartments of US donor.
**Location:** Map 19:H11. OS Ref TQ584 535. 6m E of Sevenoaks off A25. 2½m S of Ightham off A227. **Owner:** National Trust **Contact:** Pamela Westaway
**Tel:** 01732 810378 **Fax:** 01732 811029
**E-mail:** ighthammote@nationaltrust.org.uk
**Open:** 1 Mar-2 Nov Mon-Sun, 11-5pm 3 Nov -31 Dec, Mon-Sun, 11-3pm. Closed Jan, Feb, 24-25 Dec. **Admission:** Adult £11.50*, Child £5.75, Family £29.00, Groups 15 + Adult £8.80, Child £4.40. (Reduced entry prices for Nov & December) *includes voluntary donation visitors can pay standard prices displayed at property.
**Key facts:** 🛈 No flash photography. Volunteer 8 seated electric buggy. 🖼 🅿 🎏 🔲 WCs. 3 wheelchairs ground floor access only. Photograph album available of upstairs. 🍴 Licensed. Outside patio area with views of the house. 📷 House tour £3.00pp Garden tours with Head Gardener £5.00pp. 🅿 🚌 🏫

## THE GRANGE
### St Augustine's Road, Ramsgate, Kent CT11 9NY
www.landmarktrust.org.uk

Augustus Pugin is regarded as being one of Britain's most influential architects and designers and to stay here in the home he designed for himself and his family offers a unique chance to step into his colourful and idiosyncratic world.
**Location:** Map 4:O2. OS Ref TR377 643.
**Owner:** The Landmark Trust
**Tel:** 01628 825925
**E-mail:** bookings@landmarktrust.org.uk
**Open:** Available for holidays. Parts of house open Wed afternoons; there are 8 Open Days.
**Admission:** Free, visits by appointment. Contact Catriona Blaker 01843 596401.
**Key facts:** 🛈 This house was designed as a family home and it works as well today as it did in 1844. 📷 🅿 🎏 🐕 🎬 🏫

## KNOLE 🌿
### Knole, Sevenoaks, Kent TN15 0RP
www.nationaltrust.org.uk/knole

Knole has begun a huge project to conserve and refurbish its remarkable rooms and collections, peeling back the layers of 600 years of history and sharing this work with visitors. This year, building works may affect some areas and refreshments are outdoors, in Kent's last remaining medieval deer park.
**Location:** Map 19:H10. OS Ref TQ532 543. 25m SE of London. M25/J5 (for A21). Off A225 at S end of High Street, Sevenoaks, opposite St Nicholas Church. For satnav use TN13 1HU.
**Owner:** National Trust **Contact:** Property Manager
**Tel:** 01732 462100 **E-mail:** knole@nationaltrust.org.uk
**Open:** Please see website for details.
**Admission:** Please see website for details.
**Key facts:** 🛍 NT gifts and goods. 🔲 Please ask us how we can help you visit Knole. WCs; steps with handrail to first floor showrooms. 🅿 Free to NT members. 🎬 Contact education officer. 🐕 In park only, on leads. 🅿 Car park and outdoor refreshments available all year except Dec 24 & 25. 🏫

© NT/John Miller

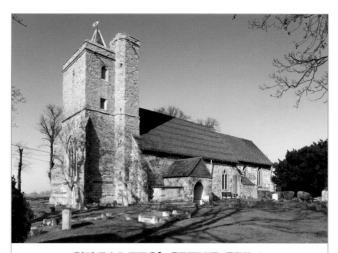

## ST JAMES' CHURCH 🔊
### Main Road, Cooling, Rochester, Kent ME3 8DG
www.visitchurches.org.uk

Charles Dickens used the churchyard of St James as his inspiration in the opening chapter of Great Expectations, where the hero Pip meets Magwitch the convict. The site - on the Hoo Peninsula with marshes stretching north to the Thames estuary, is dramatically desolate and bleak in winter, recalling the sinister opening scene in David Lean's 1946 film of the book. Inside, the church is light and spacious. There is a 500-year-old timber door that still swings on its ancient hinges. Another quirky feature is the 19th Century vestry - its walls are lined from top to bottom with thousands of cockle shells - the emblem of St James. The monuments in the church walls and floor are a fascinating record of those who once lived here. They include a slab with a brass effigy of Feyth Brook, who died in 1508 and was the wife of Lord Cobham, of nearby Cooling Castle. **Location:** OS Ref TQ756 759. 6 miles north of Rochester off B2000.
**Open:** Open daily from 10am-4pm.

## ST MARY'S CHURCH 🔊
### Manor House Lane, Capel-le-Ferne
### Folkestone, Kent CT18 7EX
www.visitchurches.org.uk

This lovely church is remote from the road and squats snugly on bleak downland above Folkestone. It has views across the channel, looking towards France.
A single Norman window, with a little delicate wallpainting in the reveal, indicates its early origins; but most notable is a 14th Century three-arched stone rood-screen with, uniquely in England, an arched opening above for the rood itself. There are also ancient roof timbers, a small brass and a 13th Century piscina.
**Location:** OS Ref TR257 400.
2 miles north east of Folkestone off B2011.
**Open:** Open daily from 10am-4pm.

Hever Castle

## ST MICHAEL'S CHURCH 🔊
### Old Church Lane, East Peckham,
### Tonbridge, Kent TN12 5NG
www.visitchurches.org.uk

When the village moved down nearer to the river, St Michael's was left romantically sited on a hilltop among beeches, with glorious views over the Medway valley to the Weald. Originally Norman, the church seems to have expanded to its present size around 1300; the piers and arches are clearly 14th Century, the windows and south porch mainly 15th Century, and the shingled spirelet has an attractive weathervane dating from 1704. Inside there are fragments of ancient glass, a Royal Arms of George II and two centuries of memorials dedicated to the Twysden family. The churchyard has some lovely 18th Century headstones.
**Location:** OS Ref TQ661 522. 2m N of East Peckham, off B2016, black and white traffic sign on B2016.
**Open:** Open daily from 10am-4pm.

South East - England

© National Trust Images / Jonathan Buckley

## ST PETER'S CHURCH 🏛
### Market Street, Sandwich, Kent  CT13 9DA
www.visitchurches.org.uk

St Peter's is the guardian of an ancient Sandwich tradition. Every day at 8pm, the curfew bell rings out, signalling that the townspeople should cover their fires to make them safe for the night. This was once known as the 'pigbell', as it also informed people they could release their animals into the street. Much of today's building dates from 800 years ago, though it has been altered many times. The handsome tower with its distinctive onion dome top is a 17th Century addition - built by Flemish protestant refugees, in the style of their homeland churches. The present church dates from the late 13th/early 14th Centuries. The atmospheric crypt - open by arrangement - was once a charnel house where bones from the graveyard were stored to make room for new graves. Inside, the church is spacious and airy with few furnishings allowing you to easily appreciate the impressive size and proportions of the lofty interior.
**Location:** OS Ref TR331 580. In centre of town; identifiable by its onion dome on top of the tower; main door on Market Street. **Open:** Open daily but occasionally closed at short notice for events; please telephone 01304 621554 in advance of your visit.

## SISSINGHURST CASTLE 🌿
### Sissinghurst, Cranbrook, Kent  TN17 2AB
www.nationaltrust.org.uk/sissinghurst

One of the world's most celebrated gardens and a sensory paradise of colour and beauty throughout the year. Vita Sackville-West, a Bloomsbury group member and her husband Sir Harold Nicolson created the garden around the surviving parts of an Elizabethan mansion.
The original design still exists today with a series of garden rooms, intimate in scale and romantic in atmosphere. See the White Garden, Lime Walk, Tower with Vita's study and Cottage Garden.
**Location:** Map 4:L4. OS Ref TQ807 383. 1m E of Sissinghurst village.
**Owner:** National Trust
**Contact:** The Administrator
**Tel:** 01580 710700
**E-mail:** sissinghurst@nationaltrust.org.uk
**Open:** Please see website for opening times and admission prices.
**Key facts:** 🔲 ♿ 🔄 💻 🍴 Licensed.
🅿 £2.00 per car. Book coaches in advance.
🐕 Gardens: Guide dogs only. Grounds: On leads.

## ALL SAINTS' CHURCH 🏛
### Church Lane, West Stourmouth, Canterbury, Kent  CT3 1HT

This picture-postcard church stands hidden by trees in a delightful setting by the Little Stour. When visiting, you first see the small spire and bell tower then the beautiful flint, ragstone and brick body of the church. There is strong evidence of Saxon origins but many alterations have left traces from most of the centuries since. Inside, the church is furnished with box pews, some with beautiful carving, a 17th Century pulpit and a handsome organ, still showing the original pumping lever. The attractive tiled flooring contains three interesting memorial stones.
**Location:** OS Ref TR256 628. 4 miles north of Wingham off B2046; signposted off minor road between Wingham and Monkton 1m north of Preston.
**Contact:** Please call The Churches Conservation Trust on 0845 303 2760 (Mon-Fri, 9am–5pm)
**Website:** www.visitchurches.org.uk
**Open:** Open daily from 10am to 4pm.

## CHURCH OF ST THOMAS A BECKET 🏛
### Church Lane, Capel, Tonbridge, Kent  TN12 6SX
www.visitchurches.org.uk

Becket himself is said to have preached in this small Norman Wealden church. The tower was partly rebuilt after a fire in 1639.
Inside, the crown-post roof is striking and there are some interesting fittings. Most significant however, are the extensive medieval wallpaintings which cover most of the nave, depicting, amongst others, Cain and Abel and Christ's entry into Jerusalem.
**Location:** OS Ref TQ637 445. 4 miles east of Tonbridge off B2017. Large car park at rear of church.
**Open:** Open daily. 10am-4pm.

Chiddingstone Castle

Register for news and special offers at www.hudsonsheritage.com

## GOODNESTONE PARK GARDENS 🏛©
**Goodnestone Park, Nr Wingham, Canterbury, Kent  CT3 1PL**
Set in 14 acres. There is a woodland area with many fine trees and woodland shrubs; a large walled garden with roses, clematis and other herbaceous plants.
**Location:** Map 4:N3. OS Ref TR254 544. 8m Canterbury, 1½m E of B2046 - A2 to Wingham Road, signposted from this road.
**Contact:** Francis Plumptre
**Tel/Fax:** 01304 840107
**E-mail:** enquiries@goodnestoneparkgardens.co.uk
**Website:** www.goodnestoneparkgardens.co.uk
**Open:** Suns only 12 noon–5pm 23 Feb–13 April. Main season with tearoom open 15 Apr–26 Sep, Tues–Fri 11am–5pm, Suns 12 noon–5pm.
Oct–Suns 12 noon–5pm.
**Admission:** Adult £6.00, Child (6-16 yrs) £2.00, OAP £5.50, Family tickets (2+2) £14.00. Groups (20+) £5.50 out of opening hours £7.50.
**Key facts:** 🖼 🚻 Suitable. WCs. 🍴 Licensed.
🎥 Partial. By arrangement. 🅿 ❌ 🔼 💷

## LULLINGSTONE CASTLE & WORLD GARDEN
**Lullingstone, Eynsford, Kent  DA4 0JA**
Fine State rooms, family portraits and armour in beautiful grounds. The 15th Century gatehouse was one of the first ever to be made of bricks.
This is also the site for the World Garden of Plants and for Lullingstone's Parish Church of St Botolph.
**Location:** Map 19:G9. OS Ref TQ530 644. 1m S Eynsford W side of A225. 600yds S of Roman Villa.
**Owner/Contact:** Guy Hart Dyke Esq  **Tel:** 01322 862114  **Fax:** 01322 862115
**E-mail:** info@lullingstonecastle.co.uk  **Website:** www.lullingstonecastle.co.uk
**Open:** Apr-Sep: Fris, Sats, Suns & BHs 12 noon-5pm. Closed Good Friday.
**Admission:** Adult £7.00, Child £4.00, OAP £6.50, Family £18.00; Groups (20+): £8.00 pp plus £40.00 for dedicated guide (Weds & Thurs).
**Key facts:** ℹ No interior photography. Wheelchairs available upon request.
🖼 🚻 Plant sales. 🚻 WCs. 🍴 Light refreshments. 🎥 Obligatory. By arrangement.
🅿 Limited for coaches. 🐕 Guide dogs only. 💷

## MOUNT EPHRAIM GARDENS 🏛©
**Hernhill, Faversham, Kent  ME13 9TX**

In these enchanting 10 acres of Edwardian gardens, terraces of fragrant roses lead to a small lake and woodland area. A grass maze, unusual topiary, Japanese-style rock garden, arboretum, herbaceous border and many beautiful mature trees are other highlights. Peaceful, unspoilt atmosphere set in Kentish orchards with magnificent views over the Thames Estuary.
**Location:** Map 4:M3. OS Ref TR065 598. In Hernhill village, 1m from end of M2. Signed from A2 & A299.  **Owner:** William Dawes & Family  **Contact:** Lucy Dawes
**Tel:** 01227 751496  **E-mail:** info@mountephraimgardens.co.uk
**Website:** www.mountephraimgardens.co.uk
**Open:** Open Apr-end Sep: Wed, Thu, Fri, Sat & Sun, 11am-5pm and BH Mons. Groups Mar-Oct by arrangement.
**Admission:** Adult £6.00, Child (4-16) £2.50. Groups (10+): £5.00.
**Key facts:** 🖼 🚻 🍴 🚻 Partial. WCs. 🍴 Licensed. 🍴 Licensed. 🎥 By arrangement. 🅿 🔼 🐕 On leads. 🔼 Licensed for civil weddings inside and out. 💷

## NURSTEAD COURT
**Nurstead Church Lane, Meopham
Kent  DA13 9AD**

Nurstead Court is a Grade I listed manor house built in 1320 of timber-framed, crownposted construction, set in extensive gardens and parkland. The additional front part of the house was built in 1825. Licensed weddings are now held in the house with receptions and other functions in the garden marquee.
**Location:** Map 4:K2. OS Ref TQ642 685. Nurstead Church Lane is just off the A227 N of Meopham, 3m from Gravesend.
**Owner/Contact:** Mrs S Edmeades-Stearns  **Tel:** 01474 812368
**E-mail:** info@nursteadcourt.co.uk  **Website:** www.nursteadcourt.co.uk
**Open:** Every Tue & Weds in Sep, 7 Oct and 8 Oct, 2-5pm.
All year round by arrangement.
**Admission:** Adult £5.00, Child £2.50, OAP/Student £4.00 Group (max 54): £4.00.
**Key facts:** 🍴 Weddings & functions catered for. 🚻 🍴 Licensed. 🎥 Obligatory, by arrangement. 🅿 Limited for coaches. 🔼 🐕 Guide Dogs only. 🔼 ❌

## RIVERHILL HIMALAYAN GARDENS 🏛©
**Sevenoaks, Kent  TN15 0RR**

Historic hillside gardens, privately owned by the Rogers family since 1840. Extensive views across the Weald of Kent.
Spectacular rhododendrons, azaleas and specimen trees. Bluebell Walk, productive Walled Garden with grass-sculpted terraces, contemporary sculpture. Shop & Cafe serving light lunches, teas and coffee.
**Location:** Map 4:J3. OS Ref TQ541 522. 2m S of Sevenoaks on A225.
**Owner:** The Rogers Family  **Contact:** Mrs Rogers
**Tel:** 01732 459777  **E-mail:** sarah@riverhillgardens.co.uk
**Website:** www.riverhillgardens.co.uk
**Open:** 23 Mar-7 Sep 2014, Weds-Sun & Bank Holiday Mons, 10.30am-5pm
**Admission:** Adult £7.50, Child £5.25, Family £22.50, Seniors £6.75. Adult Pre-booked Groups (20+) House & Garden £12.50, Garden only £6.75.
**Key facts:** 🖼 🚻 🍴 🚻 Partial. 🍴 🎥 By arrangement. 🅿 Limited for coaches. 🔼 🐕 Guide dogs only. ❌ 💷

## TONBRIDGE CASTLE
**Tonbridge & Malling Borough Council, Castle Street, Tonbridge, Kent  TN9 1BG**

Standing in landscaped gardens overlooking the River Medway, Tonbridge Castle's mighty motte and bailey Gatehouse is among the finest in England. Experience the sights and sounds of the 13th Century as we bring them to life with interactive displays, dramatic special effects and personal audio tour. We take bookings for schools, paranormal groups, weddings and other ceremonies.  **Location:** Map 19:H11. OS Ref TQ590 466. 5 mins walk from Tonbridge Train Station at the North end of Town.
**Owner:** Tonbridge & Malling Borough Council  **Contact:** Tina Levett- Gateway/ Castle Manager  **Tel:** 01732 770929  **E-mail:** tonbridge.castle@tmbc.gov.uk
**Website:** www.tonbridgecastle.org  **Open:** All year: Mon-Sat, 9am-5pm- last tour 4pm. Suns & BHs, 10.30am-4pm last tour 3.30pm.  **Admission:** 2014: Gatehouse - Adult £7.70, Child/Conc. £4.40. Family £21.00 -max 2 adults. Includes audio tour. The grounds are free.  **Key facts:** 🧸 Toys, Maps etc. 🚻 🚻 Some areas. 🍴 Close by. 🍴 Close by. 🎥 By appointment. 🖼 🅿 🔼 ❌ Grounds only. 🔼 ❌ 💷

## COBHAM HALL 🏛©
**Cobham Hall, Cobham, Kent  DA12 3BL**
Magnificent Jacobean, Elizabethan manor house with Repton designed gardens set in 140 acres of parkland. **Location:** Map 4:K2. OS Ref TQ683 689.
**Tel:** 01474 823371  **Fax:** 01474 258906  **E-mail:** enquiries@cobhamhall.com
**Website:** www.cobhamhall.com  **Open:** Specific days only. Check website or phone for details. **Admission:** Adult £5.50, Conc. £4.50, Self-guided garden tour £2.50, Historical/Conservation Grounds tour Adult £6.00, Conc. £5.00.

## OWLETTS 🌿
**The Street, Cobham, Gravesend  DA12 3AP**
Former home of the architect Sir Herbert Baker. Highlights include an impressive Carolean staircase, plasterwork ceiling and large kitchen garden.
**Location:** Map 4:K2. OS Ref TQ665687. 1m south of A2 at west end of village. Limited parking at property. Parking nearby in Cobham village. **Tel:** 01732 810378
**E-mail:** owletts@nationaltrust.org.uk **Open:** 7 Apr-28 Sep Sun only 11-5pm.
**Admission:** Adult £3.00, Child £1.50, Family £7.50. Not suitable for groups.

## ST JOHN'S JERUSALEM 🌿
**Sutton-at-Hone, Dartford, Kent  DA4 9HQ**
13 Century chapel surrounded by a tranquil moated garden, once part of the former Commandery of the Knight's Hospitallers. Occupied as a private residence, maintained and managed by a tenant on behalf of the National Trust
**Location:** Map 4:J2. OS Ref TQ558703. 3 miles south of Dartford **Tel:** 01732 810378 **Open:** 2 Apr-24 Sep 2-6pm, 1 Oct-29 Oct 2-4pm. **Admission:** £2.00.

## VISITOR INFORMATION

### ■ Owner
The Duke of Marlborough

### ■ Address
Blenheim Palace
Woodstock
OX20 1PX

### ■ Location
**Map 7:A11**
**OS Ref. SP441 161**
From London, M40, A44
(1½ hrs), 8m NW of
Oxford. London 63m
Birmingham 54m.
**Bus:** No.S3 from Oxford
Station, Gloucester Green
& Cornmarket.
**Coach:** From London
(Victoria) to Oxford.
**Rail:** Oxford Station.
**Air:** Heathrow
60m. Birmingham 50m.

### ■ Contact
Operations
**Tel:** 0800 8496500
**E-mail:**operations@
blenheimpalace.com

### ■ Opening Times
Sat 15 Feb – Sun 14 Dec 2014
Sat 15 Feb – Sun 2 Nov 2014
open daily
Wed 5 Nov – Fri 13 Dec 2014
open Wed – Sun

**Palace and Pleasure Gardens**
Open daily from
10.30am – 5.30pm
(last admission 4.45pm).
The Formal Gardens open
at 10am.

**Park**
Open daily from
9am – 6pm
(4.45pm last admission)

### ■ Admission
**Palace, Garden & Park**
9 Feb – 13 Dec
| | |
|---|---|
| Adult | £21.50 |
| Concessions | £17.00 |
| Child* | £11.80 |
| Family | £57.00 |

**Park & Gardens**
| | |
|---|---|
| Adult | £12.50 |
| Concessions | £ 9.30 |
| Child* | £ 6.50 |
| Family | £33.00 |

* (5-16 yrs )

### ■ Annual Pass Offer
Buy one day get
12 months free!
(Terms & conditions apply).

Discounts on Group
Bookings (15+) available by
contacting group sales
on 01993 815600
email groups@
blenheimpalace.com
Private tours by
appointment only,
prices on request.

# BLENHEIM PALACE 🏠 Ⓕ
www.blenheimpalace.com

## Blenheim Palace is home to the 11th Duke and Duchess of Marlborough and the birthplace of Sir Winston Churchill.

Surrounded by over 2,000 acres of 'Capability' Brown landscaped parkland and the Great Lake, the Palace was created a World Heritage Site in 1987.

Conceived in 1705 by Sir John Vanbrugh, Blenheim Palace is a masterpiece of English Baroque architecture steeped in inspirational history. Visit the room where Sir Winston Churchill was born before taking a guided tour of the gilded State Rooms graced with priceless portraits, exquisite porcelain and the magnificent tapestries.

A permanent interactive visitor experience 'Blenheim Palace: The Untold Story' is open inside the Palace bringing to life enticing tales of the last 300 years, seen through the eyes of the household staff.

Themed tours and exhibitions are also part of Blenheim Palace's offering, run on selected dates. To celebrate the WWI Centenary in 2014 a special exhibition will run from 15th February – 21st April, looking at how the lives of the people who worked and lived on the estate were impacted by the war.

The Palace is surrounded by award winning Formal Gardens, including the tranquil Secret Garden, the majestic Water Terraces, the fragrant Rose Garden, and the Grand Cascade and Lake. An audio garden tour is available to hire. The Pleasure Gardens can be reached by a miniature train, which includes the Marlborough Maze, the Butterfly House and Adventure Playground, making it a great area for the family.

Each year Blenheim Palace hosts a range of events for all to enjoy, including seasonal themed events, Jousting Tournament, The Blenheim Palace Flower Show, charity events and The Blenheim Palace International Horse Trials.

## KEY FACTS

- ℹ️ Filming, product launches, activity days. No photography inside the palace.
- 🛍️ Four shops.
- 🍽️ Corporate Hospitality includes weddings, receptions, dinners, meetings and corporate events.
- ♿ Suitable/WCs/Lift
- 🍷 Licensed.
- 🍴 Licensed.
- 📖 Guided tours except Sundays.
- 🅿️ Unlimited for cars and coaches.
- 🏆 Sandford Award holder since 1982. Teacher pre-visits welcome.
- 🐕 Dogs on leads, park only. Guide dogs welcome.

### Conference/Function

| ROOM | Size | Max Cap |
|---|---|---|
| Orangery | 36.25 x 7.1 | 250 |
| Marlborough Room | 14.3 x 7.1 | 120 |
| Great Hall, Saloon & Long Library | 13.3 x 13.1 13.3 x 9.9 45.7 x 5 | 500 |
| Great Hall & Saloon | 13.3 x 13.1 13.3 x 9.9 | 250 |
| Oudenarde Room | 7.9 x 4.9 | 20 |
| Ramillies Room | 4.9 x 4.9 | 12 |
| Malplaquet Room | 4.9 x 4.9 | 12 |
| Spencer Churchill Room | 10 x 8 | 70 |
| Courtyard | 19.4 x 10.7 | 150 |

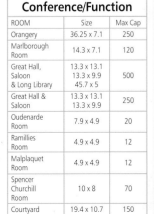

# BROUGHTON CASTLE 🏠Ⓕ
www.broughtoncastle.com

"About the most beautiful castle in all England…for sheer loveliness of the combination of water, woods and picturesque buildings." Sir Charles Oman (1898).

Broughton Castle is essentially a family home lived in by Lord and Lady Saye & Sele and their family. The original medieval Manor House, of which much remains today, was built in about 1300 by Sir John de Broughton. It stands on an island site surrounded by a 3 acre moat. The Castle was greatly enlarged between 1550 and 1600, at which time it was embellished with magnificent plaster ceilings, splendid panelling and fine fireplaces. In the 17th Century William, 8th Lord Saye & Sele, played a leading role in national affairs. He opposed Charles I's efforts to rule without Parliament and Broughton became a secret meeting place for the King's opponents. During the Civil War William raised a regiment and he and his four sons all fought at the nearby Battle of Edgehill. After

the battle the Castle was besieged and captured. Arms and armour from the Civil War and other periods are displayed in the Great Hall. Visitors may also see the gatehouse, gardens and park together with the nearby 14th Century Church of St Mary, in which there are many family tombs, memorials and hatchments.

### Gardens

The garden area consists of mixed herbaceous and shrub borders containing many old roses. In addition, there is a formal walled garden with beds of roses surrounded by box hedging and lined by more mixed borders.

## VISITOR INFORMATION

**■ Owner**
Lord Saye & Sele

**■ Address**
Broughton Castle
Broughton
Nr Banbury
Oxfordshire
OX15 5EB

**■ Location**
Map 7:A10
**OS Ref. SP418 382**
Broughton Castle is 2½m SW of Banbury Cross on the B4035, Shipston-on-Stour - Banbury Road. Easily accessible from Stratford-on-Avon, Warwick, Oxford, Burford and the Cotswolds. M40/J11.
**Rail:** From London/Birmingham to Banbury.

**■ Contact**
Manager, Mrs James
**Tel:** 01295 276070
**E-mail:** info@broughtoncastle.com

**■ Opening Times**
**Summer**
Easter Sun & Mon, 1 May-15 September Weds, Suns & BH Mons, 2-5pm. Also Thurs in July and August, 2-5pm. Last admission 4.30pm. Open all year on any day, at any time, for group bookings - by appointment only.

**■ Admission**
| | |
|---|---|
| Adult | £9.00 |
| Child (5-15yrs) | £5.00 |
| OAP/Student | £8.00 |
| Garden only | £5.00 |
| **Groups** | |
| Adult | £9.00 |
| OAP | £9.00 |
| Child (5-10yrs) | £5.00 |
| Child (11-15yrs) | £6.00 |
| Garden only | £6.00 |

**(There is a minimum charge for groups - please contact the manager for details)**

## KEY FACTS

| | |
|---|---|
| ℹ | Photography allowed in house. |
| 📷 | |
| ♿ | Partial. |
| ☕ | Teas on Open Days. Groups may book morning coffee, light lunches and afternoon teas. |
| 🎧 | Available for booked groups. |
| 🅿 | Limited. |
| 🏫 | |
| 🐕 | Guide dogs only in house. On leads in grounds. |
| ❄ | Open all year for groups. |

© NT/Paul Watson

## VISITOR INFORMATION

### ■ Owner
The National Trust
(Administered on their
behalf by Lord Faringdon)

### ■ Address
Buscot Park
Faringdon
Oxfordshire
SN7 8BU

### ■ Location
Map 6:P12
**OS Ref. SU239 973**
Between Faringdon and
Lechlade on A417.
**Bus:** Stagecoach 65/66
Oxford to Swindon, alight
Faringdon; Stagecoach 64
Swindon to Carterton,
alight Lechlade.
**Taxi:** Faringdon or
Lechlade
**Rail:** Oxford or Swindon

### ■ Contact
The Estate Office
**Tel:** 01367 240786
**Fax:** 01367 241794
**Info Line:** 01367 240932
**E-mail:**
estbuscot@aol.com

### ■ Opening Times
**House, Grounds and
Tearoom:** 2 Apr-28 Sep,
Wed-Fri and BH's and
weekends as listed below,
2.00pm-6.00pm
(last entry to
House 5.00pm,
Tearoom last
orders 5.30pm).
Apr 5/6,19/20/21
May 3/4/5, 10/11,
24/25/26
Jun 14/15, 28/29
Jul 12/13, 26/27
Aug 9/10, 23/24/25
Sep 13/14, 27/28.
**Grounds Only:**
1 Apr-30 Sep, Mon-Tues,
2.00pm-6.00pm.

### ■ Admission
**House & Grounds:**
| | |
|---|---|
| Adult | £10.00 |
| Over 65s | £8.00 |
| Child (5-15) | £5.00 |
| Under 5 Free. | |

**Grounds only:**
| | |
|---|---|
| Adult | £7.00 |
| Over 65s | £5.00 |
| Child (5-15) | £3.50 |

National Trust
members                   Free
**Groups:** Advance booking
must be made with the
Estate Office.

# BUSCOT PARK 🌿
### www.buscotpark.com

## One of Oxfordshire's best kept secrets.

Buscot Park is the family home of Lord Faringdon who looks after the property on behalf of the National Trust, as well as the collection of fine and decorative art, known as the Faringdon Collection. Consequently, despite the grandeur of their scale, the house and grounds remain intimate and idiosyncratic and very much a family home.

Built 1780-1783 Buscot Park was purchased by Lord Faringdon's great-grandfather, Alexander Henderson, a financier of exceptional skill and ability who in 1916 was created the 1st Lord Faringdon. He greatly enlarged the house, commissioned Harold Peto to design the famous Italianate water garden, and laid the foundations of the Faringdon Collection. Among his many

purchases was Rembrandt's portrait of Pieter Six, Rossetti's portrait of Pandora, and Burne-Jones's famous series The Legend of the Briar Rose.

His grandson and heir, Gavin Henderson, the 2nd Lord Faringdon, added considerably to the collection, acquiring important furniture designed by Robert Adam and Thomas Hope, and was instrumental in returning the house to its late 18th Century appearance.

The present Lord Faringdon continues to add to the collection, to improve its display, and to enliven the gardens and pleasure grounds for the continuing enjoyment of visitors.

## KEY FACTS

- ℹ️ No photography in house.
- 🌱 A selection of plants and surplus kitchen garden produce available when in season.
- ♿ Partial. WC's, some ramps, special assistance available - please contact Estate Office prior to visit for more information.
- 🍴 Homemade teas, ice cream, local cider, and honey available when house open.
- 🅿️ Ample for cars, 2 coach spaces.
- 🐕 Guide dogs only.

© David Dixon

### VISITOR INFORMATION

■ **Owner**
Lord & Lady Camoys

■ **Address**
Stonor Park
Henley-On-Thames
Oxfordshire
RG9 6HF

■ **Location**
Map 3:E1
**OS Ref. SU743 893**
1 hr from London, M4/J8/9. A4130 to Henley-on-Thames. On B480 NW of Henley. A4130/B480 to Stonor.
**Bus:** None
**Taxi:** Henley on Thames 5m
**Rail:** Henley on Thames 5m, or Reading 9m
**Air:** Heathrow

■ **Contact**
Jonathan White
**Tel:** 01491 638587
**E-mail:** administrator@stonor.com

■ **Opening Times**
1 April- mid September
Sundays and BH Mondays.
Also Wednesdays, July and August only.

**Gardens**
1-5.30pm.

**House, Tea Room & Giftshop**
2-5.30pm Last Entry 4.30pm.

Private Groups (20+) by arrangement Tuesday-Thursday, April-September.

■ **Admission**
**House, Gardens and Chapel**
| | |
|---|---|
| Adults | £9.00 |
| First Child (5-16) | £4.50 |
| 2 or more Children (5-16) | Free |
| Under 5s | Free |

**Gardens and Chapel**
| | |
|---|---|
| Adults | £4.50 |
| First Child (5-16) | £2.50 |
| 2 or more Children (5-16) | Free |
| Under 5s | Free |

**Groups**
| | |
|---|---|
| Adults | £9.00 |
| Child (5-16) | £4.50 |
| Includes guided tour. | |

■ **Special Events**
**June 1**
VW Owners' Rally.

**August 22-25**
Chilterns Craft & Design Fair.

# STONOR 🏠Ⓕ
www.stonor.com

## Stonor - a story of continuity. The same family have lived here for over 850 years and have always been Roman Catholics.

Stonor has been home to the Stonor family for over 850 years and is now home to The Lord and Lady Camoys. The history of the house inevitably contributes to the atmosphere, unpretentious yet grand. A facade of warm brick with Georgian windows conceals older buildings dating back to the 12th Century and a 14th Century Catholic Chapel sits on the south east corner. Stonor nestles in a fold of the beautiful wooded Chiltern Hills with breathtaking views of the park where Fallow deer have grazed since medieval times.

It contains many family portraits, old Master drawings and paintings, Renaissance bronzes and tapestries, along with rare furniture and a collection of modern ceramics.

St Edmund Campion sought refuge at Stonor during the Reformation and printed his famous pamphlet 'Ten Reasons', in secret, on a press installed in the roof space. A small exhibition celebrates his life and work.

Mass has been celebrated since medieval times in the Chapel. The stained glass windows were executed by Francis Eginton: installed in 1797. The Chapel decoration is that of the earliest Gothic Revival, begun in 1759, with additions in 1797. The Stations of the Cross were carved by Jozef Janas, a Polish prisoner of war in World War II and given to Stonor by Graham Greene in 1956.

The gardens offer outstanding views of the Park and valley and are especially beautiful in May and June, containing fine displays of daffodils, irises, peonies, lavenders and roses along with other herbaceous plants and shrubs.

## KEY FACTS

ℹ️ No photography in house. Dogs on leads in the park at all times. Dogs not allowed in the formal gardens.

🎁 Small gift shop.

🍽️

♿ Partial.

☕ Tea Room open from 2.00pm to 5.00pm. Group visits - all refreshments must be prebooked.

🚶 By arrangement minimum 20 maximum 54.

🅿️ 100yds away.

🛏️

🐕 Guide dogs only.

💍

## KINGSTON BAGPUIZE HOUSE 🏛ⓕ
### KINGSTON BAGPUIZE, ABINGDON, OXFORDSHIRE OX13 5AX
www.kingstonbagpuizehouse.com

This lovely family home dates from the 1660's and was remodelled in the early 1700's for the Blandy family. With English and French furniture in the elegant panelled rooms the entrance hall is dominated by a handsome cantilevered staircase. The house is surrounded by mature parkland and gardens notable for an interesting collection of cultivated plants which give year round interest including snowdrops in February, Magnolia and Fritillary in March and April, Wisteria, Cornus and roses in May and June, the herbaceous border and Albizia julibrissin in July and August, Colchicum and autumn colour from September. A raised terrace leads to the 18th Century panelled pavilion which looks over the gardens and towards the house. Venue for weddings and receptions.

**Location:** Map 7:A12. OS Ref SU408 981. In Kingston Bagpuize village, off A415 Abingdon to Witney road S of A415/A420 intersection. Abingdon 5m, Oxford 9m.

**Owner:** Mrs Francis Grant **Contact:** Virginia Grant

**Tel:** 01865 820259 **E-mail:** virginia@kbhadmin.com

**Open:** Gardens Only (Snowdrops): 2, 9, 16 & 23 Feb & 2 Mar. House & Gardens: 23 & 24 Mar. 27 & 28 Apr. 11-13, 25-27 May. 1-3, 22-24, 29 & 30 Jun. 1, 27-29 Jul. 17-19 Aug. 7, 8, 14,15, 21 & 22 Sep. All days 2.00-5.00pm. (Last entry to house 4.00pm.) Free flow visits to ground floor of house.

**Admission:** House & Garden: Adult £7.50, Child (4-16) £4.50, Family (2+3) £20. Gardens: Adult £5.00, Child (4-16) £3.00. Season tickets available. Group rates 20+ by appointment weekdays throughout the year. NB: Please visit website to confirm before travelling as dates & times may be subject to change.

**Key facts:** ℹ No photography in house on open days. 🛍 Small selection of gifts in tea room. 🎪 Rare Plant Fair 25 May 2014 www.rareplantfair.co.uk 🅣 See website. ♿ WCs. 🍴 Home made teas. 🚶 Free flow visits to ground floor only on advertised open days. Guided tours for pre-booked groups only. 🅿 🐕 Guide dogs only. 🛏 See website. ⊞ ☑

## MILTON MANOR HOUSE
### MILTON, ABINGDON, OXFORDSHIRE OX14 4EN

HOME OF THE BARRETT FAMILY FOR THE LAST QUARTER OF A MILLENIUM. At Risk, or so the querulous quangocrats of English Heritage labelled this beautiful mellow brick mansion, traditionally designed by Inigo Jones, set in its own pleasant parkland.

Come and visit and see for yourself this lived-in family home – free parking, refreshments and pony rides usually available. 2014 is the 250th Anniversary of the purchase of the estate by Bryant Barrett in 1764. To celebrate the event – FOR THIS SEASON ONLY – admission prices will be WILDLY REDUCED. It may not be perfect; but it is loved and far, far from being in a state of collapse. So come and judge for yourself.

**Location:** Map 3:D1. OS Ref SU485 924. Just off A34, village and house signposted, 9m S of Oxford, 15m N of Newbury. 3m from Abingdon & Didcot.

**Owner:** Anthony Mockler-Barrett Esq **Contact:** Alex Brakespear

**Tel:** 01235 831287 **Fax:** 01235 862321

**Open:** Easter Sun and BH Mon; Sun 4 May and BH Mon; Sun 18 May to Sun 1 Jun and Sun 17 Aug- Sun 31 Aug. Guided tours of house 2pm, 3pm and 4pm. No longer guided by Lucy Worsley, alas, who began her ascending career as a guide here, and who revisited-see both illustrations- in Jubilee Year. For weddings/events etc, please contact the Administrator. Groups by arrangement throughout the year.

**Admission:** House and Gardens: Adult £5.00; Child (under 14) Free. Gardens and grounds, for this year only: Free.

**Key facts:** 🏞 Grounds. 🎫 Obligatory. 🅿 Free. 🐕 Guide dogs only. ⊞ ☑

# ROUSHAM HOUSE
## NR STEEPLE ASTON, BICESTER, OXFORDSHIRE OX25 4QX
www.rousham.org

Rousham represents the first stage of English landscape design and remains almost as William Kent (1685-1748) left it. One of the few gardens of this date to have escaped alteration. Includes Venus' Vale, Townesend's Building, seven-arched Praeneste, the Temple of the Mill and a sham ruin known as the 'Eyecatcher'. The house was built in 1635 by Sir Robert Dormer. Dont miss the walled garden with their herbaceous borders, small parterre, pigeon house and espalier apple trees. A fine herd of Longhorn cattle are to be seen in the park. Excellent location for fashion, advertising, photography etc.
**Location:** Map 7:A10. OS Ref SP477 242. E of A4260, 12m N of Oxford, S of B4030, 7m W of Bicester.
**Owner/Contact:** Charles Cottrell-Dormer Esq

**Tel:** 01869 347110 / 07860 360407 **E-mail:** ccd@rousham.org
**Open:** Garden: All year: daily, 10am-4.30pm (last adm). House: Pre-booked groups, May-Sept. (Mon-Thur)
**Admission:** Garden: £5.00. No children under 15yrs.
**Key facts:** ℹ Rousham is an ideal Oxfordshire venue for wedding receptions, offering a site to pitch a marquee together with acres of landscape and formal gardens that can be used for photographs and pre-reception drinks. We have also held some car rallies, The Bentley, MG and Aston Martin owners clubs have all held rallies at Rousham. These events are held in the park, immediately next to the house. Open access to the house and garden can be arranged. ⬛ Partial.
🅿 ✖ ❋ ♿

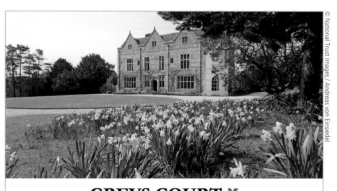

# GREYS COURT 🌿
## Rotherfield Greys, Henley-On-Thames
## Oxfordshire RG9 4PG
www.nationaltrust.org.uk/greys-court

This enchanting and intimate family home in a 16th Century mansion, is set amidst a patchwork of colourful walled gardens, courtyard buildings including a Tudor donkey wheel and medieval walls and towers. Beyond lies an estate and beech woodlands set in the rolling Chiltern Hills.
**Location:** Map 3:E1. OS Ref SU725 834.
3m W of Henley-on-Thames, E of B481.
**Owner:** National Trust **Contact:** Property Administrator
**Tel:** 01491 628529 **Infoline:** 01494 755564
**E-mail:** greyscourt@nationaltrust.org.uk
**Open:** House: 3 Mar–2 Nov 11-5. 3 Nov–31 Dec 11-4. Garden, Shop and Tea Room: 3 Mar–2 Nov 10-5. 3 Nov– 31 Dec 10-4. Property closed 7 Sep, 24 & 25 Dec. Please check website for entry details on day of visit.
**Admission:** House & Garden: Adult £12:00, Child £6.00, Family £30.00. Garden Only: Adult £9.80, Child £4.80, Family £24.20. Groups (15+) must book in advance. Free to NT members. Inc. voluntary donation but visitors can choose to pay the standard prices displayed at the property and on the website.
**Key facts:** 🔲 🔲 Partial. 🖼 ℹ By arrangement. 🅿 Limited for coaches. ♿

© National Trust Images / Andreas von Einsiedel

Gardens at Rousham House

# MAPLEDURHAM HOUSE
## Mapledurham, Reading  RG4 7TR
www.mapledurham.co.uk

Late 16th Century Elizabethan home of the Blount family. Original plaster ceilings, great oak staircase, fine collection of paintings and a private chapel in Strawberry Hill Gothick added in 1797. 15th Century watermill fully restored producing flour, semolina and bran. Hydro powered turbine producing green electricity added in 2011. Visitors may visit the Old Manor tea room where cream teas and cakes are served. A passenger boat service from nearby Caversham runs on open days. **Location:** Map 3:E2. OS Ref SU670 767. N of River Thames. 4m NW of Reading, 1½ m W of A4074.
**Owner:** The Mapledurham Trust **Contact:** Mrs Lola Andrews
**Tel:** 0118 9723350 **Fax:** 0118 9724016
**E-mail:** enquiries@mapledurham.co.uk **Open:** Easter-Sep: Sats, Suns & BHs, 2-5.30pm. Last admission 5pm. Midweek parties by arrangement only. Also Sun afternoons in Oct. **Admission:** Please call 01189 723350 for details. Mapledurham Trust reserves the right to alter or amend opening times or prices without prior notification. **Key facts:** ◎ Gift shop located in the watermill. ⊤ Ideal venue for fairs, shows and wedding receptions. ☒ Partial. ☞ Tea room serving cream teas and cakes. ⊤ Guides tours for midweek party visits. ᴘ ☞

# NUFFIELD PLACE ✻
## Nuffield Place, Huntercombe
## Henley on Thames  RG9 5RY
www.nationaltrust.org.uk/nuffield-place

The home of one of the most remarkable men of the 20th Century The time-capsule home of the philanthropist William Morris, Lord Nuffield, the founder of Morris Motor Cars and one of the richest men in the world. Lord Nuffield gave much of his wealth to good causes and his house reflects a relatively modest lifestyle. Lord and Lady Nuffield's personal possessions remain as they left them with the decor and furnishings intact, making it a perfect example of a complete 1930s country home. **Location:** Map 3:E1. OS Ref SU679 878. On the B4130 between Nettlebed and Wallingford
**Owner:** National Trust **Contact:** Property Administrator
**Tel:** 01491 641224 **E-mail:** nuffieldplace@nationaltrust.org.uk
**Open:** Wed-Sun & BH Mons. Please check website on day of visit. House, Garden, Tea Room & Shop: 11am-5pm. Last Entry at 4:30pm.
**Admission:** House & Garden: Adult £8.80, Child £4.40, Family £22.00. Free to NT members. Groups of 15+ must book in advance.
**Key facts:** ◎ ☒ Some uneven paths in garden, house ground floor accessible. ☞ Intimate tearoom-light lunches, tea, coffee & cake. ᴘ ☞

# MAPLEDURHAM WATERMILL
## Mapledurham, Reading  RG4 7TR
www.mapledurhamwatermill.co.uk

The last working watermill on the Thames still producing flour. It is a 600 year old estate mill, powered by an wooden undershot waterwheel with parts of the original wooden structure still surviving inside the building. Also the home of the first hydro powered turbine on the Thames. Constructed using an Archimedes screw system this modern addition is not only helping our planet but also ensuring the life of the watermill.
**Location:** Map 3:E2. OS Ref SU670 767. N of River Thames. 4m NW of Reading, 1½ m W of A4074.
**Owner:** The Mapledurham Trust **Contact:** Mrs Lola Andrews
**Tel:** 01189 723350 **Fax:** 01189 724016
**E-mail:** enquiries@mapledurham.co.uk **Open:** Easter -Sep Sats and Sun BHs 2-5.30pm. Midweek parties by arrangement only. Sun afternoons in Oct.
**Admission:** Please call 01189 723350 for details.
**Key facts:** ◎ A small gift shop is located within the mill - also selling flour. ☒ Partial. WCs. ☞ A tea room is located nearby in the Old Manor. ⊤ By arrangement. ᴘ ☞ School visits welcome by appointment. ☒ Dogs in grounds only. ☞

## 26A EAST ST HELEN STREET
### Abingdon, Oxfordshire
One of the best preserved examples of a 15th Century dwelling in the area. Originally a Merchant's Hall House with later alterations, features include a remarkable domestic wall painting, an early oak ceiling, traceried windows and fireplaces.
**Location:** Map 7:A12. OS Ref SU497 969.
**Owner:** Oxford Presevation Trust
**Contact:** Mrs Debbie Dance
**Tel:** 01865 242918
**E-mail:** info@oxfordpreservation.org.uk
**Website:** www.oxfordpreservation.org.uk
**Open:** By Prior appointment.
**Admission:** Small charge.

## WATERPERRY GARDENS
### Waterperry, Near Wheatley, Oxfordshire  OX33 1JZ
Beautiful eight acre Ornamental Gardens, Plant Centre Gallery, Gift Barn, Museum, Teashop. Groups welcome. **Location:** Map 7:B12. OS Ref SP610 068.
**Tel:** 01844 339226 **E-mail:** office@waterperrygardens.co.uk
**Website:** www.waterperrygardens.co.uk **Open:** All year except 17-20 Jul, 25-26 & 31 Dec 14 & 1-2 Jan 15. Low season: 10am-5pm. High season: 10am-5.30pm. **Admission:** Please see website.

Clandon parterre view

© Matthew Batchelor

## VISITOR INFORMATION

### Owner
National Trust

### Address
Hatchlands Park
East Clandon
Guildford
Surrey
GU4 7RT

### Location
**Map 19:A10**
**OS Ref. TQ065 518**
**Hatchlands:** At East Clandon off the A246 Guildford-Leatherhead road. Follow brown signs.
**Clandon:** At West Clandon on the A247, 3m E of Guildford on the A246 Guildford- Leatherhead road. Follow brown signs.
**Rail:** Clandon: Clandon Station 1m. Hatchlands: Clandon Station 2½ m, Horsley Station 3m.

### Contact
**Tel:** 01483 222482
**E-mail:** hatchlands @nationaltrust.org.uk or clandonpark @nationaltrust.org.uk

### Opening Times
**Clandon - House**
2 March-2 November Tue-Thu & Sun. Also BH Mons, Good Fri & Easter Sat, plus Mons in July & August, 11am-5pm.

**Clandon - Garden**
As house, 10.30am-5pm.

**Surrey Infantry Museum**
As house, 10.30am-5pm.

**Hatchlands - House**
1 April-30 October Tue-Thu, Sun & BH Mon, plus Fris in August, 2-5.30pm.

**Hatchlands Park Walks & NGS Quiet Garden**
1 April-2 November, daily 10.30am-6pm.

### Admission
**Clandon**
| | |
|---|---|
| House & Garden | £10.20 |
| Child | £5.00 |
| Family | £25.40 |
| Pre-booked Groups | £7.80 |

**Hatchlands**
| | |
|---|---|
| House & Grounds | £8.90 |
| Child | £4.40 |
| Family | £22.20 |
| Park Walks only | £4.70 |
| Child | £2.30 |
| Pre-booked Groups | £6.80 |

Prices include a voluntary donation but visitors can choose to pay the standard prices displayed at the property and on the website.

### Special Events
Summer theatre, walks, talks and family events throughout the year, please call 01483 222482 or visit website for details.

# CLANDON PARK 🌿 & HATCHLANDS PARK

www.nationaltrust.org.uk/clandon-park & www.nationaltrust.org.uk/hatchlands-park

## Clandon Park & Hatchlands Park, both Georgian country houses, are set amidst beautiful grounds and are just five minutes drive apart.

Clandon Park is a Palladian Mansion, built c1730 for the Onslow family and notable for its magnificent Marble Hall. The Onslows have been active in political history, being the only family to have produced three Speakers of the House of Commons. The 4th Earl of Onslow transported Hinemihi, the Maori meeting house in Clandon's garden, from New Zealand as a reminder of his time as Governor in the 1890s. There is also an intimate sunken Dutch garden and a stunning bulb field. Displayed inside the house is a superb collection of 18th century furniture, textiles and porcelain. Hatchlands Park was built in 1756 for Admiral Boscawen, hero of the Battle of Louisburg. The house is set in a beautiful 430-acre Repton park, with a variety of way-marked walks offering vistas of open parkland and idyllic views. The woodlands are a haven for wildlife and there is a stunning Bluebell wood in the spring. The house contains the Cobbe Collection of Old Master paintings and portraits and also the Cobbe Collection of keyboard instruments, the world's largest group of early keyboard instruments owned or played by famous composers such as Purcell, JC Bach, Mozart, Liszt, Chopin, Mahler and Elgar. There are frequent concerts based on the instruments in the collection (The Cobbe Collection Trust, 01483 211474, www.cobbecollection.co.uk).

## KEY FACTS

- ℹ️ No photography inside the houses.
- 📷 Clandon: Open as house plus 4 Nov -23 Dec, Tues-Thurs & Suns, 12-4pm Hatchlands: Open as house plus Sats, 10.30am-5.30pm.
- 🌱 Plant sales at Hatchlands.
- 🍽️ For Clandon weddings and receptions tel: 01483 222502.
- ♿ Please call for details. Limited lift availability at Clandon.
- 🏪 Hatchlands café- open as shop.
- 🍴 Clandon restaurant-open as shop.
- 🎧 Available at Hatchlands.
- 🅿️ Free parking.
- 🐕 Clandon - Guide dogs only. Hatchlands - dogs under close control in designated areas of parkland.
- 📅 Events throughout the year.

© James Duffy

Hatchlands Park

© National Trust Images / Chris Lacey

The Music Room at Hatchlands

### Conference/Function

| ROOM | Size | Max Cap |
|---|---|---|
| Marble Hall Clandon Pk | 40' x 40' | 160 seated 200 standing |

## VISITOR INFORMATION

■ **Owner**
Historic Royal Palaces

■ **Address**
Hampton Court Palace
Surrey
KT8 9AU

■ **Location**
**Map 19:B9**
**OS Ref. TQ155 686**
From M25/J15 or M25/J12 or M25/J10.
**Rail:** 30 minutes from Waterloo, zone 6 travelcard
**Boat:** From Richmond, Kingston or Runnymede

■ **Contact**
Historic Royal Palaces
**Tel:** 0844 482 7777
**Venue Hire and Corporate Hospitailty:** 020 3166 6507.
**E-mail:** hamptoncourt@hrp.org.uk

■ **Opening Times**
**Mar-Oct:** Daily, 10am-6pm (last admission 5pm).
**Nov-Feb:** Daily, 10am-4.30pm (last admission 3.30pm).
Closed 24-26 Dec.
Please always check website before visiting for full details.

■ **Admission**
Call 0844 482 7777 or visit www.hrp.org.uk for more information.

# HAMPTON COURT PALACE

www.hrp.org.uk/hamptoncourtpalace

## Discover the magnificence of this former royal residence, once home to the flamboyant King Henry VIII.

Marvel at the two distinct and contrasting Tudor and Baroque architectural styles and soak up the atmosphere in 60 acres of stunning gardens. Extended and developed in grand style in the 1520s by Henry VIII, the present day elegance and romance of the palace owes much to the Christopher Wren designed baroque buildings commissioned by William and Mary at the end of the 17th Century.

At the palace you are able to step back in time and relive some of the extraordinary moments in the life of Henry VIII, try on a Tudor gown and explore the majestic environment in which he entertained, celebrated and mourned. Marvel at the grandeur of the magnificent Great Hall and Great Watching Chamber, see the stunning vaulted ceiling of the Chapel Royal and explore the enormous kitchens, the most extensive surviving 16th Century kitchens in Europe today.

The palace is surrounded by formal gardens and sits in 60 acres of parkland gardens, including the 18th Century Privy Garden and world famous maze.

## KEY FACTS

- ℹ️ Information Centre.
- 🛍️
- 📞 020 3166 6507.
- ♿ WCs.
- 🍴 Licensed.
- 🎧
- 🅿️ Ample for cars, coach parking nearby.
- 🎟️ Rates on request 0844 482 7777.
- 🐕 Guide dogs only.
- 🔔
- ❄️
- ⚜️

# POLESDEN LACEY ❧
## GREAT BOOKHAM, NR DORKING, SURREY  RH5 6BD
### www.nationaltrust.org.uk/polesdenlacey

'This is a delicious house...' remarked Queen Elizabeth, the Queen Mother on her honeymoon at Polesden Lacey. This country retreat, with glorious views across the rolling Surrey Hills, was home to famous Edwardian hostess Mrs Greville, who entertained royalty and the celebrities of her time. The house has stunning interiors and contains a fabulous collection of art and ceramics. The gardens offer something for every season, including climbing roses, herbaceous borders and a winter garden. There are four waymarked countryside walks around the estate.

**Location:** Map 19:B10. OS Ref TQ136 522. 5m NW of Dorking, 2m S of Great Bookham, off A246.  **Owner:** National Trust
**Tel:** 01372 452048 **E-mail:** polesdenlacey@nationaltrust.org.uk
**Open:** Gardens, cafe & shops: daily from 10am-5pm (4pm in winter). Closed 25 Feb, 24 & 25 Dec. House: 1 Mar-2 Nov, daily 11am-5pm (weekday mornings entry by guided tour only). Jan, Feb & Nov house open for guided tours weekends only. Four weekends before Christmas house open for special event at additional charge for all visitors (inc NT members)

**Admission:** House & Grounds: Adults £12.50, Child £6.25, Family £31.25 Group (15+) £10.10. Grounds only: Adult £7.75, Child £3.90, Family £19.40, Group (15+) £6.25.

**Key facts:** ◻ ▦ ♿ Accessible toilets, catering & retail. Courtesy shuttle. Grounds mostly accessible. Free wheelchairs & powered mobility vehicles. Assistance dogs welcome. Hearing loops available. ⚲ Hot & cold food, home-made cakes & drinks made from local seasonal produce. ⚲ House tours weekday mornings Mar-Nov, weekends in winter. Free garden tours.
⌂ Gardens only. 🅿 ✕ In the grounds (excluding formal gardens).
✳ Grounds only. ♒

Polesden Lacey

# TITSEY PLACE 🏠ⓕ
## TITSEY, OXTED, SURREY  RH8 0SD
### www.titsey.org

Dating from the 16th Century, the Titsey Estate is one the largest surviving historic estates in Surrey.

Nestling under the North Downs, Titsey Place, with its stunning garden, lakes, woodland walks, walled kitchen garden and park offering panoramic views, enchants visitors. Enjoy the fine family portraits, furniture, a beautiful collection of porcelain and set of four Canaletto pictures of Venice. After visiting the mansion house and grounds, why not relax in our tea room where light refreshments are available?

Titsey dates back to the mid Sixteenth Century, though the first impression now is of a comfortable early Nineteenth Century house in a picturesque park. This well-preserved stretch of country is barely twenty miles from the centre of London: a landscape hardly changed in the last hundred years.

**Location:** Map 19:F10. OS Ref TQ406 551.

**Owner:** Trustees of the Titsey Foundation
**Tel:** 01273 715359  **Fax:** 01273 779783  **Events Organiser:** 01273 715356
**E-mail:** jo.dykes@struttandparker.com
**Open:** Open season: 14 May-28 Sep 2014. House and gardens open: 1pm-5pm every Wed and Sun. Also May and Aug BH's. Guided tours of the House at 1.30, 2.30 and 3.30pm. Gardens only open: 1pm-5pm every Sat. Also Easter Mon. Groups and coaches 20 + welcome all year Mon, Tues, Thurs & Fri only, by prior arrangement. Tea Rooms – open when house or gardens open.
**Admission:** House and Garden: £7.00, Garden Only £4.50, Children under 16 £1.00, Woodland walks Free and open 365 days. Pre-booked tours: House and garden inc. guide £8.50 per person, Garden Only £6.00 per person, Garden Guide £50.00 per group. **Key facts:** 🚻 Partial. 📷🍴 Obligatory. 🅿 Limited for coaches. 🐕 Guide dogs.

# GODDARDS LODGE
## Abinger Common, Dorking, Surrey  RH5 6TH
### www.landmarktrust.org.uk

Goddards, a masterpiece of the Arts and Crafts movement, was built by architect, Edwin Lutyens in about 1900 and has a garden laid out by his friend and collaborator, Gertrude Jekyll.

Goddards is approached by deeply sunken lanes that are almost tunnels through the wooded landscape.

**Location:** Map 19:B12.
**Owner:** The Lutyens Trust, leased to The Landmark Trust
**Tel:** 01628 825925
**E-mail:** bookings@landmarktrust.org.uk
**Open:** Garden & house by appointment, Wed 2.30-5pm, Easter - end Oct.
**Admission:** £4.00.
**Key facts:** ℹ Amid the many large, light-filled rooms a most elegant bowling alley waits for a strike.
🍴 Tours on Weds afternoons. 🅿
🏫 School visits by arrangement. 🐕❄❋♿

Titsey Place

# KEW PALACE
**Kew Gardens, Kew, Richmond, Surrey  TW9 3AB**
www.hrp.org.uk/kewpalace

Kew Palace was built as a private house in 1631 but became a royal residence between 1729 and 1818. More like a home than a palace, the privacy and intimacy of this smallest of English royal palaces made it the favourite country retreat for King George III and his family in the late 18th Century. A visit to the palace now also includes a chance to see the Royal Kitchens at Kew, the most perfectly preserved Georgian royal kitchens in existence.
**Location:** Map 19:C7. OS Ref TQ188 776.193. A307. Junc A307 & A205 (1m Chiswick roundabout M4).
**Owner:** Historic Royal Palaces
**Tel:** 0844 482 7777
**E-mail:** kewpalace@hrp.org.uk
**Open:** Apr–Sep 9.30am-5.30pm.
**Admission:** Free of charge but please note admission tickets to Kew Gardens must be purchased to gain access to Kew Palace (for gardens admission prices, please visit the Kew Gardens website).
**Key facts:** ⊤ ⌂ WCs. ☐ ⊠

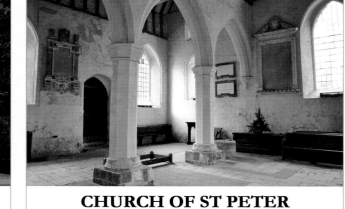

# CHURCH OF ST PETER & ST PAUL 🏛
**Albury Park, Albury, Guildford, Surrey  GU5 9BB**
www.visitchurches.org.uk

This charming, ancient church dating from Saxon and Norman times, is a flint-walled gem, set amongst the trees of beautiful Albury Park above the River Tilling. Inside, you'll find a light, limewashed uncluttered interior with a stunning medieval wall painting of St Christopher and interesting monuments including a brass of John Weston who died in 1440 and an 18th Century shingled cupola over the tower. Another highlight is the South Chapel; remodelled by renowned Victorian architect A.W. Pugin, responsible for the interior of the Palace of Westminster. He used his rich and colourful style here to create a dazzling mortuary chapel for Albury Park's Drummond family - this is lavishly decorated, with stained glass, painted walls and ceiling, and a magnificent tiled floor. **Location:** OS Ref TQ063 479. 5m SE of Guildford off A248. Turn into minor road on sharp bend and then into private drive with lodge at entrance to Albury Park. Follow drive, fork left to church.
**Open:** Open daily from 10am-5pm.

## GREAT FOSTERS
**Stroude Road, Egham, Surrey  TW20 9UR**
Set amongst 50 acres of stunning gardens and parkland Great Fosters is a fine example of Elizabethan architecture and is now a luxury hotel with 2 restaurants, The Estate Grill and The Tudor Room. Partake in afternoon tea by one of the fires or on the terrace in warmer months. Its past is evident in the mullioned windows, chimneys and brick finials, whilst the gardens include a Saxon moat, Japanese bridge, amphitheatre and knot garden designed by WH Romaine-Walker and Gilbert Jenkins.
**Location:** Map 3:G2. OS Ref TQ015 694. M25 J/13, follow signs to Egham and then brown historic signs for Great Fosters
**Owner:** The Sutcliffe family  **Contact:** Amanda Dougans
**Tel:** 01784 433822  **Fax:** 01784 472455
**E-mail:** reception@greatfosters.co.uk  **Website:** www.greatfosters.co.uk
**Open:** All year.  **Admission:** No charge.
**Key facts:** ⊡ ⊤ ⌂ WCs. ⊞ Licensed. ☐ ⊠ Guide dogs only. ⊠
⊡ ⚑ ✳ ♥

# PAINSHILL LANDSCAPE GARDEN 🏛ⓕ
**Portsmouth Road, Cobham, Surrey  KT11 1JE**
www.painshill.co.uk

Painshill is a beautiful 18th Century landscape garden. The 158 acre wonderland has something for everyone. Discover mystical follies, including the restored crystal Grotto (limited opening times), historic plantings, the John Bartram Heritage Collection of North American trees and shrubs (Plant Heritage) and spectacular views of Surrey. **Location:** Map 19:B9. OS Ref TQ 10406 60269. M25/J10/A3 to London. W of Cobham on A245. Signposted.
**Owner:** Painshill Park Trust  **Contact:** Visitor Operations Team
**Tel:** 01932 868113  **Fax:** 01932 868001  **E-mail:** info@painshill.co.uk
**Open:** All Year (Closed 25-26 Dec). Mar-Oct 10.30am-6pm or dusk (last entry 4.30pm). Nov-Feb 10.30am to 4pm or dusk (last entry 3pm).
**Admission:** Adult £7.70 Conc. £6.60, Child (5-16 yrs) £4.20, Family (2 Adults & 4 Children) £25.00, Under 5's & Disabled Carer: Free. Group rates available.
**Key facts:** ⊡ ⊠ Books, gifts, Painshill Sparkling Wine & Painshill Honey. ⊤ ⌂ WCs. Accessible route. Free pre-booked wheelchair loan. Pre-booked guided buggy tours. ⊞ Licensed. Picnic area. ⊡ Pre-book 10+ groups. ⌂ Free for disabled visitors. ☐ Free. Coaches must book. ⊠ Pre-book via Education Dept. ⊠ On short leads. ✳ ♥

Painshill Landscape Garden

# ARUNDEL CASTLE & GARDENS 🏛

www.arundelcastle.org

## Ancient Castle, Stately Home, Gardens & The Collector Earl's Garden.

A thousand years of history is waiting to be discovered at Arundel Castle in West Sussex. Dating from the 11th Century, the Castle is both ancient fortification and stately home of the Dukes of Norfolk and Earls of Arundel.

Set high on a hill, this magnificent castle commands stunning views across the River Arun and out to sea. Climb the Keep, explore the battlements, wander in the grounds and recently restored Victorian gardens and relax in the garden of the 14th Century Fitzalan Chapel.

In the 17th Century during the English Civil War the Castle suffered extensive damage. The process of structural restoration began in earnest in the 18th Century and continued up until 1900. The Castle was one of the first private residences to have electricity and central heating and had its own fire engine.

Inside the Castle over 20 sumptuously furnished rooms may be visited including the breathtaking Barons' Hall with 16th Century furniture; the Armoury with its fine collection of armour and weaponry, and the magnificent Gothic library entirely fitted out in carved Honduras mahogany. There are works of art by Van Dyck, Gainsborough, Canaletto and Mytens; tapestries; clocks; and personal possessions of Mary Queen of Scots including the gold rosary that she carried to her execution.

There are special event days throughout the season, including opera, Shakespeare, jousting, and medieval re-enactments.

Do not miss the magnificent Collector Earl's Garden based on early 17th Century classical designs.

## KEY FACTS

- ⓘ No photography or video recording inside the Castle.
- Distinctive and exclusive gifts.
- WCs.
- Licensed.
- Licensed.
- By prior arrangement. Tour time 1½-2 hrs. Tours available in various languages - please enquire.
- **P** Ample car and coach parking in town car park. Free admission and refreshment voucher for coach driver.
- Norman Motte & Keep, Armoury & Victorian bedrooms. Special rates for schoolchildren (aged 5-16) and teachers.
- Registered Assistance dogs only.
- On special event days admission prices may vary.

# GOODWOOD HOUSE 🏛ⓕ
## www.goodwood.com

## Goodwood House, ancestral home of the Dukes of Richmond and Gordon with magnificent art collection.

Goodwood is one of England's finest sporting estates. At its heart lies Goodwood House, the ancestral home of the Dukes of Richmond and Gordon, direct descendants of King Charles II. Today, it is lived in by the present Duke's son and heir, the Earl of March and Kinrara, with his wife and family. Their home is open to the public on at least sixty days a year.

The art collection includes a magnificent group of British paintings from the Seventeenth and Eighteenth Centuries, such as the celebrated views of London by Canaletto and superb sporting scenes by George Stubbs. The rooms are filled with fine English and French furniture, Gobelins tapestries and Sèvres Porcelain. Special works of art are regularly rotated and displayed and the

books can be viewed by written application to the Curator (there is a special charge for these viewings). The summer exhibition 'Nature Revisited' will look at the interest the Dukes of Richmond have taken in natural history.

Goodwood is also renowned for its entertaining, enjoying a reputation for excellence. Goodwood's own organic farm provides food for the table in the various restaurants on the estate. With internationally renowned horseracing and motor sport events, the finest downland golf course in the UK, its own aerodrome and hotel, Goodwood offers an extraordinarily rich sporting experience.

## KEY FACTS

ⓘ Conference and wedding facilities. No photography. Very well informed guides. Shell House optional extra on Connoisseurs' Days.

WCs.

Obligatory.

Ample.

Guide dogs only.

Goodwood Hotel.

Civil Wedding Licence. Telephone number for Weddings is 01243 775537 and email is estatesalesofficeenquiries@goodwood.com.

## VISITOR INFORMATION

### ■ Owner
The Goodwood Estate Co.Ltd. (Earl of March and Kinrara).

### ■ Address
Goodwood House
Goodwood
Chichester
West Sussex
PO18 0PX

### ■ Location
**Map 3:F6**
**OS Ref. SU888 088**
3½m NE of Chichester. A3 from London then A286 or A285. M27/A27 from Portsmouth or Brighton.
**Rail:** Chichester 3½m Arundel 9m.
**Air:** Heathrow 1½ hrs Gatwick ¾hr.

### ■ Contact
Assistant to the Curator
**Tel:** 01243 755048
Recorded Info: 01243 755040.
**Fax:** 01243 755005
01243 775537 (Weddings).
**Recorded Info:** 01243 755040.
**E-mail:** curator@goodwood.com
or estatesalesofficeenquiries@goodwood.com

### ■ Opening Times
**Summer**
**16 Mar-13 Oct:** Most Suns and Mons, 1-5pm (last entry 4pm).
**3-28 Aug:** Sun-Thur, 1-5pm.
Please check Recorded Info 01243 755040.
**13 May and 2 Sep 2014:** Connoisseurs' Days.
Special tours for booked groups of 20+ only.
**Closures**
Closed for some special events and for the Festival of Speed and Revival Meeting.
Please ring before travelling to check these dates and occasional extra closures.

### ■ Admission
**House**
| | |
|---|---|
| Adult | £9.50 |
| Young Person (12-18yrs) | £4.00 |
| Child (under 12yrs) | Free |
| Family | £22.00 |

**Booked Groups (20-100)**
| | |
|---|---|
| Open Day (am - by request only) | £12.00 |
| Open Day (pm) | £9.00 |
| Connoisseurs Day | £12.00 |

### ■ Special Events
**Festival of Speed**
See website for details
**Goodwood Revival Meeting**
12-14 September
**Glorious Goodwood**
29 July–2 August
Please visit our website for up-to-date information.
www.goodwood.com.

### Conference/Function
| ROOM | Size | Max Cap |
|---|---|---|
| Ballroom | 79' x 23' | 180 |

## VISITOR INFORMATION

■ **Owner**
The Great Dixter
Charitable Trust

■ **Address**
Northiam
Rye
East Sussex
TN31 6PH

■ **Location**
Map 4:L5
OS Ref. TQ817 251
Signposted off the A28 in
Northiam.

■ **Contact**
Perry Rodriguez
**Tel:** 01797 252878
**E-mail:** office@
greatdixter.co.uk

■ **Opening Times**
**1 April-26 October:** Tue-
Sun, House 2-5pm. Garden
11am-5pm.
**Specialist Nursery
Opening times:
April-October**
Mon-Fri, 9-5pm. Sat
9-5pm. Sun 10-5pm.
**November-End of March**
Mon-Fri, 9-12.30pm,
1.30-4.30pm. Sat
9-12.30pm. Sun Closed.

■ **Admission**
House & Garden    £10.00
Child                     £3.50
Garden only          £8.00
Child                     £2.50
A Gift Aid on admission
scheme is in place.

■ **Special Events**
Study days on a wide range
of subjects available. Please
check the website for
details.

# GREAT DIXTER HOUSE & GARDENS 🏠Ⓕ
www.greatdixter.co.uk

## A very special garden with a great deal of character, planted with flair, always something to see, whatever the season.

Great Dixter, built c1450, is the birthplace of the late Christopher Lloyd, gardening author. Its Great Hall is the largest medieval timberframed hall in the country, restored and enlarged for Christopher's father (1910-12). The house was largely designed by the architect, Sir Edwin Lutyens, who added a 16th Century house (moved from elsewhere) knitting the buildings together as a family home. The house retains much of the collections of furniture and other items put together by the Lloyds early in the 20th Century, with some notable modern additions by Christopher. The gardens feature a variety of topiary, ponds, wild meadow areas and the famous Long Border and Exotic Garden. Featured regularly in 'Country Life' from 1963, Christopher was asked to contribute a series of weekly articles as a practical gardener - he never missed an issue in 42 years. There is a specialist nursery which offers an array of unusual plants of the highest quality, many of which can be seen in the fabric of the gardens. Light refreshments are available in the gift shop as well as tools, books and gifts. The whole estate is 57 acres which includes ancient woodlands, meadows and ponds which have been consistently managed on a traditional basis. Coppicing the woodlands, for example, has provided pea sticks for plant supports and timber for fencing and repairs to the buildings. There is a Friends programme available throughout the year. Friends enjoy invitations to events and educational courses as well as regular newsletters.

## KEY FACTS

ℹ️ No photography in House.

🚶 Obligatory.

🅿️ Limited for coaches.

🐕 Guide dogs only.

The glorious gothic architecture of Lancing College Chapel

## VISITOR INFORMATION

■ **Owner**
Lancing College
Chapel Trust

■ **Address**
Lancing
West Sussex
BN15 0RW

■ **Location**
**Map 3:H6**
**OS Ref. TQ 196 067**
North of the A27 between
Shoreham-by-Sea and
Lancing at the Coombes
Road/Shoreham Airport
traffic lights. Filter right if
coming from the east. Turn
off Coombes Road at sign
for Lancing College and
proceed to the top of
Lancing College drive. It is
usually possible to park
outside the Chapel.
**Rail:** Train to Shoreham-by
Sea or Lancing on the
London-Littlehampton and
Portsmouth line and
take a taxi.
**Bus:** The nearest bus
routes are Brighton and
Hove Buses 2A, Compass
Buses, 106 and
Coastliner 700.

■ **Contact**
The Verger
**Tel:** 01273 465949
**Fax:** 01273 464720
Enquiries may also be
made at the Porter's Lodge,
Lancing College
on 01273 452213.
**E-mail:** ahowat
@lancing.org.uk

■ **Opening Times**
10.00am to 4.00pm
Monday to Saturday;
12noon to 4.00pm on
Sunday. Every day of the
year except for Christmas
Day and Boxing Day.

■ **Admission**
Admission Free.
Donations are requested
for the Friends of
Lancing Chapel.
Visitors are asked to sign in
for security purposes as
they enter the Chapel.
The other College buildings
are not open to the public.

■ **Special Events**
Visitors can reserve seats
for Public Carol Services by
applying in writing to
Lancing College Chapel,
Lancing, West Sussex,
BN15 0RW with a
stamped, self-addressed
envelope.
Visitors wishing to attend
other services should
contact the Verger.

# LANCING COLLEGE CHAPEL

www.lancingcollege.co.uk

## 'I know of no more spectacular post-Reformation ecclesiastical building in the kingdom.' Evelyn Waugh, former pupil.

Lancing College Chapel is the place of worship for the community of Lancing College, the Central Minster of the Woodard Schools and a well-loved Sussex landmark. The Chapel stands prominently on the South Downs. The exterior, with its pinnacles and flying buttresses, is a testament to Victorian structural bravado. Designed by Herbert Carpenter in the 13th Century French gothic style, it is the fourth tallest ecclesiastical building in England.

The foundations were laid in 1868 and the atmospheric crypt came into use in 1875. The upper chapel was dedicated in 1911 but the west wall and rose window were added in the 1970s. There is now a plan to complete the building with a west porch. A beautiful war memorial cloister was built in the 1920s.

The interior is breathtaking. Soaring columns branch out into fan vaulting, perfectly proportioned arches and vast clerestory windows. There are stained glass windows by Comper and Dykes Bower and one commemorating former pupil Fr Trevor Huddleston made by Mel Howse in 2007. Behind the high altar are superb tapestries woven on the William Morris looms in the 1920s. The oak stall canopies are by Gilbert Scott. There are two organs (Walker 1914 and Frobenius 1986) with intricately carved oak cases.

The Chapel has a fascinating history which is still unfolding and it is a treasure house of ecclesiastical art. Lancing Chapel welcomes visitors both as an important heritage landmark and as a place of quiet reflection and prayer.

## KEY FACTS

- ℹ Guide books, information leaflets & a DVD.
- Stall with guide books & postcards at entrance to the Chapel.
- ♿ The upper chapel (but not the crypt) is easily accessible for the disabled.
- Guided tours & brief talks about the Chapel can be booked with the Verger. Groups should be booked in advance.
- Ⓟ It is usually possible to park very near the entrance to the Chapel.
- School & other educational groups are welcome & may request guided tours & other information.
- Guide dogs in Chapel. Dogs on leads in College grounds.
- ❄ Open all year except Christmas Day & Boxing Day.

Interior of Lancing College Chapel looking East

The splendid rose window and Walker organ

*© National Trust Images / John Miller*

*© Geoffrey Frosh*

## BATEMAN'S ❁
### BATEMAN'S, BURWASH, ETCHINGHAM, EAST SUSSEX  TN19 7DS
www.nationaltrust.org.uk/batemans

"A good and peaceable place" was how Rudyard Kipling described Bateman's, a beautiful Sussex sandstone manor house and garden where the Kiplings lived from 1902 - 1936. Originally built in 1634 this mellow house, with its little watermill, was a sanctuary to the most famous writer in the English speaking world. Set in the glorious landscape of the Sussex Weald, the house and gardens are kept much as they were in Kipling's time and visitors can discover a fascinating collection of mementos of Kipling's time in India and illustrations from his famous Jungle Book tales of Mowgli, Baloo and Shere Khan.

**Location:** Map 4:K5. OS Ref TQ671 238.
0.5 m S of Burwash off A265.
**Owner:** National Trust

**Contact:** The Administrator
**Tel:** 01435 882302
**Fax:** 01435 882811
**E-mail:** batemans@nationaltrust.org.uk
**Open:** 1 Mar-31 Dec: 7 days/week, Closed Christmas Eve and Christmas Day. House: 11am-5pm. Garden, shop and restaurant: 10am-5pm.
**Admission:** House & Garden: Adult £9.90, Child £4.95, Family £24.90 (2+3)*. Groups: Adult £7.70, Child £3.85, Family £19.00. *Gift Aid Prices, standard prices are available at property and on website.
**Key facts:** ⬚ ⬚ ⬚ ⬚ Partial. WCs. ⬚ ⬚ Limited for coaches. ⬚ ⬚ Guide dogs only.

## FIRLE PLACE 🏛ⓕ
### FIRLE, LEWES, EAST SUSSEX  BN8 6LP
www.firle.com

Firle Place has been the home of the Gage family for over 500 years. Set at the foot of the Sussex Downs within its own parkland, this unique house of Tudor origin was built of Caen stone by Sir John Gage, friend of Henry VIII. Remodelled in the 18th Century, the house contains a magnificent collection of Old Master paintings, fine English and European furniture and an impressive collection of Sèvres porcelain. Events: Events and wedding receptions can be held in the parkland throughout the year or in the Georgian Riding School from April to October. The Great Tudor Hall can, on occasion, be used for private dinners, with drinks on the Terrace or in the Billiard Room. Please contact the Estate Office for all event and wedding reception enquiries on 01273 858567 or visit the website for further information. Tea Room: Enjoy the licensed tea room and terrace with views over the garden and parkland, serving light lunches and afternoon tea using local produce from Firle Place gardens and the wider Firle

Estate. **Location:** Map 4:J6. OS Ref TQ473 071. 4m SE of Lewes on A27 Brighton/Eastbourne Road.
**Owner:** The Rt Hon Viscount Gage
**Tel:** 01273 858307 House  **Fax:** 01273 858118  **Events:** 01273 858567
**E-mail:** enquiries@firle.com
**Open:** Jun–Sep, Sun–Thurs, 2.00–4.30 pm. Dates and times subject to change without prior notice. Tea Room open on House opening days only, from 12.00–4.30pm. Garden Open Days 18-20 Apr 2014.
**Admission:** Adult £8.50, Child £4.00, Conc. £7.50
Private Tours: Private group tours can be arranged by prior appointment. Please telephone 01273 858307 for details or visit the website.
**Key facts:** ⓘ No photography in house. ⬚ ⬚ ⬚ Ground floor & tea room. ⬚ Licensed. ⬚ ⬚ ⬚ In grounds on leads. ⬚

© National Trust Images /John Miller

# NYMANS ✿
## HANDCROSS, HAYWARDS HEATH, WEST SUSSEX  RH17 6EB

### www.nationaltrust.org.uk/nymans

In the late 1800's Ludwig Messel bought the Nymans Estate in the Sussex High Weald to make a dream family home. Inspired by the wooded surroundings he created a garden with plants collected from around the world. Today it is still a garden lovers' home - a place to relax all year round in a peaceful country garden. The house was partially destroyed by fire in 1947 and romantic ruins of a fairytale gothic mansion remain. As well as a large shop and plant centre there is a café with seasonal food, year round activities, a small gallery and a bookshop. **Location:** Map 4:I4. OS Ref SU187:TQ265 294. At Handcross on B2114, 12 miles south of Gatwick, just off London-Brighton M23.
**Owner:** National Trust  **Contact:** Nymans
**Tel:** 01444 405250  **E-mail:** nymans@nationaltrust.org.uk

**Open:** Garden, woods, cafe, shop and garden centre, gallery in the House, and second hand bookshop: 1 Jan-28 Feb, daily, 10am-4pm. 1 Mar-31 Oct, daily, 10am-5pm. 1 Nov-31 Dec, daily, 10am-4pm. House open for special events only from 1 Nov-28 Feb. Closed 25 & 26 December. Last admission to Gallery 30 minutes before closing and for short periods during the year to change exhibitions. For more information and any other changes please check the website. **Admission:** Adult £11.60, Child £6.50, Family (2 Adults, 3 Children) £29.00, Family (1 adult, 3 Children) £18.00, Booked Groups (15+) Adult £9.00, Child £4.50.
**Key facts:** ⊡ ⊞ ⊤ ⬓ WC, some level path. ⬛ Licensed. ℗ ▦
▦ Guide dogs only. ▦ No dogs in garden. ⬛ ❄ ⬓

# PARHAM HOUSE & GARDENS ⬛ⓕ
## PARHAM PARK, STORRINGTON, NR PULBOROUGH, WEST SUSSEX  RH20 4HS

### www.parhaminsussex.co.uk

One of the top twenty in Simon Jenkins's book 'England's Thousand Best Houses'. Idyllically set in the heart of a 17th Century deer park, below the South Downs, the house contains an important collection of needlework, paintings and furniture. The spectacular Long Gallery is the third longest in England. The award winning gardens include a four acre walled garden with stunning herbaceous borders. Parham has always been a much-loved family home. Now owned by a charitable trust, the house is lived in by Lady Emma Barnard, her husband James and their family.
**Location:** Map 3:G5. OS Ref TQ060 143. Midway between Pulborough & Storrington on A283. Equidistant from A24 & A29. For SatNav please enter

postcode RH20 4HR.
**Owner:** Parham Park Trust  **Contact:** Parham Estate Office
**Tel:** 01903 742021
**Fax:** 01903 746557
**E-mail:** enquiries@parhaminsussex.co.uk
**Open:** Open 6 Apr-26 Oct. Suns only in Oct. Please see website or contact property for full opening dates and details.
**Admission:** Please contact property or see website for admission prices.
**Key facts:** ⓘ No photography in house. ⊡ ⊞ ⊞ Licensed.
⒡ By arrangement. ⊡ ℗ ▦ ▦ In grounds, on leads. ⬓

# PETWORTH HOUSE & PARK ❧
## CHURCH STREET, PETWORTH, WEST SUSSEX GU28 0AE
### www.nationaltrust.org.uk/petworth

Explore this majestic mansion and beautiful landscaped deer park, forever immortalised in JMW Turner's masterpieces. Unlock the intriguing family history and marvel at the world famous painting collection, including works by Turner, Van Dyck, Reynolds and Blake amongst ancient and Neo-classical sculpture. In contrast to the lavish House, venture 'below stairs' to discover the secrets of the Servants' Quarters. Stroll the Pleasure Grounds and enjoy breathtaking views, whatever the season. On weekdays Lord and Lady Egremont kindly open private rooms for visitors to enjoy.

**Location:** Map 3:G5. OS Ref SU976 218. In the centre of Petworth town (approach roads A272/A283/A285) Car park signposted.
**Owner:** National Trust
**Contact:** The Administration Office
**Tel:** 01798 342207 **Fax:** 01798 342963
**E-mail:** petworth@nationaltrust.org.uk

**Open:** House: 15 Mar-5 Nov, Sat-Wed, 11am-5pm last admission 4pm, open on Thurs-Fri for guided snapshot tours only. Pleasure Grounds, Restaurant, Coffee Shop & Gift Shop: 11 Jan-14 Mar, Sat-Sat, 10.30am-3.30pm; 15 Mar-5 Nov, Sat-Sat, 10.30am-5pm; 6 Nov-31 Dec, Sat-Sat, 10.30am-3.30pm (closed 24 & 25 Dec).
**Admission:** House and Grounds Adult £14, Child (5-17yrs) £7, Family (2+3) £35 Groups (pre-booked) £11.20. Includes voluntary donation but visitors can choose to pay the standard prices displayed on the property.
**Key facts:** ℹ️ Events & Exhibitions throughout the year. Baby feeding and changing facilities, highchairs, pushchairs admitted in House but no prams please. 📷🎁🍽️🚻 WCs. 🍷 Licensed. 🍴 Licensed. 🎫 By arrangement. 🎧 Audio House Tours. 🅿️ 700 meters from house. Coach parties alight at Church Lodge entrance, coaches then park in NT car park. Coaches must book in advance. 🎓🐕 Guide dogs only. 🐕🏨

# ST MARY'S HOUSE & GARDENS 🏛️ⓕ
## BRAMBER, WEST SUSSEX BN44 3WE
### www.stmarysbramber.co.uk

Enchanting medieval house, winner of Hudsons Heritage 'Best Restoration' award 2011. Features in Simon Jenkins' book 'England's Thousand Best Houses'. Fine panelled interiors, including unique Elizabethan 'Painted Room'. Interesting family memorabilia. Rare Napoleonic collection. English costume-dolls. Traditional cottage-style tea room. Five acres of grounds include formal gardens with amusing topiary, exceptional example of the prehistoric tree Ginkgo biloba and the Victorian 'Secret' Garden. Original fruit-wall and pineapple pits, Rural Museum, Jubilee Rose Garden, Terracotta Garden, woodland walk and unusual circular Poetry Garden.
In the heart of the South Downs National Park, St. Mary's is a house of fascination and mystery, with picturesque charm and atmosphere of friendliness and welcome. **** CELEBRATING 30 YEARS OF CONSERVATION ****

**Location:** Map 3:H6. OS Ref TQ189 105. Bramber village off A283. From London 56m via M23/A23 or A24.
Buses from Brighton, Shoreham and Worthing.
**Owner:** Mr Peter Thorogood MBE and Mr Roger Linton MBE
**Tel:** 01903 816205
**E-mail:** info@stmarysbramber.co.uk
**Open:** May-end Sep: Suns, Thurs & BH Mons, 2-6pm. Last entry 5pm. Groups at other days and times by arrangement.
**Admission:** House & Gardens: Adult £8, Conc. £7.50, Child £4, Groups (25+) £8.50. Gardens only: Adult £5, Conc. £4.50, Child £2.00, Groups £5.
**Key facts:** ℹ️ No photography in house. 📷🎁🍽️🚻 Partial. 🍴🎫 Obligatory for groups (max 55). Visit time 2½-3 hrs. 🅿️ 20 cars, 2 coaches. 🐕🏨🎓

© NT/Chris Roe

© NT/Lisa Barnard

# SHEFFIELD PARK AND GARDEN ❧
## SHEFFIELD PARK, EAST SUSSEX  TN22 3QX
### www.nationaltrust.org.uk/sheffieldpark

A magnificent landscaped garden and historic parkland, open all year to explore and discover. In the garden, four lakes mirror the beautiful planting and colour each season. Early spring bulbs, including snowdrops, daffodils and bluebells are followed in May/June, by an outstanding exhibition of colour when our rhododendrons and azaleas display their magnificent spring colour show. Water lilies dress the lakes during the summer, whilst in the autumn the garden is transformed by the stunning autumn colour including Nyssa sylvatica, producing displays of gold, orange and crimson. The year ends with the chance to enjoy a beautiful crisp winter's walk. (Please note, house not NT).
**Location:** Map 4:I5. OS Ref TQ415 240. Midway between East Grinstead and Lewes, 5m NW of Uckfield on E side of A275.
**Owner:** National Trust
**Contact:** Property Office

**Tel:** 01825 790231
**Fax:** 01825 791264
**E-mail:** sheffieldpark@nationaltrust.org.uk
**Open:** Garden/Shop/Tearoom: Open all year (closed Christmas Day), please call 01825 790231 or log onto our website for details of times. Parkland: Open all year, dawn to dusk.
**Admission:** For 2014 prices, please call 01825 790231 or log onto our website. Groups discount available (15+ prebooked) NT, RHS Individual Members and Great British Heritage Pass holders Free. Discounts available in conjunction with the Bluebell Railway for groups.
**Key facts:** ℹ️ Garden: Accessibility dogs only. Parkland: Dogs allowed under close control. 🖥️ 📷 ♿ WCs. 🍴 Licensed. 🍴 Licensed. 🖼️ By arrangement. 🅿️ 📷 ♿ Guide dogs only. ❋ ♿

© National Trust Images / Nadia Mackenzie

© NT/Chris Hill

# STANDEN ❧
## EAST GRINSTEAD, WEST SUSSEX  RH19 4NE
### www.nationaltrust.org.uk/standen

Designed by Philip Webb in the 1890s for wealthy solicitor, James Beale, and his family, Standen is a family home with nationally important Arts & Crafts interiors most famous for its Morris & Co. designs. The house is set for a 1920s weekend with visiting members of the Beale family. You can discover how they used Standen over a 24 hour period and enjoy the house and garden as they and their guests did. The 12 acre hillside garden, is part of a 5 year project to restore lost features and conserve the historic plant collection of an important Arts & Crafts inspired garden. Our licensed café serves seasonal dishes made with produce from our Kitchen Garden. Arts & Crafts inspired gifts are available in our shop. **Location:** Map 4:I4. OS Ref TQ389 356. 2m S of East Grinstead, signposted from B2110.
**Owner:** National Trust **Contact:** The Property Manager

**Tel:** 01342 323029 **Fax:** 01342 316424 **Twitter & Facebook:** Search for StandenNT. **E-mail:** standen@nationaltrust.org.uk
**Open:** 15 Feb-2 Nov: Mon-Sun, Garden, Café, Shop 10am-5pm (House 11am–4.30pm last entry 4pm). 3 Nov–31 Dec: Garden, Café, Shop 10.00am-4.00pm (House 11am–3.30pm last entry 3pm). * Check website for full details.
**Admission:** House & Garden*: Adult £10.50, Child £5.25, Family £26.25. Pre-booked groups: £8.00 (min 15). *Includes voluntary donation but visitors can choose to pay the standard prices displayed on the property and on the website. **Key facts:** ℹ️ Year round events programme including contemporary art selling exhibitions, garden open days, lectures, demonstrations and school holiday children's activities. 🖥️ 📷 ♿ WCs. Wheelchairs available to borrow. 🍴 Licensed. 🍴 Licensed. 🅿️ 📷 ♿ Guide dogs only. ♿

# UPPARK HOUSE & GARDEN ❧
## SOUTH HARTING, PETERSFIELD, WEST SUSSEX GU31 5QR
### www.nationaltrust.org.uk/uppark

Admire the Georgian grandeur of Uppark from its stunning hilltop location on the South Downs. Discover the fascinating world of Sir Harry Fetherstonhaugh, Lady Emma Hamilton and the dairymaid who married her master.
See the famous doll's house, Victorian servants' quarters, lovely garden and breathtaking views.
**Location:** Map 3:F5. OS Ref 197 SU775 177.
Between Petersfield & Chichester on B2146.
**Owner:** National Trust **Contact:** The Property Office
**Tel:** 01730 825415 **Fax:** 01730 825873
**E-mail:** uppark@nationaltrust.org.uk

**Open:** 16 Mar-2 Nov Sun-Thu. Garden, Shop & Restaurant 11am-5pm. House 12.30-4.30pm (11am-12.30pm open for bite-sized tours only, details on arrival. Tickets limited. Not suitable for groups). Sundays only 9 Nov-21 Dec. House (some rooms only), Garden, Shop & Restaurant 11am-3pm.
**Admission:** Adult £10.40, Child (5-17yrs) £5.20, Family (2+3) £26.00.
Garden only: Adult £5.20, Child £2.60. Gift Aid prices.
**Key facts:** ⓘ No photography in the house. ⌾ ♿
🚻 WCs at carpark, in shop and in house. Lift to basement of house.
🍴 Licensed. Available for hire. 🅿
⚘ Enabling dogs only. ⌂

# BODIAM CASTLE ❧
## Bodiam, Nr Robertsbridge, East Sussex TN32 5UA
### www.nationaltrust.org.uk/bodiamcastle

Built in 1385 to defend the surrounding countryside and as a comfortable dwelling for a rich nobleman, Bodiam Castle is one of the finest examples of medieval architecture. The virtual completeness of its exterior makes it popular with adults, children and film crews alike. Inside, although a ruin, floors have been replaced in some of the towers and visitors can climb the spiral staircase to enjoy superb views from the battlements. Discover more of its intriguing past in an introductory film and new exhibition, and wander in the peacefully romantic Castle grounds.
**Location:** Map 4:K5. OS Ref TQ785 256. 3m S of Hawkhurst,
2m E of A21 Hurst Green.
**Owner:** National Trust
**Contact:** The Property Manager
**Tel:** 01580 830196
**E-mail:** bodiamcastle@nationaltrust.org.uk
**Open:** Please see website for opening times and admisson prices.
**Key facts:** ⌾ 🚻 Ground floor & grounds. 🍴 🅿
🖼 Teachers resources & education base. ⚘ ⌂

Chichester Cathedral

## CHARLESTON

**Charleston, Firle, Nr Lewes, East Sussex BN8 6LL**

www.charleston.org.uk

Charleston, with its unique interiors and beautiful walled garden, was the home of artists Vanessa Bell and Duncan Grant from 1916 and the country meeting place of the Bloomsbury group. They decorated the house, painting walls, doors and furniture and filling the rooms with their own paintings and works by artists they admired, such as Picasso, Derain and Sickert.

**Location:** Map 4:J6. OS Ref TQ490 069. 7 miles east of Lewes on A27 between Firle and Selmeston **Owner:** The Charleston Trust

**Tel:** 01323 811626 **Fax:** 01323 811628 **E-mail:** info@charleston.org.uk

**Open:** Apr-Oct: Wed-Sat, guided tours from 1pm (12pm Jul & Aug) Last entry 5pm. Sun & BH Mon open 1-5.30pm.

**Admission:** Please check website for full details of admission costs.

**Key facts:**

Obligatory, except Sunday.

## CHICHESTER CATHEDRAL

**Chichester, W Sussex PO19 1PX**

www.chichestercathedral.org.uk

Ancient and modern, this magnificent 900 year old Cathedral has treasures from every age, from medieval stone carvings to world famous contemporary artworks. Open every day and all year with free entry. Free guided tours and special trails for children. Regular exhibitions, free weekly lunchtime concerts and a superb Cloisters Restaurant and Shop. A fascinating place to visit.

**Location:** Map 3:F6. OS Ref SU860 047. West Street, Chichester.

**Contact:** Visitor Services Officer

**Tel:** 01243 782595 **Fax:** 01243 812499

**E-mail:** visitors@chichestercathedral.org.uk

**Open:** Summer: 7.15am-7pm, Winter: 7.15am-6pm. Choral Evensong daily (except Wed).

**Admission:** Free entry. Donations greatly appreciated.

**Key facts:**

## CLINTON LODGE GARDEN

**Fletching, E Sussex TN22 3ST**

www.clintonlodgegardens.co.uk

A formal but romantic garden around a Caroline and Georgian house, reflecting the gardening fashions throughout its history, particularly since the time of Sir Henry Clinton, one of Wellington's generals at Waterloo. Lawn and parkland, double blue and white herbaceous borders between yew and box hedges, a cloister walk swathed in white roses, clematis and geraniums, a Herb Garden where hedges of box envelop herbs, seats are of turf, paths of camomile. A Pear Walk bursts with alliums or lilies, a Potager of flowers for cutting, old roses surround a magnificent water feature by William Pye, and much more. Private groups by appointment.

**Location:** Map 4:I5. OS Ref TQ428 238. In centre of village behind tall yew and holly hedge.

**Owner/Contact:** Lady Collum **Tel/Fax:** 01825 722952

**E-mail:** garden@clintonlodge.com

**Open:** NGS Open Days: Sun 27 April, Mon 2 Jun & Mon 4 Aug. Other days by appointment. **Admission:** NGS Entrance £5.00, Children Free.

**Key facts:** WCs. Partial. By arrangement. Limited.

Guide dogs only.

## GLYNDE PLACE 🏠Ⓕ
### The Estate Office, Glynde, East Sussex BN8 6SX
www.glyndeplace.co.uk

Glynde Place is a magnificent example of Elizabethan architecture commanding exceptionally fine views of the South Downs. Amongst the collections of 400 years of family living can be seen 17th and 18th Century portraits of the Trevors, furniture, embroidery and silver.

**Location:** Map 4:J5. OS Ref TQ456 092. Signposted off the A27, 4m SE of Lewes at top of village. Rail: Glynde is on the London/Eastbourne and Brighton/Eastbourne mainline railway. London 1½ hours by car, Gatwick 35 mins by car.
**Contact:** The Estate Office **Tel:** 01273 858224
**E-mail:** info@glynde.co.uk **Open:** May–Jun: Wed, Thur & Sun & BHs from 1-5pm. Aug: BH and preceding Sun from 1-5pm. Visits to the House are by guided tours only starting at 2pm, 3pm and 4pm. Group bookings by prior arrangement only. **Admission:** House & Garden: Adult £5.00, Children over 12yrs & Students £3.00, Children under 12 yrs free.
**Key facts:** 🌣 House, gardens & parkland available for corporate events. 🌣 All visits to the House by guided tours only. 🅿 Limited parking for coaches 🐕 Guide dogs only. 🔔 A range of wedding options are available. Please contact the Estate Office for more information. 🌣

## HIGH BEECHES WOODLAND & WATER GARDEN 🏠Ⓕ
### High Beeches Lane, Handcross, West Sussex RH17 6HQ
www.highbeeches.com

Explore 27 acres of magically beautiful, peaceful woodland and water gardens. Daffodils, bluebells, azaleas, naturalised gentians and glorious autumn colours. Rippling streams, enchanting vistas. Four acres of natural wildflower meadows. Marked trails. Recommended by Christopher Lloyd. Enjoy lunches and teas in the tearoom and tea lawn in restored Victorian farm building.
**Location:** Map 4:I4. OS Ref TQ275 308. S side of B2110. 1m NE of Handcross
**Owner:** High Beeches Gardens Conservation Trust (Reg. Charity 299134)
**Contact:** Sarah Bray
**Tel:** 01444 400589 **E-mail:** gardens@highbeeches.com
**Open:** 15 Mar-2 Nov: daily except Weds, 1-5pm (last adm. 4.30pm). Coaches/guided tours anytime, by appointment only.
**Admission:** Adult £7.00, Child (under 14yrs) Free. Concession for groups (20+).Guided tours for groups £10pp.
**Key facts:** 🦽 Partial. WCs. Tearoom fully accessible. 🌣 Licensed. 🍽 Licensed. 🌣 By arrangement. 🅿 🐕 Guide dogs only. 🌣

## HAMMERWOOD PARK
### East Grinstead, Sussex RH19 3QE
www.hammerwoodpark.com

The best kept secret in Sussex, "untouched by a corporate plan". Built by White House architect Latrobe in Greek Revival style in 1792, left derelict by Led Zeppelin, painstakingly restored by the Pinnegar family over the last 30 years and brought to life with guided tours, concerts and filming.
**Location:** Map 4:J4. OS Ref TQ442 390. 3.5 m E of East Grinstead on A264 to Tunbridge Wells, 1m W of Holtye.
**Owner/Contact:** David Pinnegar
**Tel:** 01342 850594 **Fax:** 01342 850864
**E-mail:** antespam@gmail.com
**Open:** 1 Jun-end Sep: Wed, Sat & BH Mon, 2-5pm. Guided tour starts 2.05pm. Private groups: Easter-Jun. Coaches strictly by appointment. Small groups any time throughout the year by appointment.
**Admission:** House & Park: Adult £8.00, Child £2.00. Private viewing by arrangement. **Key facts:** ⓘ Conferences. 🌣🌣🌣 Obligatory. 🌣 In grounds. 🌣 B&B. 🌣🌣 €

## PALLANT HOUSE GALLERY
### 9 North Pallant, Chichester, West Sussex PO19 1TJ
www.pallant.org.uk

A Grade I-listed Queen Anne townhouse and landmark contemporary building holding one of the best collections of 20th Century British art in the country. An extensive exhibition programme includes international exhibitions and print shows. There is also a critically acclaimed on-site restaurant with courtyard garden and first-class art bookshop.
**Location:** Map 3:F6. OS Ref SU861 047. City centre, SE of the Cross
**Owner:** Pallant House Gallery Trust **Contact:** Reception
**Tel:** 01243 774557 **E-mail:** info@pallant.org.uk
**Open:** Tue-Sat: 10am-5pm (Thur: 10am-8pm. Sun & BH Mons: 11am-5pm)
**Admission:** Adult £9.00, Child 6-16yrs £3.50, Student £5.50*; Family £21.50* (two adults and up to four children), Groups £7.00 per person (advance booking required); Unemployed/Friends/Under 5s Free.
*Prices include voluntary donation (£1.00 per adult, £0.50 concessions).
**Key facts:** ⓘ No photography. 🌣🌣🌣 WCs. 🌣 🍽 Licensed. 🌣 Guide dogs only. 🌣🌣

© Peter Durant/arcblue.com

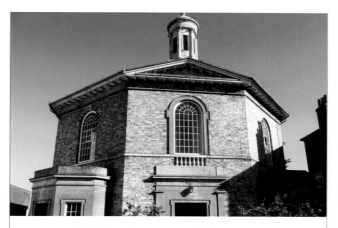

## CHURCH OF ST JOHN THE EVANGELIST 🔊
### St John's Street, Chichester, West Sussex PO19 1UR
www.visitchurches.org.uk

Built in 1812, the delightfully elegant design of St John's reflects the importance the evangelical movement. Unusually, it was not built as a parish church, but was privately funded and then run by trustees of the evangelical movement of the Church of England. Ministers were largely paid by the income from renting seats in the church. Pews in the upper gallery, where the rich sat apart from the lower orders, still have their own hire numbers. These originally had separate entrances so that the rich could enter by different doorways from the poor who sat on the benches below. The church is arranged rather like a theatre, with an impressive triple-decker pulpit with a handsome staircase and elegant handrail taking centre stage with only a small and insignificant chancel behind.

**Location:** OS Ref SU864 046. In St John's Street which is in the south-eastern quadrant of Chichester and leads off East Street.
**Open:** Open daily from 10am-4pm.

## ST PETER'S CHURCH 🔊
### Preston Drove, Preston Park, Brighton East Sussex BN1 6SD
www.visitchurches.org.uk

This simple square-towered church, built from flint rubble, is 800-years old. It stands in the beautiful landscaped park of Preston Manor. Now all looks serene but in 1906 the church was damaged by fire and nearly lost its greatest treasures - its 14th Century wallpaintings. Although fragments, you can pick out the nativity with a bowl-shaped crib and the infant Jesus. The violent scene of Thomas Becket's murder in Canterbury is clearer - you can see one of the four knights, possibly William de Tracy, plunge his sword into Becket's head and you can see blood dripping from the hand of Edward Grim, Becket's chaplain, who was injured while trying to protect him. Sumptuous 20th Century restoration brought the church new life after the fire, and today the walls, windows and floors around the altar glow with a gorgeous mix of pattern and colour.

**Location:** OS Ref TQ304 064. Immediately adjacent to Preston Manor which is at the northern tip of Preston Park on the A23 in Brighton.
**Open:** Open daily, 11am-3pm and sometimes longer in the summer.

High Beeches Woodland and Water Garden

## SACKVILLE COLLEGE
### High Street, East Grinstead, West Sussex RH19 3BX
www.sackvillecollege.co.uk

Built in 1609 for Robert Sackville, Earl of Dorset, as an almshouse and overnight accommodation for the Sackville family. Feel the Jacobean period come alive in the enchanting quadrangle, the chapel, banqueting hall with its fine hammerbeam roof and minstrel's gallery, the old common room and warden's study where "Good King Wenceslas" was composed. Chapel weddings by arrangement.

**Location:** Map 4:I4. OS Ref TQ397 380. A22 to East Grinstead, College in High Street (town centre).
**Owner:** Board of Trustees
**Contact:** College Co-ordinator
**Tel:** 01342 323414 **E-mail:** sackvillecollege@talktalkbusiness.net
**Open:** Mid Jun-Mid Sep. Groups all year by arrangement.
**Admission:** Adult £4.00, Child £1.00. Groups: (10-60) no discount.
**Key facts:** ℹ️ Large public car park adjacent to entrance. 🔲 🚻 🔲 Partial. 📷 ℹ️ Obligatory. 🅿️ 🔲 🔲 Guide dogs only. 🔲

## STANSTED PARK
### Stansted Park, Rowlands Castle, Hampshire PO9 6DX
www.stanstedpark.co.uk

Stansted Park, on the South Downs, is a beautiful Edwardian house with ancient private chapel, with spectacular views south over the Solent. The state rooms are furnished as if the 10th Earl of Bessborough was still at home, and the amazing servants' quarters are jam-packed with old-fashioned things to see.
**Location:** Map 3:F5. OS Ref SU761 103. Follow brown heritage signs from A3 (M) J2 Emsworth or A27 Havant
**Owner:** Stansted Park Foundation **Contact:** House and Events Manager
**Tel:** 023 9241 2265 **Fax:** 023 9241 3773
**E-mail:** enquiry@stanstedpark.co.uk
**Open:** House: Apr-May: Sun & BHol 1-5pm. Jun-Sep: Sun-Wed 1-5pm (last adm. 4pm). Tea Room & Garden Centre: open every day. Maze: weekends and school holidays 11-4pm (Feb-Oct). Light Railway: weekends and Wednesdays.
**Admission:** House & Chapel: Adult £7.00, Child (5-15yrs) £3.50, Conc. £6.00, Family (2+3) £18.00. Groups/educational visits by arrangement.
**Key facts:** Private & corporate hire. Suitable. WCs. Licensed. By arrangement. By arrangement. Guide dogs only. Grounds.

## WEALD AND DOWNLAND OPEN AIR MUSEUM
### Singleton, Chichester, West Sussex PO18 0EU
www.wealddown.co.uk

The Museum homes over 45 rescued historic buildings, reconstructed in beautiful parkland in the South Downs. Six historic houses include carefully researched period gardens, showcasing the plants, herbs and flowers grown by our ancestors. Enjoy the tranquillity of the Sussex downland, working Shire horses, cattle and traditional breed farm animals.
**Location:** Map 3:F5. OS Ref SZ128 875. Off A286 Chichester to Midhurst road at Singleton village
**Owner:** Weald and Downland Open Air Museum Ltd
**Contact:** Richard Pailthorpe **Tel:** 01243 811019
**Open:** Jan & Feb: Wed, Sat & Sun only with exception of ½ term week 17-21 Feb open daily. Rest of year: 10.30am-6pm BST, 10.30am-4pm rest of year.
**Admission:** Adult £11.50, Child £6.30, Over 65 £10.50, Family £32.50 (2 adults plus three children). All prices include Gift Aid option.
**Key facts:** Partial. WCs. By arrangement. On leads.

## CHURCH OF THE HOLY SEPULCHRE
### Church Park Lane, Warminghurst Ashington, West Sussex RH20 3AW
www.visitchurches.org.uk

The setting of this 13th Century sandstone church is lovely but the building itself surpasses all expectations. The unspoilt 18th Century interior contains silvery oak pews, a clerk's desk, a triple-decker pulpit, an uneven flagstone floor and a curved brace roof. There is also an elegant three arched wooden screen. Above the screen is a wonderful painting of the coat of arms of Queen Anne, with theatrical swags of painted drapery. Look for the clerk's chair. On the walls are lovely memorials to the Shelley and Butler families. James Butler bought Warminghurst Park from the Quaker, William Penn - a trustee of the American province of West Jersey (later renamed Pennsylvania). It is said that Penn wrote the first draft of Pennsylvania's constitution at Warminghurst Park. After buying Warminghurst however, James Butler demolished it, determined to remove all trace of the old Quaker.
**Location:** OS Ref TQ117 169. Off northern end of main street, just off A24.
**Open:** Usually open daily from 10am-4pm; at other times keyholder nearby.

## WILMINGTON PRIORY
### Wilmington, Nr Eastbourne, East Sussex BN26 5SW
www.landmarktrust.org.uk

The Priory is part of an outstanding now mostly ruinous monastic site in the South Downs, combined with the comfort of rooms improved by the Georgians. This area was beloved by the Bloomsbury set whose influential houses are nearby; it close to Glyndebourne and a few miles from the sea.
**Location:** Map 3:F5. OS Ref TQ544 042.
**Owner:** Leased to the Landmark Trust by Sussex Archaeological Society
**Tel:** 01628 825925
**E-mail:** bookings@landmarktrust.org.uk
**Open:** 30 days Apr-Oct, contact for details.
**Admission:** Free on Open Days, visits by appointment.
**Key facts:** A vaulted medieval entrance porch leading off the large farmhouse kitchen makes an atmospheric summer dining room and the monastic ruins are yours to wander.

© Chris Lacey

# WOOLBEDING GARDENS
## Midhurst, West Sussex GU29 9RR
### www.nationaltrust.org.uk/woolbeding

Woolbeding is a modern garden masterpiece, with constantly evolving colour-themed garden rooms surrounding the house and magical landscape garden. View the glorious River Rother and the iconic fountain, relax by the Chinese-style bridge and cascading waterfall. Booking essential; no onsite parking (apart from disabled) - free minibus service.

**Location:** Map 3:F5. OS Ref SU872 227. No access by car or parking in the local area, apart from disabled (booking essential).
**Owner:** National Trust
**Tel:** 0844 249 1895 **E-mail:** woolbedinggardens@nationaltrust.org.uk
**Open:** 24 Apr-26 Sep, 10.30am-4.30pm, Thur & Fri only. All visits must be pre-booked
**Admission:** Adult £7.50, Child (5-17yrs) £3.80, Family (2+3) £18.70. Pre-booked reduced group rate available.
**Key facts:** ⓘ Gardens only, please book all visits on 0844 249 1895. 🚻 Partial. WCs. 🖼 🐕 Assistance dogs only. 🌀

---

# ARUNDEL CATHEDRAL
## London Road, Arundel, West Sussex BN18 9AY
French Gothic Cathedral, church of the RC Diocese of Arundel and Brighton built by Henry, 15th Duke of Norfolk and opened 1873.
**Location:** Map 3:G6. OS Ref TQ015 072. Above junction of A27 and A284.
**Contact:** Rev. Canon T. Madeley
**Tel:** 01903 882297
**Fax:** 01903 885335
**E-mail:** aruncath1@aol.com
**Open:** Summer: 9am-6pm. Winter: 9am-dusk. Tues, Wed, Fri, Sat: Mass 10am; Mon and Thurs: Mass 8.30am (at Convent of Poor Clares, Crossbush); Sat: Vigil Mass 6.15pm (at Convent of Poor Clares, Crossbush); Sun: Masses 9.30am and 11.15am. Shop open in the summer, Mon-Fri, 10am-4pm and after services and on special occasions and otherwise on request.
**Admission:** Free.
**Key facts:** 🖼 ⓘ by arrangement 🌀

Stansted Park

---

# BORDE HILL GARDEN ⓡ 🏛ⓔ
## Borde Hill Lane, Haywards Heath, West Sussex RH16 1XP

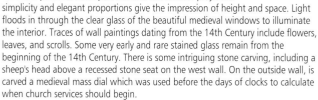

Borde Hill Garden is nestled in 200 acres of English Heritage listed woodland and parkland. The Garden was created in 1892 by the current owner's great grandfather and plant expedition sponsor, Colonel Stephenson R Clarke. The impressive Garden boasts a botanically rich and nationally important collection of trees and shrubs. The formal Garden is planted as distinctive garden 'rooms' overlooked by the Mansion House, dating back from 1598. There are woodland and lakeside walks, views of the Ouse Valley and Victorian viaduct. There is also: a café and award-winning restaurant, gallery, gift shop and plant sales. Ideal place for filming and photo shoots.
**Location:** Map 4:15. **Contact:** Aurelia Mandato
**Tel:** 01444 450326 **E-mail:** info@bordehill.co.uk **Website:** www.bordehill.co.uk
**Open:** 22 Mar-2 Nov 2014, every day from 10am-6pm (or dusk if earlier).
**Admission:** Adults £8.00, Conc. £7.50, Group £6.00, Child £5.00. Season Tickets.
**Key facts:** 🖼 🚻 T 🖼 WCs. Maps. 🖼 🍴 P 🖼 🖼 On leads. 🌀

---

# COWDRAY HERITAGE TRUST 🏛ⓔ
## River Ground Stables, Midhurst, West Sussex GU29 9AL

Cowdray is one of the most important survivals of a Tudor nobleman's house. Set within the stunning landscape of Cowdray Park, the house was partially destroyed by fire in 1793. Explore the Tudor Kitchen, Buck Hall, Chapel, Gatehouse, Vaulted Storeroom and Cellars, Visitor Centre and Shop.
**Location:** Map 3:F5. OS Ref TQ891 216. On the outskirts of Midhurst on A272.
**Owner:** Cowdray Heritage Trust **Contact:** The Manager
**Tel:** 01730 812423 **E-mail:** info@cowdray.org.uk
**Website:** www.cowdray.org.uk
**Open:** Please check our website for opening times. Groups all year round by arrangement. **Admission:** Check website for details.
**Key facts:** 🖼 🖼 Full level access, WCs, wheelchair available, limited disabled parking. 🖼 Free audio guides. Children's tour available. P In Midhurst by bus stand, a short walk along causeway. 🖼 Well behaved dogs on leads welcome.

---

# ST BOTOLPH'S CHURCH 🏛
## Annington Road, Botolphs, West Sussex BN44 3WB

St Botolph`s Church is of charming flint construction and stands on a slight rise above the River Adur. Today with just a house or two for company it is hard to imagine that 700 years ago it was at the heart of a bustling port and crossing place of the river.
The south door carries the date 1630 in delightful graffiti and leads into a homely and welcoming interior. The tall chancel arch dates from late Saxon times and is surrounded by the ghosts of medieval wall paintings whilst the three huge blocked arches in the north wall show where a north aisle has been demolished to match its reduced circumstances. The church has given its name to the place – St Botolph is patron saint of wayfarers - and today it receives many visitors walking the South Downs Way which crosses the river nearby.
**Location:** OS Ref TQ 19354 09253.
**Contact:** Please call The Churches Conservation Trust on 0845 303 2760 (Mon-Fri, 9am–5pm) **Open:** See www.visitchurches.org.uk for details.

---

# CHURCH OF ST MARY THE VIRGIN 🏛
## North Stoke, Arundel, West Sussex BN18 9LS
In an idyllic rural setting on the South Downs, in a loop of the river Arun, St Mary's is a beautiful place to stumble upon. The church remains virtually unaltered since medieval times; its calm and peaceful atmosphere evokes centuries of prayer. Its simplicity and elegant proportions give the impression of height and space. Light floods in through the clear glass of the beautiful medieval windows to illuminate the interior. Traces of wall paintings dating from the 14th Century include flowers, leaves, and scrolls. Some very early and rare stained glass remain from the beginning of the 14th Century. There is some intriguing stone carving, including a sheep's head above a recessed stone seat on the west wall. On the outside wall, is carved a medieval mass dial which was used before the days of clocks to calculate when church services should begin.
**Location:** OS Ref TQ019 108. 5 miles by road north of Arundel off B2139; signposted from Houghton Bridge. **Website:** www.visitchurches.org.uk
**Open:** Open daily; 10am-4pm.

### VISITOR INFORMATION

■ **Owner**
English Heritage

■ **Address**
Osborne House
East Cowes
Isle of Wight
PO32 6JX

■ **Location**
**Map 3:D6**
**OS Ref. SZ516 948**
1 mile SE of East Cowes.
**Ferry:** Isle of Wight ferry
terminals. Red Funnel, East
Cowes 1½ miles Tel: 02380
334010. Wightlink,
Fishbourne 4 miles Tel:
0870 582 7744

■ **Contact**
The House Administrator
**Tel:** 01983 200022
**Venue Hire and
Hospitality Tel:** 01983
203055
**E-mail:**
customers@english-
heritage.org.uk

■ **Opening Times**
Please visit www.english-
heritage.org.uk for
opening times and prices
and the most up-to-date
information.

■ **Special Events**
There is an exciting events
programme available
throughout the year, for
further details please
contact the property or visit
the website.

**Conference/Function**

| ROOM | Max Cap |
|---|---|
| Duchess of Kent Suite | Standing 70 Seated 30 |
| Durbar Hall | Standing/Seated 40 |
| Marquee | Large scale events possible |
| Upper Terrace | Standing 250 |
| Victoria Hall | Standing 120 Seated 80 |

# OSBORNE HOUSE ▦
www.english-heritage.org.uk/osborne

## Take an intimate glimpse into the family life of Britain's longest reigning monarch and the house Queen Victoria loved to call home.

Osborne House was a peaceful, seaside retreat of Queen Victoria, Prince Albert and their family. Step inside and marvel at the richness of the State Apartments including the lavish Indian Durbar Room.

The Queen died at the house in 1901 and many of the rooms have been preserved almost unaltered ever since. The nursery bedroom remains just as it was in the 1870s when Queen Victoria's first grandchildren came to stay.

Don't miss the Swiss Cottage, a charming chalet in the grounds built for teaching the royal children domestic skills. Enjoy the beautiful gardens with their stunning views over the Solent, the fruit and flower Victorian Walled Garden and Queen Victoria's private beach – now open to visitors for the first time.

Osborne hosts events throughout the year, and Queen Victoria's palace-by-the-sea offers both the superb coastal location and facilities for those who want to entertain on a grand scale in style.

## KEY FACTS

[i] Available for corporate and private hire. Suitable for filming, concerts, drama. No photography in the house.

⬚

🖥

🍸 Private and corporate hire.

♿ WCs.

♿

🍴

🏃 Nov-Mar for pre-booked guided tours only. Tours allow visitors to see the Royal Apartments and private rooms.

P Ample.

▦ Visits free, please book. Education room.

❄

♥

**ST MARGARET'S CHURCH** 🏛
Catmore, Newbury, Berkshire  RG20 7HN
**Tel:** 0845 303 2760 **E-mail:** central@thecct.org.uk

**ST MARY'S CHURCH** 🏛
Ermin Street, Woodlands St Mary, Berkshire  RG17 7SR
**Tel:** 0845 303 2760 **E-mail:** central@thecct.org.uk

**THE SAVILL GARDEN**
Windsor Great Park, Wick Lane, Windsor, Surrey  TW20 0UU
**Tel:** 01753 847518 **E-mail:** emma.twyman@thecrownestate.co.uk

**SHAW HOUSE**
Church Road, Shaw, Newbury, Berkshire  RG14 2DR
**Tel:** 01635 279279 **E-mail:** shawhouse@westberks.gov.uk

**CHURCH OF THE ASSUMPTION** 🏛
Hartwell House, Hartwell, Aylesbury  HP17 8NR
**Tel:** 0845 303 2760 **E-mail:** central@thecct.org.uk

**ST LAWRENCE'S CHURCH** 🏛
Broughton Village, Milton Keynes, Bucks  MK10 9AA
**Tel:** 0845 303 2760 **E-mail:** central@thecct.org.uk

**ST MARY'S CHURCH** 🏛
Church End, Edlesborough, Dunstable, Bucks  LU6 2EP
**Tel:** 0845 303 2760 **E-mail:** central@thecct.org.uk

**ST MARY'S CHURCH** 🏛
Fleet Marston, Aylesbury, Buckinghamshire  HP18 0PZ
**Tel:** 0845 303 2760 **E-mail:** central@thecct.org.uk

**ST MARY'S CHURCH** 🏛
Church Road, Pitstone, Leighton Buzzard  LU7 9HA
**Tel:** 0845 303 2760 **E-mail:** central@thecct.org.uk

**STOWE HOUSE** 🏛
Stowe House, Stowe, Buckingham  MK18 5EH
**Tel:** 01280 818002 **E-mail:** Houseinfo@stowe.co.uk

**WADDESDON MANOR** 🏛
Waddesdon, Nr Aylesbury, Buckinghamshire  HP18 0JH
**Tel:** 01296 653211 **E-mail:** waddesdonmanor@nationaltrust.org.uk

**WEST WYCOMBE PARK** 🏛
West Wycombe, High Wycombe, Buckinghamshire  HP14 3AJ
**Tel:** 01494 513569

**ALL SAINTS' CHURCH** 🏛
Little Somborne, Stockbridge, Hampshire  SO20 6QT
**Tel:** 0845 303 2760 **E-mail:** central@thecct.org.uk

**CHAWTON HOUSE LIBRARY** 🏛
Chawton, Alton, Hampshire  GU34 1SJ
**Tel:** 01420 541010 **E-mail:** info@chawton.net

**CHURCH OF ST JOHN THE BAPTIST** 🏛
Upper Eldon, Stockbridge, Hampshire  SO20 6QN
**Tel:** 0845 303 2760 **E-mail:** central@thecct.org.uk

**CHURCH OF ST PETER AD VINCULA** 🏛
Colemore, Alton, Hampshire  GU34 3RX
**Tel:** 0845 303 2760 **E-mail:** central@thecct.org.uk

**MOTTISFONT** 🏛
Mottisfont, Nr Romsey, Hampshire  SO51 0LP
**Tel:** 01794 340757

**PORTCHESTER CASTLE** 🏛
Portsmouth, Hampshire  PO16 9QW
**Tel:** 02392 378291 **E-mail:** customers@english-heritage.org.uk

**ST MARY THE VIRGIN OLD CHURCH** 🏛
Preston Candover, Basingstoke, Hampshire  RG25 2EN
**Tel:** 0845 303 2760 **E-mail:** central@thecct.org.uk

**ST MARY'S CHURCH** 🏛
Church Lane, Hartley Wintney, Hook, Hampshire  RG27 8EE
**Tel:** 0845 303 2760 **E-mail:** central@thecct.org.uk

**ST MARY'S CHURCH** 🏛
Ashley, Kings Somborne, Stockbridge, Hampshire  SO20 6RJ
**Tel:** 0845 303 2760 **E-mail:** central@thecct.org.uk

**ST NICHOLAS' CHURCH** 🏛
Freefolk, Laverstoke, Whitchurch, Hampshire  RG28 7NW
**Tel:** 0845 303 2760 **E-mail:** central@thecct.org.uk

**SANDHAM MEMORIAL CHAPEL** 🏛
Burghclere, Nr Newbury, Hampshire  RG20 9JT
**Tel:** 01635 278394 **E-mail:** sandham@nationaltrust.org.uk

**SIR HAROLD HILLIER GARDENS**
Jermyns Lane, Ampfield, Romsey, Hampshire  SO51 0QA
**Tel:** 01794 369318 **E-mail:** info@hilliergardens.org.uk

**THE GREAT HALL**
Castle Avenue, Winchester, Hampshire  SO23 8PJ
**Tel:** 01962 846476 **E-mail:** the.great.hall@hants.gov.uk

**WINCHESTER CATHEDRAL**
9 The Close, Winchester  SO23 9LS
**Tel:** 01962 857200 **E-mail:** visits@winchester-cathedral.org.uk

**BOUGHTON MONCHELSEA PLACE**
Boughton Monchelsea, Nr Maidstone, Kent  ME17 4BU
**Tel:** 01622 743120 **E-mail:** mk@boughtonplace.co.uk

**THE HOME OF CHARLES DARWIN** 🏛
Down House, Luxted Road, Downe, Kent  BR6 7JT
**Tel:** 01689 859119 **E-mail:** customers@english-heritage.org.uk

**CHILHAM CASTLE**
Canterbury, Kent  CT4 8DB
**Tel:** 01227 733100 **E-mail:** chilhamcastleinfo@gmail.com

**CHURCH OF ST MARY THE VIRGIN** 🏛
The Drove, Fordwich, Canterbury, Kent  CT2 0DE
**Tel:** 0845 303 2760 **E-mail:** central@thecct.org.uk

**DANSON HOUSE**
Hall Place and Gardens, Bourne Road, Bexley, Kent  DA5 1PQ
**Tel:** 020 8303 6699 **E-mail:** info@dansonhouse.org.uk

**DEAL CASTLE** 🏛
Victoria Road, Deal, Kent  CT14 7BA
**Tel:** 01304 372762 **E-mail:** customers@english-heritage.org.uk

**DODDINGTON PLACE GARDENS** 🏛
Doddington, Nr Sittingbourne, Kent ME9 0BB
**Tel:** 01795 886101

**GAD'S HILL PLACE**
Rochester Road, Higham, Gravesend, Kent ME3 7DS
**Tel:** 01474 337600 **E-mail:** info@towncentric.co.uk

**GODINTON HOUSE AND GARDENS**
Godinton Lane, Ashford, Kent TN23 3BP
**Tel:** 01233 620773 **E-mail:** info@godinton-house-gardens.co.uk

**GREAT COMP GARDEN**
Comp Lane, Platt, Borough Green, Kent TN15 8QS
**Tel:** 01732 886154 **E-mail:** info@greatcompgarden.co.uk

**GROOMBRIDGE PLACE GARDENS**
Groombridge, Tunbridge Wells, Kent TN3 9QG
**Tel:** 01892 861 444 **E-mail:** carrie@groombridge.co.uk

**HALL PLACE & GARDENS** 🏛
Bourne Road, Bexley, Kent DA5 1PQ
**Tel:** 01322 526574 **E-mail:** info@hallplace.org.uk

**HOLE PARK GARDENS** 🏛®
Rolvenden, Cranbrook TN17 4JA
**Tel:** 01580 241344 **E-mail:** info@holepark.com

**LULLINGSTONE ROMAN VILLA** ⌗
Lullingstone Lane, Eynsford, Kent DA4 0JA
**Tel:** 01322 863467 **E-mail:** customers@english-heritage.org.uk

**LYMPNE CASTLE**
Lympne Castle, Hythe, Kent CT18 7AG
**Tel:** 01303 235610 **E-mail:** info@lympnecastle.co.uk

**ST AUGUSTINE'S ABBEY** ⌗
Longport, Canterbury, Kent CT1 1TF
**Tel:** 01227 767345 **E-mail:** customers@english-heritage.org.uk

**ST BENEDICT'S CHURCH** 🏛
Paddlesworth Road, Paddlesworth, Snodland, Kent ME6 5DR
**Tel:** 0845 303 2760 **E-mail:** central@thecct.org.uk

**ST CATHERINE'S CHURCH** 🏛
Kingsdown, Sittingbourne, Kent ME9 0AS
**Tel:** 0845 303 2760 **E-mail:** central@thecct.org.uk

**ST CLEMENT'S CHURCH** 🏛
Knowlton Court, Knowlton, Canterbury, Kent CT3 1PT
**Tel:** 0845 303 2760 **E-mail:** central@thecct.org.uk

**ST MARY'S CHURCH** 🏛
Luddenham Court, Luddenham, Faversham, Kent ME13 0TH
**Tel:** 0845 303 2760 **E-mail:** central@thecct.org.uk

**ST MARY'S CHURCH** 🏛
Church Street, Lower Higham, Rochester, Kent ME3 7LS
**Tel:** 0845 303 2760 **E-mail:** central@thecct.org.uk

**ST MARY'S CHURCH** 🏛
Old Church Road, Burham, Rochester, Kent ME1 3XY
**Tel:** 0845 303 2760 **E-mail:** central@thecct.org.uk

**ST MARY'S CHURCH** 🏛
Strand Street, Sandwich, Kent CT13 9EU
**Tel:** 0845 303 2760 **E-mail:** central@thecct.org.uk

**ST PETER'S CHURCH** 🏛
The Street, Swingfield Street, Swingfield, Kent CT15 7HA
**Tel:** 0845 303 2760 **E-mail:** central@thecct.org.uk

**WALMER CASTLE AND GARDENS** ⌗
Deal, Kent CT14 7LJ
**Tel:** 01304 364288 **E-mail:** customers@english-heritage.org.uk

**ALL SAINTS' CHURCH** 🏛
Castle Road, Shirburn, Oxford, Oxfordshire OX49 5DL
**Tel:** 0845 303 2760 **E-mail:** central@thecct.org.uk

**ALL SAINTS' CHURCH** 🏛
Nuneham Park, Nuneham Courtenay, Oxfordshire OX44 9PQ
**Tel:** 0845 303 2760 **E-mail:** central@thecct.org.uk

**CHASTLETON HOUSE** 🏛
Chastleton, Nr Moreton-In-Marsh, Oxfordshire
**Tel:** 01608 674981 **E-mail:** chastleton@nationaltrust.org.uk

**ST KATHERINE'S CHURCH** 🏛
Chislehampton, Oxford, Oxfordshire OX44 7XF
**Tel:** 0845 303 2760 **E-mail:** central@thecct.org.uk

**ST MARY'S CHURCH** 🏛
Newnham Murren, Wallingford, Oxfordshire OX10 8BW
**Tel:** 0845 303 2760 **E-mail:** central@thecct.org.uk

**SULGRAVE MANOR**
Manor Road, Sulgrave, Nr Banbury, Oxfordshire OX17 2SD
**Tel:** 01295 760205 **E-mail:** wendy.barnes@sulgravemanor.org.uk

**WALLINGFORD CASTLE GARDENS**
Castle Street, Wallingford, Oxfordshire OX10 0AL
**Tel:** 01491 835373

**LOSELEY PARK** 🏛®
Events Office, Loseley Park, Guildford, Surrey GU3 1HS
**Tel:** 01483 304440 **E-mail:** enquiries @loseleypark.co.uk

**RHS GARDEN WISLEY**
Nr Woking, Surrey GU23 6QB
**Tel:** 0845 260 9000

**ST GEORGE'S CHURCH** 🏛
Esher Park Avenue, Esher, Surrey KT10 9PX
**Tel:** 0845 303 2760 **E-mail:** central@thecct.org.uk

**1066 BATTLE OF HASTINGS** ⌗
Battle, Sussex TN33 0AD
**Tel:** 01424 775705 **E-mail:** customers@english-heritage.org.uk

**BIGNOR ROMAN VILLA**
Bignor Lane, Bignor, Pulborough, West Sussex RH20 1PH
**Tel:** 01798 869259 **E-mail:** enquiries@bignorromanvilla.co.uk

**CHURCH OF ST MARY MAGDALENE** 🏛
Ford Road, Tortington, Arundel, West Sussex BN18 0FD
**Tel:** 0845 303 2760 **E-mail:** central@thecct.org.uk

## FARLEY FARM HOUSE
Muddles Green, Chiddingly, Lewes, East Sussex  BN8 6HW
**Tel:** 01825 872691 **E-mail:** tours@leemiller.co.uk

## FISHBOURNE ROMAN PALACE
Salthill Road, Fishbourne, Chichester, Sussex  PO19 3QR
**Tel:** 01243 785859 **E-mail:** adminfish@sussexpast.co.uk

## GROUNDS OF HERSTMONCEUX CASTLE
Hailsham, East Sussex  BN27 1RN
**Tel:** 01323 833816 **E-mail:** c_harber@bisc.queensu.ac.uk

## HASTINGS CASTLE
Castle Hill Road, West Hill, Hastings, East Sussex  TN34 3AR
**Tel:** 01424 444412 **E-mail:** bookings@discoverhastings.co.uk

## LEONARDSLEE LAKES & GARDENS
Lower Beeding, Horsham, West Sussex  RH13 6PP
**Tel:** 01403 891212 **E-mail:** info@leonardsleegardens.com

## LEWES PRIORY
Town Hall, High Street, Lewes, East Sussex  BN7 2QS
**Tel:** 01273 486185 **E-mail:** enquiries@lewespriory.org.uk

## PASHLEY MANOR GARDENS
Pashley Manor, Ticehurst, Wadhurst, East Sussex  TN5 7HE
**Tel:** 01580 200888 **E-mail:** info@pashleymanorgardens.com

## PEVENSEY CASTLE
Pevensey, Sussex  BN24 5LE
**Tel:** 01323 762604 **E-mail:** customers@english-heritage.org.uk

## ST ANDREW'S CHURCH
Waterloo Street, Hove, East Sussex  BN3 1AQ
**Tel:** 0845 303 2760 **E-mail:** central@thecct.org.uk

## ST WILFRID'S CHURCH
Rectory Lane, Church Norton, Selsey, West Sussex  PO20 9DT
**Tel:** 0845 303 2760 **E-mail:** central@thecct.org.uk

## SAINT HILL MANOR
Saint Hill Road, East Grinstead, West Sussex  RH19 4JY
**Tel:** 01342 317057 **E-mail:** info@sainthillmanor.org.uk

## THE ROYAL PAVILION
East Sussex  BN1 1EE
**Tel:** 01273 290900 **E-mail:** visitor.services@brighton-hove.gov.uk

## WAKEHURST PLACE
Selsfield Road, Ardingly, West Sussex  RH17 6TN
**Tel:** 01444 894054 **E-mail:** wakehurst@kew.org

## WEST DEAN COLLEGE & GARDENS
West Dean, Chichester, West Sussex  PO18 0RX
**Tel:** Gardens: 01243 818210 **E-mail:** enquiries@westdean.org.uk

## NUNWELL HOUSE & GARDENS
Coach Lane, Brading, Isle Of Wight  PO36 0JQ
**Tel:** 01983 407240 **E-mail:** info@nunwellhouse.co.uk

## CARISBROOKE CASTLE
Newport, Isle Of Wight  PO30 1XY
**Tel:** 01983 522107 **E-mail:** customers@english-heritage.org.uk

Carisbrooke Castle

Powderham Castle

Marwood Hill Gardens

Cornwall
Devon
Dorset
Gloucestershire
Somerset
Wiltshire

# South West

The South West is our most popular holiday district where the distinctive culture of Cornwall contrasts with the mansions built with wealth generated from the port of Bristol and the spa town of Bath.

*New Entries for 2014:*
• Trerice

**Find stylish hotels with a personal welcome and good cuisine in the South West. More information on page 372.**

- The Abbey
- The Berry Head Hotel
- Budock Vean
- Corse Lawn House Hotel
- The Cottage Hotel
- Dart Marina
- Farthings Country House Hotel
- Hannafore Point Hotel
- The Ilslington Country House Hotel
- Knoll House Hotel
- Penventon Park Hotel
- Plantation House Hotel
- Plumber Manor
- Tides Reach Hotel
- The White Hart Royal Hotel

## SIGNPOST
### SELECTED PREMIER HOTELS 2014

www.signpost.co.uk

**South West - England**

## VISITOR INFORMATION

■ **Owner**
English Heritage

■ **Address**
Tintagel
Cornwall
PL34 0HE

■ **Location**
Map 1:F7
OS Ref. Landranger
Sheet 200 SX048 891
On Tintagel Head, ½m
along uneven track from
Tintagel.

■ **Contact**
Visitor Operations Team
**Tel:** 01840 770328
**E-mail:** tintagel.castle@
english-heritage.org.uk

■ **Opening Times**
Please visit the website for
opening times, admission
prices and the most up-to-
date information.

■ **Special Events**
There is an exciting events
programme available
throughout the year, for
further details please
contact the property or visit
the website.

# TINTAGEL CASTLE ⌗
www.english-heritage.org.uk/tintagel

## Tintagel Castle is a magical day with its wonderful location, set high on the rugged North Cornwall coast.

Steeped in legend and mystery; said to be the birthplace of King Arthur, you can still visit the nearby Merlin's Cave. The castle also features in the tale of Tristan and Isolde.

Joined to the mainland by a narrow neck of land, Tintagel Island faces the full force of the Atlantic. On the mainland, the remains of the medieval castle represent only one phase in a long history of occupation.

The remains of the 13th Century castle are breathtaking. Steep stone steps, stout walls and rugged windswept cliff edges encircle the Great Hall, where Richard Earl of Cornwall once feasted.

## KEY FACTS

 WC. Video film shown about the Legend of Arthur.

 No vehicles. Parking (not EH) in village only.

 Dogs on leads only.

© Beth Nash

The Front of Trerice

## VISITOR INFORMATION

■ **Owner**
National Trust

■ **Address**
Kestle Mill
Nr Newquay
Cornwall
TR8 4PG

■ **Location**
**Map 1:E9**
**OS Ref. SW841 585**
3 miles SE Newquay via
A392 & A3058 signed
from Quintrell Downs
(right at Kestle Mill) or
signed from A30 at
Summercourt via A3058.

■ **Contact**
**Tel:** 01637 875404
**E-mail:** trerice@
nationaltrust.org.uk

■ **Opening Times**
15 February-2 November
daily from 10.30am -5pm.
(Garden, Shop and Barn
Restaurant open from
10.30am, House opens at
11am).

8 November-21 December
Saturday-Sunday
11am-4pm (Garden, Shop
and Barn Restaurant open
from 11am, Great Hall only
open in the House).

■ **Admission**
Adult              £7.65
Child              £3.80
Family             £19.20
1-Adult Family     £11.45
Pre-arranged Groups
(15+)              £6.85
Winter             £3.85

■ **Special Events**
Please see our website for
an action packed line up of
2014 events.

# TRERICE 🌿
www.nationaltrust.org.uk/trerice

## A grand manor on a Cornish scale.

This Elizabethan manor house lies in a secluded wooded valley, with rare examples of Dutch gables, a fine plaster ceiling and a magnificent Great Hall window. There is so much to discover about the history of this unique manor house, the families who lived here, its architecture and restoration. The story of Trerice is brought to life by a wide range of events throughout the year.

Try on our replica armour and play traditional games in the Great Hall. Take part in costumes days, Tudor and themed workshops, living history, conservation events and atmospheric evening openings. There are also family activities and trails, kayles (Cornish bowls) in the garden and our introductory and history talks. Come along and watch the transformation of our gardens as we develop our exciting new project for 2014, the Ladies Garden. Created on the site of previous formal gardens adjoining Trerice manor, our new garden will provide a modern twist on the traditional parterre, with a simple yet impactful planting scheme of yew hedging, lavender, white roses and tulips.

The new parterre will truly enhance the gardens, adding a touch of simple formality and awakening a long dormant original feature of Trerice's historic grounds.

## KEY FACTS

- ⬛ Selection of National Trust and locally produced food, drink and souvenirs.
- ⬛ Locally produced plants for sale.
- ⬛ Email trerice@nationaltrust.org.uk.
- ⬛ WCs.
- ⬛ Morning coffee, lunches made with local produce, Sunday roasts and a delicious selection of cakes and desserts.
- ⬛ Pre book for introductory talks.
- ⬛ Limited for coaches. Free parking.
- ⬛ Pre booking essential, Tudor craft activities and trails.
- ⬛ Assistance dogs only.
- ⬛ Visit www.nationaltrustcottages.co.uk.
- ⬛ Please see our website for an action packed line up of 2014 events.

© John Millar

Child playing traditional games of kayles

© Simon Riordan

# BOCONNOC 🏠
## THE ESTATE OFFICE, BOCONNOC, LOSTWITHIEL, CORNWALL PL22 0RG
### www.boconnoc.com

Boconnoc House the winner of the 2012 HHA/Sotheby's Award for Restoration and the Georgian Group Award was bought with the proceeds of the Pitt Diamond in 1717. Three Prime Ministers, a history of duels and the architect Sir John Soane play a part in the story of this unique estate. The beautiful woodland garden, the Georgian Bath House, Soane Stable Yard, 15th Century Church and naturesque landscape tempt the explorer. The Boconnoc Music Award for ensembles from the Royal College of Music, the Cornwall Spring Flower Show and fairy-tale weddings are part of Boconnoc today, in between filming, fashion shoots, corporate days and private parties. Groups by appointment (15-150).

**Location:** Map 1:G8. OS Ref 148 605. A38 from Plymouth, Liskeard or from Bodmin to Dobwalls, then A390 to East Taphouse and follow signs.

**Owner:** Anthony Fortescue Esq. **Contact:** Mrs Veryan Barneby
**Tel:** 01208 872507 **Fax:** 01208 873836
**E-mail:** info@boconnoc.com
**Open:** House & Garden: 27 Apr, 4, 11 & 18 May: Suns 2-5pm. Special Events: 8 Mar 'Glo in the Park' Run, 5 & 6 Apr CGS Spring Flower Show, 18 May Dog Show, 21 & 22 Jun EnduranceGB Ride, 18-20 Jul Steam Fair, 22-25 Jul Music Award Concerts, 26 & 27 Jul Car Rally. Group bookings daily by appointment.
**Admission:** House: £5.00, Garden: £5.00. Children under 12yrs free.
**Key facts:** 🖼 🖵 Conferences. 🚻 Partial. 🍽 Licensed.
🐕 By arrangement. 🅿 🐾 🐾 In grounds, on leads.
🛏 19 doubles (13 en suite). Holiday and residential houses to let.
💒 Church or Civil ceremony. ⚜ ♿

# CAERHAYS CASTLE & GARDEN 🏠Ⓕ
## CAERHAYS, GORRAN, ST AUSTELL, CORNWALL PL26 6LY
### www.caerhays.co.uk

One of the very few Nash built castles still left standing - situated within approximately 120 acres of informal woodland gardens created by J C Williams, who sponsored plant hunting expeditions to China at the turn of the century. As well as guided tours of the house from March to June visitors will see some of the magnificent selection of plants brought back by the intrepid plant hunters of the early 1900s these include not only a national collection of magnolias but a wide range of rhododendrons and the camellias which Caerhays and the Williams familly are associated with worldwide.

**Location:** Map 1:F9. OS Ref SW972 415. S coast of Cornwall - between Mevagissey and Portloe. 9m SW of St Austell.

**Owner:** F J Williams Esq **Contact:** Lucinda Rimmington
**Tel:** 01872 501310 **Fax:** 01872 501870 **E-mail:** enquiries@caerhays.co.uk
**Open:** House: 17 Mar-13 Jun: Mon-Fri only (including BHs), 11am- 4pm,

booking recommended. Gardens: 17 Feb-15 Jun: daily (including BHs), 10am-5pm (last admission 4pm).
**Admission:** House: £8.00. Gardens: £8.00. House & Gardens: £13.00. Group tours: £9.50 by arrangement. Groups please contact Estate Office.
**Key facts:** 🔲 No photography in house. 🛍 Selling a range of Caerhays products & many other garden orientated gifts. 🖼 Located beside entrance point. 🖵 The Georgian Hall is available for hire for meetings. 🚻
🍽 The Magnolia Tea Rooms serve a wide range of foods using locally sourced produce. 🚶 Obligatory. By arrangement. 🅿 Limited for large coaches.
🐾 🐾 On leads. 🏠 Caerhays has a selection of 5 * properties available for hire for self-catering holidays.
💒 Weddings can be held at The Vean or the Coastguard's Lookout. Please visit www.caerhays.co.uk for more information. ♿

# PORT ELIOT HOUSE & GARDENS ® 🏠ⓕ
## ST. GERMANS, SALTASH, CORNWALL PL12 5ND

www.porteliot.co.uk

Port Eliot is an ancient, hidden gem, set in stunning fairytale grounds which nestle beside a secret estuary in South East Cornwall. It has the rare distinction of being a Grade I Listed house, park and gardens. This is due in part to the work of Sir John Soane, who worked his magic on the house and Humphrey Repton, who created the park and garden. Explore the treasures in the house. Gaze at masterpieces by Reynolds and Van Dyck. Decipher the Lenkiewicz Round Room Riddle Mural. Still a family home, you will be beguiled by the warm atmosphere.

**Location:** Map 1:H8. OS Ref SX359 578. Situated in the village of St Germans on B3249 in SE Cornwall.

**Owner:** The Earl of St Germans
**Contact:** Port Eliot Estate Office
**Tel:** 01503 230211 **E-mail:** info@porteliot.co.uk
**Open:** 1 Mar 2014 to 30 Jun 2014 except Fri & 31st May, 1 Jun, 7 Jun, 8 Jun, 28 Jun & 29 Jun, 2pm-6pm (last admission 5pm) Tea Rooms available.
**Admission:** House & Garden: Adult £8.00, Student/Senior/Group (20+)/Visitors arriving by public transport £7.00, Children £4.00. Grounds only: Adult £5.00, Children £2.00.
**Key facts:** ⓘ No photography. ♿ Suitable. WCs. ▪ ⋔ ⓕ By arrangement. Ⓟ ▪ ⌂ In grounds. Guide dogs only in house. ▲ ▽

# PRIDEAUX PLACE 🏠ⓕ
## PADSTOW, CORNWALL PL28 8RP

www.prideauxplace.co.uk

Tucked away above the busy port of Padstow, the home of the Prideaux family for over 400 years, is surrounded by gardens and wooded grounds overlooking a deer park and the Camel estuary to the moors beyond. The house still retains its 'E' shape Elizabethan front and contains fine paintings and furniture. Now a major international film location, this family home is one of the brightest jewels in Cornwall's crown. The historic garden is undergoing major restoration work and offers some of the best views in the county. A cornucopia of Cornish history under one roof.

**Location:** Map 1:E8. OS Ref SW913 756. 5m from A39 Newquay/Wadebridge link road. Signposted by Historic House signs.

**Owner/Contact:** Peter Prideaux-Brune Esq
**Tel:** 01841 532411 **Fax:** 01841 532945 **E-mail:** office@prideauxplace.co.uk
**Open:** Easter Sun 20 Apr to Thu 2 Oct (closed 30 Apr & 1 May) Grounds & Tearoom: 12.30-5pm. House Tours: 1.30-4pm (last tour).
**Admission:** House & Grounds: Adult £8.50, Child £2.00.
Grounds only: Adult £4.00, Child £1.00. Groups (15+) discounts apply.
**Key facts:** ⓘ Open air theatre, open air concerts, car rallies, art exhibitions, charity events. 📷 ⋔ By arrangement. ♿ Partial. Ground floor & grounds. ▪ Fully licensed. ⓕ Obligatory. Ⓟ ▪ By arrangement. ⌂ On leads. ✳ By arrangement. ▽

## ST MICHAEL'S MOUNT 🌿
### MARAZION, NR PENZANCE, CORNWALL  TR17 0HS
www.stmichaelsmount.co.uk / www.nationaltrust.org.uk

This beautiful island has become an icon for Cornwall and has magnificent views of Mount's Bay from its summit. There the church and castle, whose origins date from the 12th Century, have at various times acted as a Benedictine priory, a place of pilgrimage, a fortress, a mansion house and now a magnet for visitors from all over the world. Following the Civil War, the island was acquired by the St Aubyn family who still live in the castle today alongside a 30-strong community of islanders.

**Location:** Map 1:C10. OS Ref SW515 300. 3 miles East of Penzance.
**Owner:** National Trust  **Contact:** Charlotte Somers, St Aubyn Estates, King's Road, Marazion, Cornwall TR17 OEL
**Tel:** 01736 710507 (710265 tide information)
**Fax:** 01736719930
**E-mail:** enquiries@stmichaelsmount.co.uk

**Open:** Castle: 30 Mar-2 Nov, Sun-Fri, 10.30am-5pm (30 Jun–31 Aug, 10.30am-5.30pm). Last admission 45 mins before castle closing time. Gardens: 14 Apr-27 Jun Mon-Fri; 3 Jul-29 Aug Thu & Fri; 4 Sep-26 Sep Thu & Fri, 10.30am-5pm (5.30pm Jul & Aug).
**Admission:** Castle: Adult £8.00, Child (under 17) £4.00, Family £20.00, 1 Adult Family £12.00. Booked Groups: £7.20. Garden: Adult £5.00, Child £2.00. Combined Castle & Garden: Adult £10.50, Child £5.00, Family £26.00, 1 Adult Family £15.50.
**Key facts:** ⓘ Parking on mainland (not NT). Dogs not permitted in the castle or gardens. For a full events calendar throughout the season, please check the website. 🖥 ⊞ ♿ Partial. WCs. ◨ Licensed. ⏇ Licensed. �👤 By arrangement. Tel for details. 🅿 On mainland, including coach parking (not NT.) 🛏 🐕 Guide dogs only. ✳ ▦

## HEARTLANDS CORNWALL
### Robinson's Shaft, Dudnance Lane, Pool, Redruth
### Cornwall  TR15 3QY
www.heartlandscornwall.com

Heartlands is a new FREE visitor attraction and World Heritage Site Gateway in Cornwall. Nestled just off the A30 in Pool, near Redruth in the former mining heart of Cornwall, there are 19 acres of eclectic fun to explore. State-of-the-art exhibitions, climb-on sculptures, gardens of epic diversity, a giant adventure playscape for kids, art and craft studios and a funky café in the old carpenter's workshop. With swathes of green outdoor space for warm, sunny days and ever-curious indoor space when it's wet, Heartlands is all-year round, all-weather entertainment for anyone and everyone. Go see, go play, go wow.
**Location:** Map 1:D10. OS Ref SW667 412. A30, take exit signposted Pool
**Owner:** Heartlands Trust
**Contact:** David Rutherford, Marketing Manager
**Tel:** 01209 722320 **E-mail:** info@heartlandscornwall.com
**Open:** Open every day of the year except Christmas and Boxing Day. 10am-5pm (Apr-Sep), 10am-4pm (Oct - Mar). **Admission:** Free.
**Key facts:** 🖥 ⊞ ⏇ ♿ WCs. ◨ Licensed. ⏇ Licensed. 👤 Obligatory. 🅿 Limited for cars and coaches. 🛏 🐕 On leads. 🔺 ✳ ▦

## PENCARROW 🏛ⓕ
### Washaway, Bodmin, Cornwall  PL30 3AG
www.pencarrow.co.uk

Owned, loved and lived in by the family. Georgian house and Grade II* listed gardens. Superb collection of portraits, furniture and porcelain. Marked walks through 50 acres of beautiful formal and woodland gardens, Victorian rockery, Italian garden, over 700 different varieties of rhododendrons, lake, Iron Age hill fort and icehouse.
**Location:** Map 1:F8. OS Ref SX040 711. Between Bodmin and Wadebridge. 4m NW of Bodmin off A389 & B3266 at Washaway.
**Owner:** Molesworth-St Aubyn family **Contact:** Administrator
**Tel:** 01208 841369 **Fax:** 01208 841722 **E-mail:** info@pencarrow.co.uk
**Open:** House: 30 Mar–2 Oct 2014, Sun-Thur, 11am-4pm (guided tour only - last tour of the House at 3pm). Café & shop 11am-5pm. (House, cafe and shop closed Fridays and Saturdays.) Gardens: 1 Mar-31 Oct, Daily, 10am-5.30pm.
**Admission:** House & Garden: Adult £10.50, Conc. £9.50, Child (5-16 years) £5.00. Grounds only: Adult £5.50, Conc. £5.00, Child (5-16 years) £2.50. Discounted family tickets and group rates available.
**Key facts:** ⓘ Cafe, Gift and plant shop, small children's play area, self-pick soft fruit. 🖥 ⊞ ⏇ ♿ ◨ 👤 Obligatory. 🅿 Free. 🛏 🐕 In grounds. 🔺 ▦

# PENTILLIE CASTLE & ESTATE ®
## Paynters Cross, St Mellion, Saltash, Cornwall PL12 6QD
### www.pentillie.co.uk

Built in 1698 by the eccentric Sir James Tillie, Pentillie Castle sits in a beautiful position above the River Tamar, surrounded by 500 acres of parkland and gardens. Originally laid out by Tillie, the gardens and parkland were extensively remodelled by Humphry Repton in 1810. The Mausoleum and Kitchen Gardens have recently been restored, and are now open to visitors. The Castle also offers award-winning 5 star luxury B&B accommodation and exclusive hire for weddings and corporate guests.

**Location:** Map 1:H8. OS Ref SX040 645. 7m West of Plymouth. Postcode: PL12 6QD **Owner:** Ted and Sarah Coryton **Contact:** Sammie Coryton **Tel:** 01579 350044 **Fax:** 01579 212002 **E-mail:** contact@pentillie.co.uk **Open:** Pentillie is open by appointment all year for B&B, exclusive hire, weddings and corporate days. Spring garden open days and Invitation to View tour dates are available to view on our website. Please visit www.pentillie.co.uk or telephone for more details. **Admission:** For updated prices please visit our website. **Key facts:** ℹ️ Visit www.pentillie.co.uk for garden open days & event details. 🏠 📷 ♿ Partial. WCs. 🍴 Licensed. 🎪 Licensed. 📷 By arrangement. 🅿️ Limited for coaches. 🚌 🐕 Guide dogs only. 🛏️ 9 luxury en-suite bedrooms with views of the parkland and River Tamar. 📷 ❄️ By appointment only. 💷

# ST ANTHONY'S CHURCH 🏠
## St Anthony-in-Roseland, Portscatho
## Truro, Cornwall TR2 5EZ
### www.visitchurches.org.uk

Behind the turreted ancestral home of the Spry family, and looking across the creek to St Mawes, St Anthony-in-Roseland is unusual in that it still has its original medieval cruciform plan, despite being extensively restored in the 19th Century. During the 12th Century, much of the land at St Anthony was owned by the Augustinian Priory at Plympton, Devon; it was during this time that the Prior established the church here. By the 19th Century the chancel was in ruins, and Samuel Spry, MP for Bodmin, employed his cousin, the Revd Clement Carlyon, an amateur architect, to oversee the restoration of the church. Carlyon rebuilt the chancel, and installed the wooden roofs, floor tiles and stained glass. He also designed many of the furnishings, including the chunky pulpit and pews, some of which he may have carved himself. In the north transept you can see impressive monuments to members of the Spry family, spanning three centuries. **Location:** OS Ref SW855 320. 20m SW of St Austell, off A3078; opposite St Mawes and 4m S of Gerrans. **Open:** Open daily.

# BURNCOOSE NURSERIES & GARDEN
## Gwennap, Redruth, Cornwall TR16 6BJ

The Nurseries are set in the 30 acre woodland gardens of Burncoose.
**Location:** Map 1:D10. OS Ref SW742 395. 2m SE Redruth on main A393 Redruth to Falmouth road.
**Owner/Contact:** C H Williams
**Tel:** 01209 860316
**E-mail:** burncoose@eclipse.co.uk
**Website:** www.burncoose.co.uk
**Open:** Mon-Sat: 9am-5pm, Suns, 11am-5pm. Gardens and Tearooms open all year (except Christmas Day).
**Admission:** Nurseries- Free. Gardens- Adult/Conc. £3.00. Child Free. Group conducted tours- £2.50 by arrangement.
**Key facts:** 📷 🏠 ♿ WCs. 🍴 📷 Obligatory. By arrangement. 🅿️ Limited for coaches. 🐕 On leads.

# FALMOUTH ART GALLERY
## Municipal Art Gallery, The Moor, Falmouth TR11 2RT

Falmouth Art Gallery is an award winning gallery with one of the most important art collections in Cornwall. The permanent collection features major artists including Thomas Gainsborough, Edward Burne-Jones, Frank Brangwyn and Charles Napier Hemy. There is a changing programme of exhibitions/events throughout the year. Family and pet friendly.
**Location:** Map 1:E10. OS Ref SW800 693. MAP 1:E10 OS Ref: SW800 693 On The Moor, in the upper floor of the Municipal Buildings above the Library.
**Tel:** 01326 313863 **E-mail:** info@falmouthartgallery.com
**Website:** www.falmouthartgallery.com
**Open:** Mon-Sat 10am to 5pm (including spring and summer bank holidays).
**Admission:** Free.
**Key facts:** 📷 Selection of prints, cards, art books and crafts. ♿ W/C. Lift. Parking. 🅿️ Short stay on The Moor, Long Stay on Quarry Hill.

# TREWITHEN 🏠®
## Grampound Road, Near Truro, Cornwall TR2 4DD

Trewithen is an historic estate near Truro, Cornwall. Owned and lived in by the same family for 300 years, it is both private home and national treasure. The woodland gardens are outstanding with 24 champion trees and famously rare and highly prized plants. The garden is one of only 30 International Camellia Society Gardens of Excellence in the world and is also RHS recommended. Tours of the house prove equally memorable. **Location:** Map 1:E9. OS Ref SW914 524. Grampound Road, near Truro, Cornwall. **Owner:** A M J Galsworthy
**Contact:** The Estate Office **Tel:** 01726 883647 **Fax:** 01726 882301
**E-mail:** info@trewithengardens.co.uk **Website:** www.trewithengardens.co.uk
**Open:** House & Gardens: Mar-Jun. House open Mon & Tue afternoons, including Aug BH Mon. Please contact us or visit website for further opening times.
**Admission:** Adult £8.50 Children U12 Free. Combined entry & group rates also available. Please contact us or visit website for more information.
**Key facts:** ℹ️ No photography in house. 📷 🏠 ♿ WCs. 🍴 📷 By arrangement. 🅿️ 🐕 On leads.

# LAWRENCE HOUSE MUSEUM 🏛️
## 9 Castle Street, Launceston, Cornwall PL15 8BA

Fine Georgian House used as a 'little jewel' of a museum and Mayor's Parlour.
**Location:** Map 1:H7. OS Ref SX330 848. Launceston **Tel:** 01566 773277
**E-mail:** lawrencehousemuseum@yahoo.co.uk
**Website:** www.lawrencehousemuseum.org **Open:** Apr-Oct Mon-Fri. 10.30am-4.30pm. Last entry 4.00pm. Occasional Sats. Open BHs.
**Admission:** Free - Donations welcomed.

## VISITOR INFORMATION

**■ Owner**
The Hon. John Rous

**■ Address**
Clovelly
Nr Bideford
N Devon
EX39 5TA

**■ Location**
Map 1:H5
OS Ref. SS248 319
On A39 10 miles W of
Bideford, 15 miles E of
Bude. Turn off at 'Clovelly
Cross' roundabout and
follow signs to car park.
**Bus:** From Bideford.
**Rail:** Barnstaple 19 miles.
**Air:** Exeter & Plymouth
Airport both 50 miles.

**■ Contact**
Visitor Centre
**Tel:** 01237 431781
**E-mail:** visitorcentre@
clovelly.co.uk

**■ Opening Times**
**High season:**
9am-6pm.
**Low season:**
10am-4.30pm.

**■ Admission**
| | |
|---|---|
| Adult | £6.50 |
| Child (7-16yrs) | £4.00 |
| (under 7yrs) | Free |
| Family (2+2) | £17.00 |
| Group Rates (20+) | |
| Adult | £5.50 |
| Child | £3.75 |
| Twin ticket rate for Clovelly and Hartland Abbey | £13.50 |

The entrance fee covers
parking, admission to the
audio-visual film,
Fisherman's Cottage,
Kingsley Museum, Clovelly
Court Gardens, and
contributes to the ongoing
maintenance of the village
to preserve its timeless
charm and magic.
Prices correct at time of
going to press.

**■ Special Events**
**May**
Celebration of Ales &
Ciders
**July**
Clovelly Maritime Festival
Woolsery Agricultural
Show
Lundy Row
**August**
Lifeboat Day
Clovelly Gig Regatta
**September**
Lobster & Crab Feast
**November**
Clovelly Herring Festival
**December**
Christmas Lights

# CLOVELLY
www.clovelly.co.uk

## Most visitors consider Clovelly to be unique. Whatever your view, it is a world of difference not to be missed.

From Elizabethan days until today, Clovelly village has been in private ownership, which has helped preserve its original character. The main traffic-free street known as 'up-a-long' and 'down-a-long', tumbles its cobbled way down to the tiny harbour, which is protected by an ancient stone breakwater. It is a descent through flower-strewn cottages broken only by little passageways and winding lanes that lead off to offer the prospect of more picturesque treasures.

At the top of the cliffs you will find the Visitor Centre in which there is a range of gift shops, a café and an audio-visual theatre where visitors are treated to a history of the village. Just beyond the centre there is the Stable Yard with a pottery and silk workshop. The steep cobbled village street is traffic-free and donkeys and sledges are the only means of transport.

The New Inn, halfway down the street, is 400 years old and the Red Lion is right on the quay. Both inns have long histories and an atmosphere rarely found in our modern world. Together with wonderful sea views, the effect is a perfect maritime experience. There are also stunning coastal and woodland walks along the cliff tops.

Next to the C13th parish church of All Saints, you can visit Clovelly Court Garden. It is a classic example of a lovingly restored Victorian walled kitchen garden and includes magnificent lean-to glasshouses sheltering Mediterranean fruits.

Access to the village is restricted to pedestrians only via the Visitor Centre with a Land Rover taxi service to and from the harbour (Easter to October) for which there is a small charge.

## KEY FACTS

 Rubber soled, low heel shoes are recommended.

Partial.

Licensed.

Licensed.

By arrangement.

On leads.

24 double, 1 single, all en suite.

Civil Wedding Licence.

# HARTLAND ABBEY

www.hartlandabbey.com

## Hartland Abbey is a family home full of history in a beautiful valley leading to a wild Atlantic cove.

Built in 1159 as an Augustinian monastery, at the Dissolution Henry VIII gifted the Abbey to the Keeper of his Wine Cellar whose descendants live here today. Visitors to Hartland Abbey can experience not only stunning architecture and interiors, fascinating collections, beautiful gardens and walks but the warmth and friendliness found only in a cherished family home. Close family connections to Poltimore House and Clovelly Court nearby are evident. BBC Antiques Roadshow was filmed here recently.

The impressive interiors span Mediaeval, Queen Anne, Georgian, Regency and Victorian periods. Of special interest are the three main Reception Rooms, the Alhambra Corridor by Sir George Gilbert Scott and the Gothic Library by Meadows with its Batty Langley fireplace. The circular table by Jupe dominates the Dining Room.

Important paintings by artists including Reynolds and Gainsborough, furniture, porcelain, early photographs, a museum, documents from 1160 and changing displays of family memorabilia fascinate visitors. The 'William Stukeley –Saviour of Stonehenge' exhibition displays the many aspects of the life of an extraordinary 18thC ancestor.

Much of the 50 acres of gardens and walks had been lost since the First World War. Since restoration, once again paths lead to woodland gardens, the Bog Garden and Fernery by Jekyll and the beautiful 18thC Walled Gardens. Here climbers, herbaceous, tender perennials and vegetables delight; glasshouses protect stunning displays.

Carpets of primroses, historic daffodils, bluebells and wildflowers lead in spring to the restored woodland Summerhouse, the Gazebo and Blackpool Mill Cottage with its rocky beach, the film location for Jane Austen's 'Sense and Sensibility' and Rosamunde Pilcher's 'The Shell Seekers'. Donkeys, black sheep and peacocks roam. Children's Quiz. Five stunning wedding venues available. Holiday cottages to rent on the Hartland Abbey Estate. 1 mile from Hartland Quay and St. Nectan's Church, the 'Cathedral of North Devon'.

## KEY FACTS

 Wedding receptions.
Partial. WC.

By arrangement.
In grounds, on leads.

© Anya Campbell

**VISITOR INFORMATION**

■ **Owner**
Sir Hugh Stucley Bt

■ **Address**
Hartland Abbey
Nr Bideford
North Devon
EX39 6DT

■ **Location**
Map 1:G5
OS Ref. SS240 249
15m W of Bideford, 15m N of Bude off A39 between Hartland and Hartland Quay on B3248.

■ **Contact**
Theresa Seligmann
**Tel:** 01237441496/234
01884 860225
**E-mail:** ha_admin@btconnect.com

■ **Opening Times**
**House, Gardens, Grounds & Beachwalk**
30 March–5 October
Sun–Thurs 11–5pm
(House 2–5pm)
Last adm 4.30pm
**Tea Room**
Light lunches and cream teas 11am–5pm.

■ **Admission**
**House, Gardens, Grounds & Beachwalk**
Adult                £11.00
OAP                  £10.50
Child (5–15ys)        £5.00
Under 5                Free
Registered disabled   £8.50
Family (2+2)         £27.00
**Gardens, Grounds, Beachwalk & Exhibition**
Adult                 £7.00
OAP                   £6.50
Child (5–15ys)        £4.00
Under 5                Free
Registered disabled   £4.50
Family (2+2)         £18.00
**Groups and coaches**
Concessions to groups of 20+. Open to coaches at other dates and times. Booking essential.
Large car park adjacent to the house.

■ **Special Events**
**February**
9, 16 Snowdrop Sundays (11am–4pm)
**March**
16 Daffodil Day (11am-4pm)
**April**
20, 27 Bluebell Sundays
**May**
4 Hartland Abbey Hartbreaker Run
**May-September**
Outdoor Theatre (Productions to be announced)
**All season Exhibition**
'Dr William Stukeley – Saviour of Stonehenge'

(See website for further details of events).

© Nick Carter

## GREAT FULFORD
### DUNSFORD, NR. EXETER, DEVON EX6 7AJ
www.greatfulford.co.uk

On a hill overlooking a lake and set in a landscaped park Great Fulford has been the home of the Fulford family since at least the 12th Century. The current house reflects the financial ups and downs of the family over the centuries, with a major rebuilding and enlargement taking place in 1530 and again in 1580 while in 1690 the house, which had been badly damaged in the Civil War, was fully restored. Internally then there is a stunning suite of Great Rooms which include a superb Great Hall replete with some of the finest surviving examples of early Tudor carved panelling as well as a William & Mary period Great Staircase which leads to the recently restored Great Drawing Room or Ballroom. Other rooms in the house are in the 'gothic' taste having been remodelled, as was the exterior, by James Wyatt in 1805.

**Location:** Map 2:J7. OS Ref SX790 917. In centre of Devon. 10m W of Exeter. South of A30 between villages of Cheriton Bishop and Dunsford.
**Owner/Contact:** Francis Fulford
**Tel:** 01647 24205 **Fax:** 01647 24401
**E-mail:** francis@greatfulford.co.uk
**Open:** All year by appointment for parties or groups containing a minimum of 10 persons, alternatively individuals can book tours on prearranged dates via www.invitationtoview.co.uk.
**Admission:** £9.00 per person.
**Key facts:** ⊤ ☕ ℹ Obligatory.
🅿 🍴 🐕 📷 🔔 ❄

## POWDERHAM CASTLE 🏛Ⓕ
### KENTON, NR EXETER, DEVON EX6 8JQ
www.powderham.co.uk

A splendid castle built in 1391 by Sir Philip Courtenay, remaining in the same family and now home to the 18th Earl of Devon. Set in a tranquil deer park alongside the Exe estuary, its stunning location offering glorious views. The Woodland Garden is delightful in the spring while the Rose Garden comes into bloom from June. Guided tours showcase the Castle's majestic rooms and stunning interiors, while fascinating stories bring its intriguing history to life. The Courtenay Cafe offers a selection of home cooked food. Gift shop, plant centre and extensive calendar of events create a wonderful day out.
**Location:** Map 2:K7. OS Ref SX965 832. 6m SW of Exeter, 4m S M5/J30. Access from A379 in Kenton village.
**Owner:** The Earl of Devon

**Contact:** Mr Simon Fishwick - Estate Director
**Tel:** 01626 890243
**Fax:** 01626 890729
**E-mail:** castle@powderham.co.uk
**Open:** 1 April 2014. Please visit our website for specific dates and times.
**Admission:** Adults £11.00, Senior £10.00, Child (4-16) £8.50, Family £33.00 (2013 prices).
**Key facts:** ℹ Available for private hire all year round.
📷 🎁 ⊤ ♿ Partial. WCs. ☕ Licensed. 🍴 Licensed.
ℹ Obligatory. Included. 1hr. 🅿 Free.
🚌 🐕 Guide dogs only. 🏨 🔔 ♿

## CADHAY 🏠Ⓕ
### Ottery St Mary, Devon  EX11 1QT
www.cadhay.org.uk

Cadhay is approached by an avenue of lime-trees, and stands in an extensive garden, with herbaceous borders and yew hedges, with excellent views over the original medieval fish ponds. The main part of the house was built in about 1550 by John Haydon who had married the de Cadhay heiress. He retained the Great Hall of an earlier house, of which the fine timber roof (about 1420-1460) can be seen. An Elizabethan Long Gallery was added by John's successor at the end of the 16th Century, forming a unique courtyard with statues of Sovereigns on each side, described by Sir Simon Jenkins as one of the 'Treasures of Devon'.
**Location:** Map 2:L6. OS Ref SY090 962. 1m NW of Ottery St Mary. From W take A30 and exit at Pattesons Cross, follow signs for Fairmile and then Cadhay. From E, exit at the Iron Bridge and follow signs as above.
**Owner:** Mr R Thistlethwayte **Contact:** Jayne Covell **Tel:** 01404 813511
**Open:** May-Sep, Fri 2pm-5pm. Also: late May + Summer BH Sat-Sun-Mon. Last tour 4pm. **Admission:** Guided tours: Adult £7.00, Child £3.00.
Gardens: Adults £3.00, Child £1.00. Parties of 15+ by prior arrangement.
**Key facts:** 🚻 🅣 🅢 Ground floor & grounds. 🅟 🅕 Obligatory. 🅟 🐕 Guide dogs only. 🏠 🔔

## CASTLE HILL GARDENS 🏠
### Castle Hill, Filleigh, Barnstaple, Devon  EX32 0RQ
www.castlehilldevon.co.uk

Set in the rolling hills of Devon, Castle Hill Gardens provide a tranquil and beautiful setting. Stroll through the spectacular gardens, dotted with mystical temples, follies, statues, vistas and a sham castle. The path through the Woodland Gardens, filled with flowering shrubs, leads you down to the river and the magical Satyr's temple.
**Location:** Map 2:I14. OS Ref SS661 362. A361, take B3226 to South Molton. Follow brown signs to Castle Hill
**Owner:** The Earl and Countess of Arran
**Contact:** Michelle White
**Tel:** 01598 760421/01598 760336 Ext 1 **Fax:** 01598 760457
**E-mail:** gardens@castlehill-devon.com
**Open:** Daily except Sats Apr-Sep 11am-5pm. Oct-Mar 11am-3pm.
Refreshments are only available from Apr to Sep. Groups and coach parties are welcome at all times by prior arrangement.
**Admission:** Adults £5.50, Senior citizens £5.00, Family £15.00, Children 5-15 £2.50, Groups (20+) £4.50. **Key facts:** 🅣 🅢 Partial. WCs. 🅕 By arrangement. 🅟 🅟 🐕 On leads. 🏠 🔔 Daily except Saturdays. 🐾

The Alhambra Corridor, Hartland Abbey

## FURSDON HOUSE 🏠Ⓕ
### Cadbury, Nr Thorverton, Exeter, Devon  EX5 5JS
www.fursdon.co.uk

Fursdon House is at the heart of a small estate where the family has lived for over 750 years. Set within a hilly and wooded landscape the gardens and grounds are attractive with walled and open areas. Family memorabilia with fine costume and textiles are displayed on informal guided tours. Two spacious apartments and a restored Victorian cottage offer holiday accommodation.
**Location:** Map 2:K6. OS Ref SS922 046. By car- Off A3072 between Bickleigh & Crediton. 9m N of Exeter signposted through Thorverton from A396 Exeter to Tiverton road **Owner:** Mr E D Fursdon **Contact:** Mrs C Fursdon
**Tel:** 01392 860860 **Fax:** 01392 860126
**E-mail:** admin@fursdon.co.uk
**Open:** Garden & Tea Room, Wed & Sun from Easter to end Sep; House Open Bank Hols & Wed & Sun in Jun, Jul & Aug.
**Admission:** House and Garden Adult £8.00, Child (10-16yrs) £4.00, Child (under 10yrs) Free. Garden only £4.00.
**Key facts:** 🅘 Conferences. No photography or video. 🅣 🅕 Obligatory. 🅟 Limited for coaches. 🏠 🔔 Self-catering.

## ST MARTIN'S CHURCH
### Cathedral Close, Exeter, Devon  EX1 1EZ
www.visitchurches.org.uk

It is one of the oldest buildings in the city, consecrated a year before the Norman Conquest, and was once one of six churches clustered in the cathedral's shadow. It is the most important and complete church in the centre of Exeter. The first church on this site was consecrated on 6th July 1065 by Bishop Leofric, the same bishop who founded the cathedral in Exeter.

The roughcast exterior of red volcanic stone with bright, white Beer stone windows makes it look a little bit like a fancy gingerbread house. Inside, it is simple and full of light. The gallery has painted on it the arms of the city and of Bishop Trelawny, a local hero in Cornwall, who was imprisoned for libel by James II.

There are also several magnificent monuments in the church including one of Philip Hooper (a benefactor who donated the reredos) - splendidly bewigged, he kneels at a prayer desk with a skull and pile of books.

**Location:** OS Ref SX922 926. Cathedral Close

**Open:** Mon-Fri: 9.30am-4.30pm. Sat: 10am-5pm.

## TIVERTON CASTLE
### Park Hill, Tiverton  EX16 6RP
www.tivertoncastle.com

Part Grade I Listed, part Scheduled Ancient Monument, few buildings evoke such an immediate feeling of history. Originally built 1106, later rebuilt and altered all ages of architecture from medieval to modern can be seen. Home of Princess Katherine Plantagenet. Fun for children, try on Civil War armour; ghost stories, secret passages, medieval loos, beautiful walled gardens, including working kitchen garden. Interesting furniture, pictures. Comfortable holiday accommodation.

**Location:** Map 2:K5. OS Ref SS954 130. Just N of Tiverton town centre.

**Owner:** Mr and Mrs A K Gordon  **Contact:** Mrs A Gordon

**Tel:** 01884 253200 **Fax:** 01884 254200 01884 255200.

**E-mail:** info@tivertoncastle.com

**Open:** Easter-end Oct: Sun, Thur, BH Mon, 2.30-5.30pm. Last admission 5pm. Open to groups (12+) by prior arrangement at any time.

**Admission:** Adult £7.00, Child (7-16yrs) £3.00, Child under 7 Free. Garden only: £2.00. **Key facts:** ⬛ ⬛ ⬛ Partial. ⬛ By arrangement. **P** Limited for coaches. ⬛ ⬛ Guide dogs only. ⬛ 4 Apartments, 2 Cottages.

## SHILSTONE
### Modbury, Devon  PL21 0TW
www.shilstonedevon.co.uk

Shilstone is a Georgian house in the heart of the Devon countryside overlooking an important historical landscape.

Recently restored, the house is now a private home and romantic wedding venue with beautiful elevations and exquisite detail that make it comfortable in its site, and timeless in its design.

**Location:** Map 2:J9. OS Ref SX674 536.

**Owner:** Lucy and Sebastian Fenwick

**Contact:** Abigail Gray

**Tel:** 01548830888

**E-mail:** abi@shilstonedevon.co.uk

**Open:** By appointment only.

**Admission:** £12.00 per person, minimum 4 people.

**Key facts:** ⬛ ⬛ Unsuitable. ⬛ Must pre-book. ⬛ Must pre-book. ⬛ Obligatory. **P** Up to 24 seaters. ⬛ ⬛ Guide dogs only. ⬛ ⬛ ⬛ €

Tiverton Castle

Castle Hill Gardens

## MARWOOD HILL GARDEN
### Marwood, Barnstaple, North Devon EX31 4EB

Marwood Hill Garden is a special private garden covering an area of 20 acres with three lakes and set in a valley tucked away in North Devon. Enjoyed by visitors of all agres looking for inspiration, relaxation or just a great day out. Awarded 'Gardens of Excellence' Marwood has extensive collection of camellias, bog garden. National collection of Astilbes. Japenese Iris and Tulbagia and Champion Trees.
**Location:** Map 2:14. OS Ref SS545 375. 4m N of Barnstaple. ½m W of B3230. Signs off A361 Barnstaple - Braunton Road. COACHES please contact us for directions **Owner:** Dr John Snowden **Contact:** Mrs Patricia Stout
**Tel:** 01271 342528 **E-mail:** info@marwoodhillgarden.co.uk
**Website:** www.marwoodhillgarden.co.uk **Open:** Mar-Oct. Please check website for opening times and events. **Admission:** Adult £6.00, Child 12-16 £2.50, Child under 12 Free. Pre-booked group of 10+ £5.00. **Key facts:** ⓘ Magical garden. ▣ Cards Jams etc. ▣ Huge selection. ▣ ▣ Partial. WCs. ▣ Lunches Teas. ▣ By arrangement. ▣ Coach/Car Park. ▣ ▣ Dogs on leads only. ▣

## CHAMBERCOMBE MANOR ▣
### Ilfracombe, Devon EX34 9RJ

Guided tours of Norman Manor House which is mentioned in Domesday Book. Hear the legend of Chambercombe and visit Haunted Room. Set in 16 acres of woodland and landscaped gardens. Ye Olde Manor Buttery Tea Rooms offering light lunches and cream teas.
**Location:** Map 2:13. OS Ref SS532 468. East of Ilfracombe between A399 and B3230, follow brown historic house signs. Private car park at end of Chambercombe Lane.
**Owner:** Chambercombe Trust **Contact:** Angela Powell **Tel:** 01271 862624
**Website:** www.chambercombemanor.co.uk
**Open:** Easter-end Oct: Guided tours Tue-Thur from 10.30am and Sun from 12noon, last tour 3.30pm. Non guided tours Mon and Fri 10.30am last entry 3.30pm closing at 4pm. **Admission:** Guided tours/non guided tours Adult £8.00/£5.00, Child £6.00/£2.50, Family 2+2 £25.00, under 5s free. Group (max 50) discount. **Key facts:** ▣ Partial. ▣ ▣ Obligatory. ▣ Limited for coaches. ▣ ▣ On leads, in grounds. ▣

## CHURCH OF ST MICHAEL & ALL ANGELS ▣
### Tavistock Road, Princetown, Yelverton, Devon PL20 6RE

This simple, slender-towered Dartmoor church was built between 1812-14 by prisoners captured in the Napoleonic Wars with France, and the War of 1812 with the United States - they were held at Dartmoor prison. Cherry and Pevsner describe the location on Dartmoor as 'unquestionably the bleakest place in Devon'. It is 436 metres above sea level and exposed to high winds and twice the national average rain fall. The walls are of local granite and the interior is as plain as the exterior. The east window contains stained glass of 1910 in memory of the American prisoners who helped to build the church.
**Location:** OS Ref SX587 737. 4 miles east of Tavistock, off B3557.
**Website:** www.visitchurches.org.uk
**Open:** Open daily, 10am-4pm.

## DOWNES ▣ ▣
### Crediton, Devon EX17 3PL

Downes is a Palladian Mansion dating originally from 1692. The former home of General Sir Redvers Buller, the house contains a large number of items relating to his military campaigns. The property is now predominantly a family home with elegant rooms hung with family portraits, and a striking main staircase.
**Location:** Map 2:K6. OS Ref SX852 997. Approx 1m from Crediton town centre.
**Owner:** Trustees of the Downes Estate Settlement
**Contact:** Judith Jones
**Tel:** 01363 775142 **E-mail:** info@downesestate.co.uk
**Website:** www.downesestate.co.uk
**Open:** Mons & Tues 21 Apr-15 Jul & Aug BH 25 & 26 Aug. Tours 2.15.Group bookings (15+) by prior appointment.
**Admission:** Adults £7.00, Children (5-16 years) £3.50, Groups (over 15) £6.00 each for Adults or £3.00 each for Children (Groups must be pre booked).
**Key facts:** ▣ ▣ Partial. ▣ Obligatory. ▣ Limited. ▣

## ST PETROCK'S CHURCH ▣
### Church Lane, Parracombe, Barnstaple, Devon EX31 4RJ

Set in glorious countryside on the edge of Exmoor, this hilltop church seems to be a modest medieval building, but it is the lovely Georgian interior with painted texts and wonderful furnishings that have hardly changed for 200 years that make it very special. The undulating slate floors and leaning arcade only add to the unforgettable charm of this church. The Ten Commandments are painted on a board above a pretty 15th Century screen, there is a three-tier pulpit with reading desk, box pews, and musicians' seats raised on steps at the west end. St Petrock's is believed to be the last church in Devon to use musicians to accompany the hymns. In 1879 there was a proposal to pull the church down and to build a new one on the same site. The poet John Ruskin led the protests and sent a £10 cheque to support the preservation of the church. The objections were successful and the church was saved. **Location:** OS Ref SS675 449. 11m NE of Barnstaple, off A39 and 4m SW of Lynton. **Website:** www.visitchurches.org.uk **Open:** Open daily.

## HOLY TRINITY CHURCH ▣
### Torbryan Hill, Torbryan, Newton Abbot, Devon TQ12 5UR

The church is a perfect example of the Gothic Perpendicular style and was unusually constructed in one 20-year building campaign between 1450 and 1470. As you enter, look up at the exquisite and rare fan-vaulted ceiling with four small angels supporting the central ribs of each fan. Inside there is a beautifully carved altar screen that spans the width of the church. Below the screen are painted panels of 40 saints - they were once whitewashed, perhaps to save them from the puritanical zeal of the Reformation. The delicacy of the wood carving is echoed by the elegant tracery of the windows, many containing medieval stained glass. Parts of the original rood-screen were reused, probably in the early 19th Century, to form the pulpit, while at the same time the original pulpit was reconstructed as the altar. The 15th Century oak benches survive but were enclosed in the 18th Century to form box pews.
**Location:** OS Ref SX820 669. 4 miles south west of Newton Abbot, off A381.
**Website:** www.visitchurches.org.uk **Open:** Open daily.

## SAND ▣ ▣
### SIDBURY, SIDMOUTH EX10 0QN

Sand is one of East Devon's hidden gems. The beautiful valley garden extends to 6 acres and is the setting for the lived-in Tudor house, the 15th Century Hall House, and the 16th Century Summer House. The family, under whose unbroken ownership the property has remained since 1560, provide guided house tours.
**Location:** Map 2:L7. OS Ref SY146 925. Well signed, 400 yards off A375 between Honiton and Sidmouth. **Contact:** Mr & Mrs Huyshe-Shires
**Tel:** 01395 597230 **E-mail:** info@SandSidbury.co.uk
**Website:** www.SandSidbury.co.uk
**Open:** Suns & Mons in Jun and BH Suns & Mons. Other dates see website. Open 2-6pm. Groups by appointment.
**Admission:** House & Garden: Adult £7.00, Child/Student £1.00.
Garden only: Adult £3.00, accompanied Child (under 16) Free.
**Key facts:** ⓘ No photography in house. ▣ Partial. ▣ ▣ Obligatory. ▣ Limited. ▣ On leads. ▣

# DORSET

## VISITOR INFORMATION

**■ Owner**
Mr & Mrs Patrick Cooke

**■ Address**
Athelhampton
Dorchester
Dorset
DT2 7LG

**■ Location**
**Map 2:P6**
**OS Ref. SY771 942**
Athelhampton House is located just 5 miles East of Dorchester, between Puddletown and Tolupddle villages.
Follow the brown tourist signs for Athelhampton from the A35.

**■ Contact**
Owen Davies or Laura Dean
**Tel:** 01305 848363
**E-mail:** enquiry @athelhampton.co.uk

**■ Opening Times**
1 Mar-1 Nov, Sun, Mon, Tue, Wed, Thurs, 10.00am-5pm. Closed every Fri & Sat (also open every Sunday throughout the Winter months).

**■ Admission**
**House & Gardens:**
| | |
|---|---|
| Adult | £12.50 |
| Senior | £10.50 |
| Child (under 16) | £2.50 |
| Disabled/Student | £7.50 |
| Gardens Only Ticket | £7.50 |

Please contact us for group booking rates and hospitality
some Fridays may be available by appointment.

**■ Special Events**
Spring Flower Festival.
MG Car Rally.
Car Auction.
Christmas Food Event.
Outdoor Theatre.
Traditional Village Fete.
Cinema Showings.
Athelhampton has a thriving Conference and Wedding business and offers exclusive use for Wedding parties and private functions on Fridays and Saturdays throughout the year.
Please see contact us by phone or visit our website for more information.

### Conference/Function

| ROOM | Size | Max Cap |
|---|---|---|
| Long Hall | 13mx6m | 80 |
| Conservatory | 16mx11m | 120 |
| Media Suite/ Cinema | fixed seating | 75 |
| Great Hall | 12mx8m | 82 |

# ATHELHAMPTON HOUSE ®🏠Ⓕ & GARDENS
www.athelhampton.co.uk

**One of the finest 15th Century Houses in England nestled in the heart of the picturesque Piddle Valley in the famous Hardy county of rural Dorset.**

Home to the Cooke family, this house dates from 1485 and is a magnificent example of early Tudor architecture. Sir William Martyn was granted a licence by Henry VII to enclose 160 acres of deer park and to build the fortified manor. His great hall, with a roof of curved brace timbers and an oriel window with fine heraldic glass is now one of the finest examples from this period. In 1891 Alfred Carte de Lafontaine (the then owner of Athelhampton) commissioned the building of the formal gardens.

The Grade 1 listed gardens which have won the HHA 'Garden of the Year' award surround the main house, with Elizabethan style ham stone courts. The famous 30 feet high yew pyramids dominate the Great Court and the 15th Century Dovecote is still home to a colony of beautiful white fantail doves. Water forms a recurring theme with pools, fountains and the River Piddle.

The house has an array of fine furniture from Jacobean to Victorian periods. The west wing gallery hosts an exhibition of paintings and sketches by the Russian Artist, Marevna (1892 - 1984) The collection of her works, painted mainly in the cubist style, includes pieces painted throughout her lifetime including her travels, life in Paris, her time whilst she lived at Athelhampton during the 1940's and 50's and her final years in Ealing. Our Historic House also has something like no other, A 77 seated plush Cinema, where we show a selection of films from September through to Easter, please visit our website for dates and screenings.

## KEY FACTS

ℹ️

📕 Books, food, DVDs, gifts & souvenirs.

🌱 Plants for sale from the gift shop.

🍽 By arrangement, for a range of activities and catering.

♿ Limited access to upper floors.

☕ Coffee, lunches & afternoon tea.

🍴 The Topiary: Home-cooked lunches, morning coffee and afternoon tea, The Long Hall: Sunday Carvery.

👤 Guided tours by arrangement. Free guidebook loan.

🅿 Free car and coach parking.

📖 Educational staff to assist available.

🐕 On leads, grounds only.

🏠 Delightful holiday cottage on the estate, sleeps 6 in 3 en-suite bedrooms.

💍 Civil wedding ceremonies inc open air.

❄️ Open all year round on a Sunday.

🛡

Register for news and special offers at **www.hudsonsheritage.com**

# SHERBORNE CASTLE 🏠F
## NEW ROAD, SHERBORNE, DORSET  DT9 5NR
### www.sherbornecastle.com

Built by Sir Walter Raleigh in 1594, Sherborne Castle has been the home of the Digby family since 1617. Prince William of Orange was entertained here in 1688, and George III visited in 1789. Splendid interiors and collections of art, furniture and porcelain are on view in the Castle. Lancelot 'Capability' Brown created the 50 acre lake in 1753 and gave Sherborne the very latest in landscape gardening, with magnificent vistas of the surrounding parklands. Today, over 30 acres of beautiful lakeside gardens and grounds are open for public viewing.

**Location:** Map 2:O5. OS Ref ST649 164. 4m SE of Sherborne town centre. Follow brown signs from A30 or A352. ½m S of the Old Castle.

**Owner:** Mr & Mrs John Wingfield Digby  **Contact:** Robert B. Smith

**Tel:** 01935 812072  **Fax:** 01935 816727

**E-mail:** castleoffice@sherbornecastle.com

**Open:** Castle, Gardens, Gift Shop and Tea Room - Tue 1 Apr-Thur 30 Oct 2014. Open daily, except Mon and Fri (but open on BH Mons), from 11.00am with last admission at 4.30pm (on Saturdays, Castle interior opens later at 2.00pm with last admission at 4.30pm). Spring Bulbs & Daffodils Weekend 22-23 Mar. Craft & Garden Fair 3-BH Mon 5 May. Sherborne Castle Country Fair Retriever Event & Rare Breeds Show BH Mon 26 May. Cancer Research UK Race for Life 22 Jun. 'Classics at the Castle' Classic Car & Supercar Show 20 Jul. Autumn Colours Weekend 25-26 Oct. Firework Extravaganza 8 Nov.

**Admission:** Castle & Gardens - Adult £11.00, Senior £10.00, Child Free (max 4 per adult). Gardens Only: Adult/Senior: £6.00, Child Free (max 4 per adult). Apply for group discount prices.

**Key facts:** ▢ T ⬓ WCs. ⬛ ⑪ Ⓕ By arrangement. 🅿 ▣ ⋈ On leads. ▲ ⬛

Highcliffe Castle

## CLAVELL TOWER
### Kimmeridge, near Wareham, Dorset  BH20 5PE
www.landmarktrust.org.uk

This four storey, circular tower stands high on the cliff overlooking one of the most striking bays on the Dorset coast. Built in 1830 its location has captivated many including writers like Hardy and PD James.

**Location:** Map 2:A7. OS Ref SY915 796.
**Owner:** The Landmark Trust
**Tel:** 01628 825925
**E-mail:** bookings@landmarktrust.org.uk
**Open:** Two Open Days per year. Other visits by appointment.
**Admission:** Free on Open Days and visits by appointment.
**Key facts:** ℹ️ A four storey tower with each room on a different floor. The bedroom, on the first floor, has a door onto a balcony that encircles the whole building. 🅿️ 🚾 🚾 ♿ ⛩

## LULWORTH CASTLE & PARK 🏠Ⓕ
### East Lulworth, Wareham, Dorset  BH20 5QS
www.lulworth.com

Stunning C17th Castle & C18th Chapel set in extensive parkland, with views towards the Jurassic Coast. Built as a hunting lodge to entertain Royalty, the Castle was destroyed by fire in 1929. Since then it has been externally restored and internally consolidated by English Heritage. The Castle provides informative displays & exhibitions on its history.

**Location:** Map 3:A7. OS Ref ST853 822.
In E Lulworth off B3070, 3m NE of Lulworth Cove.
**Owner:** The Weld Estate **Tel:** 0845 4501054
**Fax:** 01929 40563 **E-mail:** enquiries@lulworth.com
**Open:** Castle & Park: All year, Sun-Fri. Opening dates & times may vary throughout the year, check website or call before visiting. Last admission to Castle is 1hr before closing.
**Admission:** Pay & Display parking £3.00, allowing access to Park walks, Play & Picnic areas. Admission applies for Castle & Chapel - A: £5.00, C: £3.00 (4-15yrs). U4's Free, EH & HHA members Free.
**Key facts:** 🅣 Concerts, corporate & private hire/events by arrangement. ♿ WCs. Lift access to Upper Ground floor. 📷 Obligatory. By arrangement. 🅿️ 🍴 🚾 Guide dogs only. 🏠 ♿ ⛩

## HIGHCLIFFE CASTLE 🏠Ⓕ
### Highcliffe-On-Sea, Christchurch  BH23 4LE
www.highcliffecastle.co.uk

Built in the 1830s in the Romantic/Picturesque style. Although no longer with its rich interiors, the Castle now houses a Heritage Centre & Gift Shop providing a unique setting for exhibitions and events. Licenced for weddings. Available for ceremonies, receptions, banquets and corporate use. Cliff-top grounds. Access to Christchurch Coastal Path and beach.

**Location:** Map 3:B6. OS Ref SZ200 930. Off the A337 Lymington Road, between Christchurch and Highcliffe-on-Sea.
**Owner:** Christchurch Borough Council **Contact:** David Hopkins
**Tel:** 01425 278807 **Fax:** 01425 280423
**E-mail:** enquiries@highcliffecastle.co.uk
**Open:** 1 Feb-23 Dec: daily, 11am-5pm. Last admission 4.30pm (4pm Fri/Sat). Grounds: All year: daily from 7am. Tearooms daily (except Christmas Day). Coaches by appointment.
**Admission:** Adult £3.85, accompanied U16 free. Group (10+) rates available. Guided tour (including non-public areas): Adult £5.85. Grounds: Free
*Prices correct at time of going to press.
**Key facts:** 🖼️ 🅣 Wedding receptions. ♿ 🍴 📷 By arrangement. 🅿️ Limited. Parking charge. 🍴 By arrangement. 🚾 🏠 ♿ ⛩

Gardens at Sherborne Castle

# MAPPERTON 🏠F
## Beaminster, Dorset DT8 3NR
### www.mapperton.com

'The Nation's Finest Manor House'- Country Life. Jacobean manor, All Saints Church, stables and dovecote overlooking an Italianate garden, orangery, topiary and borders, descending to ponds and arboretum. A unique valley garden in an Area of Outstanding Natural Beauty with fine views of Dorset hills and woodlands.
**Location:** Map 2:N6. OS Ref SY503 997. 1m S of B3163, 2m NE of B3066, 2m SE Beaminster, 5m NE Bridport.
**Owner/Contact:** The Earl & Countess of Sandwich
**Tel:** 01308 862645 **Fax:** 01308 861082 **E-mail:** office@mapperton.com
**Open:** House: 7 Jul- 8 Aug (Mon-Fri) plus 5 May & 26 May, timed tours 2-4.30pm, booking advisable. Garden & Church: 1 Mar-31 Oct: daily (exc Sat) 11am-5pm. Café: 1 Apr-30 Sep: daily (exc. Sat) 11am-5.00pm, 01308 863 348.
**Admission:** Gardens: Adult £6.00, Child (under 18yrs) £3.00, under 5yrs free. House: £6.00. Group tours by appointment. House and Gardens combined £10.00 for groups over 20.
**Key facts:** 🖼 ⊞ ⊤ ♿ Partial. WCs. ◰ Licensed. 🎨 By arrangement. 🅿 Limited for coaches. ◼ 🐕 Guide dogs only. ▲ ♛

# ST GEORGE'S CHURCH 🏠
## Reforne, Wide Street, Portland, Dorset DT5 2JP
### www.visitchurches.org.uk

Vast and solitary, St George's is one of the most magnificent 18th Century churches in Dorset. It rises from the rocky, treeless and dramatic peninsula of Portland and is the masterwork of a local mason named Thomas Gilbert who supplied the Portland stone used to build St Paul's Cathedral.
The interior is fabulously preserved with its lectern, pulpit, box pews and galleries all surviving. It is a 'preacher's church' with all the seating facing the twin pulpits - one for reading 'the Word' (scripture), the other for lengthy sermons. The sprawling churchyard is a treasure trove of fabulous headstones and memorials that tell tales of murder, piracy and adventure in a gloriously atmospheric setting.
There are inscriptions to Mary Way and William Lano, who were shot and killed in 1803 by a press gang, and Joseph Trevitt, an assistant warder at Portland Prison who was murdered by a convict in 1869.
**Location:** OS Ref SY686 720. Easton, Isle of Portland.
Parking available close to church.
**Open:** 10am-5pm until Oct. 10am-3pm Winter Months.

# MINTERNE GARDENS ®🏠F
## Minterne Magna, Nr Dorchester, Dorset DT2 7AU
### www.minterne.co.uk

Landscaped in the manner of 'Capability' Brown, Minterne's unique garden has been described by Simon Jenkins as 'a corner of paradise.' 20 wild, woodland acres of magnolias, rhododendrons and azaleas providing new vistas at each turn, with small lakes, streams and cascades. Private House tours, dinners, corporate seminars, wedding and events.
**Location:** Map 2:O6. OS Ref ST660 042. On A352 Dorchester/Sherborne Rd, 2m N of Cerne Abbas.
**Owner/Contact:** The Hon Mr & Mrs Henry Digby **Tel:** 01300 341370
**E-mail:** enquiries@minterne.co.uk
**Open:** Mid Feb-9 Nov: daily, 10am-6pm.
**Admission:** Adult £5.00, accompanied children free. Free to RHS members.
**Key facts:** ⊤ ♿ Unsuitable. 🎨 By arrangement. 🅿 Free. Picnic tables in car park. 🐕 In grounds on leads. ▲

© Justin Barton

# ST GILES HOUSE 🏠
## Wimborne St Giles, Dorset BH21 5NA
### www.shaftesburyestates.com

Beautiful secluded setting in unspoilt Dorset, famous for the Grand Shaftesbury Run in May. Home of the Earls of Shaftesbury, the 17th Century house, gardens and landscape are under restoration. Events held in the parkland, designed by Henry Flitcroft, in the summer months; the house is available for bespoke events. The Grand Shaftesbury Run is half marathon or 10km run or 1km fun run through the pleasure grounds and woodland.
**Location:** Map 3:A5. OS Ref SU031119. In Wimborne St Giles, 4mls SE of A354, past almshouses and church.
**Owner:** The Earl of Shaftesbury
**Tel:** 01725 517214
**E-mail:** office@shaftesburyestates.com
**Open:** By appointment for groups and for bespoke events.
**Key facts:** ⊤ 🐕 ▲ ♛

## WOLFETON HOUSE 🏛Ⓕ
### Nr Dorchester, Dorset DT2 9QN

A fine medieval and Elizabethan manor house lying in the water-meadows near the confluence of the rivers Cerne and Frome. It was embellished around 1580 and has splendid plaster ceilings, fireplaces and panelling. To be seen are the Great Hall, Stairs and Chamber, Parlour, Dining Room, Chapel and Cyder House.
**Location:** Map 2:O6. OS Ref SY678 921. 1½m from Dorchester on the A37 towards Yeovil. Indicated by Historic House signs.
**Owner:** Capt N T L L T Thimbleby
**Contact:** The Steward
**Tel:** 01305 263500
**E-mail:** kthimbleby.wolfeton@gmail.com
**Open:** Jun-end Sep: Mon, Wed & Thur, 2-5pm. Groups by appointment throughout the year.
**Admission:** £7.00
**Key facts:** ⓘ Catering for groups by prior arrangement. 🍽 By arrangement. ♿ Ⓚ By arrangement. 🅿 Limited for coaches. 📷 🐕 ❄

## CHURCH OF OUR LADY & ST IGNATIUS
### North Chideock, Bridport, Dorset DT6 6LF

Built by Charles Weld of Chideock Manor in 1872 in Italian Romanesque style, it is a gem of English Catholicism and the Shrine of the Dorset Martyrs. Early 19th Century wall paintings in original barn-chapel (priest's sacristy) can be seen by arrangement. A museum of local history & village life displayed in adjoining cloister.
**Location:** Map 2:A7. OS Ref SY090 786. A35 to Chideock, turn into N Rd & ¼mile on right
**Owner:** The Weld Family Trust **Contact:** Mrs G Martelli
**Tel:** 01308 488348 **E-mail:** amyasmartelli40@hotmail.com
**Website:** www.chideockmartyrschurch.org.uk
**Open:** All year: 10am-4pm.
**Admission:** Donations welcome.
**Key facts:** ♿ Partial. 🅿 Limited for coaches. 📷 🐕 Guide dogs only ❄

## EDMONDSHAM HOUSE & GARDENS 🏛Ⓕ
### Cranborne, Wimborne, Dorset BH21 5RE

Charming blend of Tudor and Georgian architecture with interesting contents. Organic walled garden, 6 acre garden with unusual trees and spring bulbs. 12th Century church nearby.
**Location:** Map 3:A5. OS Ref SU062 116. Off B3081 between Cranborne and Verwood, NW from Ringwood 9m, Wimborne 9m.
**Owner/Contact:** Mrs Julia E Smith
**Tel:** 01725 517207
**Open:** House & Gardens all BH Mons, Weds in Apr & Oct only, 2-5pm. Gardens Apr-Oct Suns & Weds 2-5pm. Groups by arrangement (max 50).
**Admission:** House & Garden: Adult £5.00, Child £1.00 (under 5yrs free). Garden only: Adult £2.50, Child 50p (under 5yrs free).
**Key facts:** 🍽 ♿ Partial. WCs. 🍴 Only Weds Apr & Oct. Ⓚ Obligatory. 🅿 Limited. 📷 🐕 Guide dogs only. 🏠

## HIGHER MELCOMBE 🏛
### Melcombe Bingham, Dorchester, Dorset DT2 7PB

Consists of the surviving wing of a 16th Century house with its attached domestic chapel. A fine plaster ceiling and linenfold panelling. Conducted tours by owner.
**Location:** Map 2:P6. OS Ref ST749 024. 1km W of Melcombe Bingham.
**Owner/Contact:** Mr M C Woodhouse
**Tel:** 01258 880251
**Website:** www.highermelcombemanor.co.uk
**Open:** May-Sep by appointment.
**Admission:** Adult £2.00 (takings go to charity).
**Key facts:** ♿ Unsuitable. Ⓚ By written appointment only. 🅿 Limited. 🐕 Guide dogs only.

## SANDFORD ORCAS MANOR HOUSE
### Sandford Orcas, Sherborne, Dorset DT9 4SB

Tudor manor house with gatehouse, fine panelling, furniture, pictures. Terraced gardens with topiary and herb garden. Personal conducted tour by owner.
**Location:** Map 2:O5. OS Ref ST623 210. 2½m N of Sherborne, Dorset 4m S of A303 at Sparkford. Entrance next to church.
**Owner/Contact:** Sir Mervyn Medlycott Bt
**Tel:** 01963 220206
**Open:** Easter Mon, 10am-5pm. May & Jul-Sep: Suns & Mons, 2-5pm.
**Admission:** Adult £5.00, Child £2.50. Groups (10+): Adult £4.00, Child £2.00.
**Key facts:** ♿ Unsuitable. Ⓚ Obligatory. 🅿 Parking available. 🐕 In grounds, on leads.

## STOCK GAYLARD HOUSE 🏛Ⓕ
### Stock Gaylard, Sturminster Newton, Dorset DT10 2BG

Georgian house overlooking an ancient deer park with parish church of St Barnabas in garden. **Location:** Map 2:P5. OS Ref ST722 130. 1m S junction A357 & A3030 Lydlinch Common. **Tel:** 01963 23215
**E-mail:** langmeadj@stockgaylard.com **Website:** www.stockgaylard.com
**Open:** 26 Apr-5 May: 22-30 Jun and Sep: 2-5pm. Groups by appointment.
**Admission:** Adult £5.00.

Lulworth Castle

# CHAVENAGE 🏠ⓕ
### www.chavenage.com

Elizabethan Manor Chavenage House, a TV/Film location is still a family home, offers unique experiences, with history, ghosts and more.

Chavenage is a wonderful Elizabethan house of mellow grey Cotswold stone and tiles which contains much of interest for the discerning visitor. The approach aspect of Chavenage is virtually as it was left by Edward Stephens in 1576. Only two families have owned Chavenage; the present owners since 1891 and the Stephens family before them. A Colonel Nathaniel Stephens, MP for Gloucestershire during the Civil War was cursed for supporting Cromwell, giving rise to legends of weird happenings at Chavenage since that time.

There are many interesting rooms housing tapestries, fine furniture, pictures and relics of the Cromwellian period. Of particular note are the Main Hall, where a contemporary screen forms a minstrels' gallery and two tapestry rooms where it is said Cromwell was lodged.

Recently Chavenage has been used as a location for TV and film productions including a Hercule Poirot story The Mysterious Affair at Styles, episodes of The House of Elliot, Casualty and Cider with Rosie. Jeremy Musson visited in the BBC's The Curious House Guest. Chavenage has recently doubled as Candleford Manor in the BBC'S Lark Rise to Candleford. Scenes from the series Bonekickers and Tess of the D'Urbervilles and in 2013 the major new Channel 4 historical drama New Worlds, were shot at Chavenage. Chavenage is especially suitable for those wishing an intimate, personal tour, usually conducted by the owner or his family, or for groups wanting a change from large establishments. Meals for pre-arranged groups have proved hugely popular. It also provides a charming venue for wedding receptions, small conferences and other functions.

## VISITOR INFORMATION

### ■ Owner
Mr David Lowsley- Williams

### ■ Address
Chavenage
Tetbury
Gloucestershire
GL8 8XP

### ■ Location
Map 3:A1
**OS Ref. ST872 952**
Less than 20m from M4/ J16/17 or 18. 1¾m NW of Tetbury between the B4014 & A4135. Signed from Tetbury. Less than 15m from M5/J13 or 14. Signed from A46 (Stroud-Bath road).
**Taxi:** The Pink Cab 07960 036003
**Rail:** Kemble Station 7m.
**Air:** Bristol 35m. Birmingham 70m. Grass airstrip on farm.

### ■ Contact
D Lowsley-Williams or Caroline Lowsley-Williams
**Tel:** 01666 502329
**Fax:** 01666 504696
**E-mail:** info@chavenage.com

### ■ Opening Times
**Summer**
May-September
Thur, Sun, 2-5pm. Last admission 4pm. Also Easter Sun, Mon & BH Mons. NB. Will open on any day and at other times by prior arrangement for groups.
**Winter**
October-March
By appointment only for groups.

### ■ Admission
Guided Tours are inclusive in the following prices.
**Summer**
Adult                    £8.00
Child (5-16 yrs)         £4.00
**Winter**
Groups only (any date or time) Rates by arrangement.

### Conference/Function

| ROOM | Size | Max Cap |
|------|------|---------|
| Ballroom | 70' x 30' | 120 |
| Oak Room | 25 'x 20' | 30 |

## KEY FACTS

ⓘ Suitable for filming, photography, corporate entertainment, activity days, seminars, receptions and product launches. No photography inside the house.

Occasional.

Corporate entertaining. Private drinks parties, lunches, dinners, anniversary parties & wedding receptions.

Partial. WCs.

By owner. Large groups given a talk prior to viewing. Couriers/group leaders should arrange tour format prior to visit.

P Up to 100 cars. 2-3 coaches (by appointment). Coaches access from A46 (signposted) or from Tetbury via B4014, enter back gates for parking area.

Chairs can be arranged for lecturing.

## VISITOR INFORMATION

### ■ Owner
Lady Ashcombe, Henry and Mollie Dent-Brocklehurst

### ■ Address
Sudeley Castle
Winchcombe
Gloucestershire
GL54 5JD

### ■ Location
**Map 6:O10**
**OS Ref. SP032 277**
8m NE of Cheltenham, at Winchcombe off B4632. From Bristol or Birmingham M5/J9. Take A46 then B4077 towards Stow-on-the- Wold.
**Bus:** Castleways to Winchcombe.
**Rail:** Cheltenham Station 8m.
**Air:** Birmingham or Bristol 45m.

### ■ Contact
Estate Office
**Tel:** 01242 602308
**Fax:** 01242 602959
**Tel:** 01242 604244.
**E-mail:**
enquiries@sudeley.org.uk

### ■ Opening Times
Sudeley is open daily from 17th March to 2nd November; 10.30am to 5.00pm. Family events throughout the season - check the website or call for details.

### ■ Admission
**2014 Admission Prices:**
| | |
|---|---|
| Adult | £14.00 |
| Concessions | £13.00 |
| Child (5-15yrs) | £5.00 |
| Family (2 adults + 3 children) | £35.00 |
| Children under 5 | Free |
| Members of the Historic Houses Association | Free |

**Season Tickets:**
| | |
|---|---|
| Adult | £20.00 |
| Child (5–15 years) | £10.00 |
| Family (2 adults, 3 children) | £50.00 |

### ■ Special Events
Special events throughout the season. See Website, Facebook and Twitter @SudeleyCastle.

### Conference/Function
| ROOM | Size | Max Cap |
|---|---|---|
| Chandos Hall | | 60 |
| Banqueting Hall + Pavilion | | 100 |
| Marquee | | Unlimited |
| Long Room | | 80 |
| Library | | 50 |

# SUDELEY CASTLE & GARDENS 🏰Ⓕ
## www.sudeleycastle.co.uk

**The former home of Tudor Queen, Katherine Parr. Fascinating exhibitions and award-winning gardens. In 2014, the East Wing will be open to the public for the first time in over a decade.**

Award-winning gardens and medieval ruins surround Sudeley Castle, which sits nestled in the Cotswold Hills on the edge of the historic town of Winchcombe.

Sudeley Castle has played host to many royal figures throughout history. It is famously the last home and resting place of Henry VIII's sixth wife, Katherine Parr. Queen of England and Mistress of Sudeley, Katherine lived at the Castle after the death of the King, as the wife of Thomas Seymour. Here she was guardian to the young Princess Elizabeth and died tragically after childbirth. An exhibition, with a film narrated by Dr David Starkey, is testament to this exceptional woman. Katherine Parr's tomb rests in St Mary's Church within the Castle grounds; her prayer book, love letter to

Thomas Seymour and a lock of her hair feature in the exhibition. Sudeley's extensive gardens have been lovingly restored and designed to reflect the Castle's fascinating past. The Queens Garden is amongst the finest rose gardens in England, sited on an original Tudor Parterre. Nine individually designed gardens are a delight of discovery for the visitor.

General admission in 2014 will also include access to the family's private apartments in the East Wing, plus two additional fascinating exhibitions - commemorating the anniversary of WWI and 'The Plantaganets', detailing Richard III's association with Sudeley.

## KEY FACTS

| | |
|---|---|
| ℹ️ | |
| 🏛️ | Open daily - 17 Mar-2 Nov. |
| 🌱 | Plant sales at the Visitor Centre. |
| 🍸 | Weddings & events. |
| ♿ | Partial. WCs. |
| ☕ | Light lunches, afternoon tea, cakes, snacks, tea, coffee & soft drinks. |
| 🍴 | Licensed. |
| 👤 | By arrangement. Call the estate office. |
| 🅿️ | Ample parking. |
| 📷 | Contact estate office for schools materials. |
| 🐕 | Guide dogs only. |
| 🏠 | Country Cottages. |
| ▲ | The Dent Brocklehurst Family's Private Library situated within the Family's apartments is available for civil ceremonies & civil partnerships, with kind permission from the family. |
| 🔲 | See website. |

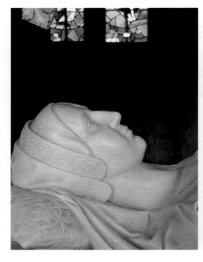

Register for news and special offers at **www.hudsonsheritage.com**

## ELMORE COURT
### ELMORE, GLOUCESTERSHIRE GL2 3NT
www.elmorecourt.com

The Guise Family have been living at Elmore for 750 years and Anselm, with his family, now live at the Grade 2* listed Elmore Court which dates back to 1580. The house and grounds have undergone extensive refurbishments and are now open for Weddings, Events, Film and Photo Shoots and other functions. A very exciting new events space, called the 'Gillyflower', has been built behind the house, constructed from rammed earth and timber sourced from the accompanying estate. It is hidden in hedgerows and trees creating a magical place for dinner, dancing and more. The house is heading back to a contemporary take on traditional estates where the land serves most of the houses needs. Food will again be grown to supply the kitchens and woodland managed to provide heat using the latest Biomass technology. Full of art and history, the house was built to entertain and everyone who visits Elmore loves its welcoming and relaxing atmosphere.

**Location:** Map 6:M11. OS Ref SO782151.
**Owner:** Mr Anselm Guise **Contact:** Anselm or Leesa
**Tel:** 01452 720293
**E-mail:** life@elmorecourt.com
**Open:** All year round, by appointment only.
**Key facts:** ⬒ Weddings, events, house parties a specialty. ⬜ ▣ Licensed. ▥ ⓟ ▦ ▥ ❋ ▽

## FRAMPTON COURT, THE ORANGERY AND FRAMPTON MANOR 🏛
### FRAMPTON-ON-SEVERN, GLOUCESTERSHIRE GL2 7EP
www.framptoncourtestate.co.uk

The Cliffords have lived in Frampton since the 11th Century. Frampton Court, built in 1731, has a superb panelled interior housing period furniture, china and 19th Century 'Frampton Flora' water-colours. The 18th Century 'Strawberry Hill gothic' Orangery sits - breath-takingly - at the end of the ornamental canal in the garden at Frampton Court, and is now a self-catering holiday house. Half-timbered Frampton Manor is said to be the birthplace of 'Fair Rosamund' Clifford, mistress of Henry II. The walled garden is a plantsman's delight. The 16th Century Wool Barn is contemporary with the main part of the house. A whole day is recommended for tours of houses and gardens.

**Location:** Map 6:M12. OS Ref SO 748080. In Frampton, ¼m SW of B4071, 3m SW of M5/J13.
**Owner:** Mr & Mrs Rollo Clifford **Contact:** Janie Clifford

**Tel:** 01452 740268 **E-mail:** events@framptoncourtestate.co.uk
**Open:** Frampton Court & Frampton Manor by appointment for groups (10+). Frampton Manor Garden: Mon & Fri 2.30-5pm, 25 Apr to 1 Aug.
**Admission:** Frampton Court: House & Garden £10.00. Frampton Manor: House, Garden & Wool Barn £10.00. Garden only £5.00. Wool Barn only £3.00. Packages available. Frampton Country Fair 14 Sep 2014.
**Key facts:** ⓘ Filming, parkland for hire. ▣ Pan Global Plants in walled garden (01452 741641). ⬒ Wedding receptions. ⬜ Partial. WCs. ▣ For groups by arrangement in the Wool Barn at Frampton Manor. ⓘ Usually by family members. ⓟ For both houses at Frampton Manor. ▦ ▣ House parties and B&B at Frampton Court contact Gillian Keightley 01452 740267; self-catering holidays at The Orangery 01452 740698. ❋ By arrangement. ▽

## RODMARTON MANOR 🏠ⓕ
### CIRENCESTER, GLOUCESTERSHIRE  GL7 6PF
www.rodmarton-manor.co.uk

A Cotswold Arts and Crafts house, one of the last great country houses to be built in the traditional way, containing beautiful furniture, ironwork, china and needlework specially made for the house. The large garden complements the architecture and contains many areas of great beauty and character including the magnificent herbaceous borders, topiary, roses, rockery and kitchen garden. Available as a film location and for small functions.

**Location:** Map 6:N12. OS Ref ST934 977. Off A433 between Cirencester and Tetbury.
**Owner:** Mr Simon Biddulph
**Contact:** John & Sarah Biddulph
**Tel:** 01285 841442  **E-mail:** enquiries@rodmarton-manor.co.uk

**Open:** House & Garden: Easter Mon, May-Sep; Weds, Sats & BHs, 2-5pm (not guided tours). Garden (snowdrops): 2, 9, 13 & 16 Feb: from 1.30pm. Guided tours of the house (approx. 1hr) may be booked for groups (15+) all year (min group charge £120). Groups (5+) may book guided or unguided tours of the garden at other times.
**Admission:** House & Garden: £8.00, Child (5-15yrs) £4.00. Garden only: £5.00, Child (5-15yrs) £1.00. Guided tour of Garden: Entry fee plus £40.00 per group.
**Key facts:** ⓘ Colour guidebook & postcards on sale. Available for filming. No photography in house. WCs in garden. ♿ Garden & ground floor. 🍽 Open days & groups by appointment. 🅵 By arrangement. 🅿 🚻 🐕 Guide dogs only. ✳

## STANWAY HOUSE & WATER GARDEN 🏠ⓕ
### STANWAY, CHELTENHAM, GLOS  GL54 5PQ
www.stanwayfountain.co.uk

'As perfect and pretty a Cotswold manor house as anyone is likely to see' (Fodor's Great Britain 1998 guidebook). Stanway's beautiful architecture, furniture, parkland and village are complemented by the restored 18th Century water garden and the magnificent fountain, 300 feet, making it the tallest garden and gravity fountain in the world. Teas available. Beer for sale. Wedding reception venue.
The Watermill in Church Stanway, now fully restored as a working flour mill, was recently re-opened by HRH The Prince of Wales. Its massive 24-foot overshot waterwheel, 8th largest waterwheel in England, drives traditional machinery, to produce stoneground Cotswold flour.
**Location:** Map 6:O10. OS Ref SP061 323. N of Winchcombe, just off B4077.

**Owner:** The Earl of Wemyss and March
**Contact:** Debbie Lewis
**Tel:** 01386 584528
**Fax:** 01386 584688
**E-mail:** stanwayhse@btconnect.com
**Open:** House & Garden: Jun-Aug: Tue & Thur, 2-5pm. Private tours by arrangement at other times.
**Admission:** Adult £7.00, Child £2.00, OAP £5.00. Garden only: Adult £4.50, Child £1.50, OAP £3.50.
**Key facts:** ⓘ Film & photographic location. 📷 🎬 Wedding receptions. 🍽 🅵 By arrangement. 🅿 🐕 In grounds on leads. ✳

## HIDCOTE MANOR GARDEN
### Hidcote Bartrim, Nr Chipping Campden, Gloucestershire GL55 6LR
### www.nationaltrust.org.uk

One of the most delightful gardens in England, created in the early 20th Century by the great horticulturist Major Lawrence Johnston; a series of small gardens within the whole, separated by walls and hedges of different species; famous for rare shrubs, trees, herbaceous borders, 'old' roses and interesting plant species.

**Location:** Map 6:O9. OS Ref SP176 429. 4m NE of Chipping Campden, 1m E of B4632 off B4081. At Mickleton ¼m E of Kiftsgate Court. Coaches are not permitted through Chipping Campden High Street.
**Owner:** National Trust
**Contact:** Visitor Services Manager
**Tel:** 01386 438333
**E-mail:** hidcote@nationaltrust.org.uk
**Open:** Visit website for full list of opening times.
**Admission:** Visit wesbite for full list of admission prices.
**Key facts:** 🖻 🗗 ⏱ 🔄 Limited. WC.
🖥 🍴 Licensed. 🅿 🎦 🐾 ♿

## KIFTSGATE COURT GARDENS 🏛ⓕ
### Chipping Campden, Gloucestershire GL55 6LN
### www.kiftsgate.co.uk

Magnificently situated garden on the edge of the Cotswold escarpment with views towards the Malvern Hills. Many unusual shrubs and plants including tree peonies, abutilons, specie and old-fashioned roses.
Winner HHA/Christie's Garden of the Year Award 2003.
**Location:** Map 6:O9. OS Ref SP173 430. 4m NE of Chipping Campden. ¼ m W of Hidcote Garden.
**Owner:** Mr and Mrs J G Chambers
**Contact:** Mr J G Chambers
**Tel:** 01386 438777
**E-mail:** info@kiftsgate.co.uk
**Open:** May, Jun, Jul, Sat-Wed, 12 noon-6pm. Aug, Sat-Wed, 2pm-6pm. Apr & Sep, Sun, Mon & Wed, 2pm-6pm.
**Admission:** Adult £7.50, Child £2.50. Groups (20+) £6.50.
**Key facts:** 🖻 🗗 🔄 Partial.
🖥 🅿 Limited for coaches.
🎦 Guide dogs only.

## PAINSWICK ROCOCO GARDEN 🏛ⓕ
### Painswick, Gloucestershire GL6 6TH
### www.rococogarden.org.uk

Painswick Rococo Garden is set in a hidden Cotswold valley. It allows you to step back into the sensual early 18th Century, when gardens were becoming theatrical and romantic backdrops for entertaining guests. Our restaurant serves a delicious range of homemade cakes and light meals using products grown here or from local producers.
**Location:** Map 6:M11. OS Ref SO864 106. 1½m NW of Painswick on B4073.
**Owner:** Painswick Rococo Garden Trust
**Contact:** P R Moir **Tel:** 01452 813204
**E-mail:** info@rococogarden.org.uk
**Open:** 10 Jan-31 Oct: daily 11am-5pm.
**Admission:** Adult £6.50, Child £3.00, OAP £5.50. Family (2+2) £17.00. Free introductory talk for pre-booked groups (20+).
**Key facts:** 🖻 🗗 ⏱ 🔄 Partial. WCs. 🖥 Licensed. 🍴 Licensed.
🗗 By arrangement. 🅿 🖥 🎦 On leads. 🔲 ❋ ♿

## SEZINCOTE 🏛ⓕ
### Moreton-In-Marsh, Gloucestershire  GL56 9AW
www.sezincote.co.uk

Exotic oriental water garden by Repton and Daniell. Large semi-circular orangery. House by S P Cockerell in Indian style was the inspiration for Brighton Pavilion.

**Location:** Map 6:P10. OS Ref SP183 324. 2 miles west of Moreton-in-Marsh on the A44 opposite entrance to Batsford Arboretum.
**Contact:** Dr E Peake
**Tel:** 01386 700444
**E-mail:** enquiries@sezincote.co.uk
**Open:** Garden: Thurs, Fris & BH Mons, 2-6pm except Dec. House: As above May-Sept. Teas in Orangery when house open.
**Admission:** House: Adult £10.00 (guided tour). Garden: Adult £5.00, Child £1.50 (under 5yrs Free). Groups welcomed weekdays, please contact for details.
**Key facts:** ⓘ Please see our website for up to date events and special openings. ♿ For full information for disabled visitors please email enquiries@sezincote.co.uk. 🎧 🎫 Obligatory. 🐕 Guide dogs only ⛪ Weddings. ❄ 🏵

## NEWARK PARK 🎗
### Ozleworth, Wotton-Under-Edge  GL12 7PZ

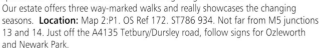

Visit Newark Park this year, with its wonderful quirky character and eclectic collections there are new discoveries at every turn. The garden provides space to play and contemplate, with spectacular views over the Cotswolds and regular garden tours.
Our estate offers three way-marked walks and really showcases the changing seasons. **Location:** Map 2:P1. OS Ref 172. ST786 934. Not far from M5 junctions 13 and 14. Just off the A4135 Tetbury/Dursley road, follow signs for Ozleworth and Newark Park.
**Tel:** 01453 842644 **E-mail:** newarkpark@nationaltrust.org.uk
**Website:** www.nationaltrust.org.uk/newarkpark **Open:** Open Wed-Sun (closed Mon and Tues, open Bank Holidays) 11am-4pm 15-23 Feb and 6 & 7 Dec, 11am-5pm 5 Mar-2 Nov. Last entry 30 minutes before closing, closes dusk if earlier. **Admission:** Adult £7.90, Child £3.90, Family £19.70.
**Key facts:** 🏬 🍴 Peak season. ♿ Ground Floor. 🎧 🎫 Garden Tours. 🅿 🐕 On leads only. 🏵

## ST NICHOLAS' CHURCH 🏛
### Westgate Street, Gloucester, Gloucestershire GL1 2PG

The church is a city landmark, known for its leaning, truncated white stone spire. The damage was caused by a direct hit by Royalist troops during the Siege of Gloucester in 1643; the spire is now topped with an attractive coronet. The existing church dates back to the 12th Century, though most of it was rebuilt in the 13th and larger windows were added later. Formerly one of Gloucester's most prosperous parish churches many of its wonderful monuments and memorial slabs commemorate significant citizens; some with alabaster figures in glorious Stuart costume reclining on chest tombs. Most important is the altar tomb of Alderman John Wallton (died 1626) and his wife Alice. On either side of the chancel are 16th Century squints, giving the congregation a view of the sanctuary and there is a Royal Arms of Charles II above the south doorway. **Location:** OS Ref SO829 188. Lower end of Westgate Street in the city centre, opposite the museum and 250 metres from the ring road.
**Website:** www.visitchurches.org.uk **Open:** Keyholder nearby.

Sudeley Castle

## ST NICHOLAS' CHURCH 🏛
### Broadway, Saintbury, Gloucestershire WR12 7PX

This medieval church has a tall and slender spire, which can be seen from all around and is a notable landmark. The building's earliest known feature is a sundial considered to be 11th Century. The early finely carved box pews are an 18th Century addition and there is a notable collection of 17th and 18th Century ledger slabs in the church. There are some interesting early post-medieval wall paintings in the chancel and visitors may also be interested in the Arts and Crafts features that were added in the early 20th Century, including the chancel and north chapel ceilings; the north chapel screen (c1904 by Ernest Gimson); the north chapel reredos (c1920 by Alec Miller) and the Chancel chandelier (1911 by Charles Ashbee). **Location:** OS Ref SP116 398. On Broadway, off the B4632 running between Weston sub Edge and Willersey. Located to the right hand side of the road.
**Website:** www.visitchurches.org.uk **Open:** Please contact the Bristol regional office on 0117 929 1766 before your visit.

## CHEDWORTH ROMAN VILLA 🎗
### Yanworth, Cheltenham, Gloucestershire  GL54 3LJ

One of the best preserved Roman sites in Britain set in beautiful Cotswold countryside. **Location:** Map 6:N11. OS Ref SP05 6136. **Tel:** 01242 890256
**E-mail:** chedworth@nationaltrust.org.uk **Website:** www.nationaltrust.org.uk/chedworth **Open:** Daily 15 Feb-30 Nov. Café and gift shop.
**Admission:** NT Members Free. Gift Aid (Standard in brackets): £9.90 (£9.00), Child £4.95 (£4.50), Family £24.75 (£22.50). Groups (15+) £8.00, Child £4.00.

## TYTHE BARN
### Tanhouse Farm, Churchend, Frampton-on-Severn, Gloucestershire  GL2 7EH

Tythe Barn Grade II* c1650 incorporating cattle byre.
**Location:** Map 6:M12. OS Ref SP014 206.
**Tel:** 01452 741072 **E-mail:** cottages@tanhouse-farm.co.uk
**Open:** By arrangement all year 10am-4pm. **Admission:** Free.

## WHITTINGTON COURT 🏛ⓕ
### Cheltenham, Gloucestershire  GL54 4HF

Elizabethan & Jacobean manor house with church
**Location:** Map 6:N11. OS Ref SP014 206. 4m E of Cheltenham on N side of A40.
**Tel:** 01242 820556 **E-mail:** jstringer@whittingtoncourt.co.uk
**Open:** 19 Apr-4 May & 9-25 Aug: 2-5pm.
**Admission:** Adult £5.00/Child £1.00/OAP £4.00.

# CHURCH OF ST JOHN THE BAPTIST

**Broad Street, Bristol, Bristol BS1 2EZ**
www.visitchurches.org.uk

In the 12th Century there were five churches built into Bristol's city walls, acting both as part of the city's defences and as places for travellers to offer prayers; St John's is the only one remaining. The sight of the Gothic city gate with the elegant perpendicular spire of St John's rising above is stunning. Walter Frampton (died 1388), who was mayor of the city three times, founded the church. His effigy lies on a tombchest decorated with heraldic shields, with a long-tailed dog at his feet. Other monuments in the chancel, and in the early 14th Century vaulted crypt beneath, testify to the wealth and business activity of the city. The interior of the church is impressively tall and graceful, with fine fittings dating from the 17th Century. On the north side of the church is a fountain, installed to bring water to the Carmelite Friary 700 years ago. **Location:** OS Ref ST587 732. Tower Lane, bottom of Broad Street at intersection with Nelson Street. **Open:** Church opened regularly, but please call the Bristol office on 0117 9291766 before you visit.

# CHURCH OF ST THOMAS THE MARTYR

**Thomas Lane, Bristol, Bristol BS1 6JG**
www.visitchurches.org.uk

Located in Bristol city centre, this handsome late 18th Century church was designed in 1789 by local architect and carver James Allen to replace a medieval church deemed unsafe for use. Allen retained the 15th Century west tower of the old church, intending it to be 'raised and modernised' in a classical fashion, but the plan was never carried out and the church is an unusual - but pleasing - blend of both periods. There is a fine ring of eight bells, all cast by local founders from 15th-19th Century. At the east end is a reredos of 1716 and at the west a gallery of 1728-32, both transferred from the previous church. On the north side of the chancel is a superb 18th Century organ case. Some of the other furnishings are 18th Century, but most date from the 1896 restoration by H Roumieu Gough. They are excellently designed and all contribute to one of the best interiors in Bristol. **Location:** OS Ref ST591 727. St Thomas Street, to south west of Bristol Bridge near intersection of Redcliff Street and Victoria Street. **Open:** Mon-Fri, 9:30am-5pm. Please call the Bristol office on 0117 9291766 for out of hour enquiries.

Sezincote

# GLASTONBURY ABBEY
## Magdalene Street, Glastonbury  BA6 9EL
www.glastonburyabbey.com

A hidden jewel in the heart of Somerset, Glastonbury Abbey is traditionally associated with the earliest days of Christianity in Britain. It is also the resting place for three Saxon kings and the legendary King Arthur. Open 364 days a year. Events held throughout the year - check out the website or follow on Twitter @glastonburyabbe.

**Location:** Map 2:N4. OS Ref ST499 388. 50 yds from the Market Cross, in centre of Glastonbury. M5/J23, A39, follow signs to Glastonbury; M4/J18 to Bath, A367 to Shepton Mallet and A361 to Glastonbury; M3/J8 A303 and head for Glastonbury. **Owner:** Glastonbury Abbey Estate
**Tel:** 01458 832267 **Fax:** 01458 836117 **E-mail:** info@glastonburyabbey.com
**Open:** Daily except Christmas Day. Nov-Feb 9am-4pm. Mar-May 9am-6pm. Jun-Aug 9am-8pm. Sep-Oct 9am-6pm. **Admission:** Adult £7.00*, Child (5-15) £4.00, Conc £6.00* Family (2+3) £18.00* *Gift Aid admission price.
**Key facts:** 🏛 ♿ 🍴 Summer. 📷 Mar-Oct (groups pre-book Nov-Feb). 🅿 Pay & display car parks nearby. 🎓 Primary to University, RE, History, tailormade workshops & activities 01458 8361103. 🐕 On leads. ⚜ Except Xmas Day. 🏨

# ROBIN HOODS HUT
## Halswell, Goathurst, Somerset  TA5 2EW
www.landmarktrust.org.uk

An 18th Century garden building with two faces, a rustic cottage and an elegant pavillion.

**Location:** Map 2:M4. OS Ref ST255 333.
**Owner:** The Landmark Trust
**Tel:** 01628 825925
**E-mail:** bookings@landmarktrust.org.uk
**Open:** 6 Open Days per year, visits by appointment.
**Admission:** Free on Open Days and visits by appointment.
**Key facts:** ℹ You may dine al fresco beneath the elegant canopy of the umbrello whilst admiring the fine views. The bathroom is housed in a separate building a few metres away from the bedroom door.
🅿 🎡 🎨 ⚜ 🏨

# MAUNSEL HOUSE 🏛
## North Newton, Nr Taunton, Somerset  TA7 0BU
www.maunselhouse.co.uk

Maunsel House is a magnificent 13th Century Manor set in 100 acres of stunning parkland at the heart of a sprawling 2,000 acre Estate comprising of lakes, orchards, Somerset wetlands, walnut groves, cottages and ancient barns. Available for luxury weddings, house hire, celebration parties, conferences, film shoots and photo shoots.

**Location:** Map 2:M4. OS Ref ST302 303. Bridgwater 4m, Bristol 20m, Taunton 7m, M5/J24, A38 to North Petherton.
**Owner:** Sir Benjamin Slade Bt
**Contact:** The Events Team
**Tel:** 01278 661076 **E-mail:** info@maunselhouse.co.uk
**Open:** Office hours are: Monday-Friday 9am-5pm.
Pre-booked viewings only. Coaches & groups welcome by appointment.
Caravan rally field available.
**Admission:** Price on application.
**Key facts:** 🍴 Functions. ♿ WCs 🅿 🎨 🏛 ⚜ 🏨

# STOBERRY HOUSE
## Stoberry Park, Wells, Somerset  BA5 3LD
www.stoberry-park.co.uk

Enjoy one of Stoberry's several special luxurious cream teas within this 6 acre garden planted sympathetically, which provides a stunning combination of vistas. Stroll around the 1.5 acre walled garden with a glass of wine or celebrate a birthday amidst sculptures in the sunken garden. Watch the sunset sitting in the secluded gazebo, wander up the romantic lime walk or picnic by the garden lake overlooking Wells, Glastonbury Tor and the Vale of Avalon. At night, enjoy the contrast of light and shadow on the plants and sculptures.

**Location:** Map 2:O4. OS Ref ST553 914. Within walking distance of Wells. From Bristol / Bath enter Wells on the A39; take first left turn into College Road; then immediately left into Stoberry Park.
**Owner:** Frances and Tim Meeres Young **Contact:** Frances Meeres Young
**Tel:** 01749 672906 **E-mail:** stay@stoberry-park.co.uk
**Open:** Open by appointment; garden guided tours can be arranged for groups.
**Admission:** Adult £5.00; Children under 12 free; enjoy a special Afternoon tea, champagne luxury teas, special cream tea, chocolate, savoury or Gentleman's tea. **Key facts:** ℹ Wedding receptions - see website www.stoberry-park.co.uk for details. 🎨 🍴 🛏 Licensed. 🅿 Ample. 🏨 All rooms en suite. ⚜ 🏨

## ALL SAINTS' CHURCH
**The Hill, Langport, Somerset TA10 9QF**

All Saints, built mainly in the 15th and 16th Centuries, stands on a hill near the River Parrett, overlooking the remains of a Benedictine abbey. Its bold, pinnacled west tower, covered with gargoyles known locally as 'Hunky Punks', is a local landmark. However, the church's special treasure is its east window, containing the largest collection of medieval stained glass in Somerset. The saints are shown in gloriously coloured robes with both animated and serene expressions.
**Location:** OS Ref ST423 267. 14 miles east of Taunton and 4 miles north east of Somerton off A378.
**Contact:** Please call The Churches Conservation Trust on 0845 303 2760 (Mon-Fri, 9am–5pm)
**Website:** www.visitchurches.org.uk
**Open:** Keyholders nearby. Open every other Wednesday from 7pm-9pm.

## FAIRFIELD
**Stogursey, Bridgwater, Somerset TA5 1PU**

Elizabethan and medieval house. Occupied by the same family (Acland-Hoods and their ancestors) for over 800 years. Woodland garden. Views of Quantocks and the sea. House described in Simon Jenkins' book 'England's Thousand Best Houses'.
**Location:** Map 2:L4. OS Ref ST187 430. 11m W Bridgwater, 8m E Williton. From A39 Bridgwater/Minehead turn North. House 1m W Stogursey.
**Tel:** 01278 732251
**Open:** 9-17 Apr, 21 Apr-26 May, 4-20 June Wed, Thur, Fri & BH Mon. Guided house tours at 2.30 & 3.30pm. Garden also open.
**Admission:** £6.00 in aid of Stogursey Church. Advisable to contact to confirm dates.
**Key facts:** ℹ No inside photography. 🖼 🎦 Obligatory. 🅿 No coach parking. ♿ Guide dogs only.

## GATCOMBE COURT
**Flax Bourton, North Somerset BS48 3QT**

This is an ancient Somerset Manor House built in the mid 13th Century by John de Gatcombe using stone from the Roman town on which it stands. The evolution is shown in the walls as described by Simon Jenkins in his book England's 1000 best houses. Occupied by the same family since 1922 we tell the story of the house's development and of the Roman inspired herb garden (with tastings!). It is surrounded by terraced gardens with old yew hedges and roses.
**Location:** Map 2:N2. OS Ref ST525 698. 4 miles West of Bristol
**Tel:** 01275 393141 / 07729729231 / 07546398901
**E-mail:** info@gatcombecourt.co.uk
**Website:** www.gatcombecourt.co.uk
**Open:** Open to groups 15 – 50 by appointment. Also Bed and Breakfast.
**Key facts:** 🖼 Farm shop. ♿ Ground floor and gardens. ☕ Tea, coffee and cake served after tour. 🍴 Carvery nearby. 🅿 🛏 B&B in one wing of the house.

## ST JAMES' CHURCH
**Cameley, Temple Cloud, Bristol
Somerset BS39 5AH**

Set in a fold of the Mendip hills, in the valley of the River Cam, St James' is an unpretentious and delightful church. This beautiful hillside landmark, with an impressive 15th Century tower built of warm red Mendip sandstone with a handsome parapet, assaults the senses and contrasts with the humbler local blue lias limestone of the rest of the church. Inside you are immediately struck by fabulous wall paintings from the 12th to the 17th Centuries. Fragments that have been identified, including the fine early 17th Century Ten Commandments over the chancel arch, framed in twining leaves with enchanting cherubs' faces peering out. There are medieval benches as well as Georgian pews, an early 17th Century pulpit, a west gallery dating from 1711 and a south gallery from 1819 inscribed in handsome lettering 'for the free use of the inhabitants'. **Location:** OS Ref ST610 576. 10 miles north east of Wells, off A37 (1 mile west from Temple Cloud) and 6 miles north west of Midsomer Norton.
**Website:** www.visitchurches.org.uk **Open:** Open daily from mid April.

## ST NICHOLAS' CHURCH
**Brockley, Backwell, Somerset BS48 3AU**

Brockley church developed from a small Norman building in the 12th and 13th Centuries.
Its fine pinnacled tower was added in the 15th Century but it owes much of its present furnishings and atmosphere to a thorough and graceful restoration in the 1820s.
The south transept has a spacious family pew with separate entrance and a fireplace, added by the Pigotts whose association with the parish lasted 300 years. There is a Norman font and a stone pulpit of c1480 and a pirate's gravestone in the churchyard.
**Location:** OS Ref ST466 670. 9 miles north east of Weston-super-Mare and 3 miles south of Nailsea, off A370.
**Website:** www.visitchurches.org.uk
**Open:** Keyholder nearby.

## DODINGTON HALL
**Nr Nether Stowey, Bridgwater, Somerset TA5 1LF**

Small Tudor manor house on the lower slopes of the Quantocks. Great Hall with oak roof. Semi-formal garden with roses and shrubs.
**Location:** Map 2:L4. OS Ref ST172 405. ½m from A39, 11m W of Bridgwater, 7m E of Williton. **Tel:** 01278 741400 **Open:** 2-12 June, 2-5pm.
**Admission:** Donations to Dodington Church. No coach parking.

## KENTSFORD
**Washford, Watchet, Somerset TA23 0JD**
**Location:** Map 2:L4. OS Ref ST058 426.
**Tel:** 01984 632309 **E-mail:** wyndhamest@btconnect.com
**Open:** Please contact for details.
**Admission:** Please contact for details.

## MILTON LODGE GARDENS 🏛️
**Old Bristol Road, Wells, Somerset BA5 3AQ**

Mature grade II listed terraced garden with stunning views of Wells Cathedral and the Vale of Avalon. **Location:** Map 2:O3. OS Ref ST549 470. ½m N of Wells from A39. **Website:** www.miltonlodgegardens.co.uk
**Open:** Easter-end Oct, Tues, Weds, Suns & BHs, 2-5pm. Coaches by prior arrangement. **Admission:** Adult £5.00, Children under 14 Free.

## ORCHARD WYNDHAM 🏛️
**Williton, Taunton, Somerset TA4 4HH**

English manor house. Family home for 700 years encapsulating continuous building and alteration from the 14th to the 20th Century.
**Location:** Map 2:L4. OS Ref ST072 400. 1m from A39 at Williton.
**Tel:** 01984 632309 **E-mail:** wyndhamest@btconnect.com **Open:** Please telephone for details. **Admission:** Please telephone for details.

## WOODLANDS CASTLE
**Ruishton, Taunton, Somerset TA3 5LU**

Woodlands is available for private functions from weddings and conferences to barbecues, birthdays and wakes.
**Tel:** 01823 444955 **E-mail:** info@woodlandscastle.co.uk
**Website:** www.woodlandscastle.co.uk
**Open:** All year to private bookings only. **Admission:** No admission.

## WILTON HOUSE 🏛ⓕ
### WILTON, SALISBURY  SP2 0BJ
www.wiltonhouse.com

Wilton House has been the Earl of Pembroke's ancestral home for 460 years. Inigo Jones and John Webb rebuilt the house in the Palladian style after the 1647 fire whilst further alterations were made by James Wyatt from 1801. Recipient of the 2010 HHA/Sotheby's Restoration Award, the chief architectural features are the 17th Century state apartments (Single and Double Cube rooms), and the 19th Century cloisters. The House contains one of the finest art collections in Europe and is set in magnificent landscaped parkland featuring the Palladian Bridge. A large adventure playground provides hours of fun for younger visitors.

**Location:** Map 3:B4. OS Ref SU099 311. 3m W of Salisbury along the A36.
**Owner:** The Earl of Pembroke  **Contact:** The Estate Office
**Tel:** 01722 746714  **Fax:** 01722 744447  **E-mail:** tourism@wiltonhouse.com
**Open:** House: 18 Apr-21 Apr inclusive, 3 May-31 Aug Sun-Thu plus BH Sats, 11.30am-5pm, last admission 4.30pm. Please check website for up to date information. Grounds: 6 Apr-21 Apr, 3 May–14 Sept daily, 11.00am-5.30pm. Private groups at other times by arrangement.
**Admission:** House & Grounds*: Adult £14.50, Child (5-15) £7.50, Concession £11.50, Family £34.00 *includes admission to Dining & South Ante Rooms when open. Grounds: Adult £6.00, Child (5-15) £4.50, Concession £5.50, Family £17.00. Group Admission: Adult £12.50, Child £6.00, Concession £9.50. Guided Tour: £6.50. Exhibition: "Cecil Beaton at Wilton". A new exhibition of photographs from The Cecil Beaton Studio Archive at Sotheby's. Opening in April 2014. **Key facts:** ⓘ Film location, equestrian events, antiques fairs, vehicle rallies. No photography in house. ▣ Open 7 days a week during the season. ♿ WCs. ▣ Licensed. ⏹ Licensed. Ⓕ By arrangement. £6.50. French, German and Spanish. Ⓟ 200 cars & 12 coaches. Free coach parking. Group rates (min 15), drivers' meal voucher. ▣ National Curriculum KS1/2. Sandford Award Winner 2002 & 2008. ▣ Guide dogs only. ▲ ▼

## CORSHAM COURT 🏛ⓕ
### Corsham, Wiltshire  SN13 0BZ
www.corsham-court.co.uk

Corsham Court is a splendid Elizabethan house dating from 1582. An internationally renowned collection of Old Masters hangs in the magnificent Picture Gallery and suite of State Rooms. Delightful gardens and parkland, designed by Brown and Repton, surround the Court.
**Location:** Map 3:A2. OS Ref ST874 706. Signposted from the A4, approx. 4m W of Chippenham. **Owner:** J Methuen-Campbell Esq **Contact:** The Curator
**Tel:** 01249 712214 / 01249 701610.
**E-mail:** staterooms@corsham-court.co.uk
**Open:** Spring/Summer 20 Mar-30 Sep. Daily, except Mon & Fri but inc Bank Holidays 2-5.30pm. Last adm 5pm. Winter 1 Oct-19 Mar (closed Dec) w/e only 2-4.30pm. Last adm 4pm. Throughout year by appointment for groups.
**Admission:** Adult £10, Child (5-15yrs) £5, Family (2 adults & 2 children) £25. Garden only Adult £5, Child (5-15yrs) £2.50. **Key facts:** ⓘ No photography in house. ▣ Guide books, postcards, etc at cash desk. ♿ Platform lift & WC. Ⓕ Max 45. If requested the owner may meet the group. Morning tours preferred. Ⓟ 120yds from house. Coaches may park in Church Square. Coach parties must book in advance. ▣ Available: rate negotiable. A guide will be provided. ▣ ▣

## LONGLEAT 🏛ⓕ
### Longleat, Warminster, Wiltshire  BA12 7NW
www.longleat.co.uk

Set in the magnificent Wiltshire countryside, Longleat House is widely regarded as one of the best examples of high Elizabethan architecture in Britain and one of the most beautiful stately homes open to the public.
Longleat House is a unique and inspiring venue for dinners, conferences, meetings, weddings and receptions.
**Location:** Map 2:P4. OS Ref ST809 430. Just off the A36 between Bath-Salisbury (A362 Warminster-Frome). 2hrs from London following M3, A303, A36, A362 or M4/J18, A46, A36.
**Owner:** Marquess of Bath  **Tel:** 01985 844328
**E-mail:** sales@longleat.co.uk
**Open:** Please see www.longleat.co.uk to confirm opening dates and times to avoid disappointment. Open for pre-booked groups of 12 + from Sat 8 Feb 2014 and throughout the year.
**Admission:** Group Prices for 12 + for Longleat House only - Adult £10.00, Child £6.50, Senior £7.50. For great online discounts for standard tickets please visit www.longleat.co.uk.
**Key facts:** ⓘ ▣ ▣ ♿ ▣ ▣ ⏹ Ⓕ Ⓟ ▣ ▣ ▲ ▼

## LYDIARD PARK 🏛
### Lydiard Tregoze, Swindon, Wiltshire  SN5 3PA
www.lydiardpark.org.uk

Lydiard Park is the ancestral home of the Viscounts Bolingbroke. The Palladian house contains original family furnishings and portraits, exceptional plasterwork and rare 17th Century window. The Georgian ornamental Walled Garden has beautiful seasonal displays of flowers and unique garden features. Exceptional monuments, including the Golden Cavalier, in the church.
**Location:** Map 3:B1. OS Ref SU104 848. 4m W of Swindon, 1½m N M4/J16.
**Owner:** Swindon Borough Council **Contact:** Lydiard Park Manager
**Tel:** 01793 770401 **E-mail:** lydiardpark@swindon.gov.uk
**Open:** House & Walled Garden: Tues-Sun, 11am-5pm (4pm Nov-Feb).
Grounds: all day, closing at dusk. Victorian Christmas decorations in Dec.
**Admission:** House & Walled Garden: Adult £4.70, Senior Citizen £4.20, Child £2.30* Pre- booked groups: Adult £4.20, Senior Citizen £3.70* *May change April 2014 **Key facts:** ℹ️ No photography in house. 🎁 Small gift shop. 🌱 Selection seasonal plants available to buy. 🅿️ Designated parking. WCs. 🍴 Forest Cafe open all year, Coach House Tea Rooms closed winter. 🎭 By arrangement. 🅿️ Free parking, limit parking for coaches. 🏫 Full programme of school sessions linked to National Curriculum. 🐕 In grounds only. ❄️ ♿

## THE MERCHANT'S HOUSE
### 132 High Street, Marlborough, Wiltshire  SN8 1HN
www.themerchantshouse.co.uk

The Merchant's House was built in 1653 following the Great Fire of Marlborough. It is a fine timber and brick building, with panelled interiors, original wall paintings and a commanding oak staircase. The ongoing restoration makes the House a special and unusual place to visit.
**Location:** Map 3:B2. OS Ref SU188 691. N side of High Street, near Town Hall.
**Owner:** Marlborough Town Council, leased to The Merchant's House (Marlborough) Trust
**Contact:** Sophie Costard **Tel:** 01672 511491
**E-mail:** admin@merchantshousetrust.co.uk
**Open:** Apr-end Oct Tue, Fri and Sat, guided tours 10.30am, 12noon, 1.30pm and 3pm. Group bookings by application.
**Admission:** Adult £6.00, Child £1.00.
**Key facts:** ℹ️ Photography only by arrangement. 🎁 ♿ Limited. 🎭 See website. 🅿️ In the High Street and public car parks in Marlborough. 🏫 Phone for details 🐕 Guide dogs only. ♿

The Merchant's House

## MOMPESSON HOUSE 🌿
### Cathedral Close, Salisbury, Wiltshire  SP1 2EL
www.nationaltrust.org.uk

Elegant, spacious house in the Cathedral Close, built 1701. Featured in award-winning film Sense and Sensibility. Magnificent plasterwork and fine oak staircase. Good period furniture and the Turnbull collection of 18th Century drinking glasses. The delightful walled garden has a pergola and traditional herbaceous borders. Garden Tea Room serves light refreshments. For 2014 Contemporary sculpture, including works by Elisabeth Frink, throughout the house and garden **Location:** Map 3:B4. OS Ref SU142 297. On N side of Choristers' Green in Cathedral Close, near High Street Gate.
**Owner:** National Trust **Contact:** The Property Manager
**Tel:** 01722 335659 **Fax:** 01722 321559 **Infoline:** 01722 420980
**E-mail:** mompessonhouse@nationaltrust.org.uk
**Open:** 15 Mar-2 Nov: Sat-Wed, 11am-5pm. Last admission 4.30pm. Open Good Fri. **Admission:** *Adult £6.30, Child £3.15, Family (2+3) £15.75, Groups £5.10. Garden only: £1.00. Tearoom vouchers when arriving by public transport. *includes voluntary donation, visitors can pay standard prices.
**Key facts:** 🎁 ♿ WCs. ♿ 🎭 By arrangement. 🏫 🐕 Guide dogs only. ♿

## THE PETO GARDEN AT IFORD MANOR 🏛Ⓕ
### Bradford-on-Avon, Wiltshire BA15 2BA
www.ifordmanor.co.uk

Unique Grade-1 Italian-style garden set on a romantic hillside above the River Frome. Designed by Edwardian architect Harold Peto, who lived at Iford from 1899-1933, the garden features terraces, colonnades, cloisters, casita, statuary, evergreen planting and magnificent rural views. Winner of the 1998 HHA/Christie's Garden of the Year Award.

**Location:** Map 2:P3. OS Ref ST800 589. 7m SE of Bath via A36, signposted Iford. 1½m SW of Bradford-on-Avon via B3109.
**Owner/Contact:** Mrs E A J Cartwright-Hignett
**Tel:** 01225 863146
**E-mail:** info@ifordmanor.co.uk
**Open:** Apr-Sep: Tue-Thu, Sat, Sun & BH Mons, 2-5pm. Oct: Sun only, 2-5pm. Tearoom at weekends May-Sep. Children under 10yrs preferred weekdays only for safety reasons.
**Admission:** Adult £5.00, Conc. £4.50. Groups (10+) welcome for exclusive use outside normal opening hours, by arrangement only.
**Key facts:** ℹ No professional photography without permission. ♿ Partial. WCs. ☕ 🅿 Limited for coaches. 🐕 On leads. ♿

The Peto Garden at Iford Manor

## ALL SAINTS' CHURCH 🏛
### Alton Priors, Salisbury, Wiltshire SN8 4LB
The Perpendicular tower of this lovely Medieval church dominates surrounding fields. It stands just across the stream from St Mary's at Alton Barnes, and the churchyard yew tree is said to be 1700 years old! Inside it is lime-washed and barn-like, with big rustic roof trusses and open timbering. The chancel arch is all that remains of the church's Norman past. The rest of the church dates from late-medieval times, except for the body of the chancel which was rebuilt in the 19th Century. The church still contains Jacobean pews, unusually tall communion rails and a 1590 tomb. A mysterious trapdoor conceals a buried Sarsen stone (a sandstone block).
**Location:** OS Ref SU109 622. 8 miles west of Marlborough, off A345.
**Contact:** Please call The Churches Conservation Trust on 020 7213 0660 (Mon-Fri, 9am–5pm) for key holder information
**Website:** www.visitchurches.org.uk
**Open:** Open daily from Apr to Oct; at other times keyholder nearby.

## CHURCH OF ST JOHN THE BAPTIST 🏛
### Inglesham, Swindon, Wiltshire SN6 7RD
www.visitchurches.org.uk

This exquisitely beautiful and fascinating 13th Century church stands on a gentle rise of land above waterside meadows near the Thames. Pioneering Victorian designer William Morris oversaw St John's restoration in the 19th Century. An amazing series of paintings, from the 13th-19th Century cover the walls often with one painted over another. While it is not always easy to puzzle out the subjects, you can see 15th Century angels above the chancel arch, an early 14th Century doom on the east wall of the north aisle and several 19th Century texts. There is an unusual and powerful Saxon stone carving of the Madonna and Child set in the south wall. The woodwork of the roofs, the 15th Century screens and the 17th and 18th Century pulpit and box pews are all original to the church, and their arrangement is still much as it would have been in Oliver Cromwell's time.
**Location:** OS Ref SU205 984. 1 mile south of Lechlade, off A361.
**Open:** Open daily.

## ST PETER'S CHURCH 🏛
### Everleigh, Marlborough, Wiltshire SN8 3HD
Built by John Morlidge of London for the Astley family in 1813 in the Gothic style, St Peter's was one of the first churches to be constructed with an iron frame.
The short chancel and narrow nave, the elegant west gallery and hammerbeam roof all emphasise its loftiness.
The church retains many of its original fittings and has monuments to the Astley family, including an enormous tablet to Francis Dugdale Astley, founder of the church, who died in 1818. There is also a ring of six bells.
**Location:** OS Ref SU198 541. 11 miles north west of Andover and 5 miles east of Upavon, on A342.
**Website:** www.visitchurches.org.uk
**Open:** Open daily.

## NEWHOUSE 🏛Ⓕ
### Redlynch, Salisbury, Wiltshire SP5 2NX
A brick, Jacobean 'Trinity' House, c1609, with two Georgian wings and a basically Georgian interior. **Location:** Map 3:B5. OS Ref SU218 214. 9m S of Salisbury between A36 & A338. **Tel:** 01725 510055 **E-mail:** events@newhouseestate.co.uk **Website:** www.newhouseestate.co.uk **Open:** 3 Mar-9 Apr, Mon-Fri & 25 Aug: 2-5pm. **Admission:** Adult £5.00, Child £3.00, Conc. £5.00. Groups (15+): Adult £4.00, Child £3.00, Conc. £4.00.

## NORRINGTON MANOR
### Alvediston, Salisbury, Wiltshire SP5 5LL
Built in 1377 it has been altered and added to in every century since, with the exception of the 18th Century. **Location:** Map 3:A5. OS Ref ST966 237. Signposted to N of Berwick St John and Alvediston road (half way between the two villages). **Tel:** 01722 780 259 **Open:** By appointment in writing.
**Admission:** A donation to the local churches is asked for.

**CHYSAUSTER ANCIENT VILLAGE** ⌗
Nr Newmill, Penzance, Cornwall TR20 8XA
**Tel:** 07831 757934 **E-mail:** customers@english-heritage.org.uk

**COTEHELE** ⚜
Saint Dominick, Saltash, Cornwall PL12 6TA
**Tel:** 01579 351346 **E-mail:** cothele@nationaltrust.org.uk

**LAUNCESTON CASTLE** ⌗
Castle Lodge, Launceston, Cornwall PL15 7DR
**Tel:** 01566 772365 **E-mail:** customers@english-heritage.org.uk

**PENDENNIS CASTLE** ⌗
Falmouth, Cornwall TR11 4LP
**Tel:** 01326 316594 **E-mail:** pendennis.castle@english-heritage.org.uk

**RESTORMEL CASTLE** ⌗
Lostwithiel, Cornwall PL22 0EE
**Tel:** 01208 872687 **E-mail:** customers@english-heritage.org.uk

**ST MAWES CASTLE** ⌗
St Mawes, Cornwall TR2 5DE
**Tel:** 01326 270526 **E-mail:** stmawes.castle@english-heritage.org.uk

**THE LOST GARDENS OF HELIGAN**
Pentewan, St Austall, Cornwall PL26 6EN
**Tel:** 01726 845100 **E-mail:** info@heligan.com

**TREBAH GARDEN** 🏛
Mawnan Smith, Nr Falmouth, Cornwall TR11 5JZ
**Tel:** 01326 252200 **E-mail:** mail@trebah-garden.co.uk

**TREWIDDEN**
Buryas Bridge, Nr Penzance, Cornwall TR20 8TT
**Tel:** 01736 351979 **E-mail:** mail@bolithoestates.co.uk

**BERRY POMEROY CASTLE** ⌗
Totnes, Devon TQ9 6LJ
**Tel:** 01803 866618 **E-mail:** customers@english-heritage.org.uk

**CASTLE DROGO** ⚜
Drewsteignton, Nr Exeter EX6 6PB
**Tel:** 01647 433306 **E-mail:** castledrogo@nationaltrust.org.uk

**CH. OF ST PETER THE POOR FISHERMAN** ⛪
Stoke Beach, Noss Mayo, Revelstoke, Plymouth PL8 1HE
**Tel:** 0845 303 2760 **E-mail:** central@thecct.org.uk

**DARTMOUTH CASTLE** ⌗
Castle Road, Dartmouth, Devon TQ6 0JN
**Tel:** 01803 833588 **E-mail:** dartmouth.castle@english-heritage.org.uk

**RHS GARDEN ROSEMOOR**
Great Torrington, Devon EX38 8PH
**Tel:** 01805 624067 **E-mail:** rosemooradmin@rhs.org.uk

**ST JAMES' CHURCH** ⛪
Luffincott, Tetcott, Holsworthy, Devon EX22 6RB
**Tel:** 0845 303 2760 **E-mail:** central@thecct.org.uk

**ST MARY'S CHURCH** ⛪
North Huish, South Brent, Devon TQ10 9NQ
**Tel:** 0845 303 2760 **E-mail:** central@thecct.org.uk

**ST NONNA'S CHURCH** ⛪
Bradstone, Tavistock, Devon PL19 0QS
**Tel:** 0845 303 2760 **E-mail:** central@thecct.org.uk

**ST PETER'S CHURCH** ⛪
Satterleigh, Umberleigh, Devon EX37 9DJ
**Tel:** 0845 303 2760 **E-mail:** central@thecct.org.uk

**TOTNES CASTLE** ⌗
Castle Street, Totnes, Devon TQ9 5NU
**Tel:** 01803 864406 **E-mail:** customers@english-heritage.org.uk

**UGBROOKE PARK** 🏛Ⓔ
Chudleigh, Devon TQ13 0AD
**Tel:** 01626 852179 **E-mail:** cliffordestate@btconnect.com

**ABBOTSBURY SUBTROPICAL GARDENS** ⊗ 🏛Ⓔ
Abbotsbury, Weymouth, Dorset DT3 4LA
**Tel:** 01305 871387 **E-mail:** info@abbotsbury- tourism.co.uk

**ALL SAINTS' CHURCH** ⛪
Nether Cerne, Dorchester, Dorset DT2 7AJ
**Tel:** 0845 303 2760 **E-mail:** central@thecct.org.uk

**CHETTLE HOUSE**
Chettle, Blandford Forum, Dorset DT11 8DB
**Tel:** 01258 830858 **E-mail:** enquiries@chettlehouse.co.uk

**DEANS COURT GARDENS** 🏛Ⓔ
2 Deans Court Lane, Wimborne, Dorset BH21 1EE
**Tel:** 01202 880515 **E-mail:** deanscourtestateoffice@deanscourt.org

**FORDE ABBEY & GARDENS** 🏛Ⓔ
Forde Abbey, Chard, Somerset TA20 4LU
**Tel:** 01460 221290 **E-mail:** info@fordeabbey.co.uk

**HOLY TRINITY OLD CHURCH** ⛪
Old Church Road, Bothenhampton, Bridport, Dorset DT6 4BP
**Tel:** 0845 303 2760 **E-mail:** central@thecct.org.uk

**PORTLAND CASTLE** ⌗
Castletown, Portland, Weymouth, Dorset DT5 1AZ
**Tel:** 01305 820539 **E-mail:** customers@english-heritage.org.uk

**ST ANDREW'S CHURCH** ⛪
Off Marsh Lane, Winterborne Tomson, Dorset DT11 9HA
**Tel:** 0845 303 2760 **E-mail:** central@thecct.org.uk

**ST CUTHBERT OLD CHANCEL** ⛪
London Road, Oborne, Sherborne, Dorset DT9 4JY
**Tel:** 0845 303 2760 **E-mail:** central@thecct.org.uk

**ST EDWOLD'S CHURCH** ⛪
Stockwood, Evershot, Dorchester, Dorset DT2 0NG
**Tel:** 0845 303 2760 **E-mail:** central@thecct.org.uk

**SMEDMORE HOUSE** 🏛
Smedmore , Kimmeridge, Wareham BH20 5PG
**Tel:** 01929 480719 **E-mail:** office@smedmore–caravansite.co.uk

**ALL SAINTS' CHURCH** ⛪
Shorncote, Cirencester, Gloucestershire GL7 6DE
**Tel:** 0845 303 2760 **E-mail:** central@thecct.org.uk

**BERKELEY CASTLE** 🏠ⓔ
Berkeley Castle, Berkeley, Gloucestershire  GL13 9BQ
**Tel:** 01453 810303 **E-mail:** info@berkeley-castle.com

**CHURCH OF ST NICHOLAS OF MYRA** 🏠
Ozleworth, Wotton-Under-Edge, Gloucestershire  GL12 7QA
**Tel:** 0845 303 2760 **E-mail:** central@thecct.org.uk

**CIRENCESTER PARK GARDENS** 🏠
Cirencester, Glocestershire  GL7 2BU
**Tel:** 01285 653135

**HAILES ABBEY** ⌗
Nr Winchcombe, Cheltenham, Gloucestershire  GL54 5PB
**Tel:** 01242 602398 **E-mail:** customers@english-heritage.org.uk

**KELMSCOTT MANOR** 🏠ⓔ
KELMSCOTT, Nr LECHLADE, GLOUCESTERSHIRE  GL7 3HJ
**Tel:** 01367 252486 **E-mail:** admin@kelmscottmanor.org.uk

**ST ARILD'S CHURCH** 🏠
Oldbury-on-the-Hill, Badminton, Gloucestershire  GL9 1EA
**Tel:** 0845 303 2760 **E-mail:** central@thecct.org.uk

**ST MARY'S CHURCH** 🏠
Little Washbourne, Tewkesbury, Gloucestershire  GL20 8NQ
**Tel:** 0845 303 2760 **E-mail:** central@thecct.org.uk

**ST MARY'S CHURCH** 🏠
Shipton Sollars, Cheltenham, Gloucestershire  GL54 4HU
**Tel:** 0845 303 2760 **E-mail:** central@thecct.org.uk

**ST MICHAEL & ST MARTIN'S CHURCH** 🏠
Eastleach Martin, Cirencester, Gloucestershire  GL7 3NN
**Tel:** 0845 303 2760 **E-mail:** central@thecct.org.uk

**ST OSWALD'S TOWER** 🏠
Lassington Lane, Highnam, Gloucester  GL2 8DH
**Tel:** 0845 303 2760 **E-mail:** central@thecct.org.uk

**ST SWITHUN'S CHURCH** 🏠
Stroud Road, Brookthorpe, Gloucester  GL4 0UJ
**Tel:** 0845 303 2760 **E-mail:** central@thecct.org.uk

**ST PAUL'S CHURCH** 🏠
Portland Square, Bristol  BS2 8SJ
**Tel:** 0845 303 2760 **E-mail:** central@thecct.org.uk

**ACTON COURT** 🏠ⓔ
Latteridge Road, Iton Acton, Bristol, Gloucestershire  BS37 9TL
**Tel:** 01454 228 224 **E-mail:** info@actoncourt.com

**ALL SAINTS' CHURCH** 🏠
Otterhampton, Bridgwater, Somerset  TA5 2PT
**Tel:** 0845 303 2760 **E-mail:** central@thecct.org.uk

**CHURCH OF ST MARTIN OF TOURS** 🏠
Silverdown Hill, Elworthy, Taunton, Somerset  TA4 3PY
**Tel:** 0845 303 2760 **E-mail:** central@thecct.org.uk

**CHURCH OF ST THOMAS A BECKET** 🏠
Old Road, Pensford, Bristol, Somerset  BS39 4AL
**Tel:** 0845 303 2760 **E-mail:** central@thecct.org.uk

**CHURCH OF THE BLESSED VIRGIN MARY** 🏠
Chapel Hill, Emborough, Wells, Somerset  BA3 4SG
**Tel:** 0845 303 2760 **E-mail:** central@thecct.org.uk

**COMBE SYDENHAM HALL** 🏠ⓔ
Monksilver , Taunton, Somerset  TA4 4JG
**Tel:** 0800 7838572

**COTHAY MANOR & GARDENS**
Greenham, Wellington, Somerset  TA21 0JR
**Tel:** 01823 672283 **E-mail:** cothaymanor@btinternet.com

**FARLEIGH HUNGERFORD CASTLE** ⌗
Farleigh Hungerford, Bath, Somerset  BA2 7RS
**Tel:** 01225 754026 **E-mail:** customers@english-heritage.org.uk

**FLEET AIR ARM MUSEUM**
RNAS Yeovilton, Ilchester, Somerset  BA22 8HT
**Tel:** 01935 840565 **E-mail:** marketing@fleetairarm.com

**HOLY SAVIOUR'S CHURCH** 🏠
Puxton, Hewish, Weston-Super-Mare, Somerset  BS24 6TF
**Tel:** 0845 303 2760 **E-mail:** central@thecct.org.uk

**KILVER COURT SECRET GARDENS** Ⓡ
Kilver Street, Shepton Mallet, Somerset  BA4 5NF
**Tel:** 01749 340410 **E-mail:** info@kilvercourt.com

**NO 1 ROYAL CRESCENT**
Bath  BA1 2LR
**Tel:** 01225 428126 **E-mail:** admin@bptrust.org.uk

**ST ANDREW'S CHURCH** 🏠
Roman Road, Northover, Yeovil, Somerset  BA22 8JR
**Tel:** 0845 303 2760 **E-mail:** central@thecct.org.uk

**ST ANDREW'S CHURCH** 🏠
Holcombe, Radstock, Somerset  BA3 5ES
**Tel:** 0845 303 2760 **E-mail:** central@thecct.org.uk

**ST MARY'S CHURCH** 🏠
Church Lane, Seavington, Ilminster, Somerset  TA19 0QP
**Tel:** 0845 303 2760 **E-mail:** central@thecct.org.uk

**ST MARY'S CHURCH** 🏠
Owl Street Lane, Stocklinch Ottersey, Ilminster  TA19 9JN
**Tel:** 0845 303 2760 **E-mail:** central@thecct.org.uk

**ST NICHOLAS' CHURCH** 🏠
Uphill Way, Uphill, Weston-Super-Mare, Somerset  BS23 4TN
**Tel:** 0845 303 2760 **E-mail:** central@thecct.org.uk

**ST THOMAS' CHURCH** 🏠
Thurlbear, Taunton, Somerset  TA3 5BW
**Tel:** 0845 303 2760 **E-mail:** central@thecct.org.uk

**ALL SAINTS' CHURCH** 🏠
Leigh, Cricklade, Wiltshire  SN6 6QY
**Tel:** 0845 303 2760 **E-mail:** central@thecct.org.uk

**ALL SAINTS' CHURCH** 🏠
Idmiston, Salisbury, Wiltshire  SP4 0AU
**Tel:** 0845 303 2760 **E-mail:** central@thecct.org.uk

### BORBACH CHANTRY
**Off Rectory Hill, West Dean, Salisbury, Wiltshire  SP5 1JJ**
**Tel:** 0845 303 2760 **E-mail:** central@thecct.org.uk

### CHURCH OF ST MARGARET OF ANTIOCH
**Leigh Delamere, Chippenham, Wiltshire  SN14 6JZ**
**Tel:** 0845 303 2760 **E-mail:** central@thecct.org.uk

### CHURCH OF ST MARY & ST LAWRENCE
**Stratford Tony, Salisbury, Wiltshire  SP5 4AT**
**Tel:** 0845 303 2760 **E-mail:** central@thecct.org.uk

### HAMPTWORTH LODGE
**Hamptworth, Landford, Salisbury, Wiltshire  SP5 2EA**
**Tel:** 01794 390700 **E-mail:** enquiries@hamptworthestate.co.uk

### HEALE HOUSE GARDENS
**Heale House, Middle Woodford, Salisbury, Wiltshire  SP4 6NT**
**Tel:** 01722 782504 **E-mail:** info@healegarden.co.uk

### OLD SARUM
**Castle Road, Salisbury, Wiltshire  SP1 3SD**
**Tel:** 01722 335398 **E-mail:** customers@english-heritage.org.uk

### OLD WARDOUR CASTLE
**Nr Tisbury, Wiltshire  SP3 6RR**
**Tel:** 01747 870487 **E-mail:** customers@english-heritage.org.uk

### ST ANDREW'S CHURCH
**Rollestone Road, Rollestone, Salisbury, Wiltshire  SP3 4HG**
**Tel:** 0845 303 2760 **E-mail:** central@thecct.org.uk

### ST GEORGE'S CHURCH
**Orcheston, Salisbury, Wiltshire  SP3 4HL**
**Tel:** 0845 303 2760 **E-mail:** central@thecct.org.uk

### ST GILES' CHURCH
**Imber, Warminster, Wiltshire**
**Tel:** 0845 303 2760 **E-mail:** central@thecct.org.uk

### ST LEONARD'S CHURCH
**Duck Street, Sutton Veny, Warminster, Wiltshire  BA12 7AL**
**Tel:** 0845 303 2760 **E-mail:** central@thecct.org.uk

### ST MARY'S CHURCH
**Shipton Road, South Tidworth, Tidworth, Wiltshire  SP9 7ST**
**Tel:** 0845 303 2760 **E-mail:** central@thecct.org.uk

### ST MARY'S CHURCH
**Old Dilton, Westbury, Wiltshire  BA13 4DB**
**Tel:** 0845 303 2760 **E-mail:** central@thecct.org.uk

### ST MARY'S CHURCH
**Chute Forest, Andover, Wiltshire  SP11 9DF**
**Tel:** 0845 303 2760 **E-mail:** central@thecct.org.uk

### ST MARY'S CHURCH
**Maddington, Shrewton, Salisbury, Wiltshire  SP3 4JE**
**Tel:** 0845 303 2760 **E-mail:** central@thecct.org.uk

### THE ABBEY HOUSE GARDENS
**Market Cross, Malmesbury, Wiltshire  SN16 9AS**
**Tel:** 01666 822212/827650 **E-mail:** info@abbeyhousegardens.co.uk

Church of St John the Baptist, Bristol

Elton Hall

Knebworth House

Bedfordshire
Cambridgeshire
Essex
Hertfordshire
Norfolk
Suffolk

# East of England

18th century reformers carved big estates out of the reclaimed lands of East Anglia, leaving great country houses to vie for attention with remote moated manors and great gardens thriving on the rich soils.

*New Entries for 2014:*
• Hindringham Hall & Gardens

221

## VISITOR INFORMATION

### ■ Owner
The Duke and Duchess of Bedford & The Trustees of the Bedford Estates

### ■ Address
Woburn
Bedfordshire
MK17 9WA

### ■ Location
**Map 7:D10**
**OS Ref. SP965 325**
Signposted from M1 J12/J13 and A412. Easy access from A5 via Hockliffe, follow signs to Woburn village.
**Rail:** London Euston to Leighton Buzzard, Bletchley/Milton Keynes. Kings Cross Thameslink to Flitwick.
**Air:** Luton 14m. Heathrow 39m. Please note there is no public transport to the Abbey.

### ■ Contact
Woburn Abbey
**Tel:** 01525 290333
**E-mail:**
admissions@woburn.co.uk

### ■ Opening Times
**Woburn Abbey, Gardens and Deer Park**
Please telephone or visit our website for details.

### ■ Admission
Please telephone or visit our website for details. Group rates available.

### ■ Special Events
**Events in 2014 include:**
The Woburn Abbey Garden Show 21/22 June. Classic car shows. Outdoor theatre performances. Horticulture study days. Children's activities during school holidays. Maze is open on Bank Holidays.

### Conference/Function

| ROOM | Size | Max Cap |
|------|------|---------|
| Sculpture Gallery | 128' x 24' | 300 Gallery 250 (sit-down) |
| Lantern Rm | 44' x 21' | 60 |
| Howland Rm | 58' x 21' | 50 |
| Russell Rm | 34' x 21' | 30 |

# WOBURN ABBEY

www.woburnabbey.co.uk

## Visit the home of Afternoon Tea to enjoy priceless treasures, uncover fascinating stories, and explore the beautiful gardens.

Set in a 3,000 acre deer park with nine free roaming species of deer, Woburn Abbey has been the home of the Russell Family for nearly 400 years, and is now home to the 15th Duke of Bedford and his family.

Touring the house reveals centuries of the family's stories and English history over three floors including the State Rooms, gold and silver vaults and porcelain display in the crypt. The stunning art collection includes over 250 pictures by artists such as Rembrandt, Gainsborough, Reynolds, Van Dyck and even Queen Victoria.

The Abbey also houses the largest private collection of Venetian views by Canaletto (pictured). The English tradition of Afternoon Tea was reportedly popularised by Duchess Anna Maria, wife of the 7th Duke, who entertained her friends in the Abbey.

Explore the 28 acres of gardens and enjoy elegant horticultural designs, glades, ponds and architectural features; much of which were the inspiration of Humphry Repton who contributed to their design. The restoration of Repton's original Pleasure Grounds from 200 years ago continues today with the rockery and Children's Garden recently recreated.

Woburn Abbey provides a magnificent backdrop for a myriad of events throughout the year which, in 2014, includes classic car shows, sport events, open air theatre and the annual Woburn Abbey Garden Show.

As part of the centenary anniversary of World War I, there will be an exhibition exploring the roles played during the war by the 11th Duke and Duchess and the Abbey itself.

## KEY FACTS

- ⓘ Suitable for tv/film location, fashion shows, product launches and company 'days out'. No photography by visitors in House.
- Conferences, exhibitions, banqueting, luncheons, dinners.
- Limited access in the house. Good access in the gardens.
- Licensed Tea Room. Serves food, hot and cold drinks, and afternoon tea.
- By arrangement. Tours in French, German & Italian available.
- Guide book and audio guide available (additional charge).
- **P** Please telephone for details.

# QUEEN ANNE'S SUMMERHOUSE
## Shuttleworth, Old Warden, Bedfordshire SG18 9DU
### www.landmarktrust.org.uk

Hidden in a pine wood on the edge of the Shuttleworth estate is this intriguing folly with high quality 18th Century brickwork. Inside is the most elegant bedsit and a staircase in which one of the turrets winds up to the roof terrace or down to the vaulted basement, now a bathroom, where the servants once prepared refreshments. Surrounded by the flora and fauna of beautiful woodland, this is a magical spot.

**Location:** Map 7:E10.
**Owner:** The Landmark Trust
**Tel:** 01628 825925
**E-mail:** info@landmarktrust.org.uk
**Open:** 10am until 4pm.
**Admission:** Free.
**Key facts:** ⓘ A bedsit with kitchen, dining, sitting and sleeping on the ground floor. A spiral staircase leads down to the bathroom.

🅿 ⬛
⬛ ⬛ ⬛

# CHICKSANDS PRIORY
## Nr Shefford, Bedfordshire SG17 5PR

The only surviving remains of a Gilbertine monastic cloister in England, founded circa 1150. Medieval roof timbers, 13C vaulting, stained glass are shown; alterations by Isaac Ware and James Wyatt. Ancestral home of the Osborn Baronets, 1599-1936. Substantially restored by the Ministry of Defence 1997-98. Visited by the Time Team, 2001. Conducted tours by Friends of Chicksands Priory by appointment only.

**Location:** Map 7:E10. OS Ref TL123 397.
**Contact:** Mrs Julia Benson
**Tel:** 01525 860497
**E-mail:** tours@chicksandspriory.co.uk
**Website:** www.chicksandspriory.co.uk
**Open:** 1st and 3rd Sun afternoons Apr-Oct.
**Admission:** Free, donations invited.
**Key facts:** ⬛ Refreshments given. ⓧ By appointment only.

# MOGGERHANGER PARK 🏛ⓔ
## Park Road, Moggerhanger, Bedfordshire MK44 3RW

Award Winning Georgian Grade I listed Country House designed by Sir John Soane, recently restored, in 33 acres of Humphry Repton designed parkland and woodland. Moggerhanger House has 3 executive conference suites and 2 function rooms, making an ideal venue for conferences, promotions, corporate entertainment, family functions and weddings. Bed and breakfast accommodation available in our beautifully refurbished bedrooms. **Location:** Map 7:E9. OS Ref TL048 475. On A603, 3m from A1 at Sandy, 6m from Bedford.
**Owner:** Moggerhanger House Preservation Trust **Contact:** Reception
**Tel:** 01767 641007 **E-mail:** enquiries@moggerhangerpark.com
**Website:** www.moggerhangerpark.com
**Open:** House Tours: See website or telephone for current information. Grounds, Tearooms & Visitors Centre: Open all year. **Admission:** Please telephone 01767 641007. **Key facts:** ⓘ No photography. No smoking. ⬛ ⓣ ⬛ WCs, ramp, lift. ⬛ Licensed. ⓣ Licensed. ⓧ By arrangement. 🅿 ⬛ ⬛ On leads. ⬛ 21 bedrooms. ⬛ ⬛

# TURVEY HOUSE 🏛ⓔ
## Turvey, Bedfordshire MK43 8EL

A neo-classical house set in picturesque parkland bordering the River Great Ouse. The principal rooms contain a fine collection of 18th and 19th Century English and Continental furniture, pictures, porcelain, objets d'art and books. Walled Garden.
**Location:** Map 7:D9. OS Ref SP939 528.
Between Bedford and Northampton on A428.
**Owner:** The Hanbury Family
**Contact:** Daniel Hanbury
**Tel:** 01234 881244
**E-mail:** danielhanbury@hotmail.com
**Open:** 22 Feb, 19 & 22 Mar, 2, 5, 16, 19 & 30 Apr, 3, 5, 14, 17, 26, 28 & 31 May, 11, 14, 25 & 28 Jun, 9, 12, 23 & 26 Jul, 6, 9, 20, 23 & 25 Aug.
Last admission 4.30pm.
**Admission:** Adult £6.00, Child £3.00.
**Key facts:** ⓘ No photography in house. ⬛ ⓧ Obligatory. 🅿 Ample for cars, none for coaches. ⬛

Deer at Woburn Abbey

# CAMBRIDGE UNIVERSITY BOTANIC GARDEN
## 1 BROOKSIDE, CAMBRIDGE CB2 1JE
www.botanic.cam.ac.uk

The Cambridge University Botanic Garden was opened in 1846 by John Henslow, mentor to Charles Darwin, and today showcases over 8000 plant species from around the globe, including nine National Plant Collections and the best arboretum in the region. Landscape highlights include the Winter Garden, the richly-fragranced Scented Garden, the buzzing Bee Borders and the unique Systematic Beds. The Glasshouse displays range from architectural cactus to flamboyant, tropical rainforests. Opening daily at 10am, the Cambridge University Botanic Garden is an inspiration year-round, and an exciting introduction to the natural world for families (children can borrow the free Young Explorer backpacks).

**Location:** Map 7:G9. OS Ref TL453 573. ¾m S of Cambridge city centre, some pay & display parking along Trumpington Road.

**Owner:** University of Cambridge

**Contact:** Enquiries Desk
**Tel:** 01223 336265
**Fax:** 01223 336278
**E-mail:** enquiries@botanic.cam.ac.uk
**Open:** Apr-Sep, daily, 10am-6pm; closes 5pm in Feb, Mar & Oct, and 4pm from Nov-Jan. Closed over Christmas and New Year, please telephone for details.
**Admission:** From 1 Mar 2012: Gift aid admission £4.95, Standard admission £4.50, Concession Gift Aid £4.35, Concession £3.95. Children 16 and under; free admission, but must be accompanied at all times. Groups must pre-book with at least one week's notice.
**Key facts:** 🛈 🎁 ♿ 🛗 WCs. ▣ 🎥 By arrangement. 🅿 Street/Pay & Display. ▣ Schools and leisure groups must book. ♿ Assistance dogs only. ⊞ ▣

# PECKOVER HOUSE & GARDEN ✤
## NORTH BRINK, WISBECH, CAMBRIDGESHIRE PE13 1JR
www.nationaltrust.org.uk/peckover

Peckover House is an oasis hidden away in an urban environment. A classic Georgian merchant's townhouse, it was lived in by the Peckover family for 150 years and reflects their Quaker lifestyle. The house is open over three floors, including the basement service area and our Banking Wing. The gardens are outstanding - two acres of sensory delight, complete with summerhouses, over 60 varieties of roses, specimen trees. Our fully restored Orangery is now open for visitors to enjoy. There is a croquet lawn for use in the summer and free garden tours may be available. Behind the Scenes tours run two weekends a month for a small additional charge. We have a varied and full events programme running throughout the year, so please visit our website for up-to-date information.

**Location:** Map 7:G6. OS Ref TF458 097. N bank of River Nene, Wisbech B1441.

**Owner:** National Trust **Contact:** The Property Secretary

**Tel:** 01945 583463 **Fax:** 01945 587904
**E-mail:** peckover@nationaltrust.org.uk
**Open:** House: 1 Mar-2 Nov, Sat-Wed 1-5pm. Garden: As house, 12-5pm. Garden & tea room between 4 Jan & 23 Feb, 12-4pm at weekends only for visitors to enjoy the garden in winter. Conservation 'Winter Clean' tours of house at 1.30pm & 3pm. Tours have limited spaces, so booking is advised. Please call for details of 7 day opening during holidays. Also open 6-14 Dec (weekends only) for Christmas event. **Admission:** Adult £7.50, Child £3.75, Family £18.75. NT members free. Groups discount: (min 15 people) book in advance with Property Secretary. **Key facts:** 🛈 PMV available for loan in grounds. Free garden tours daily and Behind the Scenes tours on selected weekends. 🎁 🎥 🛗 ♿ Partial. WCs. ▣ Licensed. 🎥 By arrangement. 🅿 Signposted. ▣ 🦮 Guide dogs only. ▣ see www.nationaltrustcottages.co.uk ▣ ▣

## ALL SAINTS' CHURCH
### Jesus Lane, Cambridge
### Cambridgeshire CB5 8BP
www.visitchurches.org.uk

All Saints' stands opposite the gates of Jesus College in the heart of Cambridge, its pale stone spire a prominent city landmark. It was built in the 1860s to the plans of the famous 19th Century architect G.F. Bodley and is a triumph of Victorian art and design. Light gleams through stained-glass windows, designed by leading Arts and Crafts artists, including William Morris, Edward Burne-Jones and Ford Madox Brown. What's more, almost every surface has painted, stencilled or gilded decoration. Pomegranates burst with seeds; flowers run riot over the walls. There is a glorious painting of Christ, Mary and St John, with throngs of angels. The north aisle features three fine windows by C.E. Kempe and Co (1891-1923) together with glass by Douglas Strachan.
**Location:** OS Ref TL453 587. In Jesus Lane opposite Jesus College, 250 yards from roundabout on A1303 at south end of Victoria Avenue.
**Contact:** Please call The Churches Conservation Trust on 0845 303 2760 (Mon-Fri, 9am–5pm) **Open:** Open daily.

## ELTON HALL
### Nr Peterborough PE8 6SH
www.eltonhall.com

Elton Hall is a fascinating mixture of styles and every room contains treasures – magnificent furniture and fine paintings from early 15th Century Old Masters to the remarkable 19th Century work of Alma Tadema and Millais. Great British artists are well represented by Gainsborough, Constable and Reynolds
**Location:** Map 7:E7. OS Ref TL091 930. Close to A1 in the village of Elton, off A605 Peterborough - Oundle Road.
**Owner:** Sir William Proby Bt, CBE
**Contact:** The Administrator
**Tel:** 01832 280468 **E-mail:** office@eltonhall.com
**Open:** 2-5pm: May: Last May Bank Holiday, Sun & Mon. Jun & Jul: Weds, Thurs. Aug: Weds, Thurs, Sun & BH Mon. Private groups by arrangement daily Apr-Sep. **Admission:** House & Garden: Adult £9.00, Conc. £8.00. Garden only: Adult £6.50, Conc. £6.00. Accompanied child under 16 Free.
**Key facts:** ⓘ No photography in house. Garden suitable. Obligatory. Guide dogs in gardens only.

Elton Hall

## ISLAND HALL
### Godmanchester, Cambridgeshire PE29 2BA
www.islandhall.com

An important mid 18th Century mansion of great charm, owned and restored by an award-winning interior designer. This family home has lovely Georgian rooms, with fine period detail, and interesting possessions relating to the owners' ancestors since their first occupation of the house in 1800. A tranquil riverside setting with formal gardens and ornamental island forming part of the grounds in an area of Best Landscape. Octavia Hill wrote 'This is the loveliest, dearest old house, I never was in such a one before.'
**Location:** Map 7:F8. OS Ref TL244 706. Centre of Godmanchester, Post Street next to free car park. 1m S of Huntingdon, 15m NW of Cambridge A14.
**Owner:** Mr Christopher & Lady Linda Vane Percy **Contact:** Mr C Vane Percy
**Tel:** Groups 01480 459676. Individuals via Invitation to View 01206 573948.
**E-mail:** enquire@islandhall.com
**Open:** Groups by arrangement: All year round. Individuals via Invitation to View. **Admission:** Groups (40+) £7.50 per person, (30+) £8.00 and Parties under 20 a minimum charge of £160.
**Key facts:** ⊤ See website for more details. ☞ Home made teas. 🗷 🗷 🗷 ❋

## THE MANOR, HEMINGFORD GREY
### Norman Court, High Street, Hemingford Grey, Cambridgeshire PE28 9BN
www.greenknowe.co.uk

Built about 1130 and one of the oldest continuously inhabited houses in Britain. Made famous as 'Green Knowe' by the author Lucy Boston. Her internationally known patchwork collection is also shown. Four acre garden, laid out by Lucy Boston, surrounded by moat, with topiary, old roses, award winning irises and herbaceous borders. **Location:** Map 7:F8. OS Ref TL290 706. A14, 3m SE of Huntingdon. 12m NW of Cambridge. Access via small gate on riverside.
**Owner:** Mrs D S Boston **Contact:** Diana Boston **Tel:** 01480 463134
**E-mail:** diana_boston@hotmail.com **Open:** House: All year (except May), to individuals or groups by prior arrangement. May guided tours daily at 2pm (booking advisable). Garden: All year, daily, 11am-5pm (4pm in winter).
**Admission:** House & Garden: Adult £7.00, Child £2.00, OAP £5.50 Family £18.00. Garden only. See website.
**Key facts:** ⓘ No photography in house. 🗷 🗷 🗷 Partial. ☞ The Garden Room, High Street. 🏠 The Cock Pub, High Street. 🗷 Obligatory. 🅿 Cars: Disabled plus a few spaces if none in High Street. Coaches: Nearby. 🗷 🗷 ❋

## ST PETER'S CHURCH
### Castle Hill, Cambridge, Cambridgeshire CB3 0AJ
www.visitchurches.org.uk

Originally built in the 11th Century, this tiny, tall-spired St Peter's is tucked away in a quiet corner of Cambridge with ancient trees in the churchyard. Traces of its Saxon past survive in the form of two carved doorways and the stone font, decorated with four mermen grasping their split tails. Mermen may have an ancient link to St Peter, patron saint of fishermen. There is a charming weathervane outside with the initials AP on it; these are said to be those of Andrew Perne, an 18th Century Dean of Ely. With the homely domestic architecture of the neighbouring houses, including Kettle's Yard Museum next door, and the quaint buildings of the Cambridge Folk Museum nearby, this corner of Cambridge has an almost rural feel, in contrast to the grandeur of the city's more famous sights. **Location:** OS Ref TL445 592. In centre of Cambridge, off Castle Street. **Open:** Tues - Sun, 11.00am - 5.00pm & Mon 9am -12pm. At other times key is available from Kettle's Yard Gallery.

### KIMBOLTON CASTLE
**Kimbolton, Huntingdon, Cambridgeshire PE28 0EA**

Vanbrugh and Hawksmoor's 18th Century adaptation of 13th Century fortified house. Katherine of Aragon's last residence. Tudor remains still visible. Courtyard by Henry Bell of Kings Lynn. Outstanding Pellegrini murals. Gatehouse by Robert Adam. Home of Earls and Dukes of Manchester, 1615-1950. Family portraits in State Rooms. Now Kimbolton School. **Location:** Map 7:E8. OS Ref TL101 676. 7m NW of St Neots on B645. **Owner:** Governors of Kimbolton School
**Contact:** Mrs N Butler **Tel:** 01480 860505 **Fax:** 01480 861763
**Website:** www.kimbolton.cambs.sch.uk/thecastle **Open:** 2 Mar & 2 Nov, 1-4pm.
**Admission:** Adult £5.00, Child £2.50, OAP £4.00. Groups by arrangement throughout the year, including evenings, special rates apply.
**Key facts:** ⊤ 🗷 Unsuitable. ☞ 🗷 By arrangement. 🅿 Parking for coaches limited. 🗷 🗷 On leads. In grounds only. 🗷

© English Heritage

## VISITOR INFORMATION

■ **Owner**
English Heritage

■ **Address**
Audley End House
Audley End
Saffron Walden
Essex
CB11 4JF

■ **Location**
Map 7:G10
OS Ref. TL525 382
1m W of Saffron Walden
on B1383, M11/J8 & J10.
**Rail:** Audley End 1¼ m.

■ **Contact**
Visitor Operations Team
**Tel:** 01799 522842
**E-mail:** customers@
english-heritage.org.uk

■ **Opening Times**
Please visit www.english-
heritage.org.uk for
opening times, admission
prices and the most up-to-
date information.

■ **Special Events**
There is an exciting events
programme available
throughout the year, for
further details please
contact the property or visit
the website.

# AUDLEY END ⊞
www.english-heritage.org.uk/audleyend

## One of England's finest country houses, Audley End is also a mansion with a difference. Enjoy a great day out.

Experience the daily routine of a Victorian stable yard as it is brought to life. Complete with resident horses and a costumed groom, the stables experience includes an exhibition where you can find out about the workers who lived on the estate in the 1880s, the tack house and the Audley End fire engine. There is also a children's play area and Café which are ideal for family visitors.

Every great house needed an army of servants and the restored Victorian Service Wing shows a world 'below stairs' that was never intended to be seen. Immerse yourself in the past as you visit the kitchen, scullery, pantry and laundries with film projections, introductory wall displays and even original food from the era.

The cook, Mrs Crocombe, and her staff can regularly be seen trying out new recipes and going about their chores.

Audley End House is itself a magnificent house, built to entertain royalty. Among the highlights is a stunning art collection including works by Masters Holbein, Lely and Canaletto. Its pastoral parkland is designed by 'Capability' Brown and there is an impressive formal garden to discover. Don't miss the working Organic Kitchen Garden with its glasshouses and vinery growing original Victorian varieties of fruit and vegetables. Audley End also boasts Cambridge Lodge a two storey detached holiday cottage. The sitting room enjoys magnificent views of the grounds of Audley End House.

## KEY FACTS

ℹ️ Open air concerts and other events. WCs.

🏪 Service Yard and Coach House Shops.

🎧

🍽️

🚶 By arrangement for groups.

🅿️ Coaches to book in advance. Free entry for coach drivers and tour guides.

🚌 School visits free if booked in advance. Contact the Administrator or tel 01223 582700 for bookings.

🐕 Dogs on leads only.

🏠

📹

© English Heritage

© National Trust Images / David Levenson

**■ Owner**
National Trust

**■ Address**
25 West Street
Coggeshall
Near Colchester
Essex
C06 1NS

**■ Location**
**Map 8:I11**
**OS Ref. TL848 225**
On West Street, parking available nearby or at The Grange Barn (also NT), a five minute walk away.

**■ Contact**
The Manager
**Tel:** 01376 561305
**E-mail:** paycockes @nationaltrust.org.uk

**■ Opening Times**
**26 March - 2 November:**
11am-5pm (last admission 4:30pm) Wed-Sun and BH Mons.

**■ Admission**
Adults          £5.00
Children:       £2.50
National Trust
Members         Free
Joint discount tickets available with The Grange Barn.

# PAYCOCKE'S HOUSE & GARDEN ❧
www.nationaltrust.org.uk/paycockes

## "One of the most attractive half-timbered houses of England" - Nikolaus Pevsner

A magnificent half-timbered Tudor wool merchant's house with a beautiful and tranquil arts-and-crafts style cottage garden. Visitors can follow the changing fortunes of the house over its five hundred year history as it went from riches to rags and discover how it was saved from demolition and restored to its former glory as one of the earliest buildings saved by the National Trust.

Thomas Paycocke was an affluent merchant whose home reflected the wealth of the wool industry in Coggeshall. The House passed to the Buxton family, descendents of Paycocke but after the decline of the wool trade it saw harder times passing through different hands and uses and by the Nineteenth Century was used

as tenements and a haulier's store and office and threatened with dereliction. In 1904 it was bought by Noel Buxton, a descendent of the family who owned the House from the late Sixteenth Century. He began a twenty year renovation of the building to restore it to how he thought it might have looked in 1509 when it was built. During this time it was lived in by friends and relatives of Buxton including Conrad Noel the 'red' vicar of Thaxted and composer Gustav Holst. Buxton bequeathed Paycocke's to the National Trust on his death in 1924.

The House has a charming Coffee Shop and relaxing garden. 2014 marks the ninetieth anniversary of bequest to the National Trust.

## KEY FACTS

ℹ️ 📷 🍴 🍽️ ☕ 🚶
**P** At The Coggeshall Grange Barn.
🏛️ 🐕 Guide dogs only in Garden.

© National Trust Images/David Levenson

Coffee Shop

Study

## BRENTWOOD CATHEDRAL
### INGRAVE ROAD, BRENTWOOD, ESSEX CM15 8AT

The new (1991) Roman Catholic classical Cathedral Church of St Mary and St Helen incorporates part of the original Victorian church. Designed by classical architect Quinlan Terry with roundels by Raphael Maklouf. Architecturally, the inspiration is early Italian Renaissance crossed with the English Baroque of Christopher Wren. The north elevation consists of nine bays divided by Doric pilasters. This is broken by a half-circular portico. The Kentish ragstone walls have a rustic look, which contrasts with the smooth Portland stone of the capitals and column bases. Inside is an arcade of Tuscan arches with central altar with the lantern above.

**Location:** Map 4:J1. OS Ref TQ596 938. A12 & M25/J28. Centre of Brentwood, opposite Brentwood School.
**Owner:** Diocese of Brentwood
**Tel:** 01277 232266
**E-mail:** bishop@dioceseofbrentwood.org
**Open:** All year, daily.
**Admission:** Free.
**Key facts:** ⬚ Suitable. 🅿 Limited. None for coaches. ✳ ✳

© Peter Gamble

## COPPED HALL
### Crown Hill, Epping, Essex CM16 5HS
www.coppedhalltrust.org.uk

Mid 18th Century Palladian mansion under restoration. Situated on ridge overlooking landscaped park. Ancillary buildings including stables and racquets court. Former elaborate gardens being rescued from abandonment. Large 18th Century walled kitchen garden - adjacent to site of 16th Century mansion where 'A Midsummer Night's Dream' was first performed. Ideal film location.
**Location:** Map 7:G12. OS Ref TL433 016. 4m SW of Epping, N of M25.
**Owner:** The Copped Hall Trust
**Contact:** Alan Cox
**Tel:** 020 7267 1679
**E-mail:** coxalan1@aol.com
**Open:** Ticketed events and special open days. See website for dates. Private tours by appointment.
**Admission:** Open Days £7.00. Guided Tour Days £7.00. Gardens Only £3.50.
**Key facts:** ▣ ⚑ ⬚ Partial. ▤ ⚑ 🅿 ▤ ▣ In grounds on leads. ✳ ☗

## HYLANDS HOUSE & ESTATE
### Hylands Park, London Road, Chelmsford CM2 8WQ
www.chelmsford.gov.uk/hylands

Hylands House is a beautiful Grade II* listed building, set in 574 acres of historic landscaped parkland. Built c1730, the original House was a Queen Anne style mansion. Subsequent owners modernised and enlarged the property. The Stables Visitor Centre, incorporates a Gift Shop, Café, Artist Studios and a second-hand bookshop.
**Location:** Map 7:H12. OS Ref TL681 054. 2m SW of Chelmsford. Signposted on A414 from J15 of A12, near Chelmsford.
**Owner:** Chelmsford City Council
**Contact:** Ceri Lowen
**Tel:** 01245 605500
**E-mail:** hylands@chelmsford.gov.uk
**Open:** House: Suns & Mons, 10am-5pm Apr-Sep, Stable Visitor Centre & Park: Daily. Guided Tours, Talks and Walks are available by arrangement.
**Admission:** House: Adult £3.80, Conc. £2.80, Accompanied Children under 16 Free. Visitor Stables Centre and Park: Free.
**Key facts:** ⓘ Visitor Centre. ▣ ⚑ ▭ ⬚ ▣ Daily. ⟐ ▣ By arrangement. ⌂ 🅿 ▣ By arrangement. ▥ In grounds. Guide dogs only in house. ▣ ✳ ☗

# INGATESTONE HALL
### Hall Lane, Ingatestone, Essex CM4 9NR
### www.ingatestonehall.com

16th Century mansion, with 11 acres of grounds (formal garden and wild walk), built by Sir William Petre, Secretary of State to four Tudor monarchs, which has remained in his family ever since. Furniture, portraits and memorabilia accumulated over the centuries - and two Priests' hiding places .
**Location:** Map 7:H12. OS Ref TQ654 986. Off A12 between Brentwood & Chelmsford. **Owner:** The Lord Petre **Contact:** The Administrator
**Tel:** 01277 353010 **Fax:** 01245 248979 **E-mail:** house@ingatestonehall.co.uk
**Open:** 20 Apr-28 Sep: Wed, Suns & BH Mons (not Weds in Jun), 12noon-5pm.
**Admission:** Adult £6.00, Child £2.50 (under 5yrs Free), Conc. £5.00. (Groups of 20+ booked in advance: Adult £5.00, Child £1.50, Conc. £4.00).
**Key facts:** ⓘ No photography in house. Partial. WCs. By arrangement. 🅿 Free parking. Guide dogs only.

# ST MARTIN'S CHURCH
### West Stockwell Street, Colchester, Essex CO1 1HN
### www.visitchurches.org.uk

St Martin's lies southeast of Colchester Town Hall, a spectacular medieval survivor with a massive truncated tower. Many reused Roman bricks may be seen in its exterior, especially in its tower.
Although there is evidence of 11th Century work, most of the present building grew during the 14th Century. Treasures include a wagon roof, Jacobean woodwork and a green man carving.
**Location:** OS Ref TL996 255.
West Stockwell Street - turn off the High Street at the Town Hall, church found on the right.
**Open:** Open Saturdays only, 9am until dusk. At other times Keyholder nearby.

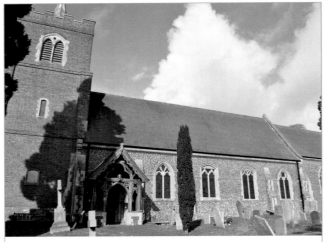

# CHURCH OF ST MARY THE VIRGIN
### Off Church Road, Burton End
### Stansted Mountfitchet, Essex CM24 8UB
### www.visitchurches.org.uk

This medieval church, with parts dating from the 1100s, has a bold brick tower and stands next to the grounds of Stansted Hall in a peaceful setting despite the nearby motorway and airport. It contains two exceptional 17th Century tomb figures - wasp-waisted Hester Salusbury in her hunting clothes and her father, Sir Thomas Middleton.
**Location:** OS Ref TL521 242. 3 miles north east of Bishop's Stortford off B1383; follow signs to 'Norman Castle and The House on the Hill Toy Museum' in village centre and then keep right on Church Road, after 0.8 miles you pass the school on your right, church shortly afterwards down lane on your left.
**Open:** Open daily 11am-3pm.

## ALL SAINTS' CHURCH
### East Horndon, Brentwood, Essex CM13 3LL

This fascinating church is built of mellow red Tudor brick and stands in magnificent isolation with wide views to the Thames. The Tyrells of nearby Heron Hall rebuilt the Norman church in the 15th Century and were buried here for four centuries. Years of decay, theft and vandalism followed until the All Saints Society and the Trust rescued the church in the 1970s. There is an exquisite memorial slab to Lady Alice Tyrell (who died in 1422) and a little chantry containing the tomb of Sir Thomas Tyrell (who died in 1476) and his wife. Also to be seen are curious galleried upper rooms in the transepts, one with a Tudor fireplace which may have housed a resident priest. **Location:** OS Ref TQ636 894. 4 miles south of Brentwood, near junction of A127 and A128 on top of the hill.
**Contact:** Please call The Churches Conservation Trust on 0845 303 2760 (Mon-Fri, 9am–5pm) **Website:** www.visitchurches.org.uk
**Open:** Open Apr to Sep on Saturdays from 10.30am to 3.30pm. At other times the key is kept at the Halfway House Pub on the A127 below the church.

## ST MARY'S CHURCH
### Chickney, Broxted, Dunmow, Essex CM6 2BY

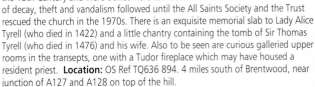

This atmospheric and remote pre-Conquest church is set within a ring of trees, beside a lane leading to Chickney Hall.
Approaching from the west one first sees the 14th Century tower, capped by an elegant pyramid-style shingled spire.
Beyond are the Saxon nave and chancel, extended eastwards early in King Henry III's reign.
The unspoilt interior is a delight, with its brick floors, 14th Century king-post roof, richly carved 15th Century font, Georgian pulpit, and squint giving a view to the altar with its Medieval mensa slab.
**Location:** OS Ref TL575 280. 4 miles south west of Thaxted, off B1051.
**Website:** www.visitchurches.org.uk
**Open:** Open daily. 10am-4pm.

# HATFIELD HOUSE
www.hatfield-house.co.uk

## Over 400 years of culture, history and entertainment.

Hatfield House is the home of the 7th Marquess and Marchioness of Salisbury and their family. The Estate has been in the Cecil family for over 400 years. Superb examples of Jacobean craftsmanship can be seen throughout the House.

In 1611, Robert Cecil, 1st Earl of Salisbury built his fine Jacobean House adjoining the site of the Old Palace of Hatfield. The House was splendidly decorated for entertaining the Royal Court, with State Rooms rich in paintings, fine furniture and tapestries.

Superb examples of Jacobean craftsmanship can be seen throughout Hatfield House such as the Grand Staircase with its fine carving and the rare stained glass window in the private chapel. Displayed throughout the House are many historic mementos collected over the centuries by the Cecils, one of England's foremost political families.

The garden at Hatfield House dates from the early 17th Century when Robert Cecil employed John Tradescant the Elder to collect plants for his new home. Tradescant was sent to Europe where he found and brought back trees, bulbs, plants and fruit trees, which had never previously been grown in England.

In the Park, an oak tree marks the place where the young Princess Elizabeth first heard of her accession to the throne. Visitors can enjoy extensive walks in the park, following trails through the woods and along the Broadwater. The Veteran Tree Trail also provides the opportunity to learn more about our ancient oaks.

## VISITOR INFORMATION

### ■ Owner
The 7th Marquess of Salisbury

### ■ Address
Hatfield House
Hatfield
Hertfordshire
AL9 5NQ

### ■ Location
**Map 7:F11**
**OS Ref. TL237 084**
21 miles north of London, M25 Jct 23, A1(M) Jct 4. Pedestrian Entrance directly opposite Hatfield Railway Station.
**Bus:** Nearest stop at Hatfield Station, also regular buses from surrounding towns.
**Rail:** Kings Cross to Hatfield 25mins. Station is opposite entrance to Park. Underground links to main line at Finsbury Park.

### ■ Contact
Visitors Department
**Tel:** 01707 287010
**E-mail:** visitors@hatfield-house.co.uk

### ■ Opening Times
**House**
5 April to 30 September 2014 Wed-Sun & BH 11-5pm (last admission 4pm).
**Garden, Park, Farm, Shops and Restaurant**
Tues-Sun & BH 10am to 5.30pm.

### ■ Admission
**House, Park and West Garden:**
Adults          £15.50
Seniors         £14.50
Children        £8.50
Group rates available.
**East Garden:**
(Wednesday only) £4.00 per person.

### Conference/Function

| ROOM | Size | Max Cap |
|---|---|---|
| The Old Palace | 112' x 33' | 280 |
| Riding School Conference Centre | 100' x 40' | 170 |

## KEY FACTS

ℹ️ No flash photography in house.

🏪 The newly refurbished Stable Yard is now home to a variety of independent retailers as well as our own Hatfield House Gift Shop.

☎ Tel 01707 262055.

♿

☕

🍴 Tel: 01707 262030.

🚶 Group tours by prior arrangement.

🎧

🅿️

👜

🐕 In park only, on leads.

🔔

♨️

Hatfield House

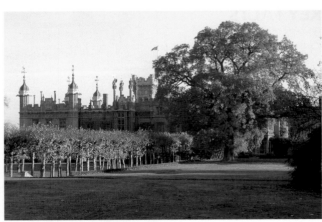

Knebworth House

## KNEBWORTH HOUSE 🏠ⓕ
### Knebworth, Hertfordshire SG1 2AX
www.knebworthhouse.com

Originally a Tudor manor house, rebuilt in gothic style in 1843. Contains rooms in various styles, which include a Jacobean banqueting hall. Home of the Lytton family since 1490. Set in 250 acres of parkland, the historic formal gardens cover 28 acres and include a dinosaur trail and walled vegetable garden. Events programme throughout the year. Knebworth is well known for its rock concerts and as a popular TV/feature film location.
**Location:** Map 7:E11. Direct access off the A1(M) J7 Stevenage, SG1 2AX, 28m N of London, 15m N of M25/J23.
**Contact:** The Estate Office **Tel:** 01438 812661
**E-mail:** info@knebworthhouse.com
**Open:** Mar-Sep, check website for open dates and times.
**Admission:** Adults: £12.00, Child*/Conc: £11.50, Family (4): £42.00. *4-16 yrs, under 4s Free. HHA members free on non-event days.
**Key facts:** ⓘ 🏠 🎫 🍽 🖾 🖥 🎦 Obligatory 🅿 🖥 🖼 In grounds. 🔔 🐕

## BENINGTON LORDSHIP GARDENS 🏠ⓕ
### Stevenage, Hertfordshire SG2 7BS

7 acre garden overlooking lakes in a timeless setting. Features include Norman keep and moat, Queen Anne manor house, James Pulham folly, formal rose garden, renowned herbaceous borders, walled vegetable garden, grass tennis court and verandah. Spectacular display of snowdrops in February. All location work welcome. **Location:** Map 7:F11. OS Ref TL296 236. In village of Benington next to the church. 4m E of Stevenage.
**Owner:** Mr R R A Bott **Contact:** Mr or Mrs R R A Bott **Tel:** 01438 869668
**E-mail:** garden@beningtonlordship.co.uk
**Website:** www.beningtonlordship.co.uk
**Open:** Snowdrops 8 Feb-2 Mar 2014 daily 12-4pm, Easter and May BH Suns & Mons 12-4pm, Floral Festival 28 & 29 Jun 12-5pm, Chilli Festival 24 & 25 Aug 10-5pm (admission £7.50).
**Admission:** Adult £5.00, Conc £4.00, Child under 12 Free.
**Key facts:** ⓘ February only. 🖾 Partial. 🖥 🎦 By arrangement. 🅿 Limited. 🖼 🐕

## GORHAMBURY 🏠ⓕ
### St Albans, Hertfordshire AL3 6AH

Late 18th Century house by Sir Robert Taylor. Family portraits from 15th-21st Centuries.
**Location:** Map 7:E11. 2m W of St Albans. Access via private drive off A4147 at St Albans. For SatNav please enter AL3 6AE for unlocked entrance to estate at Roman Theatre.
**Owner:** Gorhambury Estates Co Ltd
**Contact:** The Administrator
**Tel:** 01727 854051
**Open:** May-Sep: Thurs, 2-5pm (last entry 4pm).
**Admission:** House: Adult £8.00, Senior £7.00, Disabled, Carer, Child £5.00 including guided tour. Special groups by arrangement (Thurs am preferred).
**Key facts:** ⓘ No photography. 🖾 Partial. 🎦 Obligatory. 🅿 🖼

## ST JAMES' CHURCH 🏠
### Roydon Road, Stanstead Abbotts, Ware, Hertfordshire SG12 8JZ

St James' has been a landmark for seven centuries. Built on a hillside above the River Lea, its embattled buttressed tower was a steering point for those on the water and a waymark for those on the ancient route to London. The church's unspoiled interior has hardly been touched since Georgian times and features unusually high box pews and a three-decker pulpit. Monuments include that of a local nobleman, Sir Edward Baesh, who is shown kneeling opposite his wife.
**Location:** OS Ref TL399 111. 4 miles south east of Ware on B181.
**Website:** www.visitchurches.org.uk
**Open:** Open from Jun to Sep on Sundays from 2.30pm to 5pm.

# HOLKHAM HALL ▥Ⓕ

www.holkham.co.uk

## A breathtaking Palladian house with an outstanding art collection, panoramic landscapes and the best beach in England.

At the heart of a thriving 25,000 acre estate on the north Norfolk coast, this elegant 18th Century Palladian style house, based on designs by William Kent, was built by Thomas Coke 1st Earl of Leicester and is home to his descendants.

The Marble Hall is a spectacular introduction to this imposing building, with its 50ft pressed plaster dome ceiling and walls of English alabaster, not marble as its name implies. Stairs lead to magnificent state rooms displaying superb collections of ancient statuary, original furniture, tapestries and paintings by Rubens, Van Dyck, Claude, Gaspar Poussin and Gainsborough.

The original stables, brew and malt houses, laundry and a building that once housed the huge machines generating electricity, are now home to a fascinating museum displaying 20th Century agricultural and domestic appliances, steam engines and vintage cars, as well as being home to a gift shop offering souvenirs and crafts made by skilled local artisans and a café where you can relax and enjoy delicious, local produce.

Surrounded by parkland, discover the wildlife and landscape with nature trails, cycle and boat hire. Or visit the 18th Century walled gardens to see the restoration project to sensitively restore the gardens to their former glory. Children will have great fun exploring the woodland adventure play area with its tree house, high-level walkways and zip wire.

At the north entrance to the park lies Holkham village, with the estate-owned inn, The Victoria, a selection of shops and the entrance to the award-winning Holkham beach and National Nature Reserve, renowned for its endless golden sands and panoramic vista.

## KEY FACTS

- ℹ️ Photography allowed in hall. Stair climbing machine in hall offers unrestricted access for most manually operated wheelchairs. Elsewhere, full disabled access.
- 🎁 Gift shop in the park.
- 👶 In gift shop and at walled gardens.
- ☂ Hall & grounds.
- ♿ WC in park.
- 🍴 Stables Café. Licensed. Local produce.
- 🍽️ Licensed. The Victoria, Holkham village.
- 🚶 Private guided tours by arrangement.
- 🅿️ Ample. Parking charge.
- 🎓 Education programme on request.
- 🐕 Guide dogs only in hall.
- 💒 Weddings and civil partnerships.
- 📅 Full events programme throughout year.

## VISITOR INFORMATION

### ■ Owner
Trustees of the Holkham Estate. Home of the Coke Family.

### ■ Address
Holkham Estate Office
Wells-next-the-Sea
Norfolk
NR23 1AB

### ■ Location
**Map 8:14**
**OS Ref. TF885 428**
London 120m Norwich 35m King's Lynn 30m.
**Bus:** King's Lynn to Cromer Coasthopper route.
**Coach:** Access south gates only, follow brown/white signs 'Holkham Hall Coaches'.
**Rail:** Norwich 35m. King's Lynn 30m.
**Air:** Norwich Airport 32m.

### ■ Contact
Marketing Manager
Laurane Herrieven
**Tel:** 01328 710227
**E-mail:**
enquiries@holkham.co.uk

### ■ Opening Times
**Hall:** 1 Apr-31 Oct 12-4pm, Sun, Mon, Thur, plus Good Fri & Easter Sat. NB. Chapel, Libraries and Strangers' Wing form part of private accommodation, open at the family's discretion.
**Bygones Museum, Walled Gardens, Gift Shop, Café & Woodland Play Area:** 1 Apr-31 Oct 10am-5pm, every day.

### ■ Admission
**Hall, Museum & Walled Gardens:**
Adult £13.00
Child (5-16yrs) £6.50
Family (2 adults & up to 3 children) £35.00
**Museum & Walled Gardens:**
Adult £7.00
Child (5-16yrs) £3.50
Family (2 adults & up to 3 children) £19.00
**Car Parking:**
Per day £2.50
Redeembale in shop on £10+ purchases
**Groups:** (20+) 10% discount, free parking, organiser free entry, coach driver's refreshment voucher.
**Private Guided Tours:**
Minimum 12 people, price per person £20.00.
**Cycle Hire:** See www.cyclenorfolk.co.uk
**Lake Activities:** See www.norfolkadventure.co.uk

### ■ Special Events
Grounds for corporate events, shows, rallies, product launches, filming and weddings.

### Conference/Function
Corporate events in hall.

## HOUGHTON HALL
### HOUGHTON, KING'S LYNN, NORFOLK  PE31 6UE
www.houghtonhall.com

Houghton Hall is one of the finest examples of Palladian architecture in England. Built in the 18th Century by Sir Robert Walpole, Britain's first prime minister. Original designs by James Gibbs & Colen Campbell, interior decoration by William Kent. The House has been restored to its former grandeur, containing many of its original furnishings. Award-winning 5-acre walled garden divided into 'rooms'. Stunning 120 yard double-sided herbaceous borders, formal rose garden with over 150 varieties, mixed kitchen garden, fountains and statues. Unique Model Soldier Collection, over 20,000 models arranged in various battle formations. Contemporary Sculptures in the Gardens.

**Location:** Map 8:15. OS Ref TF792 287. 13m E of King's Lynn, 10m W of Fakenham 1½m N of A148.

**Owner:** The Marquess of Cholmondeley
**Contact:** Susan Cleaver
**Tel:** 01485 528569
**Fax:** 01485 528167
**E-mail:** info@houghtonhall.com
**Open:** Sun May 4 - Sun Oct 19, 2014. Wednesdays, Thursdays, Sundays and Bank Holiday Mondays.
**Admission:** See website for opening times/prices/booking details. www.houghtonhall.com.
**Key facts:** 🏠 🎫 ♿ WCs. Allocated parking near the House. ▣ Licensed. 🍴 Licensed. 📷 By arrangement. 🅿 🐕 On leads.

## OXBURGH HALL ❧
### OXBOROUGH, KING'S LYNN, NORFOLK  PE33 9PS
www.nationaltrust.org.uk

A romantic, moated manor house built by the Bedingfeld family in the 15th Century, they have lived here ever since. Inside, the family's Catholic history is revealed, complete with a secret priest's hole. See the astonishing needlework by Mary, Queen of Scots, original medieval documents and royal letters, and reproduction costumes of King Henry VII and Elizabeth of York, who stayed at Oxburgh in 1487. Outside, enjoy panoramic views from the gatehouse roof, explore the Victorian parterre and woodland trails. The late winter drifts of snowdrops are not to be missed.

**Location:** Map 8:16. OS Ref TF742 012. At Oxborough, 7m SW of Swaffham on S side of Stoke Ferry road.

**Owner:** National Trust **Contact:** The Property Administrator
**Tel:** 01366 328258 **Fax:** 01366 328066
**E-mail:** oxburghhall@nationaltrust.org.uk

**Open:** House, Garden Shop & Tearoom: 1 Mar-1 Oct Sat-Wed 11am-5pm (7 days Easter & August), 4 Oct-2 Nov open 11am-4pm (last entry 3.30pm). Garden Shop and Tearoom Weekends: 4 Jan-16 Feb and 3 Nov-21 Dec 11am-4pm, Mon-Wed 17 Feb-26 Feb 11am-4pm, 7 days 27 Oct-2 Nov. House Timed Tours: 15 Feb-26 Feb 12pm-2.30pm
*Check website for detailed information.
**Admission:** House & Garden: (Gift Aid in brackets) Adult £8.50 (£9.40), Child £4.25 (£4.70), Family £21.25 (£23.50). Garden & Estate: Adult £4.70 (£5.20), Child £2.35 (£2.60), Family £11.75 (£13.00). Groups (booked in advance): House & Garden: Adult £7.65, Child £3.80. Garden & Estate: Adult £4.20, Child £2.10. **Key facts:** ℹ Free garden tours daily. Souvenir guides, gift shop, second-hand bookshop. 🏠 🎫 🍴 ♿ WCs. ▣ Licensed. 📷 By arrangement. 🅿 Limited for coaches. 🔊 🐕 Guide dogs only. ❄ ♿

# CASTLE RISING CASTLE
## Castle Rising, King's Lynn, Norfolk PE31 6AH
www.castlerising.co.uk

Possibly the finest mid-12th Century Keep in England: it was built as a grand and elaborate palace. It was home to Queen Isabella, grandmother of the Black Prince. Still in good condition, the Keep is surrounded by massive ramparts up to 120 feet high. Picnic area, adjacent tearoom. Audio tour.

**Location:** Map 7:H5. OS Ref TF666 246.
Located 4m NE of King's Lynn off A149.
**Owner:** Lord Howard **Contact:** The Custodian
**Tel:** 01553 631330
**Fax:** 01533 631724
**Open:** 1 Apr-1 Nov: daily, 10am-6pm (closes at dusk if earlier in Oct). 2 Nov-31 Mar: Wed-Sun, 10am-4pm. Closed 24-26 Dec.
**Admission:** Adult £4.00, Child £2.50, Conc. £3.30, Family £12.00. 15% discount for groups (11+). Opening times and prices are subject to change.
**Key facts:** ⓘ Picnic area. ▣ ⬚ Suitable. ▤ ▣ **P** ✳

# HINDRINGHAM HALL AND GARDENS 🏛
## Blacksmiths Lane, Hindringham, Norfolk NR21 0QA
www.hindringhamhall.org

House: Tudor Manor House surrounded by 12th Century moat. Gardens: Three acres of peaceful gardens within and without the moat surrounding the house. Working walled vegetable garden, herb parterre, daffodil walk, bluebell and cyclamen copse, stream garden, bog garden, herbacious borders, autumn border, victorian nut tunnel, rose and clematis pergolas.

**Location:** Map 8:J4. Turn off the A148 halfway between Fakenham & Holt signposted Hindringham & follow brown signs.
**Owner/Contact:** Mr & Mrs Charles Tucker **Tel:** 01328 878226
**E-mail:** info@hindringhamhall.org **Open:** House: 4 times a year for a 2 hr guided history tour. See website for dates and times. Groups on other days by arrangement. 01328 878226. Gardens and tearoom: Suns and/or Weds Mar-Oct. See website www.hindringhamhall.org for dates and times.
**Admission:** House: 2hr guided history tour £17.00 including refreshments. Garden: Adults £6.00, Children under 15 Free.
**Key facts:** 🏛 Many plants for sale from seeds & cuttings from the gardens. ⬚ No hills or steps but some gravel paths. ☕ Teas, coffee and other beverages and cakes. 🅵 **P** ♿

Holkham Hall

## RAVENINGHAM GARDENS ⓘⒻ
### Raveningham, Norwich, Norfolk NR14 6NS
www.raveningham.com

Superb herbaceous borders, 18th Century walled kitchen garden, Victorian glasshouse, herb garden, Edwardian rose garden, contemporary sculptures, 14th Century church and much more.
**Location:** Map 8:L7. OS Ref TM399 965. Between Norwich & Lowestoft off A146 then B1136.
**Owner:** Sir Nicholas Bacon Bt
**Contact:** Diane Hoffman
**Tel:** 01508 548152
**Fax:** 01508 548958
**E-mail:** diane@raveningham.com
**Open:** Tue, Wed and Thur from Easter Day to end Aug. Special 2 week openings for snowdrops, agapanthus, rose and Autumn weeks - see website for full details.
**Admission:** Adult £4.00, Child (under 16yrs) Free, OAP £3.50.
Groups by prior arrangement.
**Key facts:** 🅿 🖼 🎦

## CHURCH OF ST JOHN MADDERMARKET 🔊
### Maddermarket, Norwich, Norfolk NR2 1DS
www.visitchurches.org.uk

Built in the 15th Century, the handsome flint tower of St John's rises above Maddermarket in the city centre. The best view of it is from the north, where its tower stands over Maddermarket Alley, affording one of the city's most attractive townscapes. It is believed that an original chancel may have been demolished as part of a road-widening scheme when Queen Elizabeth I came to visit Norwich. It survived a gas explosion in 1876 during a choir practice that stunned the rector, singed the choirboys and shattered windows. Today's stained-glass windows are Victorian; 20th Century replacements which flood the church with light. The church's interior is filled with marvellous monuments, from elegant plaques to detailed little figures in Tudor dress. All around are rich furnishings - part of an interesting and eccentric collection assembled by William Busby (rector from 1898 to 1923). **Location:** OS Ref TG229 087. In centre of Norwich off Pottergate. **Open:** Open Weds: 10.30am - 1.00pm. Please call 01223 324442 at other times.

Raveningham Gardens

## ST MARGARET'S CHURCH 🔊
### Church Lane, Hales, Norwich, Norfolk NR14 6QL
www.visitchurches.org.uk

St Margaret's, with its round tower and thatched roof, is a church from another time, standing in an isolated setting, as if still in its 12th Century Norman world. The magnificent carved doorway with bands of richly carved patterns zigzags, stars and rosettes over the arch is breathtaking; there is another similar doorway, though less richly carved, in the south wall.
Inside the church is simple and rustic. Medieval faces painted on the walls peer out from across the centuries - look for St Christopher carrying Christ and St James, holding his pilgrim's staff, with a delicate band of twining foliage. The 500-year-old font is carved with angels, lions and roses - and there are memorials in the brick floor.
**Location:** OS Ref TM384 962. 12 miles south east of Norwich, east of the A146 after Loddon bypass.
**Open:** Open daily.

Sandringham

## ST NICHOLAS' CHAPEL
### St Ann's Street, King's Lynn, Norfolk PE30 1NH
www.visitchurches.org.uk

From the tip of its 19th Century spire to its Norman foundations, everything about this town centre church is dazzling. Light floods from its magnificent windows into the interior. The vividly coloured picture panels to the east depict 32 scenes from the life of Jesus. Monuments from the 17th and 18th Centuries, some with startlingly life-like painted figures, celebrate King's Lynn's seamen, merchants, mayors and shopkeepers and illustrate the town's long history as a busy commercial centre and port. Among these monuments is a marble urn designed by famous Scottish architect, Robert Adam. Up in the 15th Century wooden roof, carved angels with outstretched wings sing and play musical instruments. One holds a recorder - the earliest ever portrayal of the instrument in church carving. At your feet is a fantastic collection of ledger stones including one dedicated to Robinson Cruso.
**Location:** OS Ref TF618 204. The chapel is to the north of the centre of King's Lynn, close to the Saturday Market Place on St Ann's Street.
**Open:** Mid Jun until end of Sept: Tue and Sat, 10.30am-4.30pm.

## BLICKLING ESTATE
### Blickling, Norwich, Norfolk NR11 6NF

For four centuries, the Blickling Estate has been home to many, from the Boleyn family to the RAF, stationed here during the Second World War. Cooks and butlers, gardeners and scullery maids have all made their mark on this beautiful country estate and you can follow in their footsteps. Built in the early C17th, it boasts one of England's finest Jacobean houses, famed for its important book collection. Explore the spectacular 55 acre gardens and enjoy the tranquillity of a ramble around the lake and parkland. **Location:** Map 8:K5. 1½m NW of Aylsham on B1354. Signposted off A140 Norwich (14m) to Cromer. **Owner:** National Trust
**Tel:** 01263 738030 **E-mail:** blickling@nationaltrust.org.uk
**Website:** www.nationaltrust.org.uk/blickling **Open:** Please see website or contact us for up to date information. **Admission:** NT members free. Please see website or contact us for up to date admission prices.
**Key facts:** 🛈 📷 🎫 🔽 🛎 🍴 👶 🅿 🏨 ♿ ✳ 🐕

## CHURCH OF ST MICHAEL THE ARCHANGEL
### Booton, Norwich, Norfolk NR10 4NZ

This amazingly decorative and extraordinary church was the creation of eccentric clergyman Reverend Whitwell Elwin; a descendant of Pocahontas of Hiawatha fame. Elwin not only raised the funds for the building, he also designed it. Some of his models can be identified; the west doorway was inspired by Glastonbury Abbey, for example, but the slender twin towers which soar over the wide East Anglian landscape and central pinnacle, seem to have sprung solely from his imagination. Inside, he filled his fairy-tale creation with angels modelled on the rector's young female friends. The wooden carved angels holding up the roof are the work of James Minns, a well-known master-carver whose carving of a bull's head is still the emblem on Colman's Mustard. You may love the church; you may be outraged by it, but you cannot remain unmoved by such an exuberant oddity. **Location:** OS Ref TG123 224. 12 m NW of Norwich, off B1145 SE of Reepham & SW of Cawston. **Website:** www.visitchurches.org.uk **Open:** Daily, 9am-4pm (winter), 10am-5pm (summer).

## SANDRINGHAM
### The Estate Office, Sandringham, Norfolk PE35 6EN

Sandringham House, the Norfolk retreat of Her Majesty The Queen, is set in 60 acres of beautiful gardens. The main ground floor rooms used by The Royal Family, still maintained in the Edwardian style, are open to the public, as well as the fascinating Museum and the charming parish church.
**Location:** Map 7:H5. OS Ref TF695 287. 8m NE of King's Lynn on B1440 off A148. **Owner:** H M The Queen
**Contact:** The Public Enterprises Manager
**Tel:** 01485 545408 **Fax:** 01485 541571 **E-mail:** visits@sandringhamestate.co.uk
**Website:** www.sandringhamestate.co.uk
**Open:** 19 Apr - late Jul & early Aug - 2 Nov.
**Admission:** House, Museum & Gardens, Adult £13.00, Child £6.50, Conc. £11.00. Museum & Gardens, Adult £9.00, Child £4.50, Conc. £8.00.
**Key facts:** 🛈 No photography in house. 📷 🌱 Plant Centre. 🎫 Visitor Centre only. ♿ WCs. 🍽 Licensed. 🍴 Licensed. 📷 By arrangement. Private evening tours. 🅿 Ample. 🐕 Guide dogs only. 🐕

## CLIFTON HOUSE
### Queen Street, King's Lynn PE30 1HT

Magnificent Grade 1 listed merchant's house. Elizabethan watch-tower, 14th Century vaulted cellars. **Location:** Map 7:H5. OS Ref TF615 198.
**E-mail:** anna@kingstaithe.com **Website:** www.cliftonhouse.org.uk
**Open:** Sat 17 May (Tower only), Sat 20 Jul & Sat 27 Jul 11-4pm. Pre-booked guided tours throughout the year. **Admission:** Adult admission open days £3.50.

## MANNINGTON GARDENS & COUNTRYSIDE
### Mannington Hall, Norwich NR11 7BB

The gardens around this medieval moated manor house feature thousands of roses, especially classic varieties. **Location:** Map 8:K5. OS Ref TG144 320.
**Tel:** 01263 584175 / 768444 **E-mail:** admin@walpoleestate.co.uk
**Website:** www.manningtongardens.co.uk
**Open:** Please contact us for 2014 opening times and admission prices.

## WALSINGHAM ABBEY GROUNDS & SHIREHALL MUSEUM
### Common Place, Little Walsingham, Norfolk NR22 6BP

Ruins of the medieval Augustinian Priory, tranquil gardens. Spectacular snowdrops in February. **Location:** Map 8:J4. OS Ref TF934 367. **Tel:** 01328 820510
**Website:** www.walsinghamabbey.com **Open:** Feb 10am-4pm. Mar: weekends, 11am-4pm. 31 Mar-2 Nov: 11am-4pm. **Admission:** Adult £4.00, child £2.50.

## WOLTERTON PARK
### Norwich, Norfolk NR11 7LY

18th Century Hall. Portrait collection annual exhibitions. Historic park with lake.
**Location:** Map 8:K5. OS Ref TG164 317. **Tel:** 01263 584175 / 768444
**E-mail:** admin@walpoleestate.co.uk
**Website:** www.manningtongardens.co.uk
**Open:** Please contact us for 2014 opening times and admission prices.

# KENTWELL HALL & GARDENS
## LONG MELFORD, SUFFOLK CO10 9BA
### www.kentwell.co.uk

A beautiful mellow redbrick Tudor Mansion, surrounded by a broad moat, with rare service building of c1500. Interior 'improved' by Thomas Hopper in 1820s. Still a lived-in family home

Restoration - Famed for the long-time, long term, ongoing works in House & Gardens.

Gardens - Over 30 years' endeavour has resulted in gardens which are a joy in all seasons. Moats, massed spring bulbs, mature trees, delightful walled garden, with potager, herbs and ancient espaliered fruit trees. Much topiary from massive ancient yews to the unique 'Pied Piper' Story.

Re-Creations - Renowned for its award-winning Re-Creations of Tudor Life. Also occasional Re-Creations of Victorian life including A Dickensian Christmas (Saturday 14th to Sunday 22nd December). Re-Creations take place on selected weekends from April to October.

Corporate - House and upgraded 2500 sq ft Function Room for conferences, dinners, banquets of all sizes and Corporate Activity Days of originality.

Schools - Perhaps the biggest, most original and stimulating educational programme in the region enjoyed by over 10,000 schoolchildren each year.

Filming - used for Medieval & Tudor periods for its range of suitably equipped locations and access to Kentwell's 700 Tudors as extras.

Scaresville - Award-winning Halloween Scare Event. Selected evenings Oct 10 to Nov 1.

**Location:** MAP 8:I9, OS Ref. TL864 479. Off the A134. 4m N of Sudbury,
**Owner:** Patrick Phillips Esq   **Contact:** The Estate Office
**Tel:** 01787 310207 **Fax:** 01787 379318 **E-mail:** info@kentwell.co.uk
**Open:** For full details see our website or call for Opening Leaflet.
**Admission:** Charges apply according to the Event (if any) on. Call for details.
**Key facts:** ⓘ No photography in house. 🄫 🅣 Conferences, dinners, Tudor feasts for groups of 40 or more. Car rallies. 🄪 🄬 Home-made food. Ⓟ 🄰 🄷 🄰 Including themed ceremonies. 🅥 Open-air theatre, opera and concert season Jul–Aug.

Lavenham: The Guildhall of Corpus Christi

# LAVENHAM: THE GUILDHALL OF CORPUS CHRISTI ❧
## THE MARKET PLACE, LAVENHAM, SUDBURY  CO10 9QZ
### www.nationaltrust.org.uk

Once one of the wealthiest towns in Tudor England, Lavenham oozes charm and character. The rich clothiers who thrived here left a legacy of buildings that now make up the streets of crooked timber-framed houses that are so beloved of visitors today.

With its timber-framed houses and magnificent church, a visit to picturesque Lavenham is a step back in time. The Sixteenth Century Guildhall is the ideal place to begin with its exhibitions on local history bringing to life the fascinating stories behind this remarkable village.

Once you have explored the Guildhall and sampled some home-made fare in our tearoom, why not visit some of the unique shops and galleries in the village. Lavenham truly has something for everyone.

**Location:** Map 8:J9. OS Ref OS155, TL915 942. 6m NNE of Sudbury. Village centre. A1141 & B1071.
**Owner:** National Trust
**Contact:** Jane Gosling
**Tel:** 01787 247646
**E-mail:** lavenhamguildhall@nationaltrust.org.uk
**Open:** 8-30 Mar, Wed-Sun 11am-4pm. 31 Mar-2 Nov, Daily, 11am-5pm. 8-30 Nov, Sat/Sun, 11am-4pm. Parts of the building may be closed occasionally for community use. **Admission:** Adult £5.95, Child £2.95, Family £14.85, Groups £4.80. School parties by arrangement.
**Key facts:** 🖼 ♿ ▣ ℹ By arrangement. ✖ ♿

## FRESTON TOWER
### Nr Ipswich, Suffolk IP9 1AD
#### www.landmarktrust.org.uk

Freston Tower is a six-storey Tudor folly that looks out over the River Orwell. There is a single room on each floor with the sitting room at the top to take advantage of the unrivalled views.
**Location:** Map 8:K9. OS Ref TM177 397.
**Owner:** The Landmark Trust
**Tel:** 01628 825925
**E-mail:** bookings@landmarktrust.org.uk
**Open:** Open Days on 8 days per year, other visits by appointment.
**Admission:** Free on Open Days and visits by appointment.
**Key facts:** ℹ Six storeys joined by a steep spiral staircase. There is a room on each floor and a roof terrace.
🅿 ♿ ▣ ✳ ♿

## GAINSBOROUGH'S HOUSE
### 46 Gainsborough St, Sudbury, Suffolk  CO10 2EU
#### www.gainsborough.org

Gainsborough's House is the birthplace museum of Thomas Gainsborough RA (1727-1788) and displays an outstanding collection of his paintings, drawings and prints. A varied programme of temporary exhibitions is also shown throughout the year. The historic house dates back to the 16th Century and has an attractive walled garden.
**Location:** Map 8:I10. OS Ref TL872 413. 46 Gainsborough St, Sudbury town centre. **Owner:** Gainsborough's House Society
**Contact:** Rosemary Woodward
**Tel:** 01787 372958 **Fax:** 01787 376991
**E-mail:** mail@gainsborough.org
**Open:** All year: Mon-Sat, 10am-5pm. Closed: Suns, Good Fri and Christmas to New Year. **Admission:** Please telephone 01787 372958 for details of admission charges.
**Key facts:** ℹ No photography in the House. 🖼 ♿ ♿ Suitable. WCs. ▣
ℹ By arrangement. ▦ 🐕 Guide dogs only. ✳

# ★★★★★
# THE OLD RECTORY COUNTRY HOUSE

## Located in a quiet hamlet near Lavenham, Suffolk

Offering spaciousness and graciousness, this charming grade II listed country house is steeped in over 600 years of fascinating history. Relax in one of our six luxurious ensuite bedrooms, enjoy our elegant drawing room with honesty bar and look forward to an award winning Suffolk breakfast by a roaring fire. The delightful grounds have a swimming pool and tennis court.

**The Old Rectory Country House**
Rectory Road, Great Waldingfield, Suffolk CO10 0TL

www.theoldrectorycountryhouse.co.uk
info@theoldrectorycountryhouse.co.uk
01787 372428

VisitEngland
★★★★★
BED & BREAKFAST

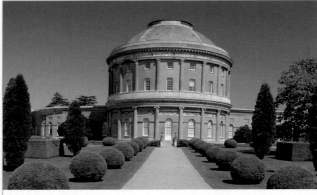

## ICKWORTH HOUSE, PARKLAND, WOODLAND & GARDENS ❧
### Horringer, Bury St Edmunds, Suffolk IP29 5QE
www.nationaltrust.org.uk/ickworth

Enjoy an entertaining day at this idiosyncratic country estate in the heart of Suffolk. The grand Georgian Rotunda, filled with treasures collected by generations of Hervey's, sits in beautiful parkland where you can wander freely. Discover one of the earliest Italianate Gardens in England and experience 1930's life in the newly restored Servants' basement.
**Location:** Map 8:19. OS Ref TL816 611. In Horringer, 3m SW of Bury St Edmunds on W side of A143. **Owner:** The National Trust **Contact:** Property Administrator **Tel:** 01284 735270 **E-mail:** ickworth@nationaltrust.org.uk
**Open:** House: 14 Mar-1 Nov, Fri-Tue, 11am-5pm (Tours only until 1pm, last entry 4pm), Thur 12-3pm. Parkland & Gardens: Daily Dawn-Dusk. Shop & Restaurant: Daily 10.30am-5pm (4pm Winter). Closed Christmas Day.
**Admission:** Gift Aid Admission (standard in brackets): House, Park & Gardens £14.00 (£12.60), Child £7.00 (£6.35), Family £35.00 (£31.55). Groups (15+) £11.00 per person. For other prices visit www.nationaltrust.org.uk/ickworth
**Key facts:** ▢ ⬚ ⊤ ⬚ ⬚ ⊞ Licensed. ⬚ ℙ ⬚ In grounds only. ⬚ ⬚ ⬚ ⬚

## HELMINGHAM HALL GARDENS ⬚ⓕ
### Helmingham, Suffolk IP14 6EF
www.helmingham.com

Grade 1 listed gardens, redesigned by Lady Tollemache (a Chelsea Gold Medallist) set in a 400 acre deer park surrounding a moated Tudor Hall. Visitors are enchanted by the stunning herbaceous borders, the walled kitchen garden, herb, knot, rose and wild gardens. A delicious range of local food is served in the Coach House Tearooms and the Stable Shops offer a wide range of local produce, plants, garden accessories and local crafts.
Coach bookings warmly welcomed. There are a variety of events throughout the season including The Festival of Classic & Sports Cars and Suffolk Dog Day.
**Location:** Map 8:K9. OS Ref TM190 578. B1077, 9m N of Ipswich, 5m S of Debenham. **Owner:** The Lord & Lady Tollemache **Contact:** Events Office
**Tel:** 01473 890799 **E-mail:** events@helmingham.com
**Open:** Gardens only 1 May-21 Sep 2014 (12-5pm Tue, Wed, Thu, Sun and all Bank Holidays).
**Admission:** Adults £6.00, Child (5-15yrs) £3.50. Groups (30+) £5.00.
**Key facts:** ▢ ⬚ ⊤ ⬚ WCs. ⬚ Licensed. ⬚ By arrangement. ℙ ⬚ Pre-booking required. ⬚ Dogs on leads only. ⬚ ⬚

## OTLEY HALL
### Hall Lane, Otley, Suffolk IP6 9PA
www.otleyhall.co.uk

Stunning medieval Moated Hall (Grade I) frequently described as 'one of England's loveliest houses'. Noted for its richly carved beams, superb linenfold panelling and 16th Century wall paintings. The unique 10-acre gardens include historically accurate Tudor re-creations and were voted among the top 10 gardens to visit in Great Britain.
**Location:** Map 8:K9. OS Ref TM207 563. 7m N of Ipswich, off the B1079.
**Owner:** Dr Ian & Reverend Catherine Beaumont
**Contact:** Karen Gwynne - Vince
**Tel:** 01473 890264
**Fax:** 01473 890803 **E-mail:** events@otleyhall.co.uk
**Open:** Open Gardens every Wed May-Sep. 11am-5pm. £3.00 entrance, café serving light lunches and afternoon tea also open every Wed May-Sep. The House and grounds are available for wedding ceremonies and receptions where we offer exclusive access to the venue on the wedding day. For more information please visit our website. **Admission:** By appointment only.
**Key facts:** ⊤ ⬚ Partial. ⬚ Licensed. ⬚ By arrangement. ℙ ⬚ ⬚ ⬚

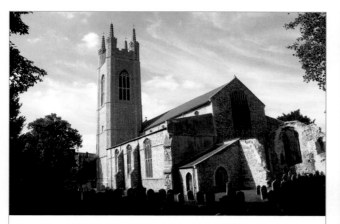

## ST MARY'S CHURCH 🔊
### St Mary's Street, Bungay, Suffolk  NR35 1AX
www.visitchurches.org.uk

The graceful and elegant tower of this grand church, with its tall pinnacles, stands 33.5 metres high. If you look up as you approach you can see intriguing carved heads under the parapet of the north aisle. Built in the late 15th Century as part of the church of the Benedictine priory, St Mary's remained the parish church after the priory was closed by Henry VIII in 1536.

Inside, the church is flooded with light from the plain glass windows, especially the west window and has an amazing display of tracery design in its upper half. The splendid carvings on the roof bosses include angels, a lion, two-headed eagles and a splendid bat. Look out for a wooden dole-cupboard near the entrance which was given by the curate in 1675 where bread was left for collection by the poor - it has religious worthies and a perky rat carved on it. There is also a fine 17th Century carved Flemish panel of the Resurrection in the War Memorial Chapel.

**Location:** OS Ref TM337 898. In Bungay town centre.
**Open:** Open daily.

## ST PETER'S CHURCH 🔊
### Church Lane, Claydon, Ipswich, Suffolk  IP6 0EQ
www.visitchurches.org.uk

On a commanding site above the Gipping Valley, St Peter's was commissioned by eccentric High Church rector, George Drury.

It is stunning, full of vibrant stained glass and extravagant carvings.

Drury himself was responsible for the design of the stained glass in the east and west windows and he may also have carved some of the stonework.

The surviving 19th Century fittings are all of high quality and also bear the stamp of Father Drury's personality.

**Location:** OS Ref TM137 499.
4 miles north west of Ipswich, off A14.
**Open:** Open daily.

## ST MARY'S CHURCH 🔊
### Churchway, Redgrave, Diss, Suffolk  IP22 1RJ
www.visitchurches.org.uk

Five centuries of parishioners have worshipped at St Mary's, a vast country church set in open fields. Everything is on a grand scale: the east window is stunning, with glorious stained-glass images of saints and angels. The collection of hatchments and monuments is of national importance. Tombs have life-size statues in elaborate 17th Century fashions and there are 13 hatchments - wood and canvas coats of arms - more than any other church in Suffolk. The north-east brick vestry is a rare survival from the 16th Century, and a wander round the churchyard reveals many 18th Century gravestones, some with little carved skulls peeping over the top.

**Location:** OS Ref TM057 782. 4 miles west of Diss, off B1113; 1 mile from village centre.
**Open:** First Sat of month: Dec-Mar, 10am-12pm; Apr & May, 10am-2pm; Jun-Sep, 10am-4pm; Oct & Nov, 10am-2pm.

## SUTTON HOO 🦋
### Woodbridge, Suffolk  IP12 3DJ
www.nationaltrust.org.uk/suttonhoo

Home to one of the world's greatest archaeological discoveries. Walk around the ancient mounds and discover the incredible story of the royal Anglo-Saxon ship burial. Enjoy beautiful period interiors of Mrs Pretty's Country House. Site includes exhibition hall, café, shop, site walks. Special events all year.
**Location:** Map 8:L9. OS Ref TM288 487. Off B1083 Woodbridge to Bawdsey road. Follow signs from A12. Train ½m Melton.
**Owner:** National Trust **Contact:** The Property Manager **Tel:** 01394 389700
**E-mail:** suttonhoo@nationaltrust.org.uk
**Open:** 1-5 Jan: 11-4pm, Wed-Sun, 11 Jan-9 Feb: 11-4pm, weekends, 15 Feb-23 Feb: 11-4pm, Mon-Sun, 1 Mar-9 Mar: 11-4pm, weekends, 15 March-2 Nov: 10.30-5pm, Mon-Sun, 8 Nov-28 Dec: 11-4pm, weekends, 29 Dec-31 Dec: 11-4pm, Mon-Wed. BH Mons. Estate walks open daily all year, 9-6 (except for some Thurs, Nov-end Dec). **Admission:** NT members free. Adult £8.25, Child £4.15, Family £20.60. Voluntary donation included, standard prices available at property and on website. **Key facts:** 🖻 🖶 🖾 Suitable. WCs. 🍽 Licensed. 🍴 Licensed. 🖊 By arrangement. 🅿 Limited for coaches. 🐕 🚾 ❄ ♿

## YAXLEY HALL 🏛
### Hall Lane, Yaxley, Suffolk IP23 8BY
www.yaxleyhall.com

Yaxley Hall is an intimate and historic Suffolk country house which effortlessly combines classic with contemporary refinement, providing a stylish, peaceful and unforgettable wedding and events venue.

Our delightful silk lined Banqueting House is available throughout the year and can accommodate up to 150 dining guests for all occasions.

**Location:** Map 8:K8. OS Ref TM122 735. Located between Yaxley and Eye, close to the market town of Diss, the Hall is easily accessible from the main A140 trunk road between Ipswich and Norwich.

**Owner:** Dominic Richards Esq.

**Contact:** Richard Orton

**Tel:** 01379 788869

**E-mail:** enquiries@yaxleyhall.com

**Open:** Private functions, weddings and events only.

**Admission:** Closed to public.

**Key facts:** T P ▲ ✳

---

## FLATFORD BRIDGE COTTAGE 🌿
### Flatford, East Bergholt, Suffolk CO7 6UL

In the heart of the beautiful Dedham Vale, the hamlet of Flatford is the location for some of John Constable's most famous paintings. Discover more about the work of John Constable in our exhibition, explore Bridge Cottage then relax in our riverside tea room and gift shop. Note: No public entry inside Flatford Mill.

**Location:** Map 8:J10. OS Ref TM076 332. On N bank of Stour, 1m S of East Bergholt B1070. **Owner:** National Trust **Contact:** Visitor Services

**Tel:** 01206 298260 **E-mail:** flatfordbridgecottage@nationaltrust.org.uk

**Website:** www.nationaltrust.org.uk **Open:** 4 Jan–2 Mar 10:30–3:30 Sat & Sun, 5 Mar–30 Mar 10:30–5 Wed-Sun, 31 Mar–27 Apr 10:30–5 open all week, 28 Apr–28 Sep 10:30–5:30 open all week, 29 Sep–26 Oct 10:30–5 open all week, 29 Oct–21 Dec 10:30–3:30 Wed-Sun.

**Key facts:** ℹ Parking free for NT members. ▢ ♿ WCs. ▣ Licensed. P Charge applies. Limited parking for coaches, advanced booking recommended. Please be aware that between the car park and Bridge Cottage is a flight of steps. ⛨ ✳

---

## HAUGHLEY PARK 🏛®
### Stowmarket, Suffolk IP14 3JY

Grade 1 listed red-brick manor house of 1620 set in gardens, park and woodland. Original five-gabled east front, north wing rebuilt in Georgian style, 1820. Varied six acre gardens including walled kitchen garden. Way-marked woodland walks. 17th Century barn bookable for Weddings, Meetings etc.

**Location:** Map 8:J8. OS Ref TM005 618. Signed from J47a and J48 on A14.

**Owner:** Mr & Mrs Robert Williams

**Contact:** Barn Office

**Tel:** 01359 240701 **E-mail:** info@haughleyparkbarn.co.uk

**Website:** www.haughleyparkbarn.co.uk

**Open:** Garden only: May-Sep: Tues, 2-5.30pm. For Bluebell Sunday dates, see website.

**Admission:** Garden £4.00 Child under 16 Free.

**Key facts:** ℹ Picnics allowed. ✳ Bluebell Sun. T ♿ WCs. 🎦 By arrangement. P Limited for coaches. ⛨ On leads. ▲ ▣

---

## ST EDMUNDSBURY CATHEDRAL
### Angel Hill, Bury St Edmunds, Suffolk IP33 1LS

The striking Millennium Tower, completed in 2005, is the crowning glory of St Edmundsbury Cathedral. Further enhanced with the stunning vaulted ceiling in 2010, the 150ft Lantern Tower, along with new chapels, cloisters and North Transept, completes nearly fifty years of development in a style never likely to be repeated.

**Location:** Map 8:I8. OS Ref TL857 642. Bury St Edmunds town centre.

**Owner:** The Church of England **Contact:** Sarah Friswell

**Tel:** 01284 748720

**E-mail:** cathedral@stedscathedral.org

**Website:** www.stedscathedral.co.uk

**Open:** All year: daily 8.30am-6pm.

**Admission:** Donations invited.

**Key facts:** ▢ Open daily. ▣ 🍴 Open Mon-Sat. 🎦 11.30am. ▣ ⛨ ✳

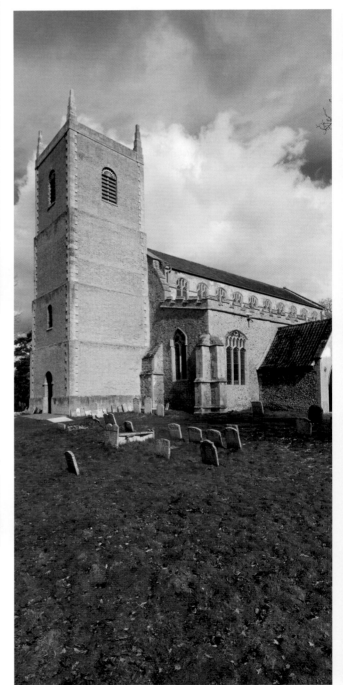

St Mary's Church, Redgrave

**CHURCH OF ST MARGARET OF ANTIOCH** 🏛
Melchbourne Road, Knotting, Bedfordshire  MK44 1AF
**Tel:** 0845 303 2760 **E-mail:** central@thecct.org.uk

**OLD WARDEN PARK** 🏛
Old Warden, Bedfordshire  SG18 9EA
**Tel:** 01767 626200

**ST DENY'S CHURCH** 🏛
Little Barford, St Neots, Bedfordshire  PE19 6YE
**Tel:** 0845 303 2760 **E-mail:** central@thecct.org.uk

**ST GEORGE'S CHURCH** 🏛
Edworth, Biggleswade, Bedfordshire  SG18 8QX
**Tel:** 0845 303 2760 **E-mail:** central@thecct.org.uk

**ST MARY'S CHURCH** 🏛
Lower Gravenhurst, Gravenhurst, Bedfordshire  MK45 4JR
**Tel:** 0845 303 2760 **E-mail:** central@thecct.org.uk

**ST MARY'S CHURCH** 🏛
Potsgrove, Milton Keynes, Bedfordshire  MK17 9HG
**Tel:** 0845 303 2760 **E-mail:** central@thecct.org.uk

**ST MICHAEL'S CHURCH** 🏛
Farndish, Wellingborough, Bedfordshire  NN29 7HJ
**Tel:** 0845 303 2760 **E-mail:** central@thecct.org.uk

**THE LUTON HOO WALLED GARDEN**
Luton Hoo Estate, Luton, Bedfordshire  LU1 3TQ
**Tel:** 01582 879089 **E-mail:** office@lhwg.org.uk

**WREST PARK** ⌗
Silsoe, Luton, Bedfordshire  MK45 4HS
**Tel:** 01525 860152 **E-mail:** customers@english-heritage.org.uk

**ALL SAINTS' CHURCH** 🏛
Church Lane, Conington, Peterborough, Cambs  PE7 3QA
**Tel:** 0845 303 2760 **E-mail:** central@thecct.org.uk

**ANGLESEY ABBEY, GARDENS & LODE MILL** 🌿
Quy Road, Lode, Cambridgeshire  CB25 9EJ
**Tel:** 01223 810080 **E-mail:** angleseyabbey@nationaltrust.org.uk

**CHURCH OF ST CYRIAC & ST JULITTA** 🏛
High Street, Swaffham Prior, Cambridge  CB25 0LD
**Tel:** 0845 303 2760 **E-mail:** central@thecct.org.uk

**CHURCH OF ST JOHN THE BAPTIST** 🏛
Main Road, Parson Drove, Wisbech, Cambridgeshire  PE13 4LF
**Tel:** 0845 303 2760 **E-mail:** central@thecct.org.uk

**ST ANDREW'S CHURCH** 🏛
Steeple Gidding, Huntingdon, Cambridgeshire  PE28 5RG
**Tel:** 0845 303 2760 **E-mail:** central@thecct.org.uk

**ST JOHN'S CHURCH** 🏛
Green Street, Duxford, Cambridge, Cambridgeshire  CB22 4RG
**Tel:** 0845 303 2760 **E-mail:** central@thecct.org.uk

**ST MARGARET'S CHURCH** 🏛
High Street, Abbotsley, St Neots, Cambridgeshire  PE19 6UJ
**Tel:** 0845 303 2760 **E-mail:** central@thecct.org.uk

**ST MICHAEL'S CHURCH** 🏛
Longstanton, Cambridge, Cambridgeshire  CB24 3BZ
**Tel:** 0845 303 2760 **E-mail:** central@thecct.org.uk

**ST PETER'S CHURCH** 🏛
High Street, Offord D'Arcy, St Neots, Cambs  PE19 5RH
**Tel:** 0845 303 2760 **E-mail:** central@thecct.org.uk

**BETH CHATTO GARDENS**
Elmstead Market, Colchester, Essex  CO7 7DB
**Tel:** 01206 822007 **E-mail:** info@bethchatto.fsnet.co.uk

**CHURCH OF ST MARY THE VIRGIN** 🏛
Barlon Road, Little Bromley, Manningtree, Essex  CO11 2PP
**Tel:** 0845 303 2760 **E-mail:** central@thecct.org.uk

**HEDINGHAM CASTLE**
Bailey Street, Castle Hedingham, Essex  CO9 3DJ
**Tel:** 01787 460261 **E-mail:** corporate@hedinghamcastle.co.uk

**HOLY TRINITY CHURCH** 🏛
Trinity Street, Halstead, Essex  CO9 1JH
**Tel:** 0845 303 2760 **E-mail:** central@thecct.org.uk

**LAYER MARNEY TOWER** 🏛ⓔ
Nr Colchester, Essex  CO5 9US
**Tel:** 01206 330784 **E-mail:** info@

**MARKS HALL ARBORETUM & GARDEN**
Coggeshall, Essex  CO6 1TG
**Tel:** 01376 563796 **E-mail:** enquiries@markshall.org.uk

**RHS GARDEN HYDE HALL**
Creephedge Lane, Rettendon, Chelmsford, Essex  CM3 8ET
**Tel:** 0845 265 8071 **E-mail:** hydehall@rhs.org.uk

**ST LEONARD-AT-THE-HYTHE CHURCH** 🏛
Hythe Hill, Colchester, Essex  CO1 2NP
**Tel:** 0845 303 2760 **E-mail:** central@thecct.org.uk

**ST MARY'S CHURCH** 🏛
Hall Road, West Bergholt, Colchester, Essex  CO6 3DU
**Tel:** 0845 303 2760 **E-mail:** central@thecct.org.uk

**SALING HALL GARDEN** 🏛
Great Saling, Braintree, Essex  CM7 5DT
**Tel:** 01371 850 243

**THE MUNNINGS COLLECTION**
Castle House, Castle Hill, Dedham, Essex  CO7 6AZ
**Tel:** 01206 322127 **E-mail:** info@siralfredmunnings.co.uk

**ASHRIDGE GARDENS** 🏛ⓔ
Berkhamsted, Hertfordshire  HP4 1NS
**Tel:** 01442 843491 **E-mail:** reception@

**CASSIOBURY PARK**
Cassiobury Avenue, Watford  WD17 2DT
**Tel:** 01923 235946

**CHURCH OF ST MARY THE VIRGIN** 🏛
Little Hormead, Buntingford, Hertfordshire  SG9 0LS
**Tel:** 0845 303 2760 **E-mail:** central@thecct.org.uk

## OXHEY CHAPEL 🏛
Gosforth Lane, South Oxhey, Watford, Herts  WD19 7AX
**Tel:** 0845 303 2760 **E-mail:** central@thecct.org.uk

## ST ANDREW'S CHURCH 🏛
Rectory Close, Buckland, Buntingford, Hertfordshire  SG9 0PT
**Tel:** 0845 303 2760 **E-mail:** central@thecct.org.uk

## SHAW'S CORNER 🌿
Ayot St Lawrence, Welwyn, Hertfordshire  AL6 9BX
**Tel:** 01438 820307 **E-mail:** shawscorner@nationaltrust.org.uk

## ALL SAINTS' CHURCH 🏛
West Harling, Thetford, Norfolk  NR16 2SE
**Tel:** 0845 303 2760 **E-mail:** central@thecct.org.uk

## ALL SAINTS' CHURCH 🏛
Thurgarton, Norwich, Norfolk  NR11 7HT
**Tel:** 0845 303 2760 **E-mail:** central@thecct.org.uk

## BAYFIELD HALL
Glandford, Holt, Norfolk  NR25 7JN
**Tel:** 01263 712219 **E-mail:** info@bayfieldhall.com

## CASTLE ACRE PRIORY ⚏
Stocks Green, Castle Acre, King's Lynn, Norfolk  PE32 2XD
**Tel:** 01760 755394 **E-mail:** customers@english-heritage.org.uk

## CHURCH OF ST JOHN THE BAPTIST 🏛
Hellington Hill, Hellington, Norwich, Norfolk  NR14 7BS
**Tel:** 0845 303 2760 **E-mail:** central@thecct.org.uk

Somerleyton Hall

## EUSTON HALL
Thetford, Suffolk  IP24 2QP
**Tel:** 01842 766366

## FELBRIGG HALL 🌿
Felbrigg, Norwich, Norfolk  NR11 8PR
**Tel:** 01263 837444 **E-mail:** felbrigg@nationaltrust.org.uk

## HOVETON HALL GARDENS 🏛
Wroxham, Norwich, Norfolk  NR12 8RJ
**Tel:** 01603 782798 **E-mail:** info@hovetonhallgardens.co.uk

## RAINTHORPE HALL AND GARDENS
Tasburgh, Norwich  NR15 1RQ
**Tel:** 01508 470618

## ST AUGUSTINE'S CHURCH 🏛
St Augustine's Street, Norwich, Norfolk  NR3 3BY
**Tel:** 0845 303 2760 **E-mail:** central@thecct.org.uk

## ST FAITH'S CHURCH 🏛
Little Witchingham, Norwich, Norfolk  NR9 5PA
**Tel:** 0845 303 2760 **E-mail:** central@thecct.org.uk

## ST GEORGE'S CHURCH 🏛
Shimpling, Diss, Norfolk  IP21 4UF
**Tel:** 0845 303 2760 **E-mail:** central@thecct.org.uk

## ST GREGORY'S CHURCH 🏛
Norton Road, Heckingham, Norwich, Norfolk  NR14 6QT
**Tel:** 0845 303 2760 **E-mail:** central@thecct.org.uk

## ST LAURENCE'S CHURCH 🏛
St. Benedict's Street, Norwich, Norfolk  NR2 3PE
**Tel:** 0845 303 2760 **E-mail:** central@thecct.org.uk

## ST MARY'S BELL TOWER 🏛
School Road, West Walton, Wisbech, Norfolk  PE14 7ET
**Tel:** 0845 303 2760 **E-mail:** central@thecct.org.uk

## ST MARY'S CHURCH 🏛
Reedham Road, Moulton, Norwich, Norfolk  NR13 3NW
**Tel:** 0845 303 2760 **E-mail:** central@thecct.org.uk

## ST MARY'S CHURCH 🏛
Islington Green, Tilney, King's Lynn, Norfolk  PE34 4SB
**Tel:** 0845 303 2760 **E-mail:** central@thecct.org.uk

## ST MARY'S CHURCH 🏛
Boughton Long Road, Barton Bendish, Norfolk  PE33 9DN
**Tel:** 0845 303 2760 **E-mail:** central@thecct.org.uk

## ST MARY'S CHURCH 🏛
Church Street, East Bradenham, Thetford, Norfolk  IP25 7QL
**Tel:** 0845 303 2760 **E-mail:** central@thecct.org.uk

## ST MARY'S CHURCH 🏛
East Ruston, Norwich, Norfolk  NR12 9HN
**Tel:** 0845 303 2760 **E-mail:** central@thecct.org.uk

## ST MICHAEL'S CHURCH 🏛
Church Lane, Coston, Norwich, Norfolk  NR9 4DT
**Tel:** 0845 303 2760 **E-mail:** central@thecct.org.uk

Register for news and special offers at **www.hudsonsheritage.com**

### ST NICHOLAS' CHURCH ⋒
**School Road, Buckenham, Norwich, Norfolk  NR13 4HN**
**Tel:** 0845 303 2760 **E-mail:** central@thecct.org.uk

### ST PETER'S CHURCH ⋒
**North Barningham, Norwich, Norfolk  NR11 7LB**
**Tel:** 0845 303 2760 **E-mail:** central@thecct.org.uk

### SHERINGHAM PARK ⅍
**Upper Sheringham, Norfolk  NR26 8TL**
**Tel:** 01263 820550 **E-mail:** sheringhampark@nationaltrust.org.uk

### ALL SAINTS' CHURCH ⋒
**Ellough, Beccles, Suffolk  NR34 7TR**
**Tel:** 0845 303 2760 **E-mail:** central@thecct.org.uk

### ALL SAINTS' CHURCH ⋒
**Little Wenham, Ipswich, Suffolk  CO7 6PU**
**Tel:** 0845 303 2760 **E-mail:** central@thecct.org.uk

### ALL SAINTS' CHURCH ⋒
**The Street, Icklingham, Bury St Edmunds, Suffolk  IP28 6PL**
**Tel:** 0845 303 2760 **E-mail:** central@thecct.org.uk

### ALL SAINTS' CHURCH ⋒
**Church Road, Newton Green, Sudbury, Suffolk  CO10 0QP**
**Tel:** 0845 303 2760 **E-mail:** central@thecct.org.uk

### ALL SAINTS' CHURCH ⋒
**Wordwell, Bury St Edmunds, Suffolk  IP28 6UN**
**Tel:** 0845 303 2760 **E-mail:** central@thecct.org.uk

Ashridge Gardens

### CHURCH OF ST JOHN THE BAPTIST ⋒
**Stanton, Bury St Edmunds, Suffolk  IP31 2XD**
**Tel:** 0845 303 2760 **E-mail:** central@thecct.org.uk

### CHURCH OF ST MARY THE VIRGIN ⋒
**Church Lane, Stonham Parva, Stowmarket, Suffolk  IP14 5JL**
**Tel:** 0845 303 2760 **E-mail:** central@thecct.org.uk

### CHURCH OF ST MARY-AT-THE-QUAY ⋒
**Foundation Street, Ipswich, Suffolk  IP4 1BU**
**Tel:** 0845 303 2760 **E-mail:** central@thecct.org.uk

### FRAMLINGHAM CASTLE ⌗
**Framlingham, Suffolk  IP13 9BP**
**Tel:** 01728 724189 **E-mail:** customers@english-heritage.org.uk

### MELFORD HALL ⅍
**Long Melford, Sudbury, Suffolk  CO10 9AA**
**Tel:** 01787 379228 **E-mail:** melford@nationaltrust.org.uk

### ORFORD CASTLE ⌗
**Orford, Woodbridge, Suffolk  IP12 2ND**
**Tel:** 01394 450472 **E-mail:** customers@english-heritage.org.uk

### ST ANDREW'S CHURCH ⋒
**Covehithe, Lowestoft, Suffolk  NR34 7JW**
**Tel:** 0845 303 2760 **E-mail:** central@thecct.org.uk

### ST ANDREW'S CHURCH ⋒
**Sapiston, Thetford, Suffolk  IP31 1RY**
**Tel:** 0845 303 2760 **E-mail:** central@thecct.org.uk

### ST MARY'S CHURCH ⋒
**Washbrook, Ipswich, Suffolk  IP8 3HQ**
**Tel:** 0845 303 2760 **E-mail:** central@thecct.org.uk

### ST MARY'S CHURCH ⋒
**Akenham, Ipswich, Suffolk  IP1 6TQ**
**Tel:** 0845 303 2760 **E-mail:** central@thecct.org.uk

### ST MARY'S CHURCH ⋒
**Badley, Ipswich, Suffolk  IP6 8RU**
**Tel:** 0845 303 2760 **E-mail:** central@thecct.org.uk

### ST MARY'S CHURCH ⋒
**Rickinghall Superior, Diss, Suffolk  IP22 1EZ**
**Tel:** 0845 303 2760 **E-mail:** central@thecct.org.uk

### ST PETER'S CHURCH ⋒
**Market Square, Sudbury, Suffolk  CO10 2TP**
**Tel:** 0845 303 2760 **E-mail:** central@thecct.org.uk

### SOMERLEYTON HALL & GARDENS ⌂ⓔ
**Somerleyton, Lowestoft, Suffolk  NR32 5QQ**
**Tel:** 08712 224244(office) **E-mail:** carolyn.ashton@somerleyton.co.uk

### THE RED HOUSE - ALDEBURGH
**Golf Lane, Aldeburgh, Suffolk  IP15 5PZ**
**Tel:** 01728 452615 **E-mail:** enquiries@brittenpears.org

### WYKEN HALL GARDENS
**Stanton, Bury St Edmunds, Suffolk  IP31 2DW**
**Tel:** 01359 250287

Burghley House

Derbyshire
Leicestershire &
Rutland
Lincolnshire
Northamptonshire
Nottinghamshire

# East Midlands

Derby-shire Nottingham-shire Lincolnshire
Leicestershire & Rutland
Northampton-shire

The treasure house of Chatsworth is not the only great house and garden in the East Midlands, which offers some of the most interesting houses and gardens in the country for the discerning visitor.

### VISITOR INFORMATION

■ **Owner**
Chatsworth House Trust

■ **Address**
Chatsworth
Bakewell
Derbyshire
DE45 1PP

■ **Location**
**Map 6:P2**
**OS Ref. SK260 703**
From London 3 hrs M1/
J29, signposted via
Chesterfield. 3m E of
Bakewell, off B6012,10m
W of Chesterfield.
**Rail:** Chesterfield Station,
11m
**Bus:** Chesterfield - Baslow
1½m

■ **Contact**
The Booking Office
**Tel:** 01246 565300
**Fax:** 01246 583536
**E-mail:**
visit@chatsworth.org

■ **Opening Times**
House, garden and
farmyard open daily, from
16 March-23 December
2014. The park is open
every day and the stables,
gift shops and Carriage
House Restaurant open
from 6 January 2014. The
farmyard and adventure
playground will open for
half term, 15–23 February
2014.

■ **Admission**
The admission prices for
the house, garden and
farmyard are listed on our
website at
www.chatsworth.org.
Online tickets available.

### Conference/Function

| ROOM | Size | Max Cap |
|------|------|---------|
| Hartington Rm | | 80 |
| Burlington Rm | | 80 |
| Racing Rm | | 22 |

# CHATSWORTH
www.chatsworth.org

## The home of the Duke and Duchess of Devonshire is one of the country's greatest Treasure Houses.

The house is renowned for the quality of its art, landscape and hospitality. Home of the Cavendish family since the 1550s, it has evolved through the centuries to reflect the tastes, passions and interests of succeeding generations. Today Chatsworth contains works of art that span 4000 years, from ancient Roman and Egyptian sculpture, and masterpieces by Rembrandt, Reynolds and Veronese, to work by outstanding modern artists, including Lucian Freud, Edmund de Waal and David Nash.

The garden is famous for its rich history, historic and modern waterworks and sculptures, the Victorian rock garden and the maze. Younger visitors also enjoy the farmyard and adventure playground and the 1000 acre park is open every day.

In 2014 we will be hosting a number of special events including our annual Food and Drink fair, summer flower festival 'Florabundance', Country Fair and Christmas markets; and from November the house will be transformed for Christmas.

In addition to our busy events programme we will be hosting a number of special exhibitions included with your admission. We are excited to be welcoming the works of Michael Craig Martin and Jacob van der Beugel, as well as introducing 'Chatsworth in Wartime', marking the centenary of the outbreak of the First World War. In the autumn we play host to the Sotheby's Beyond Limits sculpture exhibition in the garden, as well as our rolling programme of showcasing Old Master Drawings which will continue through the year.

## KEY FACTS

- 5 gift shops and Farm shop.
- Available for conferences and private functions. Contact Catering.
- WCs.
- Licensed.
- Licensed.
- Small charge for daily tours. Groups pre-book.
- Handheld and audio guides available to hire in English.
- Cars 100 yds, Coaches drop off at house.
- Guided tours, packs, and self guiding materials. Free preliminary visit.
- Dogs on leads only.
- Holiday cottages.

# HADDON HALL 🏛ⓕ
www.haddonhall.co.uk

## Haddon Hall sits on a rocky outcrop above the River Wye near the market town of Bakewell, looking much as it would have done in Tudor times.

There has been a dwelling here since the 11th Century but the house we see today dates mainly from the late 14th Century with major additions in the following 200 years and some alterations in the early 17th Century including the creation of the Long Gallery. William the Conqueror's illegitimate son Peverel, and his descendants, held Haddon for 100 years before it passed to the Vernon family. In the late 16th Century the estate passed through marriage to the Manners family, in whose possession it has remained ever since. When the Dukedom of Rutland was conferred on the Manners family in 1703, they moved to Belvoir Castle, and Haddon was left deserted for 200 years. This was Haddon's saving grace as the Hall thus escaped the major architectural changes of the 18th and 19th Centuries ready for the great restoration at the beginning of the 20th Century by the 9th

Duke of Rutland. Henry VIII's elder brother Arthur, who was a frequent guest of the Vernons, would be quite familiar with the house as it stands today. Haddon Hall is a popular location for film and television productions. Recent ones include 'Pride and Prejudice', and both the BBC dramatization of 'Jane Eyre' and the 2011 feature film 'Jane Eyre' in which Haddon Hall doubled as Mr Rochester's Thornfield.

### Gardens
Magnificent terraced gardens, adorned with roses, clematis and beautiful herbaceous borders, provide colour and scent throughout the summer. Fountain Terrace recently re-designed by award winning garden designer, Arne Maynard.

## KEY FACTS

ⓘ Haddon Hall is ideal as a film location due to its authentic and genuine architecture requiring little alteration. Suitable locations are also available on the Estate.

📷

🍴

♿ WCs.

🎥

🍽 Licensed.

🚶 Special tours £12.00pp minimum of 10, 7 days' notice.

🅿 Ample. 450 yds from house. £1.50 per car.

🎭 Tours of the house bring alive Haddon Hall of old. Costume room also available, very popular!

🐕 Assistance dogs only.

### ■ VISITOR INFORMATION

**■ Owner**
Lord Edward Manners

**■ Address**
Estate Office
Haddon Hall
Bakewell
Derbyshire
DE45 1LA

**■ Location**
Map 6:P2
OS Ref. SK234 663
From London 3 hrs
Sheffield ½hr Manchester
1 hr Haddon is on the E
side of A6 1½m S of
Bakewell. M1/J29.
**Bus:** Chesterfield Bakewell.
**Rail:** Chesterfield Station,
12m.

**■ Contact**
Vikki Castenbauer
**Tel:** 01629 812855
**E-mail:**
info@haddonhall.co.uk

**■ Opening Times**
**April:** Saturday,
Sunday & Monday.
**Easter:** 18-22 Apr.
**May to September:** open
daily (except 19 & 20 Jul).
**October:** Saturday,
Sunday & Monday.
**Opening times:**
12 noon - 5 pm (last
admission 4 pm).
**Christmas:** 3-14
December (opening times
10.30 am - 4 pm (last
admission 3.30 pm).

**■ Admission**
**Summer**
Adult                           £10.00
Child (5-15yrs)          £5.50
Family (2+3)              £28.00
Regular Visitor
Pass                            £18.00
**Groups (15+)**
Adult                           £9.00
Child (5-15yrs)          £4.50
Parking                       £1.50

Due to age and nature of Haddon, there are many uneven floors and steps within the house and gardens and this should be borne in mind when visiting. Please telephone in advance for further information and to hear about the assistance we can give.

**■ Special Events**
Regular programme of special events - check website for details.

© c. Renishaw Hall & Gardens

# RENISHAW HALL AND GARDENS 🏛Ⓕ
## RENISHAW, NR SHEFFIELD, DERBYSHIRE  S21 3WB
### www.renishaw-hall.co.uk

Renishaw Hall and Gardens have been home to the Sitwell family for over 400 years. Its present owner, Alexandra, welcomes you. Renishaw Hall is set in eight acres of Italianate gardens, designed over 115 years ago by Sir George Sitwell and featuring statues and yew hedges alongside beautiful herbaceous borders and ornamental ponds. Mature woodlands and lakes offer wonderful walks. The hall offers an intriguing insight into the Sitwell family's history, with a fascinating collection of paintings including work by John Piper and photographs by Cecil Beaton. The hall and gardens are open for group and public tours, see our website for details. The stables house the Gallery Café and shop. Plant sales are available. Tours of the historic vineyard are available throughout the season. The hall, gardens and estate can be hired for film and photo shoots. **Location:** Map 7:A2. OS Ref SK435 786. On A6135, 3m from M1/J30, located between Sheffield and Chesterfield. **Owner:** Mrs Hayward

**Contact:** The Operations Manager  **Tel:** 01246 432310  **Fax:** 01246 430760
**E-mail:** enquiries@renishaw-hall.co.uk  **Open:** 2014 29 Mar-28 Sep. Gardens open Wed-Sun & BH Mons, 10.30am-4.30pm. Hall open to public on Fridays throughout season 1pm or 2.30pm & weekends in Aug, pre-booking advisable for guided tours. Hall & garden & vineyard tours available throughout year for private groups & coach tours, by appointment only.
**Admission:** HHA /RHS members free entry to gardens. Guided hall tours £6.50. Discounts for coach/group bookings over 25 people. Parking £1.00. Non member entry gardens £6.50 Adults, £5.50 Concessions, £3.25 Children, under 5s free. Non member guided hall tour £12.75 Adults, £11.75 Concessions.
**Key facts:** ℹ Gallery Cafe, Gift Shop, WC available during garden opening. 📷 🐕 ☂ ♿ Partial. WCs. 🍽 Licensed. 🎧 By arrangement throughout season for groups & on Fridays to public 🅿 £1 per car for the day 🚌 ♿ On leads. 🔔 ♿

## ALL SAINTS' CHURCH
### Kedleston Hall, Kedleston, Quarndon
### Derbyshire DE22 5JH
www.visitchurches.org.uk

All Saints' church is all that remains of the medieval village of Kedleston, razed in 1759 by Sir Nathaniel Curzon to make way for the magnificent Kedleston Hall. Today, the hall is a beautiful National Trust property and you can easily combine a trip to both attractions at once. The Curzon family has lived at Kedleston for 700 years and their stunning memorials - created by several famous designers including Robert Adam - fill the church. The grandest was erected in 1909, commissioned by Lord Curzon, Viceroy of India, for his wife Mary. A dazzling marble tomb - with lifesize figures and watching angels - floats on a sea of green translucent quartz in its own little chapel with superb stained glass windows. **Location:** OS Ref SK313 404. Travel from Derby to Ashbourne on A52 for 5 miles, then follow brown National Trust signs to Kedleston Hall; the church is directly next to the Hall. **Contact:** Please call The Churches Conservation Trust on 0845 303 2760 (Mon-Fri, 9am–5pm)
**Open:** From 26 Mar to 30 Oct: Mon-Wed and on weekends, 11am to 5pm.

## MELBOURNE HALL & GARDENS
### Melbourne, Derbyshire DE73 8EN
www.melbournehall.com

This beautiful house of history, in its picturesque poolside setting, was once the home of Victorian Prime Minister William Lamb. The fine gardens, in the French formal style, contain Robert Bakewell's intricate wrought iron arbour and a fascinating yew tunnel. Upstairs rooms available to view by appointment. **Location:** Map 7:A5. OS Ref SK389 249. 8m S of Derby. From London, exit M1/J24. **Owner:** Lord & Lady Ralph Kerr **Contact:** Mrs Gill Weston **Tel:** 01332 862502 **Fax:** 01332 862263 **E-mail:** melbhall@globalnet.co.uk **Open:** Hall: Aug only (not first 3 Mons) 2-5pm. Last admission 4.15pm. Gardens: 1 Apr-30 Sep: Weds, Sats, Suns, BH Mons, 1.30-5.30pm. Additional open days possible in Aug. Additional days in Aug whenever the Hall is open. **Admission:** Hall: Adult £4.50, Child £3.00, OAP £3.50. Gardens: Adult £4.50,Child/OAP £3.50. Hall & Gardens: Adult £6.50, Child £4.50, OAP £5.50. **Key facts:** ⓘ Crafts. No photography in house. ⌕ Visitor centre shops inc. picture framer, gift shop, antiques, jewellery, cakes, furniture restorer. ⓚ Partial. WCs. ⓦ Melbourne Hall Tea room. ⓕ Obligatory in house Tue-Sat. ⓟ Limited. No coach parking. ⓗ Guide dogs only. ⓧ

## HARDWICK ESTATE ⚜
### Doe Lea, Chesterfield, Derbyshire S44 5QJ

One of the most splendid houses in England. Built by the extraordinary Bess of Hardwick in the 1590's, and unaltered, yet its huge windows and high ceilings make it feel strikingly modern. Rich tapestries, plaster friezes and alabaster fireplaces colour the rooms. Walled courtyards enclose fine gardens, orchards and a herb garden. The Parkland has circular walks, fishing ponds and rare breed animals. **Location:** Map 7:A3. OS Ref OS120 SK456 651. 7½m NW of Mansfield, 9½m SE of Chesterfield: approach from M1/J29 via A6175 From M1/J29 take A6175, signposted to Clay Cross then first left and left again to Stainsby Mill. **Owner:** National Trust **Contact:** Support Service Assistant **Tel:** 01246 850430 **Fax:** 01246 858424 **Shop/Restaurant:** 01246 858409 **E-mail:** hardwickhall@nationaltrust.org.uk **Website:** www.nationaltrust.org.uk/hardwick **Open:** Please see website or contact us for up-to-date information. **Admission:** Please see website or contact us for up-to-date information. **Key facts:** ⓘ ⌕ ⓣ ⓚ Partial. WCs. ⓦ ⓘⓘ Licensed. ⓕ By arrangement. ⓟ Limited for coaches. ▦ ⓗ Guide dogs only. ▣ ⓥ

## CATTON HALL
### Catton, Walton-On-Trent, South Derbyshire DE12 8LN
www.catton-hall.com

Catton, built in 1745, has been in the hands of the same family since 1405 and is still lived in by the Neilsons as their private home. This gives the house a unique, relaxed and friendly atmosphere, with its spacious reception rooms, luxurious bedrooms and delicious food and wine. Catton is centrally located for residential or non-residential business meetings/seminars, product launches and team-building activities, as well as for accommodation for those visiting Birmingham, the NEC, the Belfry - or just for a weekend celebration of family and friends. The acres of parkland alongside the River Trent are ideal for all types of corporate and public events.
**Location:** Between Lichfield & Burton-on-Trent (8m from each). Birmingham NEC 20m. **Owner/Contact:** Robin & Katie Neilson **Tel:** 01283 716311 **E-mail:** r.neilson@catton-hall.com **Open:** By prior arrangement all year, for corporate hospitality, shooting parties, or private groups. Tours of the house every Monday in August and all Bank Holiday Mondays. **Key facts:** ⓘ Conference facilities. ⓣ By arrangement. ⓚ ⓕ By arrangement. ▦ 4 x four posters, 5 twin, all en-suite. ⓥ

Renishaw Hall

# STANFORD HALL 🏛ⓕ
## STANFORD HALL, LUTTERWORTH, LEICESTERSHIRE  LE17 6DH
### www.stanfordhall.co.uk

Stanford has been the home of the Cave family, ancestors of the present owner. since 1430. In the 1690s, Sir Roger Cave commissioned the Smiths of Warwick to pull down the old Manor House and build the present Hall. Throughout the house are portraits of the family and examples of furtniture and objects which they collected over the centuries. There is also a collection of Royal Stuart portriats. The Hall and Stables are set in an attractive Park on the banks of Shakespeare's Avon. There is a walled Rose Garden and an early ha-ha.

**Location:** Map 7:B7. OS Ref SP587 793. M1/J18 6m,M1/J19 (from/to the N only) 2m, M6 exit/access at A14/M1(N)J 2m, A14 2m. Historic House signs.
**Owner:** Mr & Mrs N Fothergill
**Contact:** Sarah Maughan
**Tel:** 01788 860250  **Fax:** 01788 860870
**E-mail:** s.maughan@stanfordhall.co.uk

**Open:** Special 3 week Easter opening – Mon 7 Apr-Sun 27 Apr 2014. Open other days in conjunction with park events. See our website or telephone for details. House open any weekday or weekday evening for pre-booked groups.
**Admission:** House & Grounds: Adult £8.00, Child (5-15 yrs) £2.50. Private group tours (20+): Adult £8.50, Child £2.50.
Special admission prices will apply on event days.
**Key facts:** ⓘ Craft centre (most Suns). Corporate days, clay pigeon shoots, filming, photography, small conferences, accommodation. Parkland, helicopter landing area, lecture room, Stables cafe. Caravan site. ⬚ ⊤ Lunches, dinners & wedding receptions. ⬚ Partial. WCs. ⬚ ⓕ Tour time: ¾ hr in groups of approx 25. ⓟ 1,000 cars and 6-8 coaches. Free meals for coach drivers, coach parking on gravel in front of house. ⬚ ⬚ Dogs on leads only. ⬚ Accommodation available. ⬚

# BELVOIR CASTLE 🏛ⓕ

**Belvoir, Grantham, Leicestershire  NG32 1PE**
Belvoir Castle, the home of the Duke and Duchess of Rutland, stands high on a hill overlooking 16,000 acres of woodland and farmland. Visitors from all over the world are welcomed here to events in the park, weddings, our world famous pheasant and partridge shoot, tours of the Castle and its art collection and our recently renovated gardens. Whatever draws you to Belvoir will enable you to share the magic of this estate.

**Location:** Map 7:C4. OS Ref SK820 337. A1 from London 110m. Leicester 30m. Grantham 7m.
**Owner:** Their Graces The Duke and Duchess of Rutland
**Contact:** Harvey Proctor
**Tel:** 01476 871001  **E-mail:** Harvey@belvoircastle.com
**Website:** www.belvoircastle.co.uk
**Open:** Please see website for details.  **Admission:** Please see website for details.
**Key facts:** ⬚ ⊤ Banquets, private rooms available. ⬚ Ground floor. ⬚ ⓕ ⓟ Ample. ⬚ ⬚ Guide dogs only. ⬚ Wedding Venue. ⬚

Stanford Hall Library

# BURGHLEY HOUSE ⓘⒻ
www.burghley.co.uk

## Burghley House, home of the Cecil family for over 400 years is one of England's Greatest Elizabethan Houses.

Burghley was built between 1555 and 1587 by William Cecil, later Lord Burghley, principal adviser and Lord High Treasurer to Queen Elizabeth. During the 17th and 18th Centuries, the House was transformed by John 5th Earl of Exeter and Brownlow, the 9th Earl; travelling to the cultural centres of Europe and employing many of the foremost craftsmen of their day. Burghley contains one of the largest private collections of Italian art, unique examples of Chinese and Japanese porcelain and superb items of 18th Century furniture. Principal artists and craftsmen of the period are to be found at Burghley: Antonio Verrio, Grinling Gibbons and Louis Laguerre all made major contributions to the beautiful interiors.

### Park and Gardens

The house is set in a 300-acre deer park landscaped by 'Capability' Brown. A lake was created by him and delightful avenues of mature trees feature largely in his design. The park is home to a large herd of Fallow deer, established in the 16th Century. The Garden of Surprises is a modern oasis of flowing water and fountains, statues, and obelisks. The contemporary Sculpture Garden was reclaimed from 'Capability' Brown's lost lower gardens in 1994 and is dedicated to exhibiting innovative sculptures. The private gardens around the house are open in March for the display of spring bulbs.

## KEY FACTS

 Suitable for a variety of events, large park, golf course, helicopter landing area, cricket pitch. No photography in house.

🖭
🎁
🍷
♿ WCs.
📷 Licensed.
🍴 Licensed.
🧗 By Arrangement.
🎧
🅿 Ample. Free refreshments for coach drivers.
🎦 Welcome. Guide provided.
🐕 Guide dogs only.
💒 Civil Wedding Licence.

### VISITOR INFORMATION

■ **Owner**
Burghley House
Preservation Trust Ltd

■ **Address**
House Manager
Stamford
Lincolnshire
PE9 3JY

■ **Location**
Map 7:E7
OS Ref. TF048 062
Burghley House is 1m SE of Stamford. From London, A1 2hrs. Visitors entrance is on B1443.
**Rail:** London - Peterborough 1hr (East Coast mainline). Stamford Station 12mins, regular service from Peterborough.
**Taxi:** Direct line 01780 481481

■ **Contact**
The House Manager
**Tel:** 01780 752451
**Fax:** 01780 480125
**E-mail:**
burghley@burghley.co.uk

■ **Opening Times**
**Summer**
**House & Gardens:**
15 March-2 November (closed 4-7 September) Open Daily (House closed on Fridays), 11am-5pm, (last admission 4.30pm).

■ **Admission**
**House & Gardens**
| | |
|---|---|
| Adult | £14.50 |
| Child (3-15yrs) | £7.20 |
| Conc. | £13.00 |
| Family | £38.50 |

**Groups (20+)**
| | |
|---|---|
| Adult | £11.50 |
| School (up to 14 yrs) | £6.50 |

**Gardens only**
| | |
|---|---|
| Adult | £8.50 |
| Child (3-15yrs) | £5.50 |
| Conc. | £7.20 |
| Family | £28.00 |

*Includes a voluntary Gift Aid donation but visitors can choose to pay the standard prices displayed on our website.

■ **Special Events**
The Burghley Horse Trials 4-7 September 2014.

### Conference/Function

| ROOM | Size | Max Cap |
|---|---|---|
| Great Hall | 70' x 30' | 160 |
| Orangery | 100' x 20' | 120 |

# ALL SAINTS' CHURCH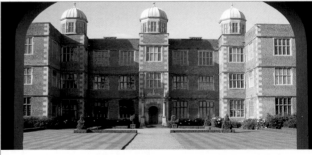
## Old Church Lane, Great Steeping, Spilsby
### Lincolnshire PE23 5PR
#### www.visitchurches.org.uk

Built in 1748, this riverside church stands proudly on lush marshland.
It is surrounded by a complex and undisturbed medieval field system, revealed by aerial photography.
Its distinctively Georgian design is elegant yet simple - essentially just a nave topped with an attractive wooden bell turret.
**Location:** OS Ref TF434 639.
3 miles south east of Spilsby, off the B1195.
**Contact:** Please call The Churches Conservation Trust on 0845 303 2760 (Monday-Friday, 9am–5pm)
**Open:** Keyholder nearby.

# AYSCOUGHFEE HALL MUSEUM & GARDENS
## Churchgate, Spalding, Lincolnshire PE11 2RA
### www.ayscoughfee.org

Ayscoughfee Hall, a magnificent grade I listed building, was built in the 1450s. The Hall is set in extensive landscaped grounds which include amongst other features a memorial designed by Edwin Lutyens. The Museum features the history of the Hall, the people who lived there and the surrounding Fens.
**Location:** Map 7:F5. OS Ref TF249 223. E bank of the River Welland, 5 mins walk from Spalding town centre.
**Owner:** South Holland District Council
**Contact:** Museum Officer
**Tel:** 01775 764555
**E-mail:** museum@sholland.gov.uk
**Open:** Hall 10.30am-4pm Wed-Sun (open on BH Mon), closed over Christmas period. Gardens 8am until dusk
**Admission:** Free.
**Key facts:** ⓘ Photography allowed. ▣ Small shop in Hall. ☎ Email for info. ♿ WCs, lift. ▣ Open 7 days a week. ⓕ By arrangement. ▣ ▣ Email for info. 🦮 Guide dogs only. ⚑ Email for info. ❄ Closed at Christmas ▣

# ALL SAINTS' CHURCH
## Thacker Bank, Theddlethorpe, Louth
### Lincolnshire LN12 1PE
#### www.visitchurches.org.uk

A 14th to 15th Century church with Norman origins, All Saints is known as the Cathedral of the Marsh - a testament to its impressive length and spacious light-filled interior, as well as the quality of the interior carvings.
Despite its lonely grandeur, the outside of the church has a colourful appearance as the local north Lincolnshire Greens and is patched with brick and limestone.
**Location:** OS Ref TF464 882.
7 miles east of Louth, off A1031.
**Contact:** Please call The Churches Conservation Trust on 0845 303 2760 (Mon-Fri, 9am–5pm)
**Open:** Keyholder nearby.

# DODDINGTON HALL & GARDENS ▣ⓕ
## Lincoln LN6 4RU
### www.doddingtonhall.com

Romantic Smythson house standing today as it was built in 1595. Still a family home. Georgian interior with fascinating collection of porcelain, paintings and textiles. Five acres of wild and walled formal gardens plus kitchen garden provide colour and interest year-round. Award-winning Farm Shop, Café & Restaurant. Country Clothing, Farrow & Ball and India Jane Interiors Store.
**Location:** Map 7:D2. OS Ref SK900 710. 5m W of Lincoln on the B1190, signposted off the A46 AND b1190 **Owner:** Mr & Mrs J J C Birch
**Contact:** The Estate Office **Tel:** 01522 812510
**E-mail:** info@doddingtonhall.com **Open:** Gardens Only: From 16 Feb-13 Apr & throughout Oct. Suns only, 11am-4pm. Last admission 3.30pm. House & Gardens: 20 Apr-28 Sep, Suns, Weds and BH Mons. 1-5pm (Gardens open at 11am) Last admission 4.15pm. 2014 -Sculpture in the Garden Exhibition, Gardens open daily 2 Aug-7 Sep inclusive. **Admission:** Gardens only: Adult £6.00, Child £3.00. House & Gardens: Adult £9.50, Child £4.75. U4 free. Family & Season Tickets available. Group visits (guided tours for 20+) £9.50 per head.
**Key facts:** ⓘ Photography permitted, no flash. No stilettos. ▣ Farm Shop - Doddington & local produce. ❄ Seasonal. ☎ ♿ Virtual tour. Garden accessible -mixed surface. ▣ Open 7 days. Breakfast, lunches and teas. No booking. 🍴 Open 7 days and Fri/Sat eve. ⓕ By arrangement. ▣ Ⓟ ▣ Workshops for KS1/2. 🦮 Guide dogs only. ▣ ⚑ ❄ ▣

# GRIMSTHORPE CASTLE, PARK AND GARDENS 🏛Ⓕ
## Grimsthorpe, Bourne, Lincolnshire PE10 0LZ
### www.grimsthorpe.co.uk

Building styles from 13 Century. North Front is Vanbrugh's last major work. State Rooms and picture galleries including tapestries, furniture and paintings. 3,000 acre park with lakes, ancient woods, cycle trail, hire shop. Extensive gardens. Groups can explore the park in their own coach by booking a one-hour, escorted park tour. **Location:** Map 7:D5. OS Ref TF040 230. 4m NW of Bourne on A151, 8m E of Colsterworth Junction of A1. **Owner:** Grimsthorpe & Drummond Castle Trust Ltd. A Charity registered in England, Wales & Scotland SCO39364. **Contact:** Ray Biggs **Tel:** 01778 591205
**E-mail:** ray@grimsthorpe.co.uk **Open:** Castle - Apr & May: Suns, Thurs & BH Mons. Jun-Sep: Sun-Thur. 1-5pm (last admission 4pm). Park & Gardens - As Castle, 11am-6pm (last admission 5pm). Groups: Apr-Sep: by arrangement. **Admission:** Castle, Park & Garden: Adult £10.50, Child £4.00, Conc. £9.50, Family (2+3) £25.00. Park & Gardens: Adult £5.50, Child £2.00, Conc. £4.50, Family (2+3) £13.00. Group rates on application. **Key facts:** 🛈 No photography in house. 📷 🖵 Conferences (up to 40), inc catering. 🅰 WCs. 🍽 🎫 Obligatory except Suns. 🅿 Ample. 🎞 🐾 Dogs on leads only. 🎗

# ST MICHAEL'S CHURCH 🅰
## Burwell, Louth, Lincolnshire LN11 8PR
### www.visitchurches.org.uk

The brick-and-greensand church tower of St Michael's can be seen on a hillside above the main road and the church has great views over gently rolling countryside.
The walls show clear signs of alterations over the centuries: there was once a south aisle and the near windowless north wall may have been adjacent to monastic buildings.
Prominent inside is the exquisite Norman chancel arch with carved capitals; above it, a medieval wallpainting depicts a crowned head. There is also a 17th Century pulpit and some interesting monuments.
**Location:** OS Ref TF356 797.
5 miles south of Louth on A16.
**Open:** Open daily.

# ST BENEDICT'S CHURCH 🅰
## Church Lane, Haltham-on-Bain, Horncastle Lincolnshire LN9 6JF
### www.visitchurches.org.uk

A lovely Norman church, with a stunning decorated east window and a beautifully simple interior.
Look out for the 17th Century pulpit and the unusual Norman carving above the south doorway.
There are also old pews with carved ends in various directions facing the 17th Century pulpit, a screen adapted as a family pew, Royal Arms of Charles I and lovely old tiled floors.
The wooden-fenced churchyard is filled with wildflowers in spring.
**Location:** OS Ref TF246 638. 4 miles south of Horncastle, on A153.
**Open:** Open daily.

# ST PETER'S CHURCH 🅰
## South Somercotes, Louth Lincolnshire LN11 7BW
### www.visitchurches.org.uk

This 13th Century church has a tall, slender spire, which for centuries has guided sailors along the Lincolnshire coast, giving the church the nickname of 'The Queen of the Marsh'.
The building is mainly 13th Century, but the tower and spire were added somewhat later, and many windows were inserted in the 15th Century.
Its spacious interior contains a superb 15th Century font carved with the instruments of the Passion.
**Location:** OS Ref TF416 938.
8 miles north east of Louth, off A1013.
**Open:** Open daily.

© S Haines

## WOOLSTHORPE MANOR ✤
### Water Lane, Woolsthorpe by Colsterworth
### Grantham NG33 5PD
www.nationaltrust.org.uk/woolsthorpe-manor

Isaac Newton, scientist, Master of the Royal Mint and President of the Royal Society, was born in this modest 17th Century manor house in 1642 and developed his ideas about light and gravity here. Visit the apple tree, explore his ideas in the Science Discovery Centre, see the short film.

**Location:** Map 7:D5. OS Ref SK924 244. 7m S of Grantham, ½m NW of Colsterworth, 1m W of A1. **Owner:** National Trust **Contact:** Visitor Services
**Tel:** 01476 862823 **Fax:** 01476 862826
**E-mail:** woolsthorpemanor@nationaltrust.org.uk
**Open:** See website www.nationaltrust.org.uk/woolsthorpe-manor for up-to date opening times and prices. Manor house closed to the public on Tuesdays, available for group visits - please contact the property for details and prices.
**Admission:** Adult £6.65*, Child £3.35*, Family £16.65*, reduction for pre-booked groups on public open days. *includes voluntary donation; visitors may pay standard prices displayed at the property and on the website.
**Key facts:** 🖼 ⬇ Partial. WCs. ◉ 🅿 Limited for coaches. ◫ 🐾 Assistance dogs only. ✖ ❄ Closed Christmas Day.

## ALL SAINTS' CHURCH 🏠
### Haugham, Louth, Lincolnshire LN11 8PU

The spire of All Saints soars above a round of trees in the open country of the Wolds, visible for miles around. As you reach All Saints on foot down a green lane, you might expect a rustic church - in fact, the building is an example of ecclesiastical elegance. It was built in 1840, modelled on the church of St James in nearby Louth. Inside, the church is solid and welcoming. There are handsome pews and a timber roof, and several memorials to Lincolnshire people. Outside, wildlife skitters around the quiet churchyard.
**Location:** OS Ref TF330 810. 4 miles south of Louth and West of A16; travelling from Louth on A16 Haugham is signposted to the right.
**Contact:** Please call The Churches Conservation Trust on 0845 303 2760 (Mon-Fri, 9am–5pm)
**Website:** www.visitchurches.org.uk
**Open:** Open daily.

## ALL SAINTS' CHURCH 🏠
### Saltfleetby, Louth, Lincolnshire LN11 7TU
The tall, square tower of this marshland church leans dramatically to the west, as if trying to stretch away from the long, low nave below. Inside, the church is striking for its light and stillness - it has an air of peace in contrast to its wild, marshy setting. All Saints is sparsely but beautifully furnished with a gorgeous 15th Century carved screen and two pulpits, one Elizabethan and rustic, the other 17th Century from Oriel College, Oxford. The heavy timbered roof demonstrates the good, honest craftsmanship of medieval builders.
**Location:** OS Ref TF455 905. 6 miles east of Louth, off B1200.
**Contact:** Please call The Churches Conservation Trust on 0845 303 2760 (Mon-Fri, 9am–5pm)
**Website:** www.visitchurches.org.uk
**Open:** Open daily.

## AUBOURN HALL 🏠
### Lincoln LN5 9DZ
Almost 5 acres of lawns and floral borders surround this homely Jacobean manor house. The Rose and Prairie Gardens are new favorites and the Turf Maze, Dell Garden and Stumpery all add to the fascination of this much loved family home. Guided tours available throughout the season.
**Location:** Map 7:D3. OS Ref SK928 628. 6m SW of Lincoln. 2m SE of A46.
**Owner:** Mr & Mrs Christopher Nevile **Contact:** Rachel Jerram, Estate Office
**Tel:** 01522 788224 **Fax:** 01522 788199
**E-mail:** estate.office@aubournhall.co.uk **Website:** www.aubournhall.co.uk
**Open:** Garden open for Events, Groups and Garden visits from May-Sep. Please contact the Estate Office for details.
**Admission:** Adults £4.50. Children Free.
**Key facts:** 🖼 ⬇ Partial. WCs. ◉ 🐾 By arrangement. 🅿 Limited for coaches. ✖ Guide dogs only.

## FULBECK MANOR 🏠
### Fulbeck, Grantham, Lincolnshire NG32 3JN
Built c1580. 400 years of Fane family portraits. Open by written appointment. Guided tours by owner approximately 1¼ hours. Tearooms at Craft Centre, 100 yards, for light lunches and teas.
**Location:** Map 7:D3. OS Ref SK947 505. 11m N of Grantham. 15m S of Lincoln on A607. Brown signs to Craft Centre & Tearooms and Stables.
**Owner/Contact:** Mr Julian Francis Fane
**Tel:** 01400 272231
**Fax:** 01400 273545
**E-mail:** fane@fulbeck.co.uk
**Open:** By written appointment.
**Admission:** Adult £7.00. Groups (10+) £6.00.
**Key facts:** ℹ No photography. ⬇ Partial. WCs. ◉ 🍴 🐾 Obligatory. 🅿 Ample for cars. Limited for coaches. ✖ Guide dogs only. ✖

## MARSTON HALL 🏠
### Marston, Grantham NG32 2HQ
The ancient home of the Thorold family. The building contains Norman, Plantaganet, Tudor and Georgian elements through to the modern day. Marston Hall is undergoing continuous restoration some of it which may be disruptive. Please telephone in advance of intended visits.
**Location:** Map 7:D4. OS Ref SK893 437. 5m N of Grantham and 1m E of A1.
**Owner/Contact:** J R Thorold
**Tel:** 07812 356237
**Fax:** 0208 7892857
**E-mail:** johnthorold@aol.com
**Open:** 22, 23, 24 & 25 Feb. 18, 19, 20, 21 & 22 Apr. 3, 4, 5, 6, 24, 25 & 26 May. 21, 22, & 23 Jun. 11, 12, 13, 14 & 15 Jul. 23, 24, 25 & 26 Aug.
**Admission:** Adult £4.00, Child £1.50. Groups must book.
**Key facts:** ℹ No photography.

## ST BOTOLPH'S CHURCH 🏠
### Skidbrooke, Louth, Lincolnshire LN11 7DQ
Set in magnificent isolation in the Lincolnshire marshland, this early Medieval church has the feel of a Great Hall. The bare and unadorned interior has several wonderful arcades, giving the church its wonderful charm and character.
**Location:** OS Ref TF439 932. 7 miles east of Louth, off B1200.
**Website:** www.visitchurches.org.uk
**Open:** Open daily.

Grimsthorpe Castle, Park and Gardens

## ST MARY'S CHURCH
**Church Lane, Alvingham, Louth, Lincolnshire LN11 0QD**

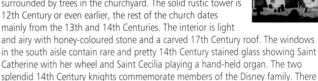

Unusually, the square-towered St Mary's shares a churchyard with another church, St Adelwold's.
The bulk of St Mary's dates from the 13th and 14th Centuries, although a blocked-up window in the chancel could date from before the Norman Conquest in 1066. It also has box pews and improving texts from the early 19th Century, when the tower was rebuilt. There is a working watermill nearby, accessible through a farmyard.
**Location:** OS Ref TF367 914. 3 miles north east of Louth; the church is in the village of Alvingham; follow Church Lane to Abbey Farm.
**Website:** www.visitchurches.org.uk
**Open:** Open daily.

## ST PETER'S CHURCH
**Kingerby, Market Rasen, Lincolnshire LN8 3PU**
Located in the fields at the end of a twisting lane, St Peter's is surrounded by trees in the churchyard. The solid rustic tower is 12th Century or even earlier, the rest of the church dates mainly from the 13th and 14th Centuries. The interior is light and airy with honey-coloured stone and a carved 17th Century roof. The windows in the south aisle contain rare and pretty 14th Century stained glass showing Saint Catherine with her wheel and Saint Cecilia playing a hand-held organ. The two splendid 14th Century knights commemorate members of the Disney family. There is exquisite detail in the carving of the armour, belt and sword. An even more extraordinary monument is a slab with a figure of a knight in relief. His head and praying hands at the top and his feet at the bottom are separated by an elaborate cross where his lower body and legs would be.
**Location:** OS Ref TF057 929. 5m NW of Market Rasen; along the A631 towards Market Rasen; after 5m turn left on road signposted to Kingerby; church is on the left after 3m. **Website:** www.visitchurches.org.uk **Open:** Open daily.

## ARABELLA AUFRERE TEMPLE
**Brocklesby Park, Grimsby, Lincolnshire DN41 8PN**
Garden Temple of ashlar and red brick with coupled doric columns.
**Location:** Map 11:E12. OS Ref TA139 112. Off A18 in Great Limber Village.
**Tel:** 01469 560214 **E-mail:** office@brocklesby.co.uk
**Open:** 1 Apr–31 Aug: viewable from permissive paths through Mausoleum Woods at all reasonable times. **Admission:** None.

## BROCKLESBY MAUSOLEUM
**Brocklesby Park, Grimsby, Lincolnshire DN41 8PN**
Family Mausoleum designed by James Wyatt and built between 1787 and 1794.
**Location:** Map 11:E12. OS Ref TA139 112. Off A18 in Great Limber Village.
**Tel:** 01469 560214 **E-mail:** office@brocklesby.co.uk
**Open:** By prior arrangement with Estate Office.
**Admission:** Modest admission charge for interior.

## ST HELEN'S CHURCH
**Watery Lane, Little Cawthorpe, Louth, Lincolnshire LN11 8LZ**
Built in red brick, with contrasting bands of black brick, St Helen's stands on a mound near the centre of an attractive village. This charming Victorian church with its contrasting bricks, vibrant stained glass and elegant spire is in the style of the early 14th Century. It was considered to be a model for parishes of modest means.
**Location:** OS Ref TF356 837. 3 miles south east of Louth, off A157.
**Website:** www.visitchurches.org.uk
**Open:** Open daily.

## LEADENHAM HOUSE
**Leadenham House, Lincolnshire LN5 0PU**
Late Eighteenth Century house in park setting. **Location:** Map 7:D3. OS Ref SK949 518. Entrance on A17 Leadenham bypass (between Newark and Sleaford).
**Tel:** 01400 273256 **E-mail:** leadenhamhouse@googlemail.com
**Open:** 1-4, 7-11, 22 - 25, 28-30 Apr; 5-9, 12-16 May, Spring & Aug Bank Hols. All 2-5pm. **Admission:** £5.00. Please ring door bell.
Groups by prior arrangement only.

## SCAWBY HALL
**Brigg, N. Lincolnshire DN20 9LX**
Early Jacobean manor house. WW1 Centenary exhibit.
**Location:** Map 11:D12. OS Ref SE966 058. **Tel:** 01652 654 272
**E-mail:** info@scawbyhall.com **Website:** www.scawbyhall.com
**Open:** Tours conducted between 1.30-4.30pm, May 25-28, Jun 7-14, Jul 7-16, Aug 1-4, and Aug 24-27. **Admission:** Adults: £7.00, Concessions: £5.50, Child (under 16): £3.00, Child (under 5): Free, Family: £17.00.

## ST MARTIN'S CHURCH
**Church Lane, Waithe, Grimsby, Lincolnshire DN36 5PR**
St Martin's, with its beautiful square tower, dates back to the 11th Century. The building is a fascinating combination of Romanesque work and Victorian Gothic.
It was restored exquisitely in 1861 by noted local architect James Fowler for the Haigh family (local landowners).
The wonderfully colourful interior has elaborately patterned Minton tiles on the floor, walls and reredos, stunning stained glass and a number of monuments to members of the Haigh family.
**Location:** OS Ref TA283 007. 5 miles south of Grimsby, just off the A16.
**Website:** www.visitchurches.org.uk
**Open:** Open daily.

East Midlands - England

## VISITOR INFORMATION

### ■ Owner
E Brudenell Esq

### ■ Address
Deene Park
Corby
Northamptonshire
NN17 3EW

### ■ Location
**Map 7:D7**
**OS Ref. SP950 929**
6m NE of Corby off A43.
From London via M1/J15
then A43, or via A1, A14,
A43 - 2 hrs. From
Birmingham via M6, A14,
A43, 90 mins.
**Rail:** Corby Station 10 mins
and Kettering Station
20mins.

### ■ Contact
The Administrator
**Tel:** 01780 450278
**Fax:** 01780 450282
**E-mail:**
admin@deenepark.com

### ■ Opening Times
Easter Sun and Mon &
Bank Hols, Suns from May-
Sept and Weds in Sept
2.00pm to 5.00pm.
Last admission 4.00pm.
Refreshments available in
the Old Kitchen.
Open at other times by
arrangement for groups.

### ■ Admission
**Public Open Days**
**House & Gardens**
| | |
|---|---|
| Adult | £9.00 |
| Conc. | £8.00 |
| Child (5-16yrs) | £5.00 |

**Under 5 free with an adult**
**Gardens only:**
| | |
|---|---|
| Adult & Conc. | £6.00 |
| Child (5-16yrs) | £3.00 |

Under 5 free with an adult.

**Groups (20+)**
**by arrangement:**
Weekdays, Suns
| & BHs | |
|---|---|
| (Min 20 | £8.00 |
| | £160.00) |
| Saturdays | £9.00 |
| (Min 20 | £180.00) |

Under 5 free with an adult.

### ■ Special Events
**17 & 24 February:**
Snowdrop Sundays
(Gardens Only),
11am-4pm.
**7 April:** Daffodil Day
(Gardens Only),
11am-4pm.
For more information
please visit our website.

### Conference/Function
| ROOM | Size | Max Cap |
|---|---|---|
| Great Hall | | 150 |
| Tapestry Rm | | 75 |
| East Room | | 18 |

# DEENE PARK
www.deenepark.com

## Home of the Brudenell family since 1514, this sixteenth century house incorporates a medieval manor with important Georgian additions.

Seat of the 7th Earl of Cardigan who led the charge of the Light Brigade at Balaklava in 1854, today the house is the home of Mr. Edmund Brudenell and his son and daughter-in-law, Mr and Mrs Robert Brudenell and the rooms on show are regularly used by their family and friends. It has grown in size as generations have made their own mark through the years, providing the visitor with an interesting yet complementary mixture of styles. There is a considerable collection of family portraits and possessions, including memorabilia from the Crimean War.

The gardens are mainly to the south and west of the house and include long borders, old-fashioned roses and specimen trees. Close to the house there is a parterre designed by David Hicks in

the 1990s. The topiary teapots, inspired by the finial on the Millenium obelisk, form a fine feature as they mature.

Open parkland lies across water from the terraced gardens providing enchanting vistas in many directions. The more energetic visitor can discover these during a rewarding walk in the tranquil surroundings. As well as the flora, there is also a diversity of bird life ranging from red kites to kingfishers and black swans to little grebes. On public open days home-made scones and cakes are available in the Old Kitchen and souvenirs can be found in the Courtyard Gift Shop. Group visits are available at anytime by prior arrangement, with booked lunch and dinners available.

## KEY FACTS

ℹ️ Suitable for events, filming and lectures. No photography in house.

🗄️

🍽 Including buffets, lunches and dinners by arrangement.

♿ Partial. Visitors may alight at the entrance, access to ground floor & garden.

💷 Special rates for groups, bookings can be made in advance, menus on request.

🍴 By arrangement.

🚶 Available for group visits by arrangement (approx 90 mins).

🅿️ Unlimited for cars, space for 3 coaches 10 yds from house.

🐕 In car park only.

🏨 Residential conference facilities by arrangement.

❄️

⚜️

Register for news and special offers at **www.hudsonsheritage.com**

## COTTESBROOKE HALL & GARDENS 🏛ⓕ
### COTTESBROOKE, NORTHAMPTONSHIRE NN6 8PF
www.cottesbrooke.co.uk

Dating from 1702 the Hall's beauty is matched by the magnificence of the gardens and the excellence of the picture, furniture and porcelain collections. The Woolavington collection of sporting pictures is possibly the finest of its type in Europe and includes paintings by Stubbs, Ben Marshall and artists renowned for works of this genre. Portraits, bronzes, 18th Century English and French furniture and fine porcelain are among the treasures.

The formal gardens are continually being updated and developed by influential designers. The Wild Gardens, a short walk across the Park, are planted along the course of a stream.

**Location:** Map 7:B8. OS Ref SP711 739. 10m N of Northampton near Creaton on A5199 (formerly A50). Signed from Junction 1 on the A14.

**Owner:** Mr & Mrs A R Macdonald-Buchanan
**Contact:** The Administrator
**Tel:** 01604 505808  **Fax:** 01604 505619
**E-mail:** welcome@cottesbrooke.co.uk
**Open:** May-end of Sep. May & Jun: Wed & Thur, 2-5.30pm. Jul-Sep: Thur, 2-5.30pm. Open BH Mons (May-Sep), 2-5.30pm.
The first open day is Thur 1 May 2014.
**Admission:** House & Gardens: Adult £8.00, Child £4.50, Conc £7.00. Gardens only: Adult £5.50, Child £3.50, Conc £5.00. Group & private bookings by arrangement.
**Key facts:** ℹ No large bags or photography in house. Filming & outside events. 🚻 ♿ Partial. WCs. 🍴 🔊 Hall guided tours obligatory. 🅿 🏨 🐕 Guide dogs only. 💷

## HOLDENBY HOUSE 🏛ⓕ
### HOLDENBY HOUSE, NORTHAMPTON NN6 8DJ
www.holdenby.com

Once the largest private house in England and subsequently the palace of James I and prison of Charles I, Holdenby has recently been seen in the BBC's acclaimed adaptation of 'Great Expectations'. Its suite of elegant state rooms overlooking beautiful Grade I listed gardens and rolling countryside make it an enchanting and ever popular venue for weddings. Its combination of grandeur and intimacy make it a magnificent location for corporate dinners, parties and meetings, while the spacious grounds have accommodated many large events, from Civil War battles and concerts to The Northamptonshire Food Show. Ask about visiting Holdenby's remarkable Falconry Centre and special interest days in the Garden in addition to the normal Sunday openings.

**Location:** Map 7:B8. OS Ref SP693 681. M1/J15a. 7m NW of Northampton off A428 & A5199.
**Owner:** James Lowther
**Contact:** Gilly Wrathall, Commercial Manager
**Tel:** 01604 770074  **Fax:** 01604 770962  **E-mail:** gilly@holdenby.com
**Open:** Gardens open: Apr-Sept; Suns & Bank Holiday Mons; 1-5pm.
**Admission:** Adult £5.00, Child £3.50, Conc £4.50, Family (2+3) £15.00; Different prices on event days. Groups must book.
**Key facts:** ℹ Children's play area. 🎁 🚻 ♿ 🔊 Obligatory, by arrangement. 🅿 Limited for coaches. 🏆 6 times Sandford Award Winner. 🐕 On leads. 🏨 💷

## KELMARSH HALL AND GARDENS 🏛ⓕ
### KELMARSH, NORTHAMPTON  NN6 9LY
www.kelmarsh.com

Built in the Palladian style to a James Gibbs design, 18th Century Kelmarsh Hall is set in beautiful gardens with views over the surrounding parkland. The former home of society decorator, Nancy Lancaster, Kelmarsh still reflects the essence of her panache and flair. Within the Hall is the Croome Exhibition, showcasing furniture and paintings on loan from Croome Court in Worcestershire. The award-winning gardens include a formal terrace, horse chestnut avenues, rose gardens and the historic walled kitchen garden. Kelmarsh Hall, gardens and parkland can be hired exclusively for weddings, corporate events and private parties. **Location:** Map 7:C8. OS Ref SP736 795. 1/3 m N of A14-A508 jct 2. Rail & Bus: Mkt Harborough.
**Owner:** The Kelmarsh Trust

**Tel/Fax:** 01604 686543  **E-mail:** enquiries@kelmarsh.com
**Open:** Apr 20-Sep 25 2014. Hall 2pm-5pm Thurs, BH Suns, BH Mons & 1st Sun of the month (Croome collection open 1st Sun of month). Gardens & tearoom 11am-5pm Weds, Thurs, Suns & BH Mons. Winter Walk–Feb 23, 11am-4pm.
**Admission:** House tour with garden admission: Adult £7.50, Conc £7.00, Child (5-14 years) £4.50. House tour with Croome exhibition and garden admission (1st Sun of month only): Adult £12.50, Conc £12.00, Child £5.50. Gardens only: Family (2 adults & 2 children) £15, Adult £5.50, Conc £5.00, Child £3.50. Garden season tickets available.
**Key facts:** ⬚ 🏆 🇹 Suitable for corporate events & functions. 🅢 WCs. ⬛ Licensed. 🍴 🎥 Obligatory. 🅿 🚼 On leads. ⬆ ⬇ €

## LAMPORT HALL & GARDENS 🏛ⓕ
### LAMPORT HALL, NORTHAMPTONSHIRE  NN6 9HD
www.lamporthall.co.uk

The home of the Isham family for 400 years, Lamport Hall contains an outstanding collection of furniture and paintings. The west front is by John Webb and the Smiths of Warwick. Surrounded by beautiful parkland, the 10-acre gardens are world famous as the home of the first garden gnome, and there are fascinating examples of changes in garden fashion from across the centuries.
**Location:** Map 7:C8. OS Ref SP759 745. Entrance on A508. Midway between Northampton and Market Harborough, 3m S of A14 J2.
**Owner:** Lamport Hall Preservation Trust  **Contact:** Executive Director
**Tel:** 01604 686272  **Fax:** 01604 686224

**E-mail:** admin@lamporthall.co.uk
**Open:** Open from Easter Sun to 12 Oct: Guided house tours at 2.15 and 3pm every Wed & Thurs. Also open every BH Sun/Mon (free-flow). Private tours at other times by arrangement. Please check website for opening times and prices.
**Admission:** House & Garden: Adult £8.50, Senior £8.00, Child (11-18) £3.00. Gardens Only: Adult £5.00, Senior £4.50, Child (11-18) £2.50. Private groups: House and gardens £8.50, Gardens only £5.00. Minimum charges apply.
**Key facts:** ⓘ No photography in house. Available for filming. 🇹 🅢 Partial. WCs. ⬛ Licensed. 🎥 Obligatory other than Fair Days. 🅿 Limited for coaches. 🔲 🚼 Guide dogs only. ⬆ ✳ Groups only. ⬇

# ROCKINGHAM CASTLE Ⓜ Ⓕ
## ROCKINGHAM, MARKET HARBOROUGH, LEICESTERSHIRE LE16 8TH
### www.rockinghamcastle.com

Rockingham Castle stands on the edge of an escarpment giving dramatic views over five counties and the Welland Valley below. Built by William the Conqueror, the Castle was a royal residence for 450 years. In the 16th Century Henry VIII granted it to Edward Watson and for 450 years it has remained a family home. The predominantly Tudor building, within Norman walls, has architecture, furniture and works of art from practically every century. Surrounding the Castle are 18 acres of gardens following the foot print of the medieval castle. The 400 year old 'Elephant Hedge' bisects the formal terraced gardens.

**Location:** Map 7:D7. OS Ref SP867 913. 1m N of Corby on A6003. 9m E of Market Harborough. 14m SW of Stamford on A427.
**Owner:** James Saunders Watson **Contact:** Nicola Moss, Operations Manager
**Tel:** 01536 770240 **Fax:** 01536 771692

**E-mail:** estateoffice@rockinghamcastle.com **Open:** Easter Sun, 20 Apr-end of May, Suns & BH Mons. Jun-Sep, Tues, Suns & BH Mons. Open noon-5pm. Grounds open at noon. Castle opens at 1pm. Last entry 4.30pm.
**Admission:** House & Gardens: Adults £9.50, Children (5-16 years) £5.50, Family (2+2) £24.50. Grounds only: (Incl. Gardens, Salvin's Tower, Gift Shop & Licensed Tea Room) Adult or Child £5.50 (Not when special events held in grounds). Groups: (min 20) Adults £9.50 (on open days), Adults £11.00 (private guided tour), Children (5-16 years) £4.75. School groups: (min 20) Adult £9.50, Children £4.75 (1 Adult free with 15 Children). Groups/school parties on most days by arrangement.
**Key facts:** ⓘ No photography in Castle. ⬛ Ⓣ ⬛ Partial. WCs. ⬛ Licensed. ⬛ Licensed. Ⓕ By arrangement. ⬛ Ⓟ Limited for coaches. ⬛ ⬛ On leads. ⬛

Haddonstone Show Gardens

# HADDONSTONE SHOW GARDENS
## The Forge House, Church Lane, East Haddon
## Northampton NN6 8DB
### www.haddonstone.com

See Haddonstone's classic garden ornaments in the beautiful setting of the walled manor gardens including: planters, fountains, statues, bird baths, sundials and balustrades - even an orangery, gothic grotto and other follies. As featured on BBC Gardeners' World. New features include a statue walk, contemporary garden and wildflower meadow. Gastro pub nearby.
**Location:** Map 7:B8. OS Ref SP667 682. 7m NW of Northampton off A428. Signposted.
**Tel:** 01604 770711 **Fax:** 01604 770027
**E-mail:** info@haddonstone.co.uk
**Open:** Mon-Fri, 9am-5.30pm. Closed weekends, BHs & Christmas period. Check press or website for details of NGS weekend openings.
**Admission:** Free. Groups by appointment only. Not suitable for coach parties.
**Key facts:** ⓘ No photography without permission. ⬛ Ⓕ By arrangement. Ⓟ Limited. ⬛ Guide dogs only ⬛ ⬛

## ST PETER'S CHURCH
### Marefair, Northampton, Northamptonshire NN1 1SR
www.visitchurches.org.uk

St Peter's stands in a pretty grass churchyard in Northampton town centre, beside the buried remains of a Saxon palace. This 900-year-old Norman church is filled with glorious carved treasures. Inside, great Norman arches of plain and banded stone rise and flow with zig-zag waves. They are supported by beautiful carved capitals, each overflowing with foliage, scrollwork, birds and beasts. These carvings were plastered over in the 17th Century and were carefully unpicked with a bone knife in the early 19th Century by local antiquarian Anne Elizabeth Baker, a labour of love lasting 11 years. Other highlights include a handsome brass lectern and carved wooden pews and monuments. Outside, strange half-human faces glare out from under the eaves, together with cruder, timeworn figures. There are other delights to be found include the 14th Century font, a 12th Century grave slab with astonishingly clear relief carving and some fine Victorian stained glass. **Location:** OS Ref SP749 603. Northampton city centre, south side of Marefair adjoining St. Peter's Way/Marefair junction. **Open:** Nov-Feb: Wed-Sat, 11am-3pm. Mar-Oct: Wed-Sat, 10am-4pm.

## 78 DERNGATE: THE CHARLES RENNIE MACKINTOSH HOUSE & GALLERIES
### 82 Derngate, Northampton NN1 1UH
Northamptonshire's Award Winning House and Galleries. 78 Derngate was remodelled by the world-famous architect and designer, Charles Rennie Mackintosh, in his iconic modernist style. Free entry to the Gallery, café, gift and craft shop. Style, inspiration and innovation, truly is a must-see venue.
**Location:** Map 7:C9. OS Ref SP759 603. In the heart of Northampton close to The Royal & Derngate Theatres. **Owner:** 78 Derngate Northampton Trust
**Contact:** House Manager **Tel:** 01604 603407
**E-mail:** info@78derngate.org.uk **Website:** www.78derngate.org.uk
**Open:** 1 Feb-21 Dec 2014, Tue-Sun & BH Mons: 10am-5pm. Group and school bookings are also available.
**Key facts:** 🛈 🗐 🗵 🛆 WCs. We offer partial mobility access. 🖻 Licensed. 🗵 Guided tours subject to availability, booking advised. 🛏 🗵 Guide dogs only. 🐾

## ALTHORP 🏛
### Northampton NN7 4HQ
Althorp is the Spencer Family's home, which they have owned since its construction in 1508. Visit the house and gardens, set in 550 acres of parkland, and see the paintings, furniture, and porcelain collected by 19 generations of the Spencer Family. Open for 60 days between 1 May and 30 September.
**Location:** Map 7:C9. OS Ref SP682 652. From the M1/J16, 7m J18, 10m. Situated on A428 Northampton - Rugby. Rail: 5m from Northampton station. 14m from Rugby station. **Owner:** The Rt Hon The 9th Earl Spencer **Contact:** Althorp
**Tel:** 01604 770107 **E-mail:** mail@althorp.com
**Website:** www.spencerofalthorp.com
**Open:** May-Sep. Please visit www.spencerofalthorp.com for 2014 opening days.
**Admission:** House & Grounds. Please visit website for up to date admission prices and rates.
**Key facts:** 🛈 No indoor photography with still or video cameras. 🗐 🗵 🛆 WCs. 🖻 🗵 🅿 🗵 Guide dogs only. 🔺 🐾

Althorp

## SOUTHWICK HALL 🏛🇪
### Southwick, Nr Oundle, Peterborough PE8 5BL
Well off the beaten track, Southwick Hall- a family home for 700 years- offers a friendly and informal welcome. Featuring an unusual variety of family and local village artefacts and with building alterations and additions throughout its history, the house vividly illustrates the development of the English Manor House.
**Location:** Map 7:E7. OS Ref TL022 921. 3m N of Oundle, 4m E of Bulwick.
**Owner:** Christopher Capron
**Contact:** G Bucknill
**Tel:** 01832 274064 **E-mail:** southwickhall@hotmail.co.uk
**Website:** www.southwickhall.co.uk
**Open:** BH Suns & Mons: 20 & 21 April /24 & 25 August & the Sunday of the Heritage Open Day scheme all 2-5pm; last admission 4.30pm.
**Admission:** House & Grounds: Adult £7.00, Child £3.50. **Key facts:** 🛆 Partial. 🖻 🗵 Groups welcome by arrangement. 🅿 🗵

## STOKE PARK PAVILIONS
### Stoke Bruerne, Towcester, Northamptonshire NN12 7RZ
The two pavilions, dated c1630 and attributed to Inigo Jones, formed part of one of the first Palladian country houses built in England. They have extensive gardens and overlook parkland. **Location:** Map 7:C10. OS Ref SP740 488. 7m S of Northampton. **Tel:** 01604 862329 **Open:** Aug: daily, 3-6pm. Other times by appointment only. **Admission:** Adult £3.00, Child £1.50.

## WAKEFIELD LODGE 🏛
### Potterspury, Northamptonshire NN12 7QX
Georgian hunting lodge with deer park. **Location:** Map 7:C10. OS Ref SP739 425. 4m S of Towcester on A5. Take signs to farm shop for directions. **Tel:** 01327 811395 **Open:** House: 18 Apr-31 May: Mon-Fri (closed BHs), 12 noon-4pm. Appointments by telephone. Access walk open Apr & May. **Admission:** £5.00.

## WESTON HALL 🏛
### Towcester, Northamptonshire NN12 8PU
A Queen Anne Northamptonshire manor house with an interesting collection associated with the literary Sitwell family.
**Location:** Map 7:B10. OS Ref SP592 469. 5 miles W of Towcester **Tel:** 07710 523879 **E-mail:** george@endven.com **Open:** Most weekends by appointment. **Admission:** £8.00. Free on Open Days.

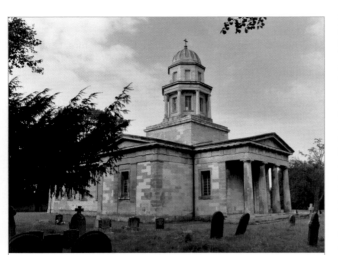

## MILTON MAUSOLEUM

**Markham Clinton, Newark, Nottinghamshire  NG22 0PJ**

www.visitchurches.org.uk

Completed in 1833, this splendid classical building with its domed tower was designed by Sir Robert Smirke for the 4th Duke of Newcastle as a mausoleum for his wife. The nave is separated from the mausoleum by an elegant Ionic reredos screen. Inside there are some stunning marble effigies.

**Location:** OS Ref SK715 730. 1 mile north west of Tuxford off A1 and B1164; access via country lane to West Markham, off B1164. Take High Street and Milton Road to Milton; mausoleum adjoins Milton Road before village.

**Open:** 1 May-30 Sep: 2nd and 4th Sun of each month, 2.30pm-4.30pm.

## MR STRAW'S HOUSE

**5-7 Blyth Grove, Worksop  S81 0JG**

This ordinary semi-detached house, with original interior decorations from 1923, was the home of the Straw family. For 60 years the family threw little away and chose to live without many of modern comforts. Photographs, letters, Victorian furniture and household objects spanning 100 years can still be seen exactly where their owners left them.

**Location:** Map 7:B4. OS Ref SK592802.

**Owner:** National Trust  **Tel:** 01909 482380

**E-mail:** mrstrawshouse@nationaltrust.org.uk  **Open:** 11 Mar - 1 Nov.

**Key facts:** ⓘ Entry by booked timed ticket only-please ring before travel for times and prices. Groups welcome-please contact us before you visit. ⬛ Small shop area with snacks and souvenirs. ⬛ Braille guide, sensory experience, large print guide available. Three steps to access back gardens and greenhouse. Number of stairs in the house. Ⓕ Tours available - please contact before you visit. Ⓟ Free parking, located across the road. Mobility car park located in main car park across road.

## PAPPLEWICK HALL

**Papplewick, Nottinghamshire  NG15 8FE**

A beautiful classic Georgian house, built of Mansfield stone, set in parkland, with woodland garden laid out in the 18th Century. The house is notable for its very fine plasterwork, and elegant staircase. Grade I listed.

**Location:** Map 7:B4. OS Ref SK548 518. Halfway between Nottingham & Mansfield, 3m E of M1/J27. A608 & A611 towards Hucknall. Then A6011 to Papplewick and B683 N for ½m.

**Owner/Contact:** Mr & Mrs J R Godwin-Austen  **Tel:** 0115 9632623

**E-mail:** mail@papplewickhall.co.uk

**Website:** www.papplewickhall.co.uk

**Open:** 1st, 3rd & 5th Wed in each month 2-5pm, and by appointment.

**Admission:** Adult £5.00. Groups (10+): £4.00.

**Key facts:** ⓘ No photography. Ⓕ Obligatory. Ⓟ Limited for coaches. In grounds on leads.

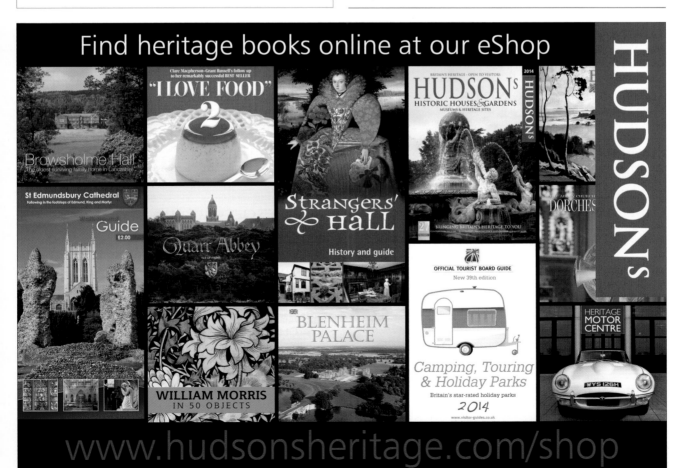

## BOLSOVER CASTLE ⌗
Castle Street, Bolsover, Derbyshire  S44 6PR
**Tel:** 01246 822844 **E-mail:** customers@english-heritage.org.uk

## CALKE ABBEY ⁂
Ticknall, Derbyshire  DE73 7LE
**Tel:** 01332 863822 **E-mail:** calkeabbey@nationaltrust.org.uk

## EYAM HALL
Eyam, Hope Valley, Derbyshire  S32 5QW
**Tel:** 01433 631976 **E-mail:** nicolawright@eyamhall.co.uk

## HARDWICK OLD HALL ⌗
Doe Lea, Nr Chesterfield, Derbyshire  S44 5QJ
**Tel:** 01246 850431 **E-mail:** customers@english-heritage.org.uk

## HOPTON HALL ⌂ℹ
Hopton, Wirksworth, Matlock, Derbyshire  DE4 4DF
**Tel:** 01629 540923 **E-mail:** bookings@hoptonhall.co.uk

## PEVERIL CASTLE ⌗
Market Place, Castleton, Hope Valley  S33 8WQ
**Tel:** 01433 620613 **E-mail:** customers@english-heritage.org.uk

## ST WERBURGH'S CHURCH ⌂
Friar Gate, Derby, Derbyshire  DE1 1UZ
**Tel:** 0845 303 2760 **E-mail:** central@thecct.org.uk

## TISSINGTON HALL ⌂ℹ
Ashbourne, Derbyshire  DE6 1RA
**Tel:** 01335 352200 **E-mail:** events@tissingtonhall.co.uk

## ALL SAINTS' CHURCH ⌂
Highcross Street, Leicester, Leicestershire  LE1 4PH
**Tel:** 0845 303 2760 **E-mail:** central@thecct.org.uk

## ASHBY DE LA ZOUCH CASTLE ⌗
South Street, Ashby De La Zouch  LE65 1BR
**Tel:** 01530 413343 **E-mail:** customers@english-heritage.org.uk

## CHURCH OF ST MARY MAGDELENE ⌂
Stapleford Park, Stapleford, Melton Mowbray, Leics  LE14 2EF
**Tel:** 0845 303 2760 **E-mail:** central@thecct.org.uk

## CHURCH OF ST MICHAEL & ALL ANGELS ⌂
Main Street, Edmondthorpe, Melton Mowbray, Leics  LE14 2JU
**Tel:** 0845 303 2760 **E-mail:** central@thecct.org.uk

## HOLY CROSS CHURCH ⌂
Burley-on-the-Hill, Burley, Oakham, Rutland  LE15 7SU
**Tel:** 0845 303 2760 **E-mail:** central@thecct.org.uk

## ST MARY'S CHURCH ⌂
Saxby Road, Garthorpe, Melton Mowbray, Leics  LE14 2RS
**Tel:** 0845 303 2760 **E-mail:** central@thecct.org.uk

## ST MICHAEL'S CHURCH ⌂
Rectory Lane, Stretton-en-le-Field, Swadlincote  DE12 8AF
**Tel:** 0845 303 2760 **E-mail:** central@thecct.org.uk

## ST PETER'S CHURCH ⌂
Main Street, Allexton, Oakham, Leicestershire  LE15 9AB
**Tel:** 0845 303 2760 **E-mail:** central@thecct.org.uk

## STAUNTON HAROLD HALL ⌂
Staunton Harold, Ashby de la Zouch, Leicestershire  LE65 1RT
**Tel:** 01332 862 599 **E-mail:** rowan@stauntonharoldhall.co.uk

## WITHCOTE CHAPEL ⌂
Oakham Road, Withcote, Oakham, Leicestershire  LE15 8DP
**Tel:** 0845 303 2760 **E-mail:** central@thecct.org.uk

## BELTON HOUSE ⁂
Grantham, Lincolnshire  NG32 2LS
**Tel:** 01476 566116 **E-mail:** belton@nationaltrust.org.uk

## CHURCH OF ST JOHN THE BAPTIST ⌂
Main Road, Yarborough, Louth, Lincolnshire  LN11 0PN
**Tel:** 0845 303 2760 **E-mail:** central@thecct.org.uk

## CHURCH OF ST JOHN THE BAPTIST ⌂
High Street, Burringham, Scunthorpe, Lincolnshire  DN17 3LY
**Tel:** 0845 303 2760 **E-mail:** central@thecct.org.uk

## EASTON WALLED GARDENS ⌂ℹ
Easton, Grantham, Lincolnshire  NG33 5AP
**Tel:** 01476 530063 **E-mail:** info@eastonwalledgardens.co.uk

## ELLYS MANOR HOUSE ⌂ℹ
Dallygate, Great Ponton, Lincolnshire  NG33 5DP
**Tel:** 01476 530023 **E-mail:** ellysmanor@btinternet.com

## ELSHAM HALL GARDENS & COUNTRY PARK ⌂ℹ
Elsham Hall, Brigg, Lincolnshire  DN20 0QZ
**Tel:** 01652 688698 **E-mail:** enquiries@elshamhall.co.uk

## HARLAXTON MANOR
Harlaxton, Grantham, Lincolnshire  NG32 1AG
**Tel:** 01476 403000 **E-mail:** lmees@harlaxton.ac.uk

## ST ANDREW'S CHURCH ⌂
Redbourne, Gainsborough, Lincolnshire  DN21 4QN
**Tel:** 0845 303 2760 **E-mail:** central@thecct.org.uk

## ST JOHN'S CHURCH ⌂
St John's Street, Stamford, Lincolnshire  PE9 2DB
**Tel:** 0845 303 2760 **E-mail:** central@thecct.org.uk

## ST LAWRENCE'S CHURCH ⌂
Snarford, Market Rasen, Lincolnshire  LN8 3SL
**Tel:** 0845 303 2760 **E-mail:** central@thecct.org.uk

## ST MARY'S CHURCH ⌂
Church Hill, Barnetby-Le-Wold, Barnetby, Lincs  DN38 6JL
**Tel:** 0845 303 2760 **E-mail:** central@thecct.org.uk

## ST NICHOLAS' CHURCH ⌂
Normanton-on-Cliffe, Grantham, Lincolnshire  NG32 3BH
**Tel:** 0845 303 2760 **E-mail:** central@thecct.org.uk

## ST PETER'S CHURCH ⌂
Main Street, Normanby-by-Spital, Lincoln  LN8 2HF
**Tel:** 0845 303 2760 **E-mail:** central@thecct.org.uk

## ALL SAINTS' CHURCH ⌂
Holdenby Rd, Holdenby, Northamptonshire  NN6 8DJ
**Tel:** 0845 303 2760 **E-mail:** central@thecct.org.uk

## ALL SAINTS' CHURCH
Thorpe Rd, Aldwincle, Kettering, Northamptonshire  NN14 3EA
Tel: 0845 303 2760 E-mail: central@thecct.org.uk

## CHURCH OF ST PETER & ST PAUL
Preston Deanery, Northampton, Northamptonshire  NN7 2DX
Tel: 0845 303 2760 E-mail: central@thecct.org.uk

## COTON MANOR GARDEN
Nr Guilsborough, Northamptonshire  NN6 8RQ
Tel: 01604 740219 E-mail: pasleytyler@cotonmanor.co.uk

## HOLY TRINITY CHURCH
Main Street, Blatherwycke, Stamford, Northants  PE8 6YW
Tel: 0845 303 2760 E-mail: central@thecct.org.uk

## KIRBY HALL
Deene, Corby, Northamptonshire  NN17 3EN
Tel: 01536 203230 E-mail: customers@english-heritage.org.uk

## ST ANDREW'S CHURCH
Grafton Road, Cranford, Kettering, Northants  NN14 4AD
Tel: 0845 303 2760 E-mail: central@thecct.org.uk

## ST BARTHOLEMEW'S CHURCH
Furtho, Old Stratford, Milton Keynes, Northants  MK19 6NR
Tel: 0845 303 2760 E-mail: central@thecct.org.uk

## ST MICHAEL'S CHURCH
Upton Lane, Upton, Northampton  NN5 4UX
Tel: 0845 303 2760 E-mail: central@thecct.org.uk

## ST PETER'S CHURCH
Deene, Corby, Northamptonshire  NN17 3EJ
Tel: 0845 303 2760 E-mail: central@thecct.org.uk

## CHURCH OF ST MARTIN OF TOURS
Gainsborough Road, Saundby, East Retford, Notts  DN22 9ER
Tel: 0845 303 2760 E-mail: central@thecct.org.uk

## ELSTON CHAPEL
Old Chapel Lane, Elston, Newark, Nottinghamshire  NG23 5NY
Tel: 0845 303 2760 E-mail: central@thecct.org.uk

## HOLME PIERREPONT HALL
Holme Pierrepont, Nr Nottingham  NG12 2LD
Tel: 0115 933 2371

## NEWSTEAD ABBEY
Ravenshead, Nottingham, Nottinghamshire  NG15 8GE
Tel: 01623 455900 E-mail: sallyl@newsteadabbey.org.uk

## ST MICHAEL'S CHURCH
Cotham, Newark, Nottinghamshire  NG23 5JS
Tel: 0845 303 2760 E-mail: central@thecct.org.uk

## ST NICHOLAS' CHURCH
Littleborough Road, Littleborough, Retford, Notts  DN22 0HD
Tel: 0845 303 2760 E-mail: central@thecct.org.uk

## ST WILFRID'S CHURCH
Holme Lane, Low Marnham, Tuxford, Notts  NG23 6SL
Tel: 0845 303 2760 E-mail: central@thecct.org.uk

Ragley Hall

Bagots Castle

Herefordshire
Shropshire
Staffordshire
Warwickshire
West Midlands
Worcestershire

# Heart of England

Tourists throng to the Cotswolds, but this region has many treasures, unusual houses, ancient churches, border fortresses and heritage gardens.

*New Entries for 2014:*
• Bagots Castle
• Hill Close Gardens
• Chedworth Roman Villa

## EASTNOR CASTLE ⓘⒻ
### EASTNOR CASTLE, NR LEDBURY, HEREFORDSHIRE HR8 1RL
www.eastnorcastle.com

Eastnor Castle was built 200 years ago by John, 1st Earl Somers, and is an example of Norman Revival. Standing at the southern end of the Malvern Hills, the castle is still a family home. The inside is dramatic: a 60' high Hall leads to the State Rooms, including the Pugin Gothic Drawing Room and an Italian-style Library, each with a view of the lake. There is a collection of mature specimen trees in the grounds, with a maze, tree trail, children's adventure playground, Burma Bridge tree top walkway and junior assault course. Exclusive use offered for weddings, private and corporate events.

**Location:** Map 6:M10. OS Ref SO735 368. 2m SE of Ledbury on A438 Tewkesbury road. M50/J2 & from Ledbury take the A449/A438. Tewkesbury 20 mins, Malvern 20 mins, Hereford 25 mins, Cheltenham 30 mins, B'ham 1 hr.
**Owner:** Mr J Hervey-Bathurst  **Contact:** Castle Office
**Tel:** 01531 633160  **Fax:** 01531 631776  **E-mail:** enquiries@eastnorcastle.com

**Open:** Easter weekend Fri 18, Sat 19, Sun 20 & BH Mon 21 Apr. May BH Weekends Sun 4, BH Mon 5 & Sun 25, BH Mon 26 May. Every Sun from 1 Jun–28 Sep. Sun-Thur from 20 Jul–28 Aug.
**Admission:** Castle & Grounds: Adult £9.50, Seniors £8.50, Child (3-15yrs) £6.00, Family (2+3) £25.00. Grounds Only: Adult £6.00, Seniors £5.00, Child (3-15yrs) £4.00, Family (2+3) £16.00, Groups (20+) Guided £11.00, Self-guided £8.00, Schools £6.75 Groups (40+) Guided £10.50, Self-guided £7.75.
**Key facts:** ⓘ Corporate events - off-road driving, team building, private dinners, exclusive hire, public events. 🛍 Gift shop open on public open days. 🎬 Product launches, TV & feature films, concerts & charities. ♿ Wheelchair stairclimber to main state rooms. 🍴 Licensed. 📷 By arrangement, Mons & Tues all year, outside normal opening hours. 🅿 Ample 10-200 yds from Castle. 🔲 Guides available. 🐕 Dogs on leads. 🛏 Exclusive use accommodation. 🔲 🔲

## HELLENS ⓘⒻ
### MUCH MARCLE, LEDBURY, HEREFORDSHIRE HR8 2LY
www.hellensmanor.com

Built as a monastery and recorded in the Domesday Book survey of 1086, with Tudor, Jacobean and Stuart additions. Occupied by Mortimer, Earl of March and visited by the Black Prince and Bloody Mary. A wealth of period furnishings, paintings and decorations. Relics from the Civil War and possessions of the Audleys, Walwyns and Whartons as well as Anne Boleyn. Beautiful 17th Century woodwork by the 'King's Carpenter', John Abel. Formal and wild gardens with a labyrinth and dovecote. These historical stories are incorporated into guided tours, revealing the loves and lives of those who lived and died here.

**Location:** Map 6:M10. OS Ref SO661 332. Off A449 at Much Marcle. Ledbury 4m, Ross-on-Wye 4m.
**Owner:** Pennington-Mellor-Munthe Charity Trust  **Contact:** The Administrator
**Tel:** 01531 660504
**Open:** Easter-3 Oct Weds, Thurs, Sun and BH Mon at 2, 3 & 4pm.
**Admission:** Adult £7.00, Child £4.00, Concession £5.00, Students £4.00, Family £15.00 (2 adults and children).
**Key facts:** ⓘ No photography inside house. 🎬 ♿ 🍴 📷 Obligatory. 🅿 🔲 🔲

# HERGEST CROFT GARDENS 🏠ⓕ
## Kington, Herefordshire HR5 3EG
www.hergest.co.uk

Garden for all seasons; from bulbs to spectacular autumn colour, including spring and summer borders, roses, azaleas and an old-fashioned kitchen garden growing unusual vegetables. Brightly coloured rhododendrons 30ft high grow in Park Wood. Over 60 champion trees set in 70 acres of spectacular countryside of the Welsh Marches.

**Location:** Map 6:J9. OS Ref SO281 565. Follow brown tourist signs along A44 to Rhayader.

**Owner:** Mr E J Banks  **Contact:** Mrs Melanie Lloyd

**Tel:** 01544 230160  **E-mail:** gardens@hergest.co.uk

**Open:** Mar: Sats & Suns. 29 Mar-2 Nov: daily, 12 noon-5.30pm. Season tickets and groups by arrangement throughout year. Flower Fair, Mon 5 May 10.30am-5pm. Plant Fair, 12 Oct 10.30am-4.30pm. See website for events.

**Admission:** Adult £6.00, Child (under 16yrs) Free. Pre-booked groups (20+) £5.00. Season ticket £25.00.

**Key facts:** 🅾 🌸 Rare plants. ♿ Partial. WCs. 🍴 🎧 By arrangement. 🅿 🚌 Dogs on leads welcome. ✤ ♨

---

# KINNERSLEY CASTLE
## Kinnersley, Herefordshire HR3 6QF

Marches castle renovated around 1580. Still a family home; many interesting owners with unusual connections. Fine plasterwork solar ceiling. Organic gardens with specimen trees including one of Britain's largest gingkos.

**Location:** Map 6:K9. OS Ref SO3460 4950. A4112 Leominster to Brecon road, castle drive behind Kinnersley village sign on left.

**Owner/Contact:** Katherina Garratt-Adams

**Tel:** 01544 327407

**E-mail:** katherina@kinnersley.com  **Website:** www.kinnersleycastle.co.uk

**Open:** See website for dates and wedding information.

**Admission:** Adult £5.50. Child £2.00. Concs. & Groups over 8: £4.50.

**Key facts:** ℹ No indoor photography. Coach parties by arrangement throughout year. ♿ Unsuitable. 🍴 🎧 Obligatory. 🅿

---

# OLD SUFTON
## Mordiford, Hereford HR1 4EJ

A 16th Century manor house which was altered and remodelled in the 18th and 19th Centuries and again in this Century. The original home of the Hereford family (see Sufton Court) who have held the manor since the 12th Century.

**Location:** Map 6:L10. OS Ref SO575 384. Mordiford, off B4224 Mordiford - Dormington road.

**Owner:** Trustees of Sufton Heritage Trust

**Contact:** Mr & Mrs J N Hereford

**Tel:** 01432 870268/01432 850328.

**E-mail:** james@sufton.co.uk

**Open:** By written appointment to Sufton Court or by fax or email.

**Admission:** Adult £5.00, Child 50p.

**Key facts:** ♿ Partial. 🎧 Obligatory. 🅿 🏫 Small school groups. No special facilities. ✤ ✤

---

# SUFTON COURT 🏠ⓕ
## Mordiford, Hereford HR1 4LU

Sufton Court is a small Palladian mansion house. Built in 1788 by James Wyatt for James Hereford. The park was laid out by Humphry Repton whose 'red book' still survives. The house stands above the rivers Wye and Lugg giving impressive views towards the mountains of Wales.

**Location:** Map 6:L10. OS Ref SO574 379. Mordiford, off B4224 on Mordiford-Dormington road.

**Owner:** J N Hereford  **Contact:** Mr & Mrs J N Hereford

**Tel:** 01432 870268/01432 850328

**E-mail:** james@sufton.co.uk

**Open:** 13-26 May & 12-25 Aug: 2-5pm. Guided tours: 2, 3 and 4pm.

**Admission:** Adult £5.00, Child 50p.

**Key facts:** 🎧 Obligatory. 🅿 Only small coaches. 🏫 Small school groups. No special facilities. 🐕 In grounds, on leads.

---

# LANGSTONE COURT 🏠
## Llangarron, Ross on Wye, Herefordshire HR9 6NR

Mostly late 17th Century house with older parts. Interesting staircases, panelling and ceilings. **Location:** Map 6:L11. OS Ref SO534 221. Ross on Wye 5m, Llangarron 1m. **Tel:** 01989 770254 **E-mail:** richard.jones@langstone-court.org.uk **Website:** www.langstone-court.org.uk **Open:** 20 May-31 Aug: Wed & Thur, 11am-2.30pm, also spring & summer BHs. **Admission:** Free.

Eastnor Castle

## VISITOR INFORMATION

### ■ Owner
The Weston Park Foundation

### ■ Address
Weston Park
Weston-Under-Lizard
Nr Shifnal
Shropshire
TF11 8LE

### ■ Location
**Map 6:N6**
**OS Ref. SJ808 107**
Birmingham 40 mins.
Manchester 1 hr.
Motorway access M6/J12
or M54/J3 and via the M6
Toll road J11A. House
situated on A5 at Weston-
under-Lizard.
**Rail:** Nearest Railway
Stations: Wolverhampton,
Stafford or Telford.
**Air:** Birmingham, West
Midlands, Manchester.

### ■ Contact
Kate Thomas
**Tel:** 01952 852100
**E-mail:** enquiries@
weston-park.com

### ■ Opening Times
Open daily from Saturday
24th May to Sunday 7th
September (Except 13th to
20th August inc.) House is
closed on Saturdays.
Granary Deli & Cafe and
Art Gallery. Free entry and
open all year round (Deli is
closed on Mondays).
Granary Grill open daily all
year round for lunch.
Prices are correct at the
time of going to print.

### ■ Admission
**Park & Gardens:**
| | |
|---|---|
| Adult | £5.50 |
| Child (3-14yrs) | £3.50 |
| Family (2+3/1+4) | £23.00 |
| OAP | £5.00 |
| House admission + | £3.00 |

**Groups (Parks & Gardens):**
| | |
|---|---|
| Adult | £4.00 |
| Child (3-14yrs) | £3.00 |
| OAP | £4.00 |
| House admission + | £2.00 |

**Granary Deli & Cafe and Art Gallery**
Free entry and open all year round.
**Granary Grill**
Open daily, all year round, for lunch.
Prices are correct at the time of going to print.

### Conference/Function

| ROOM | Size | Max Cap |
|---|---|---|
| Dining Rm | 52' x 23' | 90 |
| Orangery | 56'1' x 22'4' | 120 |
| Music Rm | 55' x 17' | 60 |
| The Hayloft | 32' x 22' | 40 |
| Doncaster | 49' x 18'7' | 80 |

# WESTON PARK 🏛Ⓕ
www.weston-park.com

## Weston Park is a magnificent Stately Home and Parkland situated on the Shropshire/Staffordshire border.

The former home of the Earls of Bradford, the House, Park and Gardens is now owned and maintained by the Weston Park Foundation, an independent charitable trust.

Built in 1671, by Lady Elizabeth Wilbraham, this warm and welcoming house boasts internationally important paintings including works by Van Dyck, Gainsborough and Stubbs; furniture and objets d'art, providing enjoyment for all visitors.

Step outside to enjoy the 1,000 acres of glorious Parkland, take one of a variety of woodland and wildlife walks, all landscaped by the legendary 'Capability' Brown in the 18th Century.

With the exciting Woodland Adventure Playground, Orchard, Deer Park and Miniature Railway, there is plenty to keep children entertained.

Over in the Granary Grill & Deli you can enjoy home cooked seasonal dishes, light bites, freshly brewed coffee and homemade cakes and pastries. The Deli's shelves are stocked with an excellent range of delicious food and drink. Upstairs the Granary Art Gallery stages a series of exciting changing exhibitions throughout the year. (The Granary Grill & Deli and Art Gallery are open all year round. Free Entry).

The House can be hired on an exclusive use basis for business meetings, entertaining, weddings, celebrations and private parties.

## KEY FACTS

ⓘ Interior photography by prior arrangement only.

🏠 Granary Deli & Cafe is open all year round. (Closed on Mondays)

Ⓣ Full event organisation service. Residential parties, special dinners, wedding receptions.

♿

☕ The Granary Deli & Cafe serves coffee, homemade cakes and light bites.

🍽 Granary Grill. Licensed.

🚶 By arrangement.

Ⓟ Ample free parking.

🖼 Award-winning educational programme available during all academic terms. Private themed visits aligned with both National Curriculum and QCA targets.

🐕 In grounds. On leads.

🛏 Weston Park offers 28 delightful bedrooms with bathrooms (26 doubles and 2 singles). 17 en suite.

🔔

🔔

## UPTON CRESSETT HALL
### UPTON CRESSETT HALL, BRIDGNORTH, SHROPSHIRE WV16 6UH
www.uptoncressetthall.co.uk

Winner of 'Best Hidden Gem' at the Hudson's Awards, Grade 1 Upton Cressett has been described by Country Life as 'a splendid example of the English manor house at its most evocative'. The spectacular gatehouse is often compared to Sissinghurst with Simon Jenkins describing the historic property as 'an Elizabethan gem' and John Betjeman saying the romantic hamlet is 'remote and beautiful'. The young king Edward V (The Princes in the Tower) stayed in 1483. In the Civil War, Prince Rupert stayed in the gatehouse, as did Margaret Thatcher. The Grade 1 gatehouse with oak spiral staircase and secret tunnel is available for honeymoons and holiday let. The moated gardens have a new rose garden, topiary lawns, woodland walks and an Elizabethan garden. The church of St Michael has been chosen as one of the finest four Norman churches in the country. **Location:** Map 6:M7. OS Ref OS506 592. Bridgnorth 4 miles. Ludlow

17 miles. **Owner:** William Cash **Contact:** The Administrator
**Tel:** Office 01746 714616 **E-mail:** enquiries@uptoncressett.co.uk
**Open:** Weekends (May to Sep) 2pm-5pm but essential to check website.
**Admission:** Group tours all year by appointment (£10.00 per person including tour, tea & cake). Min tour 10 people, max group size 45. Individual admission: Hall, gardens & tour: Adult £7.50. Child (up to 10 years) free. Check website for tour times. Please note: we are not members of the HHA Friends' Scheme.
**Key facts:** ⓘ No large tour coaches due to narrow lane. Maximum coach size: 26 seater. New public toilets for 2014. ⬡ ⓣ ⬤ Pre-booked lunches/teas for groups. ⓟ ⬛ ⬛ Dogs on leads only. ⬛ Gatehouse accommodation booking enquiries either direct via email or through agency: www.ruralretreats.co.uk. ⬛ Grade 1 Norman church of St Michael open all year. ⬛ €

## ST ANDREW'S CHURCH
### Wroxeter, Shropshire SY5 6PH
www.visitchurches.org.uk

St Andrew's is built on the Roman site of Viroconium and the evidence for the ancient town is everywhere. The gateposts are made from two Roman columns; the walls contain massive Roman stones; and the huge font is made from an inverted Roman column base. The interior dates mostly from the 17th and 18th Centuries, with some excellent woodwork in the box pews, pulpit and altar rails. Inside the church are three wonderful 16th Century alabaster tombs - each has a life-size, and eerily life-like, painted figure lying in repose. The earliest and finest commemorates Sir Thomas Bromley and his wife Mabel. He was Lord Chief Justice, and is shown in his lawyer's attire, while his wife wears a fine headdress. On the front of the tomb is the charming figure of their daughter Margaret. Margaret's own tomb is opposite that of her parents, alongside her husband Sir Richard Newport, who wears full armour.
**Location:** OS Ref SJ564 083. 4m SE of Shrewsbury on B4380 Shrewsbury to Ironbridge road. Church in village past Wroxeter Hotel.
**Open:** Open daily.

Upton Cressett Hall

## CHURCH OF ST MARY THE VIRGIN

St Mary's Street, Dogpole, Shrewsbury
Shropshire SY1 1DX
www.visitchurches.org.uk

The spire of St Mary's is one of the tallest in England and for over 500 years it has dominated the skyline of Shrewsbury's old town. The church is now the only complete medieval church in Shrewsbury. It dates from Saxon times and has beautiful additions from the 12th Century onwards. Inside, the atmosphere is peaceful with the soaring stone arches giving way to the church's great treasure - its stained glass. There are panels in glorious colour including the world-famous 14th Century 'Jesse window' filled with figures of Old Testament kings and prophets, and scenes from the life of St Bernard - a medieval cartoon strip that shows him ridding flies from an abbey, riding a mule and curing the sick. No other church in the country has a collection to equal it.
**Location:** OS Ref SJ494 126. Shrewsbury town centre location, off St Mary's Street. **Open:** Up to 31 Mar: Mon-Sat, 10am-4pm. 1 Apr-8 Dec: Mon-Sat, 10am-5pm.

## STOKESAY COURT

Onibury, Craven Arms, Shropshire SY7 9BD
www.stokesaycourt.com

Unspoilt and secluded, Stokesay Court is an imposing late Victorian mansion with Jacobean style façade, magnificent interiors and extensive grounds containing a grotto, woodland and interconnected pools. Set deep in the beautiful rolling green landscape of South Shropshire near Ludlow, the house and grounds featured as the Tallis Estate in award winning film 'Atonement'.
**Location:** Map 6:K7. OS Ref SO444 786. A49 Between Ludlow and Craven Arms. **Owner/Contact:** Ms Caroline Magnus
**Tel:** 01584 856238
**E-mail:** info@stokesaycourt.com
**Open:** Guided tours Apr-Oct for booked groups (20+). Groups (up to 60) can be accommodated. Tours for individuals take place on dates advertised on website. Booking essential. Tours are usually taken by the owner.
**Admission:** Please check website for up to date admission prices
**Key facts:** ⓘ No stilettos. No photography in house. Ⓣ Ⓖ Partial. WCs. ⊡ Ⓕ Obligatory. Ⓟ ▣ Dogs on leads - gardens only. ⊡ €

## HODNET HALL GARDENS

Hodnet, Market Drayton, Shropshire TF9 3NN
The 60+ acres are renowned as amongst the finest in the country. Forest trees provide a wonderful backdrop for formal gardens planted to give delight during every season, with extensive woodland walks amongst wild flowers and unusual flowering shrubs along the banks of a chain of ornamental pools.
**Location:** Map 6:L5. OS Ref SJ613 286. 12m NE of Shrewsbury on A53; M6/J15, M54/J3. **Owner:** Mr and the Hon Mrs Heber-Percy **Contact:** Secretary
**Tel:** 01630 685786 **Fax:** 01630 685853
**E-mail:** secretary@heber-percy.freeserve.co.uk
**Website:** www.hodnethallgardens.org
**Open:** Every Sun and BH Mon from Sun 6 Apr-Sun 28 Sep, 12pm-5pm. Please see our website for dates & opening times for our Craft, Food & Plant Fairs.
**Admission:** Adult £6.00. Children £3.00. Craft Fairs and Plant Fairs: Adults Half Price, Children Free. **Key facts:** ⓘ Groups of 25+ at other times by appointment. Ⓖ Partial. WCs. ⊡ Ⓣ Ⓟ ▣ Educational package linked to Key Stages 1 & 2 of National Curriculum. ▣ On leads.

## LONGNER HALL

Uffington, Shrewsbury, Shropshire SY4 4TG
Designed by John Nash in 1803, Longner Hall is a Tudor Gothic style house set in a park landscaped by Humphry Repton. The home of one family for over 700 years. Longner's principal rooms are adorned with plaster fan vaulting and stained glass.
**Location:** Map 6:L6. OS Ref SJ529 110. 4m SE of Shrewsbury on Uffington road, ¼m off B4380, Atcham.
**Owner:** Mr R L Burton **Contact:** Mrs R L Burton
**Tel:** 01743 709215
**Open:** Apr-Sep: Tues & BH Mons, 2-5pm. Tours at 2pm & 3.30pm. Groups at any time by arrangement.
**Admission:** Adult £5.00, Child/OAP £3.00.
**Key facts:** ⓘ No photography in house. Ⓖ Partial. Ⓕ Obligatory. Ⓟ Limited for coaches. ▣ By arrangement. ▣ Guide dogs only.

## ST LEONARD'S CHURCH

Linley, Barrow, Shropshire TF12 5JU
This secluded medieval delight is a near-complete 12th century church. Located in Linley, meaning Lime Wood, it is built entirely from local rubble stone except for the dressing stones and a tiled roof. The Norman church complete with late 12th century tower was built as a chapel for the beautiful medieval town of Much Wenlock. The south doorway was possibly relocated when the tower was built, and the ancient studded door has strap hinges. The north doorway is blocked but its weathered tympanum features a mysterious green man. Inside you'll find more Romanesque carving as illustrated by the round tub font. The decoration consists of carved of cable-moulding around the rim, and medallions which, on the north side, emerge from the mouths of demonic masks.
**Location:** OS Ref SO 6866098505.
**Contact:** Please call The Churches Conservation Trust on 0845 303 2760 (Mon-Fri, 9am–5pm) **Open:** See www.visitchurches.org.uk for details.

## COUND HALL

Cound, Shropshire SY5 6AH
Queen Anne red brick Hall.
**Location:** Map 6:L6. OS Ref ST560 053.
**Tel:** 01743 761721 **Fax:** 01743 761722
**Open:** Mon 21 Jul–Fri 25 Jul 2014, 10am-4pm.
**Admission:** Adult £4.50, Child £2.30, Conc. £3.40, Family £11.30.

## SHIPTON HALL

Much Wenlock, Shropshire TF13 6JZ
Elizabethan house with Georgian extensions. Fine plasterwork and panelling. Gardens, church and dovecote. **Location:** Map 6:L7. OS Ref SO563 918. 6 miles from Much Wenlock on B4378 towards Craven Arms, close to junction with B4368
**Tel:** 01746 785225 **E-mail:** mjanebishop@hotmail.co.uk **Open:** Easter-end Sep: Thurs, 2.30-5.30pm. BH Suns/Mons, 2.30-5.30pm. Groups 20+ by arrangement.
**Admission:** Adult £6.00, Child (under 14yrs) £3.00.

# CHILLINGTON HALL 🏚Ⓕ
## CODSALL WOOD, WOLVERHAMPTON, STAFFORDSHIRE   WV8 1RE
### www.chillingtonhall.co.uk

Home of the Giffards since 1178. Third house on the site. The present house was built during the 18th Century, firstly by the architect Francis Smith of Warwick adding the South Wing to the Tudor House in 1724 and then completed by John Soane in 1786 replacing the Tudor House in its entirety. Parkland laid out by 'Capability' Brown in the 1760s with additional work by James Paine and possibly Robert Woods. Chillington was the winner of the HHA/Sotheby's Restoration Award 2009 for work done on Soane's magnificent Saloon. Brown's great showpiece The Pool with its follies can be seen by those who want more than a stroll in the garden.

**Location:** Map 6:N6. OS Ref SJ864 067.
2m S of Brewood off A449. 4m NW of M54/J2.

**Owner/Contact:** Mr & Mrs J W Giffard
**Tel:** 01902 850236
**E-mail:** info@chillingtonhall.com
**Open:** House: Mon-Thur, 7 Apr-22 May, 2-4pm (last entry 3.30pm)
Grounds: as house. Parties at other times by prior arrangement.
**Admission:** Adult £6.00, Child £3.00. Grounds only: half price.
**Key facts:** ⓘ Available for corporate hospitality, meetings, weddings and other celebrations and photoshoots. The 18th Century Stableblock and Model Farm have undergone substantial renovation and are available as a meeting room/educational facility, suitable for filming as well. 🚻 ♿ WCs.
🎟 Obligatory. 🅿 Limited for coaches. 📷 🛏 In grounds. 🔔

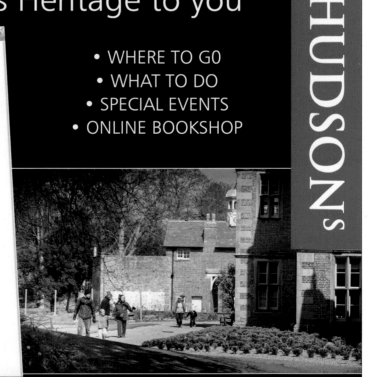

## MOSELEY OLD HALL

**Moseley Old Hall Lane, Wolverhampton WV10 7HY**

www.nationaltrust.org.uk/moseleyoldhall

This is the house that saved a king. Dating from 1600, this atmospheric farmhouse has the priest hole where Charles II hid when escaping from the Battle of Worcester in 1651. See the bed on which the royal fugitive slept while hearing the nail-biting story of his fight. Original interiors bring to life 17th Century domesticity is this friendly and fasicinating place. The 17th Century style garden has period planting and a striking knot garden.

**Location:** Map 6:N6. OS Ref SJ932 044. 4 miles North of Wolverhampton, off A449, just off jct2 of M54 **Owner:** National Trust

**Contact:** House & Visitor Services Manager **Tel:** 01902 782808

**E-mail:** moseleyoldhall@nationaltrust.org.uk

**Open:** Mon, Tues, Wed, Sat, Sun, Feb to Oct, weekends Nov & Dec, see website for times. Guided tours available most days, introductory talks and timed entry.

**Admission:** Whole property: Adult £7.50, Child £3.75, Family £18.60. Garden and woodlands: Adult £4.55, Child £2.30, Family £11.30. National Trust members and under 5s Free.

**Key facts:** No sharp heels in the Manor. Partial in house & grounds. Hearing loop available. Free. On leads outdoors.

## WHITMORE HALL

**Whitmore, Newcastle-Under-Lyme ST5 5HW**

Whitmore Hall is a Grade I listed building, designated as a house of outstanding architectural and historical interest. Parts of the hall date back to a much earlier period and for 900 years has been the seat of the Cavenagh-Mainwarings, who are direct descendants of the original Norman owners. The hall has beautifully proportioned light rooms and has recently been refurbished; it is in fine order. There are good family portraits to be seen with a continuous line dating from 1624 to the present day. The park encompasses an early Victorian summer house and the outstanding and rare Elizabethan stables.

**Location:** Map 6:M4. OS Ref SJ811 413. On A53 Newcastle-Market Drayton Road, 3m from M6/J15.

**Owner/Contact:** Mr Guy Cavenagh-Mainwaring

**Tel:** 01782 680478 or for wedding/events 01782 680868

**E-mail:** whitmore.hall@yahoo.com

**Open:** 1 May-31 Aug: Tues and Weds, 2pm-5pm (last tour 4.30pm).

**Admission:** Adult £5.00, Child 50p.

**Key facts:** Ground floor and grounds.

Afternoon teas for booked groups (15+), May-Aug. Ample.

## CASTERNE HALL

**Ilam, Nr Ashbourne, Derbyshire DE6 2BA**

Panelled manor house in own grounds in stunning Peak District location above the Manifold Valley. A seat of the Hurt family for 500 years. Georgian front, 17th Century and medieval rear. Finalist in 'Country Life' magazine's 'England's Favourite House' competition. Featured in 5 films including 'The Hound of the Baskervilles' and 'Hercule Poirot'. **Location:** Map 6:O3. OS Ref SK123 523. Leave Ilam north towards Stanshope. First left turning, signed 'Castern', & continue past No Through Road sign up steep hill. **Owner/Contact:** Charles Hurt **Tel:** 01335 310489 **E-mail:** mail@casterne.co.uk **Website:** www.casterne.co.uk **Open:** 2 Jun–16 Jun, 23 Jun–15 Jul: weekdays only for tour at 2pm prompt only. Groups of 10+ by arrangement all year. Teas & refreshments by arrangement. **Admission:** £6.00. **Key facts:** Silver service & candlelit lunches & dinners for parties of 12-22 by prior arrangement. Focus groups & corporate events welcomed. Partial. Ground floor only. Obligatory. 45 min tour. Limited for coaches. Guide dogs only. B&B by prior arrangement. Licensed. Civil ceremonies & marriages in Hall or Drawing Room. Wedding parties welcomed. €

## ERASMUS DARWIN HOUSE

**Beacon Street, Lichfield, Staffordshire WS13 7AD**

Home of Lunar Man Erasmus Darwin (1731-1802). **Location:** Map 6:P5. OS Ref SK115 098. Situated at the West end of Lichfield Cathedral Close.
**Tel:** 01543 306260 **E-mail:** enquiries@erasmusdarwin.org
**Website:** www.erasmusdarwin.org **Open:** Apr-Oct, Tues-Sun, 11am-5pm. Nov-Mar, Thur-Sun, 12-4.30pm. Check website. **Admission:** Adult £3, Conc. £2.

© Steven Gregory

Moseley Old Hall

# ARBURY HALL 🏠Ⓕ

www.arburyestate.co.uk

## Arbury Hall, original Elizabethan mansion house, Gothicised in the 18th Century surrounded by stunning gardens and parkland.

Arbury Hall has been the seat of the Newdegate family for over 450 years and is the ancestral home of Viscount Daventry. This Tudor/Elizabethan House was Gothicised by Sir Roger Newdegate in the 18th Century and is regarded as the 'Gothic Gem' of the Midlands. The principal rooms, with their soaring fan vaulted ceilings and plunging pendants and filigree tracery, stand as a most breathtaking and complete example of early Gothic Revival architecture and provide a unique and fascinating venue for corporate entertaining, product launches, fashion shoots and

activity days. Exclusive use of this historic Hall, its gardens and parkland is offered to clients. The Hall stands in the middle of beautiful parkland with landscaped gardens of rolling lawns, lakes and winding wooded walks. Spring flowers are profuse and in June rhododendrons, azaleas and giant wisteria provide a beautiful environment for the visitor. George Eliot, the novelist, was born on the estate and Arbury Hall and Sir Roger Newdegate were immortalised in her book 'Scenes of Clerical Life'.

## VISITOR INFORMATION

■ **Owner**
The Viscount Daventry

■ **Address**
Arbury Hall
Nuneaton
Warwickshire
CV10 7PT

■ **Location**
**Map 6:P7**
**OS Ref. SP335 893**
London, M1, M6/J3 (A444 to Nuneaton), 2m SW of Nuneaton. 1m W of A444. Nuneaton 5 mins. Birmingham City Centre 20 mins. London 2 hrs, Coventry 20 mins.
**Bus/Coach:** Nuneaton Station 3m.
**Air:** Birmingham International 17m.

■ **Contact**
Events Secretary
**Tel:** 024 7638 2804
**Fax:** 024 7664 1147
**E-mail:** info@ arburyestate.co.uk

■ **Opening Times**
Hall & Gardens open on BH weekends only (Sun & Mon) Easter - August. Groups/Parties (25+) by arrangement.

■ **Admission**
**Hall & Gardens**
| | |
|---|---|
| Adult | £8.00 |
| Child (up to 14 yrs) | £4.50 |
| Family (2+2) | £20.00 |

**Gardens Only**
| | |
|---|---|
| Adult | £5.50 |
| Child (up to 14 yrs.) | £4.00 |

### Conference/Function

| ROOM | Size | Max Cap |
|---|---|---|
| Dining Room | 35' x 28' | 120 |
| Saloon | 35' x 30' | 70 |
| Room 3 | 48' x 11' | 40 |
| Stables Tearooms | 31' x 18' | 80 |

## KEY FACTS

ⓘ Corporate hospitality, film location, small conferences, product launches and promotions, marquee functions, let day shooting. No cameras or video recorders indoors.

🍽 Exclusive lunches and dinners for corporate parties in dining room, max. 50, buffets 80.

♿ Partial, WCs.

🚶 Obligatory. Tour time: 50min.

🅿 200 cars and 3 coaches 250 yards from house. Follow tourist signs. Approach map available for coach drivers.

🐕 Dogs on leads only. Guide dogs only.

## VISITOR INFORMATION

**■ Owner**
The Shakespeare Birthplace Trust

**■ Address**
Henley Street
Stratford-upon-Avon
CV37 6QW

**■ Location**
Map 6:P9
OS Ref.
**Birthplace:** SP201 552
**New Place:** SP201 548
**Hall's Croft:** SP200 546
**Hathaway's:** SP185 547
**Arden's:** SP166 582
2 hrs from London 45 mins from Birmingham by car. 4m from M40/J15 and well signed from all approaches.
**Rail:** Direct service from London (Marylebone).

**■ Contact**
The Shakespeare Birthplace Trust
**Tel:** 01789 204016 (General Enquiries)
**Tel:** 01789 201806 (Group Visits).
**E-mail:** info@shakespeare.org.uk
groups@shakespeare.org.uk

**■ Opening Times**
The Shakespeare houses are open daily throughout the year except Christmas Day and Boxing Day (Shakespeare's Birthplace is open on Boxing Day).

Opening times vary throughout the year. Please see www.shakespeare.org.uk for more information.

**■ Admission**
Tickets to the Shakespeare Houses are valid for a full year, with unlimited entry. For the price of one ticket, you can enjoy days out at the Shakespeare Houses all year round -for free! Plus a visit to Shakespeare's grave at Holy Trinity Church included in multi-house passes.
Visit the website for further details
www.shakespeare.org.uk.

# THE SHAKESPEARE HOUSES
### www.shakespeare.org.uk

Five beautifully preserved Tudor Houses and gardens telling the complete Shakespeare story and all directly linked with William Shakespeare and his family.

**Shakespeare's Birthplace:**
This is where it all began, where William Shakespeare was born, grew up and spent the first years of his married life. Discover the Tudor town house that was the Shakespeare family home and glove making business. It's a special place that everyone should see at least once in their lifetime.

**Mary Arden's Farm - A real working Tudor farm:**
Visit the childhood home of Shakespeare's mother and see the farm's history brought to life. Step back in time and encounter the authentic sights, sounds and smells of a working farm in Shakespeare's day. Get involved with our Tudor residents and have a go at traditional rural skills.

**Hall's Croft - The Jacobean doctor's house:**
Wander through the elegant home of Susanna Shakespeare and her husband, Dr John Hall. Enjoy the luxurious rooms and beautiful decoration of this fascinating house, befitting a wealthy physician of Dr John Hall's status.
Relax in the beautiful gardens, breathe in the fragrant herbs as used by Dr Hall in his remedies.

**Nash's House & New Place - The site of Shakespeare's final home:**
Visit Nash's House, a well preserved Tudor house and the site of Shakespeare's last home at New Place where he died in 1616. Enjoy the grounds including a traditional knot garden and get involved in family activities throughout the summer holidays.

**Anne Hathaway's Cottage - The most romantic Shakespeare house:**
Fall in love with this beautiful, quintessentially English thatched cottage, the family home of Shakespeare's wife. Discover traditional orchards, woodland walks and explore the nine acres of grounds and gardens.

## KEY FACTS

 City Sightseeing bus tour connecting town houses with Anne Hathaway's Cottage and Mary Arden's Farm. No photography inside houses.

Gifts available.

Plants for sale at Anne Hathaway's Cottage.

Available, tel for details.

Partial. WCs.

Mary Arden's Farm, Anne Hathaway's Cottage, Hall's Croft, Shakespeare's Birthplace.

By special arrangement.

**P** Free coach terminal for groups drop off and pick up at Birthplace. Max stay 30 mins. Parking at Mary Arden's Farm. Pay & display parking at Anne Hathaway's Cottage.

Available for all houses. For information 01789 201804.

Guide dogs only.

Register for news and special offers at **www.hudsonsheritage.com**

## LORD LEYCESTER HOSPITAL
### HIGH STREET, WARWICK CV34 4BH
www.lordleycester.com

This magnificent range of 14th and 15th Century half-timbered buildings was adapted into almshouses by Robert Dudley, Earl of Leycester, in 1571. The Hospital still provides homes for ex-Servicemen and their wives. The Guildhall, Great Hall, chantry Chapel, Brethren's Kitchen and galleried Courtyard are still in everyday use. The regimental museum of the Queen's Own Hussars is housed here. The historic Master's Garden was featured in BBC TV's Gardener's World, and the Hospital buildings in many productions including, most recently, 'Dr Who' and David Dimbleby's 'How We Built Britain'.
**Location:** Map 6:P8. OS Ref 280 468. 1m N of M40/J15 on the A429 in town centre. Rail: 10 minutes walk from Warwick Station.

**Owner:** The Governors
**Contact:** The Master
**Tel:** 01926 491422
**Open:** All year: Tue-Sun & BHs (except Good Fri & 25 Dec), 10am-5pm (4pm in winter). Garden: Apr-Sep: 10am-4.30pm.
**Admission:** Adult £5.90, Child £4.90, Conc. £5.40. Garden only £2.00.
**Key facts:** ⬛ ⬛ ⬛ ⬛ Partial. WCs.
⬛ ⬛ ⬛ By arrangement.
⬛ Limited for cars. No coaches.
⬛ ⬛ Guide dogs only. ⬛ ⬛

## ALL SAINTS' CHURCH ⬛
### Billesley, Stratford Upon Avon, Warwickshire B49 6NF
www.visitchurches.org.uk

All Saints rises from a lovely wooded churchyard in the hamlet of Billesley near Stratford-upon-Avon. From its approach through an avenue of limes, it looks like a Georgian country church - but its origins go back 1,000 years. The church served the thriving village of Billesley for centuries, but by 1428 only four parishioners were left and the church's north aisle was demolished. Tradition has it that William Shakespeare married Anne Hathaway here in 1582 and that his granddaughter's wedding also took place at Billesley. Sadly no parish registers survive from this time to prove it. In 1692, Bernard Whalley rebuilt the church to create a fashionable classical addition to his Billesley estate. He installed a gallery for his staff complete with a butler's boxed seat. Whalley's own pew had a fine classical fireplace. His body lies, with his wife Lucy, in a sealed vault beneath the sanctuary floor.
**Location:** OS Ref SP148 568. 4 miles west of Stratford-upon-Avon, off A46. Follow signs to Billesley and Billesley Manor Hotel.
**Contact:** Please call The Churches Conservation Trust on 0845 303 2760 (Mon-Fri, 9am–5pm) **Open:** Open daily.

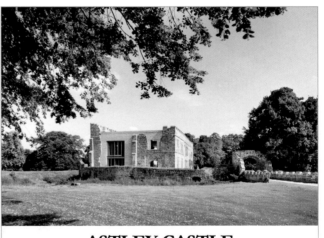

## ASTLEY CASTLE
### Nuneaton, Warwickshire CV10 7QS
www.landmarktrust.org.uk

Groundbreaking modern accommodation has been inserted within the ruined walls of this ancient moated site to combine the thrill of modern architecture with the atmosphere of an ancient place. Large glass walls now frame views of medieval stonework and the adjacent church and surrounding countryside.
**Location:** Map 7:A7. OS Ref SP310 894.
**Owner:** The Landmark Trust
**Tel:** 01628 825925
**E-mail:** bookings@landmarktrust.org.uk
**Open:** Part of grounds open Mon and Fri, 8 Open Days per year, contact office.
**Admission:** Free on Open Days and visits by appointment.
**Key facts:** ⬛ The living accommodation is on the first floor and the bedrooms and bathrooms on the ground floor. A lift enables easy access for all.
⬛ ⬛ ⬛ ⬛ ⬛ ⬛

# BAGOTS CASTLE
### Bagots Castle, Church Road, Baginton  CV8 3AR
www.bagotscastle.org.uk

History brought to life at Bagot's Castle, a 14thC ruin. The present castle is thought to have been built in the 1380's by Sir William Bagot, a distinguished nobleman, it is thought he entertained Richard II here. The castle was desolate in 1540. In 1933-48 Coventry Archaeological Society partially excavated the site but again nature took over. In 2005 the present Custodian took over and carried out restoration works with the help of a grant from English Heritage. Display of Artefacts from 1933-48 Excavations. Remains of Summer House. Two Medieval fish ponds. Medieval Saxon Village. Bluebell Glade in May. Picnic Area. Former Tank Testing Area used in World War II.
**Location:** Map 6:P8. **Contact:** David Hewer **Tel:** 07786 438711
**E-mail:** delia@bagotscastle.org.uk **Open:** Apr-Oct Weekends: 12-5pm. Bank Holidays. Weekdays by appointment through our website.
**Admission:** Full Admission £4.00. Concessions £2.00. Family (2 Adults and up to 4 children) £10.00 (children under 5 free). English Heritage Members Half Price. Group Guided Tours arranged POA. **Key facts:** ⓘ Education Visitor Centre opened April 2013. ⬚ Books for sale. ⚲ ⓟ ⬚ On leads.

# RAGLEY HALL, PARK & GARDENS ⬚ⓕ
### Alcester, Warwickshire  B49 5NJ
www.ragley.co.uk

Ragley Hall was designed in 1680 and remains the family home of the Marquess and Marchioness of Hertford, managing to retain its family charm despite the thousands of people who visit each year. Ragley offers beautiful gardens, guided tours of the majestic state rooms, adventure playground, art gallery, boat hire and woodland walk.
**Location:** Map 6:O9. OS Ref SP073 555. Off A46/A435 1m SW of Alcester, From London 100m, M40 via Oxford and Stratford-on-Avon.
**Owner:** The Marquess of Hertford
**Tel:** 01789 762090
**Fax:** 01789 764791
**E-mail:** info@ragley.co.uk
**Open:** Please see website for details.
**Admission:** Please see website for details.
**Key facts:** ⓘ No video in the house. ⬚ ⬚ Access available. ⬚ ⬚ Drinks & Light Snacks available. ⓕ By arrangement. ⓟ Free. ⬚ ⬚ In Park on leads. ⬚ ⬚

# COMPTON VERNEY
### Compton Verney, Warwickshire  CV35 9HZ
www.comptonverney.org.uk

Set within a Grade I listed mansion remodelled by Robert Adam in the 1760s, Compton Verney offers a unique art gallery experience. Relax and explore the 120 acres of 'Capability' Brown landscaped parkland, discover a collection of internationally significant art, enjoy free tours and a programme of popular events.
**Location:** Map 7:A9. OS Ref SP312 529. 9m E of Stratford-upon-Avon, 10 mins from M40/J12, on B4086 between Wellesbourne and Kineton.
Rail: nearest station is Banbury or Leamington Spa. Air: Nearest airport Birmingham International.
**Owner:** Compton Verney House Trust **Contact:** Ticketing Desk
**Tel:** 01926 645500 **Fax:** 01926 645501
**E-mail:** info@comptonverney.org.uk
**Open:** Open from 15 Feb-14 Dec 2014, Tue-Sun & BH Mons, 11am-5pm. Last entry to Gallery 4.30pm. Groups welcome, please book in advance.
**Admission:** Please call for details. Group discounts are available.
**Key facts:** ⓘ No photography in the Gallery. ⬚ ⬚ ⬚ WCs. ⬚ Licensed. ⬚ Licensed. ⓕ By arrangement. ⓟ Ample. ⬚ ⬚ Guide dogs only. ⬚ ⬚

## HILL CLOSE GARDENS
### Bread and Meat Close, Warwick  CV34 6HF

Hedged Victorian gardens overlooking the racecourse with listed brick summerhouses. Spring bulbs, old varieties of soft fruit and vegetables, unusual fruit trees and extensive herbaceous borders. Glasshouse for tender plants. Plant, produce and gift sales. Cafe at weekends in summer. Events throughout the year listed on website. **Location:** Map 6:P8. Follow A429 & signs for racecourse, enter main racecourse gate off Friars Street. Bear right to entrance to Gardens.
**Owner:** Hill Close Gardens Trust **Contact:** Patttie Hall **Tel:** 01926 493 339 Margaret Begg, Publicity Officer - mbegg@cbegg.com.
**E-mail:** centremanager@hcgt.org.uk **Website:** www.hillclosegardens.com
**Open:** Apr-Oct Gardens everyday 11am-5pm. Café Sat & Sun & BH Mons. Nov-Mar Gardens Mon-Fri 11am-4pm. **Admission:** Adults £3.50, Child £1.00 (to include garden trail). **Key facts:** ⬚ Gifts, cards, jam. ⬚ Plants produce. ⬚ Centre for hire. ⬚ Access parking. ⬚ Drinks, cakes. ⓕ On request. ⓟ 2 hours free. ⬚ On request. ⬚ Assistance only. ⬚ Weekdays in winter. ⬚

## HONINGTON HALL ⬚
### Shipston-On-Stour, Warwickshire  CV36 5AA

This fine Caroline manor house was built in the early 1680s for Henry Parker in mellow brickwork, stone quoins and window dressings. Modified in 1751 when an octagonal saloon was inserted. The interior was also lavishly restored around this time and contains exceptional mid-Georgian plasterwork. Set in 15 acres of grounds.
**Location:** Map 6:P9. OS Ref SP261 427. 10m S of Stratford-upon-Avon. 1½m N of Shipston-on-Stour. Take A3400 towards Stratford, then signed right to Honington.
**Owner/Contact:** Benjamin Wiggin Esq
**Tel:** 01608 661434 **Fax:** 01608 663717
**Open:** By appointment for groups (10+).
**Admission:** Telephone for details.
**Key facts:** ⓕ Obligatory. ⬚

## WIGHTWICK MANOR & GARDENS 🌿
### Wightwick Bank, Wolverhampton, West Midlands WV6 8EE
www.nationaltrust.org.uk/wightwickmanor

Wightwick Manor was the haven of a romantic industrialist. With its timber beams and barley-twist chimneys, gardens of wide lawns, yew hedges and roses, rich William Morris furnishings and Pre-Raphaelite paintings, Wightwick is in every way an idyllic time capsule of Victorian nostalgia for medieval England.
**Location:** Map 6:N6. 3m W of Wolverhampton, off the A454. SatNav postcode WV6 8BN. Brown signs from Wolverhampton ring road
**Owner:** National Trust **Tel:** 01902 761400
**E-mail:** wightwickmanor@nationaltrust.org.uk
**Open:** Garden, shop and tearoom open everyday except Christmas day, 11am-5pm. House open 12noon-5pm (closed Tue). 1 Jan-14 Feb & 3 Nov-31 Dec site closes at 4pm. Last entry to house 1 hour before closing.
**Admission:** Gift Aid Admission: £9.80, Child £4.90, Family £24.50, Family (1 adult) £14.70. Garden only: £4.90, Child £2.50, Family £12, Family (1 adult) £7.40. **Key facts:** ⓘ No internal photography. No sharp heeled shoes. ⬚ Specialising in William Morris products and fabric. ♿ ⓣ ⬚ WCs. ☞ ⓟ 400 yds. ⬚ ⬚ ✳ ⬚

## WINTERBOURNE HOUSE AND GARDEN 🏠Ⓕ
### University of Birmingham, 58 Edgbaston Park Road, Birmingham B15 2RT
www.winterbourne.org.uk

Winterbourne is set in 7 acres of botanic garden, just minutes from Birmingham city centre. Ground and first floor exhibition spaces tell the history of the previous owners and the garden has a beautiful Japanese bridge, tea house and walled garden, all designed in the Arts and Crafts style.
**Location:** Map 6:O7. OS Ref SP052 839. Minutes away from A38.
**Owner:** The University of Birmingham
**Tel:** 0121 414 3003 **E-mail:** enquiries@winterbourne.org.uk
**Open:** Jan-Mar/Nov-Dec 10am-4pm weekdays, 11am-4pm weekends Apr-Oct 10am-5.30pm weekdays, 11am-5.30pm weekends.
We are closed over the Christmas period.
**Admission:** Adult £5.50, Concession £4.50, Family £16.00. Group prices on request. **Key facts:** ⓘ Organised professional photography including family or wedding portraiture must be notified to management in advance and will incur a charge. ⬚ ♿ ⓣ ⬚ WCs. ☞ Licensed. 🍴 Licensed. ⓕ Pre-booked ⓟ ⬚ ⬚ Guide dogs only. ✳ ⬚

## BIRMINGHAM BOTANICAL GARDENS AND GLASSHOUSES
### Westbourne Road, Edgbaston, Birmingham B15 3TR
15 acres of beautiful historic landscaped gardens with 7000 shrubs, plants and trees. Four glasshouses, Roses and Alpines, Woodland and Rhododendron Walks, Rock Pool, Herbaceous Borders, Japanese Garden. Children's playground, aviaries, gallery, bandstand, tearoom giftshop, parking.
**Location:** Map 6:O7. OS Ref SP048 855. 2m W of city centre. Follow signs to Edgbaston then brown tourist signs. **Owner:** Birmingham Botanical & Horticultural Society **Contact:** Mr James Wheeler **Tel:** 0121 454 1860
**Fax:** 0121 454 7835 **E-mail:** admin@birminghambotanicalgardens.org.uk
**Website:** www.birminghambotanicalgardens.org.uk
**Open:** Daily: 10am-dusk. Closed Christmas Day and Boxing Day. Refer to website for details. **Admission:** Adult £7.00, Family £22.00. Groups, Conc. £4.75, Children under 5 free.
**Key facts:** ⬚ ♿ ⓣ ♿ ⬚ ⓕ On application. ⓟ ⬚ ⬚ Guide dogs only. ⬚ ✳ Closed just Christmas Day and Boxing Day. ⬚

## CASTLE BROMWICH HALL GARDENS
### Chester Road, Castle Bromwich, Birmingham B36 9BT
A unique survival of English formal garden design of the late 17th and early 18th Century – containing plants of the period and a holly maze making them one of the most important historic gardens in the country.
**Location:** Map 6:O6. OS Ref SP141 899. Off B4114, 5m E of Birmingham City Centre, 1 mile from M6/J5 exit N only.
**Owner:** Castle Bromwich Hall & Gardens Trust **Contact:** Sue Brain
**Tel:** 0121 749 4100 **E-mail:** admin@cbhgt.org.uk **Website:** www.cbhgt.org.uk
**Open:** 1 Apr-31 Oct: Tues-Thurs, 11am-4pm, Sat, Sun BH Mon 12.30-4.30pm. 1 Nov-31 Mar: Tues-Thur 11am-3pm.
**Admission:** Summer: Adults £4.50, Concs £4.00, Child £1.00. Winter: All Adults £4.00, Child £1.00.
**Key facts:** ⬚ ♿ ♿ WCs. ☞ ⓕ By arrangement. ⓟ Limited for coaches. ⬚ ⬚ On leads. ✳ ⬚

## KINVER EDGE AND THE HOLY AUSTIN ROCK HOUSES 🌿
### Compton Road, Kinver, Nr Stourbridge, Staffordshire DY7 6DL
These wonderful cave houses were inhabited until the 1950's and are now open to the public. Whilst you're here visit our new tea rooms and enjoy a 'rock cake at the rock houses'.
**Location:** Map 6:N7. 4m W of Stourbridge, 4m N of Kidderminster,
**Owner:** National Trust **Contact:** The Custodian
**Tel:** 01384 872553
**Open:** Kinver Edge: all year. House grounds: daily 10am-4pm. Open BH Mons. Rockhouses: Mar-Nov, Thur-Sun 11am-4pm. Tea Rooms: Mar-Nov, Thur-Sun 11am-4pm.
**Admission:** Adult £3.70 Child £1.70, Family £7.40.
**Key facts:** ☞ ⓟ ⬚ ✳ ⬚

## CROOME
### NEAR HIGH GREEN, WORCESTERSHIRE  WR8 9DW
www.nationaltrust.org.uk/croome

Step into what remains of a secret wartime air base, now our Visitor Centre, where thousands of people lived and worked in the 1940s. Walk through a masterpiece in landscape design, which is 'Capability' Brown's very first. Over the last 17 years we have painstakingly restored what was once a lost and overgrown 18th Century parkland and we're continuing this work today. Find Croome Court, the home of the Earls of Coventry, at the heart of the park, which has been patiently waiting for its revival. Its time has come in 2014 as Croome Redefined starts to pull this glorious yet faded house back from the brink. Explore un-restored spaces and the intricate repair works which will see the house change forever. **Location:** Map 6:N9. OS Ref SO878 448. 8m S of Worcester. Signposted from A38 and B4084.

**Owner:** National Trust  **Contact:** House & Visitor Services Manager
**Tel:** 01905 371006  **Fax:** 01905 371090
**E-mail:** croome@nationaltrust.org.uk
**Open:** See National Trust website for full opening times. Park, Restaurant & Shop open every day except 24 & 25 Dec. House open every day except Tuesdays throughout the year.
**Admission:** House and Park: £9.50, Child £4.70, Family £23.50. Groups (15+) £7.30, Child £3.55. Park only: £7.00, Child £3.50, Family £17.50. Groups (15+) £5.35, Child £2.60.
**Key facts:** 🅿️ 🚻 WCs. 🍽️ Licensed. 🍴 Licensed. 🎧 By arrangement. 🅿️ 🐕 On leads. ❄️ 🏅

## HARVINGTON HALL 🏛️⒡
### HARVINGTON, KIDDERMINSTER, WORCESTERSHIRE  DY10 4LR
www.harvingtonhall.com

Harvington Hall is a moated, medieval and Elizabethan manor house. Many of the rooms have their original Elizabethan wall paintings and the Hall contains the finest series of priest hides in the country. During the 19th Century it was stripped of furniture and panelling and the shell was left almost derelict but is now restored. The Hall has walled gardens surrounded by a moat, a gift shop and a tea room serving morning coffees, light lunches and afternoon teas. A programme of events throughout the year including outdoor plays and music, candlelight tours and a pilgrimage is available.
On many weekends the Hall is enhanced by Living History events when the Hall's re-enactment group depict one of the many significant periods throughout its long history.
**Location:** Map 6:N8. OS Ref SO877 745. On minor road, ½m NE of A450/

A448 crossroads at Mustow Green. 3m SE of Kidderminster.
**Owner:** Roman Catholic Archdiocese of Birmingham
**Contact:** The Hall Manager  **Tel:** 01562 777846  **Fax:** 01562 777190
**E-mail:** harvingtonhall@btconnect.com
**Open:** Mar: Sats & Suns; Apr-Oct: Wed-Sun & BH Mons (closed Good Fri), 11.30am-4pm. Also open throughout the year for pre-booked groups and schools. Occasionally the Hall may be closed for a private function, please ring for up to date information.
**Admission:** Adult £8.50, Child (5-16) £5.50, OAP £7.50, Family (2 adults & 3 children) £24.00, Garden and Malt House Visitor Centre: £3.50.
**Key facts:** 🅿️ 🚻 Partial. WCs. 🍽️ 🎧 🅿️ Limited for coaches. 🐕 Guide dogs only. 🏅

## ST LAWRENCE'S CHURCH 🏛
### Market Place, Evesham,
### Worcestershire  WR11 4BG
www.visitchurches.org.uk

St Lawrence, the parish church of All Saints' and the great Perpendicular bell tower of the Abbey at Evesham together form a spectacular architectural group. This large and imposing church is of Norman foundation, though it now appears entirely Perpendicular, having been rebuilt in the 16th Century. It fell into ruin in the 18th Century and but was rescued and restored again by the local architect H Eginton in 1836.

Outside, the east end has a great six-light window with elaborate tracery. Inside, the early 16th Century chantry chapel of St Clement has richly panelled arches and a beautiful fan vaulted ceiling. The windows contain fabulous glass by many of the major stained glass artists of the last 150 years.

**Location:** OS Ref SP037 436. Evesham town centre; from A4184 Abbey Road, take Vine Street and Market Place; from the B4035 Waterside, turn left into Bridge Street, shopping centre multi storey car park; church next to priory bell tower and parish church.

**Open:** Summer: Daily, 9.30am-4.30pm. Winter: 9.30am-3.30pm.

## CHURCH OF ST MARY MAGDELENE 🏛
### Croome Park, Croome D'Abitot, Worcester,
### Worcestershire  WR8 9DW
www.visitchurches.org.uk

The original church at Croome was demolished by the 6th Earl of Coventry when he decided to replace his adjacent Jacobean house in the 1750s. His new house and park were designed and laid out by Capability Brown as was the church. The views out to the Malvern Hills on a clear day are spectacular. The interiors of both house and church are attributed to Robert Adam and were completed in 1763. Built by some of the finest craftsmen in England, every detail has been considered, from pretty plaster mouldings to handsome carved pews - the church is a perfect fantasy of the period, with elegant Gothick windows and plasterwork, pulpit, communion rails, commandments and creed boards. Opulent monuments brought from the old church, long since demolished, show the former Barons and Earls of Coventry in their full glory.

**Location:** OS Ref SO 886 450. 4m W of Pershore off A38 & A44; follow National Trust signs to Croome Park. **Open:** Open when Croome Park is open. For detailed opening times, see the Croome Park website.

## LITTLE MALVERN COURT 🏛®
### Nr Malvern, Worcestershire  WR14 4JN

Prior's Hall, associated rooms and cells, c1489. Former Benedictine Monastery. Oak-framed roof, 5 bays. Library, collection of religious vestments and relics. Embroideries and paintings. Gardens: 10 acres of former monastic grounds with spring bulbs, blossom, old fashioned roses and shrubs. Access to Hall only by flight of steps.

**Location:** Map 6:M9. OS Ref SO769 403. 3m S of Great Malvern on Upton-on-Severn Road (A4104).  **Owner:** Trustees of the late T M Berington

**Contact:** Mrs T M Berington  **Tel:** 01684 892988  **Fax:** 01684 893057

**E-mail:** littlemalverncourt@hotmail.com  **Website:** www.littlemalverncourt.co.uk

**Open:** 16 Apr until 17 Jul, Weds and Thurs, 2.15-5pm, last admission 4.00pm. Open for NGS Sunday 16 Mar and Mon 5 May.

**Admission:** House & Garden - Adult £7.00, Child £2.00. Garden only - Adult £6.00, Child £1.00. Groups by prior arrangement.

**Key facts:** 🚻 ♿ Garden (partial). 🅿 🐾

## MADRESFIELD COURT
### Madresfield, Malvern  WR13 5AJ

Elizabethan and Victorian house with medieval origins. Fine contents. Extensive gardens and arboretum.

**Location:** Map 6:M9. OS Ref SO808 472. 6m SW of Worcester. 1½ m SE of A449. 2m NE of Malvern.

**Owner:** The Trustees of Madresfield Estate

**Contact:** Mrs Wendy Carruthers

**Tel:** 01684 573614  **E-mail:** madresfield@btconnect.com

**Open:** Guided tours on specific dates between Apr and Sep. Numbers are restricted and prior booking is essential to avoid disappointment.

**Admission:** £12.00.

**Key facts:** ♿ WCs. 🐕 Obligatory. 🐾 Dogs in grounds only.

## THE TUDOR HOUSE MUSEUM
### 16 Church Street, Upton-On-Severn,
### Worcestershire  WR8 0HT

Upton past and present, exhibits of local history.

**Location:** Map 6:N10. OS Ref SO852 406. Centre of Upton-on-Severn, 7miles SE of Malvern by B4211.

**Owner:** Tudor House Museum Trust

**Tel:** 01684 592447

**Open:** Please contact us for up to date opening times and admission prices.

**Key facts:** ♿ Garden and ground floor only. 🔲 Prebooked. 🐾

Croome

## BERRINGTON HALL ❧
**Nr Leominster, Herefordshire HR6 0DW**
Tel: 01568 615721 E-mail: berrington@nationaltrust.org.uk

## BROCKHAMPTON ESTATE ❧
**Bringsty, Nr Bromyard WR6 5TB**
Tel: 01885 488099 E-mail: brockhampton@nationaltrust.org.uk

## CHURCH OF ST COSMAS & ST DAMIAN ⋒
**Stretford, Leominster, Herefordshire HR6 9DG**
Tel: 0845 303 2760 E-mail: central@thecct.org.uk

## CHURCH OF ST JOHN THE BAPTIST ⋒
**Llanrothal, Monmouth, Herefordshire NP25 5QJ**
Tel: 0845 303 2760 E-mail: central@thecct.org.uk

## GOODRICH CASTLE ⌗
**Ross-On-Wye HR9 6HY**
Tel: 01600 890538 E-mail: customers@english-heritage.org.uk

## MOCCAS COURT
**Moccas, Nr. Hereford HR2 9LH**
Tel: 01981 500019 E-mail: info@moccas-court.co.uk

## ST BARTHOLEMEW'S CHURCH ⋒
**Richards Castle, Nr Ludlow, Herefordshire SY8 4ET**
Tel: 0845 303 2760 E-mail: central@thecct.org.uk

## ST CUTHBERT'S CHURCH ⋒
**Church Road, Holme Lacy, Hereford, Herefordshire HR2 6LX**
Tel: 0845 303 2760 E-mail: central@thecct.org.uk

Mawley Hall

## ST MARY'S CHURCH ⋒
**Wormsley, Hereford, Herefordshire HR4 8LY**
Tel: 0845 303 2760 E-mail: central@thecct.org.uk

## CHURCH OF ST MARY MAGDELENE ⋒
**Battlefield, Shrewsbury, Shropshire SY1 1DX**
Tel: 0845 303 2760 E-mail: central@thecct.org.uk

## DUDMASTON HALL
**Quatt, Bridgnorth, Shropshire WV15 6QN**
Tel: 01746 780838 E-mail: wendy.barton@nationaltrust.org.uk

## HAWKSTONE HALL & GARDENS
**Marchamley, Shrewsbury SY4 5LG**
Tel: 01630 685242 E-mail: hawkhall@aol.com

## LUDLOW CASTLE
**Castle Square, Ludlow, Shropshire SY8 1AY**
Tel: 01584 874465 E-mail: info@ludlowcastle.com

## MAWLEY HALL
**Cleobury Mortimer DY14 8PN**
Tel: 0208 298 0429 E-mail: rsharp@mawley.com

## MUCH WENLOCK PRIORY ⌗
**Much Wenlock, Shropshire TF13 6HS**
Tel: 01952 727466 E-mail: customers@english-heritage.org.uk

## ST JAMES' CHURCH ⋒
**Off Stirchley Road, Stirchley Village, Telford, Shrops TF3 1DY**
Tel: 0845 303 2760 E-mail: central@thecct.org.uk

## ST LEONARD'S CHURCH ⋒
**St Leonards Close, Bridgnorth, Shropshire WV16 4EJ**
Tel: 0845 303 2760 E-mail: central@thecct.org.uk

## ST MARTIN'S CHURCH ⋒
**Preston Gubbals, Shrewsbury, Shropshire SY4 3AN**
Tel: 0845 303 2760 E-mail: central@thecct.org.uk

## ST MICHAEL'S CHURCH ⋒
**Upton Cressett, Bridgnorth, Shropshire WV16 6UH**
Tel: 0845 303 2760 E-mail: central@thecct.org.uk

## ST PETER'S CHURCH ⋒
**Adderley Road, Adderley, Market Drayton, Shropshire TF9 3TD**
Tel: 0845 303 2760 E-mail: central@thecct.org.uk

## STOKESAY CASTLE ⌗
**Nr Craven Arms, Shropshire SY7 9AH**
Tel: 01588 672544 E-mail: customers@english-heritage.org.uk

## TALBOT CHAPEL ⋒
**Longford Road, Longford, Newport, Shropshire TF10 8LR**
Tel: 0845 303 2760 E-mail: central@thecct.org.uk

## WROXETER ROMAN CITY ⌗
**Wroxeter, Shrewsbury, Shropshire SY5 6PH**
Tel: 01743 761330 E-mail: customers@english-heritage.org.uk

## BIDDULPH GRANGE GARDEN ❧
**Grange Road, Biddulph, Staffordshire ST8 7SD**
Tel: 01782 517999 E-mail: biddulph.grange@nationaltrust.org.uk

Register for news and special offers at **www.hudsonsheritage.com**

### BOSCOBEL HOUSE & THE ROYAL OAK ⊞
**Bishop's Wood, Brewood, Staffordshire  ST19 9AR**
**Tel:** 01902 850244 **E-mail:** customers@english-heritage.org.uk

### ST MARY'S CHURCH ⋒
**Patshull Hall, Burnhill Green, Wolverhampton  WV6 7HY**
**Tel:** 0845 303 2760 **E-mail:** central@thecct.org.uk

### SANDON HALL ⋔
**Sandon, Staffordshire  ST18 OBZ**
**Tel:** 01889 508004 **E-mail:** info@sandonhall.co.uk

### SHUGBOROUGH ESTATE ⋇
**Milford, Stafford, Staffordshire  ST17 0XB**
**Tel:** 0845 459 8900 **E-mail:** enquiries@shugborough.org.uk

### THE TRENTHAM ESTATE
**Stone Road, Trentham, Staffordshire  ST4 8AX**
**Tel:** 01782 646646 **E-mail:** enquiry@trentham.co.uk

### BADDESLEY CLINTON ⋇
**Rising Lane, Knowle, Solihull, West Midlands  B93 0DQ**
**Tel:** 01564 783294 **E-mail:** baddesleyclinton@nationaltrust.org.uk

### HAGLEY HALL
**Hall Lane, Hagley, Nr. Stourbridge, Worcestershire  DY9 9LG**
**Tel:** 01562 882408 **E-mail:** joycepurnell@hagleyhall.com

### CHURCH OF ST JOHN THE BAPTIST ⋒
**Avon Dassett, Southam, Warwickshire  CV47 2AH**
**Tel:** 0845 303 2760 **E-mail:** central@thecct.org.uk

### CHURCH OF ST MICHAEL & ALL ANGELS ⋒
**Brownsover Lane, Brownsover, Rugby, Warwicks  CV21 1HY**
**Tel:** 0845 303 2760 **E-mail:** central@thecct.org.uk

### KENILWORTH CASTLE & GARDEN ⊞
**Kenilworth, Warwickshire  CV8 1NE**
**Tel:** 01926 852 078 **E-mail:** customers@english-heritage.org.uk

### ST PETER'S CHURCH ⋒
**Wolfhamcote, Rugby, Warwickshire  CV23 8AR**
**Tel:** 0845 303 2760 **E-mail:** central@thecct.org.uk

### STONELEIGH ABBEY
**Kenilworth, Warwickshire  CV8 2LF**
**Tel:** 01926 858535 **E-mail:** enquire@stoneleighabbey.org

### WARWICK CASTLE
**Warwick  CV34 4QU**
**Tel:** 0870 442 2000 **E-mail:** customer.information@warwick-castle.com

### ALL SAINTS' CHURCH ⋒
**Spetchley, Worcester, Worcestershire  WR5 1RS**
**Tel:** 0845 303 2760 **E-mail:** central@thecct.org.uk

### BROADWAY TOWER
**Broadway, Worcestershire  WR12 7LB**
**Tel:** 01386 852390 **E-mail:** info@broadwaytower.co.uk

### CHURCH OF ST JOHN THE BAPTIST ⋒
**Church Road, Strensham, Pershore, Worcestershire  WR8 9LW**
**Tel:** 0845 303 2760 **E-mail:** central@thecct.org.uk

Kenilworth Castle

### HANBURY HALL ⋇
**Droitwich, Worcestershire  WR9 7EA**
**Tel:** 01527 821214 **E-mail:** hanburyhall@nationaltrust.org.uk

### ST BARTHOLEMEW'S CHURCH ⋒
**Lower Sapey, Worcester, Worcestershire  WR6 6HE**
**Tel:** 0845 303 2760 **E-mail:** central@thecct.org.uk

### ST MICHAEL'S CHURCH ⋒
**Edwards Lane, Churchill, Worcester, Worcestershire  WR7 4QE**
**Tel:** 0845 303 2760 **E-mail:** central@thecct.org.uk

### ST SWITHUN'S CHURCH ⋒
**Church Street, Worcester, Worcestershire  WR1 2RH**
**Tel:** 0845 303 2760 **E-mail:** central@thecct.org.uk

### SNOWSHILL MANOR
**Snowshill, Broadway  WR12 7JU**
**Tel:** 01386 852410 **E-mail:** dominic.hamilton@nationaltrust.org.uk

### SPETCHLEY PARK GARDENS ⋔⊚
**Spetchley Park, Worcester  WR5 1RS**
**Tel:** 01453 810303 **E-mail:** hb@spetchleygardens.co.uk

### THE CHURCH ⋒
**Pendock, Sledge Green, Worcestershire  GL19 4QL**
**Tel:** 0845 303 2760 **E-mail:** central@thecct.org.uk

### WITLEY COURT & GARDENS ⊞
**Great Witley, Worcestershire  WR6 6JT**
**Tel:** 01299 896636 **E-mail:** customers@english-heritage.org.uk

Visit **www.hudsonsheritage.com** for special events and wedding venues

Wentworth Woodhouse

East Yorkshire
North Yorkshire
South Yorkshire
West Yorkshire

# *Yorkshire & The Humber*

Yorkshire

A region long famed for the extraordinary range of its country houses from medieval survivors like Markenfield Hall to treasure houses like Harewood and Castle Howard and some of the finest gardens in the land.

*New Entries for 2014:*
- East Riddlesden Hall
- Oakwell Hall
- Wentworth Woodhouse
- Red House

## VISITOR INFORMATION

■ **Owner**
Burton Agnes Hall
Preservation Trust Ltd

■ **Address**
Driffield
East Yorkshire
YO25 4NB

■ **Location**
Map 11:E9
OS Ref. TA103 633
Off A614 between Driffield
and Bridlington.

■ **Contact**
Mr Simon Cunliffe-Lister
**Tel:** 01262 490324
**Fax:** 01262 490513
**E-mail:**
office@burtonagnes.com

■ **Opening Times**
9th February-2nd March
11am-4pm
1st April-31st October
11am-5pm
14th November-23rd
December 11am-5pm.

■ **Admission**
**Hall & Gardens**
| | |
|---|---|
| Adult | £9.00 |
| OAP | £8.50 |
| Child | £4.50 |

**Gardens only**
| | |
|---|---|
| Adult | £6.00 |
| OAP | £5.50 |
| Child | £3.50 |

■ **Special Events**
Snowdrop Spectacular 8th
February-2nd March.
Orchid Festival
1st & 2nd March.
Easter Egg Trail
12th-27th April.
Easter Egg Hunt 20th &
21st April.
Classic Car Rally 11th May.
Gardeners' Fair
7th & 8th June.
Jazz and Blues Festival 27,
28, 29 June.
Family Fun Weekend 16th
& 17th August.
Michaelmas Fair 25th &
26th October.
Pumpkin Trail 25th
October-2nd November.
Christmas Opening 14th
November-23rd December.

# BURTON AGNES HALL & GARDENS 🏛Ⓕ
www.burtonagnes.com

## A magnificent Elizabethan Hall containing treasures collected over four centuries, from the original carving and plasterwork to modern and impressionist paintings.

Simon Jenkins, author of 'England's Thousand Best Houses', described Burton Agnes Hall as 'the perfect English house' and one of England's twenty finest alongside Windsor Castle, Buckingham Palace and Chatsworth House. To the Cunliffe-Lister family the Hall is home, which is filled with treasures collected or commissioned by the family over the centuries and they delight in sharing it with their visitors.

Outside, the gardens offer a feast for the senses. Lawns with more than a hundred yew topiary bushes surround the house. There is a classical pond, Woodland Walk and through the seasons, the

Elizabethan walled garden contains a magnificent floral display with several thousand plant varieties; a potager filled with fruit, vegetables and herbs; herbaceous borders, giant board games, a maze, a jungle garden and a magnificent collection of campanulas.

Many treats await visitors in the courtyard. Unique, handcrafted gifts and souvenirs can be found in the 'Home and Garden' Shop and Gift Shop and the café offers home-made meals using the garden's fruit and vegetables and local ingredients.

## KEY FACTS

Gift Shop and home and garden shop.

WCs.

Licensed.

Licensed.

Dogs on leads only.

Register for news and special offers at **www.hudsonsheritage.com**

# WASSAND HALL
## SEATON, HULL, EAST YORKSHIRE HU11 5RJ
www.wassand.co.uk

Fine Regency house 1815 by Thomas Cundy the Elder. Beautifully restored walled gardens, woodland walks, Parks and vistas over Hornsea Mere, part of the Estate since 1580. The Estate was purchased circa 1520 by Dame Jane Constable and has remained in the family to the present day, Mr Rupert Russell being the great nephew of the late Lady Strickland-Constable. The house contains a fine collection of 18/19th Century paintings, English and Continental silver, furniture and porcelain. Wassand is very much a family home and retains a very friendly atmosphere. Homemade afternoon teas are served in the conservatory on Open Days.

**Location:** Map 11:F9. OS Ref TA174 460. On the B1244 Seaton-Hornsea Road. Approximately 2m from Hornsea.

**Owner/Contact:** R E O Russell - Resident Trustee
**Tel/Fax:** 01964 534488 **E-mail:** reorussell@lineone.net
**Open:** 23-26 May (26 Vintage Car Rally); 5-9, 20-24 Jun; 11, 12 & 13 Jul (East Yorkshire youth Wind band concert), 25, 26, 27 & 28 Jul; 1, (2 Closed)3, 4, 22, 23, 24 (24 Rolls Royce Car Rally) & 25 Aug. **Admission:** Hall, all grounds & walks: Adult £5.50, OAP £5.00, Child (11-15yrs) £3.00, Child (under 10) Free. Hall: Adult £3.50, OAP £3.00, Child (11-15yrs) £1.50, Child (under 10) Free. Grounds & Garden: Adult £3.50, OAP £3.00, Child (11-15yrs) £3.00, Child (under 10) Free. Guided tours and groups by arrangment - POA.
**Key facts:** ⬚ Limited. ⬚ ⬚ By arrangement. 🅿 Ample for cars, limited for coaches. ⬚ In grounds, on leads.

Burton Agnes Hall

# BURTON CONSTABLE ⓡ 🏛ⓕ
## Skirlaugh, East Yorkshire HU11 4LN
www.burtonconstable.com

As East Yorkshire's best kept secret this truly hidden gem nestled in 300 acres of natural parkland offers visitors unrivalled access to 30 rooms of faded splendor filled with fine furniture, paintings and sculpture, a library of 5,000 books and a remarkable 18th Century 'Cabinet of Curiosities'.

**Location:** Map 11:E10. OS Ref TA 193 369. Beverley 14m, Hull 10m. Signed from Skirlaugh.
**Owner:** Burton Constable Foundation
**Contact:** Mrs Helen Dewson **Tel:** 01964 562400
**E-mail:** helendewson@burtonconstable.com
**Open:** Easter Sat-26 Oct, Hall: 1-5pm, 22 Nov-7 Dec 11-4pm, Jul, Aug & BH weekends 12-5pm.
**Admission:** Adult £8.75, Child £4.50, OAP £8.25, Family £22.00 (2 adults & 4 children). Prices include 10% Gift Aid.
**Key facts:** ⓘ Photography 🏠 Small gift shop. 🎦 Seminars/meetings ⬚ mostly accessible 🍽 Stables Tea Room. ⬚ must be pre booked 🅿 Ample free parking ⬚ indoor and outdoor ⬚ Guide dogs only. ⬚

## VISITOR INFORMATION

### ■ Owner
The Hon Simon Howard

### ■ Address
Castle Howard
York
North Yorkshire
YO60 7DA

### ■ Location
**Map 11:C8**
**OS Ref. SE716 701**
**From the North:** From the A1 take the A61 to Thirsk then the A170 to Helmsley. Before Helmsley turn right onto the B1257 and follow the brown signs.
**From the South:** Take the A1M to Junction 44 and follow the A64 east to York. Continue past York and follow the brown signs.
**Bus:** Service from York.
**Rail:** London Kings Cross to York 1hr. 50 mins. York to Malton Station 30 mins.

### ■ Contact
Visitor Services
**Tel:** 01653 648333
**E-mail:**
house@castlehoward.co.uk

### ■ Opening Times
**House:**
22 March-2 November & 29 November-21 December 2014.
Open daily from 11am (last admission 4pm).
**Grounds:**
Open all year except Christmas Day, from 10am until 5.30pm (dusk in winter).
**Stable Courtyard Shops, Café & Garden Centre:**
Open daily all year except Christmas Day from 10am until 5pm (4pm in winter)
For more information please contact Castle Howard Estate Office on 01653 648444.

### ■ Admission
**Summer**
**House & Grounds:**
| | |
|---|---|
| Adult | £14.00 |
| Conc | £12.00 |
| Child (5 to 16 yrs) | £7.50 |
| Under 5 yrs | Free |

**Grounds Only:**
| | |
|---|---|
| Adult | £9.50 |
| Conc | £9.00 |
| Child (5 to 16 yrs) | £6.00 |
| Under 5 yrs | Free |

**Winter (when the House is closed):**
| | |
|---|---|
| Adult | £6.00 |
| Conc | £5.00 |
| Child (5 to 16 yrs) | £3.00 |
| Under 5 yrs | Free |

### Conference/Function
| ROOM | Size | Max Cap |
|---|---|---|
| Long Gallery | 197' x 24' | 200 |
| Grecian Hall | 40' x 40' | 70 |

# CASTLE HOWARD ▥Ⓕ
www.castlehoward.co.uk

## Designed by Sir John Vanbrugh in 1699 Castle Howard is undoubtedly one of Britain's finest private residences.

Built for Charles Howard the 3rd Earl of Carlisle, Castle Howard remains home to the Howard family. Its dramatic interiors - with impressive painted and gilded dome - contain world-renowned collections including furniture, porcelain, sculpture and paintings; all gathered by succeeding generations. In each room friendly and knowledgeable guides will share with you the stories of the family and their influence in shaping the fortunes of Castle Howard.

The High South apartments, so tragically destroyed by fire in 1940, are now open to the public. This once bare shell is now a film set, complete with props and painted scenery, following the 2008 film remake of Brideshead Revisited. An accompanying exhibition tells the story of the great fire of 1940 and why Evelyn Waugh's famous novel was filmed, not just once, but twice at Castle Howard.

Designed on a monumental scale, the breathtaking grounds reflect the grandeur of the house. With statues, lakes, temples and fountains, memorable sights include The Temple of the Four Winds, the Mausoleum and New River Bridge. Garden enthusiasts will enjoy the 18th Century Walled Garden with its collection of roses and ornamental vegetable garden. While Ray Wood, the woodland garden widely acknowledged as a 'rare botanical jewel', features a unique collection of trees, shrubs, rhododendrons, magnolias and azaleas.

Attractions include a changing programme of exhibitions and family events, plus free outdoor tours and illustrated children's trail. There is also an adventure playground, summer boat trips on the Great Lake (weather permitting), and a choice of cafés and shops, including garden centre, farm shop and gift shops.

## KEY FACTS

- ℹ Photography allowed.
- ♟ Licensed for civil weddings.
- ♿ Access to all areas except High South, Exhibition Wing and Chapel.
- 🍽 Choice of four Cafés.
- 🚶 Guides in each room.
- 🅿 Free parking.
- 🏫 School parties welcome.
- 🐾 Dogs welcome.
- 🏕 Camping and caravanning.
- ❄ Gardens, shops and cafés open all year.
- 🛡 Full programme for all the family.

# SKIPTON CASTLE
### www.skiptoncastle.co.uk

## Skipton Castle, over 900 years old, one of the best preserved, most complete medieval castles in England.

Guardian of the gateway to the Yorkshire Dales for over 900 years, this unique fortress is one of the most complete, well-preserved medieval castles in England. Standing on a 40-metre high crag, fully-roofed Skipton Castle was founded around 1090 by Robert de Romille, one of William the Conqueror's Barons, as a fortress in the dangerous northern reaches of the kingdom.

Owned by King Edward I and Edward II, from 1310 it became the stronghold of the Clifford Lords withstanding successive raids by marauding Scots. During the Civil War it was the last Royalist bastion in the North, yielding only after a three-year siege in 1645. 'Slighted' under the orders of Cromwell, the castle was skillfully restored by the redoubtable Lady Anne Clifford and today visitors can climb from the depths of the Dungeon to the top of the Watch Tower, explore the Banqueting Hall, Kitchens, the Bedchamber and even the Privy!

Every period has left its mark, from the Norman entrance and the medieval towers, to the beautiful Tudor courtyard with the great yew tree planted by Lady Anne in 1659.

In the grounds visitors can see the Tudor wing built as a royal wedding present for Lady Eleanor Brandon, niece of Henry VIII, the beautiful Shell Room decorated in the 1620s with shells and Jamaican coral and the ancient medieval chapel of St. John the Evangelist. The Chapel Terrace, with its delightful picnic area, has fine views over the woods and Skipton's lively market town.

## VISITOR INFORMATION

### ■ Address
Skipton Castle
Skipton
North Yorkshire
BD23 1AW

### ■ Location
Map 10:09
OS Ref. SD992 520
In the centre of Skipton, at the N end of High Street. Skipton is 20m W of Harrogate on the A59 and 26m NW of Leeds on A65.
**Rail:** Regular services from Leeds & Bradford.

### ■ Contact
Judith Parker
**Tel:** 01756 792442
**Fax:** 01756 796100
**E-mail:** info@skiptoncastle.co.uk

### ■ Opening Times
**All year**
(closed 25 December)
Mon-Sat 10am-6pm
Suns 12 noon-6pm
(October-February 4pm).

### ■ Admission
| | |
|---|---|
| Adult | £7.30 |
| Child (0-4yrs) | Free |
| Child (5-17yrs) | £4.50 |
| OAP | £6.50 |
| Student (with ID) | £6.50 |
| Family (2+3) | £23.50 |
| Groups (15+) | |
| Adult | £6.20 |
| Child (0-17yrs) | £4.50 |

Includes illustrated tour sheet in a choice of ten languages, plus free badge for children.

Groups welcome- Guides available for booked groups at no extra charge.

### ■ Special Events
Historical Re-enactments. Plays. Art Exhibitions. For up-to-date information and coming events, see our website www.skiptoncastle.co.uk.

### Conference/Function
| Room | Size | Max Cap |
|---|---|---|
| Oak Room | | 30 |
| Granary | | 100 |

## KEY FACTS

- ⓘ Fully roofed. Photography allowed for personal use only.
- Specialist books, cards, gifts. Online shop.
- Unusual plants grown in grounds.
- Corporate hospitality. Wedding ceremonies. Champagne receptions.
- Unsuitable.
- Licensed. Open all year.
- Licensed. Open all year.
- By arrangement.
- Ⓟ Large public coach and car park nearby.
- Tour guides, educational rooms and teachers packs available.
- Dogs on leads only.
- Civil Wedding Licence. Max 80 guests.
- Open all year except 25th December.

## FAIRFAX HOUSE 🏠Ⓕ
### FAIRFAX HOUSE, CASTLEGATE, YORK, NORTH YORKSHIRE YO1 9RN
www.fairfaxhouse.co.uk

Unlock the splendour within the finest Georgian townhouse in England. A classical architectural masterpiece of the 18th Century featuring exceptional stuccowork, Fairfax House was the winter home of Viscount Fairfax. Its richly decorated interior was designed by York's most distinguished architect, John Carr. Today, Fairfax House reveals the elegance of city living in Georgian York. The superb collection of 18th Century furniture, clocks, paintings and decorative arts perfectly complements the house, bringing it to life and creating a special lived-in feeling. With an exciting programme of events and exhibitions, there is always a reason to come and savour Fairfax House.

**Location:** Map 11:B9. OS Ref SE605 515. In the centre of York between Castle Museum and Jorvik Centre.

**Owner:** York Civic Trust  **Contact:** Hannah Phillip
**Tel:** 01904 655543  **Fax:** 01904 652262
**E-mail:** info@fairfaxhouse.co.uk
**Open:** 7 Feb-31 Dec, Tue-Sat & Bank Holidays: 10am-5pm. Sun: 12.30-4pm. Mon: Guided tours at 11am and 2pm. Last admission half an hour before stated closing times. Closed 1 Jan-6 Feb & 24, 25 & 26 Dec.
**Admission:** Adult £6.00, Conc. £5.00, Children under 16 Free with full paying adult. Groups from £4.50 pp (min 10 persons).
**Key facts:** ⓘ Suitable for filming. No photography in house. ▣
▣ The dining facilities can accommodate up to 30 people (min of 15).
♿ Partial. 🅧 By arrangement. ▣ 🅿 ▥ ♨ Guide dogs only. ✱ ▨

© National Trust Images / Andrew Butler

## FOUNTAINS ABBEY & STUDLEY ROYAL 🌿
### RIPON, NORTH YORKSHIRE HG4 3DY
www.nationaltrust.org.uk/fountainsabbey

Come and discover for yourself why Fountains Abbey & Studley Royal is a World Heritage Site. Experience the beauty, history and tranquillity of this inspirational place in the heart of the beautiful North Yorkshire countryside. Explore the spectacular ruin of a 12th Century Cistercian Abbey, one of the best surviving examples of a Georgian Water Garden, Elizabethan Manor House, Monastic Watermill and Medieval Deer Park home to over 500 wild deer.
Enjoy exhibitions, guided tours, family activities and wildlife walks throughout the year.

**Location:** Map 10:P8. OS Ref SE275 700. Abbey entrance: 4m W of Ripon off B6265. 8m W of A1.
**Owner:** National Trust  **Contact:** The National Trust
**Tel:** 01765 608888  **E-mail:** fountainsabbey@nationaltrust.org.uk
**Open:** Apr-Sep Daily: 10am-5pm. Oct-Mar Daily: 10am-4pm or dusk if earlier. Closed 24/25 Dec, & Fri from Nov-Jan. Deer Park: All year, daily during daylight (closed 24/25 Dec).

**Admission:** Adult £10.50, Child (5-16yrs) £5.25, Family £26.25, Groups (15+) Adult £8.55, Groups (31+) Adult £8.30. Group discount applicable with prior booking. Telephone in advance, 01765 643197.
NT, EH Members & Under 5s Free. Group visits and disabled visitors, please telephone in advance.
Includes voluntary donation, visitors can choose to pay standard prices displayed at property and website. Does not apply to group prices.
**Key facts:** ⓘ Events held throughout the year. Exhibitions. Seminar facilities. The Abbey is owned by English Heritage. St Mary's Church is owned by English Heritage and managed by the National Trust. ▣ Two shops. ✱ ▣ Dinners.
♿ WCs. ▣ Licensed. ▥ Licensed. 🅧 Free, but seasonal. Groups (please book on 01765 643197), please use Visitor Centre entrance. ▣ Audio tour £2.00.
🅿 Drivers must book groups. ▥ ♨ Dogs on leads only.
▣ Fountains Hall, an Elizabethan Mansion is an ideal setting for weddings. For details or a Wedding pack tel: 01765 643198. ✱ ▨

## KIPLIN HALL AND GARDENS 🏠ⓕ
### NR SCORTON, RICHMOND, NORTH YORKSHIRE  DL10 6AT
www.kiplinhall.co.uk

Winner of Hudson's Hidden Gem & Best New Discovery awards. Jacobean country seat of founder of Maryland, George Calvert. 'Gothic' wing added in the 1820s & redesigned in 1887 by W.E. Nesfield. This intriguing house is furnished as a comfortable Victorian home with an eclectic mix of previous owners' furniture, paintings, portraits and personalia, including many Arts and Crafts items. Numerous original paintings from 16th–19th centuries include works by Beuckelaer, Carlevarijs, Kauffman, Lady Waterford & Watts. Ornamental Gardens, Walled Garden, Woodland/Lakeside Walks. Award-winning Tea Room. Children's Play Ship. Exhibition – Duty Calls: Kiplin Hall in Times of War.

**Location:** Map 11:A7. OS Ref SE274 976. Midway between Richmond & Northallerton, 5 miles east of A1, on B6271 Scorton – Northallerton road.

**Owner:** Kiplin Hall Trustees
**Tel:** 01748 818178
**E-mail:** info@kiplinhall.co.uk
**Open:** Gardens & Tea Room: Sun, Mon, Tue & Wed from 2 Feb until 29 Oct,10am–5pm (4pm Feb & Mar). Also Good Fri & Easter Sat. Hall: Sun, Mon, Tue & Wed from 30 Mar-29 Oct., 2pm–5pm. Also Good Fri & Easter Sat. Christmas: Fri, Sat, Sun 28-30 Nov & 5–8 Dec, 10am–4pm.
**Admission:** Hall/Gardens/Grounds: Adult £8, Conc. £7, Child £4, Family (2+3) £23. Gardens/Grounds only: Adult £5, Conc. £4, Child £2, Family (2+3) £13.
**Key facts:** ⓘ Special Events - see website for details.
🖼 ♿ 🚻 ♿ Partial. WCs. ⬤ ⓕ By arrangement. 🅿 🅿 🐕 In grounds only. ⬤

Bolton Castle

## MARKENFIELD HALL 🏠ⓕ
### NR RIPON, NORTH YORKSHIRE  HG4 3AD
www.markenfield.com

"This wonderfully little-altered building is the most complete surviving example of the medium-sized 14th century country house in England" John Martin Robinson The Architecture of Northern England. Tucked privately away down a mile-long winding drive, Markenfield is one of the most astonishing and romantic of Yorkshire's medieval houses: fortified, completely moated, and still privately owned. Winner of the HHA and Sotheby's Finest Restoration Award 2008. **Location:** Map 10:P8. OS Ref SE294 672. Access from W side of A61. 2½ miles S of the Ripon bypass.

**Owner:** Mr Ian & Lady Deirdre Curteis  **Contact:** The Administrator
**Tel:** 01765 692303  **Fax:** 01765 607195  **E-mail:** info@markenfield.com
**Open:** Open 3 - 18 May and 14 - 29 Jun daily 2pm - 5pm. Last entry 4:30pm. Groups bookings can be accepted all year round by appointment.
**Admission:** Prices £5.00 Adult, £4.00 conc. Booked groups £6.00 per person for a guided tour (min charge £100).
**Key facts:** ⓘ ◻ ▣ ⊤ ⬩ Partial. Wheelchair access to the ground floor only. ⓕ ℗ ▦ ⬩ Dogs in grounds only. ▣ ⬩

© Peter Packer

## NEWBY HALL & GARDENS 🏠ⓕ
### NEWBY HALL, RIPON, NORTH YORKSHIRE  HG4 5AE
www.newbyhall.com

Designed under the guidance of Sir Christopher Wren, this graceful country house, home to the Compton family, epitomises the Georgian 'Age of Elegance'. Its beautifully restored interior presents Robert Adam at his best and houses rare Gobelins tapestries and one of the UK's largest private collections of classical statuary. The award winning gardens, created in the early 1920s boast one of Europe's longest double herbaceous borders and are of interest to specialist and amateur gardeners alike. Newby also offers a large, thoughtfully designed Adventure Garden for children, a miniature railway, excellent restaurant, shop and plant centre. Events: 11 May-Spring Plant Fair, 25/26 May Yorkshire Game Fair, 7/8 Jun-Yorkshire Vintage Association - Tractor Fest, 20 Jul-Historic Vehicle Rally, 28 Sep-Apple Day & final day of season.
**Location:** Map 11:A8. OS Ref SE348 675. Midway between London and Edinburgh, 4m W of A1, towards Ripon. S of Skelton 2m NW of (A1) Boroughbridge. 4m SE of Ripon.
**Owner:** Mr Richard Compton  **Contact:** The Administrator

**Tel:** 01423 322583 opt 3  **Fax:** 01423 324452  **E-mail:** info@newbyhall.com
**Open:** Summer- House*, 1 Apr-28 Sep. Apr, May, Jun & Sep: Tue-Sun & BH Mons; Jul-Aug: Daily. See website for tour times. *Areas of the House can be closed to the public from time to time, please check website for details. Garden, dates as House, 11am-5.30pm. last admission 5pm. Winter, Oct-end Mar closed. **Admission:** See website for further information.
**Key facts:** ⓘ Allow a full day for viewing house and gardens. Suitable for filming and for special events. No indoor photography. ◻ 'The Shop @ Newby Hall' - Modern British Art and Craftsmanship. Quality toys. ▣ Quality plants available, reflecting the contents of the garden. ⊤ Wedding receptions & special functions. ⬩ Suitable. WCs. Parking. Wheelchairs available - booking essential. ⬛ Licensed. ▥ Licensed. ⓕ Obligatory. ℗ Ample. Hard standing for coaches. ▦ Welcome. Rates on request. Grantham Room for use as wet weather base subject to availability. Woodland discovery walk, adventure gardens and train rides. ⬩ Guide/hearing dogs only. Dog exercise area. ▣ ⬩

## ALL SAINTS' CHURCH
### Church Lane, Skelton-in-Cleveland, Saltburn-By-The-Sea North Yorkshire  TS12 2HQ
### www.visitchurches.org.uk

This secluded Georgian church, is set in parkland with views to Skelton Castle. Graves with skull-and-crossbone motifs mingle with wild cherry and garlic in the churchyard.

The church was mostly rebuilt in 1785 and probably two previous churches were sited there. Pulpit, box pews and other furnishings seem to date from the rebuilding, with slightly earlier text boards and some older monuments on a remaining medieval wall.

The herringbone tooling of the outside stonework gives the church a strong local feel, in contrast to the 'Venetian' east window and the dark rose colouring of the interior.

**Location:** OS Ref NZ653 191. Off A173 on to Church Lane.
**Contact:** Please call The Churches Conservation Trust on 0845 303 2760 (Mon-Fri, 9am–5pm)
**Open:** Keyholder nearby.

## BROUGHTON HALL ESTATE
### Skipton, Yorkshire  BD23 3AE
### www.broughtonhall.co.uk

Broughton Hall Estate has been nurtured by the Tempest Family for over 900 years. Guests can exclusively hire any one of the three exquisite venues from contemporary Utopia, luxury holiday retreat Eden and the stately home itself, available all year round for residential stays, celebrations and corporate events. Our sister estate offers similar hospitality packages: Aldourie Castle Estate, Loch Ness, Scotland www.aldouriecastle.co.uk.
**Location:** Map 10:N9. OS Ref SD943 507. On A59, 2m W of Skipton.
**Owner:** The Tempest Family **Contact:** The Estate Office
**Tel:** 01756 799608 **Fax:** 01756 700357 **Email:** info@broughtonhall.co.uk
**E-mail:** tempest@broughtonhall.co.uk
**Open:** Show rounds by prior arrangement. **Admission:** P.O.A
**Key facts:** ⊤ Meetings & Events space in the Hall or Utopia. 🖼 💻 Licensed. 🍽 Licensed. 📷 By arrangement. 🅿 Ample car parking onsite. 🔲 Available only at short notice & depending on availability. 🛏 Both Broughton Hall & Aldourie Castle. 🛌 15 luxury en suite bedrooms sleeping 29 guests. ❄ Please enquire for Christmas & New Year packages. ♨

## BOLTON CASTLE
### Bolton Castle, Nr Leyburn, North Yorkshire  DL8 4ET
### www.boltoncastle.co.uk

Bolton is one of the country's best preserved medieval castles. Completed in 1399, its scars bear testament to over 600 years of fascinating history, including Mary Queen of Scots' imprisonment and a Civil War siege. Enjoy our magnificent falconry experience, fascinating archery demonstrations and exciting Wild Boar feeding time. Explore our beautiful medieval gardens and maze and visit our wonderful tea room serving homemade and locally sourced light lunches, cakes and refreshments.
**Location:** Map 10:07. OS Ref SE034 918. Approx 6m W of Leyburn. 1m NW of Redmire **Owner:** Lord Bolton **Contact:** Katie Boggis
**Tel:** 01969 623981 **E-mail:** info@boltoncastle.co.uk
**Open:** Open daily 10am-5pm from Sat 15th Feb - Sun 2nd Nov (10am-4pm in Feb/Mar), 2pm closure on occasional Sat/Sun.
**Admission:** Castle and Garden: Adults: £8.50,
Concessions/children: £7.00, Family: £30.00
**Key facts:** ℹ Group discounts and guided tours available when booked in advance. 🛍 Gift and souvenir shop. 🔲 📷 📹 Audio Visual Tours available. 🅿 Parking fee is refundable. 🔲 🛏 No Dogs. 🔲 ♨

## CHURCH OF CHRIST THE CONSOLER
### Newby Hall, Skelton-cum-Newby, Ripon, North Yorkshire  HG4 5AE
### www.visitchurches.org.uk

With its colourful and vibrant interior, this Victorian church seems the very celebration of life, yet it stands as a testament to tragedy. It is a memorial to Frederick Vyner who, age 23, was captured and murdered by brigands in Greece in 1870. His mother used the money collected for his ransom to commission British architect William Burges to design this church (built 1871-76) in the grounds of her home at Newby Hall. Standing inside the gates of the park and surrounded by huge beech trees, the outside is impressive, with its lofty spire, pinnacles and fine rose window. The interior is wonderfully rich and colourful with stained glass, fine marble and gilded mosaics. Exquisite carvings on the corbels and on the organ case bring stone and wood to life.
**Location:** OS Ref SE360 679. 4m SE of Ripon, off B6265; follow brown signs to Newby Hall; go through main gateway, follow road towards the Hall. Church on right. **Contact:** Please call The Churches Conservation Trust on 0845 303 2760 (Mon-Fri, 9am–5pm)

## CONSTABLE BURTON HALL GARDENS 🏛Ⓕ
### Leyburn, North Yorkshire DL8 5LJ
www.constableburton.com

A delightful terraced woodland garden of lilies, ferns, hardy shrubs, roses and wild flowers surrounds this beautiful Palladian house designed by John Carr. Garden trails and herbaceous borders and stream garden with large architectural plants and reflection ponds.
Stunning seasonal displays of snowdrops and daffodils. An annual Tulip Festival takes place over the early May Bank Holiday weekend. Group tours of the House and Gardens are invited by prior arrangement.
**Location:** Map 10:P7. OS Ref SE164 913.
3m E of Leyburn off the A684.
**Owner/Contact:** M C A Wyvill Esq
**Tel:** 01677 450428
**Fax:** 01677 450622
**E-mail:** gardens@constableburton.com
**Open:** Garden only: Sat 22 Mar-Sun 21 Sep.
**Admission:** Adult £4.00, Child (5-16yrs) 50p, OAP £3.00.
**Key facts:** 🍴 ♿ WCs. 📷 🅿 Limited for coaches. 🐕 On leads only. 🏠

## THE FORBIDDEN CORNER
### Tupgill Park Estate, Coverham, Nr Middleham
### North Yorkshire DL8 4TJ
www.theforbiddencorner.co.uk

A unique labyrinth of tunnels, chambers, follies and surprises created in a four acre garden in the heart of the Yorkshire dales. The Temple of the Underworld, The Eye of the Needle, a large pyramid made of translucent glass paths and passageways that lead nowhere. Extraordinary statues at every turn.
**Location:** Map 10:07. OS Ref SE094 866. A6108 to Middleham, situated 2½ miles west of Middleham on the Coverham Lane.
**Owner:** Colin R Armstrong CMG, OBE **Contact:** John or Wendy Reeves
**Tel:** 01969 640638 **Fax:** 01969 640687 **E-mail:** forbiddencorner@gmail.com
**Open:** 1 Apr-31 Oct daily, then every Sun until Christmas. Mon-Sat 12-6pm. Suns & BHs 10am-6pm (or dusk if earlier). **Admission:** See www.theforbiddencorner.co.uk for up to date info & prices.
**Key facts:** ℹ️ 🖼 Gifts & mementos. ♿ Partial. WCs. Ramps into shop. 🍴 Own blend coffee, locally sourced food & award winning pies & teas. 🅿 Limited spaces for coaches. 🎫 Special rates (see our website). 🐕 Guide dogs only. 🏠 Self catering cottages all year. Free day pass with all stays. ✱

## DUNCOMBE PARK 🏛Ⓕ
### Helmsley, North Yorkshire YO62 5EB
www.duncombepark.com

The sweeping grass terraces, towering veteran trees, and classical temples are described by historian Christopher Hussey as 'the most spectacularly beautiful among English landscape conceptions of the 18th Century'. Beside superb views over the Rye valley, visitors will discover woodland walks, ornamental parterres, and a 'secret garden' at the Conservatory. **Location:** Map 11:B7. OS Ref SE604 830. Entrance just off Helmsley Market Square, signed off A170 Thirsk-Scarborough road. **Owner/Contact:** Hon Jake Duncombe
**Tel:** 01439 770213 **Fax:** 01439 771114 **E-mail:** info@duncombepark.com
**Open:** Garden Only: 20 Apr-31 Aug, Sun-Fri, 10:30am-5pm. The garden may close for private events and functions - please check website for information.
**Admission:** Gardens & Parkland: Adult £5.00, Conc £4.50, Child (5-16yrs) £3.00, Child (0-5yrs) Free, Groups (15+) £4.00, Group guided tour £5.00. Parkland: Adult £1.00, Child (0-16yrs) Free.
**Key facts:** ℹ️ Wedding receptions, conferences, corporate hospitality, country walks, nature reserve, orienteering, film location, product launches, vehicle rallies. 🍴 Banqueting facilities. 🎫 📷 For 15+ groups only. 🅿 🖼 🏠 🐕

## HOLY TRINITY CHURCH 🏛
### Low Lane, Wensley, Leyburn
### North Yorkshire DL8 4HX
www.visitchurches.org.uk

Built on 8th Century Saxon foundations, this 13th Century church sits on the bank of the river Ure at the eastern end of picturesque Wensleydale. Inside, its rich history is all around, with good examples of medieval wallpaintings, fine Flemish brasses and a 15th Century reliquary, which is claimed to have once held the relics of St Agatha.
Sit and marvel at the sumptuous richness of the Scrope family pew (who were local landowners) and imagine life as the Lord or Lady of nearby Bolton Castle.
**Location:** OS Ref SE092 895.
2 miles south of Leyburn, on A684.
**Open:** Open daily.

## HOLY TRINITY CHURCH
### 70 Goodramgate, York, North Yorkshire YO1 7LF
www.visitchurches.org.uk

Holy Trinity Goodramgate has the air of a hidden treasure. It stands in a small, secluded, leafy churchyard, with the Minster towering behind, tucked away behind Goodramgate. To visit, you pass through an 18th Century archway tacked on to buildings that served as artisans' workshops in the 14th Century. Light filters through the windows, illuminating honey-coloured stone. The east window especially has marvellous stained glass that was donated in the early 1470s by the Reverend John Walker, rector of the church. On sunny days, transient gems of coloured light are scattered on the walls, and various medieval faces stare out from the windows. The building dates chiefly from the 15th Century, but has features from its foundation in the 12th Century right up to the 19th Century. The box pews, unique in York, are exceptionally fine, and an interesting collection of monuments and memorials paint a picture of life in this busy city throughout the ages. **Location:** OS Ref SE605 522. York city centre, off Goodramgate; King's Square and Shambles 200 yards.
**Open:** Mon, 12pm-4pm; Tue-Sat 10am-4pm; Sun 12pm-4pm.

## NEWBURGH PRIORY
### Coxwold, North Yorkshire YO61 4AS

Home to the Earls of Fauconberg and the Wombwell family the house was built in 1145 with alterations in 1538 and 1720 and contains the tomb of Oliver Cromwell. The beautiful grounds contain a lake, water garden, walled garden, amazing topiary yews and woodland walks set against the White Horse.
**Location:** Map 11:B8. OS Ref SE541 764.
4m E of A19, 18m N of York, ½ m E of Coxwold.
**Owner/Contact:** Sir George Wombwell Bt **Tel:** 01347 868372
**Open:** 2 Apr-29 Jun, Wed & Sun. BH Mons 21 Apr & 25 Aug. Gardens 2-6pm, House 2.30-4.45pm. Tours every ½ hour. Bus parties by arrangement.
**Admission:** House & Gardens: Adult £6.00, Child £2.00. Gardens only: Adult £3.00, Child Free. Special tours of private apartments Wed 2, 9, 16, 23 & 30 Apr, £5.00pp.
**Key facts:** i No photography in house. T S Partial. ⚅ ⚆ Obligatory. P Limited for coaches. 🐕 In grounds, on leads. ⚅ And wedding receptions.

## HOVINGHAM HALL
### York, North Yorkshire YO62 4LU
www.hovingham.co.uk

Attractive Palladian family home, designed and built by Thomas Worsley. The childhood home of Katharine Worsley, Duchess of Kent. It is entered through a huge riding school and has beautiful rooms with collections of pictures and furniture. The house has attractive gardens with magnificent Yew hedges and cricket ground.
**Location:** Map 11:C8. OS Ref SE666 756. 18m N of York on Malton/Helmsley Road (B1257).
**Owner:** Sir William Worsley
**Contact:** The Administrator
**Tel:** 01653 628771 **Fax:** 01653 628668
**E-mail:** office@hovingham.co.uk
**Open:** 1 Jun-28 Jun inclusive 12.30pm-4.30pm (last admission 3.30pm).
**Admission:** Adult £8.50, Conc. £8.00, Child £4.00. Gardens only: £4.00.
**Key facts:** i No photography in house. T S Ground floor only. ⚆ Tea room. ⚆ Obligatory. P Limited. None for coaches. 🐕 Guide dogs only.

## ST PETER'S CHURCH
### Church Lane, Wintringham, Malton
### North Yorkshire YO17 8HU
www.visitchurches.org.uk

This beautiful and peaceful church, with an elegant spire, was built from the Norman period to the 15th Century. The oldest part of the church is the Norman chancel with its priest's door and corbel table; the nave and west tower are of the 14th Century, although externally the tower has crenellated parapets and perpendicular tracery of the 15th Century.
The graveyard is filled with 18th and 19th Century monuments to the former inhabitants of this sleepy village. The church is full of interesting furnishings including Jacobean bench pews, medieval carvings and stained glass. Look carefully and you might also find green men, mythical beasts and sword markings.
**Location:** OS Ref SE887 731.
11 miles east of Malton, off the A64.
**Open:** Open daily.

## ST STEPHEN'S CHURCH
### Robin Hood's Bay, Fylingdales, Whitby
### North Yorkshire  YO22 4PN
www.visitchurches.org.uk

Likened to an old mariner gazing out to sea, St Stephen's stands majestically on the hillside between Whitby and Ravenscar, overlooking Robin Hood's Bay. Built in 1821, its appearance can be severe but the church resonates with the history of a resilient North Sea fishing community. Inside, painted box pews, a full-length gallery and a three-decker pulpit, designed for the preaching of the Word, have all survived. The sea is a recurring theme throughout and there are memorials to the shipwrecked in both the church and churchyard. Successful lifeboat rescue missions are listed and there is also a touching display of rare maiden's garlands used in the funeral processions of young and chaste women. Outside, windswpet gravestones huddle tightly round the church walls.
**Location:** OS Ref NZ942 059.
5 miles south east of Whitby; take the B1447, the church is on the right before the road descends into Robin Hood's Bay.
**Open:** Keyholder nearby.

## SION HILL
### Kirby Wiske, Thirsk, North Yorkshire  YO7 4EU
www.sionhillhall.co.uk

Sion Hill was designed in 1912 by the renowned York architect Walter H Brierley, 'the Lutyens of the North', receiving an award from the Royal Institute of British Architects as being of 'outstanding architectural merit'.
The house is furnished with a fine collection of antique furniture, paintings ceramics and clocks.
**Location:** Map 11:A7. OS Ref SE373 844. 6m S of Northallerton off A167. 4m W of Thirsk.
**Owner:** H W Mawer Trust **Contact:** R M Mallaby
**Tel:** 01845 587206 **E-mail:** sionhill@btconnect.com
**Open:** Group visits only, available througout the year. Please contact the house for booking arrangements.
**Admission:** £10.00 per person to include guided tour and admission to the grounds.
**Key facts:** ⓘ No photography in the house. Ⓛ Partial. WC.
Ⓕ By arrangement. Ⓟ Ample for cars and coaches. Ⓜ Guide dogs only.

## SCAMPSTON WALLED GARDEN
### Scampston Hall, Malton, North Yorkshire  YO17 8NG
www.scampston.co.uk/gardens

A contemporary garden with striking perennial meadow planting that explodes with colour in the summer. Created by acclaimed designer and plantsman Piet Oudolf, the garden also contains traditional spring/autumn borders, a green "silent garden", and a dramatic use of grasses, bulbs and unusual shrubs that extend the season.
**Location:** Map 11:D8. OS Ref SE865 755.
5m E of Malton, off A64.
**Owner:** Christopher Legard
**Contact:** The Administrator
**Tel:** 01944 759111
**Fax:** 01944 758700
**E-mail:** info@scampston.co.uk
**Open:** 18 Apr-2 Nov, Tues-Sun plus BHols 10am-5pm, last adm. 4.30pm.
**Admission:** Adult £7.00, Child (5-16) £3.50, Under 5s Free. Groups (15+) welcome by arrangement.
**Key facts:** ⓘ Spring Plant Fair 1 Jun. Please see website for exhibitions and other events. Ⓖ Ⓕ Ⓣ Ⓛ Suitable. WCs. Ⓦ Ⓣ Licensed. Ⓟ Ⓜ Ⓜ Ⓦ

## STOCKELD PARK
### Off the A661, Wetherby, North Yorkshire  LS22 4AN
www.stockeldpark.co.uk

A gracious Palladian mansion by James Paine (1763), featuring a magnificent cantilevered staircase in the central oval hall. Surrounded by beautiful gardens and set in 18th Century landscaped parkland at the heart of a 2000 acre estate. Popular for filming and photography. Stockeld Park was highly commended in the Hudson's Heritage Awards 2011 Best Event category for its seasonal attraction, The Christmas Adventure www.thechristmasadventure.com.
**Location:** Map 11:A9. OS Ref SE376 497. York 12m, Harrogate 5m, Leeds 12m. **Owner:** Mr and Mrs P G F Grant **Contact:** Mr P Grant
**Tel:** 01937 586101 **Fax:** 01937 580084 **E-mail:** office@stockeldpark.co.uk
**Open:** House: Privately booked events and tours only. Contact Estate Office 01937 586101. Please see web for further seasonal opening of the adventure site and special events. www.stockeldpark.co.uk.
**Admission:** Prices on application.
**Key facts:** Ⓖ Fantastic seasonal gift emporium filled with gift ideas. Ⓣ Private event & Wedding enquiries welcome. Ⓣ Home made & Local, Fully Licensed.
Ⓕ Groups, Tours and Groups welcome by appointment. Ⓟ
Ⓜ Schools welcome by appointment. Ⓜ Ⓦ

## SUTTON PARK 🏠Ⓔ
### Sutton-On-The-Forest, North Yorkshire YO61 1DP
www.statelyhome.co.uk

The Yorkshire home of Sir Reginald and Lady Sheffield. Early Georgian architecture. Magnificent plasterwork by Cortese. Rich collection of 18th Century furniture, paintings and porcelain. Award winning gardens attract enthusiasts from home and abroad. Tranquil Caravan and Camping Club CL Site also available for Rallies. Woodland Walk. Tearooms.
**Location:** Map 11:B9. OS Ref SE583 646. 8miles N of York on B1363 York-Helmsley Road follow brown signs **Contact:** Administrator
**Tel:** 01347 810249 **Fax:** 01347 811251
**E-mail:** suttonpark@statelyhome.co.uk
**Open:** Private parties all year by appointment (min. charge for 15). Gardens: 11am-5pm 1 May-29 Jun inclusive. House: from 1.30pm 26 May Spring BH Mon, then Sat 31 May-Sun 29 Jun inclusive. 26 Aug Summer BH Mon. Heritage Days: Thur 11 & Fri 12 Sep. For House tour times and admission prices see website for details. **Key facts:** ⓘ No photography. 📷 📹 Flower Power Fairs www.flowerpowerfairs.co.uk 🍽 Lunches & dinners in Dining Room. ⓖ Partial. WCs. 🍷 Licensed. 🍴 🎫 Obligatory. 🅿 Limited for coaches. 🐕 Woodland Walk only 🌳

## ASKE HALL 🏠
### Richmond, North Yorkshire DL10 5HJ
Tours limited to 15 people per tour. Booking advisable and ID will be required (passport, driving licence etc). For further details contact Mandy Blenkiron. A predominantly Georgian collection of paintings, furniture and porcelain in house which has been the seat of the Dundas family since 1763.
**Location:** Map 10:P6. OS Ref NZ179 035. 4m SW of A1 at Scotch Corner, 2m from the A66, on the B6274.
**Owner:** Earl of Ronaldshay
**Contact:** Mandy Blenkiron
**Tel:** 01748 822000
**E-mail:** mandy.blenkiron@aske.co.uk
**Website:** www.aske.co.uk
**Open:** 11 & 12 Sep 2014 (Heritage Open Days). Tours at 10.00, 11.00 & 12.00.
**Admission:** Free.
**Key facts:** ⓖ Partial. 🎫 Obligatory. 🅿 Limited. 🐕

## BROCKFIELD HALL 🏠Ⓔ
### Warthill, York YO19 5XJ
Georgian house (1804) by Peter Atkinson for Benjamin Agar Esq. Mrs. Wood's father was Lord Martin Fitzalan Howard, son of Lady Beaumont of Carlton Towers, Selby. Brockfield has portraits of her Stapleton family. There is a permanent exhibition of paintings by Staithes Group artists, by appointment outside August.
**Location:** Map 11:C9. OS Ref SE664 550. 5m E of York off A166 or A64.
**Owner:** Mr & Mrs Simon Wood **Contact:** Simon Wood
**Tel:** 01904 489362
**E-mail:** simon@brockfieldhall.co.uk
**Website:** www.brockfieldhall.co.uk
**Open:** Aug 1-31 inclusive except Mons (open BH Mon), 1-4pm. Conducted tours at 13.00, 14.00 and 15.00.
**Admission:** Adult £7.00.
**Key facts:** ⓘ No photography inside house. 🎫 By arrangement. 🅿 🐕 In grounds, on leads.

## NORTON CONYERS 🏠
### Nr Ripon, North Yorkshire HG4 5EQ

Visited by Charlotte Brontë, Norton Conyers, an original of 'Thornfield Hall', has belonged to the Grahams since 1624. The mid-18th Century walled garden retains its original design. Herbaceous borders flanked by yew hedges lead to central pavilion. Unusual hardy plants, PYO fruit, vegetables and seasonal flowers for sale.
**Location:** Map 11:A8. OS Ref SF319 763. 4m NW of Ripon. 3 ½ m from the A1.
**Owner:** Sir James and Lady Graham **Contact:** The Administrator
**Tel/Fax:** 01765 640333 **E-mail:** visits@nortonconyers.org.uk
**Website:** www.nortonconyers.org.uk/www.weddingsatnortonconyers.co.uk
**Open:** Garden: open every Sun, Mon and Thur 3 Apr-29 Sep. Also most Mons and Thurs throughout the year (please email to check). House: closed except for pre-booked groups (min 25) to view work in progress. **Admission:** Garden: Individual admission free - donations welcome. Entrance fee on charity days. Group tours by arrangement. **Key facts:** 🎫 🍴 Pavilion is available for functions: seats up to 25. ⓖ Partial. WC. 🎫 By arrangement. 🐕 Dogs on leads only.

## PLUMPTON ROCKS 🏠Ⓔ
### Plumpton, Knaresborough
### North Yorkshire HG5 8NA

Grade II* listed garden extending to over 30 acres including an idyllic lake, dramatic millstone grit rock formation, romantic woodland walks winding through bluebells and rhododendrons. Declared by English Heritage to be of outstanding interest. Painted by Turner. Described by Queen Mary as 'Heaven on earth'.
**Location:** Map 11:A9. OS Ref SE353 535. Between Harrogate and Wetherby on A661, 1m SE of A661 junction with Harrogate southern bypass.
**Owner/Contact:** Robert de Plumpton Hunter
**Tel:** 01289 382322
**Open:** Mar-Oct: Sat, Sun & BHs, 11am-6pm.
**Admission:** Adult £3.50, Child/OAP £2.50. (prices, subject to change).
**Key facts:** ⓖ Unsuitable. 🅿 Limited for coaches. 🍽 🐕 In grounds, on leads.

## SCAMPSTON HALL 🏠Ⓔ
### Scampston, Malton, North Yorkshire YO17 8NG
Scampston is among the best examples of the English country house, combining fine architecture with a wealth of art treasures and set in a 'Capability' Brown parkland. Guided tours around this family home are often welcomed by Sir Charles Legard. Restaurant and disabled facilities in The Walled Garden (see separate entry). **Location:** Map 11:D8. OS Ref SE865 755. 5m E of Malton, off A64 Follow Scampston Only sign **Owner:** Christopher Legard **Contact:** The Administrator
**Tel:** 01944 759111 **Fax:** 01944 758700 **E-mail:** info@scampston.co.uk
**Website:** www.scampston.co.uk/hall **Open:** 25 May-17 Aug 2014, Tue-Fri & Sun plus Spring BH Mon (26 May). 1-3.45pm. All visits by guided tour. Tours at 1pm, 2pm & 3pm. **Admission:** Adults £6.00, Child (5-16yrs) £3.00, Under 5s Free. Combined ticket inc. Walled Garden available. Group (15+) rates available for pre-booked parties. **Key facts:** ⓘ Open for range of special events. See website for details. 🍴 ⓖ Partial. Ground floor only accessible for wheelchairs 🍽 See Walled Garden entry. 🍴 See Walled Garden entry. 🎫 Obligatory. 🅿 🐕 🏠 🌳

## VISITOR INFORMATION

### ■ Owner
The Newbold Family

### ■ Address
Wentworth Woodhouse
Wentworth
South Yorkshire
S62 7TQ

### ■ Location
**Map 7:A1**
**OS Ref. SK393 978**
Located in the heart of
Wentworth village, enter
using the driveway on
Cortworth Lane, directly
opposite the end of
Clayfield Lane. Use
postcode S62 7TQ.

### ■ Contact
Wentworth Woodhouse
**Tel:** 01226 351161 or
01226 749639
**E-mail:** tours@wentworth
woodhouse.co.uk

### ■ Opening Times
Wentworth Woodhouse is
open through-out the year
for pre-booked guided
tours. For availability and
to book a tour consult our
website at
www.wentworth
woodhouse.co.uk.

### ■ Admission
Admission prices are listed
on our website at
www.wentworth
woodhouse.co.uk.
Special rates for school
groups are available.

### ■ Special Events
See the house in her
Christmas finest, join us for
a meal or for mulled wine
and mince pies. Be
haunted at our Halloween
Spooktakular. Come along
to our Easter Egg Hunt in
the private West Front
Garden. Join us for the
annual Vintage Car Show.
Or if you fancy the theatre,
watch out for our special
"Theatre in the Gardens"
events throughout the
summer.

### Conference/Function
The House is available for
corporate events, from
training days to Christmas
parties. Consider hosting
your office events
surrounded by Wentworth
Woodhouse's splendour.
House is suitable as a
filming location.

# WENTWORTH WOODHOUSE 🏛ⓕ
### www.wentworthwoodhouse.co.uk

## Having the longest façade of any English country house, Wentworth Woodhouse has awoken from its slumber.

Wentworth Woodhouse is one of the finest and grandest Georgian houses in England. A formidable mansion, it was one of the most expensive ever built and ranks amongst Britain's largest and most important country houses. The current house was built by the first Marquis of Rockingham and incorporates part of an earlier manor house, built c.1630. Intriguingly, the facades of the West and East Fronts were completed by different architects using two distinct architectural styles. The East Front is sober, precise, stark Palladianism, with its political associations with the Whig architecture. In contrast, the slightly earlier West Front is a jubilantly decorated Baroque style home on a more domestic scale.

Sadly, the vast pleasure gardens of Wentworth Woodhouse have all but disappeared, the land spilt into separate ownership, the greenhouses demolished, the beauty a faded memory. But the Newbold family have a vision for the gardens that remain, one that sees life breathed back into the historic space, a garden worthy of such a grand house. A programme of restoration is underway, removing years of neglect, re-establishing pathways and vistas. Areas destroyed by mining are being redefined, planted with rare and unusual plants sourced from specialist nurseries from around the UK. From showy rhododendrons, new hybrids of magnolia and camellias, the new nestled alongside the mature trees and shrubs. A new page opens on the gardens of Wentworth Woodhouse and you are invited to walk with us. Join us for a guided tour, be amazed by the splendour of the gardens, or come along to one of our special events. Consider Wentworth Woodhouse for your wedding venue, Christmas parties, and corporate events. There truly is something for everyone at Wentworth Woodhouse.

## KEY FACTS

 No photography within the house, visitors are encouraged to photograph the Front Façade and Gardens.

Plant Fairs Apr 13 and Jul 13.

Corporate entertaining, conferences, private parties, anniversaries, lunches, dinners, wedding ceremonies & receptions.

Interactive guided tours available for school groups.

Guide dogs only.

 Access to Wentworth Woodhouse is by pre-booked guided tours. To book a tour please consult our website.

Baroque West Front

Looking out to the "Best Stairs"

## BRODSWORTH HALL & GARDENS ⊞
### BRODSWORTH, NR DONCASTER, YORKSHIRE  DN5 7XJ
### www.english-heritage.org.uk/brodsworthhall

Time really does stand still at Brodsworth Hall. Inside this beautiful Victorian country house almost everything has been left exactly as it was when it was still a family home. Possessions that took more than 130 years to gather together, from the grandest piece of furniture to family mementoes, are still in their original places. The beautiful grounds, a collection of grand gardens in miniature, have been restored to their full Victorian splendour, and feature a colourful array of seasonal displays. With an adventure playground and cosy tearoom, Brodsworth Hall has everything you need for a family day out.

**Location:** Map 11:B12. OS Ref SE506 070. In Brodsworth, 5m NW of Doncaster off A635. Use A1(M)/J37.

**Owner:** English Heritage

**Contact:** Visitor Operations Team
**Tel:** 01302 722598
**E-mail:** brodsworth.hall@english-heritage.org.uk
**Open:** Please visit www.english-heritage.org.uk for the most up-to-date opening times and admission prices.
**Key facts:** ℹ Exhibitions about the family, the servants and the gardens. WCs. No Cameras (house only). ▣ ▣ ▣
🎦 Groups must book. Booked coach parties: 10am-1pm.
🅿 220 cars and 3 coaches. Free.
▣ Education Centre. Free if booked in advance. ▣
✳ Gardens, Tearoom and Servants' Wing only. ▣

## HOLY TRINITY CHURCH ⋔
### Main Street, Wentworth, Rotherham
### South Yorkshire  S62 7TX
### www.visitchurches.org.uk

This atmospheric, partly ruined building started life as a church in the 15th Century but was converted to a mausoleum in 1877 after a new church was commissioned. Today, only the chancel and north chapel remain intact. In the chancel, brass and stone memorials and alabaster effigies from the 16th and 17th Centuries trace the powerful Wentworth family. These include one to the Earl of Strafford, a supporter of the Crown who was beheaded on Tower Hill just before the Civil War, and Charles Watson-Wentworth, the 2nd Marquis of Rockingham, who helped to negotiate an end to the American War of Independence. Wentworth estate workers and villagers rest in the churchyard, including the 17-year-old Chow Kwang Tseay from China, baptised John Dennis Blonde. He was thought to have been rescued from 'HMS Blonde' and brought to Rotherham in 1847 as a 14-year-old.

**Location:** OS Ref SK384 983. 5 miles north west of Rotherham, on B6090.
**Open:** Open daily.

Wentworth Woodhouse

## VISITOR INFORMATION

### ■ Owner
The Earl of Harewood

### ■ Address
Harewood House
Harewood
Leeds
West Yorkshire
LS17 9LG

### ■ Location
**Map 10:P10**
**OS Ref. SE311 446**
A1 N or S to Wetherby.
A659 via Collingham,
Harewood is on A61
between Leeds and
Harrogate. Easily reached
from A1, M1, M62 and
M18. 40 mins from York,
20 mins from centre of
Leeds or Harrogate.
**Bus:** No. 36 from Leeds or
Harrogate.
**Rail:** London Kings Cross
to Leeds/Harrogate 2hrs 20
mins. Leeds/Harrogate
Station 7m.
**Air:** Leeds Bradford Airport
9m.

### ■ Contact
Harewood House
**Tel:** 0113 2181010
**E-mail:**
info@harewood.org

### ■ Opening Times
Gardens, Grounds, Bird
Garden, Courtyard and
Bookshop open from 5th
April 2014. Please see
website for House opening
dates and times.

### ■ Admission
Please see website.

**Conference/Function**
Private venue hire available.

Harewood House from the South-West

# HAREWOOD HOUSE & GARDENS 🏛
www.harewood.org

## Harewood is one of the finest Treasure Houses of England, in the setting of Yorkshire's most beautiful landscape.

The family seat of the Earl and Countess of Harewood, the house was built in the 18th Century and has magnificent interiors by Robert Adam, unrivalled collections of Chippendale furniture, and paintings by JMW Turner, Reynolds, and Titian among others.

'Below Stairs' is a fascinating insight into the servants' domain and the stories of those who lived and worked here. The former Housekeeper's Room is home to a new display dedicated to the life of HRH Princess Mary, who married the 6th Earl of Harewood and lived at Harewood from 1930 until her death in 1965.

An Italianate Terrace, designed by Charles Barry, stretches along the South Front of the House and provides stunning views of 'Capability' Brown's landscape and lake.

Harewood has over 100 acres of exquisite gardens; a plant-hunter's paradise in the Himalayan Garden including the only Bhutanese Stupa in the UK, extensive working kitchen garden and elegant parterre terrace with herbaceous and sub-tropical borders.

But that's not all. Harewood is just as much about today as it is about history. There are exhibitions of contemporary art, an award-winning educational department, renowned Bird Garden home to exotic penguins, flamingos and parrots and an adventure playground.

Whether you want to visit the House and its wonderful collections, see the latest exhibitions, or enjoy the Gardens and countryside, come to Harewood for a day of discovery.

## KEY FACTS

- ℹ Please see website for further information.
- 🎁 Homeware, gifts, souvenirs, postcards and publications.
- 🌱 Seasonal plant stall May - September.
- 🍽 Fine Dining in House & private venue hire available.
- ♿ WCs. No access to State Rooms for electric wheelchairs. Courtesy wheelchair.
- ☕ Terrace Café. Licensed.
- 🍴 Courtyard Café & Restaurant. Licensed.
- 🚶 Guided tours by arrangement. Free daily talks.
- 🅿 Free. Designated for blue badge holders.
- 🏫 Sandford Award for Education. School parties welcome.
- 🐕 On leads. Service dogs welcome except in Bird Garden.
- 💍 Wedding venue hire available.

Harewood's Terrace Borders

Gallery, Harewood House

## EAST RIDDLESDEN HALL ❧
### BRADFORD ROAD, RIDDLESDEN, KEIGHLEY, WEST YORKSHIRE  BD20 5EL
### www.nationaltrust.org.uk/riddlesdenhall

East Riddlesden Hall, Small Visitor Attraction Gold Winner at the 2012 Visit England Awards, was once the home of 17th Century merchant James Murgatroyd. Explore the changes that he made to the Tudor house and discover why his work was never completed. Friendly volunteers bring the house to life with fascinating stories of this a special place. The cosy house creates a relaxing atmosphere where you can feel at ease examining the embroideries, blackwork, oak furniture and pewter. No visit is complete without a relaxing stroll around the intimate gardens.

**Location:** Map 10:O10. OS Ref SE07914 208. On the south side of Bradford Road B6265 in Riddlesden, close to Leeds & Liverpool Canal. NW of Bradford on the A650, SE of Skipton on the A629.

**Owner:** National Trust  **Contact:** Property Office

**Tel:** 01535 607075  **E-mail:** eastriddlesden@nationaltrust.org.uk
**Open:** 15 Feb-2 Mar Sat-Wed, 8 Mar-16 Mar Sat-Sun, 22 Mar-2 Nov Sat-Wed 10.30am-4.30pm (last admission 4pm). Open Good Friday. Closed 6 July. 8 Nov-21 Dec Sat-Sun House closed. Shop and Tea room 11am-3.45pm.
**Admission:** Free to NT members and under 5's, otherwise Adult £6.30, Child £3.20, Family £15.70. Pre-booked groups of 15+ £5.00. Includes a voluntary donation. Visitors can choose to pay standard admission prices displayed at property. Does not apply to group prices.
**Key facts:** ⬚ ⬚ ⬚ WC. Garden and ground floor of house accessible. Ground floor table available for tea room. ⬚ ⬚ Pre-booked coaches and groups only. ⬚ ⬚ Dogs allowed on Riverside Walk. Dogs not permitted in the house/garden/shop or tea room ⬚ ⬚

## OAKWELL HALL & RED HOUSE
### OAKWELL HALL, NUTTER LANE, BIRSTALL WF17 9LG / RED HOUSE, OXFORD RD, GOMERSAL BD19 4JP
### www.kirklees.gov.uk/museums

Visit two stunning West Yorkshire Historic Houses located less than a mile apart! Both have unique Brontë connections and featured in Charlotte Brontë's novel Shirley. Both have gorgeous award-winning period gardens to explore. Oakwell Hall is an atmospheric Elizabethan manor house with important Civil War connections, displayed as the C17th home of the Batt family. Wander through the fine oak panelled Great Hall, decorative Parlours and evocative Kitchens. Surrounded by award winning Country Park and C17th gardens; Cafe, Play Area, Nature Trail, Arboretum & Shop.
Red House is a delightful former woollen cloth merchant's home set in enchanting 1830s gardens. From elegant Parlour to stone-flagged Kitchens, each room brings you closer to the 1830s, when Charlotte Brontë visited her friend, early feminist Mary Taylor, here. Restored Garden with scented old roses, period flowers and tree shaded lawns. Bronte & local history exhibitions. Shop.

Pre-booked Group Visits; Weddings & Venue Hire; Events & Schools programme.
**Location:** Map 10:P11. M62 Jct 26 take A58 towards Leeds, turn right on A651. M62 Jct 27 take A62 towards Huddersfield. Follow brown tourist signs.
**Owner:** Kirklees Council  **Contact:** Oakwell Hall
**Tel:** 01924 326240. Red House 01274 335100
**E-mail:** oakwell.hall@kirklees.gov.uk; red.house@kirklees.gov.uk
**Open:** Summer opening: 1 Mar-31 Oct: Tue-Thu 11am-5pm; Sat & Sun 12noon-5 pm. Winter opening: 1 Nov-end Feb: Tue-Thu 11am-4pm Sat-Sun 12noon-4pm Closed Mon & Fri.
**Admission:** At each house: Adult £2.50, Child £1.00, Family £6.00 (2 adults+4 children). 'Tourist Ticket' (entry to both houses in a day): Adult £4.00, Child £1.50, Family £10.00, 'Annual Tickets' also available.
**Key facts:** ⬚ ⬚ ⬚ ⬚ Tel for access details. ⬚ ⬚ ⬚ ⬚ ⬚ ⬚ ⬚

© Simon Warner

Harewood House

## LOTHERTON HALL ESTATE

**Aberford, Leeds, West Yorkshire LS25 3EB**

**www.leeds.gov.uk/lothertonhall**

Enjoy a fantastic day out at Lotherton Hall, a charming Edwardian house and country estate, once the home of the Gascoigne family. The house is a treasure trove of fine art collections - paintings, furniture, silver, china, costume and oriental art. The estate spreads across 52 hectares of breathtaking grounds with beautiful formal, wildflower and wooded grounds, a red deer park and one of the country's most impressive and important collections of rare and endangered birds. Visit the Medieval Chapel to find out more about the medieval past of the lost Ludderton village. Relax in the Stables cafe and treat yourself to a homemade cake or light meal, and don't forget to pick up a souvenir or beautiful homeware gift inspired by Lotherton's period collections.

**Location:** Map 11:B10. OS Ref SE450 360.

**Owner:** Leeds City Council **Contact:** Michael Thaw

**Tel:** 0113 2813259 **E-mail:** lotherton@leeds.gov.uk

**Open:** Please check the website or call 0113 2813259 for seasonal opening and admission prices. **Admission:** Please check the website for current admission prices. **Key facts:** We welcome group visits, please call to arrange your day out.

## ALL SAINTS' CHURCH

**Harewood Park, Harewood, Leeds**
**West Yorkshire LS17 9LG**

**www.visitchurches.org.uk**

Nestling in the grounds of Harewood House, All Saints' dates from the 15th Century. It is remarkable for six pairs of effigies, dating from 1419 to 1510, commemorating the owners of Harewood and the nearby Gawthorpe estate. They are some of the greatest surviving examples of alabaster carving - virtually without rival in England - and offer a fascinating glimpse into the amour, robes, jewellery and headdresses of the day. The earliest depicts the fearless judge William Gascoigne in the robes of the Lord Chief Justice with a finely carved purse on one side and a dagger on the other, while his wife wears a square head-dress and rests her feet on a little dog.

**Location:** OS Ref SE314 451. 7 miles north of Leeds off A61 in grounds of Harewood House; follow signs for Harewood House; once through ticket barrier, turn immediately right.

**Contact:** Please call The Churches Conservation Trust on 0845 303 2760 (Mon-Fri, 9am–5pm) **Open:** Apr to Oct every day from 10am to 6pm; other times call Harewood House Trust Office on 0113 218 1010 in advance of your visit.

## NOSTELL PRIORY & PARKLAND

**Doncaster Road, Wakefield, West Yorkshire WF4 1QE**

**www.nationaltrust.org.uk/nostell**

Set in over 350 acres of parkland, Nostell Priory is one of Yorkshire's jewels. It is an architectural treasure by James Paine with later additions by Robert Adam, and an internationally renowned Chippendale collection.

**Location:** Map 11:A11. OS Ref SE403 175. 6m SE of Wakefield, off A638.

**Owner:** National Trust

**Contact:** Visitor Services Manager

**Tel:** 01924 863892

**E-mail:** nostellpriory@nationaltrust.org.uk

**Open:** Please see website for opening times www.nationaltrust.org.uk/nostell.

**Admission:** Please see website for Admission charges www.nationaltrust.org.uk/nostell. Includes a voluntary donation but visitors can choose to pay the standard prices displayed at the property and on the website.

**Key facts:** Baby facilities.
WCs. Licensed By arrangement.
Coaches by prior arrangement only.
On leads.

## CHURCH OF ST JOHN THE EVANGELIST

**23 New Briggate, Leeds, West Yorkshire LS2 8JD**

www.visitchurches.org.uk

Built in 1632-34, St John's is the oldest church in Leeds city centre. The glory of the church lies in its magnificent Jacobean (Carolian) fittings, particularly the superb carved wooden screen decorated with flowers, hearts and grotesque heads of humans and animals. There is more lovely carving on the wall panels, pews and pulpit. Brightly painted angels play instruments in the roof and look down on wonderful carved pews below. The church building was entirely funded by wealthy merchant and Royalist John Harrison who also paid for the grammar school and almshouses nearby. Harrison's benevolent spirit still pervades the church; buried near the altar, and a series of stained-glass windows depicts his good works. One of the windows shows an apocryphal tale in which Harrison presents King Charles, imprisoned in Leeds, with a tankard of gold coins disguised as a draught of ale.
**Location:** OS Ref SE302 338. In Mark Lane, off New Briggate in central Leeds.
**Open:** Tue-Sat, 11am-3pm.

© John Whitaker

## YORK GATE GARDEN

**Back Church Lane, Adel, Leeds LS16 8DW**

www.yorkgate.org.uk

Inspirational one acre garden widely recognized as one of Britain's finest small gardens. A series of smaller gardens with different themes and in contrasting styles are linked by a succession of delightful vistas. Striking architectural features play a key role throughout the garden which is also noted for its exquisite detailing.
**Location:** Map 10:P10. OS Ref 275 403.
2¼m SE of Bramhope, just off A660.
**Owner:** Perennial **Contact:** The Garden Co-ordinator **Tel:** 0113 2678240
**Open:** April, May & September: Thursdays, Sundays & BH Mondays, 2pm-5pm. June, July & August: Wednesdays, Thursdays, Sundays & BH Mondays, 2pm-5pm. Evenings: Wednesdays 11, 18 & 25 June, 6.30pm-9pm.
**Admission:** Standard admission £4.50. Gift Aid admission £4.95.
Children (16 & under) Free.
**Key facts:** Please park opposite church in Church Lane. Groups welcome by appointment (see website for details).
By arrangement. Guide dogs only.

## TEMPLE NEWSAM ESTATE

**Temple Newsam Road, Leeds LS15 OAE**

www.leeds.gov.uk/templenewsamhouse

One of the great country houses of England, this Tudor-Jacobean mansion was the birthplace of Lord Darnley, husband of Mary Queen of Scots and home to the Ingram family for 300 years. Rich in newly restored interiors, paintings, furniture (including Chippendale), textiles, silver and ceramics. Temple Newsam sits within 1500 acres of grand and beautiful 'Capability' Brown parkland with formal and wooded gardens as well as national plant collections.
**Location:** Map 10:P10. OS Ref SE358 321. 4m E of city centre B6159 or 2m from M1 junction 46. 4 miles from city centre.
**Owner:** Leeds City Council **Contact:** Bobbie Robertson **Tel:** 0113 3367460
**E-mail:** temple.newsam.house@leeds.gov.uk **Open:** Please check the website or call 0113 3367460 for seasonal opening times and admission prices.
**Admission:** Please check the website or call 0113 3367460 for seasonal opening times and admission prices.
**Key facts:** We welcome group visits, please call to arrange your day out.
Obligatory.

### LEDSTON HALL

**Hall Lane, Ledston, Castleford, West Yorkshire WF10 2BB**

17th Century mansion with some earlier work, lawned grounds.
**Location:** Map 11:A11. OS Ref SE437 289. 2m N of Castleford, off A656.
**Tel:** 01423 707830 **Fax:** 01423 521373 **E-mail:** joe.robinson@carterjonas.co.uk
**Open:** Exterior only: May-Aug: Mon-Fri, 9am-4pm. Other days by appointment.
**Admission:** Free.

©John Whitaker

York Gate Garden

## SEWERBY HALL AND GARDENS
Church Lane, Sewerby, Bridlington YO15 1EA
**Tel:** 01262 673769 **E-mail:** sewerby.hall@eastriding.gov.uk

## SLEDMERE HOUSE 🏛®
Sledmere, Driffield, East Yorkshire YO25 3XG
**Tel:** 01377 236637 **E-mail:** info@sledmerehouse.com

## ALLERTON PARK
Allerton Park, Knaresborough, North Yorkshire HG5 0SE
**Tel:** 01423 330927

## BOLTON ABBEY
Skipton, North Yorkshire BD23 6EX
**Tel:** 01756 718009 **E-mail:** tourism@boltonabbey.com

## BRAITHWAITE HALL
East Witton, Leyburn, North Yorkshire DL8 4SY
**Tel:** 01723 870423 **E-mail:** yorkshirecoast@nationaltrust.org.uk

## BYLAND ABBEY ⌗
Coxwold, York YO61 4BD
**Tel:** 01347 868614 **E-mail:** customers@english-heritage.org.uk

## CHURCH OF ST JOHN THE BAPTIST 🏛
Stanwick, Richmond, North Yorkshire DL11 7RT
**Tel:** 0845 303 2760 **E-mail:** central@thecct.org.uk

## CLIFFORD'S TOWER ⌗
Tower Street, York YO1 9SA
**Tel:** 01904 646940 **E-mail:** customers@english-heritage.org.uk

## EBBERSTON HALL
Ebberston Hall, Ebberston, North Yorkshire YO13 9PA
**Tel:** 01723 859057

## GILLING CASTLE
Gilling Castle, Gilling East, North Yorkshire YO62 4HP
**Tel:** 01439 766600

## HELMSLEY CASTLE ⌗
Castlegate, Helmsley, North Yorkshire YO62 5AB
**Tel:** 01439 770442 **E-mail:** helmsley.castle@english-heritage.org.uk

## HOLY TRINITY CHURCH 🏛
Coverham, Leyburn, North Yorkshire DL8 4RN
**Tel:** 0845 303 2760 **E-mail:** central@thecct.org.uk

## JERVAULX ABBEY
Ripon, North Yorkshire HG4 4PH
**Tel:** 01677 460226

## KNARESBOROUGH CASTLE & MUSEUM
Castle Yard, Knaresborough, North Yorkshire HG5 8AS
**Tel:** 01423 556188 **E-mail:** museums@harrogate.gov.uk

## MANSION HOUSE
St Helen's Square, York YO1 9QL
**E-mail:** mansionhouse@york.gov.uk

## MOUNT GRACE PRIORY ⌗
Staddlebridge, Nr Northallerton, North Yorkshire DL6 3JG
**Tel:** 01609 883494 **E-mail:** mountgrace.priory@english-heritage.org.uk

## NUNNINGTON HALL 🌿
Nunnington, North Yorkshire YO62 5UY
**Tel:** 01439 748283 **E-mail:** nunningtonhall@nationaltrust.org.uk

## RHS GARDEN HARLOW CARR
Crag Lane, Harrogate, North Yorkshire HG3 1QB
**Tel:** 01423 565418 **E-mail:** harlowcarr@rhs.org.uk

## RICHMOND CASTLE ⌗
Tower St, Richmond, North Yorkshire DL10 4QW
**Tel:** 01748 822493 **E-mail:** customers@english-heritage.org.uk

## RIEVAULX ABBEY ⌗
Rievaulx, Nr Helmsley, N. Yorkshire YO62 5LB
**Tel:** 01439 798228 **E-mail:** rievaulx.abbey@english-heritage.org.uk

## RIEVAULX TERRACE & TEMPLES 🌿
The National Trust, Rievaulx, North Yorkshire YO62 5LJ
**Tel:** 01723 870423 **E-mail:** yorkshirecoast@nationaltrust.org.uk

## RIPLEY CASTLE 🏛®
Ripley, Harrogate, North Yorkshire HG3 3AY
**Tel:** 01423 770152 **E-mail:** enquiries@ripleycastle.co.uk

## RIPON CATHEDRAL
Ripon, North Yorkshire HG4 1QR
**Tel:** 01765 602072

## RIPON MUSEUMS & HISTORIC WORKHOUSE
Ripon HG4 1QS
**Tel:** 01765 690799 **E-mail:** info@riponmuseums.co.uk

## ST ANDREW'S CHURCH 🏛
East Heslerton, Malton, North Yorkshire YO17 8RN
**Tel:** 0845 303 2760 **E-mail:** central@thecct.org.uk

## ST LAWRENCE'S TOWER 🏛
Hull Road, York, North Yorkshire YO10 3BN
**Tel:** 0845 303 2760 **E-mail:** central@thecct.org.uk

## ST MARTIN'S CHURCH 🏛
Whenby, York, North Yorkshire YO61 4SE
**Tel:** 0845 303 2760 **E-mail:** central@thecct.org.uk

## ST MARY'S CHURCH 🏛
Birdforth, Thirsk, North Yorkshire YO61 4NW
**Tel:** 0845 303 2760 **E-mail:** central@thecct.org.uk

## ST MARTIN'S CHURCH 🏛
Allerton Park, Knaresborough, North Yorkshire HG5 0SE
**Tel:** 0845 303 2760 **E-mail:** central@thecct.org.uk

## ST MARY'S CHURCH 🏛
Lead, Saxton, Tadcaster, North Yorkshire LS24 9QN
**Tel:** 0845 303 2760 **E-mail:** central@thecct.org.uk

## ST MARY'S CHURCH 🏛
Roecliffe, Ripon, North Yorkshire YO51 9LZ
**Tel:** 0845 303 2760 **E-mail:** central@thecct.org.uk

## ST MARY'S CHURCH 🏛
Stainburn, Harrogate, North Yorkshire LS21 2LW
**Tel:** 0845 303 2760 **E-mail:** central@thecct.org.uk

## ST MICHAEL'S CHURCH 🏛
Oak Road, Cowthorpe, Wetherby, North Yorkshire  LS22 5EZ
**Tel:** 0845 303 2760 **E-mail:** central@thecct.org.uk

## SCARBOROUGH CASTLE ⌗
Castle Road, Scarborough, North Yorkshire  YO11 1HY
**Tel:** 01723 372451 **E-mail:** scarborough.castle@english-heritage.org.uk

## SHANDY HALL
Coxwold, Thirsk, North Yorkshire  YO61 4AD
**Tel:** 01347 868465 **E-mail:** shandyhall@dial.pipex.com

## THORP PERROW ARBORETUM
Bedale, North Yorkshire  DL8 2PR
**Tel:** 01677 425323 **E-mail:** enquiries@thorpperrow.com

## TREASURER'S HOUSE 🦋
Minster Yard, York, North Yorkshire  YO1 7JL
**Tel:** 01904 624247 **E-mail:** treasurershouse@nationaltrust.org.uk

## WHITBY ABBEY ⌗
Whitby, North Yorkshire  YO22 4JT
**Tel:** 01947 603568 **E-mail:** customers@english-heritage.org.uk

## WYTHERSTONE GARDENS
Wytherstone Estate, Pockley, Near Helmsley  YO62 7TE
**Tel:** 01439 770012 **E-mail:** wytherstone@nawtontowerestate.co.uk

## CHURCH OF ST JOHN THE EVANGELIST 🏛
Cadeby, Doncaster, South Yorkshire  DN5 7SW
**Tel:** 0845 303 2760 **E-mail:** central@thecct.org.uk

## CONISBROUGH CASTLE ⌗
Castle Hill, Conisbrough, Doncaster  DN12 3BU
**Tel:** 01709 863329 **E-mail:** customers@english-heritage.org.uk

## ST JOHN'S CHURCH 🏛
St John's Road, Throapham, Sheffield, South Yorks  S25 1YL
**Tel:** 0845 303 2760 **E-mail:** central@thecct.org.uk

## ST OSWALD'S CHURCH 🏛
Kirk Sandall Old Village, Doncaster, South Yorkshire  DN3 1RA
**Tel:** 0845 303 2760 **E-mail:** central@thecct.org.uk

## ST PETER'S CHURCH 🏛
Old Edlington, Doncaster, South Yorkshire  DN12 1PZ
**Tel:** 0845 303 2760 **E-mail:** central@thecct.org.uk

## WENTWORTH CASTLE GARDENS
Lowe Lane, Stainborough, Barnsley, South Yorkshire  S75 3ET
**Tel:** 01226 776040 **E-mail:** heritagetrust@wentworthcastle.org

## BRAMHAM PARK
The Estate Office, Bramham Park, Bramham  LS23 6ND
**Tel:** 01937 846000 **E-mail:** enquiries@bramhampark.co.uk

## PONTEFRACT CASTLE
Castle Chain, Pontefract, West Yorkshire  WF8 1QH
**Tel:** 01977 723 440 **E-mail:** castles@wakefield.gov.uk

## ST STEPHEN'S CHURCH 🏛
North Dean Road, Copley, Halifax, West Yorkshire  HX4 8QA
**Tel:** 0845 303 2760 **E-mail:** central@thecct.org.uk

Skipton Castle

Holker Hall

Astley Hall

Cheshire
Cumbria
Lancashire
Manchester
Merseyside

# North West

From country houses built with the industrial wealth of the 19th century to the romantic appeal of the Lake District, few areas are as varied as the North West.

*New Entries for 2014:*
- Holker Hall
- Astley Hall Museum and Art Gallery
- Swarthmoor Hall

**Find stylish hotels with a personal welcome and good cuisine in the North West. More information on page 373.**

- Borrowdale Gates Country House Hotel
- Lovelady Shield Country House Hotel
- Gibbon Bridge Hotel
- Oak Bank Hotel
- Gilpin Hotel & Lake House

## SIGNPOST
SELECTED PREMIER HOTELS 2014

www.signpost.co.uk

### VISITOR INFORMATION

■ **Owner**
Sir William and Lady
Bromley-Davenport

■ **Address**
Capesthorne Hall
Siddington
Macclesfield
Cheshire
SK11 9JY

■ **Location**
Map 6:N2
OS Ref. SJ840 727
5m W of Macclesfield.
30 mins S of Manchester
on A34. Near M6, M60
and M62.
**Rail:** Macclesfield 5m
(2 hrs from London).
**Air:** Manchester
International 20 mins.

■ **Contact**
Christine Mountney
Hall Manager
**Tel:** 01625 861221
**Fax:** 01625 861619
**E-mail:** info@
capesthorne.com

■ **Opening Times**
**Summer:**
April-Oct Suns,
Mons & BHs.
**Hall:**
1.30-4pm.
Last admission 3.30pm.
**Gardens & Chapel:**
12 noon-5pm. Groups
welcome by appointment.

■ **Admission**
**Sundays & BHs**
**Hall, Gardens & Chapel**
| | |
|---|---|
| Adult | £9.00 |
| Child (5-16 yrs) | £5.00 |
| Senior | £8.00 |
| Family | £25.00 |

**Gardens & Chapel only**
| | |
|---|---|
| Adult | £6.50 |
| Child (5-16 yrs) | £3.00 |
| Senior | £5.50 |

**Mondays Only**
**Park, Gardens & Chapel**
| | |
|---|---|
| Per Car | £10.00 |

**Hall Entrance**
| | |
|---|---|
| Per person | £3.00 |

Discounts available for
groups and private tours.

**Caravan Park 4* AA
Rated
Open March to October
inclusive**

■ **Special Events**
Please visit
www.capesthorne.com.

# CAPESTHORNE HALL ® 🏛Ⓕ
### www.capesthorne.com

## A spectacular venue for weddings, corporate functions, celebrations, park events or simply a fabulous day out.

Capesthorne Hall, set in 100 acres of picturesque Cheshire parkland, has been touched by nearly 1,000 years of English history - Roman legions passed across it, titled Norman families hunted on it and, during the Civil War, a Royalist ancestress helped Charles II to escape after the Battle of Worcester.

The Jacobean-style Hall has a fascinating collection of fine art, marble sculptures, furniture and tapestries. Originally designed by the Smiths of Warwick it was built between 1719 and 1732.

It was altered by Blore in 1837 and partially rebuilt by Salvin in 1861 following a disastrous fire.

The present Squire is Sir William Bromley-Davenport, whose ancestors have owned the estate since Domesday times when they were appointed custodians of the Royal Forest of Macclesfield.

In the grounds near the family Chapel the 18th Century Italian Milanese Gates open onto the herbaceous borders and maples which line the beautiful lakeside gardens. But amid the natural spectacle and woodland walks, Capesthorne still offers glimpses of its man-made past ... the remains of the Ice House, the Old Boat House and the curious Swallow Hole.

Facilities can be hired for corporate occasions and family celebrations including Civil Wedding ceremonies and receptions.

## KEY FACTS

ⓘ Available for corporate functions, meetings, product launches, promotions, exhibitions, seminars, activity days, still photography, clay shooting and garden parties.

🍽 Catering can be provided for groups (full menus on request). Function rooms available for corporate hospitality, meetings and other special events. 'The Butler's Pantry' serves light refreshments.

♿ Partial. WC.

🚶 Guided tours avaiable for pre-booked parties (except Sundays).

🅿 100 cars/20 coaches on hard-standing and unlimited in park, 50 yds from house.

🚐 Caravan Park 4* AA Rated, open March to October inclusive.

🔔 Licensed for Civil weddings.

🎭 Concerts, antique, craft and game fairs, car shows and triathalons.

# ADLINGTON HALL 🏠Ⓕ
## ADLINGTON HALL, MACCLESFIELD, CHESHIRE SK10 4LF
### www.adlingtonhall.com

Adlington Hall, home of the Leghs from 1315 built on the site of a Hunting Lodge in the Forest of Macclesfield in 1040. Two oaks, part of the original building, remain rooted in the ground supporting the east end of the Great Hall. Between the trees in the Great Hall stands an organ built by 'Father' Bernard Smith. Played on by Handel.

The Gardens laid out over many centuries include a Lime walk planted 1688, Regency rockery surrounding the Shell Cottage. The Wilderness, a Rococo styled landscape garden containing the chinoserie T'Ing House, Pagoda bridge and classical Temple to Diana.

**Location:** Map 6:N2. OS Ref SJ905 804. 5m N of Macclesfield, A523,13m S of Manchester. London 178m.

**Owner:** Mrs C J C Legh **Tel:** 01625 827595 **Fax:** 01625 820797

**E-mail:** enquiries@adlingtonhall.com
**Open:** Apr: 6, 13, 21 & 27. May: 4, 5, 11, 18, 25 & Plant Hunters Fair & 26. Jun: 1, 8, 15, 22 & 29. Jul: 6, 13, 27 & NGS Garden. Aug: 3, 10, 17, 24, 25 & 31. Sep: 7, 14, 21 & 28,
**Admission:** House & Gardens: Adult £9.00, Child £5.00, Student £5.00, Gardens only: Adult £6.00, Child Free, Student Free, Groups of 20+ £8.50.
**Key facts:** ⓘ Suitable for corporate events, product launches, business meetings, conferences, concerts, fashion shows, garden parties, rallies, filming and weddings. ⊤ The Great Hall and Dining Room are available for corporate entertaining. Catering can be arranged. ♿ WCs.
☕ Tea room open on Hall open days ⓚ By arrangement. 🅿 For 100 cars and 4 coaches, 100 yds from Hall. 🐾 🚆 On leads. 🔔 ❄ ♨

# CHOLMONDELEY CASTLE GARDEN 🏠Ⓕ
## MALPAS, CHESHIRE SY14 8AH
### www.cholmondeleycastle.com

Cholmondeley Castle Garden is said by many to be among the most romantically beautiful gardens they have seen. Even the wild orchids, daisies and buttercups take on an aura of glamour in this beautifully landscaped setting with extensive ornamental gardens dominated by a romantic Castle built in 1801 of local sandstone. Visitors can enjoy the tranquil Temple Water Garden, Ruin Water Garden, memorial mosaic designed by Maggy Howarth, Rose garden and many mixed borders. Lakeside walk, picnic area, children's play areas, farm animals, llamas, children's corner, Gift Shop and Tea Room. Private Chapel in the park.

**Location:** Map 6:L3. OS Ref SJ540 515. Off A41 Chester/Whitchurch Rd. & A49 Whitchurch/ Tarporley Road. 7m N of Whitchurch.

**Owner:** Lavinia, Dowager Marchioness of Cholmondeley.
**Contact:** The Secretary
**Tel:** 01829 720383 **Fax:** 01829 720877
**E-mail:** dilys@cholmondeleycastle.co.uk
**Open:** 6 Apr-28 Sep Wed, Thur, Sun and Bank Holidays. All Fris throughout Aug. Oct-Suns only 11am-5pm for Autumn Tints.
(Castle open for groups only, by pre-arrangement, on limited days).
**Admission:** Adult £6.00, Child £3.00 (reduction for groups to gardens of 25+).
For special events please refer to our website www.cholmondeleycastle.com.
**Key facts:** ⓘ 📷 🎁 ♿ Partial. WCs. ☕ 🅿 🚆 On leads. ♨

# LYME PARK, HOUSE & GARDEN ❧
## DISLEY, STOCKPORT, CHESHIRE  SK12 2NR
### www.nationaltrust.org.uk/lymepark

At Lyme there is a painting called 'The Servants' Ball', created at the height of the Edwardian age. It captures Lyme's golden era of family celebrations and hunting parties. Experience Lyme's last hoorah by dressing in Edwardian finery, re-enacting a play on the family stage and exploring newly opened rooms. Be inspired by lavish interiors, discover beautiful treasures and relax in stunning gardens. Enjoy a unique visit, experiencing a vanished age and decide for yourself... would life ever be the same again?

**Location:** Map 6:N2. OS Ref SJ965 825. Off the A6 at Disley. 6½m SE of Stockport. M60 J1.

**Owner:** National Trust  **Contact:** The Visitor Experience Manager
**Tel:** 01663 762023  **Fax:** 01663 765035

**Open:** House: 22 Feb-26 Oct, 11am-5pm (last entry 4pm), Mon, Tue, Fri-Sun. Garden: 22 Feb-26 Oct, 11am-5pm (last entry 4.30pm), Mon-Sun. Please call for winter opening times.

**Admission:** House & Gardens:* Adult £11.00, Child £5.50, Family £25.00. Park: Car £7.00, Coach £25.00. NT members free. *includes a voluntary donation but visitors can choose to pay the standard prices.

**Key facts:** ⓘ Restricted photography in house. ▢ ▨ ▢ ▨ ▨ Licensed. ▥ Licensed. ▣ ▣ Limited for coaches. ▨ ▨ Guide dogs only. ▨ East Lodge. A beautiful Edwardian cottage built in 1904, with two bedrooms, sleeps 4 (one double, one twin), dogs welcome. Enjoy spectacular views of Manchester and the Peak District. Guests have access to Lyme Hall and Gardens. ▨ ▨

Gardens at Rode Hall

# PEOVER HALL & GARDENS 🏠Ⓕ
## OVER PEOVER, KNUTSFORD  WA16 9HW
www.peoverhall.com

A Grade 2* listed Elizabethan family house dating from 1585. Situated within some 500 acres of landscaped 18th Century parkland with formal gardens designed between 1890-1900 that include a series of "garden rooms" filled with clipped box, lily ponds, Romanesque loggia, warm brick walls, unusual doors, secret passageways, beautiful topiary work, herb and walled gardens. The grounds of the Hall house working stables, estate cottages and the parish church of St Laurence which, contains two Mainwaring Chapels. The architectural jewel Grade I listed Carolean stables built in 1654, with richly carved stalls and original Tuscan columns and strap work.
**Location:** Map 6:M2. OS Ref SJ772 734. 4m S of Knutsford off A50 at

Whipping Stocks Inn. Further directions on website, satnav leads down an unsuitable road.
**Owner:** Mr R Brooks  **Contact:** Mr I Shepherd
**Tel:** Mr I Shepherd: 01565 724220  **Peover Estate Office:** 01565 724220
**E-mail:** bookings@peoverhall.com
**Open:** 2014 May-Aug, Tue & Thu afternoons. Stables & Gardens open between 2-5pm. Tours of Peover Hall at 2.30pm & 3.30pm.
**Admission:** House, Stables & Gardens £6.00, Stables & Gardens only £4.00. Children under 16 years free of charge.
**Key facts:** 💻 📷 Obligatory. 🖼

# RODE HALL 🏠Ⓕ
## CHURCH LANE, SCHOLAR GREEN, CHESHIRE  ST7 3QP
www.rodehall.co.uk

The Wilbraham family have lived at Rode since 1669; the present house was constructed in two stages, the earlier two storey wing and stable block around 1705 and the main building was completed in 1752.
The house stands in a Repton landscape and the extensive gardens include a woodland garden which has many species of rhododendrons, azaleas, hellebores and climbing roses following snowdrops and daffodils in the early spring. The formal rose garden was designed in 1860; there is a large walled kitchen garden and a new Italian garden. The icehouse in the park has been restored.
**Location:** Map 6:M3. OS Ref SJ819 573. 5m SW of Congleton between the A34 and A50. Kidsgrove railway station 2m NW of Kidsgrove.

**Owner/Contact:** Sir Richard Baker Wilbraham Bt
**Tel:** 01270 873237
**E-mail:** enquiries@rodehall.co.uk
**Open:** 1 Apr-25 Sep. House only: Wed's and BH's 2pm-5pm and groups by appointment. Garden only: Tues, Wed and Thurs 12 noon-5pm. Snowdrop walks 8 Feb-16 Mar daily except Mons, 12noon-4pm.
**Admission:** House & Garden: Adult £7.00, Conc £6.00 Children over 4 £1.00. Garden only & snowdrop walks: Adult £5.00, Conc £4.00 Children over 4 £1.00. Tickets can now be bought on our website.
**Key facts:** 📷 🍴 💻 Home-made teas.
📷 🅿 🖼 On leads.

# TABLEY HOUSE
## TABLEY HOUSE, TABLEY LANE, KNUTSFORD, CHESHIRE WA16 0HB
www.tableyhouse.co.uk

The finest Palladian House in the North West, Tabley a Grade I listing, was designed by John Carr of York for the Leicester family. It contains one of the first collections of English paintings, including works of art by Turner, Reynolds, Lawrence, Lely and Dobson. Furniture by Chippendale, Bullock and Gillow and fascinating family memorabilia adorn the rooms. Fine plasterwork by Thomas Oliver and carving by Daniel Shillito and Mathew Bertram. Interesting Tea Room and 17th Century Chapel adjoin, including Burne-Jones window.

**Location:** Map 6:M2. OS Ref SJ725 777. M6/J19, A556 S on to A5033. 2m W of Knutsford. **Owner:** The University of Manchester **Contact:** The Administrator **Tel:** 01565 750151 **E-mail:** tableyhouse@btconnect.com **Open:** House: Apr-end Oct: Thu-Sun & BHs, 2-5pm.

Last admission at 4.30 pm. Tea Room open from 12.00 noon to 5.00 pm (Tea Room Tel: 01565 651199).
**Admission:** Adult £5.00. Child/Student £1.50. Groups by arrangement.
**Key facts:** ⓘ No photography in galleries. No stilleto heels. Slippers can be provided. ⊤ Suitable for drinks receptions and presentations for up to 100 people. ⬚ Call the office before arriving to arrange for lift entrance to be opened. ⬛ Serving light lunches, afternoon teas. refreshments and homemade cakes. ⓕ By arrangement, also available outside normal opening hours, guides provided at no extra charge. Ⓟ Free ⬛ Suitable for post 16 students. ⬛ Guide dogs only. ⬛ Civil Wedding and Partnerships Licence. Naming Ceremonies & Renewal of Vows. ⬛

# ARLEY HALL & GARDENS ⓐⓕ
## Northwich, Cheshire CW9 6NA
www.arleyhallandgardens.com

Arley has been a cherished family home owned for over 550 years. Renowned features include the double herbaceous border, pleached Lime Avenues, Ilex Columns, Cruck Barn and Chapel. The Hall (Grade II*) built in the Victorian Jacobean style, with elaborate ceilings & oak panelling, impressive fireplaces, intricate stained glass and beautiful contents.

**Location:** Map 6:M2. OS Ref SJ675 809. **Owner:** Viscount & Viscountess Ashbrook **Contact:** Helen Robinson - Events & Marketing
**Tel:** 01565 777353 **E-mail:** enquiries@arleyhallandgardens.com
**Open:** Gardens: 30 Mar-29 Sep, Mon-Sun 11am-5pm. Weekends in Oct. The Hall: 31 Mar-29 Sep, Sun & BHs 11am-5pm. Pre-booked group visits Mon-Sun.
**Admission:** Gardens: Adult £7.50, Children (5-12yrs) £3.00, Senior £7.00, Family (2+2) £16.50. Groups: Adult £6.50, Senior £6.00, Children £2.00. Hall & Gardens: Adult £10.00, Child (5-12yrs) £4.00, Senior £9.00. Groups: Adult £9.00. **Key facts:** ⓘ Weddings, corporate functions, conferences, filming, photography, concerts & fairs. ⬚⬚⊤⬚ WCs. ⬛ Licensed. ⬛ Licensed. ⓕ Ⓟ Free. ⬛ Dogs on leads only. ⬛⬛

## DORFOLD HALL 🏛Ⓕ
### Acton, Nr Nantwich, Cheshire CW5 8LD

Jacobean country house built in 1616 for Ralph Wilbraham. Family home of Mr & Mrs Richard Roundell.
Beautiful plaster ceilings and oak panelling. Attractive woodland gardens and summer herbaceous borders.
**Location:** Map 6:L3. OS Ref SJ634 525.
1m W of Nantwich on the A534 Nantwich-Wrexham road.
**Owner/Contact:** Richard Roundell
**Tel:** 01270 625245
**Fax:** 01270 628723
**E-mail:** dorfoldhall@btconnect.com
**Open:** Apr-Oct: Tue only and BH Mons, 2-5pm.
**Admission:** Adult £7.00, Child £3.00.
**Key facts:** 🎥 Obligatory.
🅿 Limited. Narrow gates with low arch prevent coaches.
🐾

## GAWSWORTH HALL
### Macclesfield, Cheshire SK11 9RN
www.gawsworthhall.com

Fully lived-in Tudor half-timbered manor house with Tilting Ground. Former home of Mary Fitton, Maid of Honour at the Court of Queen Elizabeth I, and the supposed 'Dark Lady' of Shakespeare's sonnets. Fine pictures, sculpture, furniture and beautiful grounds adjoining a medieval church. Garden Theatre performances take place in the Hall courtyard in July and August.
**Location:** Map 6:N2. OS Ref SJ892 697. 3m S of Macclesfield on the A536 Congleton to Macclesfield road.
**Owner:** Mr and Mrs T Richards **Contact:** Mr J Richards
**Tel:** 01260 223456
**E-mail:** gawsworthhall@btinternet.com
**Open:** See www.gawsworthhall.com.
**Admission:** Adult £7.50, Child £3.50. Groups (20+) £6.00.
**Key facts:** 🖼 📷 Partial. WCs. 🍽 Licensed. 🍴 Licensed. 🎥 Guided tours by arrangement. 🅿 🐾 In grounds. ♿ 🌺

## DUNHAM MASSEY: SANCTUARY FROM THE TRENCHES 🌺
### Altrincham, Cheshire WA14 4SJ
www.nationaltrust.org.uk/dunhammassey

During the First World War, Dunham Massey Hall - a Georgian house, set in a magnificent deer park - was transformed into a military hospital, becoming a sanctuary from the trenches for almost 300 soldiers. To mark the centenary we are turning the clock back, allowing you to discover what life was like for the patients and how the war changed everything for those who lived and worked at Dunham. Then take a stroll in one of the North's great gardens, which includes Britain's largest winter garden and a stunning rose garden.
**Location:** Map 6:M1. OS Ref SJ735 874. 3m SW of Altrincham off A56. M6/J19. M56/J7. Station Altrincham (Train & Metro) 3m. **Owner:** National Trust
**Contact:** Visitor Services **Tel:** 0161 941 1025
**E-mail:** dunhammassey@nationaltrust.org.uk **Open:** Please see website for details. **Admission:** House & Garden: Adult £12.50, Child £6.20, Family (2+3 max) £31.20. Garden: Adult £8, Child £4, Family (2+3 max) £20. Different admission prices for groups of 15 or more. Contact for more information.
**Key facts:** 🛈 Photography permitted, no flash or tripods. 📷 🖼 ♿ Partial. Wheelchairs & self-drive powered vehicles to loan. 🍽 Indoor and outdoor seating 🍴 Licensed. 🅿 £6. Free to NT members. 🐾 🐾 In park on short lead. ❄ Garden, shop & cafe. 🌺

© NT Images/Robert Thrift

## TATTON PARK 🌺
### Knutsford, Cheshire WA16 6QN
A complete historic estate with 1,000 acres of deer park, 200 year old 50 acre gardens and Tudor Old Hall. The neo-classical mansion houses one of the finest library collections in the National Trust. Families enjoy the working rare breed farm.
Stableyard shopping and dining includes specialty shops, Stables restaurant and Gardener's Cottage tea room. Over 100 events take place each year. A perfect day out! **Location:** Map 6:M2. OS Ref SJ745 815. From M56/J7 follow signs. From M6/J19, signed on A56 & A50. **Owner:** National Trust (Managed by Cheshire East Council) **Tel:** 01625 374400/01625 374435 **E-mail:** tatton@cheshireeast.gov.uk
**Website:** www.tattonpark.org.uk **Open:** Every day except Mons in low season. Attraction times vary. See website or call 01625 374400 for all opening times.
**Admission:** See website or call 01625 374400. **Key facts:** 🛈 📷 🖼
🍽 Dinners, dances, weddings & conferences. 🍽 🍴 Licensed. 🎥 By arrangement. 🅿 Charge applies. See website, 200-300 yds. Meal vouchers for coach drivers. 🐾 Please book. 🐾 In grounds. 🏷 ♿ ❄ 🌺 €

Arley Hall

## KIRKLINTON HALL AND GARDENS 🏛ⓕ
### KIRKLINTON HALL, KIRKLINTON, CARLISLE  CA6 6BB
www.kirklintonhall.co.uk

Adjacent to the 12th Century de Boyville stronghold, Kirklinton Hall is said to have been built from its stone. Begun in the 1670's, extended in the 1870's and ruined in the 1970's, the Hall has been a Restoration Great House, an RAF base, a school, a gangsters' gambling den and worse. Walk in the footsteps of Norman Knights, Cavalier Commanders, Victorian Plutocrats and the Kray twins. Now, Kirklinton Hall and its Gardens are being restored by the Boyle family to its former glory, a painstaking and fascinating process. It is also the official home of SlowFood Cumbria and is available for weddings and events. 'Spectacularly sinister ruin' - Pevsners Buildings of England.
**Location:** Map 10:K3. OS Ref NY433672. 6 miles north east of M6 junction 44 and A7 (Carlisle north).

**Owner:** Mr and Mrs Christopher Boyle
**Contact:** Ilona Boyle
**Tel:** 01697 748292
**Fax:** 01697 748472
**E-mail:** info@kirklintonhall.co.uk
**Open:** Open 1 Apr-30 Sep, weekdays and Suns 12-5pm. Sats for private/public events. See website for events.
**Admission:** Admission £4.00 Adults, £1.00 Children under 16.
**Key facts:** 🌱 Specialising in David Austin Roses. 🅣 🔲 🖥
🅕 By arrangement.
🅿 🔲 🖼 On leads. ♿

## LEVENS HALL 🏛ⓕ
### LEVENS HALL, KENDAL, CUMBRIA  LA8 0PD
www.levenshall.co.uk

Levens Hall is an Elizabethan mansion built around a 13th Century pele tower. The much loved home of the Bagot family, with fine panelling, plasterwork, Cordova leather wall coverings, paintings by Rubens, Lely and Cuyp, the earliest English patchwork and Wellingtoniana combine with other beautiful objects to form a fascinating collection. The world famous Topiary Gardens were laid out by Monsieur Beaumont from 1694 and his design has remained largely unchanged to this day. Over 90 individual pieces of topiary, some over nine metres high, massive beech hedges and colourful seasonal bedding provide a magnificent visual impact.
**Location:** Map 10:L7. OS Ref SD495 851. 5m S of Kendal on the A6. Exit M6/J36.

**Owner:** C H Bagot  **Contact:** The Administrator  **Tel:** 015395 60321
**Fax:** 015395 60669  **E-mail:** houseopening@levenshall.co.uk
**Open:** 6 Apr-9 Oct Sun-Thu (closed Fri & Sat). Garden, Tea Room, Gift Shop & Plant Centre 10am-5pm. House 12 noon-4.30pm (last entry 4pm). Groups (20+) please book.
Winner of 'Cumbria Tourism Small Visitor Attraction of the Year 2013'
**Admission:** House & Gardens or Gardens Only. Please see www.levenshall.co.uk for full details, special offers & current events. Group Rates on application. **Key facts:** 🅘 No indoor photography. 📷 Gift shop. ♿
🔲 Partial. WCs. 🍴 Licensed. 🍽 Licensed. 🅕 By arrangement.
🅿 Free on-site parking. 🔲 🖼 Assistance dogs only. 🅐

## MUNCASTER CASTLE GARDENS & OWL CENTRE 🏛ⓕ
### MUNCASTER CASTLE, RAVENGLASS, CUMBRIA  CA18 1RQ
www.muncaster.co.uk

The Large Visitor Attraction Silver winner at the 2012 Visit England Awards, Muncaster was described by Ruskin as Heaven's Gate. The many acres of Grade II* woodland gardens are famous for rhododendrons and breathtaking views of the Lake District fells. The Castle is a treasure trove of paintings, silver, embroideries and more. Muncaster hosts wonderful weddings, dinners and family celebrations. B&B is available in the "Coachman's Quarters". The World Owl Centre reveals a thrilling insight into these magical and mysterious creatures. Enjoy the Meet the Birds display and Heron Happy Hour. MeadowVole Maze, playground, gift shop, café & church. Special events throughout the year include the Muncaster Festival, Summer of Fun, Halloween Week, Christmas at the Castle and more. See www.muncaster.co.uk for details.

**Location:** Map 10:J7. OS Ref SD103 965. See our website for details. A595 1 mile south of Ravenglass. SatNav CA18 1RD.

**Owner:** Mrs Iona Frost Pennington  **Contact:** Reception
**Tel:** 01229 717614  **E-mail:** info@muncaster.co.uk
**Open:** Full Season: last Sun in Mar-last Sun in Oct, Gardens & World Owl Centre open daily 10.30am-6pm (dusk if earlier), Castle open Sun-Fri 12-4.30pm. Winter Season: 11am-4pm (dusk if earlier), Castle open reduced hours, please see website or call for details. Closed in Jan. Open for groups, conferences and weddings by appointment. Darkest Muncaster. Explore the hauntingly beautiful illuminated gardens by night and light, see website or call for more details.

**Admission:** Please see www.muncaster.co.uk for details.

**Key facts:** ⓘ Church. Film location. 🖼 ⚑ ⊤ Wedding receptions and private parties. ♿ WCs. ☕ Licensed. 🍴 Licensed. 🎫 Private Castle and Garden Tours. 🎧 Individual audio tour. 🅿 Free Parking. Central Coach parking. ▤ Conservation and Owl tours available. 🐕 Dogs on leads only. 🏨 🏠 ⚜

## DALEMAIN MANSION & GARDENS 🏛
### Penrith, Cumbria  CA11 0HB
www.dalemain.com

A fine mixture of Mediaeval, Tudor & early Georgian architecture. Lived in by the same family since 1679 and home to the International Marmalade Festival. Award winning gardens, richly planted with unusual combinations of flowers and shrubs. Highlights include the Rose Walk, Ancient Apple Trees, Tudor Knot Garden, Blue Himalayan Poppies, Earth Sculpture and Stumpery.

**Location:** Map 10:L5. OS Ref NY477 269. On A592 1m S of A66. 4m SW of Penrith. London, M1, M6/J40. Edinburgh, A73, M74, M6/J40.

**Owner:** Robert Hasell-McCosh Esq  **Contact:** Jennifer Little - Administrator
**Tel:** 017684 86450  **Fax:** 017684 86223  **E-mail:** admin@dalemain.com
**Open:** 6 Apr-30 Oct: Gardens, Tearoom & Gift Shop: Sun-Thu 10.30am-5pm (4pm in Oct). House 11.15am-4pm (3pm in Oct). Groups (12+) please book.

**Admission:** House & Gardens or Gardens Only. Please see www.dalemain.com for details. Group Prices on application.  **Key facts:** ⓘ No photography in house. Moorings available on Ullswater. Phone for event enquiries. 🖼 ⚑ ⊤ ♿ Partial. WCs. ☕ 🍴 Licensed. 🎫 1hr tours. German and French translations. Garden tour for groups extra. 🅿 50 yds. Free. ▤ 🐕 Guide dogs only. ⚜

Gardens at Dalemain

# HOLKER HALL & GARDENS 🏛Ⓕ
## Cark-In-Cartmel, Grange-Over-Sands,
## Cumbria LA11 7PL
www.holker.co.uk

Holker is the family home of Lord and Lady Cavendish, set amongst beautiful countryside surrounding the Lake District. Steeped in history, this magnificent Victorian Mansion of neo-Elizabethan Gothic style was largely re-built in the 1870's following a fire, but origins date back to the 1600's. The glorious Gardens, Café, Food Hall & Gift Shop complete the visitor experience.
**Location:** Map 10:K8. From Motorway M6/J36, Signed Barrow A590.
**Owner:** Lord Cavendish of Furness **Contact:** Jillian Rouse
**Tel:** 015395 58328 **Fax:** 015395 58378 **E-mail:** info@holker.co.uk
**Open:** Hall: 30 Mar-2 Nov Sun-Fri (closed Sat) 11am-4pm Gardens:10.30am-4.30pm (5.30pmJul/Aug). Cafe, Food Hall & Gift Shop: Mar-Dec Daily 10.30am.
**Admission:** Hall & Gardens: Adult £12.00, Child FOC. Gardens only: Adult £8.00, Child FOC. Hall only: Adults £7.50, Child FOC. Group Rates (10+) Hall & Gardens: Adult £8.00 Gardens only: Adult £5.50.
**Key facts:** ⓘ No photography in house. 🛍 Food Hall. 🎟🚂🔗🍽🎫 For groups, by arrangement. 🅿 75 yds from Hall. ♿🐕 Dogs on leads (in park). 🎗

# SWARTHMOOR HALL
## Swarthmoor Hall Lane, Ulverston, Cumbria LA12 0JQ
www.swarthmoorhall.co.uk

16th Century country house set in beautiful gardens. Visitors speak about its tranquility. A writer commented: 'Swarthmoor Hall has all the elements of a great screenplay: love, conflict, conviction and passion.' There are six historic rooms to view with a fine selection of 17th Century furniture.
**Location:** Map 10:K8. Outskirts of Ulverston just off the A590. 25 Minutes drive from J36 of the M6 **Owner:** Religious Society of Friends
**Contact:** Jane Pearson, Manager **Tel:** 01229 583204
**E-mail:** info@swarthmoorhall.co.uk **Open:** Mon-Fri 10.30–4.30pm, Sun 1.30pm-4.30pm, from 24 Feb to 31 Oct and at other times by appointment.
**Admission:** Standard/Gift Aid admission: Adult £6.00/6.60, Child £4.00/4.40, Children under 5 free. Gardens: Free **Key facts:** ⓘ 🛍 Books and merchandise are available. 🎟 ♿ Limited access to historic hall, cafe and toilet facilties and gardens. 🍽 An honesty cafe is open during house opening hours and for special events. 🎫 We offer tour guides for groups by appointment. 🎧 Audio tour. 🅿 Free car parking. 🏫 School groups by arrangement. 🐕 Service dogs only. 🏨 Holiday accommodation available. ❋ Our gardens are open all year.

# HUTTON-IN-THE-FOREST 🏛Ⓕ
## Hutton-in-the-Forest, Penrith, Cumbria CA11 9TH
www.hutton-in-the-forest.co.uk

The home of Lord Inglewood's family since 1605. Built around a medieval pele tower with 17th, 18th and 19th Century additions. Fine collections of furniture, paintings, ceramics and tapestries. Outstanding grounds with terraces, topiary, walled garden, dovecote and woodland walk through magnificent specimen trees.
**Location:** Map 10:L5. OS Ref NY460 358. 6m NW of Penrith & 2 m from M6 Jct 41 on B5305.
**Owner:** Lord Inglewood **Contact:** Pamela Davidson **Tel:** 017684 84449
**E-mail:** info@hutton-in-the-forest.co.uk
**Open:** House: 13 Apr-5 Oct. Weds, Thurs, Suns and, BH Mons, 12.30-4pm. Tearoom as House 11am-4.30pm. Gardens & Grounds: 30 Mar-2 Nov, daily except Sat, 11am-5pm. **Admission:** Please see www.hutton-in-the-forest.co.uk or telephone 017684 84449 for details.
**Key facts:** ⓘ Picnic area. 🛍 Gift stall selling locally made crafts and produce. 🌱 Small selection of beautiful plants grown by our Head Gardener. 🎟 By arrangement. ♿ Partial. WCs. 🍽 Licensed. 🎫 Guided tours available. 🅿 ♿ 🐕 Dogs welcome on leads. 🎗

# BRANTWOOD 🏛
## Coniston, Cumbria LA21 8AD

Brantwood, the former home of John Ruskin, is the most beautifully situated house in the Lake District. Explore Brantwood's estate and gardens or experience contemporary art in the Severn Studio. Brantwood's bookshop, the Jumping Jenny restaurant combine for a perfect day out.
**Location:** Map 10:K7. OS Ref SD312 959. 2½m from Coniston village on the E side of Coniston Water. **Owner:** The Brantwood Trust **Contact:** Rachel Litten
**Tel:** 01539 441396 **Fax:** 01539 441263
**E-mail:** enquiries@brantwood.org.uk **Website:** www.brantwood.org.uk
**Open:** Mid Mar-Mid Nov: daily, 10.30am-5.00pm. Mid Nov-Mid Mar: Wed-Sun, 10.30am-4.00pm. **Admission:** House & Garden: (incudes gift aid) Adult £7.95, Students £6.30, Children Free. Gardens only: Adult £5.50, Student £4.50.
**Key facts:** ⓘ No photography in house. 🛍 Specialist book titles, crafts & gifts. 🌱 Seasonal availability. 🎟 Rooms available for business hire. ♿ Ground floor only. 🍽 🍴 Licensed. 🎫 By arrangement. 🅿 Limited for coaches. 🏫 Activities for schools. 🐕 In grounds, on leads. 🏨 Self catering accommodation. ♿ ❋ 🎗

# MIREHOUSE 🏛Ⓕ
## Keswick, Cumbria CA12 4QE

Melvyn Bragg described Mirehouse as 'Manor from Heaven'. Set in stunning landscape, Mirehouse is a literary house linked with Tennyson and Wordsworth. Live piano music and children's history trail in house. Natural playgrounds, serene bee garden and lakeside walk.
**Location:** Map 10:J5. OS Ref NY235 284. Beside A591, 3½m N of Keswick. Good bus service. **Owner:** James Fryer-Spedding
**Contact:** Janaki Spedding
**Tel:** 017687 72287 **E-mail:** info@mirehouse.com
**Website:** www.mirehouse.com
**Open:** Please see website for up to date opening times and admission prices.
**Key facts:** ⓘ No photography in house. ♿ 🍽 🎫 By arrangement. 🅿 🍴 🐕 On leads in grounds.

Register for news and special offers at **www.hudsonsheritage.com**

# LEIGHTON HALL 🏛ⓕ
## CARNFORTH, LANCASHIRE  LA5 9ST
### www.leightonhall.co.uk

Leighton Hall's setting, in a bowl of parkland against a backdrop of Lakeland Fells, can deservedly be described as spectacular. Nestled in 1,550 acres of lush grounds, this romantic, Gothic house is the lived-in home of the famous Gillow furniture making family.

Boasting priceless pieces of Gillow furniture, pictures, clocks, silver and objéts d'art, Leightons' informal guided tours appeal to all ages. Outside the Hall are woodland walks, an abundant 19th Century walled garden, herbaceous borders and roses, a fragrant herb patch and an ornamental vegetable plot.

Birds of prey are flown every day at 3:30pm (weather permitting).

Finally, visit Leighton's charming tea rooms for a quintessential English afternoon tea.

Leighton Hall are proud to hold the coveted VAQAS certificate.

**Location:** Map 10:L8. OS Ref SD494 744. 9m N of Lancaster, 10m S of Kendal, 3m N of Carnforth. 1½ m W of A6. 3m from M6/A6/J35, signed from J35A.
**Owner:** Richard Gillow Reynolds Esq
**Contact:** Mrs C S Reynolds
**Tel:** 01524 734474  **Fax:** 01524 720357
**Additional Contact:** Mrs Lucy Arthurs  **E-mail:** info@leightonhall.co.uk
**Open:** May-Sep, Tue-Fri (also BH Sun and Mon, Sun in Aug) 2-5pm.
Pre-booked groups (25+) all year by arrangement. Group rates.
**Admission:** Adult £7.75, OAP/Student £6.75, Child (5 - 12 years) £4.95, Family (2 adults and up to 3 children) £24.50, Grounds only £4.50.
**Key facts:** ⓘ No photography in house. 🖼 ▣ T
♿ Partial. WCs. 🍴 🅵 🅿 🏠 🚌 🔺 🐕

Browsholme Hall

## BROWSHOLME HALL 🏛
### Clitheroe, Lancashire BB7 3DE
www.browsholme.com

Built in 1507 and the ancestral Home of the Parker Family, Browsholme is oldest surviving home in Lancashire. This remarkable Tudor Hall has a major collection of oak furniture, portraits, glass, arms and armour.
In 2010 an 18th Century 'tithe barn' was restored for refreshments, concerts theatre, events and weddings.

**Location:** Map 10:M10. OS Ref SD683 452. 5m NW of Clitheroe off B6243.
**Owner:** The Parker Family
**Contact:** Rebecca Clarke, Events Manager
**Tel:** 01254 827166 **E-mail:** info@browsholme.com
**Open:** Gardens and Tearoom 12–4.30 pm on all open days. Hall tours from 1.30 pm. every Weds during May to Sep. Plus first Sunday in each month during June to Sep. Easter, Spring & Aug Bank Hol Mondays.
**Admission:** Adults £7.00, OAPs and Groups £6.00, Children (under 10) Free.
**Key facts:** ▢ ⬚ ⬚
▢ ▣ ▣
▨ Guide dogs only. ▣ ▣

## HOGHTON TOWER 🏛ⓕ
### Hoghton, Preston, Lancashire PR5 0SH
www.hoghtontower.co.uk

Visit award-winning Hoghton Tower. Join a tour of the staterooms to learn about the history of the house. Stroll through the walled gardens. Kids love the Family tours, dungeons and Dolls Houses. Browse the shop and finish with an afternoon tea. Luxury accommodation available. Private and school tours welcome. Venue for private parties and weddings.
**Location:** Map 10:L11. OS Ref SD622 264. M65/J3. Midway between Preston & Blackburn on A675. **Owner:** Hoghton Tower Preservation Trust
**Contact:** Office **Tel:** 01254 852986 **Fax:** 01254852109
**E-mail:** mail@hoghtontower.co.uk **Open:** Jul, Aug, Sep. Mon-Thu & Sun. BH Suns & Mons except Christmas & New Year. House open every Farmers Market Sun except in Jan, Feb & Mar. Group visits by appointment all year. Check website for variations. **Admission:** Please check website. **Key facts:** ⓘ No photography in house. No picnics. ▢ Packed with gift ideas & regional products. ▤ Conferences, wedding receptions. ▣ Imaginative, healthy menus using fresh local produce. Afternoon teas. ▥ ▨ Obligatory. Family Friendly Tours. ▣ ▣ ▨ No Dogs except guide & hearing dogs within courtyards, gardens & house. ▣ Luxury self catering accommodation for two. ▣ ▣ ▣

## ASTLEY HALL AND PARK
### Astley Hall, Astley Park, Off Hallgate, Chorley PR7 1NP
In his book, 'England's 1,000 Great Houses', Simon Jenkins calls Astley Hall "the most exhilarating house in Lancashire". Originating in the 1580s, the Grade 1-listed Hall reveals its history through stunning architecture and period rooms including some of the most exuberant plaster ceilings in Britain. It is set in extensive parkland with a walled garden and coach house cafe plus a pet's corner, children's activity area and year-long programme of events and activities for all the family.
**Location:** Map 10:L11. OS Ref SD574 183. Jct 8 on M61. Signposted from A6
**Owner:** Chorley Council **Contact:** Cultural Assets Manager
**Tel:** 01257 515151 **E-mail:** astley.hall@chorley.gov.uk
**Website:** www.chorley.gov.uk/astleyhall **Open:** Astley Hall & Chorley Remembers Gallery: Apr-Nov, Sat-Sun, 12.00pm-5pm. Check website for additional Summer opening times. Cafe Ambio: Apr-Nov, Mon-Sun 9am-5.30pm. Grounds & Park/ Walled Garden: Open all year round daily. **Admission:** Free admission. Guided tours available on request (charges apply). **Key facts:** ⓘ ▤ ▣ WCs. ▣ Licensed. ▨ By arrangement. ▣ Limited for coaches. ▣ ▨ ▣ ▣

## MARTHOLME 🏛
### Martholme Lane, Great Harwood, Blackburn, Lancashire BB6 7UJ
Medieval manor house (originally moated) with Elizabethan gatehouse.
**Location:** Map 10:M10. OS Ref SD753 338. 2 Miles NE of Great Harwood off A680 to Whalley. **Tel:** 01254 8864638 **Open:** May 2–5, 23–31; Jun 1, 20–23; Jul 25–28; Aug 22–25; Sep 27-28 Guided tours (compulsory) at 2pm & 4pm.
**Admission:** £7.00. Groups welcome throughout the year by appointment.

## CHURCH OF ST EDMUND 🏛
### Edmund Street, Falinge, Rochdale Greater Manchester OL12 6QF

Tucked away in a quiet corner of Rochdale the extraordinary church of St Edmund's contains a fascinating blend of gothic revival architecture and Masonic symbolism.
Described by Pevsner as "Rochdale's Temple to Freemasonry", this fascinating building was created for wealthy Victorian industrialist and Freemason Albert Hudson Royds in 1870-3 by the Architects James Medland and Henry Taylor. The symbolism goes beyond architecture to the very position of the church in the Rochdale landscape. Sitting in a diamond shaped churchyard at the highest point in the town it is making an overt reference to the Temple which dominated Jerusalem – casting Rochdale as the New Jerusalem.
**Location:** OS Ref SD 891 138.
**Contact:** Please call The Churches Conservation Trust on 0845 303 2760 (Mon-Fri, 9am–5pm)
**Open:** See www.visitchurches.org.uk for details.

## MANCHESTER CATHEDRAL
### Victoris Street, Manchester M3 1SX
Manchester Cathedral is an ongoing 15th Century building, famous for its mediaeval carvings and modern stained glass. **Location:** Map 6:N1. OS Ref SJ838 988. Manchester. **Tel:** 0161 833 2220 **Fax:** 0161 839 6218
**E-mail:** office@manchestercathedral.org
**Website:** www.manchestercathedral.org **Open:** Every day of the year, from 9am; various closing times. **Admission:** Donations welcome.

## MEOLS HALL 🏛ⓕ
### Churchtown, Southport, Merseyside PR9 7LZ

17th Century house with subsequent additions. Interesting collection of pictures and furniture. Tithe Barn available for wedding ceremonies and receptions all year.
**Location:** Map 10:K11. OS Ref SD365 184. 3m NE of Southport town centre in Churchtown. SE of A565.
**Owner:** The Hesketh Family
**Contact:** Pamela Whelan
**Tel:** 01704 228326 **Fax:** 01704 507185
**E-mail:** events@meolshall.com
**Website:** www.meolshall.com
**Open:** May BH Monday: 5 and 26 May and from 20 Aug-14 Sep.
**Admission:** Adult £4.00, Child £1.00. Groups welcome but Afternoon Tea is only available for bookings of 25+.
**Key facts:** ▤ Wedding ceremonies and receptions available in the Tithe Barn.
▣ ▣ ▣ ▣ ▣ ▣

## BEESTON CASTLE ⌗
Chapel Lane, Beeston, Tarporley, Cheshire  CW6 9TX
**Tel:** 01829 260464 **E-mail:** beeston.castle@english-heritage.org.uk

## CHRIST CHURCH ⋔
Bridge Street, Macclesfield, Cheshire  SK11 6EG
**Tel:** 0845 303 2760 **E-mail:** central@thecct.org.uk

## ST MARY'S CHURCH ⋔
Thornton Green Lane, Thornton-le-Moors, Chester  CH2 4HU
**Tel:** 0845 303 2760 **E-mail:** central@thecct.org.uk

## ABBOT HALL ART GALLERY
Abbot Hall, Kendal, Cumbria  LA9 5AL
**Tel:** 01539 722464 **E-mail:** info@abbothall.org.uk

## ALLAN BANK ⋙
Grasmere, Cumbria  LA22 9QZ
**Tel:** 015394 35143 **E-mail:** allanbank@nationaltrust.org.uk

## BLACKWELL, THE ARTS & CRAFTS HOUSE
Bowness on Windermere, Cumbria  LA23 3JT
**Tel:** 015394 46139 **E-mail:** info@blackwell.org.uk

## CARLISLE CASTLE ⌗
Carlisle, Cumbria  CA3 8UR
**Tel:** 01228 625600 **E-mail:** customers@english-heritage.org.uk

## DOVE COTTAGE & WORDSWORTH MUSEUM
Grasmere, Cumbria  LA22 9SH
**Tel:** 01539 435544 **E-mail:** enquiries@wordsworth.org.uk

## LOWTHER CASTLE & GARDENS TRUST
Lowther Castle, Penrith, Cumbria  CA10 2HG
**Tel:** 01931 712192

## NAWORTH CASTLE
Naworth Castle Estate, Brampton, Cumbria  CA8 2HF
**Tel:** 016977 3229. **E-mail:** office@naworth.co.uk

## OLD CHANCEL ⋔
Ireby, Cockermouth, Cumbria  CA7 1HD
**Tel:** 0845 303 2760 **E-mail:** central@thecct.org.uk

## RYDAL MOUNT & GARDENS
Rydal, Cumbria  LA22 9LU
**Tel:** 01539 433002 **E-mail:** info@rydalmount.co.uk

## ST GREGORY'S CHURCH ⋔
Marthwaite, Vale of Lune, Sedbergh, Cumbria LA10 5ED
**Tel:** 0845 303 2760 **E-mail:** central@thecct.org.uk

## ST NINIAN'S CHURCH ⋔
Brougham, Penrith, Cumbria  CA10 2AD
**Tel:** 0845 303 2760 **E-mail:** central@thecct.org.uk

## SIZERGH CASTLE AND GARDEN ⋙
Sizergh, Kendal, Cumbria  LA8 8AE
**Tel:** 015395 60951 **E-mail:** sizergh@nationaltrust.org.uk

## STOTT PARK BOBBIN MILL ⌗
Colton, Ulverston, Cumbria  LA12 8AX
**Tel:** 01539 531087 **E-mail:** stott.park@english-heritage.org.uk

## TULLIE HOUSE MUSEUM & ART GALLERY
Castle Street, Carlisle, Cumbria  CA3 8TP
**Tel:** 01228 618718 **E-mail:** enquiries@tulliehouse.org

## WORDSWORTH HOUSE AND GARDEN ⋙
Main Street, Cockermouth, Cumbria  CA13 9RX
**Tel:** 01900 820884 **E-mail:** wordsworthhouse@nationaltrust.org.uk

## ALL SOULS' CHURCH ⋔
Astley Street, Bolton, Lancashire  BL1 8EH
**Tel:** 0845 303 2760 **E-mail:** central@thecct.org.uk

## CHRIST CHURCH ⋔
Heaton Norris, Stockport, Lancashire  SK4 2LJ
**Tel:** 0845 303 2760 **E-mail:** central@thecct.org.uk

## CHURCH OF ST JOHN THE BAPTIST ⋔
School Lane, Pilling, Lancaster, Lancashire  PR3 6HD
**Tel:** 0845 303 2760 **E-mail:** central@thecct.org.uk

## CHURCH OF ST JOHN THE EVANGELIST ⋔
North Road, Lancaster, Lancashire  LA1 1PA
**Tel:** 0845 303 2760 **E-mail:** central@thecct.org.uk

## GAWTHORPE HALL ⋙
Padiham, Nr Burnley, Lancashire  BB12 8UA
**Tel:** 01282 771004 **E-mail:** gawthorpehall@nationaltrust.org.uk

## HOLY TRINITY CHURCH ⋔
Mount Pleasant, Blackburn, Lancashire  BB1 5DQ
**Tel:** 0845 303 2760 **E-mail:** central@thecct.org.uk

## LANCASTER CASTLE
Shirehall, Castle Parade, Lancaster, Lancashire  LA1 1YJ
**Tel:** 01524 64998 **E-mail:** info@lancastercastle.com

## ST LEONARD'S CHURCH ⋔
Old Langho Road, Old Langho, Blackburn, Lancs  BB6 8AW
**Tel:** 0845 303 2760 **E-mail:** central@thecct.org.uk

## ST MARY'S CHURCH ⋔
Tarleton, Preston, Lancashire  PR4 6HJ
**Tel:** 0845 303 2760 **E-mail:** central@thecct.org.uk

## ST THOMAS' CHURCH ⋔
Heights Lane, Friarmere, Oldham, Lancashire  OL3 5TU
**Tel:** 0845 303 2760 **E-mail:** central@thecct.org.uk

## SMITHILLS HALL
Smithills Dean Road, Bolton  BL7 7NP
**Tel:** 01204 332377 **E-mail:** historichalls@bolton.gov.uk

## ST GEORGE'S CHURCH ⋔
Manchester Road, Carrington, Greater Manchester  M31 4AG
**Tel:** 0845 303 2760 **E-mail:** central@thecct.org.uk

## ST WERBURGH'S CHURCH ⋔
Church Green, Warburton, Warrington  WA13 9SS
**Tel:** 0845 303 2760 **E-mail:** central@thecct.org.uk

## CHRIST CHURCH ⋔
Waterloo Road, Waterloo, Liverpool, Merseyside  L22 1RF
**Tel:** 0845 303 2760 **E-mail:** central@thecct.org.uk

Chillingham Castle

Bowes Museum

# North East

The border lands of Northumberland and Durham with their castles and pele towers bring the past to life for those lucky enough to discover this unspoilt part of the country.

*New Entries for 2014:*
• Auckland Castle
• The Bowes Museum

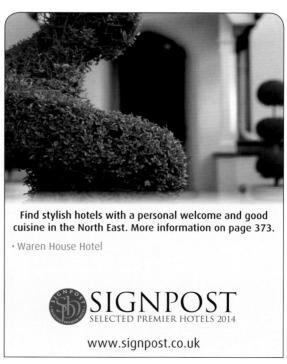

**Find stylish hotels with a personal welcome and good cuisine in the North East. More information on page 373.**

• Waren House Hotel

## SIGNPOST
SELECTED PREMIER HOTELS 2014

www.signpost.co.uk

## VISITOR INFORMATION

■ **Owner**
Auckland Castle Trust

■ **Address**
Market Place
Bishop Auckland
County Durham
DL14 7NR

■ **Location**
**Map 10:P5**
**OS Ref. NZ213 302**
From the Southbound A1, take junction 61 (Bowburn Interchange) sign posted Bishop Auckland (A688), 10 miles. From the Northbound A1 take junction 60 (Bradbury Interchange) sign posted Bishop Auckland, 8 miles. Darlington train station approx. 14 miles. Durham train station approx. 13 miles. Newcastle International Airport approx. 40 miles. Durham Tees Valley Airport approx. 20 miles.

Situated just off the Market Place in Bishop Auckland town centre.

■ **Contact**
Contact Visitor Services for opening times, group bookings, admissions etc.
**Tel:** 01388 743750
**E-mail:** enquiries @aucklandcastle.org

■ **Opening Times**
**30th March 2014 - 30th September 2014**
Open daily (except Tuesday) from 10.30am to 4.00pm. Auckland Castle is occasionally closed for private hire, please check our website for details of any planned closures.

■ **Admission**
Adults £8.00
Concession £6.00
Child 12-15 £4.00
Child under 12 Free
Family (2 Adults & 2 Children) £20.00

■ **Special Events**
Auckland Castle has a varied events programme running throughout each open season. To be kept up to date, please visit our website and subscribe to our mailing list or view the events listing.

**Conference/Function**
The Castle is available for private events ranging from initmate dinners to weddings and large outdoor events. Please contact our Events Team who will be happy to assist with your enquiry.

Auckland Castle

# AUCKLAND CASTLE 🏛
www.aucklandcastle.org

**Home to the Bishop of Durham for over 900 years and now fully open to the public, Auckland Castle is one of the best preserved medieval Bishops' palaces in Europe.**

Following the Norman Conquest and the subsequent Harrying of the North, the Bishop of Durham was granted exceptional powers to act as a political and military leader. With Auckland Castle as his seat of power in North-East England, the King allowed him to raise taxes, mint coins, and hold his own parliaments. Such royal privileges made the Bishop of Durham the second most powerful man in the country – ruling the area between the Tyne and the Tees. Wealth, power, and influence flowed through Auckland Castle and left us the treasure that we invite you to explore. Our state rooms include The Long Dining Room, remodelled by Bishop Trevor (1752-71) and home to the thirteen paintings of Jacob and his Twelve Sons by Fransisco de Zurbarán (1598-1664).

Our other impressive state apartments house an exhibition exploring power and religion in Renaissance and Tudor England, the centrepiece of which is the recently rediscovered Paradise State Bed of Henry VII & Elizabeth of York. Also on display are key examples of Counter Reformation religious art, which contextualise and compliment the Zurbaráns, including paintings by Giovanni Bilivert, Lubin Baugin and Jusepe Ribera. St Peter's Chapel, widely acknowledged as the largest private chapel in Europe, is a fine example of the influence of Bishop Cosin with its stained glass, angels, Flemish reredos and the retable with imagery of the Instruments of the Passion. Our beautiful gardens and expansive parkland are a pleasure to explore, at the heart of which is a splendid Deer House folly.

## KEY FACTS

🏠 We have a gift shop on site stocking a range of locally sourced items.

🍸 Auckland Castle is available for private hire, please visit the private hire section of our website or contact our Events Team.

☕ We have a cafe on site providing light lunches, afternoon tea and a range of hot and cold beverages.

🚶 Guided tours take place twice a day - please see the Visiting Us section of our website or contact Visitor Services on 01388 743750 for details.

📚 Auckland Castle has an active education programme and works with many schools across County Durham and the wider region. Please contact our Education and Outreach Team on 01388 743750 for more details or visit our website.

🐕 Guide Dogs Only. Dog walkers welcome in the Bishop's Park.

🛡

St Peter's Chapel

The Deer House, Bishop's Park

© Heritage House Media Ltd/Raby Castle

# RABY CASTLE 🏰ⓕ
## RABY CASTLE, STAINDROP, DARLINGTON, CO. DURHAM  DL2 3AH
### www.rabycastle.com

Surrounded by a large deer park, with two lakes and a beautiful walled garden with formal lawns, yew hedges and an ornamental pond, Raby Castle was built by the mighty Nevill family in the 14th Century, and has been home to Lord Barnard's family since 1626. Highlights include the vast Barons' Hall, where it is reputed 700 knights gathered to plot the doomed Rising of the North rebellion, and the stunning Octagon Drawing Room, which house Meissen porcelain, fine furniture and paintings by Munnings, Reynolds, Van Dyck, Batoni, Teniers, Amigoni and Vernet . Also in the grounds is the 18th Century Stable block with impressive horse-drawn carriage collection, and a delightfully converted Gift Shop and Tearooms, there is a woodland play area for children.

**Location:** Map 10:O5. OS Ref NZ129 218. On A688, 1m N of Staindrop. 8m NE of Barnard Castle, 12m WNW of Darlington.
**Owner:** The Lord Barnard  **Contact:** Clare Owen / Rachel Milner
**Tel:** 01833 660202 **E-mail:** admin@rabycastle.com

**Open:** Castle: Easter weekend Sat, Sun, Mon. 22 Apr-25 Jun, Sun-Wed. Jul & Aug, Daily except Sats, Sep Sun-Wed. 1pm-4.30pm.
Park & Gardens: As Castle, 11am-5.00pm.
**Admission:** Castle, Park & Gardens: Adult £10.00, Child (5-15yrs) £4.50, Conc. £9.00, Family discounts available. Groups (12+): Adult £7.50.
Park & Gardens: Adult £6.00, Child £2.50, Conc. £5.00. Groups (12+) Adult £4.50. Season Tickets available. Private Group Guided Tours (20+)* Adult £8.50 *Please book in advance.
**Key facts:** ⓘ Raby Estates venison and game sold in tearooms. No photography or video filming is permitted inside. Colour illustrated guidebook on sale. 🅟 ♿ WCs, designated parking, free wheelchair loan. ♿
🎟 By arrangement for groups (20+) or min charge. VIP & Standard Castle Tours available. Tour time 1½ hrs. 🅿 🍽 By arrangement (20+), weekday am. £4 a head. 🐕 Dogs on leads in deer park only. ♿

# BEAMISH, THE LIVING MUSEUM OF THE NORTH
## Beamish Museum, Beamish, County Durham  DH9 0RG
### www.beamish.org.uk

Beamish Museum is an award-winning museum vividly recreating life in North East England in Georgian, Victorian and Edwardian times. Buildings from throughout the region have been brought to Beamish, rebuilt and furnished as they once were. Costumed engagers welcome visitors and demonstrate the past way of life.

**Location:** Map 10:P3. OS Ref NZ219 541.
**Tel:** 0191 370 4000 **Fax:** 0191 370 4001
**E-mail:** museum@beamish.org.uk
**Open:** Open all year, daily in summer, closed Mondays & Fridays in winter. Special events throughout year at no extra charge.
**Admission:** 2014 rates not yet available, visit website for details.
**Key facts:** ⓘ 🛒 ♿ Partial. 🍽 🍴 Fish & Chip shop. 🅿 Free. 🏫 ♿ On leads. Not in period buildings or catering facilities. 🔺 ♿

# BINCHESTER ROMAN FORT
## Bishop Auckland, Co. Durham
### www.durham.gov.uk/archaeology

Displayed remains consist of part of commanding officer's house with attached baths-suite which includes one of best preserved examples of a hypocaust (underfloor heating) in whole of Britain. New excavations - both inside fort and in the civil settlement - can be visited weekdays beginning June until end of August. Programme of re-enactment events throughout season; for details see www.durham.gov.uk/archaeology.

**Location:** Map 10:P5. OS Ref NZ210 312. 1½m N of Bishop Auckland, signposted from A690 Durham-Crook and from A688 Spennymoor-Bishop Auckland roads. **Owner:** Durham County Council **Contact:** Archaeology Section **Tel:** 01388 663089 / 03000 267013 (outside opening hours). **Open:** Every day, Easter Sat to end Sep 11am-5pm; Jul & Aug 10am-5pm **Admission:** Adult £2.55, Concession £1.25, Children £1.15, Under 4 Free. **Key facts:** ⓘ 🛒 Publications and souvenirs for sale. 🅿 Please note: coaches should approach the fort from lane (Wear Chare) off Bishop Auckland market-place. 🏫 School visits and activitiy days by arrangement. ♿ Assistance dogs only. ♿

© The Bowes Museum

# THE BOWES MUSEUM
## Barnard Castle, County Durham  DL12 8NP
### www.thebowesmuseum.org.uk

Set in beautiful grounds, with over 20 galleries and a rolling exhibition programme. See our famous Silver Swan automaton, performing daily at 2.00pm. Complemented by regular events, tasty seasonal menus in Café Bowes and high quality gifts from the Shop. Tranquil gardens and woodland walks add to an amazing day out. **Location:** Map 10:O6. OS Ref NZ055 163. Situated on Newgate in Barnard Castle. Just off the A66 in the heart of the North Pennines. **Tel:** 01833 690606 **Fax:** 01833 637163
**E-mail:** info@thebowesmuseum.org.uk **Open:** 10.00-5.00 daily. Closed only 25 & 26 Dec & 1 Jan. **Admission:** Adults £9.50, Conc. £8.50 , 6 Month pass £14.00. Admission to all exhibitions included. Accompanied children Free (U16). Accompanying carers Free. Free access to Café Bowes, Shop & Grounds.
**Key facts:** ☐ Souvenirs & gifts. Shop open daily 10.00-4.45. ☐ hire@ thebowesmuseum.org.uk. ☐ Access to all areas. ☐ Locally produced seasonal menu, speciality teas, coffees & wines. ☐ Tours are available via group visits or selected days throughout Summer. ☐ Children's Audio available. ☐ Ample free parking, with coach & accessible parking bays. ☐ education@thebowes museum.org.uk. ☐ Except guide dogs. ☐ hire@thebowesmuseum.org.uk. ☐

# DURHAM CATHEDRAL
## Durham  DH1 3EH
### www.durhamcathedral.co.uk

A World Heritage Site. Norman architecture. Burial place of St Cuthbert and the Venerable Bede.
**Location:** Map 10:P4. OS Ref NZ274 422. Durham city centre.
**Contact:** The Cathedral Office
**Tel:** 0191 3864266
**E-mail:** enquiries@durhamcathedral.co.uk
**Open:** Daily 7.30am-6pm (8pm Summer), with Services three times daily.
**Admission:** Free, donations very welcome. Groups contact visits@durhamcathedral.co.uk www.facebook.com/DurhamCathedral
**Key facts:** ☐ ☐ ☐ ☐ Partial. ☐ ☐ ☐
☐ Limited disabled, public parking nearby.
☐ ☐ Guide dogs only. ☐ ☐

Raby Castle

# ALNWICK CASTLE 🏰Ⓕ
www.alnwickcastle.com

## Home to the Duke of Northumberland's family, the Percys, for over 700 years; Alnwick Castle offers history on a grand scale.

Alnwick Castle's remarkable past is filled with drama, intrigue, tragedy and romance, as well as a host of fascinating people including gunpowder plotters, kingmakers and England's most famous medieval knight: Harry Hotspur.

With a history beginning in the Norman age, the castle was originally built to defend England from the Scots. It was eventually transformed from a fortification into a family home for the first Duke and Duchess of Northumberland in the 1760s.

Today, Alnwick Castle is a visitor attraction of real significance, with lavish State Rooms and superb art collections, as well as engaging activities and events for all ages - all set in beautiful landscape by Northumberland-born 'Capability' Brown.

Behind the castle's iconic medieval walls are sumptuous State Rooms in Italian Renaissance style, where visitors can discover one of the country's finest private art collections, including work by Canaletto, Titian and Van Dyck. Important Meissen, Chelsea and Paris ceramics are impressively displayed in the China Gallery.

Within the towers of the Inner Bailey are museums and exhibitions which tell the story of Harry Hotspur, the Northumberland Fusiliers, and the Percy Tenantry Volunteers.

Alnwick Castle provides entertainment for Potter fans, who will recognise Alnwick as Hogwarts from the Harry Potter films, but there are also opportunities aplenty for children and families to get hands-on with history in the medieval-themed Knight's Quest arena, with dressing up, swordplay, medieval crafts and traditional games.

## KEY FACTS

- ℹ️ Storage available for suitcases. Photography is not permitted in the State Rooms.
- 📷
- 🍽️ Team-building, banqueting, dinner dances. Call 01665 511 086.
- ♿ WCs. Free wheelchair and mobility scooter hire available. Limited access in areas.
- 🍷 Licensed.
- 🚶 Free daily tours.
- 🅿️ Coach parking also available.
- 🛍️ Workshops, activities and discounted admission available. Call 01665 511 184.
- 🐕 Assistance dogs only.
- 🔔 Civil wedding ceremonies and receptions. Call 01665 511 086.
- 📋 See website for up-to-date details.

## VISITOR INFORMATION

**■ Owner**
His Grace the Duke of Northumberland

**■ Address**
Alnwick Castle
Alnwick
Northumberland
NE66 1NQ

**■ Location**
Well signposted off A1, 40 minutes north of Newcastle. 2 hours from Edinburgh, 6 hours from London.
**Bus:** Regular bus services from around the region to Alnwick Bus Station
**Rail:** 10 minutes from Alnmouth Station, 3.5 hours from London King's Cross
**Air:** 40 minutes from Newcastle Airport
**Sea:** 40 minutes from North Sea ferry terminal

**■ Contact**
**Tel:** 01665 511 100
**Group bookings:** 01665 511 184.
**E-mail:** info@alnwickcastle.com

**■ Opening Times**
**28th March - 29th October 2014**
(State Rooms close 27th October).
10.00am-5.30pm
(last admission 4.15pm).

State Rooms are open 11.00am-5.00pm (last admission 4.30pm, Chapel closes at 3.00pm).

**■ Admission**
Adult:                      £14.50
Concession:              £12.00
Child (5-16yrs):          £7.30
Family (2+up to 4):  £37.00
Discounted rates available for groups of 14 or more.

(2013 prices shown, subject to change).

**Save up to 10% online. Validate your ticket for 12 months - at no extra cost**

**■ Special Events**
See website for up-to-date details

**Medieval events**
Falconry displays, jester performances, archery, visits from skilled artisans.

**Potter-themed**
Magic shows from Potter-inspired characters, daily broomstick training sessions.

**Guided tours**
Historical grounds tours about the origins, uses, and restorations of the castle; Battleaxe to Broomsticks tours of the castle's various film locations.

### Conference/Function

| ROOM | Size | Max Cap |
|------|------|---------|
| Guest Hall | 100' x 30' | 220 |
| Hulne Abbey | varies | 500 |

### VISITOR INFORMATION

■ **Owner**
Sir Humphry Wakefield Bt

■ **Address**
Chillingham Castle
Northumberland
NE66 5NJ

■ **Location**
**Map 14:L11**
**OS Ref. NU062 258**
45m N of Newcastle
between A697 & A1.
2m S of B6348 at
Chatton.6m SE of Wooler.
**Rail:** Alnmouth or Berwick.

■ **Contact**
The Administrator
**Tel:** 01668 215359
**E-mail:**
enquiries@chillingham-
castle.com

■ **Opening Times**
**Summer**
Castle, Garden & Tearoom
Easter-31 October. Closed
Sats, 12 noon-5pm.
**Winter**
October-April. Groups &
Coach Tours any time by
appointment.
All function activities
available.

■ **Admission**
| | |
|---|---|
| Adult | £9.00 |
| Children | £5.00 |
| Conc. | £8.00 |
| Family Ticket | £22.00 |

(2 adults and 3 children
under 15)

# CHILLINGHAM CASTLE ⌂Ⓕ

www.chillingham-castle.com

## 20 Minutes from seaside or mountains. 4 stars in Simon Jenkins' 'Thousand Best Houses' and the very first of The Independent's '50 Best Castles in Britain & Ireland'.

This remarkable and very private castle has been continuously owned by just one family line since the 1200's. A visit from Edward I in 1298 was followed by many other Royal visits right down through this century. See Chillingham's alarming dungeons as well as active restoration in the Great Halls and State Rooms which are gradually brought back to life with tapestries, arms and armour. We even have a very real torture chamber.

The 1100s stronghold became a fortified castle in 1344, see the original Royal Licence to Crenellate on view. Wrapped in the nation's history Chillingham also occupied a strategic position during Northumberland's bloody border feuds being a resting place to many royal visitors. Tudor days saw additions but the underlying medievalism remains. 18th and 19th Centuries saw decorative extravagances including Capability Brown lakes and grounds with gardens laid out by Sir Jeffrey Wyatville, fresh from his triumphs at Windsor Castle. Prehistoric Wild Cattle roam the park beyond more rare than mountain gorilla (a separate tour) and never miss the family tomb in the church.

### Gardens
With romantic grounds, the castle commands breathtaking views of the surrounding countryside. As you walk to the lake you will see, according to season, drifts of snowdrops, daffodils or bluebells and an astonishing display of rhododendrons. This emphasises the restrained formality of the Elizabethan topiary garden, with its intricately clipped hedges of box and yew. Lawns, the formal gardens and woodland walks are all fully open to the public.

## KEY FACTS

 Corporate entertainment, lunches, drinks, dinners, wedding ceremonies and receptions.

By arrangement.

Avoid Lilburn route, coach parties welcome by prior arrangement. Limited for coaches.

Guide dogs only.

Self catering apartments.

# THE ALNWICK GARDEN
## DENWICK LANE, ALNWICK, NORTHUMBERLAND  NE66 1YU
www.alnwickgarden.com

The Alnwick Garden is one of the world's most extraordinary contemporary gardens. Described by The Duchess of Northumberland as "an inspiring landscape with beautiful gardens, unique features all brought to life with water." Designed by Wirtz International, The Garden is a remarkable combination of spaces, themes, quirkiness and play. Alongside being home to one of the world's largest tree houses, The Garden boasts the beauty of the Ornamental Garden, the excitement of the Grand Cascade, the mysteries of the Bamboo Labyrinth, the spell-binding water sculptures of the Serpent Garden and the intrigue of the Poison Garden.

Every visit to The Alnwick Garden is truly unique, as each season brings a new lease of life to the stunning features and specially selected plants and flowers; ensuring that no two visits are the same. Spring is an exciting time as the snowdrops, magnolias and daffodils burst into life followed by tulips in their multitudes and the blossoming of the Tai Haku Cherry Orchard. In summer,

marvel at the towering blue delphiniums in the Ornamental Garden and wind your way through scented bowers in the David Austin Rose Garden, which is home to over 200 species of roses; including the specially created Alnwick Rose. As autumn arrives, watch the chameleon-like transformation of the hornbeams bordering the Grand Cascade and the ripening of the crab apple pleaching. Winter emphasises the strong green structure of the Wirtz design, with the Sparkle light installation providing rushes of vibrant colour against the frosted backdrop of The Garden.

**Location:** Map 14:M11. OS Ref NU192 132. Just off the A1 at Alnwick, Northumberland. **Owner:** The Alnwick Garden Trust
**Tel:** 01665 511350  **E-mail:** info@alnwickgarden.com
**Open:** Please visit www.alnwickgarden.com for opening times,prices and the most up to date information. **Key facts:** ▢ ▦ ▤ ▨ WCs. ▦ ▥ Licensed. ▣ By arrangement. ▣ Cars & coaches. ▦ ▦ Assistance dogs only. ▦ ▦ ▦

Alnwick Castle, View from the Gun Terrace

### BAMBURGH CASTLE 🏛Ⓕ
**Bamburgh, Northumberland NE69 7DF**
www.bamburghcastle.com

These formidable stone walls have witnessed dark tales of royal rebellion, bloody battles, spellbinding legends and millionaire benefactors. With fourteen public rooms and over 3000 artefacts, including arms and armour, porcelain, furniture and artwork. The Armstrong and Aviation artefacts Museum houses artefacts spanning both World Wars as well as others relating to Lord Armstrongs ship building empire on the Tyne.
**Location:** Map 14:M10. OS Ref NU184 351. 42m N of Newcastle-upon-Tyne. 20m S of Berwick-upon-Tweed. 6m E of Belford by B1342 from A1 at Belford.
**Owner:** Francis Watson-Armstrong **Contact:** Chris Calvert, Director
**Tel:** 01668 214208 **E-mail:** administrator@bamburghcastle.com
**Open:** 8 Feb-2 Nov 2014, 10am-5pm. Last admission 4pm. 3 Nov 2014-13 Feb 2015, Weekends only, 11am-4.30pm. Last admission 3.30pm.
**Admission:** Adult £9.95, Senior £9.00, Child (5-15 yrs) £4.50, Family £25.00 (2 adults & up to 3 children). For group rates & bookings please call 01668 214 208. **Key facts:** ℹ No flash photography in the State Rooms. ◻ ♿ WCs. ▣ Licensed. 🎦 By arrangement at any time, min charge out of hours £150. ◻ 🅿 100 cars, coaches park on tarmac drive at entrance. ▣ Welcome. Guide provided if requested. 🦮 Guide dogs only. ▨ ▣ ▤ ▽

### CRAGSIDE ❦
**Rothbury, Morpeth, Northumberland NE65 7PX**
www.nationaltrust.org.uk

Revolutionary home of Lord Armstrong, Victorian inventor and landscape genius, Cragside sits on a rocky crag high above the Debdon Burn. Crammed with ingenious gadgets, it was the first house in the world to be lit with hydro-electricity.
**Location:** Map 14:L12. OS Ref NU073 022.
½m NE of Rothbury on B6341.
**Owner:** National Trust
**Contact:** Assistant to General Manager
**Tel:** 01669 620333
**Open:** Please see website for opening times and admission prices.
**Admission:** Please note: payment by cash only at the admission point (to maintain speed of entry). Credit/debit cards can be used for purchases in the shop. Includes a voluntary donation but visitors can choose to pay the standard prices displayed at the property and on the website.
**Key facts:** ◻ 🎦 ♿ ▣ Licensed.
🍴 🅿 ▣ 🦮 Dogs on leads only. ▽

### CHIPCHASE CASTLE 🏛Ⓕ
**Wark, Hexham, Northumberland NE48 3NT**
The Castle overlooks the River North Tyne and is set in formal and informal gardens. **Location:** Map 10:N2. 10m NW of Hexham via A6079 to Chollerton. 2m SE of Wark. **Tel:** 01434 230203 **E-mail:** info@chipchasecastle.com
**Website:** www.chipchasecastle.com **Open:** Castle: 1-28 Jun, 2-5pm daily. Gardens & Nursery: Easter-31 Aug, Thu-Sun Incl. & BH Mon, 10am-5pm.
**Admission:** Castle £6.00, Garden £4.00, concessions available. Nursery Free.

### PRESTON TOWER 🏛Ⓕ
**Chathill, Northumberland NE67 5DH**
Built by Sir Robert Harbottle in 1392.
**Location:** Map 14:M11. OS Ref NU185 253. Follow Historic Property signs on A1 7m N of Alnwick. **Tel:** 07966 150216 **Website:** www.prestontower.co.uk
**Open:** All year daily, 10am-6pm, or dusk, whichever is earlier.
**Admission:** Adult £2.00, Child 50p, Concessions £1.50. Groups £1.50.

### GIBSIDE ❦
**Nr Rowlands Gill, Burnopfield**
**Newcastle upon Tyne NE16 6BG**
Gibside is an 18th Century 'forest' landscape garden, created by wealthy coal baron George Bowes, ancestor of the Queen Mother. Gibside is a haven for wildlife with stunning Derwent Valley views, miles of woodland and riverside walks, a spectacular Palladian Chapel and exciting new adventure play area. **Location:** Map 10:P3. 5m SW of Gateshead and the A1, 20m NW of Durham. Entrance on B6314 between Burnopfield and Rowlands Gill. **Owner:** National Trust **Contact:** Visitor Services Team **Tel:** 01207 541820 **E-mail:** gibside@nationaltrust.org.uk **Website:** www.nationaltrust.org.uk/gibside **Open:** Estate: 1 Jan-28 Feb: 10am-4pm. 1 Mar-31 Oct: 10am-6pm. 1 Nov-31 Dec: 10am-4pm. Café and Shop: closes one hour earlier. **Admission:** Adult £7.95, Child £4.10, Family (2 adults+children) £19.80, Family (1 adult+children) £13.75. Booked groups £6.30. *Includes a Gift Aid donation. **Key facts:** ◻ 🎦 🍴 ♿ WCs. ▣ Licensed. 🍴 Licensed. 🎦 By arrangement. 🅿 Limited for coaches. ▣ 🦮 Dogs on leads only. ▣ ▨ ▽

## BARNARD CASTLE
Nr Galgate, Barnard Castle, Durham DL12 8PR
Tel: 01833 638212 E-mail: barnard.castle@english-heritage.org.uk

## ROKEBY PARK
Barnard Castle, Co. Durham DL12 9RZ
Tel: 01609 748612 E-mail: admin@rokebypark.com

## ST ANDREW'S CHURCH
Kiln Pit Hill, Shotley, Consett, County Durham DH8 9SJ
Tel: 0845 303 2760 E-mail: central@thecct.org.uk

## BELSAY HALL, CASTLE & GARDENS
Belsay, Nr Morpeth, Northumberland NE20 0DX
Tel: 01661 881636 E-mail: belsay.hall@english-heritage.org.uk

## DUNSTANBURGH CASTLE
Dunstanburgh Road, Craster, Northumberland NE66 3TT
Tel: 01665 576231 E-mail: dunstanburgh.castle@english-heritage.org.uk

## ETAL CASTLE
Cornhill-On-Tweed, Northumberland TD12 4TN
Tel: 01890 820332 E-mail: customers@english-heritage.org.uk

## LADY WATERFORD HALL & GALLERY
Ford, Berwick-Upon-Tweed TD15 2QA
Tel: 07971 326177 E-mail: tourism@ford-and-etal.co.uk

## LINDISFARNE CASTLE
Holy Island, Berwick-Upon-Tweed, Northumberland TD15 2SH
Tel: 01289 389244 E-mail: lindisfarne@nationaltrust.org.uk

## LINDISFARNE PRIORY
Holy Island, Berwick-Upon-Tweed, Northumberland TD15 2RX
Tel: 01289 389200 E-mail: lindisfarne.priory@english-heritage.org.uk

## MELDON PARK
Morpeth, Northumberland NE61 3SW
Tel: 01670 772341 E-mail: michelle@flyingfox.co.uk/james@flying-fox.co.uk

## NORHAM CASTLE
Norham, Northumberland TD15 2JY
Tel: 01289 304493 E-mail: customers@english-heritage.org.uk

## ST ANDREW'S CHURCH
Bywell, Stocksfield, Northumberland NE43 7AD
Tel: 0845 303 2760 E-mail: central@thecct.org.uk

## SEATON DELAVAL HALL
The Avenue, Seaton Sluice, Northumberland NE26 4QR
Tel: 0191 237 9100 E-mail: seatondelavalhall@nationaltrust.org.uk

## WALLINGTON
Cambo, Morpeth, Northumberland NE61 4AR
Tel: 01670 773600 E-mail: wallington@nationaltrust.org.uk

## WARKWORTH CASTLE
Warkworth, Alnwick, Northumberland NE65 0UJ
Tel: 01665 711423 E-mail: warkworth.castle@english-heritage.org.uk

## CAPTAIN COOK & STAITHES HERITAGE
High Street, Staithes, Cleveland TS13 5BQ
Tel: 01947 841454

## HOLY TRINITY CHURCH
Church Street East, Sunderland, Tyne & Wear SR1 2BB
Tel: 0845 303 2760 E-mail: central@thecct.org.uk

## CASTLE KEEP
St Nicholas Street, Castle Garth, Tyne & Wear NE1 1RQ
Tel: 0191 232 7938.

## ST STEPHEN'S CHURCH
Brunel Terrace, Low Elswick, Newcastle Upon Tyne NE4 7NL
Tel: 0845 303 2760 E-mail: central@thecct.org.uk

## SEGEDUNUM ROMAN FORT, BATHS & MUSEUM
Buddle Street, Wallsend NE28 6HR
Tel: 01912 772169 E-mail: caireen.butler@twmuseums.org.uk

## TYNEMOUTH PRIORY & CASTLE
Pier Road, Tynemouth, Tyne & Wear NE30 4BZ
Tel: 0191 2571090 E-mail: tynemouth.castleandpriory@english-heritage.org.uk

## WASHINGTON OLD HALL
The Avenue, Washington Village, Tyne & Wear NE38 7LE
Tel: 0191 416 6879 E-mail: washington.oldhall@nationaltrust.org.uk

The Alnwick Garden

Duart Castle

Clan Donald Skye

|  | |
|---|---|
| Borders | ■ |
| **South West Scotland,** Dumfries & Galloway, Ayrshire & The Isle of Arran | ■ |
| **Edinburgh** City, Coast & Countryside | ■ |
| **Greater Glasgow** Glasgow & The Clyde Valley | □ |
| **Tayside** Perthshire, Angus, Dundee, & The Kingdom of Fife | ■ |
| **West Highlands & Islands,** Loch Lomond, Stirling & Trossachs | ■ |
| **Grampian Highlands,** Aberdeen & North East Coast | ■ |
| **Highlands & Skye** | ■ |

# Scotland

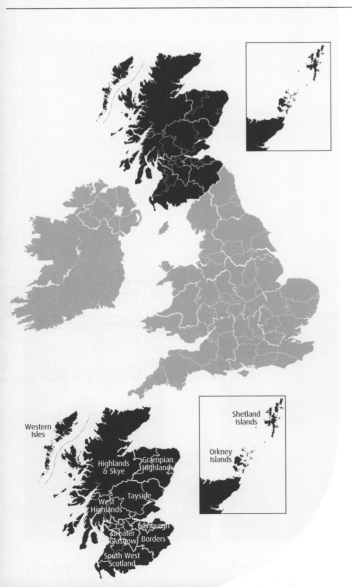

Explore Highland Scotland with its clan castles or Lowland Scotland's palaces and gardens, all linked by some of the most exciting landscape in the world.

*New Entries for 2014:*
- Arduaine Garden
- Clan Donald Skye
- Urquhart Castle
- Duff House
- Linlithgow Palace
- Crimonmogate

## VISITOR INFORMATION

■ **Owner**
The Lord Palmer

■ **Address**
Manderston
Duns
Berwickshire
Scotland
TD11 3PP

■ **Location**
**Map 14:K9**
**OS Ref. NT810 544**
From Edinburgh 47m, 1hr.
1½m E of Duns on A6105.
**Bus:** 400yds.
**Rail:** Berwick Station 12m.
**Airport:** Edinburgh or
Newcastle both 60m or
80mins.

■ **Contact**
The Lord Palmer
**Tel:** 01361 883450
**Fax:** 01361 882010
**Secretary:** 01361 882636
**E-mail:**
palmer@manderston.co.uk

■ **Opening Times**
**Summer 2014**
8 May–28 September,
Thurs and Sun only.
Gardens and tearoom
open 11.30am.
House opens 1.30–5pm;
last entry 4.15pm. BH
Mons, late May and late
August. Groups welcome
all year by appointment.

**Winter**
Group visits welcome by
appointment.

■ **Admission**
**House & Grounds**
(Open Days)

| | |
|---|---|
| Adult | £9.00 |
| Child (under 12yrs) | Free |
| Groups (15+) | £8.50 |
| Grounds only | £5.00 |

Open any other day by
appointment.

### Conference/Function

| ROOM | Size | Max Cap |
|---|---|---|
| Dining Rm | 22' x 35' | 100 |
| Ballroom | 34' x 21' | 150 |
| Drawing Rm | 35' x 21' | 150 |

# MANDERSTON 🏛 Ⓕ
### www.manderston.co.uk

## Manderston, together with its magnificent stables, stunning marble dairy and 56 acres of immaculate gardens, forms quite a unique ensemble.

Manderston is the supreme country house of Edwardian Scotland: the swansong of its era. Manderston, as it is today, is a product of the best craftsmanship and highest domestic sophistication the Edwardian era had to offer and was completely rebuilt between 1903 and 1905.

Visitors are able to see not only the sumptuous State rooms and bedrooms, decorated in the Adam manner, but also all original domestic offices, in a truly 'upstairs downstairs' atmosphere.

Manderston boasts a unique and recently restored silver staircase. There is a special museum with a nostalgic display of valuable tins made by Huntly and Palmer from 1868 to the present day. Winner of the AA/NPI Bronze Award UK 1994.

### Gardens

Outside, the magnificence continues and the combination of formal gardens and picturesque landscapes is a major attraction unique amongst Scottish houses. The stables, still in use, have been described by Horse and Hound as 'probably the finest in all the wide world'. The Marble Dairy and its unusual tower, built to look like a Border Keep, enjoys commanding views. Manderston is often used as a film location but can also cater for corporate events. It is also an ideal retreat for business groups and think-tank weekends. Manderston also lends itself very well to fashion shows, air displays, archery, clay pigeon shooting, equestrian events, garden parties, shows, rallies, filming, product launches and marathons. Two airstrips for light aircraft, approx. 5m, grand piano, billiard table, pheasant shoots, sea angling, salmon fishing, stabling, cricket pitch, tennis court, lake.

## KEY FACTS

ⓘ No photography in house.

🖼

🍴 Available. Buffets, lunches and dinners. Wedding receptions.

♿ Special parking available outside the house.

🍽 Snaffles Tearoom - home made lunches, teas, cakes and tray bakes. Can be booked in advance, menus on request.

🚶 Included. Available in French. Guides in rooms. If requested, the owner may meet groups. Tour time 1¼ hrs.

🅿 400 cars 125yds from house, 30 coaches 5yds from house. Appreciated if group fees are paid by one person.

🏫 Welcome. Guide can be provided. Biscuit Tin Museum of particular interest.

🐕 Grounds only, on leads.

🛏 6 twin, 4 double.

❄

## ABBOTSFORD ⓘⒻ
**The Abbotsford Trust, Abbotsford, Melrose, Roxburghshire  TD6 9BQ**
www.scottsabbotsford.co.uk

Abbotsford, the home that world renowned author & poet Sir Walter Scott built within the stunning landscape of the Scottish Borders. Reopened in 2013 following extensive restoration with state of the art Visitor Centre with Restaurant, Gift Shop & free to access exhibition on the life & legacy of Sir Walter Scott. Luxury accommodation in Hope Scott Wing, beautiful gardens, riverside walks & woodland play trail. **Location:** Map 14:I10. OS Ref NT508 342. 2 miles from Melrose and Galashiels. Edinburgh 35 miles, Glasgow & Newcastle approx 70 miles. Major routes: A1, A68 and A7.
**Owner:** The Abbotsford Trust **Contact:** Beverley Rutherford
**Tel:** 01896 752043 **Fax:** 01896 752916
**E-mail:** enquiries@scottsabbotsford.co.uk
**Open:** Visitors Centre: 1 Apr-30 Sep, 10am-5pm. 1 Oct-31 Mar, 10am-4pm. House & Gardens: 1 Apr-30 Sep 10am-5pm, 1 Oct-23 Dec 10am-4pm.
**Admission:** House & Gardens: £8.75, £7.50 Conc, £4.50 U17 (free for 5 years and under). Gardens only: £3.50, £2.50 Conc & U17, Group rates available.
**Key facts:** ⓘ ⬚ Ⓣ ⬚ ⬚ Licensed. Ⓕ House only. ⬚ In House. Ⓟ ⬚ ⬚ On leads except formal areas. ⬚ Hope Scott Wing. ⬚ ✳ Visitor Centre only. ⬚

Abbotsford Gardens

## FLOORS CASTLE 🏛Ⓕ
### Kelso, The Scottish Borders  TD5 7SF
www.floorscastle.com

Explore the spectacular state rooms with outstanding collections of paintings, tapestries and furniture. Find hidden treasures like the collections of porcelain and oriental ceramics. Enjoy the picturesque grounds and gardens including the beautiful walled gardens. Stop at the Courtyard Café and enjoy a morning coffee or delicious lunch. For special events, please check our website.
**Location:** Map 14:J10. OS Ref NT711 347. From South A68, A698. From North A68, A697/9 In Kelso follow signs.
**Owner:** His Grace the Duke of Roxburghe  **Contact:** Charlotte Newton
**Tel:** 01573 223333  **Fax:** 01573 226056  **E-mail:** cnewton@floorscastle.com
**Open:** Open Easter Weekend through to end Oct. Please check our website for opening times before travelling.
**Admission:** Adult £8.50, Child (5–16yrs) £4.50, OAP/Student £7.50, Family £22.50, Under 5yrs Free.
**Key facts:** ⓘ Dogs must be kept on leads and under control at all times. Photography is not permitted within the Castle. 🅾 🅵 🆃 Exclusive lunches and dinners. 🔲 Partial. WCs. 🔲 Licensed. 🍴 🅵 By arrangement. 🅿 Cars and coaches. 🔲 🔲 Dogs on leads only. 🔺 🔻

## TRAQUAIR 🏛Ⓕ
### Innerleithen, Peeblesshire  EH44 6PW
www.traquair.co.uk

Dating back to 1107, Traquair was originally a hunting lodge for the kings and queens of Scotland. Later a refuge for Catholic priests in times of terror the Stuarts of Traquair supported Mary Queen of Scots and the Jacobite cause. Today, Traquair is a unique piece of living history.
**Location:** Map 13:H10. OS Ref NY330 354. On B709 near junction with A72. Edinburgh 1hr, Glasgow 1½ hrs, Carlisle 1½ hrs.
**Owner/Contact:** Catherine Maxwell Stuart, 21st Lady of Traquair
**Tel:** 01896 830323  **Fax:** 01896 830639  **E-mail:** enquiries@traquair.co.uk
**Open:** 5 Apr-31 Oct (11am–5pm & 11am-4pm in Oct). Weekends only in Nov (11am-3pm).
**Admission:** House & Grounds: Adult £8.50; Child £4.25; Senior £7.50, Family £23 (2+3). Groups (20+): Adult £7.50; Child £3.50; Senior £6.50. Grounds only: Adults £4.00; Conc £3.00. Guide Book £4.50.
**Key facts:** ⓘ No photography in house. 🅾 Brewery & Gift Shop. 🆃 Tours, Ale Tastings & Dinners available. 🔲 🍴 Licensed. 🅵 🅿 Coaches; please book. 🔲 🔲 In grounds on leads. 🛏 Three spacious double en suite bedrooms furnished with antique furniture. 🔺 Please contact for more information. 🔻

## MELLERSTAIN HOUSE & GARDENS 🏛Ⓕ
### Mellerstain, Gordon, Berwickshire  TD3 6LG
www.mellerstain.com

Built in the 18th Century, Mellerstain is a unique eg. of William and Robert Adam design, exhibiting a treasure of paintings, period furniture, personal effects and exquisite Adam ceilings. The library is considered to be Robert Adam's finest creations. Set within acres of beautiful parkland with terraced gardens designed by Sir Reginald Blomfield, lakeside walks, coffee shop, childrens play area and holiday cottages. The perfect day out and holiday destination. **Location:** Map 14:J10. OS Ref NT648 392. From Edinburgh A68 to Earlston, turn left 5m, signed.
**Owner:** The Mellerstain Trust  **Contact:** The Trust Administrator
**Tel:** 01573 410225  **Fax:** 01573 410636  **E-mail:** enquiries@mellerstain.com
**Open:** Easter weekend (4 days), May/Jun/Jul/Aug/Sep on Fri, Sat, Sun, Mon. House: 12.30-5pm. Last ticket 4.15pm. Coffee shop and gardens: 11.30am-5pm. **Admission:** See our website or call us.
**Key facts:** ⓘ No photography or video cameras in the house. 🅾 🆃 🔲 🅵 🅵 By arrangement. 🅿 Onsite parking for vehicles and coaches. 🔲 🔲 Dogs on leads only. Guide dogs only in the house. 🛏 🔺 🔻

## MERTOUN GARDENS 🏛Ⓕ
### St. Boswells, Melrose, Roxburghshire  TD6 0EA
26 acres of beautiful grounds. Walled garden and well preserved circular dovecot.
**Location:** Map 14:J10. OS Ref NT617 318. **Tel:** 01835 823236
**Fax:** 01835 822474  **E-mail:** mertoun@live.co.uk
**Website:** www.mertoungardens.com **Open:** Apr-Sep, Fri-Mon 2-6pm. Last Admission 5.30pm. **Admission:** Adults £4.00, Conc. £3.00, Child Free.

Statue at Mellerstain House

# DUMFRIES HOUSE ⓘⓕ
www.dumfries-house.org.uk

## A Georgian Gem, nesting within 2,000 acres of scenic Ayrshire countryside in south-west Scotland.

Commissioned by William Crichton Dalrymple, the 5th Earl of Dumfries, the House was designed by renowned 18th Century architect brothers John, Robert and James Adam and built between 1754 and 1759.

Recognised as one of the Adam brothers' masterpieces it remained unseen by the public since it was built 250 years ago until it opened its doors as a visitor attraction in June 2008. The former home of the Marquesses of Bute, it was saved for the nation at the eleventh hour by a consortium of organisations and individuals brought together by HRH The Prince Charles, Duke of Rothesay.

The house holds the most important collection of works from Thomas Chippendale's 'Director' period. It is widely recognised that Scotland was a testing ground for Thomas Chippendale's early rococo furniture and the Dumfries House collection is regarded as his key project in this area.

Dumfries House also holds the most comprehensive range of pieces by Edinburgh furniture makers Alexander Peter, William Mathie and Francis Brodie. Indeed, the Scottish furniture together with the Chippendale collection is of outstanding worldwide historical significance.

## KEY FACTS

ⓘ Pre-booking of tours is recommended (Online at www.dumfries-house.org.uk or via the Booking Line 01290 421742). Tour times may vary.

ⓗ ⓣ

ⓖ Stairlift. WCs. 1 wheelchair per tour.

ⓚ Obligatory.

ⓟ Cars ample. Coaches ample.

ⓡ

ⓧ On leads in grounds only. Guide dogs only in the house.

❄ Grounds only.

ⓦ

### ■ VISITOR INFORMATION

### ■ Owner
The Great Steward of Scotland's Dumfries House Trust

### ■ Address
Dumfries House
Cumnock
East Ayrshire
Scotland
KA18 2NJ

### ■ Location
Map 13:C11
OS Ref. NS539 200
**Car:** Cumnock, East Ayrshire. Sat Nav KA18 2LN. Visitors Entrance on Barony Road (B7036)
**Rail:** Auchinleck
**Air:** Prestwick

### ■ Contact
The Wedding & Events Administrator
**Tel:** Booking Line 01290 425959
**Fax:** 01290 425464
**E-mail:** info@dumfries-house.org.uk

### ■ Opening Times
**Summer season:**
Mar - Oct (inclusive)
7 days/week 10.00am to 4.00pm (check website for Sat openings)
Guided tours at frequent intervals
**Winter season:**
Nov - Feb (inclusive)
Sat and Sun 11.00am to 2.00pm
**Please note:** The House is closed for Christmas and New Year
Please be advised that you should call the Booking Line on 01290 421742 or go onto www.dumfries-house.org.uk to confirm any House closures before your visit.

### ■ Admission
**Ticket Price for the House Tour**
Adults £8.50
Child (5-16 yrs) £4.00
Children under 5 Free
Historic Scotland Members 25% discount
Art Fund Members Free
**Grand Tour**
Adults £12.50
Child (5-16 yrs) £4.00
Children under 5 Free
Art Fund Members 50% discount
**Art Tour**
Wednesday Only £12.50
Art Fund Members 50% discount.

### ■ Special Events
Grounds available all year. House may close for private functions.
Please check with the property before travelling any distance.
Special Events information available at www.dumfries-house.org.uk.
House available for private functions and corporate events. Minister license for weddings.

## AUCHINLECK
### Ochiltree, Ayrshire  KA18 2LR
www.landmarktrust.org.uk

Once diarist James Boswell's family seat, this grand 18th Century country house has its own grounds, river, ice-house and grotto. The large dining room and its elaborate plasterwork makes any meal special while the library lends itself to conversation and contemplation, just as it did for James Boswell and Dr Johnson.

**Location:** Map 13:C11. OS Ref NS510 226.
**Owner:** The Landmark Trust
**Tel:** 01628 825925
**E-mail:** bookings@landmarktrust.org.uk
**Open:** Parts of house open Easter-Oct, Wed afternoons. The Grounds are open dawn-dusk Spring and Summer.
**Admission:** Visits by appointment.
**Key facts:** ⓘ This building has grand, elegant rooms, a sweeping staircase, large dining and sitting rooms and plenty of open fires.
🅿 ♿ ⧆ ❋ ♛

## CASTLE KENNEDY GARDENS
### Castle Kennedy, Stranraer
### Dumfries and Galloway  DG9 8SJ
www.castlekennedygardens.co.uk

Famous 75-acre gardens situated between two large natural lochs. Ruined Castle Kennedy at one end overlooking beautiful herbaceous walled garden; Lochinch Castle at the other. Proximity to the gulf-stream provides an impressive collection of rare trees, including 21 Champion Trees, magnolias, and spectacular rhododendron displays. Guided walks, children's activities, regular ranger activities, open air theatre, bird hide, gift shop, plant centre and charming tearoom - a 'must-visit'. **Location:** Map 9:D3. OS Ref NX109 610. 3m E of Stranraer on A75. **Owner:** The Earl and Countess of Stair
**Contact:** Stair Estates **Tel:** 01776 702024/01581 400225 **Fax:** 01776 706248
**E-mail:** info@castlekennedygardens.co.uk
**Open:** Gardens and Tearoom: 1 Apr-31 Oct: daily 10am-5pm. Feb & Mar: Weekends only. Gardens open all year. **Admission:** Adult £5.00, Child £1.50, OAP £3.50. Groups of 20 or more 10% discount.
**Key facts:** ⓘ ⧉ ⧆ Ⓣ ♿ WCs ☕ ⛪ 🅿 ♿ On leads only. ⧆ ▲ ❋ ♛

Gardens at Dumfries House

© National Trust for Scotland

## CULZEAN CASTLE
## & COUNTRY PARK ♛
### Maybole, Ayrshire  KA19 8LE
www.nts.org.uk

Robert Adam's 18th Century masterpiece - a real 'castle in the air' - is perched on a cliff high above the crashing waves of the Firth of Clyde. The Castle itself boasts a spectacular Oval Staircase, the impressive Armoury and the Circular Saloon, with its panoramic views over the Clyde. The extensive grounds encompass Scotland's first country park where you can explore the deer park, swan pond and miles of woodland walks.

**Location:** Map 13:B11. OS Ref NS232 103.
On A719, 4m west of Maybole and 12m south of Ayr. KA19 8LE
**Owner:** The National Trust for Scotland
**Tel:** 0844 493 2149 **E-mail:** information@nts.org.uk
**Open:** Please see our website or call us for up to date opening times.
**Admission:** Please see our website or call us for up to date prices.
**Key facts:** ⧉
🍴 ♛

Register for news and special offers at **www.hudsonsheritage.com**

# GLENMALLOCH LODGE
## Newton Stewart, Dumfries And Galloway  DG8 6AG
### www.landmarktrust.org.uk

A fairytale cottage in a wild and beautiful glen, this diminutive former schoolroom makes a perfect hideaway or writing retreat for two, or even one.
**Location:** Map 9:F3.
**Owner:** The Landmark Trust
**Tel:** 01628 825925
**E-mail:** bookings@landmarktrust.org.uk
**Open:** Visits by appointment.
**Admission:** Free for visits by appointment.
**Key facts:** Ⓘ Although not far from Newton Stewart, the Lodge feels remote and looks out over the unspoilt and geologically interesting Galloway landscape.
Ⓟ ⊞ ⊞ ⊛ ⊡

# KELBURN CASTLE
# & COUNTRY CENTRE ⓕ
## Fairlie, By Largs, Ayrshire  KA29 0BE
### www.kelburnestate.com

Kelburn is the home of the Earls of Glasgow and has been in the Boyle family for over 800 years. It is notable for its waterfalls, historic gardens, romantic glen and unique trees. The castle continues to be the venue of a major graffiti art installation, now considered to be in the top 10 graffiti installations in the world. **Location:** Map 13:B9. OS Ref NS210 580. A78 to Largs, 2m S of Largs.
**Owner:** The Earl of Glasgow **Tel:** 01475 568685/568595
**Fax:** 01475 568121 **E-mail:** admin@kelburncountrycentre.com
**Open:** Country Centre: Easter-Oct: daily. Castle: Jul and Aug. Open by arrangement for groups at other times of the year.
Now available for Weddings and Special Events.
**Admission:** Country Centre: Adult £8.50, Child/Conc. £6.00, Under 3s Free, Family £25.00. Groups (10+): Adult, £4.50, Conc. £3.50. Castle: £2.00 extra pp. **Key facts:** ⊞ ⊞ ⊞ Partial. ⊞ ⊞ Licensed. Ⓕ Jul and Aug. By arrangement at other times of the year. Ⓟ ⊞ ⊞ In grounds, on leads. ⊛

## CRAIGDARROCH HOUSE ⓕⓕ
### Moniaive, Dumfriesshire  DG3 4JB
Built by William Adam in 1729, over the old house dating from 14th Century (earliest records). The marriage home of Annie Laurie, the heroine of 'the world's greatest lovesong', who married Alexander Fergusson, 14th Laird of Craigdarroch, in 1720 and lived in the house for 33 years.
**Location:** Map 9:G1. OS Ref NX741 909.
S side of B729, 2m W of Moniaive, 19m WNW of Dumfries.
**Owner/Contact:** Mrs Carin Sykes
**Tel:** 01848 200202
**Open:** Jul: daily, 2-4pm. Please note: no WCs.
**Admission:** £3.00.

## RAMMERSCALES ⓕⓕ
### Lockerbie, Dumfriesshire  DG11 1LD
Georgian house, with extensive library and fine views over Annandale.
**Location:** Map 10:I2. OS Ref NY080 780. W side of B7020, 3m S of Lochmoben.
**Owner/Contact:** Mr M A Bell Macdonald
**Tel:** 01387 810229
**Fax:** 01387 810940
**E-mail:** malcolm@rammerscales.co.uk
**Website:** www.rammerscales.co.uk
**Open:** Later half of Jul for 25 days: daily (excluding Sat), 2-5pm. Bus tours by appointment.
**Admission:** Adult £5.00, Concessions £2.50.
**Key facts:** Ⓕ Obligatory. Ⓟ ⊞

## VISITOR INFORMATION

■ **Owner**
The Earl of Rosebery

■ **Address**
Dalmeny House
South Queensferry
Edinburgh
EH30 9TQ

■ **Location**
**Map 13:G8**
**OS Ref. NT167 779**
From Edinburgh A90,
B924, 7m N, A90 ½m.
On south shore of Firth of
Forth.
**Bus:** From St Andrew
Square to Chapel Gate 1m
from House.
**Taxi:** Hawes Cars
0131 331 1077.
**Rail:** Dalmeny station 3m.

■ **Contact**
The Administrator
**Tel:** 0131 331 1888
**Fax:** 0131 331 1788
**E-mail:**
events@dalmeny.co.uk

■ **Opening Times**
**Summer**
1st Jun to 30 Jul on Sun -
Wed afternoons 2pm-5pm.
Entry by Guided Tours only.
Tours are 2.15pm and
3.30pm.

**Winter**
Open at other times by
appointment only.

■ **Admission**
**Summer**
| | |
|---|---|
| Adult | £9.50 |
| Child (14-16yrs) | £6.50 |
| OAP | £8.50 |
| Student | £8.50 |
| Groups (20+) | £8.50 |

# DALMENY HOUSE 🏠Ⓕ
www.dalmeny.co.uk

## Welcome to a family home which contains Scotland's finest French treasurers. Dine in splendor, and enjoy sea-views over superb parkland.

Dalmeny House rejoices in one of the most beautiful and unspoilt settings in Great Britain, yet it is only seven miles from Scotland's capital, Edinburgh, fifteen minutes from Edinburgh airport and less than an hour's drive from Glasgow. It is an eminently suitable venue for group visits, business functions, and special events, including product launches. Outdoor activities, such as off-road driving, can be arranged.

Dalmeny House, the family home of the Earls of Rosebery for over 300 years, boasts superb collections of porcelain and tapestries,

fine paintings by Gainsborough, Raeburn, Reynolds and Lawrence, together with the exquisite Mentmore Rothschild collection of 18th Century French furniture. There is also the Napoleonic collection, assembled by the 5th Earl of Rosebery, Prime Minister, historian and owner of three Derby winners.

The Hall, Library and Dining Room will lend a memorable sense of occasion to corporate receptions, luncheons and dinners. A wide range of entertainment can also be provided, from a clarsach player to a floodlit pipe band Beating the Retreat.

## KEY FACTS

**ℹ** Fashion shows, product launches, archery, clay pigeon shooting, shows, filming, background photography, and special events. Lectures on House, contents and family history. Helicopter landing area.

**☰** Conferences and functions, buffets, lunches, dinners.

**♿** WCs.

**☕**

**🚶** Obligatory. Special interest tours can be arranged outside normal opening hours.

**P** 60 cars, 3 coaches. Parking for functions in front of house.

**🐕** Dogs in grounds only.

**❄**

# HOPETOUN HOUSE 🏛️ⓕ

www.hopetoun.co.uk

## Hopetoun House is a unique gem of Europe's architectural heritage and undoutedly 'Scotland's Finest Stately Home'.

Situated on the shores of the Firth of Forth, it is one of the most splendid examples of the work of Scottish architects Sir William Bruce and William Adam. The interior of the house, with opulent gilding and classical motifs, reflects the aristocratic grandeur of the early 18th Century, whilst its magnificent parkland has fine views across the Forth to the hills of Fife. The house is approached from the Royal Drive, used only by members of the Royal Family, notably King George IV in 1822 and Her Majesty Queen Elizabeth II in 1988. Hopetoun is really two houses in one, the oldest part of the house was designed by Sir William Bruce and built between 1699 and 1707. It shows some of the finest examples in Scotland of carving, wainscotting and ceiling painting.

In 1721 William Adam started enlarging the house by adding the magnificent façade, colonnades and grand State apartments which were the focus for social life and entertainment in the 18th Century. The house is set in 100 acres of rolling parkland including fine woodland walks, the red deer park, the spring garden with a profusion of wild flowers, and numerous picturesque picnic spots. Hopetoun has been home of the Earls of Hopetoun, later created Marquesses of Linlithgow, since it was built in 1699 and in 1974 a charitable trust was created to preserve the house with its historic contents and surrounding landscape for the benefit of the public for all time.

## VISITOR INFORMATION

### ■ Owner
Hopetoun House Preservation Trust

### ■ Address
Hopetoun House
South Queensferry
Edinburgh
West Lothian
EH30 9SL

### ■ Location
Map 13:F7
**OS Ref. NT089 790**
2½m W of Forth Road Bridge. 12m W of Edinburgh (25 mins. drive). 34m E of Glasgow (50 mins. drive).

### ■ Contact
Maree Brown
**Tel:** 0131 331 2451
**Fax:** 0131 319 1885
**E-mail:** marketing@hopetoun.co.uk

### ■ Opening Times
**Summer**
Easter - End Sept; Daily, 10.30am-5pm. Last admission 4pm.

**Winter**
By appointment only for Groups (20+).

### ■ Admission
**House and Grounds**
| | |
|---|---|
| Adult | £9.20 |
| Child (5-16yrs)* | £4.90 |
| Conc/Student | £8.00 |
| Family (2+2) | £25.00 |
| Groups | £8.00 |

**Grounds only**
| | |
|---|---|
| Adult | £4.25 |
| Child (5-16yrs)* | £2.50 |
| Conc/Student | £3.70 |
| Family (2+2) | £11.50 |
| Groups | £3.70 |

**School Visits**
| | |
|---|---|
| Child | £5.50 |
| Teachers | Free |

*Under 5yrs Free. Winter group rates on request. Admission to Tearoom Free.

### ■ Special Events
**Horse Trials**
June 26-29
**Fireworks**
Nov 1
**Christmas Shopping Fayre**
Nov 14-16.

### Conference/Function

| ROOM | Size | Max Cap |
|---|---|---|
| Ballroom | 92' x 35' | 300 |
| Tapestry Rm | 37' x 24' | 150 |
| State Dining Rm | 39' x 23' | 20 |
| Stables | 92' x 22' | 200 |

## KEY FACTS

ℹ️ Private functions, special events, antiques fairs, concerts, Scottish gala evenings, conferences, wedding ceremonies and receptions, grand piano, helicopter landing. No smoking or flash photography in house.

🍽️ Receptions, gala dinners.

♿ Suitable. WCs.

🍴 Licensed.

🧑‍🏫 Obligatory. By arrangement.

🅿️ Close to the house for cars and coaches. Book if possible, allow 1-2hrs for visit (min).

📷 Special tours of house and/or grounds for different age/interest groups.

🐕 No dogs in house, on leads in grounds.

Edinburgh City, Coast & Countryside

## EDINBURGH CASTLE
### Castle Hill, Edinburgh EH1 2NG
www.edinburghcastle.gov.uk

Edinburgh Castle, built on an extinct volcano, dominates the skyline of Scotland's capital city. Attractions include: The Honours of Scotland, The Stone of Destiny, The Great Hall, Laich Hall and St Margaret's Chapel, Prisons of War Experience, National War Memorial, the famous One O'clock Gun - fired daily Mon-Sat.

**Location:** Map 13:G8. OS Ref NT252 736. At the top of the Royal Mile in Edinburgh **Owner:** Historic Scotland **Tel:** 0131 225 9846
**E-mail:** hs.explorer@scotland.gsi.gov.uk **Open:** 1 Apr-30 Sep 9.30am to 6pm. 1 Oct-31 Mar 9.30am to 5pm. Last tickets sold 1 hour before closing. Closed Christmas Day and Boxing Day. Visit the website for New Year opening times.
**Admission:** Adult £16.00 Conc £12.80 Child £9.60.
**Key facts:** ⓘ Disabled parking only, blue disabled badge required. ⬚ ⊤ Private evening hire. ⬚ WCs. ⬚ ⫴ ⨍ Regular tours included in admission price. Check website for details. ⬚ In 8 languages. ⬚ ⬚ Guide dogs only. ⬚ ⬚ ⬚ €

## LINLITHGOW PALACE
### Linlithgow, West Lothian EH49 7AL
www.historicscotland.gov.uk

The royal pleasure palace was the birthplace of Mary Queen of Scots. The high towers look down over the palaces grounds - the Peel - and Linlithgow Loch, an important refuge for wildlife. A ranger service operates on site. Visit the great hall where Monarchs hosted banquets tour James IV suite of chambers. Back by popular demand, our spectacular jousting event returns in the summer.
**Location:** Map 13:F8. OS Ref NS 996774. In Linlithgow off the M9.
**Owner:** Historic Scotland
**Tel:** 01506 842896
**E-mail:** hs.explorer@scotland.gsi.gov.uk
**Open:** 1 Apr-30 Sep 9.30am to 5.30pm. 1 Oct-31 Mar 9.30am to 4.30pm. Last ticket sold 45 minutes before closing.
**Admission:** Adult £5.50 Conc £4.40 Child £3.30.
**Key facts:** ⬚ ⬚ The ticket office, shop and courtyard are accessible to visitors with disabilities. ⬚ ℙ Parking is available at the cobbled entrance. ⬚ Booked in advance. ⬚ €

## GOSFORD HOUSE
### Longniddry, East Lothian EH32 0PX
www.gosfordhouse.co.uk

1791 the 7th Earl of Wemyss, aided by Robert Adam, built one of the grandest houses in Scotland, with a 'paradise' of lakes and pleasure grounds. New wings, including the celebrated Marble Hall were added in 1891 by William Young. The house has a fine collection of paintings and furniture.
**Location:** Map 14:17. OS Ref NT453 786. Off A198 2m NE of Longniddry.
**Owner/Contact:** The Earl of Wemyss
**Tel:** 01875 870201
**Open:** Please check www.gosfordhouse.co.uk for most up to date opening times/days.
**Admission:** Adult £6.00, Child under 16 Free.
**Key facts:** ⊤ ⨍ By arrangement. ℙ Limited for coaches. ⬚

Edinburgh Castle

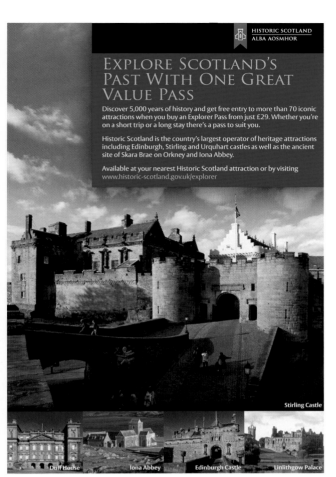

Stirling Castle

Duff House    Iona Abbey    Edinburgh Castle    Linlithgow Palace

© VisitBritain/Britain on View

# PALACE OF HOLYROODHOUSE
## Edinburgh EH8 8DX
### www.royalcollection.org.uk

The Palace of Holyroodhouse, the official residence of Her Majesty The Queen, stands at the end of the Royal Mile against the spectacular backdrop of Arthur's Seat. Visitors can explore Mary, Queen of Scots' historic chambers, the ten magnificent State Apartments used by The Queen, and the romantic ruins of Holyrood Abbey.

**Location:** Map 13:G8. OS Ref NT110 735. Central Edinburgh, end of Royal Mile. **Owner:** Official Residence of Her Majesty The Queen
**Contact:** Ticket Sales & Information Office
**Tel:** +44 (0)131 556 5100
**E-mail:** bookinginfo@royalcollection.org.uk
**Open:** Please see website for opening times.
**Admission:** Visit www.royalcollection.org.uk for details.
**Key facts:** Assistance dogs welcome.

---

### NEWLISTON
**Kirkliston, West Lothian EH29 9EB**
Late Robert Adam house. 18th Century designed landscape, rhododendrons, azaleas and water features. On Sundays there is a ride-on steam model railway from 2-5pm.
**Location:** Map 13:G8. OS Ref NT110 735. 9miles W of Edinburgh, 4miles S of Forth Road Bridge, off B800.
**Owner/Contact:** Mrs Caroline Maclachlan
**Tel:** 0131 333 3231
**Open:** 1 May–4 Jun: Wed–Sun, 2–6pm. Also by appointment.
**Admission:** Adult: £3.00, Children under 12: Free of charge.
**Key facts:** In grounds, on leads.

---

### AMISFIELD MAINS
**Nr Haddington, East Lothian EH41 3SA**
Georgian farmhouse with gothic barn and cottage. **Location:** Map 14:I8. OS Ref NT526 755. Between Haddington and East Linton on A199.
**Tel:** 01875 870201 **Fax:** 01875 870620
**Open:** Exterior only: By appointment, Wemyss and March Estates Office, Longniddry, East Lothian EH32 0PY. **Admission:** Please contact for details.

---

### ARNISTON HOUSE
**Gorebridge, Midlothian EH23 4RY**
Magnificent William Adam mansion started in 1726. Beautiful country setting beloved by Sir Walter Scott. **Location:** Map 13:H9. OS Ref NT326 595.
**Tel:** 01875 830515 **Website:** www.arniston-house.co.uk **Open:** May & Jun: Tue & Wed; 1 Jul-14 Sep: Tue, Wed & Sun, guided tours at 2pm & 3.30pm. Pre-arranged groups accepted. **Admission:** Adult £6.00, Child £3.00, Conc. £5.00.

---

### BEANSTON
**Nr Haddington, East Lothian EH41 3SB**
Georgian farmhouse with Georgian orangery.
**Location:** Map 14:I8. OS Ref NT450 766. Between Haddington and East Linton on A199. **Tel:** 01875 870201 **Open:** Exterior only: By appointment, Wemyss and March Estates Office, Longniddry, East Lothian EH32 0PY.
**Admission:** Please contact for details.

---

### HARELAW FARMHOUSE
**Nr Longniddry, East Lothian EH32 0PH**
Early 19th Century 2-storey farmhouse built as an integral part of the steading. Dovecote over entrance arch. **Location:** Map 14:I8. OS Ref NT450 766. Between Longniddry and Drem on B1377. **Tel:** 01875 870201
**Open:** Exteriors only: By appointment, Wemyss and March Estates Office, Longniddry, East Lothian EH32 0PY. **Admission:** Please contact for details.

---

### RED ROW
**Aberlady, East Lothian EH32 0DE**
Terraced Cottages **Location:** Map 14:I7. OS Ref NT464 798. Main Street, Aberlady, East Lothian.
**Tel:** 01875 870201 **Fax:** 01875 870620
**Open:** Exterior only. By appointment, Wemyss and March Estates Office, Longniddry, East Lothian EH32 0PY. **Admission:** Please contact for details.

Corehouse

## NEW LANARK WORLD HERITAGE SITE
### New Lanark Mills, S Lanarkshire  ML11 9DB
www.newlanark.org

Close to the famous Falls of Clyde, this cotton mill village c1785 became famous as the site of Robert Owen's radical reforms. Beautifully restored as a living community and attraction, the fascinating history of the village has been interpreted in New Lanark Visitor Centre.

**Location:** Map 13:E9. OS Ref NS880 426. 1m S of Lanark. Sat Nav code ML11 9BY. Bus service between Buchanan Bus Station in Glasgow and Lanark. Nearest train station is Lanark (1m). **Owner:** New Lanark Trust **Contact:** Trust Office **Tel:** 01555 661345 **E-mail:** visit@newlanark.org
**Open:** Open daily, 10–5pm Apr-Oct, 10–4pm Nov-Mar. Shops/catering open until 5pm daily. Closed 25 Dec and 1 Jan.
**Admission:** Visitor Centre: Adult £8.50, Conc. (senior/student) £7.00, Child £6.00. Groups: 1 free/10 booked. **Key facts:** ⬛ ⊤ ⬛ Suitable. WC. ⬛ Licensed. ⬛ Licensed. ⬛ Obligatory. By arrangement. ⬛ P Cars & coaches. 5 min walk. ⬛ ⬛ Guide dogs. ⬛ Double, single & ensuite. ⬛ ⬛

## COREHOUSE 🏠℗
### Lanark  ML11 9TQ
Designed by Sir Edward Blore and built in the 1820s, Corehouse is a pioneering example of the Tudor Architectural Revival in Scotland.
**Location:** Map 13:E9. OS Ref NS882 416. On S bank of the Clyde above village of Kirkfieldbank. **Tel:** 01555 663126 **Open:** 3-21 May & 6-17 Sep: Sat–Wed. Tours: weekdays: 1 & 2pm, weekends: 2 & 3pm. Closed Thurs & Fri.
**Admission:** Adult £7.00, Child (under 16yrs)/OAP £4.00.

New Lanark World Heritage Site

# SCONE PALACE & GROUNDS 🏛 Ⓕ
www.scone-palace.co.uk

## Scone Palace is home to the Earls of Mansfield and is built on the site of an ancient abbey.

1500 years ago it was the capital of the Pictish kingdom and the centre of the ancient Celtic church. In the intervening years, it has been the seat of parliaments and crowning place of Scottish kings, including Macbeth, Robert the Bruce and Charles II. The State Rooms house a superb collection of objets d'art, including 17th and 18th Century ivories, mostly collected by the fourth Earl of Mansfield. Notable works of art are also on display, including paintings by Sir David Wilkie, Sir Joshua Reynolds, and Johann Zoffany. The Library boasts one of Scotland's finest collections of porcelain, including Sèvres, Ludwigsburg and Meissen, whilst the unique 'Vernis Martin' papier mâché may be viewed in the Long Gallery. An audio visual presentation explores centuries of Scone's history.

### Gardens
The grounds of the Palace house magnificent collections of shrubs, with woodland walks through the Wild Garden containing David Douglas' original fir and the unique Murray Star Maze. An informative pavilion dedicated to Douglas and other Scottish plant hunters is situated in the Pinetum. New for 2014 we are developing a Kitchen Garden to supply our Old Servants' Hall Coffee Shop. There are Highland cattle and peacocks to admire and an adventure play area for children. The 100 acres of mature Policy Parks, flanked by the River Tay, are available for a variety of events, including weddings, corporate and private entertaining.

We also hold events and activities such as receptions, fashion shows, war games, archery, clay pigeon shooting, equestrian events, garden parties, shooting, fishing, floodlit tattoos, highland games, parkland, helicopter landing, croquet, racecourse, polo field, firework displays and adventure playground.

## KEY FACTS

ℹ️ No photography in state rooms.

🏠 Gift shop and food shop.

🖼 Grand dinners in state rooms (inc. buffets and cocktail parties).

♿ WCs.

🍴 By Arrangement. Guides in each room. Private tours.

🅿️ 300 cars and 15 coaches (coaches - booking preferable). Couriers/drivers free meal and admittance.

🎦 Welcome.

🐕 Dogs in grounds only.

🔔 By Appointment.

## VISITOR INFORMATION

### ■ Owner
The Earl of Mansfield

### ■ Address
Scone Palace
Perth
PH2 6BD

### ■ Location
Map 13:G5
OS Ref. NO114 266
From Edinburgh Forth Bridge M90, A93 1hr.
**Bus:** Regular buses from Perth.
**Road:** M90 from Edinburgh.
**Taxi:** 01738 444000
**Rail:** Perth Station 3m.

### ■ Contact
The Administrator
**Tel:** 01738 552300
**Fax:** 01738 552588
**E-mail:** visits@
scone-palace.co.uk

### ■ Opening Times
**Summer**
1st Apr-31st Oct.
Gates open at 9.30am-last admission 5.00pm, Mon-Fri and Sun.
9.30am-last admission 4.00pm, Sat.
**Winter**
Free Grounds admission each Fri, Sat and Sun from November-March. Coffee Shop and Food Shop Open.
Please check our website for details of Winter Events.

### ■ Admission
**Palace & Grounds**
| | |
|---|---|
| Adult | £10.50 |
| Conc. | £9.80 |
| Child (5-16yrs) | £7.60 |
| Family | £33.00 |

**Groups (20+)**
| | |
|---|---|
| Adult | £9.80 |
| Conc. | £8.30 |
| Child (5-16yrs) | £7.60 |

**Grounds only**
| | |
|---|---|
| Adult | £6.30 |
| Conc. | £5.70 |
| Child (5-16yrs) | £4.40 |
| Family | £20.00 |
| Private Guide | £60.00 |

Season tickets are available.

### ■ Special Events
**2014 Events**
**Potfest - International Ceramics Festival:**
6th-8th June
**The GWCT Scottish Game Fair:**
4th-6th July
**80s Rewind Festival:**
18th-21st July
**Chilli Festival:**
21st-22nd September

For details of our 2013 event programme please visit www.scone-palace.co.uk and www.facebook.com/sconepalace.
All information correct at time of going to print.

### ■ Conference/Function
| ROOM | Size | Max Cap |
|---|---|---|
| Long Gallery | 140' x 20' | 200 |
| Queen Victoria's Rm | 20' x 20' | 20 |
| Balvaird Rm | 29' x 22' | 50/60 |
| Tullibardine | 19' x 23' | 40/50 |

## DRUMMOND CASTLE GARDENS 🏛Ⓕ
### Muthill, Crieff, Perthshire PH7 4HZ
www.drummondcastlegardens.co.uk

Scotland's most important formal gardens. The Italianate parterre is revealed from a viewpoint at the top of the terrace. First laid out in the 17th Century and renewed in the 1950s. The perfect setting to stroll amongst the manicured plantings and absorb the atmosphere of this special place.

**Location:** Map 13:E5. OS Ref NN844 181. 2m S of Crieff off the A822.
**Owner:** Grimsthorpe & Drummond Castle Trust A registered charity
**Contact:** The Caretaker
**Tel:** 01764 681433
**Fax:** 01764 681642
**E-mail:** thegardens@drummondcastle.sol.co.uk
**Open:** Easter weekend, 1 May-31 Oct: Daily, 1-6pm. Last admission 5pm.
**Admission:** Adult £5.00, Child £2.00 Conc. £4.00, Groups (20+) 10% discount. **Key facts:** 🔲 🔄 Partial. WCs. 🔣 By arrangement. 🅿 🔄 Dogs on leads only. 🔳

## GLAMIS CASTLE & GARDENS 🏛Ⓕ
### Glamis By Forfar, Angus DD8 1RJ
www.glamis-castle.co.uk

Glamis Castle is the family home of the Earls of Strathmore and Kinghorne, and has been a royal residence since 1372. It was the childhood home of Her Majesty Queen Elizabeth The Queen Mother, the birthplace of HRH Princess Margaret and the legendary setting of Shakespeare's play Macbeth.

**Location:** Map 13:H4. OS Ref NO386 480. Off A94.
**Owner:** The Earl of Strathmore & Kinghorne
**Contact:** Doreen Stout **Tel:** 01307 840393
**Fax:** 01307 840733 **E-mail:** enquiries@glamis-castle.co.uk
**Open:** Apr-Oct, daily; 10-6pm, last admission 4.30pm. Nov-Mar groups and private tours welcome by prior arrangement.
**Admission:** Please see website for details.
**Key facts:** ℹ Visit website for details. 🔲 🔣 🔅 🔄 WCs. 🔳 Licensed. 🔟 Licensed. 🔣 🅿 Cars and coaches. 🔳 🔄 Grounds only. Guide dogs only. 🔺 ❄ By appointment Jan-Mar. 🔳 €

Scone Palace

## BALCARRES
**Colinsburgh, Fife  KY9 1HN**

16th Century tower house with 19th Century additions by Burn and Bryce. Woodland and terraced gardens.

**Location:** Map 14:I6. OS Ref NO475 044. ½m N of Colinsburgh.
**Owner:** Balcarres Heritage Trust
**Contact:** Lord Balniel
**Tel:** 01333 340520
**Open:** Woodland & Gardens: 1 Mar-30 Sep, 2-5pm. House not open except by written appointment and 1-30 Apr, excluding Sun.
**Admission:** House £6.00, Garden £6.00. House & Garden £10.
**Key facts:** 🔲 Partial. 🔳 By arrangement. 🐾 Dogs on leads only.

## CORTACHY ESTATE
**Cortachy, Kirriemuir, Angus  DD8 4LX**

Countryside walks including access through woodlands to Airlie Monument on Tulloch Hill with spectacular views of the Angus Glens and Vale of Strathmore. Footpaths are waymarked and colour coded.  **Location:** Map 13:H3. OS Ref N0394 596. Off the B955 Glens Road from Kirriemuir.  **Owner:** Trustees of Airlie Estates
**Contact:** Estate Office  **Tel:** 01575 570108  **Fax:** 01575 540400
**E-mail:** office@airlieestates.com  **Website:** www.airlieestates.com
**Open:** Walks all year. Gardens 18 -21 Apr; 5 and 12 May-1 Jun inclusive; 4 and 25 Aug. Last admission 3.30pm.
**Admission:** Please contact estate office for details.
**Key facts:** 🔳 The estate network of walks are open all year round. The gardens and grounds can be hired for the location and setting of wedding ceremonies and photographs. 🔲 🔳 Unsuitable. 🔳 By arrangement. 🅿 Limited.
🐾 Dogs on leads only. 🏛 Licensed to hold Civil Weddings and can offer wedding receptions, either a marquee in the grounds or a reception within the Castle. 🔳

## CHARLETON HOUSE
**Colinsburgh, Leven, Fife  KY9 1HG**

**Location:** Map 14:I6. OS Ref NO464 036. Off A917. 1m NW of Colinsburgh. 3m NW of Elie.
**Tel:** 01333 340249 **Fax:** 01333 340583
**Open:** 30 Aug-28 Sep: daily, 12 noon-3pm. Guided tours obligatory, admission every ½hr. **Admission:** £12.00.

## GLENEAGLES
**Auchterarder, Perthshire  PH3 1PJ**

Gleneagles has been the home of the Haldane family since the 12th Century. The 18th Century pavilion is open to the public by written appointment.
**Location:** Map 13:F6. OS Ref NS931 088. 0.75 miles S of A9 on A823. 2.5m S of Auchterarder.
**Tel:** 01764 682388 **Open:** By written appointment only.

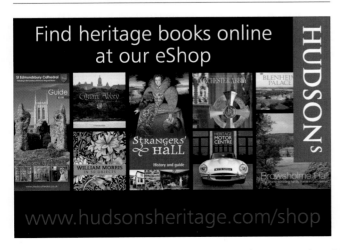

Glamis Castle

## MONZIE CASTLE 🏛ⓔ
**Crieff, Perthshire  PH7 4HD**

Built in 1791. Destroyed by fire in 1908 and rebuilt and furnished by Sir Robert Lorimer. **Location:** Map 13:E5. OS Ref NN873 244. 2miles NE of Crieff.
**Tel:** 01764 653110 **Open:** 17 May-15 Jun: daily, 2-4.30pm. By appointment at other times. **Admission:** Adult £5.00, Child £1.00. Group rates available, contact property for details.

## STRATHTYRUM HOUSE & GARDENS 🏛
**St Andrews, Fife  KY16 9SF**

**Location:** Map 14:I5. OS Ref NO490 172. Entrance from the St Andrews/Guardbridge Road which is signposted when open. **Tel:** 01334 473600
**E-mail:** info@strathtyrumhouse.com **Website:** www.strathtyrumhouse.com
**Open:** 5-9 May, 2-6 Jun, 7-11 Jul, 4-8 Aug, 1-5 Sep: 2-4pm. Guided tours at 2pm and 3pm. **Admission:** Adult £5.00, Child + Concessions £2.50.

## TULLIBOLE CASTLE
**Crook Of Devon, Kinross  KY13 0QN**

Scottish tower house c1608 with ornamental fishponds, a roofless lectarn doocot, 9th Century graveyard. **Location:** Map 13:F6. OS Ref NO540 888. B9097 1m E of Crook of Devon. **Tel:** 01577 840236 **E-mail:** visit@tulbol.demon.co.uk **Website:** www.tulbol.demon.co.uk **Open:** Last week in Aug-30 Sep: Tue-Sun, 1-4pm.
**Admission:** Adult £5.50, Child/Conc. £3.50. Free for Doors Open weekend.

West Highlands & Islands, Loch Lomond, Stirling and Trossachs

# INVERARAY CASTLE & GARDEN

www.inveraray-castle.com

## Inveraray Castle & Garden - Home to the Duke & Duchess of Argyll and ancestral home of the Clan Campbell.

The ancient Royal Burgh of Inveraray lies about 60 miles north west of Glasgow by Loch Fyne in an area of spectacular natural beauty. The ruggedness of the highland scenery combines with the sheltered tidal loch, beside which nestles the present Castle built between 1745 and 1790. The Castle is home to the Duke and Duchess of Argyll. The Duke is head of the Clan Campbell and his family have lived in Inveraray since the early 15th Century. Designed by Roger Morris and decorated by Robert Mylne, the fairytale exterior belies the grandeur of its gracious interior. The Clerk of Works, William Adam, father of Robert and John, did much of the laying out of the present Royal Burgh, which is an unrivalled example of an early planned town. Visitors enter the famous Armoury Hall containing some 1,300 pieces including

Brown Bess muskets, Lochaber axes, 18th Century Scottish broadswords, and can see preserved swords from the Battle of Culloden. The fine State Dining Room and Tapestry Drawing Room contain magnificent French tapestries made especially for the Castle, fabulous examples of Scottish, English and French furniture and a wealth of other works of art. The unique collection of china, silver and family artifacts spans the generations which are identified by a genealogical display in the Clan Room.

The castle's private garden which was opened to the public in 2010 for the first time is also not to be missed, especially in springtime with it's stunning displays of rhododendrons and azaleas.

## KEY FACTS

ℹ️ No flash photography. Guide books in French and German translations.

♿ Partial. WCs.

🍴 Licensed.

👥 Available for up to 100 people at no additional cost. Groups please book. Tour time: 1 hr.

🅿️ 100 cars. Car/coach park close to Castle.

🎒 ?3.50 per child. A guide can be provided. Areas of interest include a woodland walk.

🐕 Guide dogs only.

# MOUNT STUART 🏛ⓕ
## ISLE OF BUTE  PA20 9LR
### www.mountstuart.com

One of the World's finest houses - Mount Stuart, ancestral home of the Marquess of Bute, is a stupendous example of Victorian Gothic architecture set amidst 300 acres of gloriously landscaped gardens. Spectacular interiors include the stunning White Marble Chapel and magnificent Marble Hall complete with kaleidoscopic stained glass. A Fine Art Collection and astounding architectural detail presents both stately opulence and unrivalled imagination. With something for all the family, this Award winning Visitor Attraction offers excellent restaurant facilities, Gift Shop, Tearooms, way-marked walks, picnic areas, Adventure Play Area and Contemporary Visual Arts Exhibition.

**Location:** Map 13:A9. OS Ref NS100 600. SW coast of Scotland, 5 miles S of Rothesay.
**Owner:** Mount Stuart Trust  **Contact:** Mount Stuart Office
**Tel:** 01700 503877  **Fax:** 01700 505313
**E-mail:** contactus@mountstuart.com
**Open:** Please our website for 2014 opening times.
**Admission:** Please see our website for up-to-date information.
**Key facts:** ⓘ No photography. 🔲🔲🔲🔲 Suitable. 🔲🔲🔲 🅿 Ample. 🔲
🔲🔲 Exclusive - House/Self Catering - Grounds. 🔲🔲

Stirling Castle

Sea Room at Duart Castle

## DUART CASTLE 🏠Ⓕ
### Isle Of Mull, Argyll  PA64 6AP
www.duartcastle.com

The Castle of the Clan Maclean. Brought back from ruin in 1911, the sentinel Clan home proudly guards the sea cliffs of the Isle of Mull. Explore the ancient Keep, ghostly Dungeons, magnificent Banqueting Hall, Edwardian State Rooms and breathtaking views from the Battlements. Homegrown, homemade cakes and savouries are available in the Castle Tearoom and Gift Shop. Most recently made famous by the film "Entrapment" (1999) with Sean Connery.

**Location:** Map 12:O4. OS Ref NM750 350. Off A849, 3.5 miles from Craignure Ferry Terminal, eastern side of Isle of Mull.

**Owner/Contact:** Sir Lachlan Maclean Bt

**Tel:** +44(0)1680 812309 **E-mail:** guide@duartcastle.com

**Open:** Castle & Tearoom open 1 April Sun-Thur 11am-4pm. Daily from 1 May (inc. Shop) 10.30am-5pm. Castle closes 18 Oct (Tearoom & Shop close 11 Oct)

**Admission:** Adult: £5.75, Child (4-15) £2.85, Conc. £5.10, Family (2+2) £14.35. **Key facts:** 🛍 Duart Shop/Maclean Gifts. 🔳 Unsuitable in areas. 📷 Duart Tearoom/Homemade baking. 🎟 Guided Tours available. 🅿 50m from Castle. 🔳 🐕 Dogs welcome. 🔔 Weddings available at Duart. 🔳

## ARDENCRAIG GARDENS
### Ardencraig, Rothesay, Isle Of Bute, West Highlands  PA20 9ZE

Walled garden, greenhouses, aviaries. Woodland walk from Rothesay 1 mile (Skippers Wood.)

**Location:** Map 13:A8. OS Ref NS105 645. 2m from Rothesay

**Owner:** Argyll and Bute Council

**Contact:** Joe McCabe

**Tel:** 01700 504644

**Open:** Mon-Thurs 9pm-4pm. Fri 9pm-3:30pm. Sat and Sun 1pm-4:30pm.

**Admission:** Free.

**Key facts:** 🔳 🔳 WCs. 🎟 By arrangement. 🅿 🔳 🐕 Guide dogs only.

## STIRLING CASTLE 🔔
### Stirling  FK8 1EJ
www.stirlingcastle.gov.uk

Experience the newly refurbished Royal Palace where you can explore the richly decorated King's and Queen's apartments. Other highlights include the Great Hall, Chapel Royal, Regimental Museum, Tapestry Studio and the Great Kitchens. Don't miss our guided tour where you can hear tales of the castle's history.

**Location:** Map 13:E7. OS Ref NS790 941. Leave the M9 at junction 10. and follow road signs for the castle.

**Owner:** Historic Scotland

**Tel:** 01786 450 000 **E-mail:** hs.explorer@scotland.gsi.gov.uk

**Open:** 1 Apr-30 Sep. 9.30am- 6pm. 1 Oct-31 Mar 9.30am to 5pm. Last ticket is sold 45 minutes before closing. Visit website for New Year opening times.

**Admission:** Adult £14.00, Concessions £11.00, Child £7.50.

**Key facts:** 🛍 🔳 Private hire. 🔳 Partial. WCs. 📷 Licensed. 🍽 Licensed. 🎟 Obligatory. 🔳 🅿 Limited for coaches. Car parking is available £4.00. 🔳 🐕 Guide dogs only. 🔳 🔳 €

## ARDUAINE GARDEN 🏆
### Arduaine, Oban  PA34 4XQ

This tranquil garden oasis can surprise and delight visitors all year. In spring and summer, the renowned rhododendrons attract enthusiasts from far and wide. Azaleas, magnolias and other beautiful plants fill the garden with scent and colour and the magnificent perennial collection flowers well into autumn.

**Location:** Map 12:O6. OS Ref NM794103. Off A816, 20 miles south of Oban/19 miles north of Lochgilphead.

**Owner:** The National Trust for Scotland  **Contact:** Property manager

**Tel:** 0844 493 2216 **E-mail:** information@nts.org.uk

**Website:** www.nts.org.uk

**Open:** Garden open all year. Reception centre Apr to Sep.

**Admission:** Please visit our website or call us for admission prices.

**Key facts:** ℹ Refreshments available in adjacent Loch Melfort Hotel. 📷 Licensed. 🍽 🅿 🐕 Guide dogs only. 🔳 Accommodation available in adjacent Loch Melfort Hotel. 🔳 Garden open all year 9.30 to sunset.

## ARDTORNISH GARDENS
### Ardtornish, Morvern, Argyll  PA80 5UZ

30 acres of garden including over 200 species of rhododendron, extensive planting for year round interest. **Location:** Map 12:O4. OS Ref NM702 472. In Ardtornish (Highland region, nr Loch Aline) which is just off the A884 to Mull.

**Tel:** 01967 421 288 **Website:** www.ardtornishgardens.co.uk

**Open:** Mar - Nov, Mon - Sun, 9am - 6pm.

## CASTLE STALKER
### Portnacroish, Appin, Argyll  PA38 4BL

Early 15th Century tower house and seat of the Stewarts of Appin. Set on an islet 400 yds off the shore of Loch Linnhe. **Location:** Map 12:P3. OS Ref NM930 480.

**Tel:** 01631 730354 **E-mail:** rossallward@madasafish.com

**Website:** www.castlestalker.com **Open:** 12-16 May; 26-30 May; 9-13 June; 7-11 July and 25-29 Aug. Phone for app. **Admission:** Adult £12.50, Child £5.00.

## CRATHES CASTLE, GARDEN & ESTATE ♛
### Banchory, Aberdeenshire  AB31 3QJ
#### www.nts.org.uk

Fairytale-like turrets, gargoyles of fantastic design and the ancient Horn of Leys given in 1323 by Robert the Bruce are just a few of the features of this historic castle. The Crathes gardens and estates are ideal for a family day out.
A delight at any time of year, the famous gardens feature great yew hedges and a colourful double herbaceous border. Further afield the 595-acre estate offers six separate trails to enjoy.

**Location:** Map 17:D12. OS Ref NO735 967.
On A93, 3 miles east of Banchory. AB31 5QJ
**Owner:** The National Trust for Scotland
**Tel:** 0844 493 2166
**E-mail:** information@nts.org.uk
**Open:** Please see website for opening times.
**Admission:** Please see our website or call us for up to date prices.
**Key facts:** 🖻
🍴 ♨

## DELGATIE CASTLE
### Turriff, Aberdeenshire  AB53 5TD
#### www.delgatiecastle.com

'Best Visitor Experience' Award Winner. Dating from 1030 the Castle is steeped in Scottish history yet still has the atmosphere of a lived in home. It has some of the finest painted ceilings in Scotland, Mary Queen of Scots' bed-chamber. Clan Hay Centre. Scottish Home Baking Award Winner. Victorian Christmas Fayre last weekend November and first weekend December. The castle is decorated throughout with decorations, Christmas trees and much more. Santa is here for the children with a pre-christmas present, crafters in many of the rooms throughout the Castle, staff in period costume.

**Location:** Map 17:D9. OS Ref NJ754 506. Off A947 Aberdeen to Banff Road.
**Owner:** Delgatie Castle Trust  **Contact:** Mrs Joan Johnson
**Tel:** 01888 563479  **E-mail:** joan@delgatiecastle.com
**Open:** Daily, 10am-5pm. Closed from the 20 Dec and reopens 8 Jan.
**Admission:** Adult £8.00, Child/Conc. £5.00, Family £21.00 (2 Adults & 2 Children), Groups (10+): £5.00.
B&B in Symbister apartment £50 per person per night.
**Key facts:** ℹ️ No photography. 🖻 📟 🖻 WCs. 🍴 🔲 🔲 By arrangement. 🅿️
🔲 🔲 Guide dogs only. 🏠 6 x houses for self catering. ❋ ♨

Drum Castle

## DUFF HOUSE
### Banff AB45 3SX
www.duffhouse.org.uk

One of the finest houses built in Scotland, Duff House is a magnificent Georgian mansion designed by William Adam. Standing in extensive parkland, today it houses a beautiful collection of paintings and furniture on loan from the National Galleries of Scotland. The setting is impressively situated amid lawns fringed by woodland and enchanting follies.

**Location:** Map 17:D8. OS Ref NJ 690 633. Off the A97
**Owner:** Historic Scotland
**Tel:** 01261 818181
**E-mail:** hs.explorer@scotland.gsi.gov.uk
**Open:** 1 Apr-31 Oct. Open daily 11am-5pm. 1 Nov-31 Mar. Open Thurs-Sun 11am-4pm.
**Admission:** Adult £7.10, Concession £5.70, Child £4.30 Exhibition only £4.40.
**Key facts:** ⬛ 🔲 Lift available.
💻 🅿️ 🖥 ✂ ❄

## CRAIGSTON CASTLE ▥
**Turriff, Aberdeenshire AB53 5PX**

Built between 1604 and 1607 by John Urquhart Tutor of Cromarty. Two wings were added in the early 1700s. The beautiful sculpted balcony, unique in Scottish architecture, depicts a piper, two grinning knights and David and Goliath. Remarkable carved oak, panels of Scottish kings' biblical heroes, originally from the family seat at Cromarty castle on the Black Isle were mounted in doors and shutters in the early 17th Century. The house is a private home and is still owned and lived in by the Urquhart family.

**Location:** Map 17:D8. OS Ref NJ762 550. On B9105, 4.5m NE of Turriff.
**Owner:** William Pratesi Urquhart **Contact:** The Housekeeper
**Tel:** 01261 839014 **E-mail:** wu-gen01@craigston.co.uk
**Open:** Sat May 10-Sun May 25 (inclusive) 1-3 pm. Sat Oct 18-Mon Oct 27 (inclusive) 1-3 pm. Groups by appointment throughout year. **Admission:** Adult £6.00, Child £2.00, Conc. £4.00. Groups: Adult £5.00, Child/School £1.00.
**Key facts:** 🔲 Very limited wheelchair access. 🔲 Obligatory. 🅿️ 🖥 ✂

## CRIMONMOGATE
**Lonmay, Fraserburgh, Aberdeenshire AB43 8SE**

Situated in Aberdeenshire, Crimonmogate is a Grade A listed mansion house and one of the most easterly stately homes in Scotland, it is now owned by William and Candida, Viscount and Viscountess Petersham. Pronounced 'Crimmon-moggat', this exclusive country house stands within beautiful and seasonally-changing parkland and offers one of Aberdeenshire's most outstanding and unusual venues for corporate events, parties, dinners and weddings.

**Location:** Map 17:F8. OS Ref NK043 588.
**Owner/Contact:** Lord Petersham **Tel:** 01346 532401
**E-mail:** info@cmg-events.co.uk
**Open:** 1-8 May. 18-30 June. Aug 27-1 Sep. Tours at 10.30, 11.30, and 12.30, or by appointment.
**Admission:** Adult £7.00, Conc. £6.00, Child £5.00. Max of 12 at any one time, guided tours only.
**Key facts:** 🔲 Weddings & special events: max 60 in hall & up to 200 in Marquee. 🔲 Only the principal rooms are part of the tour. ✂ No dogs. ⬛ ▥

## BALFLUIG CASTLE
**Alford, Aberdeenshire AB33 8EJ**

Small 16th Century tower house, restored in 1967. Its garden and wooded park are surrounded by farmland.
**Location:** Map 17:D11. OS Ref NJ586 151. Alford, Aberdeenshire.
**Tel:** 020 7624 3200
**Open:** Please write to M I Tennant Esq, 30 Abbey Gardens, London NW8 9AT.

## CRAIG CASTLE
**Rhynie, Huntly, Aberdeenshire AB54 4LP**

The Castle, a Gordon stronghold for 300 years; built round a courtyard and consists of a 16th Century L-shaped Keep, a Georgian house and an 19th Century addition. **Location:** Map 17:C10. OS Ref NJ472 259. 3m W of Rhynie and Lumsden on B9002. **Tel:** 01464 861705 **Open:** May-Sep: Wed & every 2nd weekend in each month, 2-5pm. **Admission:** Adult £5.00, Child £1.00.

## DRUMMUIR CASTLE
**Drummuir, By Keith, Banffshire AB55 5JE**

Castellated Victorian Gothic-style castle built in 1847 by Admiral Duff. 60ft high lantern tower with fine plasterwork, family portraits and interesting artefacts. **Location:** Map 17:B9. OS Ref NJ372 442. Between Keith and Dufftown, off the B9014. **Tel:** 01542 810332 **Open:** Sat 30 Aug-Sun 28 Sep: daily, 2-5pm (last tour 4.15pm). **Admission:** Adult £4.00, Child £2.50. Groups by arrangement.

## LICKLEYHEAD CASTLE
**Auchleven, Insch, Aberdeenshire AB52 6PN**

Beautifully restored Laird's Castle, built by the Leslies c1450, renovated in 1629 by John Forbes of Leslie. Boasts many interesting architectural features.
**Location:** Map 17:C10. OS Ref NJ628 237. 2m S of Insch on B992.
**Tel:** 01651 821276 **Open:** 6-9 May, 12-16 May, 19-23 May. Suns 22 & 29 Jun & Sats only from 5 Jul-2 Aug, 16 Aug-30 Aug. 12-2pm. **Admission:** Free.

Crathes Castle Gardens

# CAWDOR CASTLE 🏠Ⓕ
www.cawdorcastle.com

## A must see romantic fairy-tale Castle of historical beauty and one of the most outstanding Stately Homes in Scotland.

This splendid romantic castle, dating from the late 14th Century, was built as a private fortress by the Thanes of Cawdor, and remains the home of the Cawdor family to this day. The ancient medieval tower was built around the legendary holly tree. Although the house has evolved over 600 years, later additions, mainly of the 17th Century, were all built in the Scottish vernacular style with slated roofs over walls and crow-stepped gables of mellow local stone. This style gives Cawdor a strong sense of unity, and the massive, severe exterior belies an intimate interior that gives the place a surprisingly personal, friendly atmosphere. Good furniture, fine portraits and pictures, interesting objects and outstanding tapestries are arranged to please the family rather than to echo fashion or impress.

Memories of Shakespeare's Macbeth give Cawdor an elusive, evocative quality that delights visitors.

### Gardens

The flower garden also has a family feel to it, where plants are chosen out of affection rather than affectation. This is a lovely spot between spring and late summer. The walled garden has been restored with a holly maze, paradise garden, knot garden and thistle garden. The wild garden beside its stream leads into beautiful trails through spectacular mature mixed woodland, in which paths are helpfully marked and colour-coded. The Tibetan garden and traditional Scottish vegetable garden are at the Dower House at Auchindoune.

## VISITOR INFORMATION

### ■ Owner
The Dowager Countess Cawdor

### ■ Address
Cawdor Castle
Nairn
Scotland
IV12 5RD

### ■ Location
**Map 16:O9**
**OS Ref. NH850 500**
From Edinburgh A9, 3.5 hrs, Inverness 20 mins, Nairn 10 mins. Main road - A9, 14m.
**Bus:** Unfortunately there is no longer a bus service throughout the season but a service may be available from Inverness over the Scottish school holidays (TBC; check our website)
**Taxi:** Cawdor Taxis 01667 404315.
**Rail:** Nairn Station 5m.
**Air:** Inverness Airport 5m.

### ■ Contact
Administrator - Lorraine Thomson
**Tel:** 01667 404401
**Fax:** 01667 404674
**E-mail:** info@cawdorcastle.com

### ■ Opening Times
1st May - 5th Oct 2014
Daily 10am-5.30pm. Last admission 5pm.
Groups by appointment.

### ■ Admission
| | |
|---|---|
| Adult | £10.00 |
| Child (5-15yrs) | £6.50 |
| Senior Citizens and Disabled | £9.00 |
| Student | £9.00 |
| Family (2+5) | £29.00 |
| Gardens, Grounds and Nature Trails | £5.50 |

**Groups**
| | |
|---|---|
| Adult Groups (20+ people) | £8.75 |
| Child Groups (20+ children, 1 teacher/adult free) | £6.00 |
| Auchindoune Gardens (May - Jul only) | £3.00 |

### ■ Special Events
Check website for annual event programme.

## KEY FACTS

- 🛈 9 hole golf course, putting green, golf clubs for hire, conferences, whisky tasting, musical entertainment, specialised garden visits, private off-season tours. No photography, video taping or tripods inside. No large day sacks inside castle.

- 🛍 Gift, Highland and Wool shops.

- 🍽 Lunches, sherry/champagne receptions.

- ♿ Visitors may alight at the entrance. WC. Parts of the ground floor are accessible to wheelchair users and the gardens.

- ☕ Licensed Courtyard Cafe, May-Oct, groups should book.

- 🚶 By arrangement.

- 🅿 250 cars and 25 coaches.

- 🎒 £6.00 per child. Room notes, quiz and answer sheet can be provided.

- 🐕 Guide dogs only in castle and grounds. Dog walking trail available.

€

**Highlands & Skye**

## VISITOR INFORMATION

■ **Owner**
Hugh Macleod of Macleod

■ **Address**
Dunvegan Castle
Isle Of Skye
Scotland
IV55 8WF

■ **Location**
Map 15:F9
OS Ref. NG250 480
1m N of village. NW corner of Skye. Kyle of Lochalsh to Dunvegan via Skye Bridge.
**Rail:** Inverness to Kyle of Lochalsh
**Ferry:** Maillaig to Armadale

■ **Contact**
Janet Wallwork Clarke, Executive Director
**Tel:** 01470 521206
**Fax:** 01470 521205
**E-mail:**
info@dunvegancastle.com

■ **Opening Times**
**1 April - 15 October**
Daily 10am-5.30pm
Last admission 5pm
**16 October - 31 March**
Open by appointment weekdays only.
Castle and Gardens closed Christmas and New Year.

■ **Admission**
**Summer**
**Castle & Gardens**
| | |
|---|---|
| Adult | £10.00 |
| Child (5-15yrs) | £7.00 |
| Senior/Student/Group (Group min. 10 adults) | £8.00 |
| Family Ticket (2 Adults, 3 Children) | £28.00 |

**Gardens only**
| | |
|---|---|
| Adult | £8.00 |
| Child (5-15yrs) | £5.00 |
| Senior/Student/Group | £7.00 |

**Seal Boat Trips**
| | |
|---|---|
| Adult | £6.00 |
| Child (5-15yrs) | £4.00 |
| Senior/Student/Group | £5.00 |
| Infant (under 2yrs) | Free |

**Loch Cruises & Fishing Trips**
| | |
|---|---|
| Adult | £40.00 |
| Child (5-15yrs) | £30.00 |

Dunvegan Castle

# DUNVEGAN CASTLE & GARDENS 🏰Ⓕ
www.dunvegancastle.com

## Experience living history at Dunvegan Castle, the ancestral home of the Chiefs of Clan MacLeod for 800 years.

Any visit to the Isle of Skye is incomplete without savouring the wealth of history on offer at Dunvegan Castle & Gardens, the ancestral home of the Chiefs of Clan MacLeod for 800 years. Originally designed to keep people out, it was first opened to visitors in 1933 and is one of Skye's most famous landmarks. On display are many fine oil paintings and Clan treasures, the most famous of which is the Fairy Flag. Legend has it that this sacred Banner has miraculous powers and when unfurled in battle, the Clan MacLeod will defeat their enemies. Another of the castle's great treasures is the Dunvegan Cup, a unique 'mazer'

dating back to the Middle Ages. It was gifted by the O'Neils of Ulster as a token of thanks to one of the Clan's most celebrated Chiefs, Sir Rory Mor, for his support of their cause against the marauding forces of Queen Elizabeth I of England in 1596. Today visitors can enjoy tours of an extraordinary castle and Highland estate steeped in history and clan legend, delight in the beauty of its formal gardens, take a boat trip onto Loch Dunvegan to see the seal colony, enjoy an appetising meal at the MacLeods Table Café or browse in one of its four shops offering a wide choice to suit everyone.

## KEY FACTS

ℹ️ Boat trips to seal colony. Fishing trips and loch cruises. No photography in the castle.

🏪 Gift and craft shops.

♿ Partial. WCs.

🍽️ MacLeod Table Café (seats 76).

🧑‍🦯 By appointment. Self Guided.

🅿️ 120 cars and 10 coaches. If possible please book. Seal boat trip dependent upon weather.

🏫 Welcome by arrangement. Guide available on request.

🐕 Dogs on leads only.

🏡 3 self-catering holiday cottages in Castle grounds.

📷 Film & TV. A unique location for film, TV or advertising. Check website for details.

Dunvegan Castle Gardens

Boat Trips to Seal Colony

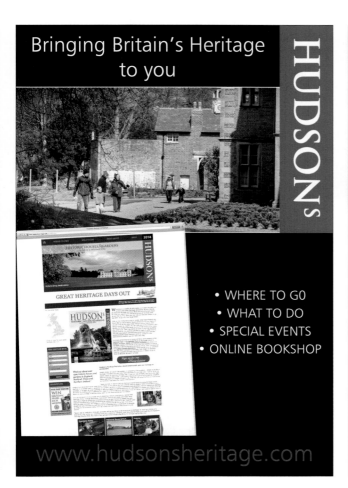

## CLAN DONALD SKYE
### Armadale, Sleat, Isle of Skye  IV45 8RS
www.clandonald.com

Be inspired by the magic of the restored historical gardens and walking trails threading through 40 acres of ancient woodland around the striking ruins of Armadale Castle. Discover 1500 years of the history and culture of the Highlands and the Isles in the award-winning Museum of the Isles. Explore your Scottish ancestry in the Museum's Study Centre.

**Location:** Map 15:H11. OS Ref NG633036. From Skye Bridge, 16 miles south of Broadford on the A851; or, take ferry from Mallaig to Amadale and follow signs. **Owner:** Clan Donald Lands Trust **Contact:** Mags Macdonald **Tel:** 01471 844305 **E-mail:** office@clandonald.com

**Open:** Apr-Oct, 9:30am-5:30pm. Nov-Mar, gardens open dawn to dusk; Museum & Study Centre by appointment. Please check our website for any changes.

**Admission:** Adults £8.00, Children & Conc. £6.50, Family (2 adults & 2 children) £25.00. Groups (10 or more) £6.50 per person. Children under 5 free.

**Key facts:** 2 shops featuring Scottish designers. Local cuisine. Various languages & visually impaired. 9 units; 4 - 6 persons each. All self-catering.

## CASTLE OF MEY
### Thurso, Caithness  KW14 8XH
www.castleofmey.org.uk

The home of The Queen Mother in Caithness. She bought the Castle in 1952, developed the gardens and it became her holiday home because of the beautiful surroundings and the privacy she was always afforded. There is a Visitor Centre with shop and tearoom and an Animal Centre for children.

**Location:** Map 17:B2. OS Ref ND290 739. On A836 between Thurso and John O'Groats, just outside the village of Mey.

**Owner:** The Queen Elizabeth Castle of Mey Trust **Contact:** Shirley Farquhar **Tel:** 01847 851473 **Fax:** 01847 851475 **E-mail:** enquiries@castleofmey.org.uk

**Open:** 7 May-30 Sep: daily, 10.20am-last entries 4pm. Closed end of Jul early Aug. Check website or please telephone for details.

**Admission:** Adult £11.00, Child (5-16yrs) £6.50, Concession £9.75. Family £29.00. Booked groups (15+): £9.75. Gardens and grounds only: Adult £6.50. Garden and Grounds family ticket £19.00.

**Key facts:** No photography in the Castle. Partial. WCs. Licensed. By arrangement. Guide dogs only.

## DUNROBIN CASTLE
### Golspie, Sutherland  KW10 6SF
www.dunrobincastle.co.uk

Dates from the 13th Century with additions in the 17th, 18th and 19th Centuries. Wonderful furniture, paintings, library, ceremonial robes and memorabilia. Victorian museum in grounds with a fascinating collection including Pictish stones. Set in fine woodlands overlooking the sea. Magnificent formal gardens, one of few remaining French/Scottish formal parterres.

**Location:** Map 16:O6. OS Ref NC850 010. 50m N of Inverness on A9.

**Owner:** The Sutherland Dunrobin Trust **Contact:** Scott Morrison **Tel:** 01408 633177 **Fax:** 01408 634081 **E-mail:** info@dunrobincastle.co.uk

**Open:** 1 Apr–15 Oct: Apr, May, Sep and Oct, Mon-Sat, 10.30am-4.30pm, Sun, 12 noon-4.30pm. No Falconry on Suns. Jun, Jul and Aug, daily, 10.00am-5.00pm. Falconry displays every day. Last entry half an hour before closing. Falconry displays at 11.30am and 2pm.

**Admission:** Adult £10.50, Child £5.75, OAP/Student. £8.25, Family (2+3) £27.50. Groups (minimum 10): Rates on request. Rates include falconry display, museum and gardens. **Key facts:** Unsuitable for wheelchairs. By arrangement.

### IONA ABBEY ⌂
**Iona, Mull PA76 6SQ**
www.ionahistory.org.uk

This ancient holy place remains a vibrant centre of Christianity. Founded by St Columba in 563. Highlights include the abbey church, iconic high crosses, Columba's shrine and the site of the saints writing cell. New in 2013, visit the new Abbey Museum featuring the stunning redisplay of magnificent high crosses and stones.

**Location:** Map 12:L5. OS Ref NM 286245. on the island of Iona
**Tel:** 01681 700 512
**E-mail:** hs.explorer@scotland.gsi.gov.uk
**Open:** 1 Apr-30 Sep, 9.30am to 5.30pm 1 Oct-31 Mar, 9.30am to 4.30pm. Last ticket sold 30 min before closing time. Check website for any closures.
**Admission:** Adult £7.10, Concession £5.70, Child £4.30.
**Key facts:** 🖸 🔊 Check website for full information.
🎞 🖸 🅿 ❄ €

### URQUHART CASTLE ⌂
**Drumnadrochit, Loch Ness, Inverness-shire IV63 6XJ**
www.historic-scotland.gov.uk

Discover 1,000 years of drama, experience a glimpse of medieval life and enjoy stunning views over Loch Ness. Climb the Grant Tower that watches over the iconic loch. Peer into a miserable prison cell and imagine the splendid banquets staged in the great hall. A more comfortable view of the iconic ruin against a backdrop of lock ness and the hills of the great glen can be enjoyed from the cafe. **Location:** Map 16:M10. OS Ref NH2908 5150. On Loch Ness near Drumnadrochit
**Owner:** Historic Scotland
**Tel:** 01456 450551
**E-mail:** hs.explorer@scotland.gsi.gov.uk
**Open:** 1 Apr-30 Sep 9.30am-6pm. 1-31 Oct 9.30am-5pm. 1 Nov-31 Mar 9.30am to 4.30pm. Last entry 45 minutes before closing.
**Admission:** Adult £7.90, Concession £6.40, Child £4.80.
**Key facts:** ⓘ Disability buggies are available. Photographic guide for those who have mobility difficulties. 🖸 🖻 🅿 🎞 ❄

### BALLINDALLOCH CASTLE 🏠ⓔ
**Ballindalloch, Banffshire AB37 9AX**

Ballindalloch Castle has been occupied by its original family, the Macpherson-Grants, since 1546. Filled with memorabilia, 17th Century Spanish paintings, china, furniture and family photographs. Beautiful rock and rose gardens, a grass labyrinth and river walks. The estate is home to the famous Aberdeen-Angus cattle breed. A superb family day out. **Location:** Map 17:A9. OS Ref NJ178 366. 14m NE of Grantown-on-Spey on A95. 22m S of Elgin on A95.
**Owner:** Mr & Mrs Oliver Russell **Contact:** Mrs Clare Russell
**Tel:** 01807 500205 **E-mail:** enquiries@ballindallochcastle.co.uk
**Website:** www.ballindallochcastle.co.uk
**Open:** Good Fri-30 Sep: 10.30am-4.45pm (last entry). Closed on Sats (except Easter Sat). Coaches outwith season by arrangement.
**Admission:** Castle & Grounds: Adult £10.00, Child (6-16) £5.00, OAP £8.00, Family (2+3) £25.00, Season Ticket £35.00. Grounds Only: Adults £5.00, Children £2.50, OAP £4.00. **Key facts:** 🖸 🅣 Please enquire. 🔊 Partial. 🖻 🖸 Short film. 🅿 Cars & coaches. 🎞 Designated area

### THE DOUNE OF ROTHIEMURCHUS
**By Aviemore PH22 1QP**

The family home of the Grants of Rothiemurchus since 1560, described by Elizabeth Grant, (born 1797), in 'Memoirs of a Highland Lady is stunningly situated beside the River Spey. Visit partial restoration, exterior & grounds or the Ranger led 'Highland Lady Experience' includes completed rooms.
**Location:** Map 16:P11. OS Ref NH900 100. 2m S of Aviemore.
**Owner:** John Grant of Rothiemurchus, Earl of Dysart
**Contact:** Rothiemurchus Centre open daily 9.30–5.30 **Tel:** 01479 812345
**E-mail:** info@rothie.net **Website:** www.rothiemurchus.net
**Open:** Exhibition: two partly restored rooms, exterior and grounds: Apr-Aug: Mon 10-12.30pm and 2-4.30pm (or dusk) and first Mon in the month, Sep–Dec, Feb & Mar. House: Wed as part of Highland Lady Experience (booking essential) or by special arrangement excl. Xmas and New Year. Groups by arrangement.
**Admission:** Restoration and grounds, voluntary charitable donation; Ranger led Tours:£30.00pp (min 2 people) 2 hours; Specialist groups: on application.
**Key facts:** ⓘ 🖸 🎞 Obligatory. 🅿 Limited.

### EILEAN DONAN CASTLE 🏠
**Dornie, Kyle Of Lochalsh, Wester Ross IV40 8DX**

A fortified site for eight hundred years, Eilean Donan now represents one of Scotland's most iconic images. Located at the point where three great sea lochs meet amidst stunning highland scenery on the main road to Skye. Spiritual home of Clan Macrae with century old links to Clan Mackenzie.
**Location:** Map 16:J10. OS Ref NG880 260. On A87 8m E of Skye Bridge.
**Contact:** David Win - Castle Keeper
**Tel:** 01599 555202
**E-mail:** eileandonan@btconnect.com
**Website:** www.eileandonancastle.com
**Open:** Open 1 Mar - 31 Oct.
**Admission:** Adult £6.50, Concession £5.50, Family £16.50.
**Key facts:** ⓘ 🖸 🖻 🎞 Eilean Donan holiday cottage. 🔲

© Britain On View

Iona Abbey

## BOWHILL HOUSE & COUNTRY ESTATE
Bowhill, Selkirk  TD7 5ET
Tel: 01750 22204

## DUNS CASTLE
Duns, Berwickshire  TD11 3NW
Tel: 01361 883211

## FERNIEHIRST CASTLE
Jedburgh, Roxburghshire, Scottish Borders  TD8 6NX
Tel: 01450 870051 E-mail: curator@clankerr.co.uk

## NEIDPATH CASTLE
Peebles, Scotland  EH45 8NW
Tel: 01721 720 333

## SMAILHOLM TOWER
Smailholm, Kelso  TD5 7PG
Tel: 01573 460365

## THIRLESTANE CASTLE
Lauder, Berwickshire  TD2 6RU
Tel: 01578 722430 E-mail: admin@thirlestanecastle.co.uk

## ARDWELL GARDENS
Ardwell House, Ardwell, Stranraer, Wigtownshire  DG9 9LY
Tel: 01776 860227 E-mail: info@ardwellestate.co.uk

## BLAIRQUHAN CASTLE
Maybole, Ayrshire, Scotland  KA19 7LZ
Tel: 01655 770239

## CAERLAVEROCK CASTLE
Glencaple, Dumfries  DG1 4RU
Tel: 01387 770244

## DRUMLANRIG CASTLE
Thornhill, Dumfriesshire, Scotland  DG3 4AQ
Tel: 01848 331555

## SORN CASTLE
Ayrshire  KA5 6HR
Tel: 01290 551555

## GLASGOW CATHEDRAL
Castle Street, Glasgow  G4 0QZ
Tel: 0141 552 6891

## ARBROATH ABBEY
Arbroath, Tayside  DD11 1EG
Tel: 01241 878756

## ARBUTHNOTT HOUSE & GARDEN
Arbuthnott, Laurencekirk  AB30 1PA
Tel: 01561 361226

## BLAIR CASTLE & GARDENS
Blair Castle, Blair Atholl, Pitlochry, Perthshire, PH18 5TL
Tel: 01796 481207 E-mail: bookings@blair-castle.co.uk

## BRECHIN CASTLE
Brechin, Angus  DD9 6SG
Tel: 01356 624566 E-mail: enquiries@dalhousieestates.co.uk

## HOUSE OF DUN
Montrose, Angus  DD10 9LQ
Tel: 0844 493 2144 E-mail: information@nts.org.uk

## HOUSE OF PITMUIES GARDENS
Guthrie, By Forfar, Angus  DD8 2SN
Tel: 01241 828245

## HILL OF TARVIT MANSION HOUSE
Cupar, Fife  KY15 5PB
Tel: 0844 493 2185 E-mail: information@nts.org.uk

## KELLIE CASTLE & GARDEN
Pittenweem, Fife  KY10 2RF
Tel: 0844 493 2184 E-mail: information@nts.org.uk

## ST ANDREWS CASTLE
The Scores, St Andrews  KY16 9AR
Tel: 01334 477196

## ST ANDREWS CATHEDRAL
St Andrews, Fife  KY16 9QL
Tel: 01334 472563

## STOBHALL
Stobhall, Cargill, Perthshire  PH2 6DR
E-mail: info@stobhall.com

## ARDCHATTAN PRIORY GARDENS
Connel, Argyll, Scotland  PA37 1RQ
Tel: 01796 481355

## BRODICK CASTLE
Isle Of Arran  KA27 8HY
Tel: 0131 243 9300

## CRARAE GARDEN
Inveraray, Argyll, Bute & Loch Lomond  PA32 8YA
Tel: 0844 493 2210 E-mail: CraraeGarden@nts.org.uk

## BALMORAL CASTLE
Balmoral, Ballater, Aberdeenshire  AB35 5TB
Tel: 013397 42534 E-mail: info@balmoralcastle.com

## CASTLE FRASER & GARDEN
Sauchen, Inverurie  AB51 7LD
Tel: 0131 243 9300

## DRUM CASTLE & GARDEN
Drumoak, By Banchory, Aberdeenshire  AB31 3EY
Tel: 0844 493 2161 E-mail: information@nts.org.uk

## HADDO HOUSE
Tarves, Ellon, Aberdeenshire  AB41 0ER
Tel: 0844 493 2179 E-mail: information@nts.org.uk

## PITMEDDEN GARDEN
Ellon, Aberdeenshire  AB41 7PD
Tel: 0844 493 2177 E-mail: information@nts.org.uk

## SKAILL HOUSE
Breckness Estate, Sandwick, Orkney, Scotland  KW16 3LR
Tel: 01856 841 501

Powis Castle
©National Trust Images

Dyffryn Gardens
©National Trust Images

# Wales

North Wales

Mid Wales

South Wales

The coast, mountains and hillsides of Wales all attract visitors who are drawn to its castles, manor houses and gardens.

*New Entries for 2014:*
- Penrhyn Castle
- Powis Castle & Garden
- Aberglasney Gardens
- Tredegar House & Park
- Dyffryn Gardens
- Llandaff Cathedral

357

© Fonmon Castle

© The Hall

## FONMON CASTLE ▥ⓕ
### FONMON, BARRY, VALE OF GLAMORGAN  CF62 3ZN
www.fonmoncastle.com

Just 25 minutes from Cardiff and the M4, Fonmon is one of few mediaeval castles still lived in as a home, since being built c1200, it has only changed hands once. Visitors are welcomed by an experienced guide and the 45 minute tour walks through the fascinating history of the Castle, its families, architecture and interiors. The Fonmon gardens are an attraction in their own right for enthusiasts and amateurs alike and visitors are free to wander and explore. Available as an exclusive wedding and party venue, corporate and team building location, visitor attraction and host for product launches and filming.
**Location:** Map 2:L2. OS Ref ST047 681. 15miles W of Cardiff, 1miles W of Cardiff airport. **Owner:** Sir Brooke Boothby Bt **Contact:** Casey Govier

**Tel:** 01446 710206 **Fax:** 01446 711687 **E-mail:** Fonmon_Castle@msn.com
**Open:** Public opening: 1 Apr- 30 Sep on Tue & Wed afternoons for individuals, families & small groups. Midday-5pm, no need to book. Tours at 2pm, 3pm & 4pm & last 45 mins, last entrance to gardens at 4pm. Groups 20+ welcome by appointment throughout the year. Varied hospitality options with very popular Afternoon Teas. **Admission:** Entry and tour of the Castle priced at £6.00, Children free. Access to garden and grounds is free.
**Key facts:** ⓘ Conferences. ⊤ By arrangement. ⬓ Suitable. WCs. ⓕ Guided Tour obligatory. ℙ Ample free parking for cars and coaches. ▣ ⬚ Guide dogs only. ⬕ Licensed for Civil Ceremonies for up to 110 people.

© National Trust Images/Andrew Butler

© National Trust Images/Andreas von Einsiedel

## TREDEGAR HOUSE & PARK ❧
### NEWPORT, SOUTH WALES  NP10 8YW
www.nationaltrust.org.uk/tredegarhouse

Tredegar House is one of the most significant late 17th Century houses in Wales, if not the whole of the British Isles. This delightful red brick house is situated within 90 acres of beautiful gardens and parkland and is the ideal setting for a fantastic day out. Take a look around the house, stroll in the gardens, explore the park, indulge in the tea rooms and pick up a treat or two in the shop. Not to be missed are the impressive Grade 1 listed stables and the series of three walled formal gardens, including the distinctive parterre garden which lies adjacent to The Orangery. For more than 500 years the house was home to one of Wales' greatest families, The Morgans, later the Lords Tredegar.
**Location:** Map 2:M1. OS Ref ST290 852. M4 - J28 signposted. From London 2 1/2hrs, from Cardiff 30 mins. 2m SW of Newport town centre.
**Owner:** Leased to the National Trust by Newport City Council
**Tel:** 01633 815880 **E-mail:** tredegar@nationaltrust.org.uk

**Open:** Tea room & shop open, 1 Jan-2 Feb (Sat & Sun only),
House (below stairs), gardens, tea room & shop open, 8 Feb-28 Feb (7 days),
House, gardens, tea room & shop open, 1 Mar-2 Nov (7 days),
Tea room & shop open, 8 Nov-28 Dec (Sat & Sun only),
House, gardens, tea room & shop, 29 Nov-21 Dec (Sat & Sun only).
Park open all year from dawn until dusk.
For times please check website: www.nationaltrust.org.uk/tredegarhouse
**Admission:** 2014 prices - Gift Aid Admission (Standard Admission prices in brackets). Adult £8.00 (£7.20). Child £4.00 (£3.60). Family £20.00 (£18). Groups (10+) £6.10, child £3.05. Park: admission Free.
**Key facts:** ▦ ⓣ ⊤ ⬓ ▣ ℙ Pay and display, free to National Trust members. ▣ ⬚ Dogs on leads welcome in gardens, and park. ⬕ ✳ ⬗

# ABERGLASNEY GARDENS
### Llangathen, Carmarthenshire
### SA32 8QH
### www.aberglasney.org

Aberglasney is one of Wales' finest gardens - a renowned plantsman's paradise of more than 10 acres with a unique Elizabethan cloister garden at its heart. The gardens and the fully restored ground floor of Aberglasney's grade II* listed mansion are open 364 days a year.

**Location:** Map 5:F10. OS Ref SN579 221. 4m W of Llandeilo. Follow signs from A40.
**Owner:** Aberglasney Restoration Trust
**Contact:** Booking Department
**Tel/Fax:** 01558 668998 **E-mail:** info@aberglasney.org
**Open:** All year: daily (except Christmas Day). Apr-Sep: 10am-6pm, last entry 5pm. Oct-Mar: 10.30am-4pm.
**Admission:** Adult £8, Child £4, Conc. £8, Booked groups (10+) Adult £6.80.
**Key facts:** ⊙ Free entry. ⚒ Free entry. ☎ Contact us for info. ⬇ Mostly suitable. ☕ Licensed. 🍴 Licensed. 🎓 Pre-booked for group. 🅿 Also coach park. ⬛ ⬛ Guide dogs only. ⬛ ❋ ♿

# DYFFRYN GARDENS ❧
### St Nicholas, Vale of Glamorgan  CF5 6SU
### www.nationaltrust.org.uk/dyffryngardens

These Grade I listed gardens feature a collection of formal lawns, intimate garden rooms an extensive arboretum and reinstated glasshouse. Designed by Thomas Mawson, the vision of industrialist John Cory and son Reginald Cory. Now open is the recently restored, Grade II* late-Victorian Dyffryn House.
**Location:** Map 2:L2. OS Ref ST094 717. M4 - J33 to A4232 (to Barry), exit & follow A48 (to Cowbridge) & brown signs.
**Owner:** Leased to the National Trust by the Vale of Glamorgan Council
**Tel:** 02920 593328
**E-mail:** dyffryn@nationaltrust.org.uk
**Open:** Gardens, tea-room & shop, 1 Jan–31 Dec (open 7 days) *closed 25 & 26 Dec. House: 4 Jan–28 Feb (Sat & Sun only); 1–30 Mar (Thurs–Sun only); 31 Mar–2 Nov (7 days); 6 Nov–14 Dec (Thurs–Sun only).
For times please check website: www.nationaltrust.org.uk/dyffryngardens.
**Admission:** 2014 prices – Gift Aid Admission (Standard Admission in brackets). Adults £8.40 (£7.40). Child £4.20 (£3.70). Family £21.00 (£18.50). Groups (15+) £6.25. **Key facts:** ⊙ ⚒ ☎ ⬇ ☕ 🍴 🎓 🅿 ⬛ ⬛ ⬛ ❋ ♿

# CARDIFF CASTLE
### Castle Street, Cardiff  CF10 3RB
### www.cardiffcastle.com

2000 years of history has shaped Cardiff Castle into a spectacular and fascinating site at the heart of one of the UK's most vibrant cities. From Roman fort and Norman stronghold to a Victorian fairytale Castle, find a surprise around every corner.
**Location:** Map 2:M1. OS Ref ST181 765. Cardiff city centre, signposted from M4.
**Owner:** City and County of Cardiff
**Contact:** Booking Office
**Tel:** 029 2087 8100
**Open:** Please see website for opening and admission.
**Key facts:** ⊙ ☎ ⬇ ☕ 🍴 🎓 ⬛ ⬛ ⬛ ❋ ♿

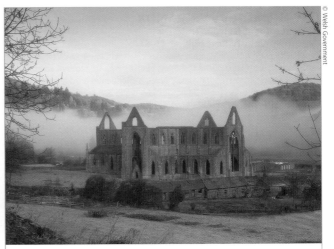

# TINTERN ABBEY ✤
### Tintern, Monmouthshire  NP16 6SE
### www.cadw.wales.gov.uk

Tintern is the best-preserved abbey in Wales and ranks among Britain's most beautiful historic sites. The great Gothic abbey church stands almost complete to roof level. Turner sketched and painted here, while Wordsworth drew inspiration from the surroundings.
**Location:** Map 6:L12. OS Ref SO533 000. Tintern via A466, from M4/J23. Chepstow 6m. **Owner:** In the care of Cadw **Contact:** The Custodian
**Tel:** 01291 689251 **Open:** Please visit www.cadw.wales.gov.uk for 2014 opening times and admission prices or download the free Cadw app.
**Admission:** Please visit www.cadw.wales.gov.uk for 2014 opening times and admission prices or download the free Cadw app.
**Key facts:** ⓘ Induction loop. Toilets. Baby changing. Guidebook. Cycle stands. ⊙ ⬇ WCs. 🅿 Charges apply. ⬛ ⬛ Dogs on leads only. ❋ €

## ABERCAMLAIS HOUSE
**Abercamlais, Brecon, Powys LD3 8EY**

Splendid Grade I mansion dating from middle ages, altered extensively in early 18th Century with 19th Century additions, in extensive grounds beside the river Usk. Still in same family ownership and occupation since medieval times. Exceptional octagonal pigeon house, formerly a privy.
**Location:** Map 6:I10. OS Ref SN965 290. 5m W of Brecon on A40.
**Owner/Contact:** Mrs S Ballance
**Tel:** 01874 636206 **Fax:** 01874 636964
**E-mail:** info@abercamlais.co.uk
**Website:** www.abercamlais.co.uk
**Open:** Apr-Oct: by appointment.
**Admission:** Adult £5.00, Child Free.
**Key facts:** ⓘ No photography in house. ⌘ ⓕ Obligatory. Ⓟ ⌘ Dogs on leads only. ⊡

## CRESSELLY ⋒
**Kilgetty, Pembrokeshire SA68 0SP**

Home of the Allen family for 250 years. The house is of 1770 with matching wings of 1869 and contains good plasterwork and fittings of both periods. The Allens are of particular interest for their close association with the Wedgwood family of Etruria and a long tradition of foxhunting.
**Location:** Map 5:C11. OS Ref SN065 065. W of the A4075.
**Owner/Contact:** H D R Harrison-Allen Esq MFH
**E-mail:** hha@cresselly.com
**Website:** www.cresselly.com
**Open:** May 5-18 inclusive and Sep 1-14. Guided tours only, on the hour. Coaches at other times by arrangement.
**Admission:** Adult £4.00, no children under 12.
**Key facts:** ⌘ Ground floor only. ⓕ Obligatory. Ⓟ Coaches by arrangement. ⌘ ⊡ ⊡

## LLANCAIACH FAWR MANOR
**Gelligaer Road, Nelson, Treharris, Caerphilly County Borough CF46 6ER**

Llancaiach Fawr is a Tudor Manor restored as it was during the Civil War year of 1645. Visitors are guided by the costumed 'servants' who love to chat about the lives of ordinary people in extraordinary times. Visitor Centre provides modern amenities and also caters for weddings, functions and B2B.
**Location:** Map 2:M1. OS Ref ST114 967. S side of B4254, 1m N of A472 at Nelson. **Owner:** Caerphilly County Borough Council
**Contact:** Lesley Edwards **Tel:** 01443 412248 **Fax:** 01443 412688
**E-mail:** llancaiachfawr@caerphilly.gov.uk **Website:** www.llancaiachfawr.co.uk
**Open:** 10am-5pm Tue to Sun and BH Mons all year round. Last entry to the Manor 4.00pm Closed 24 Dec-1 Jan inclusive. **Admission:** £7.50 Adults, £6.00 Concessions, £6.00 Child, £22.00 Family Ticket (2ad+2ch), Group discounts available (20+). **Key facts:** ⓘ No photography in Manor House. ⊡ ⊞ ⊡ ⌘ Partial, WCs. ⊡ Licensed. ⊞ Licensed ⓕ Obligatory. Ⓟ ⊡ ⌘ Dogs in grounds only. Not allowed in walled gardens of the manor. ⊡ ⊡

## LLANDAFF CATHEDRAL
**Llandaff Cathedral, Llandaff Cathedral Green, Cardiff CF5 2LA**

Discover Llandaff Cathedral. A holy place of peace and tranquility art, architecture and music with a very warm welcome. Over 1500 yrs of history. Works include Epstein, Piper, Pace, Rossetti, William Morris and Goscombe John. Services daily some sung by the Cathedral Choir with the Nicholson organ. Discover one of the most important buildings in Wales, you will be glad that you came!
**Location:** Map 2:L2. OS Ref ST155 397. At Cardiff Castle, drive West and cross River Taff; turn right into Cathedral Road (A4119) and follow signs to Llandaff
**Owner:** Representative body of the Church In Wales **Contact:** Cathedral Office
**Tel:** 02920 564554 **E-mail:** admin@llandaffcathedral.org.uk
**Website:** www.llandaffcathedral.org.uk
**Open:** Every week day 9:30am-6pm, Sun 7:30am-6pm.
**Admission:** Free. Donations gratefully received.
**Key facts:** ⊡ ⌘ ⓕ By arrangement. Ⓟ Nearby. ⊡ ⌘ Guide dogs only. ⊡ ⊞ ⊡

## LLANVIHANGEL COURT ⋒
**Nr Abergavenny, Monmouthshire NP7 8DH**

Grade I Tudor Manor. The home in the 17th Century of the Arnolds who built the imposing terraces and stone steps leading to the house. The interior has a fine hall, unusual yew staircase and many 17th Century moulded plaster ceilings. Delightful grounds. 17th Century features, notably Grade I stables.
**Location:** Map 6:K11. OS Ref SO433 139. 4m N of Abergavenny on A465.
**Owner/Contact:** Julia Johnson
**Tel:** 01873 890217
**E-mail:** jclarejohnson@googlemail.com
**Website:** www.llanvihangelcourt.com
**Open:** 3 May-17 May, 11 Aug-20 Aug inclusive, daily 2.30-5.30pm. Last tour 5pm.
**Admission:** Entry and guide, Adult £6.00, Child/Conc. £3.00.
**Key facts:** ⓘ No inside photography. ⌘ Partial. ⓕ Obligatory. Ⓟ Limited, no coaches. ⌘ Dogs on leads only. ⊡

## TREBINSHWN
**Nr Brecon, Powys LD3 7PX**

16th Century mid-sized manor house. Extensively rebuilt 1780. Fine courtyard and walled garden.
**Location:** Map 6:I10. OS Ref SO136 242. 1½m NW of Bwlch.
**Owner/Contact:** R Watson
**Tel:** 01874 730653
**Fax:** 01874 730843
**Open:** Easter-31 Aug: Mon-Tue, 10am-4.30pm.
**Admission:** Free.
**Key facts:** Ⓟ

## USK CASTLE ⋒
**Usk Castle, Monmouth Rd, Usk, Monmouthshire NP5 1SD**

Best kept secret, romantic ruins overlooking Usk. **Location:** Map 6:K12. OS Ref SO3701SE. Off Monmouth Road in Usk. **Tel:** 01291 672563
**E-mail:** info@uskcastle.com **Website:** www.uskcastle.com
**Open:** Castle open:All year, see website. House Open: May (not Mons), 2-5pm and BHs. Guided tours only. **Admission:** £7.00; Gardens £4.00.

Llancaiach Fawr Manor

Register for news and special offers at **www.hudsonsheritage.com**

# THE HALL AT ABBEY-CWM-HIR
## Nr Llandrindod Wells, Powys  LD1 6PH
### www.abbeycwmhir.com

In a breathtaking Mid Wales setting, the 52 room, Grade II* Hall offers tours to the public combining outstanding architecture, stunning interiors and fascinating collections. - all in a family atmosphere. It is one of Wales` finest examples of Victorian Gothic Revival arcitecture, and is surrounded by beautiful and notable 12 acre gardens.

**Location:** Map 6:I8. OS Ref SO054 711. 7m NW of Llandrindod Wells, 6m E of Rhayader, 1m north of Crossgates on A483.
**Owner:** Paul and Victoria Humpherston **Contact:** Paul Humpherston
**Tel:** 01597 851727 **E-mail:** info@abbeycwmhir.com
**Open:** All year daily for prebooked tours only at 10.30am and 2pm for couples, small parties or groups. The Hall is decorated in all 52 rooms for Christmas (1 Nov-6 Jan) and Easter (April). **Admission:** House Tour and Gardens: Adult £15.00 Child (under 12) £5.00 Groups (10+) or repeat visitors £13.00. Gardens only: Adult £5.00. **Key facts:** ⓘ Visitors are asked to remove outside shoes for house tours, slippers can be provided. 🍴 ♿ Partial. 🍽 Licensed. ⚜ Licensed. 🎟 Obligatory. 🅿 Cars and coaches. 🐕 In grounds on leads. ⚜ ♿

---

# HAFOD
### Hafod Estate, Pontrhydygroes, Ystrad-Meurig, Ceredigion  SY25 6DX

Picturesque landscape, one of the most significant in Britain located in a remote valley and improved by Col Thomas Johnes 1780-1816. Ten miles of restored walks featuring cascades, bridges and wonderful views in 500 acres of wood and parkland. The epitome of the Picturesque and Sublime. Georgian Group Award winner.

**Location:** Map 5:G8. OS Ref SN768 736. 15 miles E of Aberystwyth near Devils Bridge, car park, off B4574.
**Owner:** Natural Resources Wales **Contact:** The Hafod Trust
**Tel:** 01974 282568 **Fax:** 01974282579
**E-mail:** trust@hafod.org **Website:** www.hafod.org
**Open:** All year, daylight hours.
**Admission:** Free - guide book available at local shops or website.
**Key facts:** ♿ WC. 🎟 Obligatory by arrangement. 🅿 🍽
🐕 Dogs allowed in grounds on leads. ⚜

---

# THE JUDGE'S LODGING
### Broad Street, Presteigne, Powys  LD8 2AD

Explore the fascinating world of the Victorian judges, their servants and felonious guests at this award-winning, totally hands-on historic house. Through sumptuous judge's apartments and the gas-lit servants' quarters below, follow an 'eavesdropping' audio tour featuring actor Robert Hardy. Damp cells, vast courtroom and new interactive local history rooms included.

**Location:** Map 6:K8. OS Ref SO314 644. In town centre, off A44 and A4113. Easy reach from Herefordshire and mid-Wales.
**Owner:** Powys County Council **Contact:** Gabrielle Rivers **Tel:** 01544 260650
**E-mail:** info@judgeslodging.org.uk **Website:** www.judgeslodging.org.uk
**Open:** 1 Mar-31 Oct: Tues-Sun, 10am-5pm. 1 Nov-31 Nov: Wed-Sun, 10am-4pm, 1 Dec-22 Dec: Sat-Sun 10am-4pm. Open BH Mons.
**Admission:** Adult £6.95, Child £3.50, Conc. £5.95, Family £18.00. Groups (10-80): Adult £6.50, Conc. £5.50, Schools £4.50. **Key facts:** ⓘ 📷 🍴 ♿ Partial. 🎟 By arrangement. 📷 🅿 In town. 🍽 🐕 Guide dogs only. ⚜ ♿

---

# POWIS CASTLE & GARDEN 🌿
## Welshpool, Powys  SY21 8RF

Visit the Castle, Clive museum and stunning garden

**Location:** Map 6:J6. 1 mile south of Welshpool. Signed from main road to Newtown (A483) **Tel:** 01938 551929 **E-mail:** powiscastle@nationaltrust.org.uk
**Website:** www.nationaltrust.org.uk/powis-castle **Open:** Castle (open 7 days): 1-31 Mar 11-4; 1 Apr-30 Sep 11-5; 1 Oct-2 Nov 11-4; 3 Nov-23 Dec 12-4.
**Admission:** Castle & garden Adult £13.00.

---

# TREWERN HALL
## Trewern, Welshpool, Powys  SY21 8DT

A grade II* listed building standing in the Severn Valley. It has been described as 'one of the most handsome timber-framed houses surviving in the area'.
**Location:** Map 6:J6. OS Ref SJ269 113. Off A458 Welshpool-Shrewsbury Road, 4m from Welshpool. **Tel:** 01938 570243 **Open:** Please contact us for up to date opening times and admission prices.

Gardens at Powis Castle

## ISCOYD PARK 🏛
### NR WHITCHURCH, SHROPSHIRE  SY13 3AT
www.iscoydpark.com

A red brick Georgian house in an idyllic 18th Century parkland setting situated on the Welsh side of the Shropshire/Welsh border. After extensive refurbishment of the house and gardens we are now open for Weddings, parties, photography and film shoots, conferencing and corporate events of all kinds.

The house is only let on an exclusive basis meaning there is never more than one event occurring at any time. We offer a wide range of B&B and self catering accommodation, The Secret Spa and beautiful gardens all within the context of a family home.

**Location:** Map 6:L4. OS Ref SJ504 421. 2m W of Whitchurch off A525.
**Owner:** Mr P C Godsal
**Contact:** Mr P L Godsal
**Tel:** 01948 780785
**E-mail:** info@iscoydpark.com
**Open:** House visits by written appointment.
**Key facts:** 🍽 Private dinners a speciality. ♿ WCs. 📷 Licensed. 🍴 Licensed. 🎦 Obligatory. 🅿 Limited for coaches. 🛏 🛌 ❄ ⛲

## BODNANT GARDEN 🌿
### Tal-Y-Cafn, Colwyn Bay  LL28 5RE
www.nationaltrust.org.uk/bodnant-garden

Bodnant Garden is one of the finest gardens in the country not only for its magnificent collections of rhododendrons, camellias and magnolias but also for its idyllic setting above the River Conwy with extensive views of the Snowdonia range. **Location:** Map 5:H2. OS Ref SH801 723. 8 miles S of Llandudno and Colwyn Bay, off A470. Signposted from A55, exit at Junction 19.
**Owner:** National Trust
**Tel:** 01492 650460
**E-mail:** bodnantgarden@nationaltrust.org.uk
**Open:** Please see website for opening times.
**Admission:** Please visit website for a full list of admission prices.
**Key facts:** 📷 🎦 ♿ Partial. WCs. 📷 🅿 Ample. 🦮 Guide dogs only.

© Welsh Government

## CAERNARFON CASTLE ✤
### Castle Ditch, Caernarfon  LL55 2AY
www.cadw.wales.gov.uk

The most famous and perhaps the most impressive castle in Wales, built by Edward I. Distinguished by polygonal towers and colour-banded stone, the castle hosted the 1969 investiture of the current Prince of Wales, HRH Prince Charles. Part of a World Heritage Inscribed site.
**Location:** Map 5:F3. OS Ref SH477 626. In Caernarfon, just W of town centre.
**Owner:** In the care of Cadw
**Contact:** The Custodian **Tel:** 01286 677617
**Open:** Please visit www.cadw.wales.gov.uk for 2014 opening times or download the free Cadw app.
**Admission:** Please visit www.cadw.wales.gov.uk for 2014 admission prices or download the free Cadw app.
**Key facts:** ℹ Induction loop. Toilets. 📷 ♿ Partial. 🦮 Assistance dogs only. ❄ €

## CONWY CASTLE ✤
### Conwy LL32 8AY
### www.cadw.wales.gov.uk

The impressive castle and town walls were built as a single entity by Edward I between 1283 and 1287. Explore both and enjoy the spectacular views. Experience the Conwy Quest and explore the castle. Part of a World Heritage Inscribed site.

**Location:** Map 5:H2. OS Ref SH783 774. Conwy by A55 or B5106
**Owner:** In the care of Cadw
**Contact:** The Custodian
**Tel:** 01492 592358
**Open:** Open/Admission: Please visit www.cadw.wales.gov.uk for 2014 opening times and admission prices or download the free Cadw app.
**Admission:** Open/Admission: Please visit www.cadw.wales.gov.uk for 2014 opening times and admission prices or download the free Cadw app.
**Key facts:** ⓘ Induction loop. Toilets. ⬚ ♿ Partial. WCs. ✗ By arrangement. ⬛ 🐕 Assistance dogs only. ❀ €

## GWYDIR CASTLE
### Llanrwst, Conwy LL26 0PN
### www.gwydircastle.co.uk

Gwydir Castle is situated in the beautiful Conwy Valley and is set within a Grade I listed, 10 acre garden. Built by the illustrious Wynn family c1500, Gwydir is a fine example of a Tudor courtyard house, incorporating re-used medieval material from the dissolved Abbey of Maenan. Further additions date from c1600 and c1828. The important 1640s panelled Dining Room has now been reinstated, following its repatriation from the New York Metropolitan Museum.
**Location:** Map 5:H3. OS Ref SH795 610. ½m W of Llanrwst on B5106.
**Owner/Contact:** Mr & Mrs Welford
**Tel:** 01492 641687 **E-mail:** info@gwydircastle.co.uk
**Open:** 1 Apr-31 Oct: daily, 10am-4pm. Closed Mons & Sats (except BH weekends). Limited openings at other times. Please telephone for details.
**Admission:** Adult £6.00, Child £3.00, Concessions £5.50. Group discount 10%. **Key facts:** ⬚ ♿ Partial. ⬛ By arrangement. ✗ By arrangement. 🅿 ⬛ 🐕 2 doubles. ⬛

## DOLBELYDR
### Trefnant, Denbighshire LL16 5AG
### www.landmarktrust.org.uk

Set in a timeless, quiet valley this 16th Century gentry house has many of its original features, including a first floor solar open to the roof beams. It also has good claim to be the birthplace of the modern Welsh language.
**Location:** Map 6:I2. OS Ref SJ027 698.
**Owner:** The Landmark Trust
**Tel:** 01628 825925
**E-mail:** bookings@landmarktrust.org.uk
**Open:** Open days on 8 days per year. Other visits by appointment.
**Admission:** Free on open days and visits by appointment.
**Key facts:** ⓘ There is an open plan kitchen and dining area in front of a huge inglenook fireplace.
🅿 ⬛
⬛ ❀ ⬛ ⬛

## PLAS MAWR ✤
### High Street, Conwy LL32 8DE
### www.cadw.wales.gov.uk

The best-preserved Elizabethan town house in Britain, Plas Mawr reflects the status of its builder Robert Wynn. A fascinating house and garden allowing visitors to sample the lives of the Tudor gentry and their servants, Plas Mawr is famous for its colourful plasterwork and authentic furnishings.
**Location:** Map 5:H2. OS Ref SH781 776. Conwy by A55 or B5106 or A547.
**Owner:** In the care of Cadw
**Contact:** The Custodian **Tel:** 01492 580167
**Open:** Please visit www.cadw.wales.gov.uk for 2014 opening times and admission prices or download the free Cadw app.
**Admission:** Please visit www.cadw.wales.gov.uk for 2014 opening times and admission prices or download the free Cadw app.
**Key facts:** ⓘ Toilets. Induction loop. Video presentation. Garden. ⬚ ♿ Partial. ⬚ 🅿 Charges apply. 🐕 Assistance dogs only. ⬛ €

## TOWER 🏠ⓕ
### Nercwys Road, Mold, Flintshire CH7 4EW
www.towerwales.co.uk

Tower, which had been in the same family for over 500 years, is a Grade 1 listed building steeped in Welsh history and has been witness to the continuous warfare of the time. A fascinating place to visit, host a wedding or corporate event at or for an overnight stay. Bed and Breakfast – was graded 5-star in 2012-13 by Visit Wales.

**Location:** Map 6:J3. OS Ref SJ240 620. 1m S of Mold. SAT NAV - use CH7 4EF.
**Owner:** Executors of the late Charles Wynne-Eyton
**Contact:** Mrs Mairi Wynne-Eyton
**Tel:** 01352 700220
**E-mail:** enquiries@towerwales.co.uk
**Open:** May: Mon-Fri inclusive. Aug Bank Holiday – Sat, Sun & Mon. Groups by appointment. **Admission:** Adult £5.00, Child £3.00.
**Key facts:** ⓘ Opening dates etc. correct at time of going to press. If travelling significant distance please phone to check details. 🅣 🅕 Obligatory. 🅟 Limited for coaches. 🖼

## FFERM
### Pontblyddyn, Mold, Flintshire CH7 4HN

17th Century farmhouse. Viewing is limited to 7 persons at any one time. Open by appointment. No toilets or refreshments.
**Location:** Map 6:J3. OS Ref SJ279 603. Access from A541 in Pontblyddyn, 3½m SE of Mold.
**Owner:** Dr M.C. Jones-Mortimer Will Trust
**Contact:** Mrs Miranda Dechazal
**Tel:** 01352 770204
**Open:** 2nd Wed in every month, 2-5pm. Open by appointment.
**Admission:** £4.00.
**Key facts:** 🖼 ✳

## HARTSHEATH 🏠ⓕ
### Pontblyddyn, Mold, Flintshire CH7 4HP

18th and 19th Century house set in parkland. Viewing is limited to 7 persons at any one time. Open by appointment. No toilets or refreshments.
**Location:** Map 6:J3. OS Ref SJ287 602. Access from A5104, 3.5m SE of Mold between Pontblyddyn and Penyffordd.
**Owner:** Dr M.C. Jones-Mortimer Will Trust
**Contact:** Mrs Miranda Dechazal
**Tel/Fax:** 01352 770204
**Open:** 1st, 3rd & 5th Wed in every month, 2-5pm. Open by appointment.
**Admission:** £4.00.
**Key facts:** 🖼 ✳

## PLAS BRONDANW GARDENS, CAFÉ & SHOP
### Plas Brondanw, Llanfrothen, Gwynedd LL48 6SW

Italianate gardens with topiary.
**Location:** Map 5:G4. OS Ref SH618 423. 3m N of Penrhyndeudraeth off A4085, on Croesor Road.
**Owner:** Trustees of the Clough Williams-Ellis Foundation.
**Tel:** 01766 772772  01743 239236.
**E-mail:** info@brondanw.org
**Website:** www.brondanw.org
**Open:** Mar-Sep daily,10.00am-5.00pm.
Coaches accepted, please book.
**Admission:** Adult £4.00, Children under 12 £1.00.
**Key facts:** 🗋 🎁 🅣 🍽 🅕 🅟 🖼 ✉ ▲ 🎗

## WERN ISAF
### Penmaen Park, Llanfairfechan, Conwy LL33 0RN

This Arts and Crafts house was built in 1900 by the architect H L North as his family home and contains much of the original furniture and William Morris fabrics. Situated in a woodland garden with extensive views over the Menai Straits and Conwy Bay.
**Location:** Map 5:G2. OS Ref SH685 753. Off A55 midway between Bangor and Conwy.
**Owner/Contact:** Mrs P J Phillips
**Tel:** 01248 680437
**Open:** 2-16 Mar and 1-13 May: daily 12-2pm, except Wednesdays.
**Admission:** Free.

## PENRHYN CASTLE 🌿
### Bangor, Gwynedd LL57 4HN

Built by famed architect Thomas Hopper in the 19th Century Penrhyn Castle is a fantastical neo-Norman Castle that sits in the glorious surroundings of Snowdonia and the Menai Strait. **Location:** Map 5:G2. 1m E of Bangor, at Llandygai (J11, A55). **Tel:** 01248 353084 **E-mail:** penrhyncastle@nationaltrust.org.uk
**Website:** www.nationaltrust.org.uk/PenrhynCastle
**Open:** Grounds: All year. Castle from Mar-Nov. See website for latest information.

National Botanic Garden of Wales

Register for news and special offers at **www.hudsonsheritage.com**

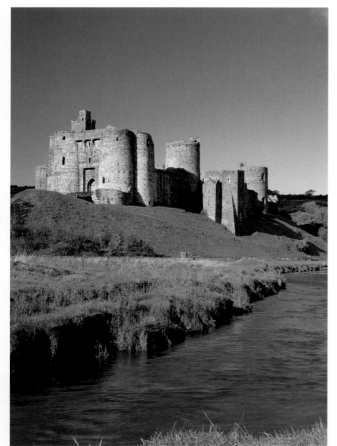
Kidwelly Castle

## PICTON CASTLE & WOODLAND GARDENS ⬛ⓔ
The Rhos, Nr Haverfordwest, Pembrokeshire SA62 4AS
**Tel:** 01437 751326 **E-mail:** info@pictoncastle.co.uk

## ST FAGANS: NATIONAL HISTORY MUSEUM
Cardiff CF5 6XB
**Tel:** 029 2057 3500

## STRADEY CASTLE
Llanelli, Carmarthenshire, Wales SA15 4PL
**Tel:** 01554 774 626 **E-mail:** info@stradeycastle.com

## ABERYSTWYTH CASTLE
Aberystwyth, Ceredigion SY23 2AG
**Tel:** 01970 612125

## CARDIGAN CASTLE
Green Street, Cardigan, Ceredigion SA43 1JA
**Tel:** 01239 615131 **E-mail:** cadwganbpt@btconnect.com

## GLANSEVERN HALL GARDENS
Glansevern, Berriew, Welshpool, Powys SY21 8AH
**Tel:** 01686 640644 **E-mail:** glansevern@yahoo.co.uk

## BEAUMARIS COURT
Beaumaris Court, Castle Street, Beaumaris LL58 8BP
**Tel:** 0870 121 1251 **E-mail:** info@visitwales.com

## BODRHYDDAN HALL
Bodrhyddan, Rhuddlan, Rhyl, Denbighshire LL18 5SB
**Tel:** 01745 590414

## CRICCIETH CASTLE ✚
Castle Street, Criccieth, Gwynedd LL52 0DP
**Tel:** 01766 522227

## ERDDIG ⚘
Wrexham LL13 0YT
**Tel:** 01978 355314 **E-mail:** erddig@nationaltrust.org.uk

## HARLECH CASTLE ✚
Castle Square, Harlech LL46 2YH
**Tel:** 01766 780552

## PENMON PRIORY
Penmon, Beaumaris LL58 8RW
**Tel:** 01443 336031 **E-mail:** cadw@wales.gsi.gov.uk

## PLAS NEWYDD
Hill Street, Llangollen, Denbighshire LL20 8AW
**Tel:** 01978 861314

## PLAS NEWYDD COUNTRY HOUSE & GARDENS ⚘
Llanfairpwll, Anglesey LL61 6DQ
**Tel:** 01248 714795 **E-mail:** plasnewydd@nationaltrust.org.uk

## PORTMEIRION
Minffordd, Penrhyndeudraeth, Gwynedd LL48 6ER
**Tel:** 01766 772311 **E-mail:** enquiries@portmeirion-village.com

## TREVOR HALL
Trevor Hall Road, Llangollen, Debighshire, Wales LL20 7UP
**Tel:** 01978 810505 **E-mail:** info@trevorhall.com

## ABERDEUNANT ⚘
Taliaris, Llandeilo, Carmarthenshire SA19 6DL
**Tel:** 01588 650177 **E-mail:** aberdeunant@nationaltrust.org.uk

## CHEPSTOW CASTLE ✚
Chepstow, Monmouthshire NP16 5EY
**Tel:** 01291 624065

## KIDWELLY CASTLE ✚
Kidwelly, Carmarthenshire SA17 5BQ
**Tel:** 01554 890104

## LAUGHARNE CASTLE
Laugharne, Carmarthen SA33 4SA
**Tel:** 01994 427906

## MARGAM COUNTRY PARK & CASTLE
Margam, Port Talbot, West Glamorgan SA13 2TJ
**Tel:** 01639 881635 **E-mail:** margampark@npt.gov.uk

## NATIONAL BOTANIC GARDEN OF WALES
Llanarthne, Carmarthenshire SA32 8HG
**Tel:** 01558 667149 **E-mail:** info@gardenofwales.org.uk

## OXWICH CASTLE ✚
Oxwich, Swansea SA3 1NG
**Tel:** 01792 390359

## PEMBROKE CASTLE
Pembroke SA71 4LA
**Tel:** 01646 681510 **E-mail:** info@pembrokecastle.co.uk

Castle Coole

Montalto Estate Carriage House

Antrim
Armagh
Down
Fermanagh
Londonderry
Tyrone

# Northern Ireland

For the country house visitor, Northern Ireland is a little known wonderland where Palladian houses of singular beauty provide an unrivalled backdrop for days out, weddings and special events.

Northern Ireland

## ANTRIM CASTLE GARDENS
### RANDALSTOWN ROAD, ANTRIM  BT41 4LH
www.antrim.gov.uk/antrimcastlegardens

Antrim Castle Gardens and Clotworthy House is a hidden gem waiting to be explored. After a recent £6 million restoration, the Gardens have been transformed into a unique living museum. With some features restored to their original 17th Century condition, the Gardens and Clotworthy House are now a must see attraction. Antrim Castle Gardens offers a breathtaking walk into history, but also much more, with a programme of events running all year round. While you are here why not stay for a coffee or lunch and browse the visitor shop. **Location:** Map 18:N4. OS Ref J186 850. Outside Antrim town centre off A26 on A6. **Owner:** Antrim Borough Council

**Contact:** Samuel Hyndman - Garden Heritage Development Officer
**Tel:** 028 9448 1338
**E-mail:** culture@antrim.gov.uk
**Open:** All year: Mon, Wed and Fri 9.30am-5pm. Tues and Thurs 9.30am–9.30pm. Sat and Sun 10am-5pm.
**Admission:** Free. Guided group tours by arrangement only.
**Key facts:** ⓘ Photographic shoots and filming by written permission only. ⓒ ⓣ Ⓛ WCs. ⓔ Ⓜ Licensed. Ⓟ ▣
Ⓗ Dogs on leads only. Ⓐ ⓧ Ⓥ

## BALLYWALTER PARK 🏛
### Ballywalter, Newtownards, Co Down  BT22 2PP
www.ballywalterpark.com

Ballywalter Park was built, in the Italianate Palazzo style, by Sir Charles Lanyon for Andrew Mulholland. A Gentleman's wing, was added in 1870 for Andrew's son, John Mulholland, later 1st Baron Dunleath. The house has a fine collection of original furniture and paintings, complemented by contemporary pieces.
**Location:** Map 18:P4. OS Ref J610 723. Off A2 on unclassified road, 1 km S of Ballywalter village.
**Owner:** The Lord and Lady Dunleath
**Contact:** Mrs Sharon Graham, The Estate Office
**Tel:** 028 4275 8264
**E-mail:** enq@dunleath-estates.co.uk
**Open:** By prior appointment only; please contact The Estate Office.
**Admission:** House or Gardens: £8.50. House & Gardens: £12.00. Groups (max 50): £8.50. Refreshments by arrangement.
**Key facts:** ⓘ No photography indoors. Ⓣ Ⓔ Ⓕ Obligatory. Ⓟ
Ⓗ Guide dogs only. ▣ Ⓥ €

Antrim Castle Gardens

## CASTLE COOLE

**Enniskillen, Co Fermanagh BT74 6JY**

www.nationaltrust.org.uk/castlecoole

Surrounded by its stunning landscape park on the edge of Enniskillen, this majestic 18th Century home of the Earls of Belmore, designed by James Wyatt, was created to impress. The surrounding wooded landscape park sloping down to Lough Coole is ideal for long walks.

**Location:** Map 18:J5. OS Ref H245 436.
On A4, 1½m from Enniskillen on A4, Belfast-Enniskillen road.
**Owner:** National Trust
**Contact:** House Steward
**Tel:** 028 6632 2690
**E-mail:** castlecoole@nationaltrust.org.uk
**Open:** Please see website for up to date opening times.
**Admission:** Please see website for up to date admission prices.
**Key facts:** Partial. WC.
In grounds, on leads.

## CASTLE WARD HOUSE & DEMESNE

**Strangford, Downpatrick, Co Down BT30 7LS**

www.nationaltrust.org.uk/castleward

Situated in a stunning location within an 820 acre walled demesne overlooking Strangford Lough, the lawns rise up to the unique 18th Century house and its Gothic façade. This fascinating house features both Gothic and Classical styles of architectural treatment, internally and externally.

**Location:** Map 18:P6. OS Ref J573 498.
On A25, 7m from Downpatrick and 1½m from Strangford.
**Owner:** National Trust
**Contact:** Visitor Services Manager
**Tel:** 028 4488 1204
**E-mail:** castleward@nationaltrust.org.uk
**Open:** Please see website for opening times and admission prices.
**Key facts:** WCs.
By arrangement.
On leads only. Caravan park. Holiday cottages. Basecamp.
€

### BARONS COURT

**Newtownstewart, Omagh, Co Tyrone BT78 4EZ**

The home of the Duke and Duchess of Abercorn, Barons Court was built between 1779 and 1782, and subsequently extensively remodelled by John Soane (1791), William and Richard Morrison (1819-1841), Sir Albert Richardson (1947-49) and David Hicks (1975-76).

**Location:** Map 18:M3. OS Ref H236 382. 5km SW of Newtownstewart.
**Contact:** The Agent
**Tel:** 028 8166 1683 **Fax:** 028 8166 2059
**E-mail:** info@barons-court.com
**Website:** www.barons-court.com
**Open:** By appointment only.
**Admission:** Adult £10.00. Groups max. 50.
**Key facts:** No photography. The Carriage Room in the Stable Yard.
Partial. By arrangement.
Holiday cottages, 4 star rated by Northern Ireland Tourist Board. €

### DOWN CATHEDRAL

**Cathedral Office, English Street, Downpatrick**
**County Down BT30 6AB**

Built in 1183 as a Benedictine monastery, Down Cathedral is now a Cathedral of the Church of Ireland. Prominent and majestic, the cathedral is believed to have the grave of St Patrick in its grounds. There is also wonderful stained glass and a pulpit and organ of highest quality.

**Location:** Map 18:O6. OS Ref SB583 989. Located in Downpatrick, in the heart of English Street. Follow brown signs.
**Owner:** Church of Ireland **Contact:** Joy Wilkinson
**Tel:** 028 4461 4922 **Fax:** 028 4461 4456 **E-mail:** info@downcathedral.org
**Website:** www.downcathedral.org
**Open:** Open all year round. Mon-Sat: 9.30am - 4.00pm.
Sun: 2-4pm.
**Admission:** Donations. Guided tours by arrangement.
**Key facts:** By arrangement. Limited for cars and coaches.
Guide dogs only.

### KILLYLEAGH CASTLE

**Killyleagh, Downpatrick, Co Down BT30 9QA**

Oldest occupied castle in Ireland. Self-catering towers available, sleeps 4-13. Swimming pool and tennis court available by arrangement. Access to garden.
**Location:** Map 18:O5/6. OS Ref J523 529. **Tel:** 028 4482 8261 **E-mail:** grh@gmail.com **Website:** www.killyleaghcastle.com **Open:** By arrangement.
**Admission:** Groups (30-50) by arrangement. Around £2.50 pp.

Barons Court Estate

## ANTRIM ROUND TOWER
16 High Street, Antrim, County Antrim  BT41 4AN
Tel: 028 94428331

## ARTHUR ANCESTRAL HOME
Cullybackey, County Antrim  BT42 1AB
Tel: 028 2563 8494 E-mail: devel.leisure@ballymena.gov.uk

## BELFAST CASTLE
Cave Hill, Antrim Road, Belfast  BT15 5GR
Tel: 028 9077 6925

## BENVARDEN GARDEN
Benvarden, Dervock, County Antrim  BT53 6NN
Tel: 028 20741331

## BOTANIC GARDENS
Stransmillis Road, Belfast  BT7 1LP
Tel: 028 9031 4762

## CARRICKFERGUS CASTLE
Marine Highway, Carrickfergus, County Antrim  BT38 7BG
Tel: 028 9335 1273

## CATHEDRAL OF CHRIST CHURCH, LISBURN
24 Castle Street, Lisburn  BT28 1RG
Tel: 028 9260 2400 E-mail: sam@lisburncathedral.org

## DUNLUCE CASTLE
87 Dunluce Road, Portrush, County Antrim  BT57 8UY
Tel: 028 20731938

## MONTALTO HOUSE
5 Craigaboney Road, Bushmills, County Antrim  BT57 8XD
Tel: 028 2073 1257 E-mail: montaltohouse@btconnect.com

## GLENARM CASTLE WALLED GARDEN
2 Castle Lane, Glenarm, Larne, County Antrim  BT44 0BQ
Tel: 028 28841305

## SENTRY HILL
Ballycraigy Road, Newtownabbey  BT36 5SY
Tel: 028 90340000

## ST. ANNE'S CATHEDRAL
Donegall Street, Belfast  BT12 2HB
Tel: 028 9032 8332

## ST. PETER'S CATHEDRAL
St Peters Square, Falls Road, Belfast  BT12 4BU
Tel: 028 9032 7573

## ARDRESS HOUSE ❧
64 Ardress Road, Portadown, Co Armagh  BT62 1SQ
Tel: 028 8778 4753 E-mail: ardress@nationaltrust.org.uk

## BENBURB CASTLE
Servite Priory, Main Street, Benburb, Co, Tyrone  BT71 7JZ
Tel: 028 37548241 E-mail: servitepriory@btinternet.com

## DERRYMORE ❧
Bessbrook, Newry, Co Armagh  BT35 7EF
Tel: 028 8778 4753 E-mail: derrymore@nationaltrust.org.uk

## GILFORD CASTLE ESTATE
Banbridge Road, Gilford  BT63 6DT
Tel: 028 40623322 E-mail: gilford@irishfieldsports.com

## AUDLEYS CASTLE
Strangford, County Down  UK
Tel: 028 9054 3034

## BANGOR ABBEY
Bangor, County Down  BT20 4JF
Tel: 028 91271200

## BANGOR CASTLE
Bangor, County Down  BT20 4BN
Tel: 028 91270371

## CLOUGH CASTLE
Clough Village, Downpatrick, County Down  UK
Tel: 028 9054 3034

## DUNDRUM CASTLE
Dundrum Village, Newcastle, County Down  BT33 0QX
Tel: 028 9054 3034

## GREENCASTLE ROYAL CASTLE
Cranfield Point, Kilkeel, County Down  UK
Tel: 028 90543037

## GREY ABBEY
9-11 Church Street, Greyabbey, County Down  BT22 2NQ
Tel: 028 9054 6552

## GREY POINT FORT
Crawfordsburn Country Park, Helens Bay, Co Down  BT19 1LD
Tel: 028 9185 3621

## HELENS TOWER
Clandeboye Estate, Bangor  BT19 1RN
Tel: 028 91852817

## INCH ABBEY
Downpatrick, County Down  UK
Tel: 028 9181 1491

## KILCLIEF CASTLE
Strangford, County Down  UK
Tel: 028 9054 3034

## MAHEE CASTLE
Mahee Island, Comber, Newtownards  BT23 6EP
Tel: 028 91826846

## MOVILLA ABBEY
63 Movilla Road, Newtownards  BT23 8EZ
Tel: 028 9181 0787

## NEWRY CATHEDRAL
38 Hill Street, Newry, County Down  BT34 1AT
Tel: 028 3026 2586

## PORTAFERRY CASTLE
Castle Street, Portaferry, County Down  BT22 1NZ
Tel: 028 90543033

**QUOILE CASTLE**
Downpatrick, County Down  BT30 7JB
**Tel:** 028 9054 3034

**RINGHADDY CASTLE**
Killyleagh, County Down  UK
**Tel:** 028 90543037

**ROWALLANE GARDEN** ❧
Ballynahinch, Co Down  BT24 7LH
**Tel:** 028 9751 0721 **E-mail:** rowallane@nationaltrust.org.uk

**SKETRICK CASTLE**
Whiterock, County Down  BT23 6QA
**Tel:** 028 4278 8387

**STRANGFORD CASTLE**
Strangford, County Down  UK
**Tel:** 028 9054 3034

**THE PRIORY**
Newtownards, County Down  UK
**Tel:** 028 90543037

**CROM ESTATE** ❧
Newtownbutler, County Fermanagh  BT92 8AP
**Tel:** 028 6773 8118

**ENNISKILLEN CASTLE** ❧
Castle Barracks, Enniskillen, County Fermanagh  BT74 7HL
**Tel:** 028 6632 5000 **E-mail:** castle@fermanagh.gov.uk

**FLORENCE COURT** ❧
Enniskillen, Co Fermanagh  BT92 1DB
**Tel:** 028 6634 8249 **E-mail:** florencecourt@nationaltrust.org.uk

**BELLAGHY BAWN**
Castle Street, Bellaghy, County Londonderry  BT45 8LA
**Tel:** 028 7938 6812

**DUNGIVEN CASTLE**
Main Street, Dungiven, Co Londonderry  BT47 4LF
**Tel:** 028 7774 2428 **E-mail:** enquiries@dungivencastle.com

**DUNGIVEN PRIORY AND O CAHANS TOMB**
Dungiven, County Londonderry  UK
**Tel:** 028 777 22074

**KINGS FORT**
7 Connell Street, Limavady, Co Londonderry  BT49 0HA
**Tel:** 028 77760304 **E-mail:** tourism@limavady.gov.uk

**MOUNTSANDAL FORT**
Mountsandal Road, Coleraine, Co Londonderry  BT52 1PE
**Tel:** 027 7034 4723 **E-mail:** coleraine@nitic.net

**PREHEN HOUSE**
Prehen Road, Londonderry  BT47 2PB
**Tel:** 028 7131 2829 **E-mail:** colinpeck@yahoo.com

**ROUGH FORT**
Limavady TIC, 7 Connell Street, Limavady  BT49 0HA
**Tel:** 028 7084 8728

**SAINT COLUMBS CATHEDRAL**
London Street, Derry, County Londonderry  BT48 6RQ
**Tel:** 028 71267313 **E-mail:** stcolumbs@ic24.net

**SAMPSONS TOWER**
Limavady TIC, 7 Connell Street, Limavady  BT49 0HA
**Tel:** 028 7776 0307

**SPRINGHILL HOUSE** ❧
20 Springhill Road, Moneymore, Co Londonderry  BT45 7NQ
**Tel:** 028 8674 8210 **E-mail:** springhill@nationaltrust.org.uk

**THE GUILDHALL**
Guildhall Square, Londonderry  BT48 6DQ
**Tel:** 028 7137 7335

**CASTLEDERG CASTLE**
Castle Park, Castlederg, County Tyrone  BT81 7AS
**Tel:** 028 7138 2204

**HARRY AVERYS CASTLE**
Old Castle Road, Newtownstewart  BT82 8DY
**Tel:** 028 7138 2204

**KILLYMOON CASTLE**
Killymoon Road, Cookstown, County Tyrone  UK
**Tel:** 028 86763514

**NEWTOWNSTEWART CASTLE**
Townhall Street, Newtownstewart  BT78 4AX
**Tel:** 028 6862 1588 **E-mail:** nieainfo@doeni.gov.uk

**OMAGH GAOL**
Old Derry Road, Omagh, County Tyrone  UK
**Tel:** 028 82247831 **E-mail:** omagh.tic@btconnect.com

**SAINT MACARTAN'S CATHEDRAL**
Clogher, County Tyrone  BT76 0AD
**Tel:** 028 0478 1220

**SIR JOHN DAVIES CASTLE**
Castlederg, County Tyrone  BT81 7AS
**Tel:** 028 7138 2204

**THE ARGORY** ❧
Moy, Dungannon, Co Tyrone  BT71 6NA
**Tel:** 028 8778 4753 **E-mail:** argory@nationaltrust.org.uk

**THE KEEP OR GOVERNORS RESIDENCE**
Off Old Derry Road, Omagh, County Tyrone  UK
**Tel:** 028 82247831 **E-mail:** omagh.tic@btconnect.com

**TULLYHOGUE FORT**
B162, Cookstown, County Tyrone, Northern Ireland  UK
**Tel:** 028 86766727

# SIGNPOST

## RECOMMENDING THE UK'S FINEST HOTELS SINCE 1935

Motoring conditions may have changed since the founder of Signpost first took to the road in 1935, but inspectors' standards are still the same. Inspected annually, Signpost features the UK's Premier hotels who possess that something special – style, comfort, warmth of welcome, cuisine, location – which really make them worth the visit. Here are Signpost's recommendations, by region, of fantastic places to stay while you are visiting Britain's historic sites. A wonderful combination.

## www.signpost.co.uk

### LONDON

**The Gainsborough Hotel**
7-11 Queensferry Place
South Kensington
London SW7 2DL
Tel: 0207 9757 0000

**The Mayflower Hotel & Apartment**
26-28 Trebovir Road
Earls Court
London SW5 9NJ
Tel: 0207 370 0991

**New Linden Hotel**
59 Leinster Square
London W2 4PS
Tel: 0207 221 4321

**San Domenico House**
29-31 Draycott Place
Chelsea
London SW3 2SH
Tel: 0207 581 5757

**Searcys Roof Garden Rooms**
30 Pavilion Road
London SW1X 0HJ
Tel: 0207 584 4921

**Twenty Nevern Square Hotel**
20 Nevern Square
London SW5 9PD
Tel: 0207 565 9555

### SOUTH EAST

**Deans Place Hotel**
Seaford Road
Alfriston
East Sussex BN26 5TW
Tel: 01323 870248

**Drakes Hotel**
44 Marine Parade
Brighton
East Sussex BN2 1PE
Tel: 01273 696934

**Flackley Ash Hotel & Spa**
Peasmarsh
Nr. Rye
East Sussex TN31 6YH
Tel: 01797 230651

**Hotel Una**
55-56 Regency Square
Brighton
East Sussex BN1 2FF
Tel: 01273 820464

**The Marquis at Alkham**
Alkham Valley Road
Dover
Kent CT15 7DF
Tel: 0130 487 3410

**The Millsteam Hotel & Restaurant**
Bosham Lane
Bosham
Chichester
West Sussex PO18 8HL
Tel: 01243 573234

**Newick Park Hotel & Country Estate**
Newick
Nr. Lewes
East Sussex BN8 4SB
Tel: 01825 723633

**The Priory Bay Hotel**
Priory Drive
Seaview
Isle of Wight PO34 5BU
Tel: 01983 613146

**Romney Bay House Hotel**
Coast Road
Littlestone
New Romney
Kent TN28 8QY
Tel: 01797 364747

**Stone House**
Rushlake Green
Heathfield
East Sussex TN21 9RJ
Tel: 01435 830553

**White Horse Hotel & Brasserie**
Market Place
Romsey
Hampshire SO51 8ZJ
Tel: 01794 512431

### SOUTH WEST

**The Abbey**
Abbey Street
Penzance
Cornwall TR18 4AR
Tel: 01736 366906

**The Berry Head Hotel**
Berry Head Road
Brixham
Devon TQ5 9AJ
Tel: 01803 853225

**Budock Vean**
Helford Passage
Mawnan Smith
Nr. Falmouth
Cornwall TR11 5LG
Tel: 01326 252100

**Corse Lawn House Hotel**
Corse Lawn
Nr. Tewkesbury
Gloucestershire
GL19 4LZ
Tel: 01452 780771

**The Cottage Hotel**
Hope Cove
Kingsbridge
Devon TQ7 3HJ
Tel: 01548 561555

**Dart Marina**
Sandquay Road
Dartmouth
Devon TQ6 9PH
Tel: 01803 832580

**Farthings Country House Hotel & Restaurant**
Hatch Beauchamp
Taunton
Somerset TA3 6SG
Tel: 01823 480664

**Hannafore Point Hotel**
Marine Drive
West Looe
Cornwall PL13 2DG
Tel: 01503 263273

**The Ilsington Country House Hotel**
Ilsington Village
Nr. Newton Abbot
Devon TQ13 9RR
Tel: 01364 661452

**Knoll House Hotel**
Studland Bay
Dorset BH19 3AH
Tel: 01929 450450

**Penventon Park Hotel**
Redruth
Cornwall TR15 1TE
Tel: 01209 203000

**Plantation House Hotel**
Totnes Road
Ermington
Dorset PL21 9NS
Tel: 01548 831100

**Plumber Manor**
Sturminster Newton
Dorset DT10 2AF
Tel: 01258 472507

**Tides Reach Hotel**
South Sands
Salcombe
South Devon TQ8 8LJ
Tel: 01548 843466

**The White Hart Royal Hotel**
High Street
Moreton in Marsh
Gloucestershire
GL56 0BA
Tel: 01608 650731

### EASTERN REGION

**Beechwood Hotel**
Cromer Road
North Walsham
Norfolk NR28 0HD
Tel: 01692 403231

**Broom Hall Country Hotel**
Richmond Road
Saham Toney
Thetford
Norfolk IP25 7EX
Tel: 01953 882125

**Maison Talbooth**
Stratford Road
Dedham
Colchester
Essex CO7 6HN
Tel: 01206 322367

**Milsoms Kesgrave Hall**
Hall Road
Kesgrave
Ipswich
Suffolk IP5 2PU
Tel: 01473 333741

**Norfolk Mead Hotel**
Church Loke
Coltishall
Norfolk NR12 7DN
Tel: 01603 737531

**The Pier at Harwich**
The Quay
Harwich
Essex CO12 3HH
Tel: 01255 241212

**Redcoats Farmhouse Hotel**
Redcoats Green
Nr. Hitchen
Hertfordshire SE4 7JR
Tel: 01438 729500

**Wentworth House Hotel**
Wentworth Road
Aldeburgh
Suffolk IP15 5BD
Tel: 01728 452312

## EAST MIDLANDS

**Barnsdale Lodge Hotel**
The Avenue
Rutland Water
Oakham
Rutland LE15 8AH
Tel: 01572 724678

**Biggin Hall Hotel**
Biggin-by-Hartington
Buxton
Derbyshire SK17 0DH
Tel: 01298 84451

**Cavandish Hotel**
Church Lane
Baslow
Derbyshire DE45 1SP
Tel: 01246 582311

**The George**
Main Road
Hathersage
Derbyshire S32 1BB
Tel: 01433 650436

**Langar Hall**
Langar
Nr. Nottingham
Nottinghamshire
NG13 9HG
Tel: 01949 860559

**Losehill House Hotel & Spa**
Edale Road
Hope
Derbyshire S33 6RF
Tel: 01433 621219

**The Manners Arms**
Croxton Road
Knipton
Nr. Grantham
Lincolnshire NG32 1RH
Tel: 01476 879222

**The Peacock Hotel**
Rowsley
Matlock
Derbyshire DE4 2EG
Tel: 01629 733518

**The Talbot Hotel**
New Street
Oundle
Northamptonshire
PE8 4EA
Tel: 01832 273632

**Whittlebury Hall**
Conference Training
Centre, Hotel & Spa
Whittlebury
Nr. Towcester
Northamptonshire
NN12 8QH
Tel: 01327 857857

## HEART OF ENGLAND

**Aylestone Court**
2 Aylestone Hill
Hereford
Herefordshire HR1 1HS
Tel: 01432 359342

**Castle House**
Castle Street
Hereford
Herefordshire
HR1 2NW
Tel: 01432 356321

**The Chase Hotel**
Gloucester Road
Ross-on-Wye
Herefordshire HR9 5LH
Tel: 01989 763161

**The Mytton & Mermaid Hotel**
Atcham
Shrewsbury
Shropshire SY5 6QG
Tel: 01743 761220

**Soulton Hall**
Wem
Nr. Shrewsbury
Shropshire SY4 5RS
Tel: 01939 232786

## YORKSHIRE & THE HUMBER

**The Blue Bell Inn & Champagne Rooms**
Main Street
Weaverthorpe
North Yorkshire
YO17 8EX
Tel: 01944 738204

**The Coniston Hotel & Country Estate**
Coniston Cold
Skipton
North Yorkshire
BD23 4EA
Tel: 01756 748080

**The Devonshire Arms**
Bolton Abbey
Skipton
North Yorkshire
BD23 6AJ
Tel: 01756 718111

**The Devonshire Fell**
Burnsall Village
Skipton
North Yorkshire
BD23 6BT
Tel: 01756 718111

**Lastingham Grange Hotel**
Lastingham
Nr. Kirkbymoorside
York YO62 6TH
01751 417345

**The Sportsman's Arms Hotel & Restaurant**
Wath in Nidderdale
Pateley Bridge
Harrogate HG3 5PP
Tel: 01423 711306

**The Traddock**
Austwick
Settle
North Yorkshire
LA2 8BY
01524 251224

## NORTH WEST

**Borrowdale Gates Country House Hotel**
Grange-in-Borrowdale
Keswick
Cumbria CA12 5UQ
Tel: 01768 777204

**Gibbon Bridge Hotel**
Chipping
Forest of Bowland
Lancashire PR3 2TQ
Tel: 01995 61456

**Gilpin Hotel & Lake House**
Crook Road
Nr. Windermere
Cumbria LA23 3NE
Tel: 01539 488818

**Lovelady Shield Country House Hotel**
Nenthead Road
Nr. Alston
Cumbria CA9 3LF
Tel: 01434 381203

**Oak Bank Hotel**
Broadgate
Grasmere Village
Grasmere
Cumbria LA22 9TA
Tel: 01539 435217

## NORTH EAST

**Waren House Hotel**
Waren Mill
Belford
Northumberland
NE70 7EE
01668 214581

## SCOTLAND

**Atholl Palace Hotel**
Pitlochry
Perthshire PH16 5LY
Tel: 01796 472400

**Blackaddie Country House Hotel**
Blackaddie Road
Sanquhar
Dumfries & Galloway
DG4 6JJ
Tel: 01659 50270

**Coul House Hotel**
Contin
By Strathpeffer
Highlands IV14 9ES
Tel: 01997 421487

**Craigadam House**
Crocketford
Kirkpatrick Durham
Castle Douglas
Dumfries & Galloway
DG7 3HU
Tel: 01556 650233

**Eddrachilles Hotel**
Badcall Bay
Scourie
Sutherland
Highlands IV27 4TH
Tel: 01971 502080

**The Four Seasons Hotel**
St. Fillans
Perthshire PH6 2NF
Tel: 01764 685333

**Roman Camp Country House & Restaurant**
High Street
Callander
Perthshire FK17 9BG
Tel: 01877 330003

**Viewfield House**
Portree
Isle of Skye
Highlands IV51 9EU
Tel: 01478 612217

## WALES

**Glen-yr-Afon House Hotel**
Pontypool Road
Usk
Monmouthshire
NP15 1SY
Tel: 01291 672302

**The Groes Inn**
Tyn-y-Groes
Nr. Conwy LL32 8TN
Tel: 01492 650545

**Miskin Manor Hotel & Health Club**
Miskin
Llantrisant
Nr. Cardiff CF72 8ND
Tel: 01443 224204

**Palé Hall House**
Palé Estate
Llanderfel
Bala
Gwynedd LL23 7PS
Tel: 01678 530285

**Penally Abbey**
Penally
Nr. Tenby
Pembrokeshire
SA70 7PY
Tel: 01834 843033

**Royal Oak Hotel**
Holyhead Road
Betws-y-Coed
Conwy County
LL24 0AY
Tel: 01690 710219

**St. Tudno Hotel**
The Promenade
Llandudno
Conwy LL30 2LP
Tel: 01492 874411

**Trefeddian Hotel**
Aberdovey
Gwynedd LL35 0SB
Tel: 01654 767213

**Tre-Ysgawen Hall Country House Hotel & Spa**
Capel Coch
Llangefni
Anglesey
Wales LL77 7UR
Tel: 01248 750750

**Warpool Court**
St. David's
Wales SA62 6BN
Tel: 01437 720300

**Wolfscastle Country Hotel**
Wolfscastle
Haverfordwest
Wales SA62 5LZ
Tel: 01437 741225

Arley Hall

Elton Hall

# *Indexes*

# *Plant Sales*

## Properties where plants are offered for sale

Hartland Abbey, ©Anya Campbell

© Giles Rocholl

Boconnoc

George Bell House

# *Accommodation*

## Properties where accommodation can be arranged

# *Open All Year*

Properties and / or their grounds that are open for all or most of the year

Otley Hall

Dumfries House

Harewood House
©Anthony Hicks

Pentillie Castle

# Civil Weddings

Properties at which wedding or civil partnership ceremonies can take place

Lulworth Castle

Chiddingstone Castle

# Corporate Hospitality

Properties able to accommodate corporate functions, wedding receptions and events

# Guided Tours

Properties that offer informative guided tours

Chatsworth House

Beamish Museum

# Special Events

Historical re-enactments, festivals, country and craft fairs, concerts, fireworks, car and steam rallies, and much more...
(please check dates before visiting)

Leeds Castle

## JANUARY

**25**

Alnwick Castle, Northumberland
Burns Night Party

## FEBRUARY

**8 Feb - 2 March**

Burton Agnes Hall & Gardens,
East Yorkshire
Snowdrop Spectacular

**9 & 16**

Hartland Abbey, Devon
Snowdrop Sundays 11am-4pm

**15-23**

Leeds Castle, Kent
Just Jesting

**17 & 24**

Deene Park, Northamptonshire
Snowdrop Sundays (Gardens Only)
11am-4pm

## MARCH

**1-30 (closed Mondays)**

Chiswick House, London
Camellia Festival, (Closed Mondays)

**1 & 2**

Burton Agnes Hall & Gardens,
East Yorkshire
Orchid Festival

**2**

Harvington Hall,
Worcestershire
Living History Weekend

**8**

Boconnoc,
Cornwall
Glo in the Park Run

**16**

Hartland Abbey,
Devon
Daffodil Day 11am-4pm

**22 & 23**

Sherborne Castle,
Dorset
Spring Bulbs and Daffodils Weekend

**28**

Harvington Hall,
Worcestershire
Murder Mystery Evening

**28 March-29 October**

Alnwick Castle, Northumberland
Broomstick Training, State Rooms Tours
(ends 27 Oct), Historical Grounds Tours,
Battleaxe to Broomsticks Tours, Medieval
Crafts and Dressing Up, Dragon Quest

**30**

Chiddingstone Castle, Kent
Mothering Sunday Teas 12noon-4pm,
pre booking essential.

## APRIL

**April-October**

Kentwell Hall & Gardens, Suffolk
Victorian Re-Creations on
selected weekends

**5 & 6**

Boconnoc, Cornwall
CGS Spring Flower Show

**7**

Deene Park, Northamptonshire
Daffodil Day (Gardens Only) 11am-4pm

**12-27**

Burton Agnes Hall & Gardens, East
Yorkshire
Easter Egg Trail

**13**

Chiddingstone Castle, Kent
Ancient Egypt Family Day

**18-21**

Eastnor Castle, Herefordshire
Easter Treasure Hunt

**20 & 21**

Burton Agnes Hall & Gardens,
East Yorkshire
Easter Egg Hunt

**20 & 27**

Hartland Abbey, Devon
Bluebell Sundays

**21 April, Easter Monday**

Chenies Manor House, Buckinghamshire
House & Garden 2-5pm. Children's Egg
Races, Chenies resident magician Dee
Riley, plants for sale, homemade teas

**27**

Beaulieu, Hampshire
Boatjumble

## MAY

Clovelly, Devon
Celebration of Ales and Ciders

**May - September**

Hartland Abbey, Devon
Outdoor Theatre

**3-5**

Sherborne Castle,
Dorset
Craft & Garden Fair

**4**

Hartland Abbey, Devon
Hartland Abbey Heartbreaker Run

**5 May, Bank Holiday Monday**

Penshurst Place and Gardens, Kent
Weald of Kent Craft Show
Chenies Manor House,
Buckinghamshire
Tulip Festival. House & Garden 2-5pm

**11**

Burton Agnes Hall & Gardens,
East Yorkshire
Classic Car Rally

Shakespeare at Skipton Castle

**11**

Newby Hall & Gardens,
North Yorkshire
Spring Plant Fair

**13**

Goodwood, Sussex
Connoisseur's Day, special tours for
booked groups of 20+ only

**17 & 18**

Beaulieu, Hampshire
Autojumble

**18**

Boconnoc, Cornwall
Dog Show

**18-22**

Athelhampton House and Gardens,
Dorset
Flower Festival 10:30am-5pm

**25**

Kingston Bagpuize House, Oxfordshire
Rare Plant Fair

**25 & 26**

Newby Hall & Gardens, North Yorkshire
Yorkshire Game Fair

**26 May, Bank Holiday Monday**

Chenies Manor House,
Buckinghamshire
Carriage Driving Day 10am-4pm.
House & Garden 2-5pm

Sherborne Castle, Dorset
Sherborne Castle Country Fair Retriever
Event & Rare Breeds Show

## JUNE

**First week in June**

Penshurst Place and Gardens,
Kent
Glorious Gardens Week

**1**

Stonor, Oxfordshire
VW Owner's Rally

**6-8**

Scone Palace and Grounds, Tayside
Potfest: International Ceramics Festival

**7 & 8**

Burton Agnes Hall & Gardens,
East Yorkshire
Gardeners Fair

Newby Hall & Gardens,
North Yorkshire Yorkshire
Vintage Association - Tractor Fest.

**14 & 15**

Beaulieu, Hampshire
Custom and Hot Rod Festival

**15**

Chiddingstone Castle,
Kent
Japanese Day

**19**

Athelhampton House and Gardens,
Dorset
Dorset Vintage and Classic Auctions.

**21 & 22**

Boconnoc, Cornwall
Endurance GB Ride

Woburn Abbey,
Bedfordshire
The Woburn Abbey Garden Show

**22**

Sherborne Castle,
Dorset
Cancer Research UK Race for Life

**26-29**

Hopetoun House,
Edinburgh
Horse Trials

**27/28/29**

Burton Agnes Hall & Gardens,
East Yorkshire
Jazz and Blues Festival

**28 & 29**

Leeds Castle, Kent
Leeds Castle Triathlon

## JULY

Clovelly, Devon
Clovelly Maritime Festival,
Woolsery Agricultural Show,
Lundy Row

**4-6**

Scone Palace and Grounds,
Tayside
The GWCT Scottish Game Fair.

**13**

Beaulieu, Hampshire
Motorcycle Ride In Day

**18-20**

Boconnoc, Cornwall
Steam Fair

**18-21**

Scone Palace and Grounds
Tayside
80s Rewind Festival

**20**

Chenies Manor House, Buckinghamshire
Famous Plant and Garden Fair 10-5pm
House 2pm

Newby Hall & Gardens, North Yorkshire
Historic Vehicle Rally.

Sherborne Castle, Dorset
'Classics at the Castle' Classic Car
and Supercar Show.

**22-25**

Boconnoc, Cornwall
Music Awards Concerts.

**23**

Chiddingstone Castle, Kent
Best of West Kent Veteran Car Run

**26 & 27**

Boconnoc, Cornwall, Car Rally

**29 July-2 August**

Goodwood, Sussex
Glorious Goodwood.

## AUGUST

Clovelly, Devon
Lifeboat Day, Clovelly Gig Regatta

**10**

Athelhampton House and Gardens,
Dorset
MG Owners Rally 10:30am-4pm.

**16 & 17**

Burton Agnes Hall & Gardens,
East Yorkshire
Family Fun Weekend

**22-25**

Stonor, Oxfordshire
Christmas Craft and Design Fair

**25 August, Bank Holiday Monday**

Athelhampton House and Gardens,
Dorset
5 Churches Fete 12pm-4:30pm.

Chenies Manor House, Buckinghamshire
Dahlia Festival. House & Garden 2-5pm

**29**

Athelhampton House and Gardens,
Dorset
Outdoor Theatre- Sense and Sensibility,
Chapterhouse Theare Company
6pm-9pm.

## SEPTEMBER

Clovelly, Devon - Lobster & Crab Feast.

Penshurst Place and Gardens, Kent
Weald of Kent Craft Show.

Alnwick Castle

**2**

Goodwood, Sussex
Connoisseur's Day, special tours for
booked groups of 20+ only.

**4-7**

Burghley House,
Lincolnshire
Burghley Horse Trials.

**6 & 7**

Beaulieu, Hampshire
International Autojumble.

**12-14**

Goodwood, Sussex
Goodwood Revival Meeting

**14**

Chiddingstone Castle, Kent
Country Fair

**18**

Athelhampton House and Gardens,
Dorset
Dorset Vintage and Classic Auctions.

**21 & 22**

Scone Palace and Grounds,
Tayside
Chilli Festival

**28**

Newby Hall & Gardens, North Yorkshire
Apple Day

## OCTOBER

**10 October-1 November**

Kentwell Hall & Gardens,
Suffolk
Scaresville, selected evenings.

**25**

Beaulieu,
Hampshire
Fireworks Spectacular.

**25 & 26**

Burton Agnes Hall & Gardens,
East Yorkshire
Michaelmas Fair.

**8**

Sherborne Castle, Dorset
Autumn Colours Weekend.

**25 October-2 November**

Burton Agnes Hall & Gardens, East Yorkshire
Pumpkin Trail.

**29 & 30**

Chenies Manor House, Buckinghamshire
Spooks and Surprises- Special scary
tour of the house for children 2-5pm.

## NOVEMBER

Clovelly, Devon
Clovelly Herring Festival

**1**

Hopetoun House, Edinburgh
Fireworks.

**8**

Sherborne Castle, Dorset
Firework Extravaganza.

**14-16**

Hopetoun House, Edinburgh
Christmas Shopping Fayre

**28**

Chiddingstone Castle, Kent
Christmas Fair

## DECEMBER

Clovelly, Devon
Christmas Lights

**Four weeks before Christmas**

Polesden Lacey, Surrey
Christmas Event

**6-14**

Peckover House & Gardens,
Cambridgeshire
Christmas Event (weekends only)

**14-22**

Kentwell Hall & Gardens, Suffolk
A Dickensian Christmas,
Victorian Re-Creation.

# HUDSON'S HERITAGE Explorer

Hatfield House, Hertford

# An exciting touring pass

## Opening the door to the country's heritage attractions

2014

**CHILD 14-DAY PASS**

2014

**ADULT 28-DAY PASS**

3, 7, 14 or 28-day passes

Visit as many participating attractions as you wish during the fixed-day period

Prices start from just £49.00 per Adult

Complimentary full-colour guidebook

Available to buy online and in person at selected outlets

*Amazing value! Visit heritage attractions for less than £6.40 per day\* SAVE MORE WITH EVERY VISIT*

## www.hudsons-explorer.com

RHS Garden Wisley, Surrey    Bamburgh Castle, Northumberland    Roman Baths, Somerset    Portsmouth Historic Dockyard

**STATELY HOMES • HISTORIC HOUSES • CASTLES • GARDENS • ABBEYS & CATHEDRALS • WORLD HERITAGE SITES**

# Maps

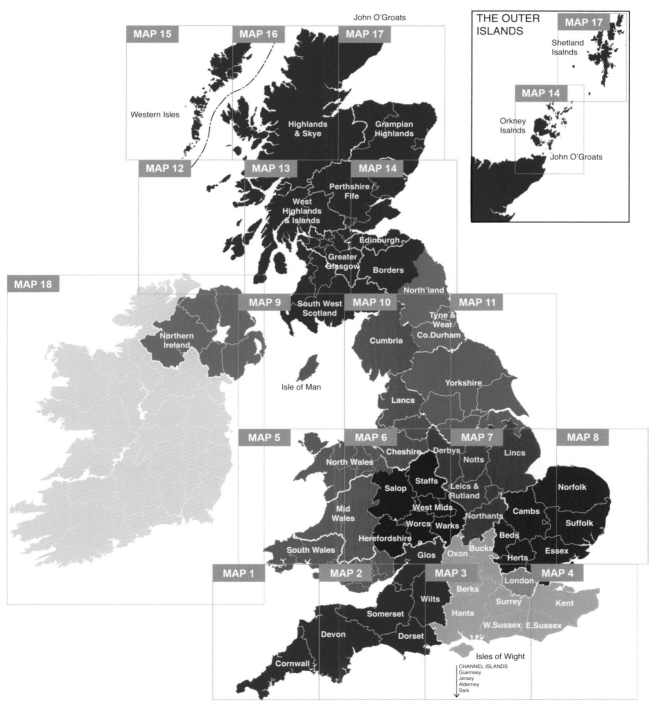

**THE OUTER ISLANDS**

MAP 15 — Western Isles

MAP 16

MAP 17

MAP 17 — Shetland Isalnds

MAP 14 — Orkney Isalnds

John O'Groats

MAP 12

MAP 13

MAP 14

Highlands & Skye

Grampian Highlands

West Highlands & Islands

Perthshire Fife

Edinburgh

Greater Glasgow

Borders

MAP 18

MAP 9 — South West Scotland

MAP 10

MAP 11

North'land

Northern Ireland

Cumbria

Tyne & Wear

Co.Durham

Isle of Man

Yorkshire

Lancs

MAP 5

MAP 6

MAP 7

MAP 8

North Wales

Cheshire

Derbys

Notts

Lincs

Mid Wales

Salop

Staffs

Leics & Rutland

Norfolk

West Mids

Worcs

Warks

Northants

Cambs

Suffolk

South Wales

Herefordshire

Beds

Glos

Oxon

Bucks

Herts

Essex

MAP 1

MAP 2

MAP 3

MAP 4

London

Berks

Surrey

Kent

Wilts

Hants

W.Sussex

E.Sussex

Somerset

Devon

Dorset

Isles of Wight

Cornwall

CHANNEL ISLANDS
Guernsey
Jersey
Alderney
Sark

©VisitBritain/Rod Edwards

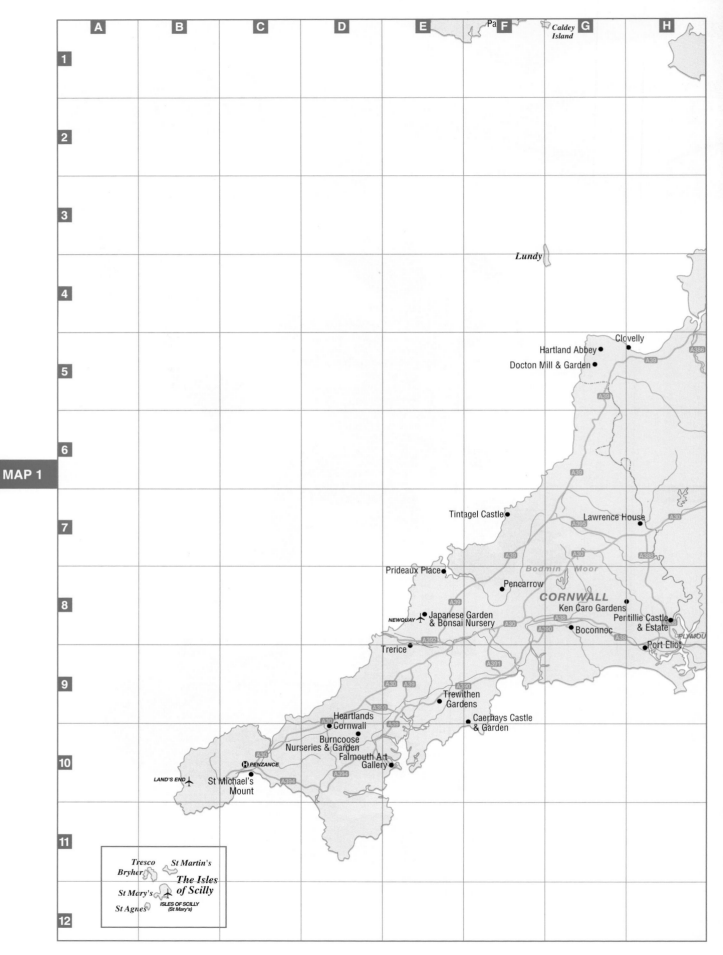

MAP 1

A B C D E F G H

1
2
3
4
5
6
7
8
9
10
11
12

Caldey Island

Lundy

Clovelly
Hartland Abbey
Docton Mill & Garden

A39
A39
A386

Tintagel Castle
Lawrence House

A39
A395
A30

Bodmin Moor

Prideaux Place
Pencarrow
CORNWALL
Ken Caro Gardens
Pentillie Castle & Estate

NEWQUAY
Japanese Garden & Bonsai Nursery
Boconnoc
PLYMOU

A39
A30
A38
A390
A38
Port Eliot

Trerice
A392
A391

Trewithen Gardens

A30
A39
A390
A350
Caerhays Castle & Garden

Heartlands Cornwall
A30
Burncoose Nurseries & Garden
Falmouth Art Gallery

A30
PENZANCE
A394
A394
LAND'S END
St Michael's Mount

Tresco St Martin's
Bryher
St Mary's
The Isles of Scilly
St Agnes
ISLES OF SCILLY (St Mary's)

Register for news and special offers at www.hudsonsheritage.com

Weobley Castle
SWANSEA
SWANSEA ✈
Oxwich Castle

BRIDGEND

RHONDDA CYNON TAFF
CAERPHILLY
Llancaiach Fawr Manor

Caerleon Roman Baths
NEWPORT
Tredegar House

Chepstow Castle
SOUTH GLOUCESTERSHIRE
M48
M4
M49
BRISTOL
M32
M4
New Park

CARDIFF
Llandaff Cathedral
A4232

VALE OF GLAMORGAN
Dyffryn Gardens
Fonmon Castle
CARDIFF ✈

NORTH SOMERSET
BRISTOL
Gatcombe Court
A4174

A371

M5

Building of Bath Museum
Crowe Hall
Holburne Museum of Art

Peto Gardens at Iford Manor

Mendip Hills

Chambercombe Manor
Exmoor
Exmoor Forest

Fairfield
Kentsford
Orchard
Wyndham
Dodington Hall

SOMERSET
Milton Lodge Gardens
Stoberry House

Nunney Castle
Longleat

Marwood Hill Garden
Brendon Hills
Quantock Hills

Robin Hood's Hut
Maunsel House

A39
Polden Hills
Glastonbury Abbey
A361

A39
A361

A377

Woodlands Castle
M5
Blackdown Hills
A358
A303
A3088

Sandford Orcas Manor H

Sherborne Castle

Castle Hill Gardens
A361

A377
Tiverton Castle

Stock Gayland House

DEVON
Fursdon House
Downes
A377
M5

A30
A35

Forde Abbey & Gardens

Higher Melcombe
Minterne Gardens
Mapperton
DORSET

Great Fulford
A30
EXETER
M5
A30
A376
Cadhay
Sand

Church of Our Lady & St Ignatius
A35
Wolfeton House
Athelhampton House & Gardens
A354

Powderham Castle
A380

Dartmoor
Dartmoor Forest
A386

A354
Chesil Beach
A354
Lulworth Castle & Park

Buckfast Abbey
TORBAY
A380
Portland Bill

Buckland Abbey
PLYMOUTH ✈
A38
A38

Shilstone

GUERNSEY

Sausmarez Manor

MAP 2

I J K L M N O P
1
2
3
4
5
6
7
8
9
10
11
12

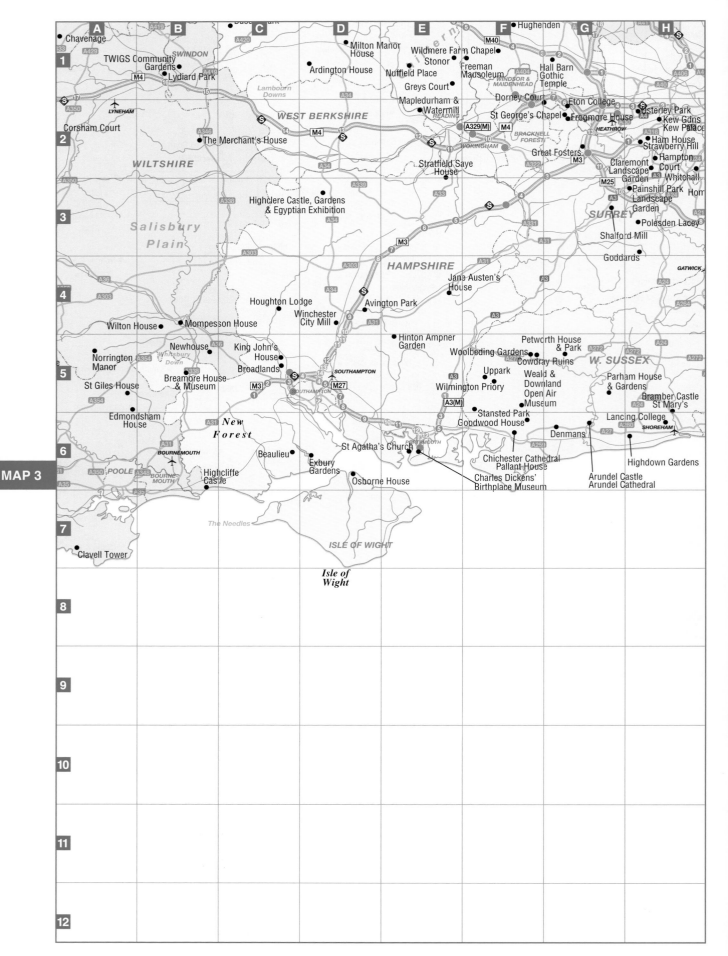

MAP 3

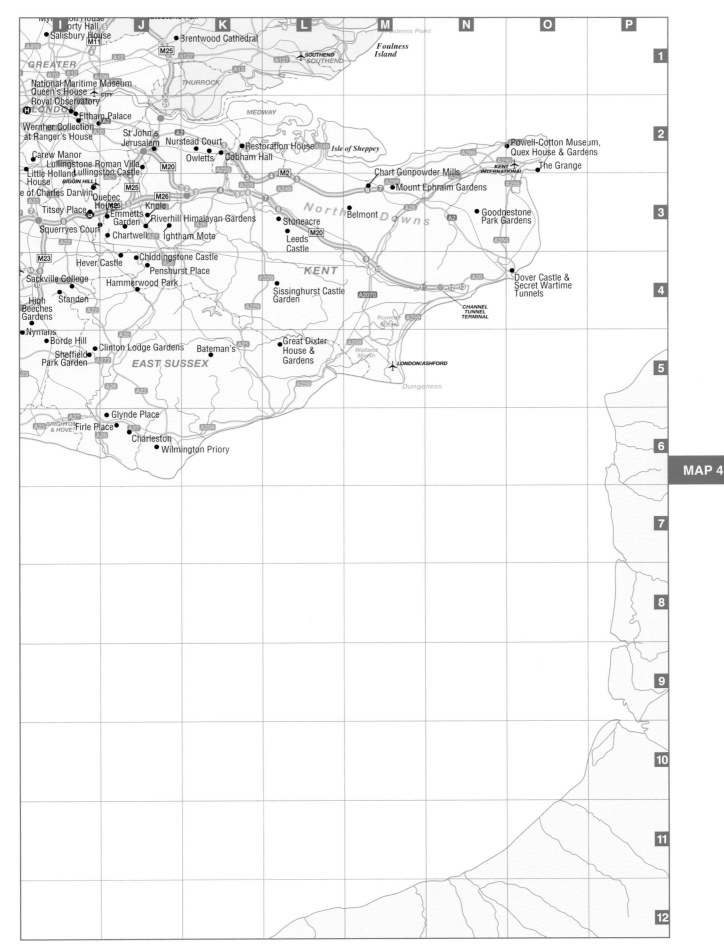

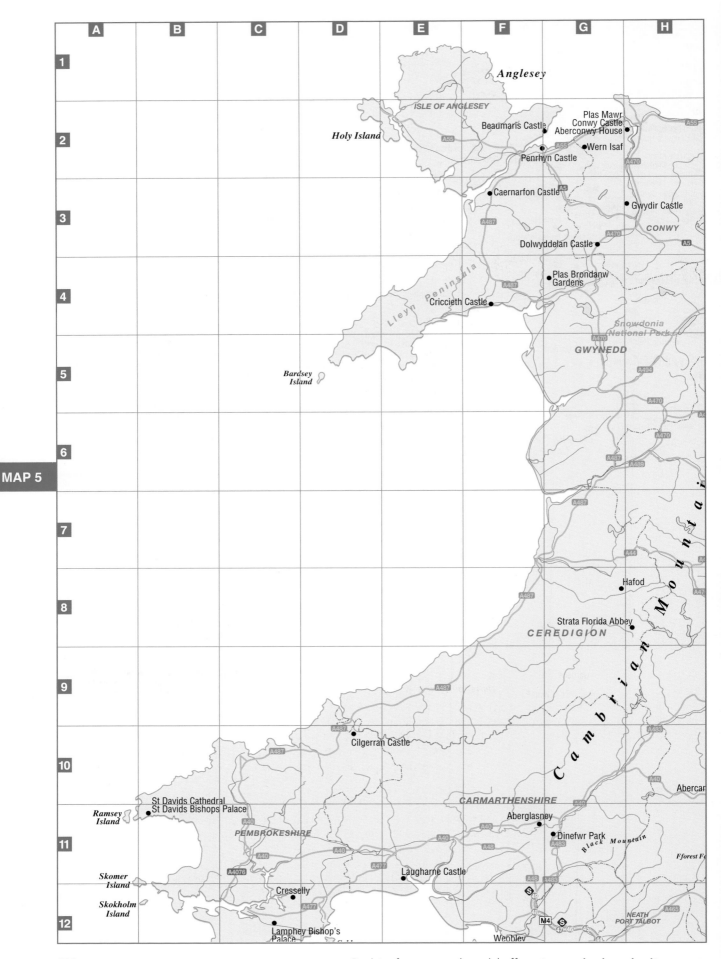

MAP 5

Anglesey

ISLE OF ANGLESEY

Holy Island

Plas Mawr
Conwy Castle
Beaumaris Castle • Aberconwy House
Wern Isaf
Penrhyn Castle

Caernarfon Castle

Gwydir Castle

CONWY

Dolwyddelan Castle

Plas Brondanw Gardens

Lleyn Peninsula

Criccieth Castle

Snowdonia National Park

GWYNEDD

Bardsey Island

Hafod

Strata Florida Abbey

CEREDIGION

Cambrian Mountains

Cilgerran Castle

St Davids Cathedral
St Davids Bishops Palace

Ramsey Island

CARMARTHENSHIRE

Aberglasney

Abercar

PEMBROKESHIRE

Dinefwr Park

Black Mountain

Fforest F

Skomer Island

Laugharne Castle

Cresselly

Skokholm Island

NEATH PORT TALBOT

Lamphey Bishop's Palace

Weobley

Register for news and special offers at www.hudsonsheritage.com

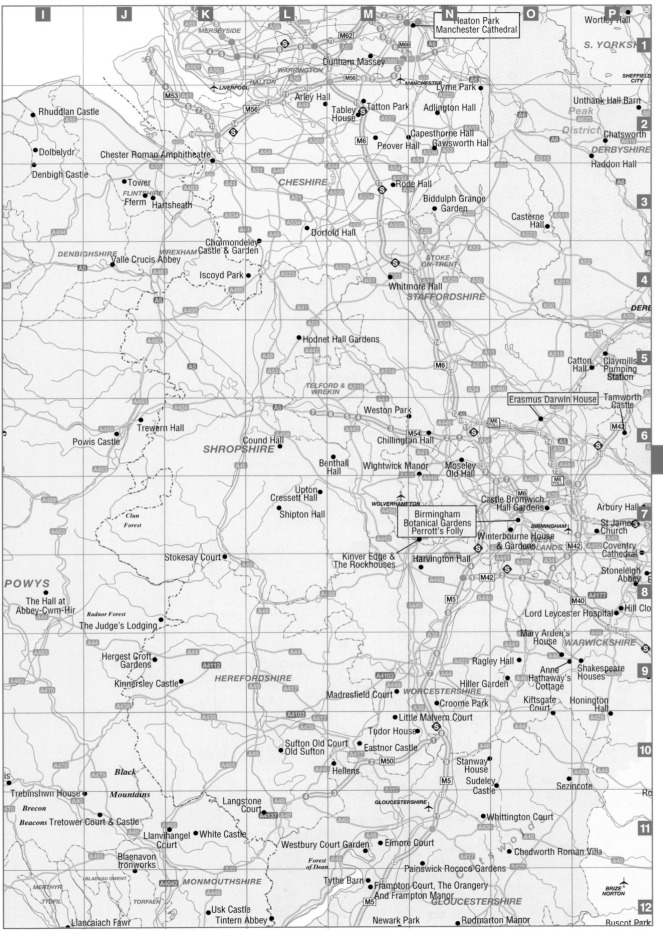

**MAP 7**

Grid references: A B C D E F G H / 1–12

Wentworth Woodhouse

Renishaw Hall Gardens

Hardwick Hall

*NOTTINGHAMSHIRE*

Doddington Hall & Gardens

*LINCOLNSHIRE*

Aubourn Hall

Pappiewick Hall

Mr Straw's House

Leadenham House

Fulbeck Manor

*NOTTINGHAM*

Marston Hall

Belvoir Castle

*NOTTINGHAM EAST MIDLANDS*

Melbourne Hall
Calke Abbey

Woolsthorpe Manor

Grimsthorpe Castle Park & Gardens

Ayscoughfee Hall Museum & Gardens

Sandringham

Castle Rising

Clifton House

*The Fens*

*LEICESTERSHIRE*

Peckover House & Garden

*RUTLAND*

Burghley House

*LEICESTER*

*PETERBOROUGH*

Ely Cathedral
Old Palace
Oliver Cromwell's House

Rockingham Castle

Elton Hall

Southwick Hall

Deene Park

Astley Castle

*CAMBRIDGESHIRE*

Stanford Hall

Cottesbrooke

Lamport Hall

*COVENTRY*

got's Castle

*NORTHAMPTONSHIRE*

Haddonstone Show Gardens

The Manor, Hemingford Grey

Kimbolton Castle

Island Hall

ose Gardens

Holdenby House

Althorp

78 Derngate

University Botanic Garden

*CAMBRIDGE*

ompton Verney

*BEDFORDSHIRE*

Turvey House

Stoke Park Pavilions

*MILTON KEYNES*

Moggerhanger Park

Wakefield Lodge

Weston Hall

Queen Anne's Summerhouse

Audley End House & Gardens

Broughton Castle

Chicksands Priory

Wrest Park

ousham House

Woburn Abbey

Benington Lordship

*STANSTED*

*BUCKINGHAMSHIRE*

Ascott

*LUTON*

*HERTFORDSHIRE*

enheim Palace

Knebworth

*OXFORDSHIRE*

Wotton House

Gorhambury House

Hatfield House

Claydon House

Copped Hall

Nether Winchendon House

Waterperry Gardens

Capel Manor

Kingston Bagquize

26A East St Helen Street

Chenies Manor House

Hyla

402    Register for news and special offers at www.hudsonsheritage.com

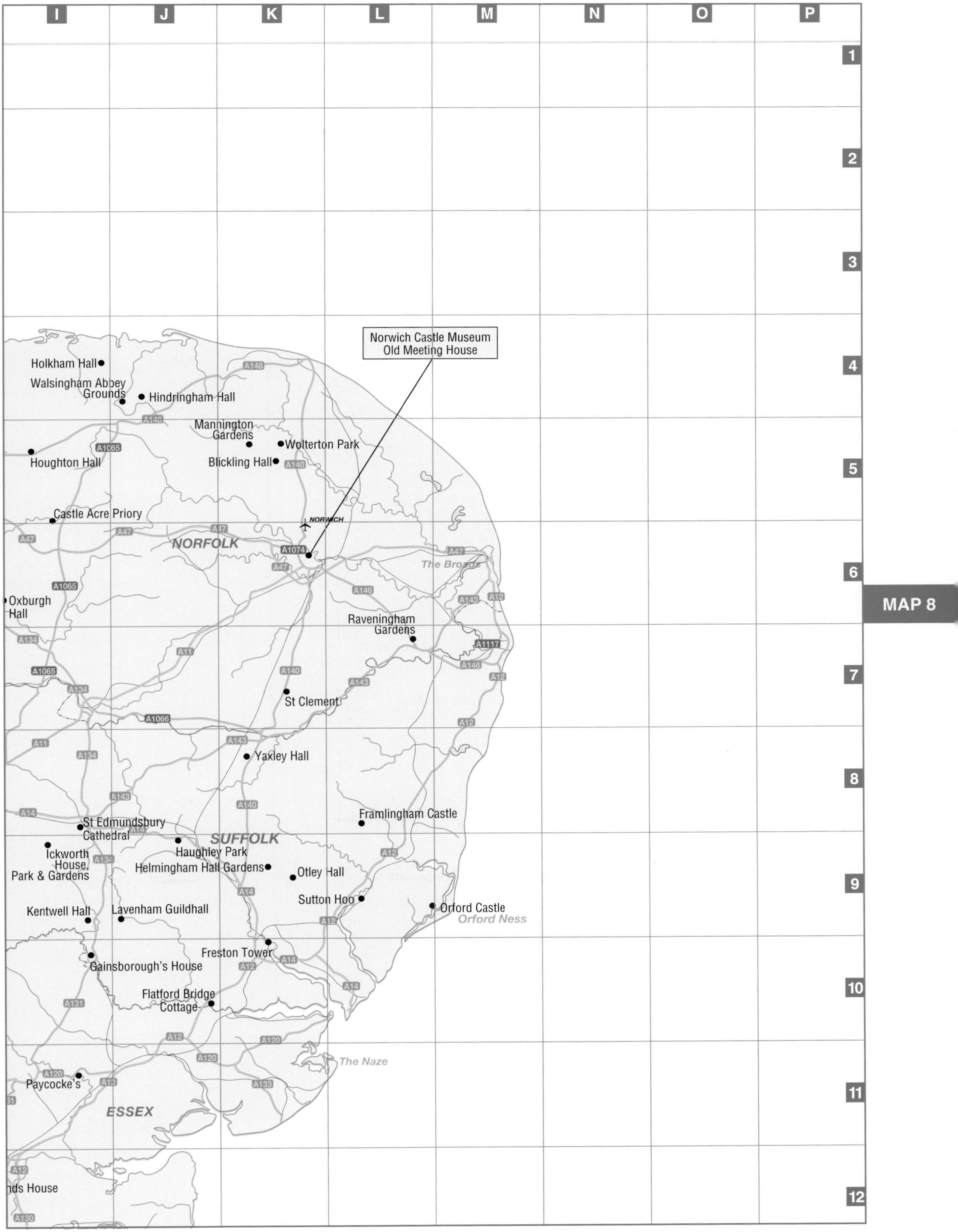

I   J   K   L   M   N   O   P

1

2

3

4

Holkham Hall●

Walsingham Abbey
Grounds
● Hindringham Hall

Norwich Castle Museum
Old Meeting House

Mannington
Gardens
● ●Wolterton Park

Houghton Hall
● Blickling Hall

A148

A148

A1065

A140

5

Castle Acre Priory
●

NORFOLK

A47

A47

NORWICH

A1074

A47

A67

The Broads

6

MAP 8

●Oxburgh
Hall

A1065

A134

A148

A143  A12

Raveningham
Gardens

A1117

7

A1065

A134

A11

A140

A143

A146

A12

● St Clement

A1066

A12

A11

A134

●Yaxley Hall

A143

8

A14

A143

A140

St Edmundsbury
Cathedral
●

Framlingham Castle
●

SUFFOLK

A12

9

Ickworth
House,
Park & Gardens
●

A134

Haughley Park
●

Helmingham Hall Gardens●

● Otley Hall

A14

Kentwell Hall
●

Lavenham Guildhall
●

Sutton Hoo
●

●Orford Castle
Orford Ness

Freston Tower
●

A14

10

Gainsborough's House
●

A12

A14

Flatford Bridge
Cottage

A131

A12

A120

A120

A120

The Naze

11

Paycocke's
●

A120

A12

A133

ESSEX

131

12

A12

ds House

A130

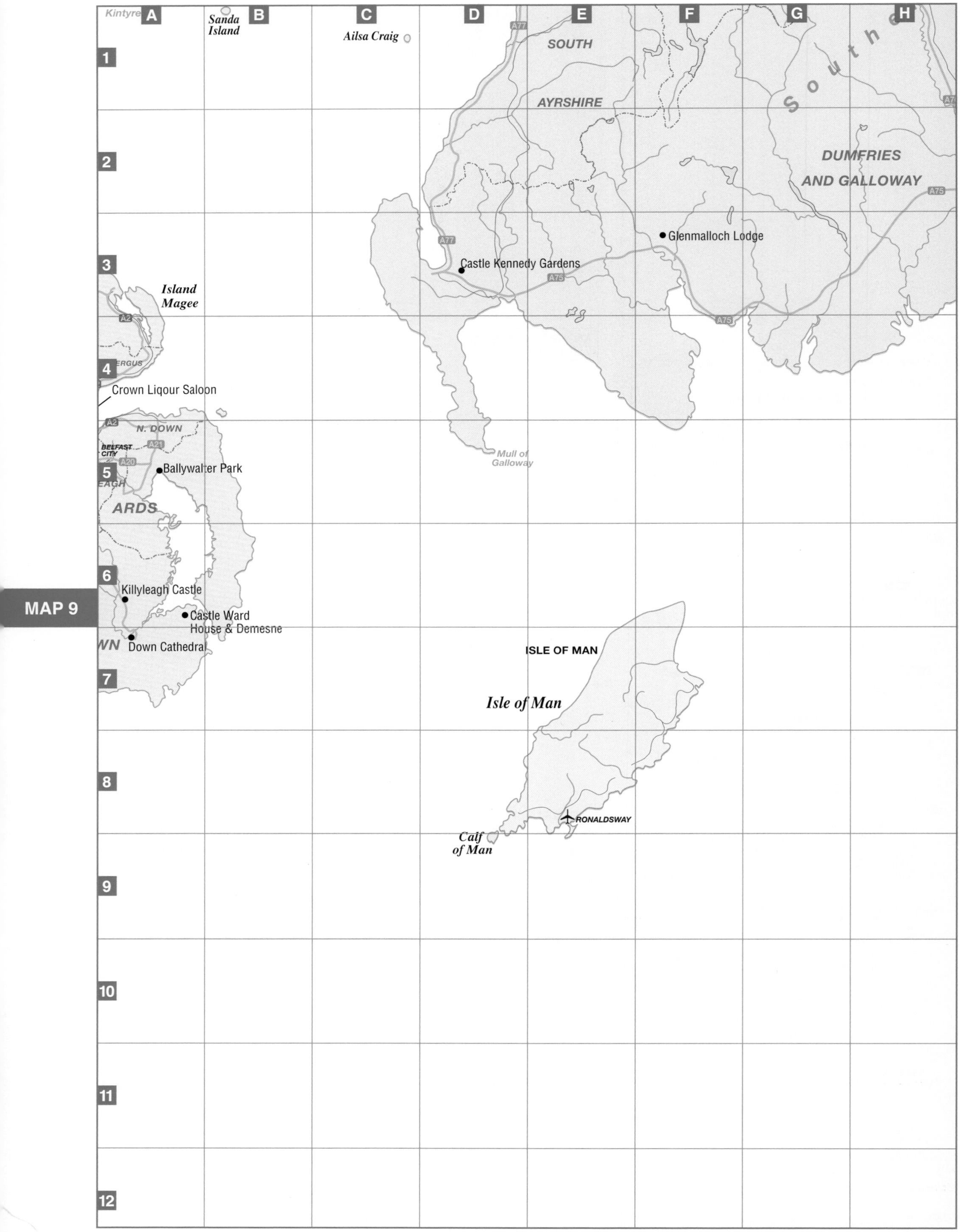

MAP 9

Kintyre

**A**  **B**  **C**  **D**  **E**  **F**  **G**  **H**

Sanda
Island

Ailsa Craig

**1**

SOUTH

AYRSHIRE

South

**2**

DUMFRIES
AND GALLOWAY

A75

A77

● Glenmalloch Lodge

**3**

Island
Magee

● Castle Kennedy Gardens

A75

A2

**4**

ERGUS

Crown Liqour Saloon

A75

A2

N. DOWN

A21

BELFAST
CITY

A20

Mull of
Galloway

**5**

EAGH

● Ballywalter Park

ARDS

**6**

● Killyleagh Castle

● Castle Ward
House & Demesne

ISLE OF MAN

WN

● Down Cathedral

**7**

Isle of Man

**8**

Calf
of Man

RONALDSWAY

**9**

**10**

**11**

**12**

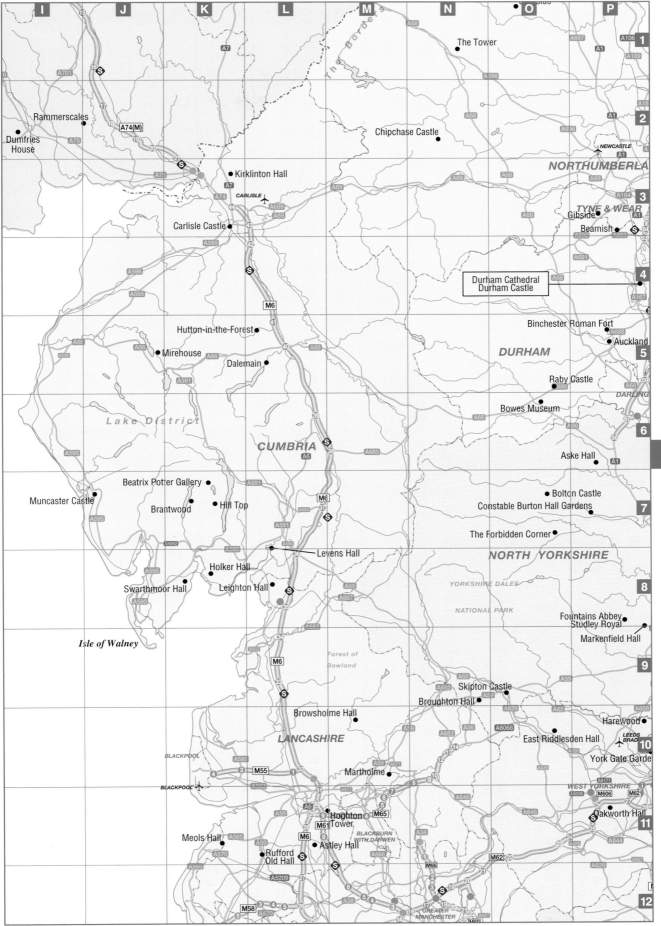

MAP 10

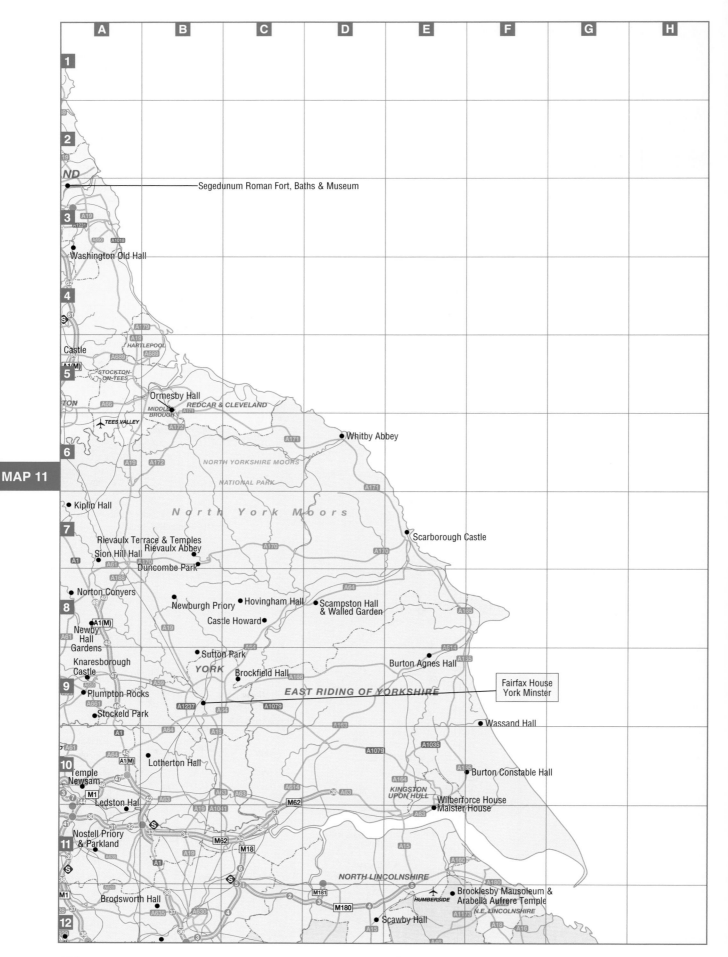

Segedunum Roman Fort, Baths & Museum

Washington Old Hall

Castle

Ormesby Hall

Whitby Abbey

MAP 11

Kiplin Hall

Scarborough Castle

Rievaulx Terrace & Temples
Rievaulx Abbey
Sion Hill Hall
Duncombe Park

Norton Conyers

Newburgh Priory
Hovingham Hall
Scampston Hall
& Walled Garden

Newby
Hall
Gardens

Castle Howard

Knaresborough
Castle

Sutton Park

Burton Agnes Hall

Brockfield Hall

YORK

EAST RIDING OF YORKSHIRE

Fairfax House
York Minster

Plumpton Rocks

Stockeld Park

Wassand Hall

Lotherton Hall

Burton Constable Hall

Temple
Newsam

KINGSTON
UPON HULL

Wilberforce House
Maister House

Ledston Hall

Nostell Priory
& Parkland

NORTH LINCOLNSHIRE

Brocklesby Mausoleum &
Arabella Aufrere Temple

HUMBERSIDE

Brodsworth Hall

N.E. LINCOLNSHIRE

Scawby Hall

Register for news and special offers at www.hudsonsheritage.com

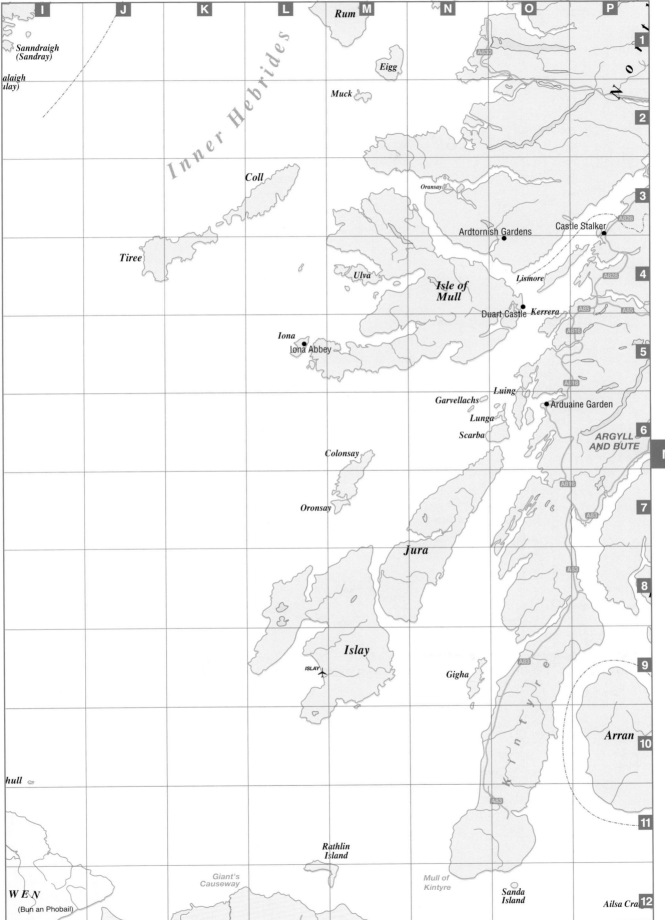

MAP 12

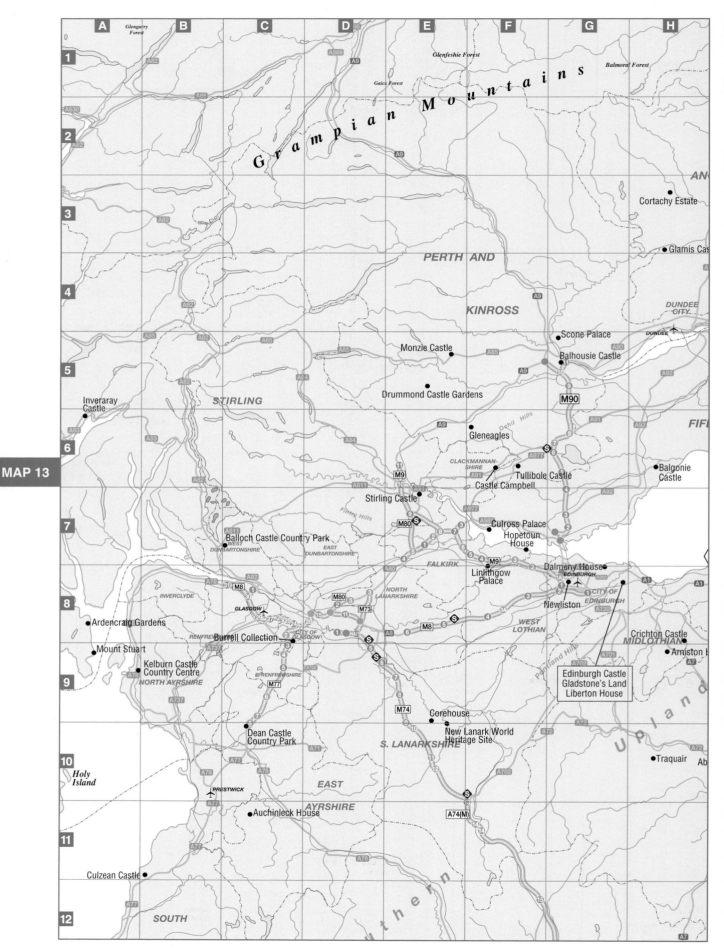

MAP 13

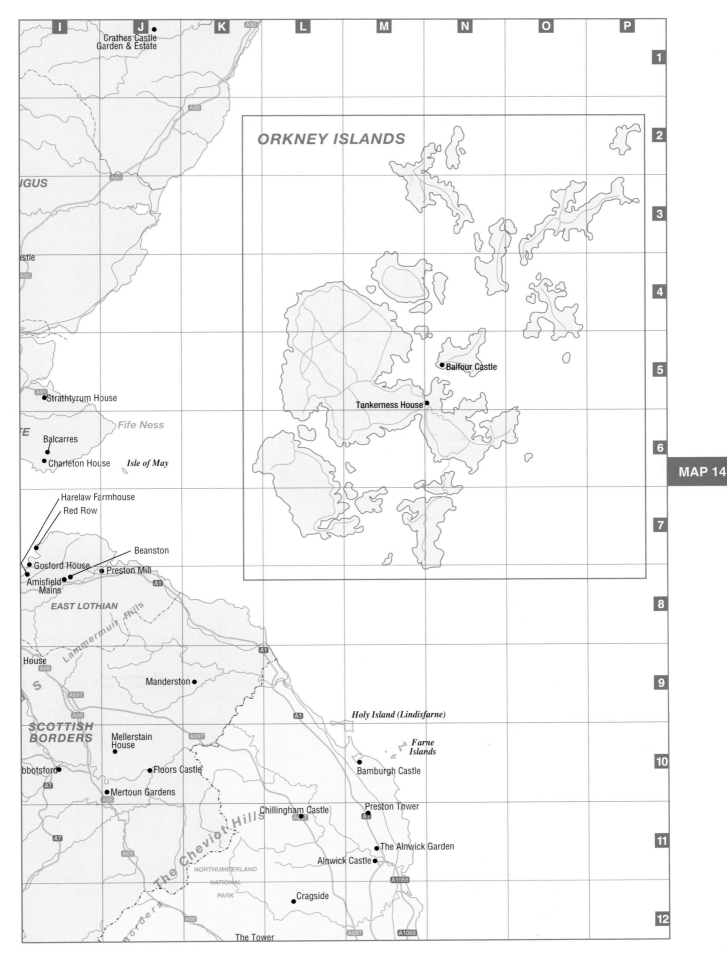

ORKNEY ISLANDS

MAP 14

Crathes Castle Garden & Estate

ANGUS

Castle

Fife Ness

Strathtyrum House

Balcarres

Charleton House    Isle of May

FE

Harelaw Farmhouse
Red Row
Beanston
Gosford House
Amisfield Mains
Preston Mill

EAST LOTHIAN

Lammermuir Hills

House

SCOTTISH
BORDERS

Manderston

Holy Island (Lindisfarne)

Mellerstain House

Farne Islands

bbotsford

Floors Castle

Bamburgh Castle

Mertoun Gardens

Chillingham Castle    Preston Tower

The Cheviot Hills

The Alnwick Garden
Alnwick Castle

NORTHUMBERLAND NATIONAL PARK

Cragside

Borders

The Tower

Balfour Castle

Tankerness House

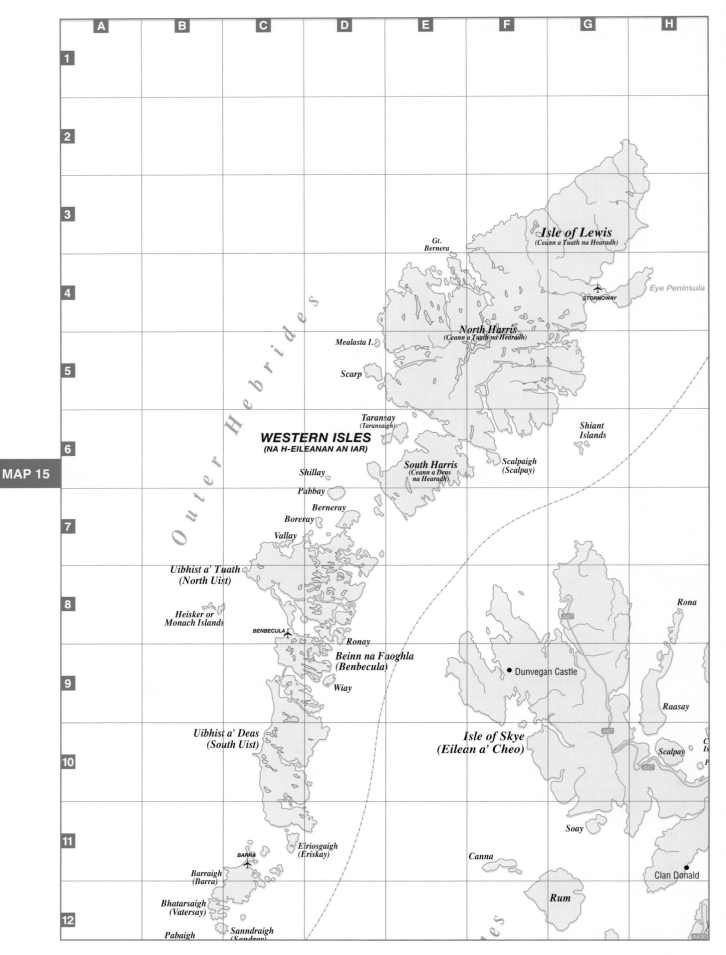

MAP 15

A  B  C  D  E  F  G  H

*Outer Hebrides*

**WESTERN ISLES**
*(NA H-EILEANAN AN IAR)*

Gt.
Bernera

*Isle of Lewis*
*(Ceann a Tuath na Hearadh)*

Eye Peninsula

STORNOWAY

Mealasta I.

*North Harris*
*(Ceann a Tuath na Hearadh)*

Scarp

*Taransay*
*(Taransaigh)*

Shiant
Islands

*South Harris*
*(Ceann a Deas na Hearadh)*

Scalpaigh
(Scalpay)

Shillay

Pabbay

Berneray

Boreray

Vallay

*Uibhist a' Tuath*
*(North Uist)*

Heisker or
Monach Islands

BENBECULA

Ronay

*Beinn na Faoghla*
*(Benbecula)*

Wiay

Rona

● Dunvegan Castle

Raasay

*Uibhist a' Deas*
*(South Uist)*

*Isle of Skye*
*(Eilean a' Cheo)*

Scalpay

Soay

Eiriosgaigh
(Eriskay)

BARRA

Canna

Clan Donald

Barraigh
(Barra)

**Rum**

Bhatarsaigh
(Vatersay)

Pabaigh

Sanndraigh
(Sandray)

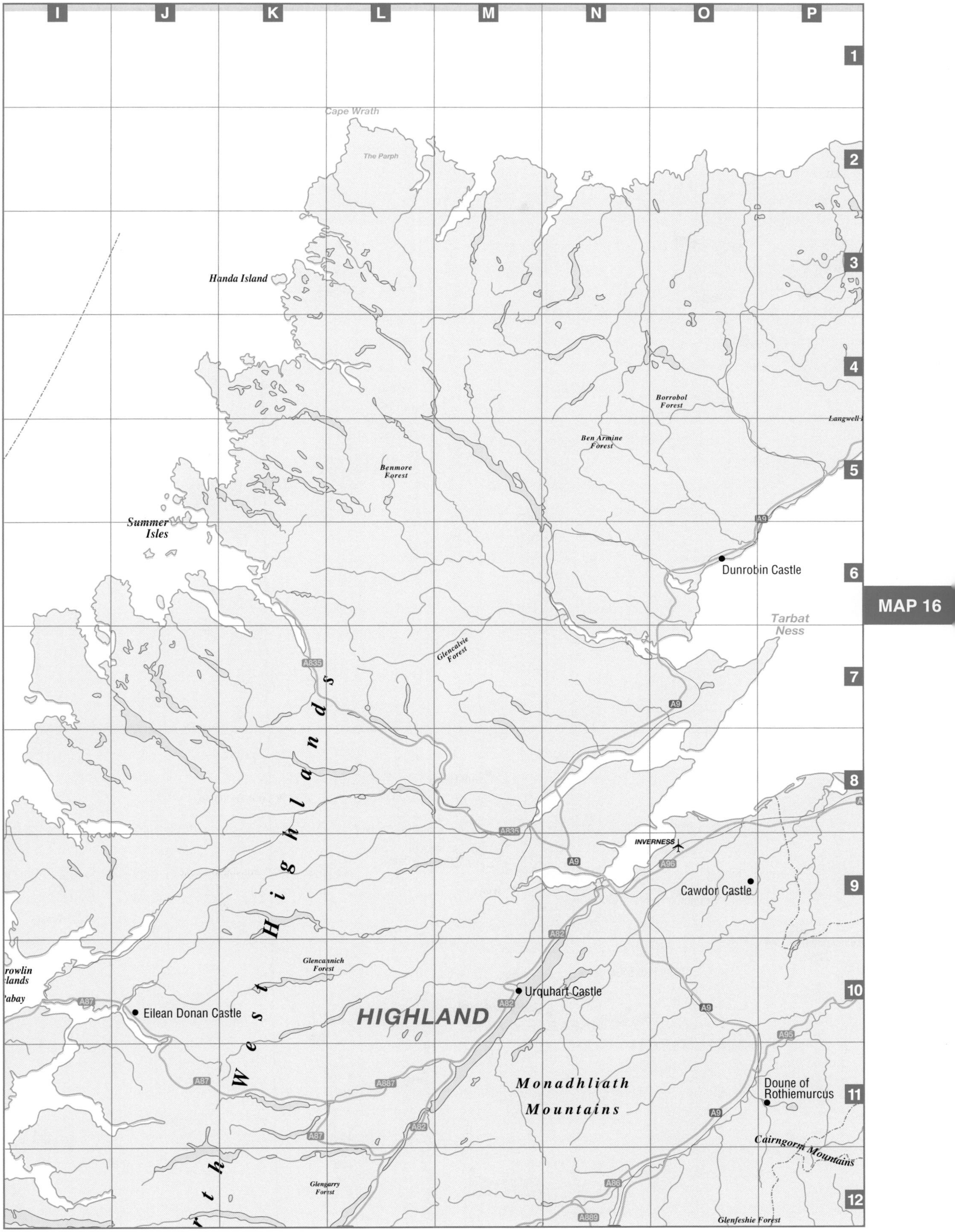

I J K L M N O P

1

Cape Wrath

The Parph

2

Handa Island

3

4

Borrobol
Forest

Langwell

Ben Armine
Forest

5

Benmore
Forest

Summer
Isles

Dunrobin Castle

6

MAP 16

Tarbat
Ness

Glencalvie
Forest

A835

7

H
i
g
h
l
a
n
d
s

A835

8

A

INVERNESS
A96

A9

9

Cawdor Castle

rowlin
lands

Glencannich
Forest

A82

abay

A87

Urquhart Castle

10

Eilean Donan Castle

W
e
s
t

HIGHLAND

A82

A9

A95

A87

Monadhliath

A887

Mountains

Doune of
Rothiemurcus

11

A87

A82

A9

Cairngorm Mountains

N
o
r
t
h

Glengarry
Forest

12

A86

A889

Glenfeshie Forest

Visit **www.hudsonsheritage.com** for special events and wedding venues

411

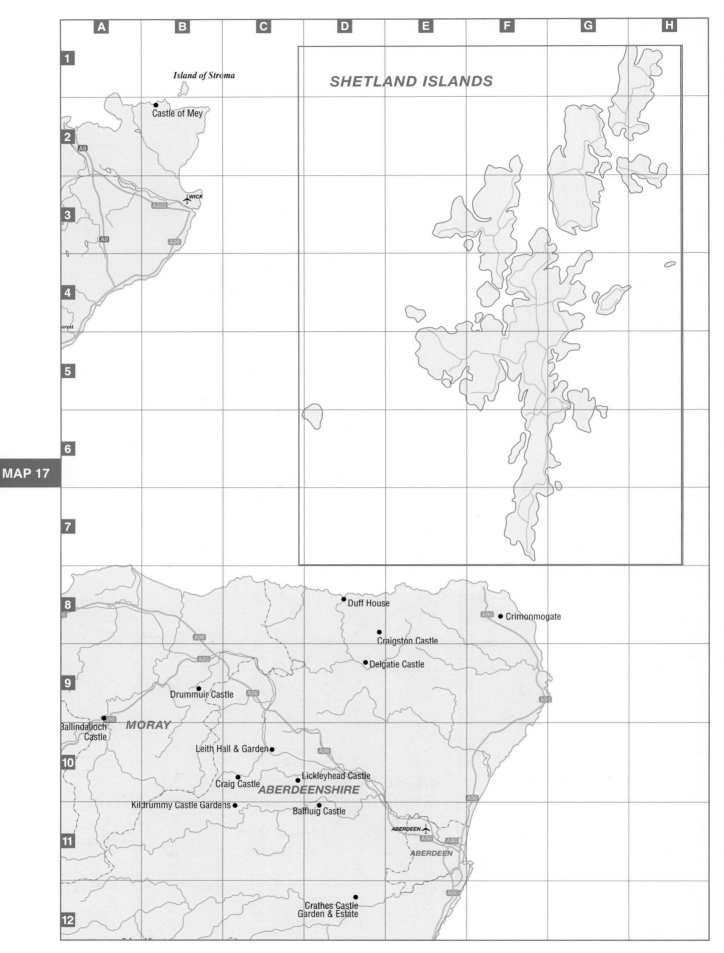

**SHETLAND ISLANDS**

Island of Stroma

● Castle of Mey

✈ WICK

Duff House ●

● Crimonmogate

● Craigston Castle

● Delgatie Castle

● Drummuir Castle

MORAY

● Ballindalloch Castle

Leith Hall & Garden ●

Craig Castle ●

● Lickleyhead Castle

ABERDEENSHIRE

Kildrummy Castle Gardens ●

● Balfluig Castle

ABERDEEN ✈

ABERDEEN

Crathes Castle
Garden & Estate ●

**MAP 17**

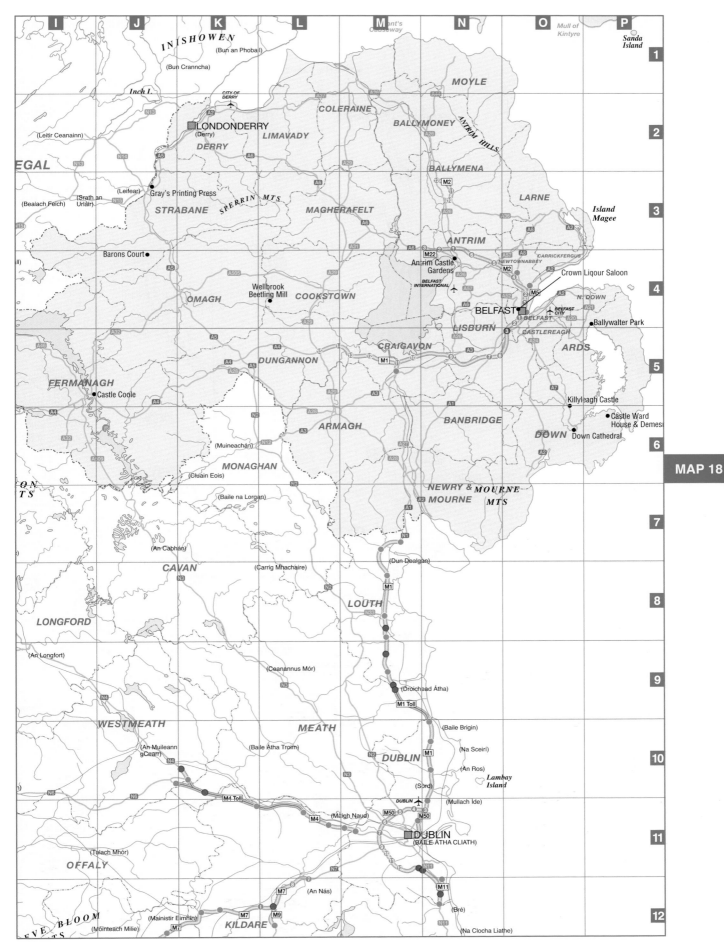

MAP 18

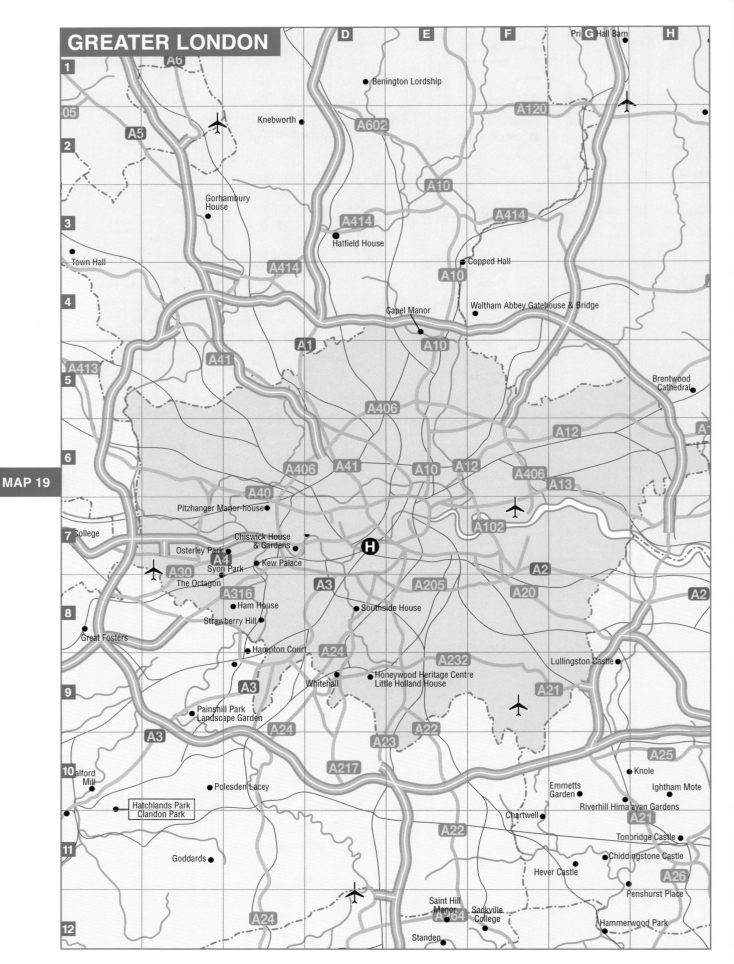

# GREATER LONDON

MAP 19

A6

05

A5

D · Benington Lordship

E    F    Pri G Hall Barn    H

A120

Knebworth

A602

A10

Gorhambury House

A414

A414

Hatfield House

Town Hall

· Copped Hall

A10

Capel Manor · Waltham Abbey Gatehouse & Bridge

A413

A41

A1

A10

Brentwood Cathedral

A406

A12

A406

A41

A10 A12

A406

A40

A13

Pitzhanger Manor-house

A102

Chiswick House & Gardens

College

Osterley Park

A4

Kew Palace

Syon Park

A30

The Octagon

A3

A205

A20

A2

A316

A2

Ham House

Southside House

Strawberry Hill

Lullingston Castle

Hampton Court

A24

A232

A21

Whitehall

Honeywood Heritage Centre
Little Holland House

Painshill Park Landscape Garden

A3

A24

A22

A25

A23

A217

Knole

Walford Mill

Polesden Lacey

Emmetts Garden

Ightham Mote

Hatchlands Park
Clandon Park

Chartwell

Riverhill Himalayan Gardens

A21

A22

Goddards

Tonbridge Castle

Chiddingstone Castle

Hever Castle

A26

Penshurst Place

Saint Hill Manor

Sackville College

Hammerwood Park

A24

A264

Standen

Register for news and special offers at **www.hudsonsheritage.com**

**CENTRAL LONDON**

I   J   Spaniards Rd   K   Highgate   L   M   Archway

1

Kenwood House

Finsbury Park

UpperHolloway

2

Burgh House

Stoke Newington

Hampstead

Holloway

Keats House

3

Finchley Road

Sutton House

Swiss Cottage

Rosslyn Hill

Kentish Town Rd

Camden Road

Islington

4

Kilburn High Road

Camden Town

Shoreditch

Kingsland Road

Kilburn

St John's Wood

King's Cross

City Rd

5

Regent's Park

Euston

Old St

Bethnal Green

Maida Vale

Euston Rd

Foundling Museum

Moorgate

6

**MAP 20**

Marylebone

Bloomsbury

Bishopsgate

Paddington

Dr Johnson's House

St Paul's Cathedral

College of Arms

Aldgate

7

Westway

Oxford St

Somerset House

Bayswater Rd

Hyde Park

Mayfair

Park Lane

Tower of London

Tower Bridge Exhibition

8

Kensington Palace

Spencer House

Banqueting House

Kensington

18 Stafford Terrace

Buckingham Palace

Palace of Westminster

Bermondse

Blewcoat School

9

Westminster Cathedral

Elephant & Castle

Old Kent Road

Sloane Sq

10

Earls Court

Pimlico

Vauxhall

Kennington

Chelsea

Chelsea Physic Garden

Oval

Camberwell

Nine Elms

11

Battersea

Kings Rd

12

Fulham

Stockwell

575 Wandsworth Rd

Fulham Palace & Museum

Clapham

WALES

Wo

Clapton-in-

Uphill

● Parracombe

● Elworthy

● Upton Tower

Lar

● Satterleigh

Stocklinch Otter

Devon

● Luffincott

Exeter ● Exeter St Martin

● Bradstone

● West Ogwell

Cornwall

Princetown ●

● Torbryan

● North Huish

Revelstoke ●

● Roseland St Anthony

# THE CHURCHES CONSERVATION TRUST

Blatherwycke •
• Deene
...cestershire

West Midlands

• Brownsover
Northamptonshire
Aldwincle •
• Cranford

Ca...

• Richards Castle
Worcestershire
Wolfhamcote •
• Holdenby
Knotting
Offord D...

• Lower Sapey
Warwickshire
• Billesley
Upton St Michael • •
Farndish •
Northampton
Ca...

• Stretford
Worcester • • Churchill
• Chadshunt
• Preston Deanery
Little Bar...

Wormsley •
Spetchley
• Avon Dassett
Bedfordshire

Yazor •
• Moreton
Jeffries
Croome D'Abitot
Furtho •
Broughton •

Herefordshire
Strensham •
• Evesham
• Thornton
Lower
Grave...

Holme Lacy •
• Pendock
Little Washbourne
• Saintbury
• Pottesgrove
H...

• Yatton
• Edlesborough

• Michaelchurch
Lassington
Shipton Sollars
Fleet Marston •
• Pitstone
Hertfor...

• Llanrothal
Gloucester
Oxfordshire
Hartwell

• Brookthorpe
Eastleach Martin • ○ Oxford
Chiselhampton •

Gloucestershire
Shorncote
• Inglesham
• Shirburn

Ozleworth •
• Tetbury • Leigh
Nuneham
Courtenay
Wallingford •
Oxhey •
Li...

Charfield •
Oldbury-on-the-Hill
Newnham Murren •
Kingsbury •

Leigh Delamere •
Catmore •
Mongewell

Bristol St Paul
• Draycot Cerne
• Lower Basildon

Bristol St John
• East Shefford
Gre...

...in-Gordano •
• Bristol St Thomas
Berwick Bassett
Lambourn Woodlands
Berkshire

• Brockley
Esher •

• Puxton
• Pensford
Wiltshire
• Alton Priors

...phill •
Cameley •
Hardington
Bampfylde
Imber •
Everleigh •
Chute Forest
• Hartley Wintney
Surrey

Emborough •
Churchill
• Albury

Holcombe
Old Dilton •
Orcheston •
Sth Tidworth • Freefolk

• Otterhampton
Sutton Veny •
Maddington
Rollestone
• Preston Candover

...hy •
• Sutton Mallet
Fisherton
Delamere
Idmiston
Little Somborne

Somerset
Berwick St Leonard •
Wilton •
○ Salisbury
• Ashley
• Itchen
Stoke
• Colemore

Langport •
Stratford Tony •
Eldon
• Privett

• Thurlbear
Northover •
West Dean
West Sussex...

...Ottersey •
Seavington •
Oborne
Hampshire

• Stockwood
○ Southampton
Chichester •
• Tortington

Nether Cerne •
Dorset
• Tarrant Crawford

Bothenhampton •
• Winterborne Tomson
• North Stoke

Winterborne Came • Whitcombe
• Church Norton

• Portland

Fledborough
Lincoln
Great Steeping
Haltham-on-Bain
**Lincolnshire**
Normanton
Haceby

North Barningham • Thurgarton
Gunton
East Ruston
**Norfolk**
Booton • Brandiston
•rthorpe
Edmondthorpe
Walpole
King's Lynn
Little Witchingham
West Walton
Islington
East
Norwich St Augustine
Burley
Wiggenhall
Bradenham **Norwich**
Norwich St John
Withcote
Stamford St John
Parson Drove
Coston
Moulton
**Rutland**
Guyhirn
Norwich
Buckenham
•herwycke•
Wakerley
Barton Bendish
St Laurence
Hellington
Deene
Heckingham
Hales
Feltwell
West
Bungay
Harling
Aldwincle •
Conington
Hockwold
Shimpling
Ellough
Steeple Gidding
Frenze
South
Covehithe
•onshire
Cranford
**Cambridgeshire**
Sapiston
Redgrave
Elmham
•enby
Knotting
Icklingham
Rickinghall
•arndish•
Offord D'Arcy
Long Stanton
Wordwell Stanton
•rthampton
Swaffham Prior
**Suffolk**
Stonham Parva
Preston Deanery
**Cambridge**
Cambridge St Peter
Badley
Little Barford
Abbotsley
Cambridge All Saints
Claydon
Akenham
Newton
**Bedfordshire**
Duxford
Sudbury
Green
Ipswich
Broughton
Edworth
St Peter
Chilton
Washbrook
•hornton
Lower
Buckland
Little Wenham
Gravenhurst
Halstead
Pottesgrove
Little •
West Bergholt
Little Bromley
Hormead
Chickney
Colchester St Leonard
•mshire
Stansted
Colchester St Martin
Edlesborough
Mountfitchet
Berechurch
Pitstone
**Essex**
•well
**Hertfordshire**
Stanstead Abbots
Willingale
•oton
•ourn
Oxhey •
•rd
Little Stanmore
East Horndon
•Murren
Kingsbury
Vange
•ll
Oseney Crescent
•sildon
**London**
Cooling
**Greater London**
Higham
Esher •
Lumley Chapel
Luddenham
Goodnestone
Paddlesworth
Burham
West Stourmouth
Hartley Wintney
Kingsdown
Fordwich
Sandwich St Mary
**Surrey**
East Peckham
Knowlton
Sandwich St Peter
Albury
Waldershare
•andover
Capel St Thomas
**Kent**
Swingfield
Capel-le-Ferne
•emore
•t
**West Sussex**
**East Sussex**
Warminghurst
North Stoke
Preston Park
•er •
Tortington
**Brighton**
Church Norton
Hove

Northumberland

Newcastle-
Low Elswick
Bywell
Tyne an
Shotley

Durham

Ireby

Brougham

Cumbria

Star

Vale of Lune

Wensley
Coverha

Blawith

Skelton-cum-Ne

Lancaster

Cov
Stainburn

Pilling

Lancashire

Langho

Leeds

Blackburn

Halifax
Copley

Becconsall
Tarleton

West Yorks

Bolton

Friarmere

Greater Manchester

Wentw
Manchester
Sou

Waterloo
Merseyside
Carrington
Heaton Norris

Liverpool
Warburton

Thornton-le-Moors

Macclesfield

Derb

Cheshire

Adderley

Northumberland

Newcastle-upon-Tyne
Low Elswick ●
Bywell ●
Tyne and Wear
● Shotley
● Sunderland

Durham

● Skelton-in-Cleveland

● Stanwick

● Fylingdales

● South Cowton

une

● Wensley
● Coverham

North Yorkshire

● Birdforth
● East Heslerton
● Wintringham
● Whenby

Skelton-cum-Newby ●
● Roecliffe

● Allerton Mauleverer

Cowthorpe ●
York ● York Holy Trinity
Stainburn ● York St Lawrence

● Harewood

East Riding of Yorkshire

● Lead
Leeds ● Leeds

● Halifax
● Copley

West Yorkshire

Burringham

ton
● Friarmere
Kirk Sandall ●
● Barnetby
● Clixby

Manchester
● Cadeby
Redbourne ●
● Waithe
South Somercotes
● Manchester
Wentworth ●
● Edlington
Yarburgh
● Skidbrooke
South Yorkshire
Kingerby ●
● N Cockerington ●
● Saltfleetby
● Heaton Norris
● Normanby-by-Spital
● Theddlethorpe
Throapham ●
● Saundby
● Buslingthorpe
Littleborough ●
Snarford ●
Haugham ●
● Little Cawthorpe
● Goltho
Burwell

● Macclesfield
Milton Mausoleum ●
● Fledborough
Low Marnham ●
● Lincoln

Derbyshire
● Great Steeping

Nottinghamshire
Haltham-on-Bain ●

Lincolnshire

Elston ● ●
Cotham
● Normanton

● Kedleston

ev

# *Index*

## Listed by property name in alphabetical order

Marwood Hill Gardens

# B

Duncan Grant's Studio, Charleston

## C

The Great Hall at Castle Howard

## D

Hughenden

Great Fulford

Elton Hall

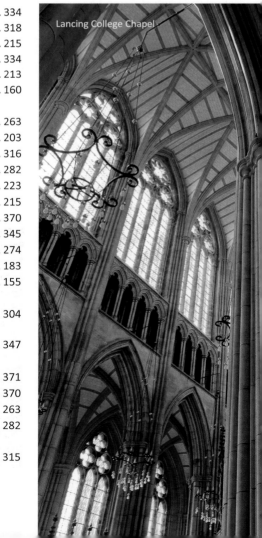

Lancing College Chapel

# Index

Holker Hall